Assessing Risk
in Adult Males
who Sexually Abuse Children

A Practitioner's Guide

KNOWLEDGE   RISKS

Martin C. Calder

with

Andy Hampson and John Skinner

RHP

Russell House Publishing

Assessing Risk in Adult Males who Sexually Abuse Children

Russell House Publishing Limited

First published in 1999 by:
Russell House Publishing Limited
4 St George's House
Uplyme Road
Lyme Regis
Dorset DT7 3LS

© Martin Calder
© Chapter six Andy Hampson

British Library Cataloguing-in-Publication Data:
A catalogue record for this manual is available from the British Library.

ISBN: 1-898924-23-6

Typeset by TW Typesetting, Plymouth, Devon.
Printed by Print in Black, Midsomer Norton, Bath.

Contents

List of Appendices

Acknowledgements

About the Authors

Chapter 1 Introduction 1

Chapter 2 Evolution and the scope of the problem 5

Chapter 3 Defining the problem: the myth of shared meaning 10

Chapter 4 Causation: an overview 20

Chapter 5 Contextualising assessments 34

Chapter 6 The management of sex offenders in the community 47
Andy Hampson

Chapter 7 A framework for comprehensive assessment 65
with John Skinner

Chapter 8 Outcome measures: separating the wood from the trees 159

References 172

Resources 194

Appendices 197

List of Appendices

	Page
Generalised Contentment Scale	198
Family of Origin Scale	198
Sex Offender Lifestyle: Cognitive Behavioral Inventory	199
Dating and Assertion Questionnaire	203
Parental Attitude Scale	204
Revised U.C.L.A. Loneliness Scale	205
Loneliness Rating Scale	205
Impulse Control Checklist	207
Multi-dimensional Anger Inventory	207
An Anger Diary	208
Anger Management and Assertiveness Skills	209
Sexual Aggression Test	210
Bakker Assertiveness-Aggressiveness Inventory	212
Index of Self-concept	213
Social Self-esteem Inventory	213
Self-control Questionnaire	214
Locus of Control Scale	215
Illness Behavior Questionnaire	216
Automatic Thoughts Questionnaire-Revised	217
The Mach Tech Sex Test: Attitude and Value Inventory	218
Behavior Inventory	219
Sexual Experiences Survey	221
Negative Attitudes toward Masturbation Inventory	222
Sexual Experiences Questionnaire	223
Miller Social Intimacy Scale	223
Fear of Intimacy Scale	224
Index of Marital Satisfaction	225
Index of Sexual Satisfaction	225
Marital Comparison Level Index	226
The Eysenck Inventory of Attitudes to Sex	227
Attitudes to Offending	229
Burt Rape Scales	230
Burt Rape Myth Acceptance Scale	231
Hanson Sex Attitudes Questionnaires	232
Sexual Attitudes for Self and Others Questionnaire	234
Dysfunctional Attitude Scale	235
Abel and Becker Sexual Interest Card Sort	236
Gender Identity and Erotic Preference in Males	239
Sexual Arousability Inventory	243
Sexual Arousal Patterns	244

Sex Anxiety Inventory   245
Fantasy Questionnaire   247
Ideal Offence Fantasy   247
Bumby Cognitive Distortion Scales   248
Abel and Becker Cognitions Scale   250
The Sex Offender Cognitive Disowning Behavioral Distortion Scale   251
SOIQ-r   254
Thinking Errors/Cognitive Distortions   255
Why Deny it?   257
Making Excuses   257
Sexual Offence Attitudes Questionnaire   258
Sex Offence Attitudes Questionnaire   259
Developing Effective Communication Skills   261
Carich-Adkerson Victim Empathy and Remorse   261
    Self Report Inventory   262
    Inventory   262
Levinson Victim Empathy Scale   264
Selfism (NS)   266
Sexual Offense Assessment Questions   267
Generalised Scale of Acceptance (GSA)   268
Offence Analysis (Calder)   269
Reasons to Change   269
Risk Assessment Rating Scale   270
Bays and Freeman-Longo Evaluation of Dangerousness for Sexual Offenders   271
Risk Assessment Checklist Scale   274
Risk Assessment Checklist Scale Protocol   277
10 FC Profile   278
Sex Offender Treatment Needs Assessment and Progress Summary   279
Evolution of Recovery   279
Standard Protocol for Conducting Recovery Evaluation   281
15 Factor Sex Offender Recovery Scale   283
Sex Offender Recovery Inventory   287
Recovery Risk Assessment Scale   289
The Eleven Point Treatment Plan   292

*This book is dedicated to my daughter Stacey Laura
and to the memories of my sons and daughter,
Liam Martin, Adam Charles and Laura.*

Acknowledgements

Thanks to Leigh Library for persevering with both my handwriting and the endless stream of requests for this book. To my wife Janet for allowing me the space to complete the task and for her typing skills and patience. This book is as much hers as it is mine. To Andy Hampson for his tutorage over the last five years, and his chapter. To John Skinner for his constructive comments and guidance on the backbone chapter within this text. To those individuals who have offered constructive comments and suggestions on early drafts of the book. To Geoffrey Mann at Russell House Publishing for his continued support and investment in me. To all those authors who have allowed me to reproduce their materials in the text, especially Mark Carich, and to the social workers in Salford who have unwittingly piloted some of these ideas in their daily pursuit of child protection.

Martin C. Calder

About the Authors

Martin C. Calder is a Child Protection Co-ordinator with the City of Salford Community and Social Services Directorate. He has interests in making materials accessible to fieldwork staff, and has published widely on a range of child protection matters. His interests include children, juveniles and adults who sexually abuse; child protection core group practice; and child protection theory.

John Skinner is a Child Protection Officer with the NSPCC in the North West. He was previously a social worker in Salford and Lancashire focusing on child protection. Between 1992–1998 he was a practitioner in the Salford, Bolton and Wigan Adult Sex Offender Groupwork Treatment Programme and the G-MAP Adolescent Sex Offender Treatment Programme. In addition to groupwork, his experience also includes individual risk assessments and treatment to both adult and adolescent sex offenders, he provides consultation to sex offender groupwork programmes, and he currently co-ordinates the NSPCC partnership initiative with Greater Manchester Probation Service—providing assessment, treatment and consultancy service to work with adolescent sex offenders.

Andy Hampson is a Principal Officer with Salford Social Services Department. He was appointed to the post of Child Protection Co-ordinator in 1989 and now manages the Child Protection and Reviewing Unit. He has been actively involved for many years in the development of inter-agency responses to the management of sex offenders in the community and is a founder member of Salford's Multi-Agency Risk Panel.

A pre-publication review of *Assessing Risk in Adult Males who Sexually Abuse Children*.

This excellent book can be warmly recommended for use by a variety of professionals working in different settings which bring them into contact with sexually abused children, and the men who have abused them. It will also serve as a valuable textbook for social work, probation and child care educators.

The text by Martin Calder moves seamlessly between the review of and synthesis of a growing body of academic studies in this field, and their practical application. The text is learned yet easy to read, and after 160 fascinating pages the reader has the satisfying feeling that he or she has become an expert in the field. Supplementary chapters by experts, and an impressive array of instruments in the appendices mean that the fortunate person who owns this book can both initiate and evaluate programmes of assessment and treatment for this problematic group of clients.

Christopher Bagley
Professor of Social Work Studies
University of Southampton

Chapter 1
Introduction

"The abusive adult understands children better than the rest of us. The child can come to depend on victimisation with terrible assurance, much more surely than our protection. It is the perfect fit between the child's needs and the adult's desires that we must consider if we are to comprehend the incomprehensible and empower our interventions on behalf of the powerless" (Summit, 1990).

This text is designed to complement my previous book on the risk assessment of juveniles and children who sexually abuse (Calder, 1997), and is driven by a need to provide workers at the coalface with accessible materials within a structured and coherent framework. This is needed so we can try and narrow the huge gap between aspiration and delivery as well as helping workers to understand the fit between the adult's desires and the child's needs so they can be more effective in their interventions.

The mountains of articles and books in relation to sexual abuse continue to provide very real practical (cost and time) and emotional obstacles to workers: largely because of their inaccessibility and the variability in their quality. Picking up the wrong texts in isolation can create new problems for the recipient families rather than helping to resolve them. For example, McMillan et al. (1995) wrote an article on the perceived benefits of child sexual abuse, which they broke down into four categories: protecting children from abuse, self-protection, increased knowledge of child sexual abuse, and having a stronger personality. They went on to cite support for their findings from Finkelhor (1979), Kilpatrick (1992) and Okami (1991). The worker could review their approach to the work on the basis of adopting such material wholeheartedly and without balancing it against the extensive literature on the effects of sexual abuse on its victims (see Beitchman et al., 1991; 1992; Gomes-Schwartz et al., 1990; Wyatt and Powell, 1988). The aim of this book is, therefore, to guide workers through this mountain of material and organise it in a clear and accessible manner. The worker has responsibility for ultimately deciding what material they choose to accept, reject or search out more information on. The book is designed to wet your appetite to learn more about the complexities of sexual abuse and sexual offending.

The book does aim to integrate theory, research and practice wisdom and provide a blend of all three elements. It does not aim to prepare workers to go out and do the task in isolation: it is, at best,

a stepping stone, and should normally only be used with workers who have some experience in this area. It does aim to offer workers guidance to instil confidence and direction for those thinking about, or actually undertaking, this work. We need to empower workers if we are to begin to shift the balance of power from the offender to the worker. This should ideally be through co-working with someone experienced in the work until they have served their 'apprenticeship' (Calder, 1995). It should not allow agencies to displace their anxieties onto workers willing to invest some of their time into learning to understand this dangerous group of men.

This book is being written at a time of unprecedented public debate and concern about the dangers posed by sex offenders, reinforced through extensive media coverage of high profile individual cases, such as Sidney Cooke and his accomplice Robert Oliver, who raped and killed Jason Swift. There has also been the introduction of the Sex Offenders Act (1997) after the issue hit the political agenda, and the government is currently considering indeterminate sentencing for child sex offenders. The focus on monitoring sexual offenders in the community has had a spectacular rise in the realm of public concerns and a remarkably quick response in terms of legislation coming onto the statute books. This legislation requires those convicted or cautioned for specified sexual offences to notify the police of their names, and addresses and any subsequent changes. Andy Hampson discusses this issue in more detail in Chapter 6. What is clear is that this increased profile has led to community vigilantism when members of the public have been notified about the whereabouts of a paedophile. Such responses can be described as 'society suddenly being woken from its sleep of denial'. This is important. The enforcement of silence has been and remains the most potent weapon of the offender, both individually and collectively. The breaking of this silence can thus be seen as the first crucial step towards bringing about change and a safer environment (Nelson, 1998). We are only now shifting from the traditional wall of silence and professional denial of the problem to a new position of proactive searching, investigation and disclosure of the problem (Edwards and Soetenhorst, 1994). We need to educate the public as well as many of the professionals on the issues relating to sexual abuse. If we educate them through providing essential information and clear messages, then there is more chance of them understanding and thus supporting our responses. This book can help in this task. It seems likely that the interest in sexual offending will continue to generate a lot more interest in the coming years, and the prospect of moving into a new phase of our work with sex offenders as the millenium approaches looks more likely. Let us hope that this new explosion of interest does not add to the problems of the victims by increasing the likelihood of discovery whilst subjecting them to the secondary assaults of an inconsistent intervention system (Summit, 1983).

Workers continue to face very real problems in the management of those believed to have committed sexual abuse against children, especially where this does not result in a criminal conviction. The title of the book was chosen with this circumstance in mind. The terms *abuser*, *offender* and *perpetrator* are frequently used interchangeably in the literature and this causes confusion. Most people would agree that the difference between the three terms is as follows: *abuser* covers those accused, but not convicted of a crime; *offender* covers those who have been convicted of, or have admitted to committing a schedule one offence; whilst the term *perpetrator* embraces both of these possibilities. The term offender will be used throughout this book although it takes on its broadest remit in that it covers all those behaviours that result in sexual abuse. This is important as it opens up the proposed assessment framework to the broadest group of adult males who sexually abuse.

The material in the book is for application *only* with adult males who have committed sexual abuse against children. There is a need to look elsewhere for guidance on assessing adult females who sexually abuse (see Elliott, 1993; Matthews et al., 1989; Saradjian and Hanks, 1996) and juveniles and children who sexually abuse (Calder, 1997; Calder, forthcoming). This is an important book as it has the potential to influence the assessment and processing of the largest group of sex offenders: adult males. Studies have indicated that most offenders are men, with 90 per cent being repeatedly quoted (Furniss, 1991; MacLeod and Saraga, 1988) and the gendered component of sexual offending is covered in more detail in Chapter 4.

Sex offenders are an extremely heterogeneous group that cannot be characterised by single motivational or etiological factors, but this has not halted numerous attempts to create typological frameworks which aim to split this broad group into more homogeneous sub-groups (see Chapter 3). In doing so, there is often an acknowledgement that sexually offensive behaviour is varied, complex, and multiply determined. The aim for workers in the process of their initial and then comprehensive assessment, is to identify the specific factors pertinent to the offender in question, as this is a preface to constructing an individually tailored treatment and relapse prevention package. This book also aims to address both familial and extra-familial sexual abuse, exploring the shifting sands in relation to the 'crossover' between the two, as well as crossover between ages and genders (see Chapter 7). This is a crucial area for workers to understand and apply when undertaking risk assessments of sex offenders as it does point to elevated or lowered risk in a variety of different contexts and situations.

The book does briefly address both the issue of black sexual offenders (as the evidence suggests that ethnic groups differ in their patterns of sexual offending, for example see Bancroft, 1991) and mentally handicapped offenders, although this book does not claim to offer the necessary adaptation or new material for risk assessment of this group (see Chapter 7 and O'Callaghan, forthcoming).

The book does aim to address selection issues for workers thinking of embarking on this work and it considers organisational issues that influence the work. Sexual abuse and sexual offending are complex and multi-determined problems that do not fall exclusively within the remit of any individual agency. No single theory and no single agency are able to provide either all the resources or all the answers. As such, a co-ordinated and multi-disciplinary approach is needed if we are to effectively address the problem. Insular practice by professionals can allow the offender to continue unchecked in their pattern of escalating behaviour.

One of the greatest dangers involving sexual abuse is that the emphasis becomes one of punishing the offender rather than remaining child-focussed (some achieve both). Atollo et al. (1991) defined a child-centred service as one that:

- Takes children seriously as individuals.
- Gives primary attention to their needs and experiences.
- Provides opportunities and such representation as may be necessary for children to be heard in matters pertaining to them, when children are capable of such expression.
- Responds flexibly to the diversity of their cultural backgrounds and the circumstances in which they find themselves.

It is essential, therefore, that workers engaged in the work with the offender have regular liaison with those working with the children and their mother. The work with the offender is important, but not at the expense of the children. The offender assessment is only one piece of the jigsaw, and the issues surrounding the context of the assessments is explored in Chapter 5.

The backbone of the book is a framework for conducting the comprehensive risk assessment of the sex offender, which I wrote with the assistance of John Skinner. We break this down into smaller areas and then provide an overview of the issues, including relevant research findings, as well as a range of tools and questionnaires for use in the identified areas. The chapter is structured in such a way that workers can dip in and out as required and it is formatted in such a way as to allow the sections to be photocopied for the face-to-face work or for training purposes. Where any of the material is photocopied, full acknowledgement of the source is needed. We do need to acknowledge that working with adult male sex offenders is a more recent development in the evolution of our response to the sexual abuse of children, and we are still in an early stage of developing assessment tools and techniques with sex offenders. This has already led to a change of direction from a confrontational to a motivational interviewing approach, explored in more detail in Chapter 7.

Child protection work is a risky business and working with sex offenders is about the management of uncertainty. The book thus moves on from the extensive material on comprehensive risk assessments to a framework for using the information collected in a structured and considered way. Outcomes are an integral part of our interventions, and we have to be clear about issues such as offender contact with birth children, place of residence, eligibility and suitability for treatment, and risks associated with future offending. The notion of recovery assessments is explored as an additional part of the work. These issues are explored further in Chapter 8.

The book cannot provide a 'black and white' text that will always enable workers to choose the right material and route for each case, but it can educate and guide us in this difficult task. Just as the assessment process is dynamic, so must our practice and knowledge base evolve over time and with the benefit of both hindsight and experience.

The ultimate goal has to be the prevention of all sexual abuse of children. At the present time, our sexual abuse interventions can be characterised as primary, secondary or tertiary. Primary prevention involves preventing the abuse from happening in the first place. Secondary prevention includes the early detection and reporting of offenders for the purpose of stopping them and minimising the negative effects for the child. Finally, tertiary prevention focuses on the treatment of abused children and adults who have developed signs and symptoms of distress. Historically, the focus has been on altering the behaviour of the victim rather than that of the offender—arguably displacing the problem (Swift, 1979). Chapter 2 explores both the size as well as the evolution of the problem, and it is clear that this book finds its niche at the second level. Hopefully, this book will some day become redundant as we move into primary prevention rather than control.

Whilst we need to continue to work with offenders, it is essential that we are clear why. Bagley (1997) has articulated the case against adult sexual involvement with children as follows:

- Young children are in a dependent state, and deserve the care and protection of adults. They are unable to give informed consent to a sexual relationship with an adult who, because of their seniority and power in the relationship, can require the child to perform duties against his or her will. The age at which a young person is free to give consent to a sexual relationship in most European countries is 16.
- When an adult imposes a sexual relationship upon a child or young person against their wishes, long-term psychological harms can result.
- Sexuality imposed on a child can cause physiological harm, such as cervical cancer, pregnancy or sexually transmitted diseases.
- The sexual abuse of children is illegal, thus reflecting the moral code of the majority of common people. Sexual abuse is a selfish act designed to meet the needs of the male adult rather than being for the benefit of the child.
- Incestuous relationships can lead to biological harms for the offspring.
- A child seduced by an adult may, in adolescence and adulthood go on to become an abuser himself.
- The imposition of sexuality upon a child is an act of power by which the child is ritually subjugated. Male victims may be brutalised by this misuse of power, and internalise the role of the abuser. As adults these men may become abusers of both male and female children.

Finally, it is important that we are clear about the principles underlying our work with sex offenders. The Home Office (1998) set out some core principles, which I have expanded upon:

- Sexual assault is always unacceptable and should be investigated as a crime.
- Where it is in the victim's interests, sexual offenders should be prosecuted.
- Sexual assault is damaging to the victims, in some ways.
- Sexual assault results from an intention on the part of the offender to seek both sexual and emotional gratification from the victim.
- Sexual abuse represents an abuse of power.
- The overarching aim of intervention is to protect victims and potential victims.
- Intervention must be based on the offender taking full responsibility for the feelings, thoughts and behaviour, which support his offending. Male sexual arousal is controllable.
- The goal of intervention is to ensure that sex offenders can control their behaviour so that they do not re-offend or sexually abuse others.

- The management of offenders requires a co-ordinated response involving criminal justice and child protection agencies.
- In the longer term the prevention of sexual offences has to address the sex role expectations of males in our society.
- Victims are not responsible for their abuse— under any circumstances.
- Before any risk assessment can begin, children must be protected and the offender controlled.

We also need to believe that the majority of sex offenders can learn how to manage and control their sexually deviant behaviours. We need to concede that not all sex offenders are amenable to treatment and, whilst these will not always be eligible for community-based programmes, we do need to consider the ongoing risks they present. Andy Hampson covers the management of sex offenders in the community in detail in Chapter 6. Finally, treatment of sexual offenders reduces future victimisation and is prevention (Cumming and Buell, 1997).

Chapter 2
Evolution and the scope of the problem

Child sexual abuse is not a new phenomenon, but our response to it is. The earliest response in England was in the 16th century when legislation was introduced to protect children from sexual abuse: boys were protected from forced sodomy and girls under ten from forcible rape. There were harsh punishments for both the offender as well as the victim, and it was not uncommon for men to be executed and children whipped for their part in the crime. Thus protection was offered on the one hand, yet the victim blamed to some degree on the other hand. In the 1700s some educators began warning parents to supervise their children at all times, and to ensure they were never nude in front of other adults, in order to protect them from sexual abuse. Whilst this represented an early indication that society accepted the potential for children to be sexually abused, the emphasis was on the child's behaviour rather than on the offender's. The case of Mary Ellen in 1874 in New York (seriously mistreated by her parents) led to the establishment of the New York Society for the Prevention of Cruelty to Children. This was quickly followed in the UK, with the establishment in 1884 of the British National Society for the Prevention of Cruelty to Children (the NSPCC).

By the late 1900s, the most common form of sexual abuse was familial abuse, although this gave way to extra-familial abuse in the 1920s, although the responsibility was displaced from the stranger to the child as 'temptress'. Victims were regarded as engaging in seductive behaviour or as being unusually attractive (and therefore irresistible). There was no further response until after the rediscovery of child abuse by Kempe and colleagues in 1962. This led to a growth of recognition of the different forms of abuse, with sexual abuse being formally acknowledged as being criteria for entry into the child protection system in 1980 in the UK. Reppucci and Haugaard (1993) have pointed to the feminist movement and child advocates as the pressure groups leading to this position, but not before professionals viewed incestuous behaviour as being the product of a collusive mother (Justice and Justice, 1979).

The societal resistance to accepting the problem of sexual abuse probably existed due to the enormous difficulties associated with the threat to the family from familial sexual abuse. Despite the progress made, there remained individuals who strongly advocated sex between adults and children, citing it is being a normal and valuable experience (Tower, 1989).

Theories of evolution

The general public has become increasingly aware of the extent of child sexual abuse. Mayer et al. (1992) have pointed to the following three theories to account for this apparently magnified social problem:

- *The 'nothing new' account*: History tends to suggest that children have always been sexually abused, and the difference now is that it is recognised as a social problem worthy of our attention. It could be argued that the scope of the problem is declining just at the time when we are prepared to acknowledge and deal with it.

- *Sociological theories*: These focus on the context in which the sexual abuse occurs. Finkelhor (1984) cites several trends, which may be linked to the increase of sexual abuse, and include—divorce and remarriage, changing sexual norms and a change in expectations. For example, he argues that the traditional externalised controls over sexual behaviour such as religion and parental authority no longer have the same power to control behaviour and enforce sexual norms such that standards about what is, and what is not, permissible are hazy and in flux. Popular pornography has also contributed to the erosion of sexual taboos, and has arguably contributed to today's 'sexually saturated' environment (Calder, 1997). Finkelhor also suggests that the sexual revolution of the 1960s may have created a more dramatic rise in expectation than in actual activity, with some men turning to children in an attempt to actualise these expectations, particularly since women were also challenging their roles from sexually innocent and sexually subservient.

- *The social constructionist approach*: Suggests that problems such as child sexual abuse represent not so much 'things that happen', as they are 'ways of making sense'. Child sexual abuse is not real, in itself, but is something we have made real by the way we think and talk about it. It is, therefore, a product of the way we currently run society and construe our world (Stainton-Rogers, 1989).

Keeping the lid on the problem

The other side of the coin is understanding why there has been such a delayed recognition and action. There are a number of reasons for this, and they include:

- The view that children are miniature adults, owned by their parents.
- The view that sex with children is acceptable (see O'Carroll, 1980).
- The view that the family have a right to privacy that should only be sacrificed in certain 'exceptional' circumstances (see Calder, 1995).
- The poor knowledge base of professionals, thus downplaying the importance of child sexual abuse, as well as contributing to a fragmented and unreliable response.
- The low level of reporting and conviction continues to feed a public denial of the problem.
- The blinkered view of sexual abuse as incest or extra-familial abuse, thus narrowing the catchment and focus.
- The lack of evidence of the range and magnitude of the effects on the victims of sexual abuse.
- A belief that sexual abuse is not harmful. For example, Gebhard et al. (1965) noted that up to 60 per cent of the children fully participated, collaborated, or 'seduced' the adult partner.

Taylor-Browne (1997) examined the factors, which have enabled child sexual abuse to remain obscured and hidden, thus allowing our response to remain inadequate, unfocused and piecemeal. She argued that child sexual abuse has conformed more with the definition of a moral panic than a social problem, reinforced by the actions of the media in Cleveland and Orkney where they blamed the workers rather than the offenders, thus displacing responsibility for the problem. This response is based on misinformation and an investment in denying the true scale of the problem.

The 'issue-attention' cycle (Downs, 1972)

When a social problem is identified, we often respond with a euphoric enthusiasm about our ability to 'solve the problem' or 'do something effective' within a relatively short time. Unfortunately, in the next stage of the cycle there is a realisation of the cost of significant progress. Inevitably, solving the problem would not only take a great deal of money but would also require major sacrifices by large groups of the population. Downs attributes society's most pressing social problems to a deliberate or unconscious exploitation of one group in society by another, or the prevention of one group from enjoying something that others want to keep for themselves. In the penultimate stage of the cycle there is a gradual decline of public interest: some people get discouraged, others feel positively threatened by thinking about the problem, whilst others become bored with the issue. This is coupled with a competing and new issue, which attracts the attention of the public and this leads to a shift of focus.

This cycle sits neatly with Olafson et al.'s (1993) notion of cycles of discovery and suppression in the modern history of sexual abuse awareness. Summit (1990) has also pointed to the reality that many of us will overlook clues, blame victims and stigmatise victim's families as sick, rather than consider that trusted friends could be sexual predators. He believes that society has a 'blind spot' in that they develop views and then defend them against revision, even when they have glaring defects. Even when society is moving towards recognition, it is repelled by the prospect of newer, still more threatening discoveries, and they suppress the issue.

At the crossroads: the current period of sexual abuse awareness

"The current period has been marked by unprecedented and sustained professional and media attention of child sexual abuse, the establishment of national and international societies and journals devoted to abuse . . . [and] many-fold increases in the reporting of child sexual abuse" (Olafson et al., 1993).

Widespread current awareness of the problem in modern times is only two decades old, and has been characterised by a greater readiness to listen to children and believe what they say, which, in turn, has led to a recognition that child sexual abuse constitutes a major problem with which society must deal. Conte (1991) noted that the first phase of professional development in responding is characterised by efforts to recognise that it is a common problem. This in itself has been an ongoing struggle for the public and professionals alike. At a psychological level, it is anxiety provoking and emotionally difficult and can lead to defences such as denial and rationalisation. The next phase has been to prevent secondary abuse from the response systems, with the introduction of memorandum protocols (Home Office, 1992), witness protection and so on. This has also been accompanied by a hardening of public attitudes towards sexual offences, reflected in a push for punishment and incarceration ('just desserts'), as well as the need to develop treatment programmes for offenders in prison. There is now something of a backlash against those professionals dealing with the problem, aimed at their poor and inaccurate knowledge base, and the belief that they overstepped the mark when intruding into family life, such as Cleveland (Calder, 1995). Hechler (1988) has pointed out that there is a school of thought which maintains that the sexual abuse of children is a limited problem that is being built out of all proportion in a hysterical climate of over-concern. These are the people who direct their venom onto dirty old men in raincoats so they can continue to dissociate themselves from the sexual abuse, which does take place in all sections of our society. As Chapter 4 will illuminate, the offender cannot be isolated by any one particular characteristic. The problem with the backlash stance is that it ignores the multiple effects of sexual abuse on the victims.

It is clear that the 1990s has increasingly seen suggestions that we continue to underestimate the true scale of the problem: with the acknowledgement of ritual abuse, 'sex tourism', the child murders and abuse (Fred and Rosemary West), paedophile rings, residential and foster care sexual abuse (Calder, 1999), to name but a few. There are also huge new problems waiting round the corner for us in the face of the Internet and the video recorder. Child sexual abuse appears to be endemic and deeply embedded in our social fabric.

Despite greatly heightened public and professional awareness, the task of reducing the incidence of child sexual abuse and formulating more effective intervention strategies remains a huge one for us all. We may be ready to prohibit the sexual abuse of children, but do not know how to. Hopefully, by working with more sex offenders we will target the true focus of our preventive efforts, and will learn more about effective as well as cost-effective interventions. As Bray (1997) has pointed out, 'The pretence that child sexual abuse does not exist has become an untenable position to maintain with credibility. This in itself has been a considerable achievement'.

The scope of the problem: uncovering the hidden reservoir of suffering

It is very difficult to accurately determine the true scale of the child sexual abuse problem. This is due to a number of factors and includes the secrecy of the abuse, the consequences of disclosure for the victim, societal denial of the problem and the lack of any standardised definition. This is compounded further when you consider the limitations of the two principal mechanisms for collecting statistical information: incidence and prevalence. These two terms mean quite different things although they are often used interchangeably. Prevalence studies attempt to estimate the proportion of a population that has been sexually abused during childhood; while incidence studies seek to estimate the number of new cases occurring in a given period of time, usually a year. Both the incidence and prevalence of child sexual abuse, in the family and outside of it, are unknown—although the available information does support it as a significant problem. Davies (1998) has pointed out that whilst we do not know the true numbers, to construct a picture is to watch 'an arithmetical explosion'. For example, there has been a 111 per cent increase in sex offender incarceration in this country in the period 1979–1990 (HMP Risley, 1994). There has also been an 800 per cent increase in child protection registration for sexual abuse in the period 1983–1987 (Morrison, 1994), whilst in the US there has been a 2,100 per cent increase in sexual abuse reports in the decade 1976–1986 (Koester-Scott, 1994). In 1993, there was estimated to be 260,000 men in the population of England and Wales with a conviction for a sexual offence (Marshall, 1994). Of these, 110,000 were convicted of an offence against a child. Of these, 100,000 were liable for registration as part of the Sex Offenders Act (1997) and 10,000 were exempt because of either their age or the nature of their offence.

Prevalence studies involve asking an adult population, by questionnaire or interview, whether they experienced sexual abuse in childhood. These studies usually reveal fairly high rates for abuse, but they are usually inflated in two ways: all incidents including the relatively minor are usually counted, and all figures reflect a childhood lifetime perspective, i.e. around ten years of reliable recall—all problems can appear large if we aggregate over a long period of time (Gillham, 1996). Incidence rates are thus usually lower than prevalence rates.

Information on prevalence is available from several developed countries, including the USA, Canada, England, Sweden, Australia and New Zealand. In the UK, the key prevalence studies are those conducted by Baker and Duncan (1985) and Liz Kelly and colleagues (1991). Baker and Duncan found a prevalence rate of 10 per cent of subjects reporting having been sexually abused before the age of 16 years (12 per cent females, 8 per cent males). Their nationally representative sample of 2,019 men and women also found that whilst 63 per cent reported only a single experience, 23 per cent were repeatedly abused by the same person and 14 per cent subjected to multiple abuse by a number of people. This figure is considerably higher than an earlier study in the UK by Beesley-Mrazek et al. (1983) who suggested a prevalence rate of 0.3 per cent, although Baker and Duncan believe their finding to be a conservative one. Extrapolation of these findings to the UK in general would give the following estimates: over 4.5 million adults will have been sexually abused as children; a potential 1,117,000 children will be sexually abused before the age of 15; and at least 143,000 of these will be abused within the family.

Kelly revealed that roughly one in two girls (59 per cent) and one in four boys (27 per cent) will experience some form of sexual abuse before reaching the age of 18. The abuse was committed by peers as well as adults, and almost a third of the incidents occurred before the children were 12 years of age.

In the latest Australian national statistics of the prevalence of child sexual abuse, 19 per cent of

28,711 substantiated cases were labelled as sexual abuse. Of these substantiated cases, the rate of sexual abuse for the nation was 1.1 per 1,000 children aged 0–16 years. This compared to a higher rate of 2.0 per 1,000 children aged 0–16 years in the Aboriginal and Torres Strait Islander population— showing that this small group was over-represented (Angus and Woodward, 1995).

In the United States, Finkelhor (1984) estimated that the proportion of children that were exposed to some form of sexual abuse was between 9 and 52 per cent for females and between 3 and 9 per cent for males (depending on the definition of sexual abuse and methodology used). Russell (1983) in a prevalence study of the sexual abuse of women found that the most serious forms of abuse were more than twice as likely to occur outside the family. The aggregate figures produced for a collection of US research projects has indicated a broader range of figures, ranging from 6–62 per cent for girls and 3–31 per cent for boys (Peters et al., 1986). Prevalence rates can be broken down further. Burkhardt and Rotatori (1995) reported that for sexual abuse involving contact between the offender and the victim under 18 range from 7–45 per cent for females and 3–5 per cent for males. Other non-contact estimates range from 10–62 per cent for females and 3–6 per cent for males. In the US, Crewdson (1988) estimated that there were as many as 38 million sexually abused Americans.

The Canadian research on sexual abuse which involved over 1,000 females and 1,000 males, revealed that 15 per cent of females under 16 years and 22 per cent of females under 18 years had been sexually abused. The figures for males were 6 and 9 per cent respectively (Bagley et al., 1984).

Davies (1998) pointed out that the current prevalence studies would cover 1.5 million girls and 520,000 boys in the UK: a figure that is consistent with the projection of 1.1 million offenders.

Incidence studies are more systematically biased and less representative than prevalence studies. For example, this may be due to the researchers particular view of causation and their view of sexual abuse. Incidence figures will also be influenced by local criteria for registration and its application. Only 1 per cent of the annual incidence of reported crime refers to sexual offences (Fisher, 1994).

The NSPCC, on the basis of the number of children registered with them, estimate the national incidence in England and Wales of childhood sexual abuse for children under 14 years of age is 5,850 and 6,600 under 16 years. Of the registered cases, 78 per cent involve female children and 22 per cent involve males.

Beesley-Mrazek et al.'s (1983) study drew its information from several hundred questionnaire returns from a number of different professional groups. Extrapolating their findings to the general population indicated an annual incidence of over 1,500 cases per year, that is an incidence of about one case per 6,000 children per year, and about 3 per 1,000 over childhood. These figures are low but do reflect the experience of the professional sample group.

ChildLine reported receiving nearly 6,000 calls alleging sexual abuse in the period 1 November 1988 to 31 October 1989. Over 90 per cent of these involved abuse within the family. More recent figures (Madge, 1998) show that over 15,000 children and young people a year ring ChildLine to talk about physical or sexual abuse and some 800 adults seek help for their own past or continuing childhood abuse.

In the US, the National Incidence Study estimated that a rate of 0.7 cases of child sexual abuse per 1,000 children per year (Russell, 1988).

Whilst there has been a significant increase in the recognition of child sexual abuse, reflected in the substantial increase in the number of reports made to the child protection agencies, it is only more recently that the substantiation rate increased accordingly. In 1995 in Australia, only 44 per cent of all finalised cases were substantiated (Angus and Woodward, 1995).

Reports of sexual abuse have increased by a factor of ten over the last decade (Templeman and Stinnett, 1991). The number of reports being filed is due to a range of factors and include:

● Greater public awareness of the problem.
● A greater willingness for the public and victims to report.
● Willingness for professionals to listen and believe.

These factors probably explain the increased reporting rather than a huge increase in the amount of child sexual abuse. Indeed, the actual level of abuse is arguably on the decline when considering the historical context.

The tip of the iceberg: hidden victims and undetected offenders

It is conceded universally that the problem is far greater than the statistics reflect. This is attributable to a number of issues and include:

● The number of offences for which men are charged is significantly lower than that which they have committed. Abel et al. (1987) provided us with an estimate of the number of sexual acts committed by a sample of sex offenders. The 561 offenders committed a total of 291,737 acts. The lifetime number of victims were estimated for each of the major paraphilias represented in their sample. The 224 non-incestuous paedophiles targeting female children had a total of 4,435 victims; 155 non-incestuous paedophiles targeting male children a total of 29,981 victims; 158 incestuous paedophiles targeting female children a total of 286 victims; and 44 incestuous paedophiles targeting male children a total of 75 victims. This study again highlighted that the average number of crimes per offender had previously been significantly underestimated. Victim data generally supports this picture.

- The various definitions used in the studies, sampling differences and methodological variation conspire to prevent any consistent approach or comparison.
- The Home Office figures only record the number of offences and not the number of offenders (Fisher, 1994). This is important. The current prison population for sex offenders is 2,100 and there are 108,000 convicted paedophiles in the community. Yet the projected number of paedophiles in Britain today is 1.1 million (Davies, 1998). There is a huge discrepancy between official records and the actual target population size. The statistics also do not allow for the probability that the offender is sentenced in a different year than the charges were brought.
- The official figures do not account for a large number of offenders (52 per cent) who plead to a lesser charge or a non-sexual offence, or where the charges refer to 'specimen' rather than total charges (Stewart and Young, 1992).
- The police have a huge discretion in determining which cases are liable for prosecution (Warwick, 1991).
- The vast majority of sexual crimes go unreported (e.g. 90 per cent). This is acutely so for familial offences given the consequences of disclosure (more so for children from ethnic backgrounds—see Calder, 1998). Even where children do disclose to family members, this rarely leads to third party reports to official agencies. Clark (1993) has challenged this view, pointing out that the number of notifiable sexual offences in 1990 was some 37.4 per cent higher than those reported in 1990, although he doesn't refer to the fact that this was consistent with other recorded offences, remaining at under 1 per cent of the total (Lancaster, 1996).
- Boys are more unlikely to disclose sexual abuse because of the stigma attached to disclosure. The average time lapse from being abused to seeking help is 20 years (Etherington, 1995). Finkelhor (1979) found that 63 per cent of his sample of 530 college women and 73 per cent of 266 college males had never told anyone about the sexual abuse before the researchers, much less disclosed to anyone in a position of authority when they were children. It has been found that 70 per cent of adult survivors never tell anyone about their abuse as a child. Indeed *The Los Angeles Times* study of 1985 found that fewer

than half of the children told anyone about the abuse within a year, whilst only 3 per cent reported it to the police or other public agency (Timnick, 1985a and b).
- Even where cases are reported, the conviction rate is low at around 5–10 per cent (Willis, 1993). Many cases fall short of the demands of the judicial process.
- Many cases are inaccurately determined not to have been abused (Chaffin, 1994).
- Child victims often retract their initial disclosures when they become aware of the consequences of their actions (for a fuller discussion of this issue, please refer to Marx (1996), Rieser (1991) and Summit (1983)). Others are acutely anxious about the possibility of attending court and giving evidence.
- No figures are currently collected on civil findings of sexual abuse. Since many cases cannot proceed criminally, the child protection agencies are left with instituting care proceedings to protect the children involved. Conte (1991) has pointed to the fact that there was a parity of finding (26 per cent) in the US courts in relation to civil and criminal proceedings.
- There is little acknowledgement that whilst reports of sexual abuse are increasing, there remain a number of false allegations that skew the figures further. Raskin and Yuille (1989) have claimed that the rate of fictitious allegations is approximately 8 per cent, but in the context of divorce or child-custody battles it may be as high as 50 per cent.

Whatever the limitations of the current statistics, there is evidence that there are 1.1 million projected offenders in this country at the present time (Davies, 1998), and they commit an average of 380 crimes in their lifetime (Abel et al., 1987). This is evidence enough that we must refine our assessment and treatment strategies with this large group of dangerous men.

Chapter 3
Defining the problem: the myth of shared meaning

Sexual abuse

Definitions are very important: if they are too narrow, they restrict our understanding, figures of incidence and prevalence as well as our intervention threshold. Conversely, if they are too broad, they are all embracing and often detract from focussing in on the highest risk cases.

Sexual abuse is a cultural, social, political, economic, legal, medical, psychological, educational and a spiritual issue (Groth and Oliveri, 1989). Child sexual abuse is, therefore, a complex and multi-determined problem which can be viewed from a wide range of perspectives. This is reflected in the number and variance of definitions, most of which are rigorously defended by the originating discipline. Thus, whilst child sexual abuse falls within the remit of a wide variety of professional groups—social workers, teachers, health service workers, police and legal professionals—they rarely discuss the same phenomenon, tending to use criteria in line with the goals of their particular profession. There is often more consensus at the severe end of the continuum, whilst there are many differing and often divergent opinions when the consideration relates to non-penetrative acts. Child sexual abuse thus tends to be a blanket term for a multitude of vaguely defined acts (Haugaard and Reppucci, 1988). It is generally accepted to be any form of non-consenting interpersonal sexual behaviour that poses some risk of harm to the other individual (Groth and Oliveri, 1989). It is usually defined according to three key elements:

- The betrayal of trust and responsibility.
- The abuse of power.
- The inability of children to consent (MacLeod and Saraga, 1988).

David Finkelhor (1979) would also argue that it should embrace the community standard, although it is questionable which community should provide the standard since there will be cultural and probably regional differences.

The problem for professionals is that there are too many different definitions and this makes it difficult when they are trying to understand the problem. It also makes it very difficult when they try to interpret the findings of any 'comparative' research. The search for a definition is further compounded by the use of various terms, such as sexual assault, sexual molestation, sexual victimisation, sexual exploitation and so on.

I will try to make several points around the three key elements above by selecting a number of high profile definitions of sexual abuse. For example, Schechter and Roberge (1976) defined sexual abuse as "... *the involvement of dependent, developmentally immature children and adolescents in [sexual] activities they do not truly comprehend, to which they are unable to give informed consent, or that violate the social taboos of family roles."* The last part of this definition is unnecessary for extra-familial abuse.

This definition is general enough to allow the worker discretion in each individual case. The strength of the above definition from Schechter and Roberge is that it talks about informed consent. It is difficult to accept that children are capable of giving informed consent to sex with adults. In situations where they are threatened or fear being threatened, they may 'consent', but it is not freely given and is certainly not informed in the sense that they are unaware of the significance of their actions (Oates, 1990). What is more difficult is the age at which childhood ends. For example, a 14 year old girl can consent to an abortion in the US, but they are not deemed able to consent to the sex that resulted in their pregnancy (Haugaard and Reppucci, 1988). In the UK, a child is anyone under 18 years for child protection registration and civil proceedings, yet anyone over 17 years is an adult in criminal law (see Calder, 1989). There is a need to differentiate between true consent and legal consent as there can be consent to an unlawful sexual act, thus leaving legal/true consent in conflict. As such, true consent refers to *"being informed, not forced, in an equal relationship, without financial or other inducements, and free of any pressure to comply"* (NCH, 1992).

Many of the terms within the definition require definition in their own right. For example, 'dependent', 'developmentally immature', 'do not truly comprehend', etc. This definition also does not include any explicit breakdown of contact and non-contact abuse, which is unfortunate as it does not capture the range of abuses perpetrated against children. The range of sexual behaviours that constitute child sexual abuse is an integral part of any definition, as it acts as a boundary between acceptable and unacceptable behaviours (Calder, 1997). It also does not allow for the severity of the abuse to be assessed, whereas other writers, such as Russell (1983) have. She offered three categories of abuse in terms of its severity: very serious (e.g. vaginal intercourse or oral sex), serious (e.g. genital fondling or digital penetration), and least serious (e.g. intentional sexual touching of clothed breasts or genitals). This allows some gradient for the abuse to be considered, although it does not reflect that many children suffer several forms of sexual abuse simultaneously.

The definition is useful in that it allows for culturally relative considerations, although it does not embrace the destructiveness to the victim of the abuse—even where the offender has been seductive rather than forceful. It also does not acknowledge that the harm caused is not always predictable to an outsider, as there is not always a direct correlation between the severity of the abuse and the ensuing harm. What some may consider 'minor' abuse may have devastating and traumatic consequences for the victim. Tower (1989) advised us to consider the following variables in assessing the degree of trauma to a child: the type of abuse; the identity of the offender; the duration of the abuse; the extent of the abuse; the age at which the child was abused; the first reactions of significant others at disclosure; the point at which the abuse was disclosed; and the personality structure of the victim.

Another useful definition of sexual abuse is that of Suzanne Sgroi as it emphasises the power relationship between the offender and the child and points to the fact that the child has had no choice in the matter:

"Child sexual abuse is a sexual act imposed on a child who lacks emotional, maturational, and cognitive development. The ability to lure a child into a sexual relationship is based upon the all-powerful and dominant position of the adult or older adolescent perpetrator, which is in sharp contrast to the child's age, dependency and subordinate position. Authority and power enable the perpetrator, implicitly or directly, to coerce the child into sexual compliance." (Sgroi et al., 1982).

Baker and Duncan (1985) offered us a definition focussing on the aims of the offender:

"A child . . . is usually sexually abused when another person who is sexually mature involves the child in any activity which the other person expects to lead to their sexual arousal. This might involve intercourse, touching, exposure of the sexual organs, showing pornographic material or talking about sex in an erotic way."

We need to be sure that we are as clear as possible on what constitutes sexual abuse so it is not simply a *". . . sanitised term which protects us all from unpalatable truths"* (Hughes and Parker, 1994). Yet, as O'Hagan (1989) has pointed out, it may well be better to 'have no definition and to retain a healthy discriminatory approach to each recorded experience, than to seek a blanket definition applied to all 'experiences' if we cannot find the 'right' definition. Given that the range of definitions or descriptions varies as much as child sexual abuse itself, the latter appears highly unlikely, and it is most unhelpful to adopt all-inclusive phrases such as 'anything that appeared sexually abusive to you'.

If we are to ever agree a definition of child sexual abuse, there are certain key issues that would need to be embraced and agreement reached. They might include the following.

Community definitions

Finkelhor and Redfield (1984) used a series of vignettes to study laypersons' definitions of sexual abuse. Across vignettes, they varied nine factors selected as sources of controversy in definitions: the age and sex of the victim, the age and sex of the offender, the relationship between the victim and the offender, the sexual act, consent, the consequence of the abuse, and the sex of the respondent. Using multiple regression analysis, they analysed 9,839 vignettes from 521 adult respondents living in the Boston area and found that the age of the offender, if under 20, and the type of the act committed were the most significant components of the definitions. If the offender was over 20, there was virtually no distinction by age, but juveniles were viewed as less abusive than adults but more abusive than younger children. In terms of acts committed, intercourse, attempted intercourse, and genital fondling were all rated as highly abusive. Verbal abuse with a sexual theme was rated as the least abusive act. Other findings included less abusive ratings when the offenders were women, as well as the age of the victim: with less abusive ratings when the victims were either younger or older than pre or early adolescence. The consequence of the abuse was the least important variable.

Angus and Woodward (1995) defined child sexual abuse according to community standards:

". . . any act which exposes a child to, or involves a child in, sexual processes beyond his or her understanding or contrary to accepted community standards."

The range of sexual acts

This is a highly contentious area within the definitional debate, and largely focuses on whether we embrace non-contact abuse. There is a school of thought which advocates an all inclusive catchment of sexual acts so there is no confusion and no ambiguity. Caren and Fay (1981) offered a very graphic definition which clearly spells out exactly what sexual abuse involves:

". . . the forcing of sexual contact. This can involve handling the child's genitals or requests for sexual handling by an older child or adult. Sometimes the contact is oral sex. Sexual contact includes attempts at penetration of the vagina or anus. Sometimes actual penetration occurs. It can involve penetration by penis, but also fingers and objects can be used. Some assaults involve no physical contact. A child may be forced to look at the genitals of an older child or an adult, forced to watch adults having sex, forced to perform sexual acts in front of an adult(s), forced to undress or otherwise expose themselves."

Smith (1986) advocated the addition of *"spied on and photographed in private personal situations"*, and I would advocate the inclusion of: talking about things in an erotic way, obscene telephone calls, voyeurism, fetishism, having the child view sexually explicit magazines, films or videos, and sexual comments' (non-contact); and frottage, fondling, bestiality, handling, pornography or forcing the victim to do something to themselves, such as undress, or masturbate themselves (contact abuse). It seems clear that child sexual abuse does not require penetration, nor touch: *"it can occur through genital or non-genital fondling, or in the way a child is talked to, what the child is forced to see, hear, or do with others. It is the use of a minor to meet the sexual or sexual/emotional needs of another person"* (Blume, 1986).

Another school of thought objects to the inclusion of non-contact behaviours in the definition as they might typically reflect a family pattern and behaviour, such as a father undressing in the home. They argue that the inclusion of such behaviours is at best highly controversial, and at worst, highly misplaced—as they are not accompanied by sexual intent. More controversially, there is an argument that we should exclude all sexual activities from the definition as they have a wide range of varying impacts on the individual (Peters et al., 1986).

Elliott et al. (1995) found that all the offenders in their sample indecently assaulted their victims, sometimes in more than one way. 72 per cent of them reported that this included masturbating the child and being masturbated by the child. 31 per cent engaged in mutual oral sex and 57 per cent attempted or actually engaged in full sexual intercourse, either vaginal or anal. 8 per cent murdered or attempted to murder the child victim during or after the sexual assault. 85 per cent committed the sexual acts with one victim at a time although the remaining 5 per cent had multiple victims present. 93 per cent acted alone.

The first abusive action often involved one or two immediate sexual acts, such as sexual touching or genital kissing, whilst others desensitised the child by asking them to do something that would help the offender, such as undressing. The majority of offenders carefully tested the child's reaction to sex, by bringing up sexual matters or having sexual materials around, or by subtly increasing sexual touching. This 'normalised' sexual setting could be achieved by using sexually explicit videos, or magazines, or sexualised talking.

Waterhouse et al. (1993) reported that most sexual abuse was severe. In 40 per cent of cases children were subjected to sexual manipulation of their genitals either beneath or above their clothing, vaginal intercourse occurred in 20 per cent of cases, whilst 4 per cent of the sample were subjected to oral sex, 4 per cent to sodomy, and 5 per cent to non-contact abuse.

It is also important to consider the cultural variables regarding sex as there are huge variations of what is proper and acceptable among cultures and sub-group, although a void of knowledge in this area exists at the present time.

Age differences

Sexual activity between post-pubertal but 'under-age' children is so common as to be general (Ingham, 1994). Without mutual consent, this becomes abusive, but the distinction is rarely easy to make (see Calder, 1997). The key issue is the equality of the relationship. Any factor which, makes a relationship unequal creates a power imbalance—which can occur through differences in age, size, levels of sexual knowledge or understanding, or developmental level. Elliott et al. (1995) found that the child victim ranged from 1–18 years. The mean age of the youngest victims was 8.5 years: the mean age of the eldest victims was 13 years. 6.6 per cent also assaulted victims aged 19–45; one offender abused a 65 year old victim.

Researchers usually include an age differential between abuser and victim of five years or more (Watkins and Bentovim, 1992), and the offender is the oldest. Finkelhor (1979) defined sexual abuse according to age, occurring where: a sexual encounter between a child of 12 and under with a person of 19 or over; where the child is under 12 and the other person is under 19 but at least 5 years older; and where a child/ adolescent is 13 to 16 years old and the other person is at least 10 years older.

The narrower the age difference, the more difficult the judgement becomes. For example, the issue of informed consent usually runs into some trouble when we talk about 15- and 16-year-olds (Trowell, 1991), although the offender cannot argue with figures of 13 per cent of girls abused being under 6, and 60 per cent of girls sexually abused being under 12 when first abused (Elliott, 1986). Despite this evidence, there are those who believe that the child plays a role in their own abuse (West, 1986), regardless of the age or power imbalance.

It is rare that age differential alone will be used to differentiate an abusive from a non-abusive one. Indeed, some writers have advocated definitions which focus entirely on the behavioural component of the abuse and without specifying any age criterion. Cantwell (1988) argued that oral–genital conflict or penetration of the vagina or anus with fingers or objects is abusive whatever the age differential.

Sexual intent

Sexual gratification of the offender is the usual aim of the abuse (Hobbs, Hanks and Wynne, 1993), and this has been used as the primary focus of some definitions. For example, Fraser (1981) argued that *"sexual abuse is the exploitation of a child for the sexual gratification of an adult"*, whilst Tower (1989) has argued that it is *"the use of a child for sexual gratification by an adult or significantly older child/ adolescent."*

Coercion

Violence is not always part of child sexual abuse, yet there is evidence that offenders are exceptionally sophisticated in identifying and involving their victims in the abuse (Budin and Johnson, 1989); and violence is an appropriate description for an abuse of power by the offender. Smith (1986) referred to force as *"taking advantage of someone who is younger; bribery; threats of harming the child or their family; threats of what will happen to the offender; withdrawal of affection, love, attention; sometimes actual physical force is used but the threat of it is implicit. These types of force are frequently used in combination."*

Strategies used

- Offering to play games, teach them a sport or play a musical instrument.
- Giving bribes, taking them on outings, or giving them a lift home.
- Using affection, understanding and love.
- Telling stories involving lies, magic or treasure hunts.
- Asking a child for help (Elliott et al., 1995).

They found that 84 per cent used a strategy that had been previously successful compared to 16 per cent who adapted theirs over time. 30 per cent replayed their own experiences, whilst 14 per cent were influenced through pornography, television, films and the media.

Offenders can use one or a combination of methods to secure a child's compliance. Elliott et al. found that 19 per cent used physical force with a child, 44 per cent used coercion and persuasion, and 46 per cent used bribery and gifts in exchange for sexual touches. 39 per cent were prepared to use threats or violence to control a resisting child. 61 per cent used passive methods of control such as stopping the abuse and then coercing and persuading once again. 33 per cent specifically told the child not to tell compared to 24 per cent who used threats of dire consequences, whilst 24 per cent used anger and the threat of physical force, and 20 per cent threatened the loss of love or said the child was to blame. 61 per cent were 'very worried' about the child disclosing.

The Waterhouse research (Waterhouse et al., 1993) reported on a wide range of means sex offenders used to procure sex from naive children. Actual physical coercion and force was used in some 20 per cent of cases, verbal inducements or bribes in 14 per cent, and coercion by verbal threats of violence in 6 per cent of cases. Margolin (1992) shattered the myth of the friendly and 'gentle' grandfather approaches reported earlier by Good-

win et al. (1983), finding evidence of explicit threats and overt physical coercion (p740). Conte et al. (1989) also noted that verbal threats are based on an understanding of the child and what will be an effective threat against them. Conte et al. found that those relatively non-violent sex offenders in their sample had employed a range of coercive behaviours, for example conditioning through the use of reward and punishment, and letting the child view violence towards their mother (p299). Furniss (1991) noted that the offender will deliberately induce sexual arousal in the child/ren which can lead to loyalty from their victim(s).

Relationships

The context of the relationship in which the sexual behaviour occurs defines the harmful or abusive or illegal nature of the act (Ryan et al., 1990). Faller (1990) reported that the degree of proximity in the offender–victim relationship will have a bearing on many aspects of the sexual abuse. For example, proximity will influence the frequency and duration of the abuse. Close relationships often allow extended access to the victim, compared to stranger assaults which are usually a single episode. She also identified offender strategies being linked to the relationship. For example, offenders in a close relationship will often rely on psychological manipulation of the child, such as appeals to the offenders need for affection—whereas more distant relationships may use force or the threat of it. The child's reaction to the abuse and potential disclosure are also linked to the offender–victim relationship, as is the non-abusive carers response.

Russell (1988) differentiated intra and extra-familial abuse as follows. She defined extra-familial child sexual abuse as *"one or more unwanted sexual experiences with persons unrelated by blood or marriage, ranging from petting (touching of breasts or genitals or attempts at such touching) to rape, before the victim turned 14 years of age, and completed or attempted forcible rape experiences from the ages of 14 to 17 years (inclusive)."* Extra-familial offenders maybe neighbours, friends of the family, or persons in a professional capacity, or occasionally, complete strangers. She defined intra-familial child sexual abuse as *"any kind of exploitive sexual contact that occurred between relatives, no matter how distant the relationship, before the victim turned 18 years old. Experiences involving sexual contact with a relative that were wanted and with a peer were regarded as non-exploitive, for example, sex play between cousins or siblings of approximately the same ages. An age difference of less than 5 years was the criterion for a peer relationship."* Intra-familial offenders are usually fathers, step-fathers, grandfathers, uncles, or siblings of their victims. Incest is usually thought of as any form of sexual activity that occurs between a child and an adult family member, extended family member, or family-like member. Legal statute defines incest as specific sexual acts, usually involving intercourse, occurring between persons who would not be allowed to marry. Another common definition says that incest occurs when a family member in a more powerful position or role attempts to satisfy a sexual need with another less powerful family member (Ingersoll and Patton, 1990).

Sexual offences are often perpetrated by someone very familiar to the victim. Elliott et al. (1995) found that 46 per cent of the sex offenders felt that a 'special relationship' with the child was vital. They found that 66 per cent knew their victims. Most sex offenders can be divided into three groups based on their relationship with the victim: family members, friends or acquaintances, and strangers.

- *Family members*: Waterhouse et al. (1993) found that 40 per cent of offenders were related to the victim. In their earlier research, Waterhouse and Carnie (1992) found that the offender was the natural father in 31 per cent of cases, step-fathers in 21 per cent of cases, and cohabitees in 11 per cent of cases. Kelly et al. (1991) found that close relatives (father-figures, siblings, grandfathers, uncles and aunts) offended in 14 per cent of cases, compared to 68 per cent perpetrated by distant relatives, known adults and peers. Oates (1990) found that in 75 per cent of cases the offender was known to the child and vice-versa. In 50 per cent of the cases, the offender was a member of the child's own family, whilst 50 per cent were trusted friends who had access to the children.
- *Friends or acquantancies*: Elliott et al. (1995) found that 66 per cent of offenders knew their victims through their families, friends or ac-quantancies, e.g., babysitting. Waterhouse et al. (1993) found that 60 per cent of the sex offenders in their sample were not biologically related to their victim.
- *Strangers*: The range of offenders unknown to the child pre-abuse ranges from 18 per cent (Kelly et al., 1991) through 25 per cent (Oates, 1990) to one-third (Elliott et al., 1995).

Whilst sexual abuse is an interactive behaviour, the responsibility lies entirely with the adult. Finkelhor (1979) preferred the term sexual vic-timisation to sexual abuse as it underscored that children become victims as a result of their age, naivete and relationship with the abusive adult.

Consent

This has been covered partially earlier in this chapter, but it is very important that we have a complete understanding of consent, a term which implies full knowledge, understanding and choice. Consent as agreement should include all of the following: understanding what is proposed based on age, maturity, developmental level, functioning and experience; knowledge of societal standards of what is being proposed; awareness of potential consequences and alternatives; assumption that agreement or disagreement will be respected equally; voluntary decision; and mental compet-ence (The National Task Force, 1993).

Consent is one of the key notions around which we organise the ethics of our social interactions. Finkelhor (1984) is very clearly of the view that children are incapable of truly consenting to sex with adults because they are children. He argues that for consent to truly occur, two conditions must prevail: a person must know what it is they are consenting to, and must have some true freedom to say yes or no. Children cannot fulfil these conditions in relation to sex with adults. For example, they lack the information necessary to make an 'informed' decision about the matter. They are ignorant about sex and sexual relationships. They are unaware of the social meanings of sexuality. They do not have the freedom to say yes or no as they are under the authority of an adult and therefore have no free will. As Groth (1979) has pointed out: although the young person may be sexually mature, they are not psychologically equipped to deal with sexual situations on an equal basis with an adult. Abel et al.. (1984) have gone further. They pointed out that in most cultures children have not yet had the opportunity to learn their cultural sexual standards. Without this information, is is very difficult for them to weigh the advantages and disadvantages of adult–child sexual activity. They argue that the advocates of sexual interactions between children and adults focus on consent in a simplistic fashion, i.e. they do not look beyond consent to see if it is informed.

It is equally important not to confuse co-operation with consent. Sometimes the strong needs of the child for physical affection, attention and dependence lead to the child's apparent complicity or willingness to initiate and maintain the abuse. In any relationship involving an adult and a child, the adult is always the responsible party, if for no other reason than because the adult is the larger and more powerful of the two. Any such power imbalance precludes consent. Sgroi (1989) has identified several barriers to consent: they are aged under 16 years; the presence of a parental, custodial, or caretaking relationship be-tween the persons involved; the use of a weapon, threat of injury, or use of force by the first person; the presence of a cognitive inability in the second person to understand the basic elements of sexual behaviours or the presence of a power imbalance between them which precludes consent by the weaker person.

In the UK, the age of consent provides us with a legal framework and refers to the notion that before this age, children cannot be held to consent to sexual activity (Gillham, 1996). In English law, this relates to sexual intercourse—either heterosexual, i.e. by a man over 16 with a girl aged 16 or less; or homosexual—i.e. by a man over 18 with a male under 18. The age of consent has varied over time and between countries. It is important for workers to differentiate legal from other definitions.

Abel et al. (1984) introduced the notion of variable consent into the equation. Here, a child, under certain conditions, might, if they have have already achieved the necessary requisites, be able to give consent prior to reaching the age of majority. It assumes that the child has a conscious mind (their mental functioning is not impaired), they are rational (not delusional), can accurately perceive the world and their place within it and they possess enough intelligence and experience to determine what is in their own best interest.

The child's specific vulnerability

Summit (1990) addressed himself to the various aspects of intrinsic, specific vulnerability of children in this equation. He argued that we can only comprehend the child's abject helplessness to deal with sexual abuse as we come to see our own determined avoidance on this issue. The following factors highlight the child's specific vulnerabilities:

Children are perfect victims: if only by virtue of size and power. They are not allowed to challenge the demands of responsible adults. To the naive adult, they cannot imagine that a child would not resist and would not tell, nor imagine the extraordinary gulf of power that a large person imposes on a child. To reverse this, we "... *need to risk painful empathy with the uniquely powerless position of the child as sex object ...*". Until people can make transitions, they are 'one-down to all offenders', who know already that they can overpower the child and the trusting adult.

Children are totally dependent on adults, without whom they cannot survive. They will therefore protect their access to the victim at any price, adapting tenaciously to any mysterious conditions that adults impose on that access. Secrecy is paradoxical to our habitual trust that a child would confide their deepest concerns to a loving parent. Children may assume that mothers should know everything and, therefore must know and not care. They may then become discredited by the child due to their ineffectual protection. The intruder, having broken the rules and got away with it, assumes a kind of divine authority, and the child becomes fearfully dependent on the offender's instructions. Where the child's need for love, attention, approval and affection are thwarted at home, they search for them elsewhere. Once abused, they may fall into the trap of believing the abuse is the only reliable anchor. We should not feel that sexual abuse of children only occurs in

dysfunctional families, as many children across all types and classes of family feel alienated in their family settings.

Children are vulnerable through heir intrinsic naivety. Their need to be taught renders them vulnerable to abuse and to a position of irrelevance, as if their ideas and feelings do not count. A victimised child is therefore in no position to teach us that we must suspect someone that we know to be trustworthy. Any detraction from this is viewed as dangerous to adult authority and may lead to mockery by their peers. Thus the child who discloses child sexual abuse infects the listener with a peculiar helplessness, with the ultimate threat of being disgraced.

Children are vulnerable through their imagination. They translate reality into playful games and fantasies. We often discredit unwelcome complaints despite research that shows that children tend to be accurate witnesses (Goodman, 1984). If they found the abuse painful to remember, they will dissociate themselves as a defence. The more severe the abuse, the most effective dissociation will occur. As an offender, many will learn to manipulate dissociation, in the knowledge that the more severe the invasion, the more immune they may become from detection.

Children are vulnerable because they are sexual. As they may have a physical response to the abuse, e.g. reflex erection, even though they may not like the abuse itself. Many can become confused by this, and may feel more guilty about it. It is a maxim amongst sex offenders that a boy will never tell if he has been stimulated to erection. They glory in the illusion that sex with children is both natural and healthy.

Children are vulnerable because of their innocence:
and
Children may become vulnerable as a result of their resemblance to the offender's particular obsession, where the child prototype is considered to fit a specific gender, age, shape and colour.

Offenders also have a tendency to target vulnerable children, e.g. handicapped (Sobsey and Mansell, 1994), those with a physical or learning difficulty (Craft, 1992) those in poor parenting situations and disorganised families, those previously victims to sexual abuse (Miller, 1978), as well as children who are not assertive or outgoing, and who are trusting or withdrawn (Renvoize, 1993). Sanderson (1990) pointed out that the offender can almost instinctively pick out vulnerable children, whilst ignoring those who might resist.

Conte et al. (1989) interviewed a sample of adult sex offenders who claimed a special ability to identify such vulnerable children, and to manipulate this vulnerability as a means of sexually using them. Vulnerability was defined in terms of children's status (e.g. living in a divorced home or being young), and in terms of emotional or psychological state (e.g. a needy child, a depressed or unhappy child). Regardless of their current targeting, we all need to acknowledge that ALL children have inherent vulnerabilities. The protection of children needs to include a strategy for making children less vulnerable, recognising that all the factors remain weighted on the side of the adult, e.g. superior knowledge level and skill which will not easily be overcome by children.

Elliott et al. (1995) found the following selection characteristics used by sex offenders:

- 42 per cent felt the child had to be pretty.
- 27 per cent cited the way the child dressed was important.
- 18 per cent reported being young or small was significant for them.
- 13 per cent focused on innocent or trusting children.
- 49 per cent reported an attraction to those who lacked confidence or had low self-esteem.

Typologies of sexual offenders

Typology is the study of a class or group that has common characteristics. Sex offender typologies can be helpful in distinguishing different groupings of offenders, recognising that there may be crossover between the different types of behaviour. Two problems with typologies is the tendency to fit a particular offender into a category that may not fit or failure to acknowledge that an offender may exhibit behaviours from two or more categories (Cumming and Buell, 1997).

Because of the heterogeneity of sexual offenders, typological frameworks have been attempted to construct homogeneous sub-groups and thus categorisations of sex offender. For example, there have been 'fixated, regressed and aggressive' (Cohen et al., 1969); the 'sex-force' and 'sex-pressure' offenders (Groth and Burgess, 1977); 'fixated' versus 'regressed' paedophilia (Groth et al., 1982), and 'preferential' versus 'situational' offenders (Deitz, 1983). These are discussed in more detail below.

'Fixated, regressed and aggressive'

Here, the authors proposed that the fixated offender prefers the company of children, and seeks those that are known to them. The regressed offender has some adult heterosexual interest, but also has feelings of inadequacy, and may react to a child following a threat to his masculinity. The aggressive type engages in sadistic acts, usually with boys.

'Sex-force', 'sex-pressure' offenders

Groth and Burgess proposed a typology, which emphasised the non-sexual motives of the offender. The sex-force offender uses coercion or physical force and is either exploitive, using the child for sexual relief without any further relationship, or sadistic, obtaining pleasure from hurting and humiliating the child. The sex-pressure offender feels safer with children, and adopts enticement or persuasion with the child.

'Fixated' and 'regressed' paedophiles

In our assessment work, we need to make a determination as to whether the offender's socio-sexual development was 'fixated' (stopped or arrested) during their childhood, adolescence or early adulthood, or whether their primary socio-sexual interest had been with age-mates until their response to an identifiable stressor caused them to 'regress' to an earlier stage of development where functioning in the world was manageable. The term 'regressed' refers to an emotional regression. It occurs when an individual who has developed normally (emotionally) to a given point reverts to an earlier point of development that was in some way more comfortable or more secure than the age-appropriate developmental level. This type of offender tends to be deeply affected by interpersonal dynamics, especially family dynamics. As such, the latter play an important role in determining the situational precursors to the offence.

Sgroi (1982) provided the following framework to distinguish between the two:

- Regressed offenders primary sexual orientation is to age-mates compared to children with the fixated offender.
- Paedophilic interests of the regressed offender emerge in adulthood, whilst those of the fixated offender emerge in adolescence.
- For the regressed offender, a precipitating stressor is usually evident or identifiable, whilst there is no precipitating stressor with the fixated offender.
- For the regressed offender, sexually abusive acts may be episodic, compared to the persistence of paedophilic interest in the fixated offender.
- For the regressed offender, the initial offence may be impulsive; whilst for the fixated offender the sexual offence is pre-planned.
- The regressed offender substitutes the child for a peer, whilst the fixated offender identifies with the child victim.
- The regressed offender's primary targets are opposite-sex victims; the fixated offender's primary targets are same-sex victims.
- For the regressed offender, sexual contact with a child occur concurrent with sexual contact with age-mates; for the fixated offender there is little or no sexual contact with age-mates.
- The regressed offender tends to focus on his or her own sexual arousal and satisfaction, whilst the fixated offender tends to seek sexual arousal on the part of the child victim.
- For the regressed offender, the offence is more likely to be alcohol-related than for the fixated offender. The latter doesn't usually use either alcohol or drugs.

- The regressed offender is likely to lead a fairly traditional lifestyle, but have poorly developed peer relationships. The fixated offender exhibits chronic immaturity.
- The regressed offender offends as a response to an overwhelming life stress, whilst the fixated offender offends in response to developmental life issues.

'Situational' and 'preferential' offenders

Deitz (1983) developed this typology in order to help workers recognise, arrest and convict offenders who have sex with children. This 'law-enforcement' typology is not geared towards gaining any insight or understanding of why offenders have sex with children in order to help or treat them.

The situational offender does not have a true sexual preference for children, but engages in sex with them for varied and sometimes complex reasons. They may commit 'once in a lifetime' offences up to long-term patterns of behaviour. They usually have fewer victims, who are usually vulnerable individuals, such as the sick or disabled. Within this category, at least 4 major patterns of behaviour emerge:

- *Regressed*: They have low self-esteem and poor coping skills, and turn to children as a sexual substitute for the preferred peer sex partner. The main victim criterion is availability, hence the abuse of their own children.
- *Morally indiscriminate*: The sexual abuse of children is simply part of a general pattern of abuse in their lives. They use and abuse people. They lie, cheat and do anything they think they can get away with. Victims are chosen due to both vulnerability as well as opportunity. They are often their own children, acquaintances or strangers.
- *Sexually indiscriminate*: Such as those who experiment sexually, e.g. bondage or sado-masochism. This is his motivator. Children will be different and new to them, and may extend to group sex, swapping children, etc.
- *Inadequate*: Describes those who are suffering from psychoses and mental retardation. They engage in sex with children out of insecurity or curiosity. They may take out their problems on their victims, and this can be exceptionally cruel.

The preferential sex offender has a definite sexual preference for children: they are sexually aroused by them. They have a predictable and highly worrying pattern of behaviour, including the need for sex frequently and repeatedly. Within this category, three major patterns of behaviour occur:

- *Seduction*: Courting the child with attention, affection, and gifts over a period of time by gradually lowering their sexual inhibitions. They are often involved simultaneously with several victims. They are able to identify with children and are able to listen to them.
- *Introverted*: Describes the offender who has a preference for children but lacks the interpersonal skills necessary to seduce them. He thus molests either very young children or strangers, and may use child prostitutes. He can hang around playgrounds and other areas where children congregate, watching them, or marry someone with young children.
- *Sadistic*: Describes the offender who has a sexual preference for children but who, in order to be aroused or gratified, must inflict pain or suffering on the child victim. They may murder their victims.

Tomison (1995) has argued that these typologies are crude and unreliable due to the extensive overlap of various behaviours by offenders. Epps (1996) also argued that they often involve an over-simplification of existing data, although they can be helpful to workers when having to choose between various forms of disposal and treatment options. Willis (1993) proposed a more accurate model based on previous categorisations such that offenders are categorised according to their preferences on three scales: fixated versus regressed paedophilia, preferential versus situational offending, and homosexual versus heterosexual offending. In this model, those more strongly associated with the first term of each factor would most closely resemble a 'paedophile' profile, while those regressed, situational, heterosexual offenders would be more likely to be intra-familial offenders, and may be more accessible to changing their abusive behaviour.

The most recent typology has been developed by Knight and Prentky (1990). The MTC: CM3 typology consists of two axes. The first axis involves a dichotomous rating on two dimensions, degree of fixation and social competence, giving rise to four sub-groupings. The second axis refers to the amount of contact with children, and involves further sequential decisions according to the context, the amount of physical injury, and the meaning of aggression to the offender. The classification system is obviously complex and is currently undergoing external validation. It offers an informed way forward.

MacHovec and Wieckowski (1992) have developed a ten-factor continual/treatment model as a way to classify and categorise sex offenders. The ten factors in the classification system are physical aggression, fantasy, asocialisation, sexual arousal, offence cycle, cognitive distortions, denial-minimisation, remorse–empathy, and prognosis for further work. Also included in this assessment is victim gender, victim age, specific sexual offences, kind of contact, other deviant behaviours and other treatment issues.

For a more detailed review of sex offender typologies and characteristics, see Schwartz and Cellini (1995).

Sexual offending

The term sex offender implies a homogeneous group of individuals, yet we know that sexual offenders do not neatly fit into categories, and thus a continuum of behaviours is often a preferred method of definition. There are also as many definitions of sex offenders as there are individuals doing the defining. Schwartz (1995) noted that the definition of sex offenders is shaped largely by the sexual mores of the times. An act may be defined as a sex crime depending on the degree of consent of the partner, his/her age, kinship, sex, the nature of the act, the offender's intention, or the setting. A behaviour that in itself may be considered perfectly normal can become a serious criminal offence if it violates any of the above qualifiers.

Many feminists see sexual offending behaviour along a continuum of 'normal' male behaviour, with such offending representing one of the most extreme consequences of the socialisation of boys and men. Sexual offending is seen as a means of assuring them of their male identity as well as serving as a method of social control via the maintenance of unequal gender relations (see Chapter 4 for a further discussion).

The term 'offending' is a legal concept that refers to any sexual behaviour prohibited by law. Whilst this term implies that a criminal conviction will have been secured, it is widely recognised that many sexual assaults remain unreported, and many of these that are do not secure a successful criminal outcome. Just because allegations from a child are believed, this does not equate with legal proof that abuse has taken place. Only 2 per cent of allegations are found to be untrue (Jones, 1985), whilst close to one-third of allegations are falsely retracted (Sahd, 1980). Additional factors that inhibit successful criminal outcomes include a lack of corroborative evidence, the age of the child and the stress of participating in any criminal forum. Convicted sex offenders whose victims are children under 18 years assume the 'Schedule One' status for life (a list is included as an Appendix to Chapter 7). At the present time, Clause 3 of the Sex Offenders Act (1997) defines a sex offender as a person who:

- Has been convicted of a sexual offence to which **Part 1 of the Sex Offenders Act [1997]** applies.
- Has been found not guilty of such an offence by reason of insanity, or found to be under a disability and has done the act charged against him in respect of such an offence.
- Has been cautioned by a Constable, in England, Wales or Northern Ireland, in respect of such an offence which, at the time when the caution was given, he had admitted or

- Has been punished under the law in force in a country or territory outside the United kingdom for an act which:
    (i) constituted an offence under the law and
    (ii) would have constituted a sexual offence to which that part applies if it had been done in any part of the United Kingdom.

This definition further highlights the need for a broader definition of sexual offending to embrace all the behaviours that result in sexual abuse (see Morrison et al., 1994) and this is adopted by us in this text to open up the assessment framework to the widest catchment of adult males who commit sexual abuse on children and young people.

Summary

Definition: what's in a name?

None of the definitions referred to in this chapter are adequate in themselves, but taken collectively may serve as a useful baseline for workers. Sexual abuse is very difficult to categorise and define. It has been used to describe a range of experiences from witnessing a single instance of self-exposure at one extreme, to repeated and coercive sexual intercourse at the other. Over the last decade, the description and classification has become more complicated as further contexts and characteristics have been identified, such as professional abuse (see Calder 1992; 1998), and abuse by juveniles (see Calder, 1997; Calder, forthcoming).

Despite these observations, it is quite important to succeed in defining the concept as it carries with it implications for solutions to the problem, and more specifically determines which acts are dealt with, and in what ways (Haugaard and Reppucci, 1988). The task of communicating about an issue remains much more difficult when the same term does not convey identical meaning across professionals and in the local community. Kelly et al. (1995) have argued that the search for a universally-agreed definition is a fruitless task, whilst O'Hagan (1989) has argued that it may be far more practical to have **no** definition and retain a healthy discriminatory approach to each recorded experience. Mayers et al. (1992) then suggested that it may be more appropriate for professionals to be more aware of the differences between the professions, and an effort should be made to use specific descriptions of acts and agents, rather than the blanket term of sexual abuse.

As a closing position, I favour a broad and encompassing definition of both sexual abuse as well as sexual offending—as this ensures that we alert ourselves to the widespread nature of these abusive experiences. The definition from Drauke (1992) is useful for this purpose:

"*. . . any exploitative sexual activity, whether or not it involves physical contact, between a child and another person who by virtue of his or her power over the child due to age, strength, position, or relationship uses the child to meet his or her sexual and emotional needs . . .*"

Appendix

Paedophilia is a flexible concept, and there is an ongoing debate about its usage (see Kelly et al., 1995). Becker and Kaplan (1988) define it as "*adults whose preferred or exclusive method of achieving sexual excitement is in the act of fantasy of engaging in sexual activity with pre-pubescent children (generally age 13 or younger). The difference in age between the adult (who must be at least 16 years of age) and the pre-pubescent child is at least 5 years. For late adolescents with this disorder, no precise age difference is specified*".

Hebephiles are those who find themselves sexually attracted to young teenagers or adolescents. It is a term rarely used today.

The term paraphilia literally means 'substitute love' (Schwartz, 1985). John Money (1986) defined it as "*an erotic sexual condition of being recurrently responsive to, and obsessively dependent on, an unusual, personally or socially acceptable stimulus, perceptual or in fantasy, in order to have a state of erotic arousal initiated or maintained, and in order to achieve or facilitate orgasm*". Paraphilic imagery may be replayed in fantasy during solitary masturbation or intercourse with a partner. Recurrence is usually over six months. Whilst some sex offenders have multiple paraphilias (averaging 3–4), (Marshall and Eccles, 1991), some inappropriate sexual behaviour is not always characterised as a paraphilia. Indeed, isolated acts can be precipitated by mental problems, illness, or loneliness (Becker and Kaplan, 1988).

For an excellent dictionary of relevant terms, the reader is referred to Money (1986).

Chapter 4
Causation: an overview

The importance of theory

Many theories over the years have attempted to explain the causes of sexual offending. Such theories have tried to explain it as an individual, a family, a community (cultural) or as a societal problem. Given the breadth and increasing complexity of the problem, it is highly unlikely that a single theory can ever fully explain the origins and cause of the sexually abusive behaviour, yet they are helpful when considered in combinations. This chapter does not pretend it can do justice to the growing amount of literature relating to a theoretical understanding of sexual offending, and the reader is referred to the following if they wish to read about the issue in more detail: Lanyon, 1991; Li et al., 1990; Marshall and Barbaree, 1990; Sanderson, 1990; Schwartz, 1995. What this chapter does aim to achieve is to inform the reader about the key theories and provide a very selective flavour about what they say.

As Epps (forthcoming) has pointed out, the test of any theory is its usefulness. A useful theory is one that accounts for all the data and promotes research which, in turn, leads to further theoretical development. At the present time there is a shift in thinking, away from single-theory models towards integrated models which are able to explain more fully the diversity of sexual offending. This is important when we accept that there is no 'typical' sex offender.

In common with many other areas of scientific investigation, research has given rise to competing theories, each with its own terminology and assumptions. As Epps indicated: *"At the most simple level, a sexual offence can be construed as an interaction between the offender and the victim, in a particular situation, at a specific moment in time, associated with certain behaviours, thoughts and feelings in the offender. However, explaining why these events took place is fraught with difficulty ... Proving that one event (e.g. a particular thought) 'caused' another (e.g. a particular behaviour) is difficult. Usually there are 'hidden' variables that mediate between events. The situation becomes even more complex when events are separated by a long period of time. Rather [we] talk in terms of an 'association' between events (e.g. an association between childhood sexual abuse and ... sexual offending) and to statistically demonstrate the strength of the association through empirical research."*

In order to intervene effectively in cases of child sexual abuse, workers must have some clear and up-to-date understanding of why adults sexually abuse children. Even with some grounding in our current knowledge base, there are as many unknowns as there are knowns. Knowledge is an essential source for workers endeavouring to counter offender power: we need to ensure the offender is only one and not two or more steps ahead of us.

Our knowledge of child sexual abuse and sexual offending derives mostly from those cases that come to our attention, yet we know that most offenders who are detected and processed through the system come from the less socially advantaged groups. Hughes and Parker (1994) identified several reasons why child sexual abuse from the more affluent end of our class system are not investigated. These include the considerable ability well-dressed, articulate offenders have in avoiding detection and the few referrals of this group to social services or the police. This needs to change if children from more affluent backgrounds are to receive the protection they deserve.

What is consistently clear is that sex offenders do not present as remarkably different from others with social, personal or behavioural difficulties, except in the nature of their offending, rendering detection remarkably difficult (Willis, 1993). Wyre (1994) has noted that many sex offenders are outwardly respectable men who don't resemble 'monsters'. Indeed, 'monsters' don't get near children—'nice men' do. Pringle (1993) found that most research finds offenders functioning as 'normal' and heterosexual members of society, often in mature and stable relationships. They usually have the same emotional and psychological profile as people who do not abuse. Many of us entertain abusive thoughts, yet we restrain ourselves from acting on them. Briere and Runtz (1989) found that some 21 per cent of college males reported having some sexual attraction to children. Of these, 14 per cent reported that they would not go on to abuse, whereas 7 per cent indicated that they may act on their attraction if they could be sure that the matter would not be detected or punished.

Single factor models

Despite the limitations of each single-factor theory, each one does make a useful contribution to understanding at least some types of sexual offending. As Epps (forthcoming) points out, all behaviour is mediated through the brain and involves an interaction between the individual and the environment. Some theories have more to say about what happens inside the individual (internal factors), at either a biological level (genetics, brain and body chemistry) or psychological level (conscious and unconscious thoughts, fantasies, and feelings). Other theories are more concerned with what happens outside the individual (external, 'environmental' factors) and the effect these experiences have on thinking, feeling and behaviour. Through various learning processes human behaviour is especially open to influence from external sources.

Biological (or medical) theories

Several theories consider the possibility that some type of genetic, hormonal, chromosomal, or neurological biological process is responsible for sexual offending behaviour.

Genetic (inherited) factors have been linked to sexual offending behaviour. Some feel that the XXY chromosome pattern is related to offending behaviour given that the majority of sex offenders are male, and the 'Y' chromosome differentiates males from females and determines male characteristics, including testosterone. Rada (1978) found that offenders judged to be the most violent had higher testosterone levels, and there are several psycho-pharmocological treatments in existence, designed to reduce the sexual libido by reducing testosterone levels. The presence of an extra 'Y' chromosome has also been linked to criminal and sexual offending behaviour (Day, 1993), although the evidence remains inconclusive.

Money (1965) has argued that testosterone is the 'fuel' that drives sexual behaviour. The available data does not entirely support this argument. Heim and Hursch (1979) found that of 39 released sex offenders who agreed to voluntary castration, 31 per cent reported continued ability to engage in sexual intercourse.

Money's lovemap theory (1986; 1989) postulates that sexual interests are 'imprinted' in the brain the same way as language. As such, men with paraphilias are men with vandalised lovemaps analogous to aphasic men with strokes.

Other researchers have indicated that organic dysfunction related to epilepsy or head injuries have a bearing on sexual behaviour (Radzinowicz, 1967). Miller et al. (1986) described eight cases of either hyper-sexuality or altered sexual preference after injury to the brain. Indeed, changes in the brain chemistry may also influence the existence of intrusive, recurrent sexual fantasies (Prentky and Burgess, 1991). Lilly et al. (1983) reported that bilateral, temporal lobe dysfunction results in altered sexual orientation. Bradford (1985) suggested that changes in neurotransmitters might have an impact on sexual behaviour, and that offenders may have genetic abnormalities, which they inherit and points them towards that pattern of behaviour.

Federoff and Moran (1997) explored whether sex offenders are sex maniacs. They note that sex drive is a powerful determinant of sexual behaviour, yet it is only one of many biological drives. They also note that the drive to engage in sexual activity quickly plateaus and then decreases dramatically with increasing deprivation from sexual activity. In addition, consummated sexual activity is extremely satiating for males, and few men are capable of multiple orgasms.

Are sex offenders mentally ill? This is an ongoing debate. The general public do often believe that sexual offenders are 'weirdos', 'perverts' or 'mad'. Although the addiction model frames sexual offending as an illness, Knopp (1984) found that only 8 per cent had a known psychotic illness. Briggs (1994b) reported from a survey of sex offenders in Rampton's Special Hospital that 88 per cent suffered from a psychopathic disorder. Whilst Serin et al. (1994) noted a link between psychopathy and deviant sexual arousal, Barbaree and Marshall (1989) found that intra-familial offenders tend to have less extreme deviant sexual arousal.

I believe that it would be wrong to frame sex offending as a consequence of sickness as this allows the community to frame offenders as 'exceptions' rather than 'the rule', and this makes it easier for the offender themselves who are absolved of any responsibility (Hudson, 1992). The offender can attribute blame to a deficient part of himself over which they have little influence (Jenkins, 1990). It then becomes the job of others to take responsibility and 'cure' him. It is also not practical to identify sex offenders simply by medical testing.

As all behaviour has biological roots, it seems reasonable to speculate that biological factors play an indirect role in some sexual offences. The limitations lie in the fact that it describes static characteristics rather than exploring the ways in which the client interacts with others. For an excellent review of the medical models of sexual deviance, please refer to Grubin and Mathews (1997).

Psychoanalytical theories

Freud suggested that in the course of development, all people find children sexually attractive and need to be 'weaned' away from such perverse attractions by social conditioning and repression (Freud, 1901; 1905). He viewed paedophilia as a form of neurosis, a regression to infantile sexuality or to a phallic stage of development, which results in unresolved Oedipal conflicts.

Freud argued that our behaviour is the product of inner drives and forces (especially 'sexual drive' and 'aggressive drive') which develop during early childhood and become 'fixed' around the age of five years. Those individuals who have experienced distressing events often employ defence mechanisms in order to shield themselves from their memories, although they remain sub-consciously. Such defence mechanisms are contributory to the development and maintenance of sexually offensive behaviour (e.g. denial, projection) through the use of cognitive distortions. Quite apart from experience, sexually offensive thoughts and behaviour may be the product of 'castration anxiety' or a poorly developed superego. In 'castration anxiety', Freud theorised that young males who learn about gender differences (usually in the Oedipal stage), they conclude that their jealous fathers have cut their penises off. In fear, they decide not to compete with their fathers themselves for their mother's attention. Unresolved at this stage, they go on to develop an adversity to females, and can sexually abuse other males or rape females to reassure themselves of the power of their own organ. With the poorly developed superego, they relate to others partially as genitals rather than as a whole individual.

The importance of psychoanalytic theory lies in the recognition of childhood sexuality and early trauma, yet it remains woefully inadequate as an account for child sexual abuse.

Behavioural theories

Behavioural theory sees the external environment as the determining factor of behaviour. McGuire et al. (1965) suggested that some sexual offences are the direct result of sexually deviant behaviours that have been classically conditioned through direct experience, and reinforced through fantasy and masturbation. The learning takes place as part of an initial seduction, which supplies a basic fantasy. If this seduction is deviant in nature, it is reinforced during each masturbation and may gradually become distorted and develop into more bizarre fantasies. Sexual deviation can occur from classic conditioning in which a repetitious or traumatic pairing of sexuality and some negative experience, produces some type of intensive emotional response that distorts subsequent sexual gratification. The cause may be childhood sexual abuse (Schwartz, 1995). Operant conditioning may contribute to the learning of sexually deviant behaviour. For example, a child who is repeatedly abused and brought to orgasm will have that type of sexual conduct powerfully reinforced. As an adult, they may only be able to become sexually aroused by replaying such an experience. Modelling offending behaviour (following observation) may also contribute to the development of sexually deviant behaviour.

Cognitive behavioural theories

Cognition refers to a wide range of mental structures, processes and products, including perceptions, appraisals, beliefs, attitudes, memories, goals, standards and values, expectations, and attributions, in addition to current thoughts and self-statements (Epps, forthcoming). Cognitive functioning is to some extent determined by inherent factors (e.g. temperament and intellectual ability) and past learning (e.g. encouragement for achieving goals).

Cognitive theory is based on the assumption that an individual's thought processes, beliefs, and styles of thinking have a direct influence on emotions and behaviour and should therefore be the focus of intervention.

Theorists here explore how thoughts mitigate actions. Sex offenders may initially set up negative emotional states by interpreting experiences in a negative way. They manage the effects of these by preoccupying themselves with deviant fantasies. When the fantasies (or the transformation into actual behaviour) become difficult for them to manage, they employ cognitive distortions as a mechanism of self-justification, which inevitably leads to a repetition of the behaviour and an entrenchment of the problem.

The aim of any assessment is to identify the meaning of the sexually abusive behaviour and the extent to which it is rewarding to the offender. Relapse prevention is a cognitive behavioural technique that allows us to focus on the individual offence pattern and thus allows us to develop interventions designed to help manage any repetition. Individuals are held responsible for regulating their own thoughts, feelings and behaviour (Marlatt and Gordon, 1985).

Container theories

Jenkins (1990) argued that these explanations speculate that offenders store up or accumulate emotions such as frustration, tension, anger or sexual arousal, in response to environmental stressors or cues, until a certain threshold is reached, whereupon an explosion occurs. These explanations are deficient as they propose a passive process by which the offender is acted upon by factors, such as stress, in his environment. The filling of the container and the offence are attributed to external environmental factors (e.g. financial pressures) over which he has no influence. He thus cannot see that he has any responsibility for the filling up of his container, let alone his sexual offending behaviour.

Addiction theory

There is now almost a professional consensus that sexual offending should be viewed as an addictive problem, with a high probability of recidivism in the absence of comprehensive treatment of the problem. Sexual addiction is correlated with more than half of all sexual crimes (Blanchard, 1995). A continuum of sexual behaviour was explored by Patrick Carnes in the 1980s as he attempted to identify and treat sex offenders using the 12 step model previously associated in work with alcoholics. He did so as he became increasingly aware that there was an overlap between the addiction to drugs and alcohol, and sexual behaviour. He defined sexual addiction as a *"the substitution of a sick relationship to an event or process for a healthy relationship"* (Carnes, 1983). Sex addicts subscribe to a set of core beliefs that distort reality. They believe that sex is the most important thing in their life—their only source of nurturance, the origin of their excitement, the remedy for pain, and their reason for being.

Carnes identified a 4 step cycle which the sex addict passes through, and which intensifies with each repetition:

- *Preoccupation*: The trance or mood wherein the addict's mind is completely engrossed with thoughts of sex. This mental state creates an obsessive search for sexual stimulation.
- *Ritualisation*: The addict's own special routine which leads up to sexual behaviour. The ritual intensifies the preoccupation and ritualisation, thus adding arousal and excitement.
- *Compulsive sexual behaviour*: The actual sexual act, which is the end goal of the preoccupation and ritualisation. Sexual addicts are unable to control or stop their behaviour.
- *Despair*: The feeling of utter hopelessness addicts have about their behaviour and their powerlessness. While they experience despair, guilt and remorse, this rarely leads to reformation as it leads to an escape back into the addictive cycle.

Carnes indicated that there are three levels of addicted sexual behaviour:

- *Level one behaviours* such as masturbation, the use of pornography, and resorting to prostitution. These are generally tolerated by the public (as they exclude victims), but can be devastating when indulged in by the addict compulsively or publicly.
- *Level two behaviours* such as exhibitionism, voyeurism, indecent phone calls, and indecent sexual suggestions and touching. These have consequences for the victim, and usually involve legal sanctions.
- *Level three behaviours* such as rape, incest and child molesting. These represent profound violations of cultural boundaries.

Carnes (1990) outlined several characteristics that appear to be common to sexual addicts:

- The addictive cycle involves a variety of behaviours that form a pattern involving different levels of addiction (see previous section). Addicts can be compulsive at either one or at several levels, although they usually engage in multiple forms of sexual compulsiveness.
- Other addictions co-exist and become an intrinsic part of the sexual addiction. The most common concurrent addiction is dependence on alcohol or drugs. The co-addictive system parallels the process of the addictive system.
- The role of the family of origin and current family dynamics are important, particularly where addictive patterns of other family members as well as co-participation in the sexual addicts' behaviour support the addictive cycle.

Carnes went on to offer a 15 point code for use in the diagnosis of sex addiction:

Presence of five or more of the following:

- Sexual obsession and fantasy is a primary coping strategy.
- Sexual behaviour is a central organising principle of their daily life.
- Inordinate amounts of time are spent in obtaining sex, being sexual, or recovering from the sexual experience.
- The amount, extent, or duration of sexual behaviour often exceeds what the person intended.
- Severe mood shifts around sexual acting out are noted.
- There is an escalating pattern of increasing amounts of sexual experience because the current level of activity is no longer sufficient.
- Persistent pursuit of self-destructive or high-risk sexual behaviour.
- Persistent desire or efforts to limit sexual behaviour.
- Pattern of out-of-control (compulsive) sexual behaviour for two years.
- Inability to stop behaviour despite adverse consequences.
- Pattern of alternating excessive control and out-of-control behaviour over five years.
- Severe consequence due to sexual behaviour.
- Presence of clear hierarchy of sexual acting out behaviours.
- Important social, occupational, or recreational activities sacrificed or reduced because of sexual behaviour

The presence of any three of the following associated conditions:

- Extreme sexual shame.
- Depression.
- Other addictions.
- Has been or is currently victim of sexual abuse.
- Suicidal ideation or attempt.
- Presence of sex-negative behaviour.
- Excessive reliance on denial.
- Presence of co-dependent personality disorder.
- Has been or is a victim of emotional or physical abuse.
- Secret or 'double life' due to sexual behaviour.
- Sexualising or nurturing, and
- Few or no non-sexual relationships (Carnes, 1990).

Not all sexual offenders demonstrate sexual addiction, just as not all sex addicts commit criminal sexual offences. For a comprehensive review of sexual addiction, please refer to Carnes (1983; 1990; 1991) and Earle and Earle (1995).

Recovery from addiction requires the offender to admit his behaviour and to concede that he is powerless to overcome it alone. The very admission of the problem removes the secrecy, which can significantly contribute to the excitement.

One criticism of the addiction model is that it implies impulsive reactions leading to offending, whereas there is ample evidence to highlight the careful planning of sexual offences. A further feminist concern over the addiction model is that *"the currently fashionable description of abusers as addicted may reinforce rather than challenge their notion of being out of control"* (MacLeod and Saraga, 1991).

Family theories

There are a variety of family theories, which have contributed to our understanding of sexual offending. Each explains sexual offending differently! Some theories focus on the current family (e.g husband–wife relationship in the incest family) while others focus on the family of origin. Some family variables clearly have a direct influence on the development of sexual offending behaviour. For example, being sexually abused by family members, witnessing others being abused, or being exposed to pornography. Other indirect effects include family breakdown leading to blurred family roles and boundaries, marital violence and physical abuse, poor care and neglect, and lack of parental supervision (Epps, forthcoming). Theories also differ in whether they emphasise the pathology of the individual within a family or the pathology of the family system. It is possible that different clusters of family factors are associated with different types of sexual offending.

In the family dysfunction approach, child sexual abuse is seen as a symptom of 'dysfunctional families' (the result of a particular pattern of relationships), rather than as something that arises from any one individual (Kidd and Pringle, 1988). With the breakdown of the parental relationship as the central factor, the withdrawal of sex or general family servicing by the mother, is seen to precipitate the drawing of the eldest daughter into an inappropriate role that may well involve sex with the father. Such an approach views the family members as contributing to the abuse taking place, consciously or otherwise. They arguably have some investment and reward for it and this allows an unhealthy balance to be maintained. Bentovim et al. (1988) published a book from within the family dysfunction position, and which should be referred to for a fuller understanding of their philosophy. They suggest that certain patterns of family life are closely associated with the occurrence of child sexual abuse. They identify two patterns: very

chaotic families and very rigid families. The attraction of this model is that it suggests that sexually abusive families can thus be identified easily.

I believe that the family dysfunction model is fundamentally flawed in key areas. The family becomes dysfunctional as a result of the abuse and is not the cause of it, and it cannot explain the high level of crossover between intra and extra-familial abuse. Other criticisms of this approach include: it does not account for many dysfunctional families who have absolutely no urge to sexually abuse their children (Tonkin, 1988); it has a tendency to absolve the offender (Wilson, 1990); whilst blaming the mother (MacLeod and Saraga, 1988): whilst accommodating the distorted 'cycle of abuse' theory where offenders have accepted some (conditional) responsibility for their offences; whilst feeding incorrect assumptions about the incidence and prevalence of sexual abuse in black families, who are frequently framed as dysfunctional; and seeing that the cure lies in the strengthening of the family, thus leading to a more positive view of family rehabilitation (Kidd and Pringle, 1988). Systems theory thus appears to offer too simplistic and irresponsible an explanation for child sexual abuse and sexual offending.

Trauma theory

Tower (1989) advised us to consider the following variables in assessing the degree of trauma to a child: the type of abuse; the identity of the offender; the duration of the abuse; the extent of the abuse; the age at which the child was abused; the first reactions of significant others at disclosure; the point at which the abuse was disclosed; and the personality structure of the victim. There are those who link early trauma (such as being abused or witnessing extreme violence) with sexual offending behaviour. These explanations include simple re-enactment of the abuse, through social learning and modelling; that abusive acts are an attempt to achieve mastery over conflicts about sexuality resulting from negative sexual experiences; and that sexual arousal becomes conditioned to sexually abusive fantasies as a result of past abusive experiences which, in turn, lead to sexually abusive behaviour (Epps, forthcoming). The '*traumagenic dynamics*' model developed by Finkelhor and colleagues (Finkelhor, 1984; Finkelhor and Browne, 1986) has been particularly useful in understanding the psychological effects of sexual abuse and their relationship to sexual offending behaviour. Within this model the consequences of sexual abuse are examined under four headings: traumatic sexualization, powerlessness, betrayal, and stigmatisation. Of these, the notion of traumatic sexualization has most relevance to understanding the progression from victim to offender. This refers to the process in which abusive experiences are re-enacted cognitively (e.g. 'flashbacks') and behaviourally (e.g. engaging other children in sexual acts). Preoccupation with sexual behaviour, combined with a desire to gain control over distressing feelings of fear and helplessness, may lead the offender to victimise children, placing himself in the powerful offender role rather than the helpless victim role ('identification with the aggressor').

However, whilst trauma clearly plays an important role in the development of sexual offending behaviour in some individuals, it is unlikely to account for all sexual offending. Many sex offenders seem not to have experienced significant trauma and research is consistent in showing that many sex offenders have not been sexually abused.

The cycle of abuse

In its simplest, and most common form, the 'cycle of abuse' proposes that if you are abused as a child you will in turn abuse others. Gocke (1991) reported that early theorists such as Stoller (1975) suggested that people who have been abused in childhood are so damaged developmentally that, in an attempt to overcome the trauma, they become the abusers of the next generation. Oliver and Taylor (1971) provide a striking illustration of this with the discovery of physical abuse that ran through at least five generations of the same family. However, cycles of abuse are not the norm. The current estimate is that 10–15 per cent of the male population are victimised as children (Peters et al., 1986), yet it is highly unlikely that this percentage go on to become sex offenders. Examination of the percentage of offenders themselves who are also victims casts doubt on the role of prior victimisation in the aetiology of sex offending. Hanson and Slater (1988), in a review of 18 studies that reported rates of victimisation among offenders, found rates from 0–70 per cent. Most importantly, they found that as the sample size increased, so the rate tended to stabilise between 20–30 per cent. Although this is higher than the general population, this is much lower than in much of the literature. However, offenders who are victims may be different. Hanson (1991) found that a history of sexual abuse was associated with higher levels of overall sexual deviancy, increased psychological disturbances, and increased likelihood of coming from more dysfunctional families.

If we turn to the gendered distribution of sexual victimisation and offending, the proposition begins to fall apart. We know that girls are between three and six times more likely to experience sexual abuse, yet the vast majority of sexual abuse is perpetrated by males. If there is any kind of cycle it is a gendered one, and that in turn requires explanation (Kelly et al., 1995). Indeed, *"even if we limit our focus to offenders the data here is also equivocal. No study has yet demonstrated that there is an obvious 'cycle' even within samples of convicted offenders: the range of those reporting experiences of abuse in childhood varies between 30–80 per cent. Alongside these glaring problems in evidential support for the proposition, there is seldom any exploration of the precise mechanisms involved whereby those who have been victimised become victimisers, since this is not simple repetition, but a reversal of roles.'* Thus, rather than being an accurate theory, this popular perspective has acute limitations. The problem is that 'breaking cycles' is much easier than changing the structure of social relations, so there is some way to go before it is relegated from being a popular, neat and highly accessible concept.

For a fuller discussion of the issues, the reader is referred to Beck-Sander (1995); Buchanan (1996); Federoff and Pinkus (1996); Federoff and Moran (1997); Garland and Dougher (1996); Gilgun (1991); Kelly (1996); Romano and De Luca (1997); Sinason (1996); and Widom (1989).

Cycles of behaviour

Most (but not all) offenders do have a cycle of behaviour, which may go from masturbatory fantasy to contact with the victim. Each cycle is unique, which, if identified, allows work to focus on how it can best be interrupted and managed. Offenders can identify the points at which they are able to control and divert their thoughts and actions and consequently avoid offending. Workers need to understand that the stages are not necessarily distinct, and the sequence is not rigid: there is considerable overlap between the stages and smaller, repetitive cycles operate within the longer cycle. The length of the cycle may vary, and this is important as the frequency is an important indicator of risk. Offenders can travel through their cycle in a matter of hours, or it may take a few weeks or even years for others to reach the point of re-offending. The cyclical nature of the behaviour reinforces that it is continuous unless challenged.

Wolf (1984) provided a theory of the cycle of offending which links factors known frequently to occur in the lives of individuals identified as sexually deviant. His paper builds on earlier research to suggest a comprehensive model to explain (in part) the development and maintenance of sexually deviant orientations. His hypothesis is that there exists a positive and increasing relationship between specific environmental and developmental experiences and the acquisition and maintenance of sexual deviance. He describes a multi-dimensional model linking factors known frequently to occur in the lives of individuals identified as sexually deviant and a learning model describing the relationship between inhibition and deviant arousal.

Wolf identified a category of 'potentiators' which simplistically relate early experiences of offenders influencing their later attitudes and behaviour. The range of the latter includes witnessing sexual violence or abuse, family dysfunction, isolation, or a victim themselves from some kind of violence or abuse. He found that this group of offenders experienced significant abuse and deprivation at a rate approximately twice that of the general population. These potentiators seem to have a direct impact on the form of adult personality. These areas include low frustration, tolerance and poor social adjustment. They had a tendency to form interpersonal relationships that were shallow and lacking in true intimacy. They also commonly projected blame for whatever current difficulties they were experiencing. In terms of sexual preoccupation, Wolf noted that these individuals had developed a coping strategy for dealing with internally felt stress by translating it into sexual fantasy and behaviour. Under pressure, the sex offender will give first in the weakest area of his personality membrane, for example his sexuality.

Wolf then moved on to consider disinhibitors which he defined as transitory environmental factors or internal states that act to lower the person's inhibitions against a specified behaviour. These have an important role in weakening the inhibition (social controls) against and strengthening the attraction to sexually deviant behaviour. Disinhibitors also have a role in terms of justification or rationalisation, which serve to further the individual's development and continuation of their sexual deviation.

Wolf also considers the role that sexual fantasy plays. Firstly, it acts as a disinhibitor towards the person being thought about. Secondly, it reinforces the attraction towards the behaviour, and finally it reinforces the rationalisations used in the fantasy, which is the focus of masturbation. Fantasy acts to desensitise the offender to the behaviour. The consistent repetition of the deviant theme in association with the pleasant sensations of sexual arousal and/or ejaculation serves to reinforce the attraction to the deviance, so that the overall arousal and attraction to the deviant focus increases.

After the sexual fantasy the person may have to deal with a sense of guilt and embarrassment, so that a pattern of rationalisation is incorporated—a process known as 'cognitive distortion'. To the outsider such cognitive distortions amount to unreal excuses, although to the offender they are functional as they control the level of guilt and anxiety that the offender might otherwise experience as he repeats the abuse. Wolf points to how strong this belief system can be.

Wolf then looks at the addiction cycle, which has the advantage of being easily used in any direct work, and can be used for those who cannot read or write. Wolf developed the cycle of addiction after having looked both at the offender's past history and his presenting behaviours.

Wolf's cycle of offending can be expressed as follows:

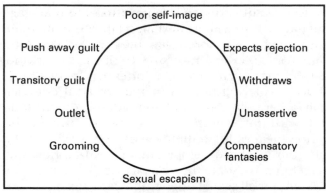

Figure 1: The offence cycle (Wolf, 1984).

This addiction cycle charts the entry level then all the points the offender must go through in order to sexually abuse, and then rationalise and continue their behaviour. The entry point of poor self-image is often related to their early life experiences and to a general dissatisfaction with their life. Indeed, Koester-Scott (1994) referred to the fact that offenders frequently present with a significantly disturbed developmental history; early feelings of emotional and social isolation, often combined with physical and sexual abuse, which leads them to distort cognitively about themselves, others and the way in which the world operates. They often present in a state of 'victim posture'. They expect rejection, so they withdraw. They compensate through needs fulfilment fantasies, which often have a sexual dimension or tone. This 'escape to sexuality' can be understood as a learned coping mechanism, which develops fairly early in life out of a realisation that sexual gratification is a way of displacing other more painful feelings. These belief systems form the beginning components of the 'offence cycle' as the offender develops a habit of using fantasy in order to manage emotional needs unmet because of a lack of connection with others. These fantasies serve as a cognitive rehearsal for deviant behaviour and may include aspirations of wealth, power, control and revenge. The escape to fantasy places the offender in control and they then start targeting victims that match their deviant sexual interest. Indeed, if the offender fixes their fantasy on a specific behaviour or individual it will increase the need for, or attraction to, that behaviour or individual. The result is that the fantasy begins to 'groom' the environment, as the offender rehearses sexual behaviours and this reinforces their belief that the primary goal of sexual relations is to feel better about themselves. Behaviourally, compulsive masturbation often follows, as does the incorporation to their fantasy of rationalisation and justification. Although guilt and embarrassment follow (particularly relating to the possibility of being caught), it is quickly pushed away, and this is symptomatic of their general inability to take responsibility for themselves. They externalise responsibility and often promise never to do it again, although we need to note that they rarely learn from their mistakes. Since the offender has not really changed and been unsuccessful in applying discontinuation strategies they are again at step one and the whole process begins anew.

It is clear from the thoroughness of this cycle, that it forms the basis of the 'relapse prevention' model utilised in most sex offender treatment. For a discussion of relapse prevention see Laws (1989), which argues that the thrust is on the maintenance of pro-social behaviour post-treatment.

For a broader discussion of the deviant cycle, the reader is referred to Eldridge and Still, 1995; Ryan et al. (1987), Salter (1995) and Ward et al. (1995).

Feminist theory

Feminist writers define sexual offending as part of a continuum of male behaviour in which *"men feel driven to act out sexually because that is how they assure themselves of their identity as men"* (Person, 1991). Brownmiller (1975) defined sexual assaults as part of a continuum of sexist behaviour which serves as a method of social control, whilst Gocke (1991) states that *"the commission of sexual offences can be viewed as part of a continuum of male behaviour within unequal gender relations, for which men must take responsibility. It represents a key aspect of their collective subjugation of women and children in order that they be serviced domestically, socially and sexually."*

In summary, most feminists see sex offending behaviour along a continuum of 'normal' male sexuality, whilst Morrison (1989) believes such offending to be *"one of the most extreme consequences of the socialisation of boys and men."* Men have considerable power in our patriarchal society (defined as *". . . a systematic set of social relationships through which men maintain power over women and children"*, and which *"varies across societies . . ."*, Kelly and Radford, 1990/1) simply because of their gender.

Kelly (1988) developed the notion of a continuum much further in relation to child sexual abuse. Here, she proposed that child sexual abuse be defined along a continuum based on *"what women and girls experience as abusive"*. She argued that the concept can enable women to make sense of their own experiences by showing how 'typical' and 'aberrant' male behaviour shade into one another (Kelly, 1988). Her use of the term is based on two of its meanings in the Oxford English Dictionary: first, *"a basic common character that underlies many different events"*, and, second, *"a continuous series of elements or events that pass into one another and which cannot be readily distinguished."* The first enables us to discuss sexual violence in a generic sense. The basic common character underlying the many different forms of violence is the abuse, intimidation, coercion, intrusion, threat and force men use to control women. The second meaning enables us to document and name the range of these different forms of violence whilst acknowledging that there are no clearly defined and discrete analytic categories into which men's behaviour can be placed.

The continuum should not be interpreted as a statement of relative seriousness given that all such violence is serious, and there are already documented reasons on the difficulties facing workers in analysing the impact on women and children.

The feminist approach thus starts from the premise that the overwhelming majority of offenders are men, and that sexual abuse happens in normal families, not deviant ones. It is not men's biology that makes them abuse women and children. Men, in learning to be men, learn that they have a right to be sexually and emotionally serviced by women; they learn that their power can ensure that this happens, and that in order to feel like a man, they have to feel powerful. Within the family women are relatively powerless in relation to men, and children even more so. 'Normal' families therefore have the opportunity for men to sexually abuse children. The ideology of the family as a private place of love, comfort, mutual care and trust makes it very difficult that anyone will know about it or intervene. The feminist approach rejects any notion that children make-up or 'fantasise' about their abuse, are 'seductive', ask for it, or are in any way responsible. They put the blame firmly and exclusively on the offender (MacLeod and Saraga, 1988).

Applying these arguments to intra-familial abuse, Smith (1986) noted that *"the issue of blood relations obscures what is at the root of all child sexual abuse: the betrayal of trust and the abuse of power to achieve personal gratification."* Family situations constitute the most common form of relationships of trust we experience. In patriarchal families, power is defined as the right of men as the controllers of the family's resources and status of the world, to impose their authority on women and children, and of adults to assert their will over that of the children. Such power should be tempered by trust where the powerless members of the family will be cared for and protected by its more powerful ones. Their failure to live up to this expectation becomes a betrayal of trust, or the abuse of power (Dominelli, 1989). MacLeod and Saraga (1991) argued that any explanation must include a number of elements: the opportunity to abuse, the motivation or desire, the objectification of the victim and a set of beliefs that make it legitimate. These are all constructed in a social structure of power inequalities, and ideologies of childhood, femininity and masculinity.

O'Hagan (1989) outlined three contributions feminism has made to this topic area: its exposure of child sexual abuse, its analysis of the cause, and the relevance of its history. I would add that it has brought much needed attention to the issues around race, religion and culture. Indeed, some writers argue that the feminist analysis is fast becoming the most widely accepted theoretical framework for professional practice, particularly as it is wholly compatible with research findings on sex offenders.

There are, however, several shortcomings to the feminist arguments, and they include:

- It does not explore the sexual abuse of male children and female offending (although his has now been attempted by Hackett, 1993). The motives of such offending are not easily explicable within the patriarchal paradigm.
- The approach is essentially sociological and as such minimises the psychological factors and motivations.
- Many sex offenders report that they are motivated by sexual feelings, whereas the feminists believe it to be grounded in the abuse of trust and power.
- The focus on the powerlessness of the mothers indulges in a form of stereotyping similar to the male developed 'collusive mother' stereotype (Hooper, 1989).
- No absolute distinctions can be drawn between the sex offending and the non-sex offending male population.
- Rape 'myths', which foster an acceptance of sexual coercion, are widely dispersed.
- Female sexuality is improperly analysed (Warwick, 1991).
- It does not explain patterns of sexual crime or why some men do and others do not commit sexual offences. At best, it does account for how patriarchy may make abuse possible. Whilst it has offered a credible strategy at a policy level, this doesn't always extend to the practice level. It has been argued that it provides us more with a compass than a map.

Hackett argued that abuse by men and women are inextricably linked. If women are perpetrating abuse, they do so in systems where men hold power and ensure that children are made vulnerable. He argues therefore, that any abuse by women can be seen as part of the web of abuse of children by men as they create the oppressive systems within which females operate, and they have probably been the victims of male abuse themselves.

More generally, Wattam et al. (1989) noted that all theories of child sex abuse are written from an adult point of view, rather than being based on the child's own experiences. The feminist approach does begin to provide us with a platform for this by eliciting information to try and promote a child's perspective.

Victim blame

Gocke (1991) noted that the strongest theme within these theories is the notion that the victim has 'led the offender on' through her dress, behaviour, or even simply spatial location. Damning personality traits are often given to the victim, e.g. precocious child, with an underlying assumption made that she could have prevented the abuse if motivated to do so. Such theory is fundamentally flawed as it fails to account for the issue of consent and the unequal power dynamics.

Sociological theories

Socio-cultural explanations locate the causes of abuse within the social structures, traditions, norms and ideologies of the culture. This section thus embraces the effects of wider and societal factors on individual and family functioning and their relationship to sexual offending. Sexual offending behaviour is often viewed as normal and acceptable in certain communities. For example, they may foster certain beliefs such as women want to be raped or present material through the media that either desensitises or sexually arouses the audience to offend sexually. Societal changes may also produce changes in the patterns of sex offences within a culture (Schwartz, 1995). Finkelhor (1982) has noted that since men occupy powerful policy making positions, the gender politics of sexual abuse can often hamper effective policies and public action around the problem.

Previously, some believed social factors such as poor housing and unemployment contributed to sexual offending. Research has discounted this view as sexual abuse clearly occurs in all social settings.

Anthropologically, we do need to acknowledge that no sexual behaviour is universally recognised as deviant, and there is virtually no sexual behaviour that some culture in some instance has not condoned (Schwartz, 1995). Sexual offending is a legal as well as a social concept and is thus not an inherent characteristic.

Sex offenders are not all the same and there are many etiological pathways to sexual offending behaviour. There is, however, one constant feature—the process of the male socialisation. Both Finkelhor (1982; 1984; 1985) and Russell (1984) have put forward reasons to explain the preponderance of males amongst sex offenders. The following represents an amalgamation of their works:

- Women as potential child carers are taught earlier and much more completely to distinguish between sexual and non-sexual forms of affection. In part, because of the preparation for motherhood, they are sensitised to appreciate the satisfactions involved in affection without a sexual component. Men are not given many legitimate opportunities to practice nurturing and to express dependency needs except through sex. As such, when men need affection and are feeling dependent they are much more likely to look for fulfilment in a sexual form, even if this is with an inappropriate partner. Women get such needs met with children without sex entering the picture (Finkelhor, 1982).

- Men are socialised to be able to focus their sexual interest around sexual acts isolated from the context of the relationship. By contrast, women fantasise about whole situations and whole relationships. For women, the fact that a partner was a child would make it more difficult to experience sexual interest in the partner. As far as a male is concerned, if a *"child has the right set of orifices to provide sexual gratification"*, they become aroused and engage in the desired sexual act (Finkelhor, 1982 and 1985).

- Men are socialised to see their appropriate sexual partners as persons who are younger, smaller, and less powerful than themselves, while women are socialised to see their appropriate sexual partners as being older and larger. It is less of a contortion for men to find a child sexually attractive (Finkelhor, 1982).

- As men do not generally express nurturing behaviours they become socialised to express their dependency needs through sex (Finkelhor, 1994), and they sexualise their expressions of emotion more than women do.

- Men grow up to see heterosexual success as much more important to their gender identities than do women. Men tend to need sex as a form of reconfirmation of their adequacy when their ego has encountered any form of rebuff (Finkelhor, 1984). If the only available sexual partner is a child, it may be weak confirmation, but it is some.

- Males are not only expected to take the initiative, but also to overcome resistance regarding sexual relationships (Russell, 1984). Women are conditioned to be more passive, and sexual abuse is unlikely to be initiated by children.

- Men appear to be more promiscuous than women and the choice of multiple partners is more likely to include under-age partners. The search for sexual opportunity seems more important to the maintenance of self-esteem in men (Russell, 1984).

- Many men experience sexual arousal outside the context of a relationship with their sexual partner (Finkelhor, 1984, Russell, 1984).

- Men may be less able to empathise with the potential harm because they are less likely to be victims, and, as they interact less frequently with young children, they do not develop the kind of protective bonding that would make them sensitive to the harm of sexual contact (Russell, 1984).

- Sexual contact with children may be more condoned by the male subculture (Russell, 1984).

The hurdle to be jumped to offend is therefore lower for men than women. Accepting that society has typed women and men into specific roles, largely through its patriarchal social structure, the question many ask is why there are not more sex offenders. The socialisation process should never remove any individual responsibility from the offender.

Brannon and David (1976) offered a useful conceptualisation of maleness in which they argue that men are required to live up to four expectations in our society:

- *The sturdy oak*—men must stand alone, and should not lean on anyone for help. They must offer protection to others, notably women and children.

- *No sissy stuff*—men should not cry, should play with motorbikes rather than children and must avoid anything feminine.

- *The big wheel*—men must be successful at work, in the public domain and master at home, and

- *Give 'em hell*—men must be aggressive, must stand up to male banter and not be put upon. Men must compete.

The male dilemma is that they know that they cannot live up to these standards, yet they still attempt to attain them. The outcome is that *"they fall prey to jealousy, paranoia, rage and violence more easily than if they had a more accepting attitude to life"* (Burnham et al., 1990). These authors then go on to provide three links between this analysis and offending behaviour:

- Because being male involves developing a tough front, males develop an investment in fooling themselves and their friends into believing they are brave and hard and manly. Offending is one rite of passage into male adulthood.

- The masculine ideal offers the perfect vehicle for an oppositional position to the conformist adult ideal of steady work, family responsibility and so on. The oppositional culture is demonstrated in group violence, violence towards minority groups etc.

- If men feel the need to compete successfully for power in the public domain, but cannot do so, or fear they are underachieving, some choose to exercise dominance where they can—over women and children. Domestic violence and many sex offenders relate to such attitudes.

The power differentials which make exploitation possible are male over female, adult over child, physically superior over physically weaker, and superior economic strength over economic dependence. In acknowledging that many sex offenders are 'ordinary' men, we need to review male socialisation and the problems that it can create. In doing so, we have to set sexual offending within the context of a society embodying unequal gender relations. Sex offenders are simply men who have the power to take what they want, and take it. For a recent exploration of the male majority in perpetrating child sexual abuse, the reader is referred to Featherstone and Lancaster (1996); Itzin (1992) and Liddle (1993). For those who wish to read further about the contrasts and similarities between male and female sexual offending, the reader is referred to Allen and Pothast (1994); Kaufman (1995); and Welldon (1996).

There is a huge gap in the information available around black sex offenders, although they do tend to be over-represented in the rapist populations (Grubin and Gunn, 1990). Gebhard (1972) conducted the most significant of comparisons between black and white sex offender groups in the 1940s and 1950s. He found that blacks individually tended to have fewer sexual offences, except that black homosexual offenders had more convictions than their male counterparts. He also found that differences between the two groups reflected the traits of the black subculture and the greater socio-economic deprivation suffered by blacks. This issue is discussed further in Chapter 7 under the section on Demographic data.

Sexual arousal

The sexual arousal theory suggests that sexual offenders have a greater than normal sexual arousal to children. Sexual offenders experience sexual feelings towards children mentally (fantasy) as well as physically (erection and ejaculation). These may be exclusive responses (e.g. paedophiles), they may co-exist with other appropriate adult arousal or they may be restricted to a particular age range, gender, appearance (e.g. blond hair) or situation (stress, opportunity). Sexual arousal often varies in frequency and intensity. For example, some offenders may experience constant and compelling feelings of sexual desire for children, or they may have mild, moderate or circumstantial arousal (Faller, 1990). There is a substantial body of evidence which suggests that sexual arousal is associated with sexual offending. Howitt (1995) points out that the evidence includes laboratory tests which show that at least some paedophiles get erections to deviant images of children; sexual abuse in childhood conditions sexual arousal to children; the experience of offenders in childhood provides a model for deviant sexual behaviour patterns; hormone abnormalities; paedophiles mistakenly interpret physiological arousal as sexual arousal; and paedophiles are socialised by child pornography or advertising to regard children as sexual objects. However, whilst sexual arousal is considered a necessary prerequisite to sexually offend, it is not sufficient unless the individual is prepared to act on the arousal. There are also questions about the differences between familial and extra-familial sexual arousal, with some suggestion that incest offenders are not as entrenched in their behaviour.

Sex offenders: what they tell us

There are a growing number of papers which set out the findings of research into why sex offenders commit sexual offences against children—in their own words. These are essential developments in our understanding and are given some status as the respondents are frequently offered confidentiality, thus removing the fear of further consequences. These are important and detailed accounts and the reader is referred to the following: Budin and Johnson (1989); Conte et al. (1989); Elliott et al. (1995); Gilgun (1994); Gilgun and Connor (1989); Lang and Frenzel (1988); Ward et al. (1993); Weinrott and Saylor (1991). Some reference has been made to the Elliott et al. paper in Chapter 3, and some reference is made to these papers throughout the next chapter as they relate to the different blocks of the assessment. We do need to acknowledge that a great deal of the available literature derives from offender account, albeit disguised in academic prose.

Social workers understanding of sexual offending

Ward et al. (1996) explored with both qualified and student social workers the reasons why they think adult males sexually abuse children. This is important as we know that social work knowledge and their attitudes toward sexual offenders correlates with the offenders' response to change (Hogue, 1993). Stermac and Segal (1989; 1991) had reported that some professionals may actually view adult sexual contact with children to be of partial benefit for the child.

Ward et al. found that the reasons given by both groups strongly paralleled factors identified in theories of child sexual abuse, such as developmental issues, power and control, dysfunctional cognitions, sexual motivation, personal inadequacy, and external contextual factors. What they did find was gender differences in the types given for sexual offending. Whilst males weighted each of the eight categories equally, the females were more likely to cite power and control as the primary reason for sexual offending, and, by contrast, rated sexual motivations less often. This is interesting when we know that the sex offender himself believes sexual motivation to be the most likely cause of their behaviour (Ward et al., 1993).

Their findings do reinforce the belief that any adequate explanation of sexual offending is likely to be multi-factorial in nature . . .

Integrated models: frameworks for practice

Individual theories restrict our vision: we see things through a microscope rather than through a set of binoculars. Despite the territorial nature of the originating discipline about their particular theory, we should accept that each may hold part of the

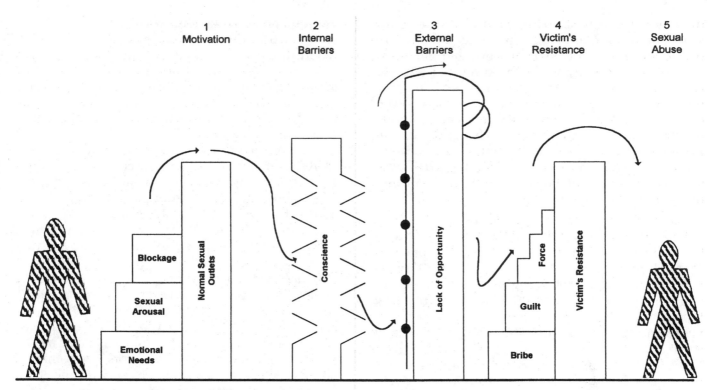

1 Motivation	2 Internal Barriers	3 External Barriers	4 Victim's Resistance	5 Sexual Abuse

Figure 2: Four preconditions of sexual abuse (Finkelhor, 1984)

larger jigsaw puzzle. To understand sexual offending, we need to identify and understand the multi-level influences and possible interactions that may lead to a sexual offence being committed.

An integrated theory of child sexual abuse (Finkelhor, 1984; Araji and Finkelhor, 1986)

Finkelhor developed a multi-factor model to explain child sexual abuse by integrating a variety of single factor theories. It incorporates characteristics of the offender, disinhibitors, the environment and the victim (see Figure 2). It operates at a high level of generality, thus allowing its use across a wide range of sexual offenders, whilst also encouraging analysis of the relative significance of the different factors in individual cases. It allows individual cases to be examined in detail, moving an offender on from asserting that his behaviour 'just happened' to an understanding of the thoughts, feelings and conscious manipulation of people and events which he undertook before the offence could take place (Lancaster, 1996). It thus emphasises that sexual abuse only takes place if the offender already has sexual feelings towards the child, and this firmly locates responsibility with the offender. Finkelhor's model accounts for both familial and extra-familial child sexual abuse, and, although widely used, there remains a paucity of hard evidence to support the model or risk factors (Oates, 1990).

Finkelhor argues that all the known factors contributing to child sexual abuse can be grouped into four preconditions, which need to be met prior to the instigation of child sexual abuse. The four preconditions are:

- *Motivation*: The potential offender needs to have some motivation to sexually abuse a child. Thus, he will need to find children erotically and sexually desirable.
- *Internal inhibitions*: The potential offender must overcome internal inhibitions that may act against his motivation to sexually abuse.
- *External inhibitions*: The potential offender also has to overcome external obstacles and inhibitions prior to sexually abusing the child.
- *Resistance*: Finally, the potential offender has to overcome the child's possible resistance to being sexually abused.

All four preconditions have to be fulfilled, in a logical, sequential order, for the abuse to commence. The presence of only one condition, such as a lack of maternal protection, social isolation or emotional deprivation is not sufficient to explain abuse.

(1) Motivation to sexually abuse.

Finkelhor argues that there are three functional components subsumed under the motivation to sexually abuse children:

(a) *Emotional congruence*—in which sexual contact with a child satisfies profound emotional needs.
(b) *Sexual arousal*—in which the child represents the source of sexual gratification for the abuser.
(c) *Blockage*—when alternative sources of sexual gratification are not available or are less satisfying.

As these components are not actual preconditions, not all three need to be present for sexual abuse to occur. They are however important in explaining the variety of motivations offenders may have for sexually abusing children. The three components explain not only the instance of offenders who aren't sexually motivated but enjoy degrading victims by wielding power, but also the paedophile, and the sexually motivated offender who looks towards children for variety, even though he has access to other sources of sexual gratification. In some instances elements from all three components may be present to account for whether the motivation is strong and persistent, weak and episodic, or whether the focus is primarily on girls or boys, or both.

(2) Overcoming internal inhibitors.

To sexually abuse, the offender needs not only to be motivated but also to be able to overcome his internal inhibitions against acting on his motivation. No matter how strong the sexual interest in children might be, if the offender is inhibited by taboos then he will not abuse. Arguably, most people do have some inhibitions towards sexually abusing children.

Dis-inhibition is not a source of motivation, it merely releases the motivation. Thus an individual who has no inhibitions against child sexual abuse, but who is not motivated, will not abuse. The second precondition aims to isolate the factors that account for how inhibitions are overcome, and whether they are temporary or not. The element of dis-inhibition is an integral part of understanding child sexual abuse.

(3) Overcoming external inhibitors.

While preconditions (1) and (2) account for the offender's behaviour, preconditions (3) and (4) consider the environment outside the offender and child which control whether and whom he abuses. External inhibitors that may restrain the offenders' actions include family constellation, neighbours, peers, and societal sanctions, as well as the level of supervision that a child receives.

Although a child cannot be supervised constantly, a lack of supervision has been shown in the clinical literature to be a contributing factor to sexual abuse, as has physical proximity and opportunity. External inhibitions against committing child sexual abuse may easily be overcome if the offender is left alone with a child who is not supervised.

(4) Overcoming the resistance of the child.

One limitation of much of the research literature is the failure to recognise that children are able to resist, or avoid abuse. The focus in the clinical literature is on children who have been sexually abused, while ignoring those who although approached were able to avoid it or resist. The feminist argument proposes that insufficient attention is paid to the fact that children do have a capacity to resist. This capacity may operate in a very subtle, covert way, and does not necessarily involve overt protestations. Offenders may sense which children

are good potential targets, who can be intimidated, and can be exhorted to keep a secret. Offenders report that they can almost instinctively pick out a vulnerable child on whom to focus their sexual attentions, while ignoring those who might resist. Frequently these children may not even be aware that they are being sexually approached, or indeed resisting such advances.

Some of the risk factors that inhibit the capacity to resist include emotional insecurity and neediness, lack of physical affection, lack of friends, lack of support and interest from parents, age, naivety, and lack of information. Knowing which factors make children vulnerable is essential in formulating prevention programmes. Isolating behaviours that continue a risk, while emphasising those that enhance resistance or avoidance, can empower children to protect themselves. This is not to say that children who are not vulnerable do not get abused. Many children may be forced or coerced despite displaying resistance or avoidance behaviours. In such instances the factors overcoming a child's resistance has nothing to do with the child, or the child's relationship with the offender, but is the result of force, threat or violence. No matter how much resistance is manifested by the child, this may not necessarily prevent abuse.

Precondition (4) has three possible outcomes: the child may resist overtly by saying no and running away, or covertly by presenting a confident assertive demeanour which conveys a strong messages to the offender not to attempt abuse for fear of detection or exposure; the child may resist but still be abused through the use of force or violence; or a child may resist but be overcome through coercion.

Acknowledging the child's capacity to resist or avoid abuse enhances our understanding of child sexual abuse. The notion that children can resist, albeit frequently covertly, is a positive one which could usefully generate more empirical research on the content of resistance behaviours, and how these can be incorporated and adopted in the preventive programmes which aim to teach children how to avoid sexual abuse (Sanderson, 1990).

An integrated theory of sexual offending (Marshall and Barbaree, 1990)

These authors developed an integrated theory as they *"believe that a proper understanding of sex offending can only be attained when these diverse processes are seen as functioning interdependently."* They go on to explore biological influences, childhood experiences, socio-cultural context and transitory situational factors, concluding that:

"Biological inheritance confers upon males a ready capacity to sexually aggress which must be overcome by appropriate training to instil social inhibitions toward such behaviour. Variations in hormonal functioning may make this task more or less difficult. Poor

parenting, particularly the use of inconsistent and harsh discipline in the absence of love, typically fails to instil these constraints and may even serve to facilitate the fusion of sex and aggression rather than separate these two tendencies. Socio-cultural attitudes may negatively interact with poor parenting to enhance the likelihood of sexual offending, if these cultural beliefs express traditional patriarchal views. The young male whose childhood experiences have ill-prepared him for a pro-social life may readily accept these views to bolster his sense of masculinity. If such a male gets intoxicated or angry or feels stressed, and he finds himself in circumstances where he is not known or thinks that he can get away with his offending, then such a male is likely to sexually offend depending upon whether he is aroused at the time or not . . ."

Dynamics of a sexual assault (Schwartz, 1995)

The model proposed by Schwartz has two components: a motive and a releaser. For the sex offender, a motive may be sexual arousal, anger, lack of power, fear of women, distorted attitudes, or a combination of these. The releaser is what allows the sex offender to engage in the behaviour despite personal or societal sanctions. Releasers include stress, lack of empathy, cognitive distortions, substance abuse, pornography, peer pressure, mental retardation, psychosis, and/or brain damage. Environmental controls and victim attributes will also factor into whether an assault actually occurs.

A quadripartite model of sexual aggression against children (Hall and Hirschman, 1992)

This model was formulated as the authors believed that sub-groups of sex offenders have a unique and complex set of characteristics, rather than being alike. They consider the combinations of physiological, cognitive, affective, and personality factors which may be more or less prominent as motivational factors depending on the typologies of the aggressor and the event. Physiological sexual arousal in sex offenders against children is higher than controls, yet does not always lead to actual offending in all cases. Not only must the physiological sexual arousal be cognitively appraised before it is acted upon, other cognitive appraisals may affect the process (such as cognitive distortions, and these are more deviant than sex offenders against adults). The offender may also balance the benefit of offending (e.g. sexual gratification) against the consequences (e.g. punishment), and act if they believe the former outweigh the latter. A third factor—affective dys-control, typically in the form of depression, and occasionally anger and hostility—is posited as a motivational factor that facilitates sexual offending against children. Physiological, cognitive, and affective factors that motivate sexual offending against children are primarily state and situation dependent, but in some cases, more enduring trait variables may interact with

these three factors to facilitate sexual aggression. For example, when the state components are operational in a person with developmentally related personality problems or disorders, sexually aggressive behaviour is more likely (than any other violation of non-sexual rules) to occur. When all four factors are present, synergistic interactions may occur, with the intensity of one precursor potentially affecting the intensity of any or all of the other precursors. They do acknowledge that environmental variables may have an indirect effect in the expression of sexually aggressive impulses.

Summary and way forward

Federoff and Moran (1997) have highlighted how important it is to question everything about the knowledge base on sex offenders, since even intuitively obvious 'facts' often turn out to reflect more about what we want to believe than about what is true.

Hudson and Ward (1997) and Ward and Hudson (1998) have recently offered a meta-theoretical framework for the construction and development of future theory in the sexual offending area. They pointed out that there has not been any integrated approach to theory building to date, resulting in an *ad hoc* proliferation of theories that often overlap as well as ignoring each other's existence. Their framework takes into account a number of different theory construction principles and ideas; it differentiates between different levels of theory and stresses the importance of distinguishing between distal and proximal causal factors. They begin to locate the existing theory within the framework and argue that an integrated approach using their framework will benefit workers and researchers significantly. This is needed if we are to neutralise the offenders' power base and further invite them to accept responsibility for their behaviour.

Finally, given that there is a need to explore theory in relation to the different kinds of sexual offences, the reader is referred to the excellent text by Laws and O'Donohue (1997) which explores theory relating to exhibitionism, fetishism, frotteurism, paedophilia, sexual sadism, transvestic fetishism, voyeurism, rape, and paraphilia not otherwise specified.

Chapter 5
Contextualising assessments

Whilst assessment is generally accepted *in principle* as the foundation of good child protection work, recent research has identified very clearly that assessments are not routinely carried out in all cases of child protection, and that there is a huge variance in what constitutes an assessment. There appears to be as many ways of doing an assessment as there are people writing papers on it. We know that the Department of Health guidance *'Protecting Children'* (DoH, 1988) neglected the issue of sexual abuse, with the outcome being the emergence of differing approaches to the task. Faller (1990) identified several ways in which sexual abuse assessments differ from other child protection assessments:

- The likelihood of recidivism is exceptionally high in such cases.
- It is the most likely form of abuse to prompt workers to remove the abuser from the home rather than the child.
- It is perceived to inflict more harm on its victims.

The process of assessment is an attempt to:

- Comprehend the key elements in the problem situation.
- Understand the meaning of the problem to the client in their situation.
- Use all of the client's understanding.
- Direct all of the professional knowledge to identify what needs to change, before
- Planning how these desired changes may be effected.

The process is as crucial as the content. The test of a good assessment is the contribution it makes to satisfactory problem resolution and in guiding any client and worker action. In this book, risk assessment is the systematic collection of information to try and predict the likely recurrence of the abuse, whether there is a need for further work, and what form this should take. It can also be used to predict the escalation of the presenting behaviour as well as the client's motivation for change.

As Adcock (1995) has pointed out, the assessment should enable the professionals to formulate preliminary answers to the following:

- To identify whether there is cause for concern for the child.
- To assess whether there is significant harm, or likely harm.
- To obtain a preliminary explanation, if there is one, of what has happened, and
- To decide whether any immediate protection for the child is necessary.

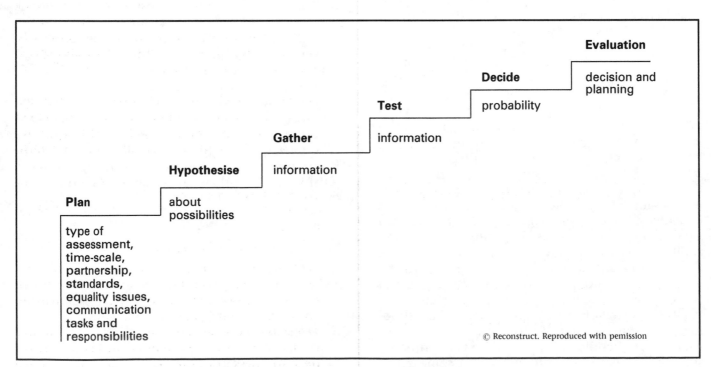

© Reconstruct. Reproduced with permission

Figure 3: A stepwise framework for undertaking assessments.

A framework for conducting assessments

Reconstruct have developed a stepwise model for conducting comprehensive assessments. Whilst this is described in detail by Samra-Tibbets and Raynes (1998), the basic structure is worthy of mention here, as it can help ensure the multiple assessments commissioned in sexual abuse cases, follow the correct process.

The first step of the stepwise model is planning. Here, the professionals need to look at the beginning of the assessment at what information they already have and what still needs to be gathered, and agree how they will work together to do this. Tasks, roles and responsibilities need to be agreed, as does inter-professional communication.

The second step attends to issues of hypotheses. No singular hypothesis should be adopted at the outset, as this usually dictates the process of the assessment and usually leads to the predetermined outcome materialising. An open-minded approach should lead to multiple hypotheses being generated, with them being graded only according to the available information. Most initial hypotheses are speculative although they should be specific as well as comprehensive. The subsequent process gathers information, which either supports or refutes individual hypotheses.

The third stage in the model is information gathering. Workers need to approach this task objectively and holistically. They must endeavour to make connections between the different pieces of information gathered, in order to consider whether any additional hypotheses need adding, or whether any original ones require amendment.

The fourth step requires that the information collected is tested out. Different professionals will come together with information around levels of risk and potential, and targets for change, and there needs to be some analysis about what evidence there is to either support or refute their views. Strategies for achieving change or the management of risk in the interim do need to be agreed, as do areas where gaps exist and further information may need to be gathered.

At the decision step, the professionals may have to make recommendations for the future protection of children in contact with the offender. This may be to the civil or criminal courts or child protection conference.

In the final step, there is a need to review the way forward. This may well include the potential for change within both the offender and his family; the viability and focus of the necessary work; any mandate needed; any relaxation of contact restrictions; and any family reconstitution.

Features of risk

The previous chapter will have reinforced that sex offenders are a heterogeneous group. It follows, therefore, that a comprehensive assessment is needed to pinpoint the specific problems within the presenting individual. Each sex offender has a specific profile that needs to be accurately identified, and the worker needs to identify the interplay of numerous factors which have predisposed the offender to abuse a child/ren. In line with this, McEwan and Sullivan (1996) have set out 21 important features of risk that need assessing:

- Level and types of denial.
- Type of offences committed.
- Category of offender—extra-familial, intra-familial, sadistic, non-sadistic.
- Target (victim) group.
- Duration of offence pattern. Age at onset of offending.
- Variation of offence pattern.
- Motivation to change. Experience of previous treatment and acceptance of worker assumptions.
- Presence of external factors affecting motivation, e.g. a collusive or 'well-groomed' family will block an offender's progress.
- Level of acceptance of responsibility for the abuse.
- Level of victim empathy.
- Mental illness.
- Drug and alcohol misuse.
- Non-sexual offending. Previous convictions.
- Sexual aggressiveness.
- Abusive personality.
- Seriousness of sexually abusive behaviour (often different from conviction or offence charged).
- Cultural issues—target group. It is important to note that the power base of most institutions is white and this may impinge on the ability of black victims to disclose.
- Learning disability—psychological testing required as many programmes are cognitive/behavioural. Relapse prevention techniques require direct consequences rather than victim empathy.
- Level of self-esteem/social isolation.
- Own victim experience.
- Links with other sexual offenders—co-defendants, paedophile rings?

The aims of the offender assessment include:

- To help them identify some of the factors that led to their offending via the process of targeting, grooming, fantasising, masturbating, abusing, regretting and rationalising.
- To establish the degree of accepted responsibility for the abuse by the offender. In particular, we need to assess just how close a match we achieve between victim account and offender admission.

- To explore any reasons for being unable to assume responsibility for the offending.
- To explore the potential for future abuse.
- Occasionally, workers are asked to assist the court in a determination of guilt or innocence. It is not the assessors' role to make this judgement. They can only offer an opinion based on the known dimensions of the problem— unless the offender openly admits the offence.
- To explore the degree of reluctance to change their attitudes and behaviour/to establish their motivation and capability to change. For example, the reuse of certain tasks and question-naires is a useful gauge of change.
- To look at their attitude towards the victim and their understanding of the harm they have caused to them.
- To assess the specific risks (short and long-term) posed to the children, and in which situations such risk becomes more or less acute. These are best 'guesstimates', as no instrumentation is specific and absolute. This may involve recom-mendations on where they live and contact issues. Retaining the offender in the community needs to consider such issues as the number of victims, the compulsiveness of the behaviour, violence in the offence, and an offender's general criminal history.
- To develop an understanding of their attitude towards their own sexuality, and that towards women and children.
- To assess the viability of, and necessity for, longer-term treatment and/or management, and what forms they may take. The offenders need for, interest in, and potential performance in treatment are important factors in these con-siderations.

The initial risk assessment has to make prelimi-nary decisions on child protection risks, placement and contact issues, whilst the comprehensive risk assessment reconsiders these issues as well as projecting forwards on risk and recidivism. Assess-ment is a continuous process rather than a discrete piece of work. The material from this book is transferable between the two areas, although the primary focus is on the structured comprehensive assessment. The aims of the offender assessment are onerous and it is important that workers do not attempt to cut corners for time or resource considerations. Superficial assessments are insuffi-cient to make decisions regarding dangerousness, contact and family reconstitution.

For a detailed analysis about the concept of risk assessment, the reader is referred to Brearley (1982); Doueck et al. (1993); Moore (1996); Murphy-Bressan (1994); Waterhouse and Carnie (1992).

Co-working: two heads are better than one

Co-working has to become the norm at the risk assessment stage of a child protection investigation in order to set the foundations for any subsequent treatment work.

It is important that any workers planning to co-work an offender assessment develop a cohesive working relationship. This is particularly important where one worker is involved in an 'apprenticeship' into such work, or where there are both sexes involved. Workers need to create an environment where open and honest communication, trust and commitment are enshrined. Understanding each other's motivation to do the work and any fears, anxieties, prejudices or stereotypes need naming and working through. They may wish to explore gender issues, sexuality and assumptions; life histories and experiences as men, women, children, parents, and professionals. It is also important to share each other's individual skills and experiences in undertaking sex offender work. They may want to develop their own strategy for managing any questioning from peers about their involvement in the work.

Co-working is useful in the face-to-face work itself as it allows work, tasks, approaches, and skills to be shared. Where one worker becomes stuck, the other worker can intervene. They can also change direction if necessary or pick up on either what is, or is not, said. Post-interview, there can be some exploration of what was elicited, what was not, and what this means. Co-working is not a substitute for supervision or consultation, which must also address the process of the assessment, self-aware-ness and personal development.

Collusion: assessing the assessors

Burnham et al. (1990) named several temptations for workers engaged in work with sex offenders:

- Some workers may fall prey to the temptation of playing up to the glamour associated with such work.
- Gender assumptions can lead to collusion, which can be difficult to extricate themselves from. For example, banter to engage the offender can create a relationship, but not one that makes the subsequent professional task very easy.
- There may be a temptation to do nothing in the belief that the offender will not accept responsi-bility.
- Isolated practice to impress colleagues often masks a worker who is struggling with the task.
- It can lead to voyeuristic practice, where the worker gets titillated by the discussion of the offences.
- Avoidance of the issues is a temptation, particularly where a supportive and directive environment is absent.

Effective work with sex offenders requires the resolution of any personal issues that could produce counter-transference issues. These might include conscious or unconscious primitive reactions such as sadistic or aggressive responses, or retaliation—which, if left unresolved, could lead to difficulties for the worker when resisting any rationalisations put forward by the offender for their behaviour. It also compromises the workers ability to assess sexual abuse in an objective manner. Working with sex offenders is thus an active process, where the workers, as well as the offenders, have to be cared for (Polson and McCulloch, 1995). This does involve assessing the assessors to be satisfied that they are able as well as willing to do the work. A workers emotional involvement in a case needs careful monitoring and management.

Linking different assessment pieces

Risk assessments conducted in isolation from other pieces of work will be fundamentally flawed. All clues are interlinked. Considering the varying elements of risk together enhances the quality of the assessment. To achieve this, the most effective method is a multi-agency approach, with various agencies working alongside, sharing knowledge and resources. Comprehensive risk assessments are necessary for agencies to be able to make safer child care decisions. Risk assessments also enable the individual agencies to focus their work in appropriate areas. In general, offenders are stereotyped, and individual assessments are a way of providing a framework for professional decision-making and increasing professional knowledge. In turn, this should increase worker confidence in the work being undertaken.

Work with adult sex offenders must be considered alongside work with the victim(s), siblings and the non-abusing carer, and that regular consideration of these assessment pieces is necessary to check information collected, and guard against mirroring the dynamics of the offender and/or a collusive family.

The assessment of the offender should be undertaken by two workers wherever possible and should run in tandem to other work with the family. Close partnerships are needed between the assessing teams to neutralise any control employed by the offender. The assessment of sexual offenders should not be considered in a vacuum, as they are inherently dependent upon a comprehensive inter-disciplinary response. The following triad sets out the wider context of risk assessments where sexual abuse is concerned:

All these different assessments need to be integrated for child protection to be achieved.

Assessment involves gathering information, identifying need and making recommendations. It also implies a willingness and ability to act on those recommendations.

The following questions also have to be answered:

- What is the risk and can the child/ren be protected by the parents? Are there risks in other

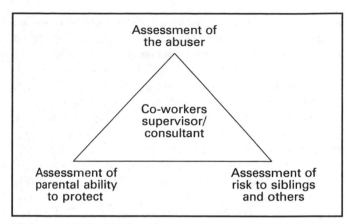

Figure 4: A triad model for sexual abuse assessments (Calder, 1997).

environments, e.g. school, baby-sitting, position of authority, such as scouts?
- Do the parents accept responsibility for what has happened to the child or the risks of what could have happened?
- Can the offender remain in the family whilst the assessment takes place?
- What are the wishes and feelings of the victim/s and/or sibling/s?
- What is the scope for work with both the offender and their family?
- What needs to change to prevent further abuse occurring?
- What is the motivation and prognosis for change?
- What is the time-scale for the proposed work and how will success or failure be measured?

No single agency has sole responsibility for child protection, nor can one agency have the necessary resources, range of skills and knowledge to effectively work with child sexual abuse. Neither can we continue to work independently: we need to see the value in each other's responsibilities, skills and knowledge and pool resources. For example, the victim may very well want the abuse to stop, but they may also report other positive offender characteristics, which they want to be noted also. Operating as isolated individuals, the workers with the offender may never be aware of this information.

Engaging the offender in the assessment work

This is a crucial area that is often overlooked in child protection work, yet it can be essential to the outcome of any assessment work. Most clients are involuntary and this leaves an uphill challenge for the workers whose initial task is to convert them to accept the planned work. Many offenders have grown up permeated with denial and projection of responsibility, and these are likely to become more entrenched in the face of immediate confrontation. It is clear, therefore, some degree of flexibility and creativity will be needed from the workers when attempting to engage the resistant client. In order to start the process, workers do need to consider where the offender is starting from, as there is frequently a discrepancy between professional and offender starting points, which contribute to the problem, rather than serving to address and resolve it (see the model of change set out in Chapter 8).

Workers clearly need to reserve the right to use authority and statutory powers where necessary, but only to the extent that it provides a mandate for the work. Punishment is not a feature that encourages family co-operation, although workers may become tempted to adopt such an approach where the offender is denying in the face of overwhelming evidence to the contrary, and where the denial serves little purpose. Any partnership between a worker and an offender is also acutely difficult where the details of the crime are very clear and graphic, as the worker may wish to adopt a punitive, non-therapeutic approach. This is particularly important as we usually start with a reluctance by the family to share information and strong negative feelings such as anxiety, anger, suspicion, guilt or despair. In sexual abuse work, great care needs to be taken in interpreting the cause of any such emotions, as misinterpretation can aggravate the tensions or conflict. It is possible to engage families from such positions, but this needs careful, considered interventions on the part of the workers. Workers new to the work do need to guard against falling for the diversionary tactics employed by the offender, and often his family.

For a full discussion of the process of engagement of men who sexually abuse children, the reader is referred to Jenkins (1990), who provides us with a 7 step model.

Choosing the assessing workers: self-selection as the starting point

Working with these groups is not something that everybody can or should do. Most workers face sexual abuse cases totally unprepared by their training, and, when coupled with the size and nature of their workloads, become anxious and disabled by the task. Workers need to acknowledge personal costs may be involved, such as conflicts and contamination invading their personal lives. Because of the nature of the work, self-selection of workers is a very important starting point, although careful managerial screening is also essential to filter out inappropriate candidates. This has particular reference to those who are to engage in longer-term assessments. Such work confronts the defences and assumptions that protect the 'average' individual from being overwhelmed by the sexual fears and confusion of our times. There are also very real problems in measuring outcomes, which frequently has a direct correlation with job satisfaction (Palmer, 1995).

O'Connell et al. (1990) have written certain guidelines for the selection of therapists in working

with sex offenders, and they point out that the choice of workers needs to be based on personal characteristics as well as a knowledge of the relevant research findings. Given the presumptive nature of the work allied with the context of structured confrontation, careful consideration needs to be given to who undertakes this area of work. Working more generally in the area of sexual abuse, workers will find their personal feelings and lives intruded, and they may become overly responsible at a personal level for the success or failure of the work with their clients (Morrison, 1994). It is for this reason that personal characteristics are considered a priority selection requirement over and above relevant experience or training. The worker needs a sense of personal values that are not overly rigid or ideologically restricted, yet must explicitly believe that sexual offending can never be excused or tolerated. They need to be comfortable in their use of authority and power to neutralise that of the offender, as well as denying confidentiality in the cause of future prevention. This is not a job for a worker who needs to play the role of 'Mr/Ms Nice Guy' (Horton, 1990). Frank MacHovec (1993) developed a self-rating 'caring–critical' grid to help workers determine which of the two approaches they are most likely to adopt in the work. He noted that even experienced workers get manipulated by the superficial charm of the sex offender, and they do need to re-ground themselves in a more critical than caring approach. In the grid (see Figure 5), a highly caring worker would be found in the upper left quadrant, whereas a highly critical worker would be somewhere in the lower left quadrant. Experienced workers report it is more effective to be more critical than caring, at least a 2–4 on the grid of moderate scepticism (4 critical) with some caring (2). A slightly biased critical approach more effectively diffuses denial and minimisation, which is much higher than the norm in the general clinical population. Traditional therapy suggests the reverse: moderate caring (4) and minimal scepticism (2). Yet caring, uncritical workers are more easily manipulated and more susceptible to becoming emotionally involved in defence of

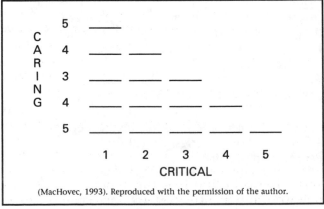

(MacHovec, 1993). Reproduced with the permission of the author.

Figure 5: The caring–critical grid.

offenders, more apt to lose their objectivity, and thus, more apt to diminish treatment effectiveness. Even a 3–3 balance increases worker susceptibility to being manipulated. A 2–4 more critical than caring posture is the 'tough love' approach more conducive to therapeutic processing, yet it has a negative side in that it can increase the probability of worker negativism and a more punitive attitude. The ideal stance is one of balance with a slight tint toward scepticism to maintain objectivity and maximal therapeutic effect.

Personal preparation

Individual workers will need to consider their motivation for undertaking work with sex offenders, and may wish to undertake a personal evaluation before putting themselves forward for any such work. They need to examine their motivation in a way that often does not apply to other areas of child protection work. Examples of the questions they may wish to ask themselves may be:

- How will I cope with the stress of the work?
- Are there any areas of sexuality or offending that I may have a problem discussing?
- What cultural, religious and gender biases would I bring to the work?
- Will I be able to remain objective in the face of detailed sex crimes?
- Would working with sex offenders reduce or enhance my sexual arousal levels?
- How will I manage a situation, which sexually arouses me? Will it cause me a problem?
- Am I frightened of working with sex offenders?
- Am I worried by professional, and personal comments and reactions regarding my work with sex offenders? How will I manage them?
- Can I accommodate any personal changes as a direct result of this work?
- What support will I need (and get) during the period of working with sex offenders?

Morrison (1994) has highlighted that the motivation for people working in this field may be variable and sometimes only partially acknowledged by the worker, and is often questioned by their peers and managers. There is evidence to suggest that males may be attracted to this work due to the confrontational style of the interviewing (Sheath, 1990), whilst others may find some sexual attraction to children, thus raising some concerns about their involvement in child sexual abuse work. The potential for voyeuristic and persecutory practice is very high (Morrison, 1994).

Hilton et al. (1995) reported on the levels of childhood sexual abuse among professionals working with sex offenders and found that over one-third of their sample reported childhood sexual abuse. They did find that this brought benefits to their work and that they often only recognised their own experiences after engaging in the work.

Gender issues

Gender issues are of vital importance, as simply allocating the duty (or first available) worker to the case is just going to generate anxieties for those chosen. Female workers may feel covertly victimised during the process, or may feel a generalised anger with men for their abusive behaviour, and may feel unable to trust any man, because of the apparent 'normality' of many offenders. Male workers may also feel covertly victimised, have feelings of identification with offenders because of gender, experience 'gender guilt', feel blamed for their own maleness, or experience other issues related to the use of power in their own lives (Lane, 1986). Erooga (1994) also warns the workers to prepare for appeals to gender, such as 'You're a man, you understand'.

We need to be alert to the use of language, recognising that it is man-made, and be sensitive to ways in which it might be used by the worker, co-worker or the offender, to reinforce or collude with gender stereotypes (Burnham et al., 1990). We need to use language that is clear and precise, avoiding euphemisms or mystification such as 'private parts' or 'down below'. These can obscure or minimise what has occurred.

Female workers need to be aware that many offenders will use their eyes and language to penetrate any defence they may have started off with for example 'visually undressing me' (Moore, 1990).

Workers anxieties

There are a number of anxieties workers may feel when confronted by sex offenders:

- There is never enough training to deal with this difficult client group.
- There is a perceived expectation of perfection, of never making mistakes and knowing everything from the research and the literature.
- The sexuality of the worker can be disturbed by such offenders, in a way that goes further than professed attitudes and values. Sex offenders can stir up very conflictual feelings about our own sexual identity and history, and the workers may find their own sexual relationships affected.
- Always achieving the desired balance between partnership and paternalism in the pursuit of child protection (see also Calder, 1995 and 1996), particularly where the worker is a victim of sexual abuse themselves, or they have children the same age as the offenders' victims.
- The notion of co-working being far more difficult (but more essential) in this area of work—as they need to carefully model what the offender should be working towards.
- A good support and supervision package to ensure that unprofessional reactions are managed and collusion addressed immediately,

recognising that sex offenders can victimise not only their victims but also the assessing social worker. We have to remember that the sex offender will often have developed a sophisticated and seductive ability with language to support their tendency towards avoidance, and that the power in the interview is held firmly with the offender (Garrison, 1992).

- They tend to fool the workers and themselves and are unrealistically optimistic about their progress (Moore, 1991).
- Failing to prevent re-offending.
- Being unable to separate the offending behaviour from the person.
- Not having the skills to work with the client.
- Colluding and mirroring the families they are striving to intervene in.
- Losing control of assessment sessions, and
- Personal, sexual and psychological vulnerability (adapted from Mark, 1992; and Morrison, 1994).

Personal impacting

Farrenkopf (1992) surveyed the personal impact on workers of working with this particular client group. Half of those reviewed experienced some emotional hardening, rising to anger and confrontation, whilst the remainder were split between frustration at the criminal justice system and society and increased suspiciousness and vulnerability. The work led to severe stress for workers, particularly when they noticed the involuntary nature of offenders presence in the process, the questionable prognosis and likely recidivism, alongside the poor support for staff (e.g. 25 per cent experienced burn-out). This might then lead to a lowering of expectations and an acceptance of the human dark-side.

Farrenkopf identified the adjustment phases to the work. Many experienced shock, bewilderment and vulnerability at the start of the process. A period of professional 'mission' followed, characterised by hopes for effectiveness, non-judgemental work ethics and empathy for their clients. This phase was soon replaced by a resurfacing of repressed emotions ranging from anger to cynicism—leading to 'erosion' and a sense of disenchantment.

Erooga (1994) explored in detail the impact on workers of working with sex offenders. He found that workers experience the same impact as the victims of the abuse themselves, and thus cannot always manage the dysfunctional impacts on their own lives without help. Work with sex offenders entails being exposed to powerful emotions in an intense worker–offender relationship that may involve a variety of roles for the worker–helper, confessor, rule-enforcer. It involves fundamental issues about the use and abuse of power and control, authority, discipline and emotional pain; clients are often both resistant and deceitful; it

involves dealing with a high level of distortion about issues of sex and sexuality. You need to add to this the social context of public attitudes to sex offenders as it is controversial, often lacking consensus from the public, media, politicians and the judiciary or indeed between professionals themselves about how it should be dealt with. In addition to these, many managers lack a knowledge base for this work and this can isolate the workers further and they can run a greater risk of collusion or breakdown. Quite simply, it is difficult to distance yourself from sex offenders given that they are not easily recognisable.

In order that collusion does not become an optional phase, workers needed to be mindful of the following: do not accept a verbatim account of offences without appraising attitudes or addressing behaviour; do not let them get away with mitigation, justification, projection or rationalisation; and accumulate all the multi-agency information to corroborate information given and also to channel denial.

In order to address these anxieties, Mark (1992) suggests that any work with offenders needs to be prefaced by some understanding of the following: a grasp of theory concerning why offenders do what they do; an awareness and openness about our own sexuality as well as our broader attitudes towards other persons sexuality; a clear stance of personal values and attitudes towards sexual abuse and offending; a willingness to co-work the case and to prepare ourselves by addressing power and gender issues; and a careful choice of methodology suited to the particular offender rather than simply suited by the assessing team.

Organisational commitment

Whilst careful consideration needs to be given to the choice of workers, it needs to be built on a departmental package of support and procedural guidance. Unfortunately, we can never underestimate the lack of support from managers on the quality of service delivery and ultimately on outcomes. More worrying is that there may well be an open questioning of personal motives and interest in this particular area of work. Such approaches only serve to challenge rather than support workers. Until recently, initiatives in sex offender work have been led by fieldworkers, often with little or no organisational or governmental support or guidance.

Effective supervision needs to look at the triad of feelings, tasks and thinking, and needs to be accompanied by consultation from someone knowledgeable in this area of work. For a fuller discussion of the challenge for managers in sex offender work, the reader is referred to Morrison (1992) and Calder (forthcoming).

A failure to pair workers together can lead to isolation, stress and secrecy which mirrors the dynamics of the offenders themselves, and leads to unsafe decisions and premature burn-out. Palmer (1995) pointed out that it is important that the work takes place in an environment which supports the sharing of knowledge and responsibility, whilst also prohibiting scapegoating and secrecy. Support of peers, managers and administrative support (procedures for referral, recording, etc.) are all extremely important. 'Normal' supervision is not really adequate for workers who are doing this work and more time is needed to address knowledge and skills, ensuring sensible workloads, monitoring the work, critically analysing the work and providing support and giving praise. 'Live' supervision using CCTV may be one option worth considering. Adequate time is necessary to do the work, which must include time for planning and debriefing. It is important that this time is not eroded and priority is given to it. This is vital if the workers are to stay in control of the sessions and in control of themselves.

For a fuller discussion of the necessary organisational building blocks, the reader is referred to Morrison (1994a and b) and Morrison (1997).

Morrison (1993) has articulated the 'professional accommodation syndrome' to provide a very coherent framework for understanding the effects of sex offender work on staff. In this framework, there are five stages: secrecy, helplessness, entrapment and accommodation, delayed or unconvincing disclosure, and retraction. The discussion reveals the massive contribution the agency can make to the workers (di)stress from the direct work itself. The stages become cyclical and this leads to a reinforcement, rather than a resolution to, the problem. Please refer to the source for a detailed discussion of the framework.

Partnerships between professionals

There are a number of different agencies potentially involved in the management of sexual abuse: social workers, the police, the courts, solicitors, psychiatrists, psychologists, probation officers, health and education providers, and so on. As McGovern and Peters (1988) have pointed out: *"Disparate reactions from these professional groups when confronted with child sexual abuse sometimes has led to chaos, confusion, and mishandling of cases."* Certainly, where agencies have worked at cross-purposes, the protection of children has been compromised. Fortunately, inter-agency initiatives are much more commonplace now than a decade ago, leading to substantial improvements in service delivery. Despite a governmental emphasis on working together, there is no set model on how it should take place although this had been redressed recently by Calder (forthcoming) and Calder and Howarth (1998). For a discussion of individual agency responsibility for sex offenders and their organisational structures, the reader is referred to Margetts (1998).

Partnerships between professionals are essential to pool skills and resources in the battle against sex offenders. Partnerships need to be forged in the context of recognition for each other's professional cultures and philosophies. There needs to be a marriage between the child protection (social service led) and the criminal justice systems (probation led) in this area of work. Any collaborative work needs to be accompanied by clearly defined roles and responsibilities as professional confusion or collusion will only serve to direct the energies and focus from the work with the offender himself. Social services can learn a great deal from probation officers who traditionally service offenders, although the probation need to shift their focus from a client-centred approach to a child-centred approach. Willis (1993) reminded us that a real danger of working with sex offenders is contamination and losing sight of the child, whilst Morrison (1994) states that a strong, co-ordinated child protection system is the best mechanism to redress denial.

Problems in inter-agency working

There are a number of problems facing inter-agency working in the child sexual abuse arena. Fargason et al. (1994) reviewed the underlying sources of conflict that impair inter-organisational functioning and provided a framework for resolving them. Without repeating the detail of the paper, they do argue that much conflict arises from differences in socialisation, goal incompatibility, task uncertainty, differences in performance expectations, and resource limitations. Pearce (1991) added the following to this list: differences between punishment and therapy; the interests of the child and the interests of the offender; the role of agencies between those agencies with, and those without, statutory responsibilities; the issue of voluntary versus involuntary intervention; individual factors of personality as well as professional differences.

Strategies to address these problems

McEwan and Sullivan (1996) set out some ideas for developing a common philosophy for managing child sexual abuse cases between agencies who are largely unfamiliar with each others structures and procedures. They include:

- Responsibility for abuse: lies exclusively with the offender. Disagreements about the management of such cases often centre around this issue.
- Assessment before intervention: assessments of risk require work with the offender, the victim and non-abusing family members before finalising interventions. This does not count for the immediate protective decision-making that is occasionally required.
- Family reconstitution is not an assessment aim: it is inappropriate to set out the outcome at the outset as this suggests the assessment is not

being objective. It can also give the family the wrong message. No discussion about the reconstitution of the family should take place before full assessments have been completed.

- Sex offenders cannot be cured and do not always offend against the same victim group: this is important when considering the breadth of future risk and associated management strategies. For a fuller discussion of crossover, the reader is referred to Chapter 7.

Interviewing approaches and strategies

The confrontational approach

The confrontational approach to interviewing is characterised by the making of assumptions, by persistence and by structured confrontation. The emphasis is on the breakdown of denial, which is believed to be a manipulative strategy employed by the offender to deceive the worker. Here, the work needs to be structured and is usually characterised by painstaking dialogue with the offender—where every step, attitude and explanation is challenged unless it is a straightforward acceptance of responsibility. Structured confrontational interviews put the offender under pressure of questioning to describe the offending in detail and then have their account systematically questioned and the cognitive distortions pointed out. Mark (1992) argues that this is the approach to get to the heart of sex offending.

The worker is able to make 'safe' assumptions based on research evidence and clinical findings. The view usually adopted is that offenders will follow and will continue to follow, if uninterrupted, an identifiable pattern of behaviour that will lead them inevitably into other offences. Despite this position, workers do need to guard against an approach, which is over-controlling, un-empathic and defensive. At times it will become difficult to continue to maintain a legitimate use of authority without being persecutory (Sheath, 1990).

Assumptions when working with sex offenders

It is considered appropriate and necessary for workers to make assumptions about sex offenders based on a combination of research findings and practice wisdom. The pioneer of this area was Wyre (1989), and I have significantly extended his earlier work to embrace newer developments. The list is not exhaustive, and the worker can usefully add to, or update, the list over time:

- Assume the offender's actions were premeditated—it is rarely a spontaneous crime, and develops through a process of establishing and normalising need.
- Assume the offender's role was active and conscious. Offending is a choice at all levels of awareness including conscious, subconscious and unconscious (Carich, 1997).
- Assume that they rehearsed the offence in fantasy.
- Assume that they perceived their victim as a sex object, and assume that the abuse was motivated by the sexual needs of the offender (Frude, 1982), although there are often many other purposes to the offending which also need identifying.
- Assume they targeted their victim.
- Assume that they groomed the environment—using seductive techniques, which surprise many workers as to why children ever tell (Wyre, 1991).
- Assume that their offending is repetitive (offender's rarely commit 'one-off' offences).
- Assume that offenders have multiple patterns, offences and victim types (Carich, 1997).
- Assume that an addictive cycle of behaviour has developed.
- Assume that offending is supported by the dysfunctional lifestyle behaviours (i.e. anti-social, narcissistic), although these will vary in both intensity and strength of pattern (Carich, 1997).
- Assume they will seek support for their rationalisations from peers, family, victim(s) and professionals, yet assume the rationalisations and excuses may not be what they actually believe—although it is easy to persuade oneself of the truth of one's own rationalisations (MacLeod and Saraga, 1991).
- Assume their motivation to adhere to the assessment will fluctuate.
- Assume they have a long-term risk of re-offending. There is no cure.
- Assume that they will be sexually aroused when they commit their offences (Abel et al., 1981), and that there is a far more fundamental sexual component to their offending pattern (Morrison, 1989).
- Assume that for every piece of information they reveal, the question arises as to what information they have thereby decided to conceal (Wyre, 1989).
- Assume that their version of events is incorrect and incomplete (Moore, 1990).
- Assume that their apparent normality is their most striking diagnostic characteristic (Lewis Herman, 1990).
- Assume they will analyse and feed the needs/ wants of the worker (Prendergast, 1991).
- Assume they know their actions are wrong because they persuade, coerce or threaten children into secrecy (MacLeod and Saraga, 1991).
- Assume they will attempt to manipulate and deceive those making the assessment (Bernard and Bernard, 1984).

- Assume they have a vested interest in silencing their victims and partners (Kelly and Radford, 1990/1).
- Assume they will portray the child as being responsible for all the above (Abel, Becker et al., 1984).
- Assume they will deny all the above.

Wyre argues that we need to make assumptions as we trust people too much and often expect too much from them. He cautions us that we will often be frightened about what we discover when assessing sex offenders. He argues that we need to be curious, think the unthinkable, imagine the unimaginable, and we might sometimes get close to the truth. He warns us that we are taking men down roads that they do not want to go, and we do so by using a certain tone of voice and level of assumption. We must believe that this behaviour is addictive. As such, we cannot accept that it is a one-off as we assume that it is deliberate. It did not 'just happen' as it is 'in character'—even though they will argue that it is not. They will reinterpret the behaviour of the victim to excuse and justify, and this will be accompanied by minimisation, normalisation, justification, and projection. We need to assume that there are clear patterns of behaviour in sexual offending and that we can identify that pattern of behaviour (Wyre, 1990). Wyre highlighted the level of risk posed by offenders who claim that something 'just happened'. Here, the fact that he has done it once does not bode well as he might just 'do it' again. Wyre (1990b) suggested that if assumptions have to be used at all, then it is probably more appropriate to operate by the most unlikely of alternatives.

These assumptions are the building blocks from which we need to build a picture of their offending history and profile. Presumption is legitimate, but persecution is not.

The disadvantage of this approach is that workers frequently see the offender withdraw further and the relationship and future work become irretrievable. It has become clear that the way offenders are interviewed will determine the extent to which they co-operate with the assessment process which, in turn, will affect both the amount and quality of information obtained (Epps, 1993).

Motivational interviewing

Motivational interviewing is a style of intervention that is designed to strengthen the offender's commitment to change. It does not negate the use of confrontation, but this needs to come after a non-collusive working relationship has developed. NOTA (The National Association for the Development of Work with Sex Offenders) have recently issued a very useful guide applying motivational interviewing to work with sex offenders (Mann, 1996), whilst Kear-Colwell and Pollock (1997);

Mann and Rollnick (1996); Miller and Rollnick (1991) and Taylor (1972) have described the approach well also.

Morrison and Print (1995) reproduced the principles of motivational interviewing stressed by Miller and Rollnick (1991):

- Motivation is the probability that a person will enter into, continue and adhere to a specific change strategy.
- Motivation does not reside within the client but involves an interpersonal context.
- Denial is a common functional behaviour not a personality trait.
- The worker is an important determinant of the client's motivation.
- Motivation is a key task for the interviewer.
- Therapist style is a major outcome of treatment success, and is often set in the very early stages of the client–worker relationship.
- Clients can be seen as unsuccessful self-changers needing help to change.
- Accurate empathy is a critical condition for an effective therapeutic relationship.
- Labelling people does not assist change, and is different to labelling behaviours.
- Confrontation is presenting a person with himself. It is a goal of intervention not a forceful/aggressive style.
- Working with the client's ambivalence about change is essential.
- The model is not personal combat with the client, and the object in motion is not a body but a perception.
- Effective interviewing controls the process not the client.

Gray and Wallace (1992) offered us lists of 'dos' and 'don'ts' within this:
Examples of things to do include:

- Do control the interview.
- Do remain objective at all times, monitoring all interactions and behaviours.
- Do be self-caring: keep your own body relaxed and comfortable.
- Do state immediately and clearly the nature of the interview.
- Do structure your interviews, or your client will.
- Do use silence for power in the interview, it can help build client anxiety.
- Do respectfully acknowledge client discomfort and anxiety and use it positively to motivate the client.
- Do change topics frequently to control the interview in an effort to elicit spontaneous responses from the client.
- Do keep the focus on the client and swiftly and repeatedly bring the client back to task.
- Do track the client's physiological changes closely (eye contact, posture, fidgeting, breathing, twitching).

- Do ask 'what' and 'how' questions, not 'why' questions.
- Do confirm the client understands the question being asked.
- Do track your feelings during the interview.
- Do respect the client as a whole individual, capable of change.
- Do respect the seriousness and harmfulness of the abusive behaviour.

To this we can add:

- Do take a break if stuck.
- Do ensure a safe formal setting.
- Do work in detail, using hypothetical questions with positive assumptions.
- Do build on 'yes' sets of questions and use successive approximation/rapid fire questions.
- Do use paradox: *"I don't expect you will tell me but . . ."*
- Do use ratings: *"on a scale of 1 to 10, how aroused were you . . .?"*
- Do give positive feedback: *"you answered that very well"* (Morrison and Print, 1995).

Examples of things not to do include:

- Don't become aggressive.
- Don't get into power struggles.
- Don't interview the offender without seeing the statements.
- Don't work harder than the offender.
- Don't continue an interview where the offender is completely unco-operative.
- Don't collude: indicate you have a different understanding.
- Don't think that admission is the same thing as taking responsibility.
- Don't think your experience will protect your feelings, and
- Don't ever work alone or unsupervised (Morrison and Print, 1995).

To this we can add:

- Do not agree to keep secrets.
- Do not ask yes/no questions: keep them open-ended.
- Do not ignore subtle changes in expression.
- Do not overlook 'thinking errors'.
- Do not make a rule you cannot enforce (but do set clear limits and act on them).
- Do not relinquish interview control.
- Do not be diverted.
- Do not abuse the client, avoid using confrontation in a manner that induces shame.
- Do not continue a weak strategy, change course, or 'up' your energy.
- Do not give up.
- Do not isolate yourself.
- Do not 'need or want' something from the client.
- Do not be exploited for what you do not know (Gray and Wallace, 1992).

Ross (1989) pointed out the three most common mistakes made by assessors:

- The assessor loses control of the interview and allows the offender to take control. This can occur for a variety of reasons: fear of the abuser, absence of accurate corroborative information about the offenders assaults prior to interview, discomfort in discussing sexual or abuse-specific issues, hostility towards the offender, pity for the offender, lack of confidence, or a lack of training to carry out the interview.
- The assessor assumes that they have the answer to the question instead of exploring in more detail. Here, excuses such as 'I can't remember', 'have a poor memory', 'it was so long ago that I can't remember' need to be tackled strongly, with us spelling out that their style of response is unacceptable, and can only lead to a conclusion that they will be an unquantified, but serious danger in the future. We can leave them to think about this for five minutes or adjourn the session.
- Assessors take sides by becoming either punitive or allied with the offender—usually when they have been severely abused themselves. Neutrality is the key and can be maintained through keeping up with theory, practice and assessment procedures.

Jones and Lewis (1990/1) argued that the middle-ground approach is optimistic when working with this client group, although the intention of shifting them from a passive to an active perspective of the offence is laudable.

The worker needs to choose their approach bearing in mind the circumstances of the individual case. The worker may want to consider the offender's motivation in choosing a particular approach, and review this throughout the risk assessment.

Strategies within approaches

Pithers et al. (1989) developed methods for assisting sex offenders to admit to their offending by developing the following:

- Attempt to create 'yes' response questions.
- Demythologise stereotypes about sex offenders.
- Mix confrontations with supportive comments.
- Emphasise relief of acknowledging his secrets.
- Discuss the strength demonstrated by disclosure.
- Stress the importance of not making a second mistake.
- Make use of strong religious beliefs.
- Ask 'successive approximation' questions, e.g. offenders may deny that a specific act occurred yet acknowledge that they approximated the act; by leading them by successive, closer proximations to the act, he may reach the point of admitting it took place.
- Confront contradictions.
- Repeat questions periodically.

Beckett (1994) made several suggestions, which can be added to this list:

- Present as confident and familiar with the dilemmas they face in admitting the extent of their offending and the consequences of doing so.
- Convey that in your experience that many offenders feel anxious about fully disclosing and co-operating, but will often feel relief having done so, and are subsequently able to change and rebuild their lives, albeit in a way different to before, and
- Explain the benefits of collaborating in the assessment and how it will create the opportunity for treatment.

Burnham et al. (1990) told us to make sure we:

- Use questions that are open and allow for exploration rather than questioning that solicit what you want to hear.
- Be behaviour specific in comment and questions. Start with the 'what', 'when' and 'with whom' before the 'why' and do not just take the description on trust.
- Avoid the rule of optimism in responding to expressions of remorse. Be realistic about what you can achieve, e.g. letting them believe you can 'cure' them.
- Avoid work which only addresses the 'what' and 'when' and not the 'why'. This risks merely displacing the behaviour, or enabling the offender to be more successful in not getting caught.
- Avoid work or techniques that collude with social constructs of gender.

McGrath (1990) added some additional interviewing strategies:

- Be familiar with the research on sex offenders.
- Remain in control of the interview.
- Don't tip your hand (about the extent of what you know until you are happy to do so).
- Interview other family members separately so the offender cannot control their responses.
- Use multiple information sources.
- Emphasise 'what happened' not 'why did it happen?'
- Use behavioural descriptors.
- Ask direct questions.
- Ignore answers believed to be untruthful.
- Place the burden of denial on the offender.
- Embed assumptions in questions.
- Avoid multiple questions.
- Ask questions in a rapid-fire manner.
- Use the fatigue factor.
- 'Test the limits'.

Prendergast (1991) used the 'four C's approach' to work with sex offenders:

- *Confrontation by the therapist*. Whatever the offender says, it must be doubted and he must always be made to back up or prove his statements. When using confrontation, it is important not to interrupt the thought processes of the offender with long-winded statements or questions. In order to achieve this, he advocates the use of the following phrases: picture you're being vague, and I don't get a clear understanding off the situation; because I don't understand the motive or reasons for your actions/conclusions; pzzzzt: I don't believe you or don't buy your explanation, reason etc. . .; show me: don't just tell me the changes you've made, give me proof that I can verify; and ?: not enough. Whatever you're telling me is incomplete; and tilt: You're off the subject or track! Get back to what we were discussing. The principle here is the less said by the therapist, the better!!
- *Cautions*—sex offenders are manipulative, seductive and con-artists. Never become too complacent or comfortable with sex offenders.
- *Confirmation*—believe nothing that they say. He coined the term 'partialisation' to reflect the persistent and compulsive practice of telling only part of the story. We should only confirm change when there is behavioural evidence to back it up.
- *Continuation/consistency*—of assessment is essential; as is the reinforcement that self-control is essential. Sex offenders are never cured and may experience recurrences both easily and frequently, at least at the thought and fantasy level.

The ABC approach

If there is a need for a more structured approach to getting further information on the offences, the work of Bliss (1990) is very useful. He formulated the 'ABC' method of interviewing sex offenders. It is a structured approach, which examines all facets of the client's sexual offending. This type of interview works on breaking down the different levels of denial and thereby enables the offender to become aware of his full and active responsibility in the offending.

It aims to establish and unpack the progression of the offenders' behaviour via looking at eliciting specific information as follows:

A—for antecedents

Here the client is encouraged to give a full account of the days, hours and minutes before the offence. The purpose of this is to set the scene and enable the offender to relive the experience; challenge any subsequent excuse of lack of recall; and to establish the progression of behaviour.

Include as much information as possible, however seemingly irrelevant:

Setting (*at home? layout of furniture? other people around?*) Time of day (*dark or light? weather?*) Events during the day (*travelled on which bus? visited which pub?*) Physical state (*any illness?*) Emotional state (*what mood?*) Stress points (*a row with partner?*) Fantasies about victim (*sexually available?*) Relationship to victim (*why this person?*) Description of victim (*age, hair, clothes*). Assumptions about victim (*married?*).

B—for behaviour

The actual offence is the focus of concern. It is important to establish the following at this point:

Degree and nature of planning, what actually happened, internal state at the time (did he feel any relief? or guilt?), efforts made to conceal the offence, degree of violence used, attitudes towards the victim at the time.

Be careful to clarify any inconsistencies and watch the tendency to slide over issues. At this stage Bliss argues it may be counter productive to start challenging or confronting the offender.

C—for consequences: which may include:

Imprisonment and Rule 43, public humiliation, losing job, family break-up, rejection by people of significance, Schedule 1 offender for life, feelings of personal shame, disgust and regret.

Consider also at this stage what the benefits were for the offender. The reality for the offender is that there will have been some pay-off for him.

The complete paper describing the exercise can be found as an appendix to Garrison (1992).

There are several other texts, which also address the interviewing process, and the reader is referred to Maple (1998) and Millar et al. (1992).

Detecting phoniness in sex offenders

Carich (1991) set out some helpful methods for evaluating phoniness in sex offenders. These include:

- Jumping from topic to topic and not focusing on, or staying with, one topic.
- Provides much verbal garbage or verbiage as if he was trying to impress others, avoid issues or present phony self.
- They keep shifting stories, demonstrating contradictions.
- Distorted, twisted information compared to other reports.
- Taking long verbal trips to nowhere or not being relevant.
- They elaborate on leads with tangential verbiage.
- When information is left out and not volunteered.
- Inconsistency in behaviour in the past and present.
- Scanning others to look for cues on how to respond.
- Keeps shifting non-verbal behaviours, cues and responses, i.e. eye movements, body posture, limbs, etc.
- They scan the room looking for any type of confirmation and reinforcement.

- They avoid eye contact.
- They answer questions by asking questions as indicated by their non-verbal (voice—tone, pitch, rate, volume, etc.) in order to get confirmation.
- Hesitation in answering very intense questions.
- Pauses in responses to intense questions, as they construct an answer.
- Strong reactions and over-exaggerated reactions.
- The split second change or appearance of non-verbal cues, usually indicated in the offender's facial expressions.
- Incogruence in verbal or non-verbal behaviour in the here and now.
- Incongruence between cognitive/affective/behavioural/psycho-physiological/social—domains of experience.
- Cutting off feelings—bland or blunted effect.
- Intellectualising.
- The 'chameleon effect'—changing feelings, behaviours or joining you or the group by mimicking what he thinks you want to hear. The changes have no meaning, and are superficial at best.
- Playing in the middle or being non-committed in responses.
- Agreeing on every topic or response.
- Presenting a superficial façade—no real depth in responses or just shallowness.

Summary

Risk assessment is notoriously difficult. Even under optimal circumstances, it is one of the most fraught and complicated tasks for professionals. There are certain strategies which can be adopted in order to make the assessments more structured and considered. This chapter has discussed issues such as worker selection, co-working, professional collusion, inter-agency and organisational issues, and how to engage the offender in the work. It has also attempted to look at what an offender assessment should aim to achieve, how a model of assessment may help us in this task, and what interviewing options are open to us. Whilst good practice does exist, this often occurs in isolation and is rarely co-ordinated and used as the basis of future work. This chapter has looked broadly at a framework within which the sex offender assessment should be contextualised.

Andy Hampson, Principal Officer, Child Protection, City of Salford Community and Social Services Directorate.

Introduction

In a recent review of arrangements for the management of sex offenders in the community (Scottish Office, 1997) the Social Work Services Inspectorate for Scotland (SWSIS) proposed that such arrangements could be broadly divided into four main categories. These were:

1. **Monitoring**: Routinised arrangements for maintaining up-to-date information about the whereabouts of convicted sex offenders. The purpose of monitoring is to know where sex offenders are and about their movements.
2. **Supervision**: Planned arrangements for overseeing sex offenders in the community, designed to manage and reduce the risk posed by the offender within the framework of a statutory order which may be either a community disposal or a post-custodial requirement. The supervision plan includes an assessment of risk and how the supervisor will check on the activities and circumstances of an offender, monitor compliance with all requirements of the order (taking action where necessary) and collaborate with other agencies in managing and reducing risk. Supervision involves assessing risk and putting in place a programme of oversight of the offender designed to minimise the risks. Supervision may take various forms and include checking on accommodation, employment and other activities.
3. **Treatment**: Medical, psychological, or psychosocial measures following a medical diagnosis that an offender is suffering from an illness or disability that may be remedied or alleviated by such treatment. In all cases treatment is provided by, or under the direction of, a registered medical practitioner.
4. **Personal change programmes**: Programmes, including residential programmes, aimed at helping offenders avoid or eradicate their criminal sexual behaviour through control or management of their drives and feelings in other ways than offending. Programmes may use a range of psychological, psycho-social or other methods, and be provided by social workers, probation officers, psychologists, doctors or other health professionals, and involve others, such as residential or prison staff.

Although in practice these categories often overlap they do provide a useful way of differentiating the various interventions and I have therefore attempted to follow the model in structuring this chapter.

The chapter begins with an examination of the main provisions of the Sex Offenders Act 1997 and a brief examination of the operation of sex offender registers. This section also includes a consideration of issues around the rehousing of sex offenders and the vexed question of community notification. It is followed by a review of those sections of the recently implemented Crime and Disorder Act which relate to the management of sex offenders, with a particular emphasis on the guidance concerning sex offender orders.

The next section is concerned largely with the role of the probation service in the supervision of sex offenders in the community and the chapter concludes with a review of community-based treatment programmes and their effectiveness.

Although this handbook is concerned exclusively with those who offend sexually against children, the legal and policy framework within which strategies for the management of such offenders in the community have been developed do not generally differentiate between the different categories of offender. I have therefore adopted the generic term, sex offender, throughout most of this chapter and the review includes the full range of provisions available for all types of sex offender in addition to those which have been specifically developed for dealing with offenders against children.

The Sex Offenders Act 1997

Introduction

The Sex Offenders Act 1997 came into force on the 1st September 1997. It requires those who have convictions for certain specified offences to register with the police in the area in which they live, and to provide, and keep up to date, information about their whereabouts.

The Act's stated purpose is to ensure the accuracy of information on sex offenders recorded on the police national computer. Prior to the introduction of the Act, this information was often limited to the address of the offender at the time of his conviction, and was therefore very often out of date.

Guidance issued in support of the Act has made

it clear, however, that the purpose is not simply to record the information but to use it proactively to undertake risk assessments of all convicted sex offenders living in the community and to monitor the activities of those who are considered to represent a significant risk.

The Act is not retrospective. It applies only to persons convicted after the 1st September 1997 and those who, on the date of implementation, were serving community or custodial sentences for relevant offences (in this respect it could be said in a limited way to be retrospective).

The Home Office estimated that there were around 4,000 offenders in prison on the 1st September 1997 to whom the provisions of the Act would apply.

Qalifying offences

Qualifying offences include rape, buggery and indecent assaults on adult men or women and incest, rape, indecent assault and other indecency offences involving children. A complete list of all the qualifying offences is set out in Schedule 1 of the Act. Schedule 1 of the Sex Offenders Act is substantially different from Schedule 1 of the Children and Young Persons Act 1933 in that, among other differences it includes sexual offences against adults and excludes offences involving physical assaults on children.

Administrative arrangements

Those convicted of a qualifying offence after the 1st September 1997 will be issued with a certificate by the court in which they are convicted. This certificate provides confirmation of the conviction or finding and contains a summary of the registration requirements with which the offender must comply. A copy of the certificate is sent to the police criminal records unit (in the area in which the offender normally resides) and, where a prison sentence is imposed, to the relevant custodial establishment. The custodial establishment will inform the police of the prisoner's release date.

All those who are liable to register must, within 14 days of conviction or release:

- Inform the local police of their name(s), date of birth and current address.
- Report any subsequent change of address within 14 days of the change.
- Notify the police of any other address at which they stay or are resident for 14 days or longer in any 12 month period.

Notification may be provided in writing or by going in person to any police station in the area where the offender is living.

Responsibility for registration lies with the offender himself. Supervising probation officers are expected to ensure that the offender is aware of the requirements but are not directly responsible for

ensuring compliance. However, agency procedures generally require confirmation of the advice given to the offender to be provided to him in writing with a copy to the local police.

The offender must register within 14 days of sentence or release. Failure to register is a criminal offence punishable by a fine and up to 6 months imprisonment.

Offenders under 18 years cannot be sent to prison for failing to comply with the registration requirements. However, the court in which the juvenile offender is convicted can impose the notification requirement on the offender's parent or guardian. In the case of young people who are looked after, the local authority can, by order of the court imposing sentence, be made responsible for discharging the registration requirements.

The length of time for which the registration requirements apply depends upon the length of the sentence imposed for the qualifying offence or offences. In the case of young people under the age of 18 years, the period of registration is half that which would apply if an adult had received a similar sentence.

Sentence	Adults	Juveniles
Life imprisonment	Indefinite	Indefinite
Hospital restriction order	Indefinite	Indefinite
> 30 months prison	Indefinite	Indefinite
6–30 months	10 years	5 years
< 6 months prison	7 years	3 ½ years
Hospital (no restriction order)	7 years	3 ½ years
Non-custodial sentence or caution	5 years	2 ½ years

The notification period starts from the date of caution, conviction or release from sentence. When a court convicts a person of one of the qualifying offences it will issue a certificate to the offender and send a copy to the police. The police will issue a similar certificate where the offender receives a caution. Following the implementation of the provisions of the Crime and Disorder Act the caution will be replaced by a reprimand or final warning.

Local arrangements for responding to the act

Home Office Circular 39/97 directs the police to undertake a risk assessment in respect of each offender in order to determine:

- Generally, the potential threat to the community;
- Specifically, the immediate threat to any persons with whom the offender may be having contact (including members of the same household).

The police will receive notification of an individual's requirement to register from a number of sources (e.g. from courts following sentence, and from prisons prior to the offender's release). Whilst specific local arrangements may vary, it is likely that most will follow a procedure similar to that operating in Greater Manchester and described below (Greater Manchester Police and Probation Joint Protocol 1998).

Within two weeks of notification (and regardless of actual registration) the local Crime Management Unit (CMU) must complete an initial intelligence check and risk assessment which will include:

- Details of all previous sex offences including sentences.
- Details of all offences involving violence.
- The method and pattern of the individual's offending.
- Details of any treatment received.
- Attitude towards victims/offences.
- Any significant relationships with other sex offenders.

In gathering information and undertaking the assessment of risk the CMU is expected to liase with other police units and with other agencies who may have a contribution to make. In particular, the local probation service will be contacted in order to establish whether the offender is currently under supervision or has been known to them in the past. The probation service is itself required to undertake an assessment of the potential for harm and the risk of re-offending for all clients with whom they are involved or on whom they have prepared a PSR.

Following the completion of the initial intelligence check and risk assessment each offender will be provisionally assigned to one of the following categories:

1. Screened out: low/moderate risk.
2. Screened in: offender in custody—high risk.
3. Screened in: offender in community—high risk.

Where an offender is screened out this decision will be reported to other agencies and the case will be reviewed in 6–12 months. Where an offender is screened in, i.e. assessed as high risk, consideration will need to be given to the development of a strategy for managing the risk. This will include consideration of whether the criteria for referral to a Multi-Agency Risk Panel (MARP) are met. All cases where there is thought to be a need for disclosure to a third party must be referred to the MARP.

Home visits by the police are considered to be an important source of information in undertaking the risk assessment and in verifying the information provided to the register by the offender

Multi-Agency Risk Panels (MARPs)

Multi-Agency Risk Panels were originally developed in West Yorkshire in response to concerns about difficulties in protecting the public from those known to represent a risk to the community.

Following a successful pilot in Rochdale in 1995 they have now been introduced throughout Greater Manchester. Lead responsibility is shared between the police and probation services with other agencies, particularly health, housing and social services also playing an important role.

The purpose of the Multi-Agency Risk Panel is to provide a forum for sharing information on potentially dangerous offenders and for developing strategies for managing the risks that they pose to individuals and to the community. The panels do not deal exclusively with sex offenders, the sole criteria for referral being that there is believed to be a high likelihood of re-offending and that the nature of the offences that are likely, constitute a serious risk of harm.

The administration of the panels is managed by the probation service at district level and all referrals are routed through a panel manager. Meetings are usually held at 6 weekly intervals but there is provision for meetings to be convened at very short notice in special cases.

In addition to the core membership, attendance is usually restricted to those who have a significant contribution to make. Issues of confidentiality are given a high priority in order to facilitate the free exchange of information within the meeting. There is an expectation that offenders who are the subject of a panel will be told of the meeting unless this would be likely to put someone's safety at risk.

The objectives for the panel in each individual case are:

- To share information at critical stages of an agency's contact with the offender, e.g. prior to his release from a custodial sentence.
- To assess the level of risk to individuals and/or the community.
- To devise strategies for managing and minimising the risks involved.
- To decide whether to include the offender's name on the MARP register.
- To agree arrangements for monitoring and review.

The MARP register operates in a similar way to the child protection register in that it includes only those who are considered to represent a continuing risk of significant harm to the community. Registration is supported by the development of a formal multi-agency plan to address the main areas of risk and these arrangements are reviewed at regular intervals to ensure that they are appropriate to the needs of the case and that registration continues to be justified.

There is a range of options available in seeking to address the concerns that may arise. These may include:

- Preventing or delaying the offender's release.
- Imposing conditions on release.
- Arranging accommodation.
- Surveillance/monitoring.
- Intelligence/information sharing.
- Victim preparation and protection.
- Contingency planning.

Wherever possible the co-operation of the offender will be sought, but unless there is the power to include conditions in an order or licence, compliance is voluntary. The range of conditions that can be included and the factors which determine the duration of post-release supervision are considered later in the chapter.

Multi-Agency Risk Panels are now well established in Greater Manchester and in a number of other areas. Although they were established well before the introduction of the Sex Offenders Act and the Crime and Disorder Act they will clearly have an important role to play in the implementation of the new legislation.

Disclosure and community notification

In the guidance that was issued by the government in support of the Sex offenders Act (HOC 39/1997) it was made very clear that they were under no illusions about the limitations of registers, by themselves, to provide the protection to the public that was intended. The purpose of the register was not simply to collect and record information, but, as indicated above, to use that information to drive a process of risk assessment and strategic intervention. Central to that process is the free exchange of information with other agencies and, in exceptional cases with third parties and the wider community.

Arrangements for the exchange of information between agencies have been well established in most areas for a number of years. Area Child Protection Committees in particular have provided a very effective forum for establishing close collaborative relationships between the key players in the child protection field and this has provided the foundation for the development of a similar partnerships in tackling wider issues of community safety. However, the sharing of sensitive information outside of these established partnerships is much more problematic.

Appendix A of the Home Office Circular provides guidance to the police on the management of the information that is acquired under the provisions of the Sex Offender Act. It describes the legal framework within which information can be exchanged and provides some examples of occasions when information exchange and disclosure to third parties may be appropriate.

The guidance sets out the following factors to be taken into account in deciding whether an offender poses such a high risk that disclosure may be indicated:

- The nature and pattern of the offender's previous offending.
- His compliance with previous sentences or court orders.
- Any predatory behaviour which may indicate a likelihood that he will re-offend.

- The probability that any further offence will be committed.
- The likely harm that such behaviour would cause.
- The extent to which potential victims, such as children, are vulnerable.
- The potential consequences of disclosure to the offender and their family.
- The potential consequences of the disclosure for other aspects of law and order.

In *R. v. The Chief Constable of North Wales Police, ex parte AB* (1997) 4 All ER 692, the court held that although there is a general presumption that the police should not disclose information about offenders to third parties, they could do so where it was necessary to prevent crime or to alert the public to a potential risk.

In this case the applicant and his wife had each served a seven year prison sentence after pleading guilty to a number of serious offences involving the sexual abuse of children. Following their release they were forced to move on two occasions after details of their offences, together with photographs, were published in local newspapers. They then took up residence on a caravan park in North Wales and were forced to move again when the police, concerned that the school holidays were approaching, informed the site owners of their convictions. The applicant sought a judicial review of the actions of the police.

Lord Bingham, in the leading judgement, supported the actions of the police but made it clear that blanket disclosure policies were not acceptable and the decision to disclose must depend on a careful consideration of all the circumstances of each individual case. It must be part of a carefully considered plan of action in which the interests of the offender and the potential impact of disclosure (i.e. risk of victimisation and loss of contact with the offender) should also be taken into account.

With regard to persons who are only suspected of offending against children, the earlier case of *R. v. Devon County Council* provides authority for disclosure in cases where a person is considered to represent a risk because of previous allegations but where there has not been a prosecution or conviction. Again each case must be carefully considered on its merits within existing arrangements for inter-agency collaboration.

There is now a small but significant body of case law which relates to the issue of disclosure and it is likely that policies which adhere to the following principles will be safe from any claim under both British law and the provisions of Article 5 of the European Convention on Human Rights:

- Disclosure to third parties of personal information about individual offenders should be exceptions to a general policy of confidentiality.
- Each decision with regard to disclosure must be justifiable on the basis of a thorough assessment

of the likelihood of the harm which might otherwise result.

- Disclosure should be only one part of a more comprehensive plan for managing the risk posed by a potential offender.
- All decisions must be based on an assessment of the potential for simply displacing the risk or compromising other elements of the risk management strategy.

Sex offender registers: lessons from America

In 1997 the Home Office commissioned a report on the operation of sex offender registers in America to assist practitioners in the UK in responding to the requirements of the Sex Offenders Act (Hebenton and Thomas, 1997).

Sex offender registers have been in operation in some States in America for many years, the first having been introduced in California in 1947. Most, however, have been established much more recently, largely in response to a federal law enacted in 1994 which required all States to have introduced a register by 1997. Further legislation including the infamous Megan's Law, requires States to allow public access to registration information and to pass information to the FBI to enable a National Sex Offender Registry to be established. This legislation, and the associated guidance, is also intended to bring about a more standardised approach to the variety of different arrangements that are currently in existence at State and county level.

Compliance rates in the US vary considerably from 30 per cent in one State to over 80 per cent in others. Similarly, the accuracy of the information recorded on registers is extremely variable. A study by the Californian Department of Justice concluded that the accuracy of addresses was 'probably quite poor'. This tends to be supported by the experience of the Los Angeles Police Department who, in 1984, during a search for a missing child, attempted to contact 4,400 registered sex offenders and found that 90 per cent of the addresses were inaccurate. One of the aims of the move towards a more consistent approach to registration arrangements is to encourage the adoption of measures which have been shown to be effective in maximising compliance rates and accuracy of information.

As is already evident in the UK, the introduction of registers in the US has encouraged the formation of multi-agency risk panels to share information, undertake assessments and develop strategies for managing and minimising risk. These may include community notification and surveillance operations.

Are registers effective?
Registers have certainly been effective in the US in promoting a more collaborative approach to the identification and management of risk. However, there is as yet very little research on their effectiveness in preventing or detecting offences or on the potential displacement effects of registration and community notification. One study which did examine re-offending and detection found no difference in the rate of re-offending in those subject to disclosure but there was a marked reduction in the interval between offending and re-conviction. Those subject to disclosure were re-arrested within an average of two years compared to five years for the non-disclosure group and is thought likely that this was attributable to the increased level of surveillance by both the police and the public.

A possible indirect benefit of the registration requirements was that high risk offenders who failed to register could be arrested for non-compliance when found in suspicious circumstances even though there was no evidence of an offence having been committed.

On the other hand, it has been suggested that an awareness of the implications of the registration and community notification requirements, not only for the offender, but also, potentially, for other members of his family, may impact on the willingness of some victims to report offences (Scottish Office, 1997).

The impact of community notification has so far been rather less problematic than might have been anticipated with estimates suggesting that some form of harassment occurs only in around 10 per cent of disclosure cases. Practice varies widely but in most States a relatively cautious approach has been adopted with decisions being taken at a very senior level, supported by measures to reassure the community about the steps being taken to address the risks posed by the offender and warning of the penalties for harassment.

As in the UK, problems arise more often in response to uninformed speculation and spontaneous vigilantism than to officially sanctioned disclosure. Agencies report that the threat of disclosure in response to non-compliance can be effective in motivating offenders to participate in treatment programmes and adhere to conditions of supervision.

What can we learn from the American experience?
As anticipated the main benefits of sex offender registers are that they:

- Provide a mechanism for the regular monitoring of known sex offenders.
- Facilitate the sharing of information and closer links between agencies.
- Provide the basis for the development of risk assessment and risk management strategies.

The most important lessons from the American experience are that high compliance rates and accurate information are critical to success in maximising the effectiveness of registers. To this end, Hebenton and Thomas make a number of recommendations and these have generally been incorporated into the guidance issued in support of the Sex Offenders Act in England and Wales. They suggest that police forces in this country should:

- Ensure that they have effective verification procedures.
- Ensure effective organisational arrangements for optimising information sharing within and between agencies.
- Introduce efficient systems for maintaining and updating information.
- Agree clear procedures for managing information on offenders moving between areas.
- Determine, where some form of third party or community notification has taken place, the frequency of review and updating.
- Anticipate and make contingency plans for minimising the risk of vigilantism.

Rehousing sex offenders

The provision of appropriate accommodation is critical to the effective management of risk in dealing with potentially dangerous sex offenders in the community. Not only does a settled address assist in monitoring and surveillance but it will also facilitate participation in a treatment programme.

The provision of social housing also ensures that careful consideration can be given to issues of risk in determining the nature and location of the accommodation to be provided.

In response to media and public concern, the Chartered Institute of Housing published a paper in February 1998 which summarises the legal and operational issues involved in the rehousing of sex offenders. The principles set out in the paper have been endorsed by both the Local Government Association and the National Housing Federation and are based on the premise that social housing providers have a significant role to play in multi-agency arrangements for the management of potentially dangerous offenders.

Acknowledging that sex offenders will always be a part of the community and therefore any risk they pose needs to be actively managed, the paper sets out to clarify some of the legal and operational issues which housing organisations need to take into account in developing policies and procedures on rehousing them.

The legal framework for the allocation of accommodation by local authorities in England and Wales is provided by the Housing Act 1996. Part VI of the Act states that local housing authorities can only provide accommodation to 'qualifying persons'. However, individual local authorities are relatively free to determine classes of person who

are, or are not, qualifying persons and the code of practice issued in support of the Act encourages authorities to exercise discretion in determining eligibility in individual cases. This has not prevented a number of local authorities from taking advantage of the provisions of Part VI to introduce a total exclusion of sex offenders against children from eligibility for social housing. The legitimacy of such policies is open to question but so far there has not been a challenge to establish the legality of such blanket exclusions.

The Institute of Housing paper suggests that indefinite blanket bans on broad classes of people are almost certainly open to legal challenge. It also points out that under Part VII of the 1996 Act, local authorities have statutory obligations towards vulnerable homeless persons from which sex offenders cannot be indiscriminately excluded. More positively, the paper suggests that the successful resettlement and reintegration of sex offenders within society, for which settled housing is a key requirement, can make an important contribution to managing the risk that they pose. Blanket exclusion policies will only make this process more difficult to achieve. It should also be noted that the Crime and Disorder Act includes requirements for local authorities and the police to produce strategies for reducing crime and disorder in their areas. These requirements apply to all local authority departments.

The adoption of an exclusion policy in one area will almost certainly result in displacement of the problem into neighbouring authorities and will force offenders on to dependence on the private sector where there is limited opportunity for regulating the type and location of the accommodation with which they are provided. On the contrary, there is a relatively high concentration within the private sector, in many areas, of the kind of households which are likely to be most vulnerable to the activities of high risk sex offenders.

The Institute therefore recommend that local authorities and housing associations (now known in England and Wales as Registered Social Landlords, RSLs) should:

- Abide by the legal requirements of the Data Protection Act 1984 and the Rehabilitation of Offenders Act 1974.
- Be active participants in forums or multi-agency panels to share information about the risks posed by individuals at an early stage.
- Negotiate agreements with the police at a local level on the sharing of information.
- Clarify or reinforce codes of conduct for staff and committee members on issues of confidentiality.
- Liase with other agencies on possible courses of action if the identity of an offender who is already a tenant is revealed to the general public.

Crime and Disorder Act 1998

Introduction

The Crime and Disorder Act 1998 received royal assent on the 31st July 1998 but its various provisions are to be implemented in stages with most being introduced on the 1st and 7th August 1998 and the 30th September 1998. A number of the Act's provisions will initially only come into force in certain areas where they will be subject to pilot trials.

A wide range of guidance is being produced to assist with implementation and draft guidance on sex offender orders was published as a consultation document on the Home Office Crime and Disorder Act website early in September. Home Office Circular 38/1998 provides an overview of the Act and a timetable for implementation.

The Introductory Guide to the Act emphasises the importance of understanding its overall objective, which is 'to tackle crime and disorder and create safer communities'. There are a number of underlying themes, which are:

- The purpose of the youth justice system is to reduce offending and to ensure that action is taken quickly to, 'nip youth offending in the bud'.
- The police and the local authority with the whole community must establish a local partnership to cut crime.
- Local authorities and other public bodies must consider the crime and disorder implications of their decisions.

The emphasis on crime prevention and community safety as a shared responsibility requiring a partnership between the police, the local authority and other public bodies and the local community is a recurring theme throughout the provisions of the Act. Sections 5 and 6 in particular place upon local authorities and the police joint responsibility for the formulation and implementation of crime and disorder reduction strategies in their areas. Police authorities, probation committees and health authorities have a legal obligation to co-operate fully in this process. The results of local reviews of the levels and patterns of crime and disorder must be published, targets must be set for tackling local issues and performance in achieving these targets must also be publicized. There is a clear expectation of consultation with local business, the voluntary sector and the community in conducting the reviews and setting the targets.

Sex offender orders

Section 2 of the Act, to be implemented in December 1998 creates new sex offender orders which are intended to fill a gap in existing provisions for dealing with the continued risk that some sex offenders may pose in the community.

The orders are preventative and require those subject to them to register under the Sex Offenders Act 1997 for as long as they are in force. The minimum duration for an order is five years and breach of an order without reasonable excuse is a criminal offence, triable either way, and with a maximum penalty on indictment of five years in prison.

The police can apply for an order against any sex offender whose behaviour in the community gives them reasonable cause for concern that an order is necessary to protect the public from serious harm from him.

Applications are to the magistrates' court acting in its civil capacity. Sex offences are defined by reference to Part 1 of the Sex Offenders Act 1997.

It is worth noting that the provisions of Section 2 apply equally to children and young people and in theory therefore an application for an order can be made in respect of a child as young as ten years old. In practice this is not very likely but there will be some older adolescent offenders for whom such an order may be appropriate. The local authority will therefore be under a responsibility to inform the police of any concerns they may have in respect of those young people with whom they are involved.

Criteria for seeking an order

The guidance identifies two basic conditions which have to be met in deciding whether to seek an order:

- The person must be a sex offender within the meaning of the Act (effectively they must have been cautioned for or convicted of one or more of the offences listed in Part 1 of the Sex Offender Act, 1997).
- He must have acted, since his conviction and since the date of implementation of this part of the Act, in a way, which gives reasonable cause to believe that an order is necessary to protect the public from serious harm from him.

By virtue of clause 17(2) of the Act the definition of 'serious harm' is the same as that set out in Part 1 of the Criminal Justice Act, 1991. Section 31(3) of the Criminal Justice Act states that, in relation to an offender convicted of a violent or sexual offence, protecting the public from serious harm from him means protecting members of the public from death or serious personal injury, whether physical or psychological, occasioned by further offences committed by the defendant. Although the guidance is no more specific than this, it is almost certain that the potential sexual abuse of a child would in circumstances constitute 'serious harm'.

The police do not need to prove an intention to cause serious harm, only that there is a probability of such harm as a result of the offender's behaviour.

In doing so it is likely that a link will need to be established between the recent actions or activities of the offender and the circumstances of his previous offending. Thus the context will be as important as the behaviour itself in making a judgement about the degree of risk.

In one of the first cases to be dealt with under the new legislation, a curfew order was imposed on a 35 year old man who had been seen by the police peering through the windows of student accommodation in south Manchester. He was carrying his shoes, gloves, a tape recorder and a condom. He had moved back into the area after serving seven years of a twelve year sentence for the rape of two students whose flats had been broken into. The curfew order barred him from entering a wide area within which most of the City's student accommodation was situated between 10.00p.m. and 7.00a.m. until the year 2007 (Manchester Evening News, 4th January 1999).

The risk of harm can be a general one and it will not be necessary to establish concerns in relation to any particular individual. It therefore follows that in the above example the fact of being found outside a school will be sufficient justification for an application for an order without the need for evidence of an approach to any individual child.

Where the police have concerns about the behaviour of a sex offender, either from their own observations or as a result of information received from another agency or a member of the public, they will be expected to undertake some form of risk assessment before deciding whether to apply for an order.

The following factors are recommended to be taken into account:

- The probability or likelihood that a further offence will be committed.
- The potential harm resulting from such behaviour; and the potential victims of the harm.
- The nature and circumstances of the previous conviction or convictions and any pattern which emerges.
- The current circumstances of an offender and how these might foreseeably change (e.g. work placements/environments; housing; family/relationships; stress/drink/drugs; proximity to schools/playgrounds, etc.).
- The disclosure implications if an order is applied for; and how the court process might affect the ability to manage the offender in the community.
- An assessment of the accuracy and currency of the information about the individual (including an assessment of the status of those expressing concern and their reasons for doing so).
- The nature and pattern of the behaviour giving rise to concern; and any predatory behaviour which may indicate a likelihood of re-offending.

- Compliance, or otherwise, with previous sentences, court orders or supervision arrangements.
- Compliance or otherwise with therapeutic help and its outcome.

It is anticipated that, although the ultimate responsibility rests with the police, the assessment of risk will be informed by consultation with other relevant agencies. It is therefore very likely that, as with disclosure, all cases where an application for a sex offender order is being considered will be referred to the multi-agency risk panel. The risk of uncontrolled disclosure as a result of publicity arising from the application is identified as an issue which will require careful handling.

The issue of the disclosure of information between agencies is directly addressed in the Act and section 115 provides that any person can lawfully disclose information *for the purposes of the Act* to the police, local authorities, probation services or health authorities even if they would not otherwise have this power. Section 115 should prove to be of considerable value in reinforcing existing protocols or in facilitating their development where they have not already been agreed.

Applying for an order

As previously indicated an application for an order is made by way of complaint to the magistrates' court, acting in its civil capacity. The standard of proof is therefore the civil standard of a balance of probabilities. Again, since these are civil proceedings, the CPS is not likely to have a role and the police will therefore have to rely on in-house lawyers or private solicitors. Legal aid will be available to defendants subject to the usual eligibility criteria.

The circumstances which are likely to give rise to an application for a sex offender order are such that the proceedings will need to be dealt with speedily and magistrates' courts will need to give consideration to how this can be assured.

What the order may contain

In addition to the requirement to register under the Sex Offender Act 1997 for a specified period, the order can also include any provisions which may be necessary for the protection of the public. Such provisions must obviously be relevant to the circumstances which gave rise to the application and they should be sufficiently specific to leave no doubt about what constitutes a breach. The conditions can only be prohibitive. There is no power to compel an offender to engage in any specified activity.

In the guidance, an example is given of a man who has a conviction for an offence of indecent assault on a young child. He is subsequently seen to be frequenting the area outside a local primary school at the end of the school day. On a number of occasions he approaches children on their way home, offers them sweets, and tries to engage them in conversation. Following complaints from parents, the police set up an observation and confirm his activities. They apply for an order which prohibits him from going within 200 yards of the named school, or any other primary school, between the hours of 8.00a.m. and 10.00a.m, 12.00p.m. and 2.00p.m. and 3.00p.m. and 5.00p.m.

The minimum duration for an order is five years and once granted the police must monitor compliance and keep under review the need for the order to remain in force. Either the police or the defendant can apply for a variation or discharge of the order. However, an order cannot be discharged within five years without the agreement of both parties.

Breach of an order

A breach of a sex offender order is an arrestable offence with a maximum penalty of up to five years imprisonment. The standard of proof is the criminal standard of 'beyond reasonable doubt'. A breach of the registration requirement alone will not formally be an arrestable offence but it is a criminal offence punishable by a fine and/or a maximum of six months imprisonment.

Comment

Sex offender orders have the potential to be a very powerful weapon in the defence of the community from a minority of high risk offenders. It is essential, if they are to be effective, that they are regarded as a credible and responsible method of intervention and that in those cases where applications are made the decision is supported by a fully informed risk assessment and inter-agency consensus. The application of a realistic standard of proof by the courts will be essential to the effectiveness of this measure and it is vitally important therefore that in the early stages of the Act's implementation, agencies are seen to be adopting a measured response to the exploitation of this power.

Forms of supervision and sentencing provisions for sex offenders in the community

Historically, sex offenders have always represented a small but significant minority in the case-load of the probation service but, until relatively recently, there has been little in the way of specialist provision for them.

Throughout the 1990s there were a series of internal and Home Office initiatives which progressively raised the profile of work with sex offenders. However, it should be acknowledged that much of the early impetus came from the activities of a relatively small group of individual staff members with a particular interest in this area of work. Thus the 1991 Thematic Inspection Report on work with sex offenders (HM Inspectorate of Probation, 1991) found that:

"Within those probation services visited, individuals or groups of POs, often on their own initiative, had in recent years developed knowledge, skills and ad hoc support systems in order to equip themselves to work with a group of offenders with whom they often feel especially vulnerable. In relation to such offenders, they have to make crucial judgements about risk and dangerousness and have to persist in confronting what at times are repulsive aspects of offending behaviour. While some 'centres of excellence' have been created within services, frequently inspired and led by middle managers or main grade staff particularly committed to such work, it is, nevertheless, the inspectors' view that while such initial development may properly be grass roots led, the long-term provision of such facilities and the support and supervision for staff is the responsibility of management and should be built into the official management systems of area and division. This was not always the case."

In July 1996 a further thematic inspection was begun with the fieldwork being undertaken in ten probation areas during late 1996 and early 1997. The report, published in March 1998 (HM Inspectorate of Probation, 1998) concluded that:

"The policy framework relating to sex offenders in probation services had developed considerably in recent years but had nonetheless in some cases been outstripped by the even faster growth of practice . . . Increasingly, work with sex offenders was taking place within the framework of services' overarching policies for assessing and managing the risk posed by all dangerous offenders which had also been considerably developed in recent years. In most of the work sampled, the development of risk management policies was positively reflected in practice."

The 1998 Inspection Report considered the full range of work undertaken by the service and includes the checking of bail arrangements, pre-sentence reports, individual supervision and group work programmes and the work of probation hostels. What follows is a summary of the report's main findings together with a brief account of the legislative and policy framework within which the service operates.

Bail

Bail Information Officers (BIOs) are employed by the probation service to provide information to the Crown Prosecution Service (CPS) to inform decisions with regard to the granting of bail. Some BIOs are qualified probation officers but most are unqualified. However, in-service training for BIOs generally includes some limited coverage of issues relating to sex offenders and some services have produced practice guidance for court based staff.

Where a defendant is charged with a sexual offence involving children, the Bail Information Officer would be expected to check if there were any children at that address (usually only by asking the householder over the phone). Checks should also be made with social services about the whereabouts of the offender's victims. Relevant information is then provided to the CPS with whom the responsibility lies for making the decision about whether to oppose the bail application or the proposed address. It is not the responsibility of the Bail Information Officers to undertake any assessment of potential risk.

The Inspectorate found that BIOs were well aware of the need to be particularly vigilant in checking the proposed accommodation arrangements for sex offenders. However such requests were, for most of them, relatively infrequent.

Pre-sentence reports

There is no centrally collected information on the number of pre-sentence reports (PSRs) prepared on sex offenders. However, an examination of 3,100 PSRs as part of a joint ACOP/HMIP quality assurance review in May/June 1996 found 1.9 per cent were for sexual offences. This suggests a national total in that year of between 4,000 and 4,500.

A total of 331 PSRs were included in the 1998 Thematic Inspection. Each area was asked to submit the last 40 reports completed prior to the 31st July 1996 on defendants convicted of a specified range of sexual offences.

The overall quality of the reports was high, with 34 per cent being rated as very good, and a further 48 per cent satisfactory. This represents an improvement on the earlier ACOP survey which found only 73 per cent of reports to be satisfactory. In both samples the quality of reports varied considerably between areas.

In 38 per cent of the reports in the HMIP inspection there was a supplemental assessment undertaken by a specialist officer and a further 29 per cent had some level of specialist input.

In some areas there was a specific requirement that only specialist officers should be involved in the preparation of reports on sex offenders though this didn't always happen in practice. The actual rate varied considerably between areas, from 56–98 per cent. Overall, 81 per cent of the reports in the sample gave the impression that they had been written by someone knowledgeable about patterns of sexual offending.

The preparation of pre-sentence reports is governed by national standards and many areas provide detailed practice guidance on the particular issues to be addressed in preparing PSRs on sex offenders. The contents of a typical PSR will include:

1. Introduction—source of information and general background.
2. Offence analysis:
   —summary of offence;
   —context;
   —culpability/premeditation;
   —attitude to victim.
3. Relevant information about the offender:
   —previous convictions;
   —pattern of offending;
   —previous sentences.
4. Conclusion and recommendations.

Home visits were only conducted in 10 per cent of the cases in the HMIP inspection even though 66 per cent of the defendants were on bail. Practice guidance in a number of services recommends home visits when preparing PSRs on sex offenders.

Similarly, practice guidance frequently emphasises the importance of obtaining detailed information from a number of sources about the nature of the offending behaviour rather than relying exclusively on the offender's own account. Documents such as witness statements were available from the CPS in 95 per cent of cases but significant information was judged not to be available in 15 per cent of the cases.

Section 44 of the Criminal Justice Act 1991 contains provision for a judge, when sentencing a sex offender to a period of custody in excess of 12 months, to extend the period of post-release supervision to the end of the full period of imprisonment imposed. National standards for PSRs require those writing reports on sex offenders to have regard to these provisions but they have not been extensively used, with less than 500 offenders being subject to them at the end of 1996.

Although only a minority of services had issued any guidance on section 44, those which had advised that extended supervision should always be recommended for sex offenders unless there were specific reasons why it was not appropriate. However, of the 248 PSRs prepared for the crown court that were examined during the inspection, only 38 per cent contained a reference to the section. This is surprising given that officers themselves frequently commented on the problems associated with the supervision of offenders subject to periods of post-release supervision that were too short to allow for their inclusion in treatment programmes.

A non-custodial sentence was recommended in 65 per cent of reports but in a quarter of these there was no detailed proposals for supervision. In nearly a fifth of cases custody was the only sentencing option considered.

Supervision in the community

Sex offenders may be subject to supervision either as an alternative to a custodial sentence immediately following conviction or following their release from prison after serving a sentence. In addition to the basic requirement to keep the supervising officer informed of their circumstances there are a number of specific requirements which may also be included.

There are three main elements to supervision:

- Advice and support to assist the offender in securing a settled lifestyle within the context of which the risk of re-offending is minimised;
- Direct work to address the factors associated with offending and the risk of re-offending;
- Monitoring compliance with supervision requirements and any other measures intended to minimise the risk to the community which the offender may pose.

A court can place an offender under the supervision of the probation service for a period of between six months and three years. Such an order would normally be granted on the basis of a recommendation in a PSR. The report will set out the requirements to be complied with and these should have been discussed and agreed with the subject during the completion of the report.

National standards require a minimum of weekly contact for the first 3 months and fortnightly contact thereafter for the first half of the order. During the second half, contact may be less frequent but should still be at least monthly. It is expected that there will be at least one home visit during the first three months of the order.

If an offender does not comply with the requirements of an order the supervising officer may issue a warning. Non-compliance or a serious breach of conditions can result in breach proceedings. In this case the offender is returned to court. If the breach is proven, the court can impose a fine, vary the conditions of the order, impose a community service order in addition to the probation order or terminate the order and impose a different sentence for the original offence.

There were around 9,000 sex offenders on the case-load of the probation service at the end of 1996 with 4,753 of these in the community and 4,338 in prison. This represents an increase of 27 per cent on the total of 7,109 sex offenders on case-loads in an ACOP survey in 1995. The increase is due at least in part to the increasing number of throughcare cases resulting from the extension of post-release supervision following implementation of the Criminal Justice Act 1991. Sex offenders therefore account for approximately 3 per cent of the total of court orders supervised by the probation service and 9 per cent of the total throughcare case-load.

The 1998 HMIP inspection Report includes a total of 343 cases under supervision in the community of which 158 were probation and combination orders and 185 were throughcare licences. Areas were asked to provide the first 20 probation and combination orders made after the 1st January 1996

and 25 throughcare licences reflecting both short-term and long-term work.

Overall 86 per cent of cases were considered to be supervised to a satisfactory standard and 40 of these were rated as 'very good'. However, in 6 per cent of cases there was no evidence that the offending behaviour itself had been directly addressed and in around 10 per cent of cases the offender's level of denial was such that any offence focussed work was effectively precluded.

National standards require a minimum of monthly contact and this was achieved in 93 per cent of cases. In many instances a higher frequency of contact was appropriate and inspectors judged that the level of contact was appropriate to the circumstances of the case in 88 per cent of the sample. However the number of home visits were only judged to be sufficient to address issues of risk in 40 per cent of probation and 65 per cent of throughcare cases. There was no evidence of any home visits at all in 25 per cent of cases and unannounced home visits were only found in 6 per cent of the cases.

Additional requirements relating to group work or contact with a psychologist or psychiatrist were examined in a sample of 120 cases. First attendance was found to be within four weeks of making the order or date of release in 46 per cent of cases but was 3 months in nearly a fifth of cases and over six months in 7 per cent. The work being undertaken as part of the additional requirement was judged to have been an enhancement to the effectiveness of supervision in 70 per cent of cases.

No sessions of individual work were directly observed but the inspectors considered that such work was less well informed by a coherent theoretical framework than was found in the group work programmes.

There was generally a high level of compliance with both supervision and additional requirements. In total over a third of the 343 in the sample failed to comply with some aspect of the order or licence but only 34 represented significant non-compliance. Of these, 13 were breached and 12 were given warnings but in 9 cases it does not appear that any action was taken.

In around 20 per cent of probation and 43 per cent of throughcare cases the offender's continued denial limited the work that the supervising officer was able to undertake. The inspectors were concerned that in 17 per cent of cases there was no evidence that this denial was being challenged.

A quarter of probation orders were for less than two years and it is questionable whether this is really long enough in the case of sex offenders. In one area where there was clear practice guidance on the issue, there was only one case where the order was for less than three years, and all orders included a requirement for group work attendance. Similarly, one of the other areas had developed a standard package for child sex offenders which included a three year order, additional requirements and weekly contact with the supervising officer. In areas where there was no such expectation the proportion of three year orders was as low as 31 per cent.

Both of the areas referred to above included within the additional requirements, conditions which prohibited unsupervised contact with children. Specifically the requirements were:

- Not to seek or undertake employment which would bring the offender into direct contact with young people under the age of 16 years;
- Not to receive visits at home from any child under the age of 16 years and not to visit the home of any child without prior written permission from the supervising officer;
- Not to undertake any leisure pursuit or hobby which brings the offender into direct contact with any child;
- To reside where approved by the supervising officer.

Community service orders

A community service order requires the offender to carry out unpaid work in the community for a specified number of hours. These may be not less than 80 and not more than 200 hours.

Although community service would not normally be considered an appropriate disposal for sex offenders, at the end of 1996 in England and Wales there were a total of 548 community service orders and 342 combination orders (which include both a probation and a community service order) on offenders charged with sexual offences. However, 437 (80 per cent) of community service orders related to offences of indecent exposure.

Most community service units had clear risk management guidelines and a number of these made specific reference to Schedule 1 and other types of sexual offence. Provisions that were typically included were:

- That the placement must be directly authorised by the community service manager;
- The offender must be supervised by someone employed by the community service unit rather than the placement provider;
- Supervising staff must be informed of the nature of the offender's conviction.

In some cases, offenders were taken to and collected from placements and were required to remain on site at all times throughout the day. Nevertheless, it remains questionable whether all the safety issues associated with the placement of such high risk offenders can be effectively addressed and there must be some concern with regard to the appropriateness of a disposal which includes no provision for treatment.

Throughcare: prisoners released on licence

Post-release supervision on licence can occur in one of three ways:

- Parole licence.
- Non-parole licence.
- Life licence.

Prisoners serving a determinate sentence which was imposed before the 1st October 1992 may be released on parole licence after having served either one-third of their sentence or 12 months, whichever is greater. They will then be supervised in the community up to the two-thirds point of the sentence unless their supervising officer applies for the parole licence to be revoked early.

Prisoners sentenced before 1st October 1992 who are not granted an early release on parole will normally be released once they have served two thirds of their sentence.

Offenders sentenced after 1st October 1992 may be released on parole licence after serving at least half of a sentence of four or more years. Supervision lasts until the sentence expiry date and may be revoked early on the recommendation of the supervising officer.

Those not granted parole will be released on non-parole licence on completion of two thirds of their sentence. Again, supervision lasts until their sentence expiry date unless the supervising officer recommends that it be ended earlier.

Life licences apply to prisoners serving indeterminate sentences, usually life sentences, where the decision with regard to release rests with the Home Secretary acting on the advice of the parole board. A life licence is without limit of time although the supervision requirement may be cancelled after ten years or more if the offender is no longer considered to be a risk to the community.

National standards require the supervising officer should see the offender within one working day of release from custody, at least weekly for the first month, at least fortnightly for the second month, and at least monthly thereafter. At least one home visit per month should take place during the first three months of supervision.

If a person re-offends during the licence period or fails to comply with the licence conditions the parole board must be informed and they may revoke the licence and recall the offender to prison.

Treatment in prison: the Sex Offender Treatment Programme (SOTP)

In 1992 the Prison Department decided to concentrate the treatment of sex offenders in selected prisons. and to introduce a standardised treatment programme (quote reference). The Sex Offender Treatment Programme (SOTP) is run in twenty-five prisons with twenty-four running the core programme and nine a booster, to reinforce, prior to release, the work undertaken earlier in the sentence. In 1996, 564 prisoners completed the core programme and 116 the booster.

The programme is not generally available to those

serving a sentence of less than two years because there would not then be sufficient time to complete the programme. Certain other categories of prisoner are also not eligible:

- Prisoners who are mentally ill.
- Of low intelligence.
- With extreme personality disorders.
- Serious suicide risks.

Participation in the programme is voluntary and it is estimated that approximately a quarter of all sex offenders receiving a custodial sentence and half of those serving a sentence long enough to enable them to complete the programme are undertaking the SOTP.

The Sex Offender Treatment Programme utilises a cognitive-behavioural approach and provides about 130 hours of group work. Individual programmes are subject to accreditation and all work to a common standard which ensures a consistent approach throughout the prison service.

Only 31 per cent of the offenders in the HMIP throughcare sample had attended a prison-based sex offender programme and in a number of cases this would have predated the introduction of the SOTP. In only 15 cases had supervising officers actually attended a transfer meeting with SOTP staff and the information sent out from the prisons was considered to be unsatisfactory in about a quarter of the cases.

In 39 of the 57 cases in the throughcare sample where no work had been undertaken in prison the reason was the offender's denial or refusal to participate in a programme. In 26 cases the prisoners were serving too short a sentence and a variety of reasons were recorded in another 12. For the remainder, there was no indication of the reason for non-participation recorded on the file.

There were not a sufficient number of offenders yet in most areas to make a programme specifically for men who had completed the SOTP programme viable. In some areas such men were required to participate in only a part of the community-based programme. There were also some cases where, although the offender had completed the SOTP programme, the risk assessment indicated a need for participation in the full community programme.

A number of staff expressed concerns at the lack of a programme for offenders serving sentences of less than two years and that offenders serving less than one year were released without any provision for supervision.

Overall the Inspectorate were concerned that the links between the SOTP and the community-based provision, 'remained far from ideal', and recommended a number of measures to improve integration.

Hostel provision

National standards for approved hostels require them not to accept residents whose admission would present an unacceptable risk of serious harm to staff, other residents or the immediate community or who may themselves be at risk from other residents. Nevertheless, sex offenders, and particularly offenders against children now account for a very high proportion of the resident population in many hostels.

The HMIP looked at a sample of hostels from nine areas and found considerable variation. Some hostels had a policy of restricting the maximum number of sex offenders and one would not take any because of opposition from the local community. In areas where there was no restriction the proportion could be as high as 89 per cent.

Files on 75 residents or former residents were examined with particular reference to issues of risk assessment and management. These aspects of the work were considered to have been satisfactorily undertaken in all but seven cases.

It is interesting to note that the report questions the appropriateness of traditional Home Office performance indicators in relation to this population and includes a quotation from one of the cases sampled which was described as an

"excellent example of risk management in a difficult case—regrettably, because he was ultimately breached, this case will be recorded as a failure in the Home Office statistics when it is a good example of successful protection of the public."

Group work

Barker and Morgan (1993) identified 63 sex offender programmes nationally but by the time of the ACOP survey in 1995 the number had risen to 109 with only seven areas lacking such a programme. This gave a total capacity of 1,907 places in treatment programmes. However, the ACOP survey estimated that the probation service had statutory responsibility for the supervision of some 3,080 convicted sex offenders in the community. It therefore follows that the service only had the capacity to provide places on treatment programmes for less than 65 per cent of offenders and less than half of available treatment programmes included a relapse prevention element, considered by the STEP review to be essential to the effectiveness of programmes for high risk offenders.

Less than half (40 per cent) of the sex offenders in the 1998 HMIP inspection were participating in group work programmes (although such programmes were available in all of the areas in the study). Of these, 60 per cent were on probation and combination orders and 40 per cent were on throughcare licences.

The relatively low proportion of throughcare offenders in groups was thought likely to be a consequence of the license period being too short in many cases for the time required to complete the group work programme. There was particular concern that offenders serving sentences of less than 2 years would be unlikely to attend either prison or community-based groups and the extended supervision provisions in the Crime and Disorder Act, 1998 were therefore welcomed.

In a few areas groups included offenders who were not subject to statutory supervision. It is likely that a significant proportion of these would have been Schedule 1 offenders wishing to be reunited with their families. In these circumstances group work programmes have the potential to provide an important contribution to child protection. However, the inclusion of offenders who are already living in households where there are children can be problematic in programmes which prohibit contact with children for the majority of group members.

It is interesting to note that although many areas encouraged men whose period of statutory supervision had ended to continue to attend group work projects on a voluntary basis there is currently no provision for this in the funding arrangements for the Probation Service.

The typical content of a probation group work programme is considered later in the chapter. However, it is interesting to note that the 1998 inspection found that there was a greater emphasis on victim empathy work and relapse prevention than had been found in the earlier STEP research and ACOP surveys.

Most group work programmes were modular with new members able to join either at any point or at the beginning of a new module. Offenders who were judged not to have made significant progress could be required to repeat a particular module, or in exceptional cases, to repeat the whole programme.

The average group size was 6–8 offenders. The average number of hours spent in group work per offender varied from 36 to over 150 with an average of around 100 to 120 hours. The number of staff, frequency of meetings, programme length and structure were more likely to reflect the priority given to work with sex offenders in a particular area than socio-demographic factors or resources.

In most areas the groups were co-led by two workers with a third acting as on observer, recorder and consultant. Whilst this was generally acknowledged to be a valid role, the inspection report suggests that the need for three staff to be involved in every session should be kept under review.

Facilities were generally good and all but two of the groups had a video link to another room.

Most areas expected individual contact with the supervising officer to be maintained throughout the offenders' involvement with the group work programme. The focus in individual sessions in these circumstances would be on reinforcing the messages from the group work sessions and dealing with any more general issues.

Supervising officers were also responsible for co-ordinating liaison with other agencies and for ensuring that appropriate risk management strategies were in place.

Frequency of contact varied and although in some areas there was a policy requirement for co-working, often with a specialist officer, in practice this did not always happen. The inspectors question whether such a requirement is always justified given the resource implications.

Specialist areas:

Sexual offenders against adults

Most groups were intended to include both offenders against adults and those who offend against children and there were few groups whose stated aim was to focus exclusively on any one category of offender.

Although there is some research evidence to suggest that offenders against adults, and particularly rapists, are less responsive to cognitive-behavioural methods there is no clear indication of the relative effectiveness of mixed groups. Nevertheless, many practitioners consider that the treatment needs of offenders against adults are sufficiently different to make it difficult to accommodate them both within the same programme without compromising its effectiveness.

Sexual offenders with learning disabilities

Very few group work projects felt able to accommodate offenders with significant learning disabilities and most were therefore worked with on an individual basis, often very imaginatively and with advice and assistance from other agencies.

The West Midlands, Leicestershire and North Wales Probation Services did offer group work programmes specifically for sex offenders with learning disabilities and these groups were run at a slower pace and with a greater emphasis on visual aids to help to explain concepts.

Female offenders

Although it is increasingly accepted that sexual abuse by women is more prevalent than first thought there are still very few prosecutions and in the sample of 370 PSRs examined as part of the inspection, only one was on a female offender.

The ACOP survey in 1995 found that only 94 female sex offenders were being supervised by the probation service nationally and this presents less than 1 per cent of the total sex offender case-load. All work with the female sex offenders in the HMIP inspection was undertaken on an individual basis.

Offenders from ethnic minority groups

At the time of the ACOP survey in the summer of 1995 there were reported to be 451 black sex offenders under supervision and this represented 6 per cent of the total sex offender case-load of the probation service nationally.

The HMIP inspectors were unable to analyse the race and ethnicity of the offenders in their sample because the information was either not recorded or not coded consistently between different areas.

In most areas there were relatively few sexual offenders from minority ethnic groups and they were either accommodated in predominantly white groups or supervised individually. Some services had made considerable efforts to ensure that their practice was non-discriminatory but there is as yet only a very limited literature concerning the most effective ways of work with offenders from ethnic minority groups.

What works in community-based group work programmes

The assessment of suitability for participation in group work programmes and a consideration of programme content are not within the scope of this chapter. These and other treatment issues are dealt with in more detail elsewhere in the book. However, it may be useful to briefly examine the typical content of a probation group work programme.

The 1994 STEP research found that most group work programmes were using some form of cognitive-behavioural approach and this was confirmed by the 1998 inspection. Beckett (1994) notes that most programmes in the UK focus on four main elements of work:

- Altering patterns of deviant arousal.
- Correcting distorted thinking.
- Increasing social competence.
- Educating offenders about both the effects of sexual abuse and theories of offending cycles.

Similarly, Proctor (1996) found that the most common goals of programmes delivered by the probation service in England and Wales were:

- Controlling sexual arousal.
- Reducing denial.
- Victim empathy.
- Improving family relationships.

The most common elements in the group work programmes examined in the 1998 HMIP inspection were:

- Identification of the offence cycle.
- Challenging cognitive distortion.
- Increasing the offenders' willingness to accept responsibility for their behaviour.
- Developing victim awareness and empathy.
- Social skills training.
- Relapse prevention.

A number of studies emphasise the importance of the offender's attitude towards treatment and acknowledge that this may vary over time. Waterhouse et al. (1994) identified four factors which they suggest might influence an offender's responsiveness to treatment. These are:

- The nature of the offence.
- The acceptance of responsibility.
- The motivation to change.
- The type of offender.

They also note that certain patterns of offending may be particularly difficult to change because of their seriousness and duration. Factors associated with a poor prognosis include:

- High intensity patterns of offending involving penetrative sexual contact and the use of force.
- A long history of offending.
- Multiple victims

Bennett et al. (1994) suggest that attempting to challenge sex offenders' beliefs about the impact of their offending before they are able to cope with the recognition of what they have done may simply push them further into denial and minimisation.

Barker and Morgan (1993) concluded that a flexible approach based on a core of cognitive-behavioural work was likely to be the most successful in working with child sex offenders. However, this type of approach was less successful with rapists and exhibitionists.

In their report for the Home Office on an evaluation of community-based treatment programmes, Barker and Morgan (ibid) identified a number of features of group work programmes that were associated with more positive outcomes. These include:

1. Sexual assault cycle

The offender should be able to:

- Describe the lead up to the offence and to give an account of the offences.
- Identify attitudinal and situational triggers to the 'cycle'.
- Identify current position in relation to the cycle.
- Describe strategies for dealing with triggers and disrupting the cycle.

2. Cognitive distortion

The offender should be able to:

- Describe what is meant by distorted thinking and give examples.
- Identify examples of the denials, minimisations and justifications he has used.
- Demonstrate changes in his thinking in response to treatment.
- Acknowledge which distortions are hardest to let go of.

3. Sexual arousal

The offender should be able to:

- Identify and acknowledge sexual thoughts, masturbation, fantasies and patterns of sexual arousal supportive of offending behaviour.
- Describe current inappropriate thoughts and identify strategies for controlling them.

4. Victim awareness

The offender should be able to:

- Identify current distortions about victims.
- Explain damage to victims of his abusive behaviour.
- Explain why children cannot give meaningful consent, what rights children have and what things look like from their perspective.
- Describe strategies for keeping a victim perspective in focus in the future.

5. Sexuality

The offender should be able to:

- Look at previous sexuality; sexual experiences (including own abuse) and links with abusive behaviour.
- Explore links between attitudes, thoughts, feelings and abusive behaviour.

6. Attitudes towards women and children

The offender should be able to:

- Examine societal attitudes towards women and children and look at how these relate to his own attitudes and behaviour.

7. Relapse prevention

The offender should be able to:

- Admit/acknowledge lapses, 'illegal' sexual thoughts etc.
- Acknowledge future risks.
- Describe strategies for dealing with lapses.

Positive indicators of change include:

- The offender's account of the abuse matches the victim's.
- He understands that he cannot undo the harm he has done and acknowledges the serious consequences for his victim.
- He does not believe that change is easy.
- He accepts he will always be a risk.
- He is able to describe antecedent thoughts and fantasies associated with offending.
- He acknowledges the planning and grooming strategies he has deployed.
- He can identify and has strategies for dealing with situational triggers.
- He has genuinely internalised guilt and experiences remorse.
- He acknowledges the need for external monitoring.

The Wolvercote Clinic

The Wolvercote Clinic is a residential treatment facility run by the Lucy Faithful Foundation. It was opened in on the 29th August 1995 and utilises an updated version of the programme that was originally developed at the Gracewell Clinic in Birmingham. It provides places for up to 21 offenders with an emphasis on assessment, treatment and relapse prevention for those who have sexually abused children after developing a relationship with them through social, family or professional contact.

Where men have abused in a family setting the clinic also offers parallel services for non-abusing parents and other family members. Where the victim is outside the family a separate service can be provided for the child and his or her family. In either case the work with the children is done on a separate site from the offender clinic. Referrals are accepted from both statutory and voluntary organisations but the services are designed to be of particular value to probation and social services.

The clinic is a secure facility, located in extensive hospital grounds, some miles away from any housing, and is surrounded by a high fence with an alarmed gate.

Placements are funded from a variety of sources including the Home Office and individual probation services. The probation element of the funding can be offset by any social security benefits to which the offender may be entitled and in some cases contributions have also been made by health authorities and social services departments.

Between August 1995 and December 1996 the clinic received 66 referrals from 30 probation services and admitted 30 new residents.

The clinic offers the following services:

- Risk assessment only which can be undertaken regardless of the offender's level of denial.
- Risk assessment with a view to placement at the clinic for intervention and relapse prevention.
- Pre-sentence assessment with a view to placement as a requiiurement of a probation order.
- Assessment with a view to placement as a requirement of a currently existing probation order or as a condition of a parole licence.

Where an offender is accepted, the referring agency will be required to:

- Maintain a minimum of quarterly contact with the offender.
- Plan the offender's resettlement and supervision back in the home area following treatment.
- Complete post-discharge monitoring forms at half yearly intervals to assist in the Foundation research.

The clinic programme includes a four week assessment and a treatment programme lasting from six to twelve months. Residents are required to comply with the following conditions:

- To live and sleep each night at the clinic.
- To participate in and co-operate fully with the treatment programme.
- To have no contact, directly or indirectly, with children under 18 years without prior written consent from the clinic.

- Not to leave the clinic without written permission or unless accompanied by a member of staff.
- To abide by any other conditions imposed by the court or the parole board.

Effectiveness research

Research into the effectiveness of treatment programmes for sex offenders is beset by a number of methodological problems. Sample sizes are usually small, allocation to treatment groups is not usually random and comparisons with matched control groups of untreated offenders is rarely an option. Outcome measures based upon re-conviction rates require long periods of follow-up with associated high rates of sample attrition and the reliability of re-conviction rates as an indicator of re-offending is problematic given the known tendency for under-reporting and low rates of prosecution and conviction.

Recidivism studies attempt to measure the incidence of re-offending. Re-conviction rates are generally used as a proxy for re-offending so figures are inevitably an underestimate. Re-arrest rates go some way to compensating for low rates of prosecution and conviction but these figures are more difficult to obtain.

There are only two major national studies which identify recidivism rates for different types of offender; one by the Home Office in England and Wales based on re-conviction rates and the other by the United States Justice Department based on re-arrest rates (Beck and Shipley, 1989).

The Home Office study found that in a two year follow-up period, sex offenders had the lowest general re-conviction rate of all offenders (25 per cent, though only 15 per cent of these were for sexual offences). This compares with a general re-conviction rate of 47 per cent for those convicted of offences involving violence (though only 27 per cent of these were for further violent crimes).

The US study involved a three year follow-up period and again found that general re-arrest rates were among the lowest for sex offenders (murderers had the lowest rates). The re-arrest rate for rapists was 52 per cent and for sexual assaulters (indecent assault) 48 per cent. This study also found that re-arrest rates for similar offences were lowest among murderers (7 per cent) and sex offenders (25 per cent).

Hanson and Bussiere (1996) looked at recidivism rates for sex offenders in 61 studies from 6 countries and found that over an average four to five year follow-up, average recidivism rates for sex offences was 13.4 per cent; 12.2 per cent for non-sexual violent offences and 36.3 per cent for all types of offence. Rapists were much more likely to commit non-sexual violent offences than child molesters.

High levels of sexual deviance and to a lesser extent a history of prior sex offences (especially when these were against unrelated and unknown male victims) were found to be the strongest predictors of re-offending.

A limitation of many studies is the relatively short follow-up period. Where studies have looked at re-conviction rates over much longer periods they tend to show significantly higher rates. They also show that many years can elapse between first conviction and re-offending, which tends to support the view that under-reporting and low detection rates lead to an under-representation of the true rates of recidivism.

An ongoing Home Office research programme (Hedderman and Sugg, 1996) has so far measured re-conviction rates over a two year follow-up period and will measure again at five and ten years.

There are a considerable number of smaller scale studies examining re-conviction rates for different types of offender and using a variety of different measures:

Marshall and Barbaree (1990) found that:

- Exhibitionists have the highest rates of recidivism (41 to 71 per cent).
- Rates for non-familial child sex abusers range from 10 to 40 per cent.
- Rates for rapists range from 7 to 35 per cent.
- Intra-familial child sex abusers have the lowest recidivism rates at 4 to 10 per cent.

They quote the following rates for untreated offenders:

Incest	4–10%
Extra-familial (girls)	10–29%
Extra-familial (boys)	13–40%
Rapists	7–35%
Exhibitionists	41–71%

Other studies show that age and gender of victims is also associated with different rates. Child molesters who target male victims have higher rates than those who target females (35 per cent compared to 18 per cent).

Conclusion

Historically, there has always been a dilemma for those who work in the field of criminal justice and nowhere is this more apparent than in the area of work with sex offenders. On the one hand, there is the evidence that the majority of those who offend are unlikely to represent a continuing risk to the community and with the right approach they can be successfully reintegrated into society. On the other, there is the grim reality that a small minority will always represent a serious threat to those with whom they come into contact. There are, therefore, no single, simple solutions to the problem of how to deal with the risks posed by sex offenders living in the community.

Traditionally, responsibility for the management of sex offenders in the community has been almost exclusively the preserve of the probation service. However, more recently, there has been an increasing emphasis on the importance of a more collaborative approach and a growing recognition that the problems posed by persistent offenders are far too complex to be tackled effectively by any one agency acting alone. In addition, public concern about the risks posed by sex offenders in the community has resulted in a variety of new legislative provisions which are only just now being assimilated by the agencies charged with their implementation.

Although there are inevitably some concerns about the most extreme manifestations of public concern it has at least resulted in the creation of a range of options which go some way towards addressing the needs of offenders who lie at both ends of the risk spectrum. The challenge for those agencies concerned with the administration of the criminal justice and child protection systems is how to deploy the resources that are available in a way which both maximises the potential for rehabilitation for those for whom this is a safe option whilst at the same time protecting the community from those for whom it is not and perhaps never will be.

Chapter 7
A framework for comprehensive assessment

Martin C. Calder—with John Skinner, NSPCC

"We see what we look for and we look for what we know" (Goethe).

A theoretical framework to inform practice

Chapters 3 and 4 will have made us aware of the complexities of understanding how male sex offenders are 'created'. Sex offenders are not born 'that way', but are the products of several interacting variables over time. One of the most important messages to bring to the assessment itself is that many sex offenders present as 'ordinary men', 'normal' and heterosexual members of society, who cannot be typified in terms of class, profession, wealth or family status. They usually have the same emotional and psychological profile as people who do not abuse. As they do not present as remarkably different from non-sexual offenders (other than in the nature of their offending), it is remarkably difficult to detect them. Sex offenders, do not present as 'monsters' as they would not get near children, but 'nice' men can, and do (Wyre, 1994). Sex offenders remain an extremely hetero-geneous group. Most theories of sexual offending emphasise multiple constructs or factors (Finkelhor, 1984; Quinsey 1984; 1986). Some of these factors include deviant sexual interests, attitudes support-ive of sexual offending, deficient sexual knowledge, sexual dysfunction, opportunities provided by exposure to potential victims, and the disinhibiting effects of deviant role models (both real and imagined). Some factors interact with others to contribute to sexual offending.

In this chapter, we will provide a comprehensive framework for assessing adult male sex offenders who target children. It is acknowledged that the material is not for use exclusively by field workers in social services or probation, as it is clear that they require the input of both health and criminal justice personnel in their task. The framework is designed to guide workers both in the conduct of an assessment as well as determining the kind of assessment they need to commission, and then how to interpret the findings. We thus present a complete and optimally desirable framework, which may be inappropriate if followed rigidly and prescriptively by workers in each case. Each offender will require an individually tailored package to suit the needs and circumstances of each case.

Pre-Assessment tasks

Given the magnitude of the task, it is important to prepare thoroughly and methodically for the comprehensive assessment to help neutralise the power and control of information held by the sex offender. In the framework recommended, it is important that we try and utilise the largest number of assessment strategies or tools available to us as a means of maximising the accuracy and detail of our findings. The more strands to the assessment there are, the more confident we can be with both our findings as well as our recommendations.

Aims of the work

Most workers will have formed a preliminary view on whether the offender has perpetrated sexual abuse before the comprehensive assessment com-mences. However it is vitally important that workers remain objective throughout the assess-ment process. It follows, therefore, that the aim of the work is to:

- Gain an understanding of the dynamics of the sexual abuse.
- Obtain a direct or indirect admission from the offender recognising that this will not always be possible.
- To make some predictions with regard to prognosis.
- Gather information helpful in formulating a child protection plan.
- Identify the motivating factors in the offending behaviour, such as protection from painful and intrusive realities.
- Work with their fear of punishment and other consequences.
- Identify and help them manage any further impacts on an often already low self-esteem (extended from Faller, 1988).

Anticipating denial

Most sex offenders referred for a comprehensive assessment will have committed acts that they deny and it is not unusual for them to be more open as the process unfolds. We should anticipate their denial and incompleteness of information before it emerges and explain that this is usually a reflection of their current lack of acceptance of the need for change, their need to feel reassured by the process and the worker(s) involved, or as a temporary memory lapse (Morrison and Print, 1995). It is important to spend some time explaining the content and process of their particular assessment and how we will expect and accept the release of more information as the process unfolds. It is important to generate self-belief that they can understand and change their presenting offending behaviours, whilst also making clear to them we have access to multiple sources of information which will allow us to compare, and challenge them, about their account as compared to others.

Identifying co-workers

When identifying the assessing co-workers, we need to consider issues of gender, culture, race, language and ability as these interpersonal factors (including client attractiveness) may have some bearing on the information elicited (Earls, 1992). Snell et al. (1989) found that men were equally willing to discuss sexual topics with therapists of either sex. As such, there needs to be some consideration of the message or model the workers wish to portray to the offender, e.g. role models with a male/female partnership.

Multi-disciplinary partnerships

It is likely that social workers and probation officers doing the work will want to use the skills of psychologists who can interpret the offender's responses to certain questionnaires. This can be done in two ways: by administering them and then sending them off for interpretation, or by using a psychologist as part of the assessment team. There are some circumstances where the workers can use some of the questions and material derived from the field of psychology to generate the necessary information around the key areas, but they should never try to interpret them using the coding systems. In this book, certain psychological measures are reproduced, yet the scoring mechanisms are left in the original sources to prevent unauthorised usage. Psychologists can of course access these and some contact points are reproduced in the resources section at the end of the book. For a fuller discussion of the utility and usefulness of the psychological evaluation in these cases see Marshall (1996).

Planning

Once the co-workers have been identified, they must be allowed sufficient time and space to both plan the work as well as constructing a viable working relationship (see previous chapter for details of how). Planning is the key to a good assessment, as it enhances the chances of the workers retaining the necessary control. Any failure to plan can result in chaotic sessions in which the initiative can revert to the offender, and the sessions do not flow. Content, process, recording and feelings need to be discussed and resolved in advance. Time to do the work needs to include preparatory tasks—particularly where homework assignments have been set and need interpreting—and debriefing time to deal with feelings and collate and interpret the new information. Whilst planning does take some considerable time at the start of the process, this does usually pay dividends later.

Working with adults with learning difficulties

The issue of assessing adult sex offenders who have some degree of learning disability is an important one. There is often a barrier to recognising that they too have sexual feelings and desires, and this has to be overcome if we are to recognise that their behaviour is both sexual and abusive in nature (Sgroi, 1989). Whilst the prevalence of offending in mentally handicapped people is lower than the general population, they are frequently over-represented (times six) in sexual offending than the general population, probably due to the increased likelihood of apprehension and conviction (Day, 1994).

Clare (1993) identified several disadvantages of utilising a traditional approach to assessment with this group:

- Poor memory: frustrates the efforts to get them to recall past experiences.
- Acquiescent and suggestible responding: where they are more likely than the intellectually average person to answer 'yes/no' questions affirmatively, regardless of their content. They are also more likely to be (mis)led by 'leading questions'.
- Reading difficulties: can be overcome through the greater use of discussion, although this does place a higher demand on their verbal memory ability, which is generally poorer than their average ability counterparts.
- Problems in understanding complex language and concepts and discriminating responses: particularly in standardised questionnaires, and in making the fine discriminations required for responding.

These limitations do point to the need for a pre-assessment screening of their cognitive ability, as this will determine the need for a particular consultant and assessment package. It is increasingly clear that we need to produce specific materials for this group (see Sgroi, 1989 for a detailed discussion of how to evaluate sexual behaviours), and there is a greater need for a co-ordinated, multi-agency response and emphasis on the initial and comprehensive assessment phases. This is due to the increased probability of additional difficulties in this group making the constellation of factors underlying and maintaining their sexual offending more complex than is normally found. For example, they may have numerous behavioural disorders in addition to their sexual offence. Some may be impulsive, showing extremely poor judgement; some may behave aggressively in many situations; and there may be a range of inappropriate behaviours such as temper tantrums (Murphy et al., 1983).

There are some suggestions for approaching the assessment with this group. Information can often best be elicited by using open questions which are general, rather than specific (e.g. 'what happened next' rather than 'what did you do next'), and we can adapt *some standard measures* so they are visual (pictures, audiotape) rather than written. Day (1994) reported that the available studies do show that there is a similarity in their overall offence patterns to non-handicapped sexual offenders; with sexual naivity, poor impulse control and lack of relationship skills as important aetiological factors. There is a need, therefore, to focus in more detail in some areas such as interpersonal social skills, sexual knowledge and their understanding of the laws relating to sexual behaviour.

For fuller discussions around this group, the reader is referred to Griffiths et al. (1989); Ho (1997); Noelly et al. (1996).

Collecting background information

Workers need to clarify the start date of the assessment, allowing a reasonable amount of time to collect and digest the relevant information. The workers need to gather substantial background information and material on the offender, from as many sources as possible, to verify or corroborate information. The offender is often an unreliable source of information as they are frequently motivated to conceal facts. Self-report, even where believed, should not be a cue to veer from the necessary assessments indicated in this text. Whilst we may not always be able to access all information, the following are essential preparatory documents: victim and abuser statements/videos/PACE interviews and those of any co-accused; full details of all members of the relevant family household—past and present; criminal records—in detail, outlining convictions, and the circumstances of each; child protection conference minutes; any previous social services, NSPCC, probation or health records. Any information from colleagues involved in parallel assessments with the family or any professional with relevant information, and interview with the victim(s) can be helpful: in providing useful information, particularly where the available reports are vague. This can relate both to the detail of the offence as well as the nature of the relationship with the victim, and the impact of the offence on the victim. The appropriateness of this needs to be carefully considered in every case, particularly if there have been prior interviews. It can, on occasions, be instigated by the victim themselves.

It is impossible to undertake an assessment without detailed accounts about the nature of the sexually abusive act, and the prior offence history (Morrison and Print, 1995), and these represent the minimum amount of information required. It is also beneficial to establish the true nature and range of the offender's problems so the potential contributions to their behaviour can be explored and examined in detail. For example, adults with learning difficulties. If anything is unclear, then it is wise to discuss the matter directly with the source. The assessment needs this to back up and offset the deceit of self-report. The keyword here is thoroughness. It is important to collect information in a number of different ways and from a number of different sources, as any conflicting information can be a useful means of generating discussion with the offender.

The written agreement

Prior to the assessment starting, the workers need to meet with the offender to establish an explicit written agreement. The work should NEVER start in the absence of this written agreement, even where the focus of the work has to be restricted more than the workers would ideally like it to. The agreement should never be conditional, and we should therefore omit any area where there is no mutual agreement.

In the establishment of a written agreement, we need to be clear about minimum expectations of the agreement and the parameters of the assessment. There are differing views about whether work can commence in the absence of any willingness to discuss the presenting concerns or allegations, as the work is arguably rendered meaningless if omitted—largely as the future risks remain un-assessed, and therefore presumed to be high. However, given the high-risk the sex offender poses, we would argue that it is worthwhile attempting to negotiate an agreement covering relevant, albeit, peripheral areas, as a starting point (e.g. attitudes to women, sex and children), and then renegotiate it after these areas have been fully explored. Progress requires patience as well as persistence and presumptive thinking. 'Peripheral' work represents a useful starting point, and is preferable to a 'one-off' admission that many see as a means of short-circuiting the system—allowing the offender to avoid facing any detailed internal examination of the motivating factors which led to their offending behaviour.

The written agreement needs to embrace the following points:

- Clarification of who the agreement is between.
- The purpose of the assessment and the commissioning body (e.g. civil or criminal court, child protection conference).
- The process and content of the assessment,

including the number of sessions, venue, time and agreed method of recording.

- Accessibility of information collected, e.g. professionals, legal advocates, offender's partner, etc.
- The limits of confidentiality need to be explicitly articulated, and periodically restated throughout the work. We should indicate the circumstances in which we are required to act.
- Consequences of non-co-operation and/or non-attendance should also be explicit.
- The centrality of homework assignments to the assessment process.
- The ground rules for the assessment sessions themselves, e.g. no drugs, alcohol or violence, punctuality, no oppressive language or behaviour, and the completion of all the homework assignments.
- The nature of any contact with children throughout the assessment process and an agreed process for reporting any breaches, e.g. to whom and in what time-scale. A schedule for review also needs to be agreed.
- Arrangements and parties to feedback (e.g. the commissioning body, the offender's partner); at which point in the process (e.g. half-way through, at the end of the work, or both); plus format (e.g. verbal, written or both). Signatures and dates from all parties to the agreement.

It is not unreasonable to allow the offender to take the proposed agreement to a solicitor for legal advice, although this should never be allowed to delay the work.

The workers should ideally videotape the assessment as this represents an accurate record of the sessions, as well as being useful in challenging things with the offender retrospectively, e.g. cognitive distortions. We need to negotiate this with the offender, and agree on how to record the sessions in the absence of consent to videotape. The refusal to videotape does not, in itself, constitute a justifiable reason to block the assessment sessions but it does cause potential problems of 'unwanted error', e.g. incomplete or incorrect recall (Earls, 1992). These tapes can be viewed by their legal representative and used at a later point with the offender's partner in order to share points and concerns arising from the work pertinent to the future protection of their child/ren. They may also be used, or directed to be used, in any civil proceedings involving the protection of children.

Confidentiality

Confidentiality should never be offered and the worker must clearly state from the onset that any new and relevant information will be referred to the police for their consideration, and possible action. The latter will only usually be possible where there is an identified victim, or they report being abused themselves (DiGeorgio-Miller, 1994). It is important to remember that general information indicating previous behaviours is important as part of the assessment of future risk and treatment viability, and we can never overlook information which points to a breach of existing orders (e.g. 'no contact' orders, prohibited steps orders, injunctions, bail or parole conditions). Confidentiality can never be assured and the less confidentiality that exists, the more complete the assessment will be (Calder, 1997). There may also be circumstances where there are concerns about an offender's presentation, or behaviour, which necessitates a referral for mental health assessment.

Homework assignments

The face-to-face work is punctuated by sessions and homework assignments, which serve several purposes: it extends the time available to the assessment team; it tests the offender's motivation; it enables the offender to record sexual thoughts, feelings and fantasies, and cognitive distortions at, or close to, the time that they actually occur; and it attempts to shift the balance of power from the offender to the workers' by allowing them preparation time in advance of the sessions. If the offender does not return the homework by the deadline, the subsequent sessions should be cancelled, but rearranged with a revised schedule of return.

Self-report: advantages and disadvantages

Self-report questionnaires are *"standardised paper-and-pencil questionnaires that can be filled out by the client in a relatively short period of time, that can be easily administered and scored by the practitioner, and that give fairly accurate pictures of the client's condition at any point in time and/or over a period of many administrations"* (Corcoran and Fischer, 1987). The self-report of sexual behaviour has always been a pivotal source of data (Andersen and Broffitt, 1988), and Malatesta and Adams (1986) have argued that we shouldn't underestimate the value of self-report or render it any less valid than other information. This should not mean that we do not scrutinise such information, if it is to remain an integral part of the total assessment package. It clearly provides us with important information on offender problem-perception as well as the related discrepancies and inconsistencies.

Self-report questionnaires have many potential advantages: they provide extensive information at little cost; thus, they are cost-effective. They allow a client thinking time to organise his or her thoughts in a reflective, considered way that is not always possible within the time constraints of an interview. This is more so when we limit ourselves to one area of assessment at a time. Some offenders cannot narrate sexual offending verbally but can when answering a questionnaire. Self-report questionnaires permit clients to disclose sensitive information that they might not reveal during a 'live' interaction, or that they might find difficult to verbalise (Corcoran and Fischer, 1987). Self-report questionnaires allow us to assess an offender's progress over time, making treatment evaluation more precise and less prone to worker-related biases. Self-report questionnaires allow us to compare the offender to other individuals (with the help of established norms). Thus, in difficult diagnostic cases, these questionnaires can provide a known measure against which to make judgements. Questionnaires can serve as an additional stimulus that encourages an offender to think through aspects of his (or her) sexuality. If used after the interview, self-report questionnaires can be used to evaluate the validity of a diagnostic or etiological formulation (see Carey et al., 1984). They also ensure important information does not get missed and can help workers formulate hypotheses regarding the problem areas to be explored during interviews. They have a distinct advantage, as they are easy to administer. Alternatively, if used before the interview, self-report measures can serve as screening devices that help us to be more efficient in getting to the heart of the presenting complaint (Wincze and Carey, 1991).

Despite the many potential advantages of self-report questionnaires, there are numerous identified problems also. These include:

- They can be ambiguous and lead to the collection of unstructured information. Many have been developed for very specific purposes and any broader application may be limited (Conte, 1983). Although numerous sex scales have been proposed, there have been few evaluative reviews of these measures. Murphy (1990) has reviewed sex history and sex attitude measures; Derogatis (1980) has reviewed sex role and sexual dysfunction measures, and Hanson et al. (1991) have reviewed sexuality, personality and attitude questionnaires for sex offenders.
- Their careful use can be time-consuming and inconvenient in busy teams. It may therefore, be better to administer a variety of relatively brief questionnaires rather than lengthy ones.
- Many useful tools remain inaccessible to busy workers, either because they are located in diverse journals or are targeted at specific professional groups, and they could select inappropriate tools for any particular purpose (particularly if using them for the first time). See Calder (1994a, b and c).
- Many offenders are defensive and distorting for

fear of the consequences of full disclosure of their offences. *The greater the consequences of disclosure, the poorer the quality of the information provided.* It is therefore hard to see that any self-report could be any more predictive than the offence histories recorded in official records. They may fake responses if they reveal a real investment in concealing aspects of either their arousal patterns or behaviour.

- Scales and check-lists often yield less useful information than those using open-ended questions or written responses of one or more sentences.
- Some offenders will not (or cannot) put anything down on paper, preferring to discuss matters with the worker directly. This should be embraced in the written agreement.
- Workers may try and draw conclusions from their completion without reference to expert psychological interpretation, particularly where technical skills and scoring scales are required (cf. Prentky and Edmunds, 1997). They are *not* indicators and have the potential for over-focus, particularly to causal explanations.
- Workers miss the non-verbal cues which are available to them in the interview situation.

In summary, it would appear that self-report questionnaires are used because of their pragmatic value rather than anything else, particularly as they are very subjective. Whilst little is known about the worth of many of these tests, they can be used to aid in the planning and progression of work, whilst not disregarding their shortcomings (Howitt, 1995). The strongest test of any measure is its ability to predict future sexual offending, yet few measures have been sufficiently researched to establish their predictive validity. In addition, recidivism studies have tended to be inconclusive.

Beckett (1994) identified three approaches, which may be used to assist in judging the reliability of self-report:

- There is a good level of agreement between the offender self-report and those of others.
- Personality scales which incorporate validity scales or procedures for adjusting self-report for social desirability bias may be used to alert workers to those who attempt to fake good or bad, or who lack insight into their general feelings and motives; and
- Scales may be deployed to enable comparison to be made between the offender and other offenders of a similar type.

Whilst we advocate their use, we cannot disregard their identified limitations and they should never be the sole means of information collection. It may be useful at the outset to ask each offender to complete the sexual self-disclosure scale (Snell et al., 1989) which was constructed to study people's willingness to communicate and discuss various sexual topics with others. It deals with 12 topics: sexual behaviours (e.g. 'my past experiences'); sexual sensations ('that arouse me'); sexual fantasies (e.g. 'my private sexual fantasies'); sexual attitudes (e.g. 'my attitudes about sexual behaviours'); the meaning of sex (e.g. 'the meaning that sexual intercourse has for me'); negative sexual affect (e.g. 'how frustrated I feel about my sex life'); positive sexual affect (e.g. 'how satisfied I feel about the sexual aspects of my life'); distressing sexual experiences (e.g. 'what I think about birth control'); sexual responsibility (e.g. 'my private notion of sexual responsibility'); sexual dishonesty (e.g. 'how I feel about sexual dishonesty'); and rape (e.g. 'my private views about rape'). It comprises 60 items whose responses are coded on a 5 point scale.

Resources

We would also recommend that workers refer to the following books, which either contain self-report questionnaires (or reviews of them), when undertaking a comprehensive assessment of a sex offender:

- CALDER MC (1997) Juveniles and children who sexually abuse: A guide to risk assessment. Dorset: Russell House Publishing.
- CORCORAN K AND FISCHER J (1987) Measures for clinical practice: A sourcebook. New York: Free Press.
- DAVIS CM, YARBER YL and DAVIS SL (1988) Sexuality-related measures: A compendium. Lake Mills, Iowa: Graphic Publishing Company.
- DAVIS CM, YARBER WL, BAUSERMAN R, SCHEER G and DAVIS SL (1998) Handbook of sexuality-related measures. Thousand Oaks, Ca.: Sage.
- PRENTKY R and EDMUNDS SB (1997) Assessing sexual abuse: A resource guide for practitioners. Brandon, VT: Safer Society Press.
- SALTER A (1988) Treating child sex offenders and their victims—A practical guide. Newbury Park, Ca.: Sage.
- WYRE R (1987) Working with sex abuse. Oxford: Perry publications.
- HANSON RK, COX B and WOSZCSYNA C (1991) Sexuality, personality and attitude questionnaires for sex offenders. Ottawa: Supply and Services.
- CARICH MS and ADKERSON DL (1995) Adult sexual offender assessment packet. Brandon, VT: Safer Society Press.
- SCHIAVI RC, DEROGATIS LR, KURIANSKY J, O'CONNOR D and SHARPE L (1979) The assessment of sexual function and marital interaction. Journal of Sex and Marital Therapy 5(3): 169-224.

There are also journals such as 'Psychological Assessment: A Journal of Consulting and Clinical Psychology', which contain useful measures, reported close to their evolution.

In this chapter, we will refer to selected questionnaires as one means of collecting information. We will briefly outline each instrument to enable the reader to make a preliminary judgement as to the potential applicability of each scale for the presenting case. We reproduce several questionnaires as appendices, and these are marked with an * in the text itself.

Limitations of assessment information

Whichever assessment tools are used, workers do need to acknowledge at the onset, that there are likely to be certain limitations to the information gathered from the offenders:

- Unwanted error, due to both worker and offender characteristics. For example, problems of recall that can lead to either a lack of information or a distortion of the information, responses to leading questions or the failure to focus questioning on pertinent areas of functioning.
- The worker is not an unbiased measurement agent—with their work influenced by a number of interpersonal factors totally unrelated to what is said by the offender, e.g. sex, client attractiveness.
- The unwillingness of the offender to disclose embarrassing or socially undesirable behaviour. The greater the consequence of disclosure, the lower the quality of information provided (Earls, 1992).

Even with a thorough assessment, it is likely that workers will not get a clear picture of all the sexual behaviours in which the individual has engaged. Offenders try to present themselves in the most favourable light possible. They tend to minimise, deny, and distort their motivation and behaviour. Part of this distortion will be conscious and part of it will be a function of distortions in perceptions, values, attitudes, and beliefs that support the sexual abuse of children (for discussions, see Conte, 1985). Disclosing this highly personal information involves a high degree of trust. In many cases, workers will gather more and more of this information as the process unfolds, particularly if we judge only their offending behaviour, rather than them as individuals. Offenders themselves may unconsciously block some of this information and the behaviours are 'remembered' in the course of the assessment. For example, it is certainly not uncommon for offenders to report having had sexual relations with one or two minors and then in the course of the work to remember others (Dwyer and Coleman, 1994).

	OFFENDER	MOTHER	CHILD
1. Legal	• Imprisonment	• Care order on child and other sibling	• Care order
2. Family	• Marital separation • Loss of children/restriction of contact • Loss of support by other relatives	• Loss of partner • Loss of child/ren • Loss of co-parent • Loss of support by other relatives	• Loss of father • Loss of mother • Loss of siblings • Fear of not being believed • Fear of retribution • Fear of violence and punishment • Fear of violence within the family • Fear of offender's and others well-being (e.g. offender's threat of suicide)
3. Psychological	• Suicide • Guilt over effects • Let down of partner • Self-respect • Self-esteem and identity • Own history of sexual abuse • Fear of loneliness and isolation • Inability to cope • Inability to face addiction and tension relief through abuse	• Self-respect • Let down of child • Self-blame • Having married an abuser • Own history of sexual abuse • Fear of loneliness and isolation • Need to care without partner • Desperation, fear, anger and loneliness	• Fear of being blamed • Fear of being scapegoated • Self-blame • Fear of loneliness and isolation • Loyalty • Desperation, fear, anger and loneliness
4. Social	• Reprisal • Reputation • Stigma • Isolation • Overcoming shame	• Reputation • Stigma • Isolation • Problems of being a single parent	• Reaction of peers • Treatment at school • Loss of friends • Behavioural changes, e.g. becoming beyond control • Assumption of parenting role
5. Financial and professional	• Loss of job • Loss of earnings • Loss of professional licence • Loss of reputation	• Financial hardship and stress • Effects on own work and professional career • Legal expenses	• Doing part-time jobs to help (e.g. paper rounds) (adapted from Furniss, 1990, and Wright, 1991)

Figure 6: The feared negative consequences of disclosure for all family members.

One of the major problems in verifying self-reports is an absence of some objective criterion by which we could compare the self-report of the offender. We are therefore highly likely to underestimate the frequency and seriousness of their sexual offending.

As already stated, any information provided by the sex offender should be verified wherever possible by accessing community-generated data such as significant police reports, interviews with others, e.g. siblings, other relatives, friends or others who have extensive knowledge of him. Whilst this can create special problems with confidentiality, it does allow us to verify any descriptions provided by the offender as well as check any values held by their families regarding sex roles, such as the roles of adults versus children. The search here is for the presence of factors potentially associated with the development of the adult sexual abuse of children (Conte, 1985).

Recognising consequences: a barrier to engagement?

It is essential that every worker has some understanding about the imbalance between the negative and the positive consequences of accepting, and working with the allegations, for the offender and his family. The thoroughness of their response will almost invariably be linked to the level of anticipated denial of their behaviour when it is tackled. The consequences may include: civil proceedings—living away from home and having supervised contact with their children; criminal proceedings—and the imposition of a Schedule One status; personal, social, psychological and financial consequences for them and their family. These consequences often become more real and personalised as the work unfolds.

The reader is asked to add further items to the list based on their own experiences of working with families where sexual abuse is a feature:

It is thus very important that we get the offender, their families, as well as ourselves and other professionals, to look at any positive consequences of disclosure. These might include:

For the offender.
1. An understanding of how their behaviour has developed as this is the start of repairing the damage and working at controlling any future repetition of their behaviour.
2. It allows the workers to identify and work on the most dangerous areas.
3. It shows the offender they are able to accept responsibility for their behaviour and the need for change.
4. A greater respect for the victims of their abuse including the immediate and extended families.

For their partner.
1. It allows them to make a more informed decision on the risk their partner poses and whether they are to continue with, or end the relationship.
2. It can encourage the offender to complete the necessary work.

For the child/ren.
1. It allows them to have a safe home environment.

2. It allows them to have their views regarding contact heard.
3. It allows them to have safe contact with their father.

It is important that the workers encourage the families they are working with to identify all the positive consequences of working on the sexual abuse, as otherwise they will be overwhelmed by the negative consequences. Reference to some of the points highlighted in components 5 and 8 can be used to elicit positives for each family.

Components of a comprehensive assessment

Each comprehensive assessment needs to be tailored to the individual circumstance of each case, the requirements of the commissioning body and the time-scale allowed. It is for this reason, that a pic 'n' mix framework is proposed, allowing workers to select identified components as deemed appropriate. Although we have compartmentalised the assessment areas for ease of access, the reader needs to be aware that there is some overlap between them. In ideal circumstances, workers should aim to meet with the offender 6–10 times, recognising that the time available is extended through the option of homework assignments. The work can be ordered as required, but the social history often allows safe areas to be explored, maximising the opportunity for trust to be developed at the outset. This chapter will explore many modules, which embrace the components set out in Figure 7 (below).

1. Social/family history	The offender's family background and early home life and support; demographic data; educational history; occupational history; religious beliefs; financial history; recreational interests; criminal history; psychiatric history; neurological and biological factors; interpersonal relationships; anger, aggression and assertiveness; self-esteem, sexual-esteem and self-concept; social skills and social competence; health and medical history.
2. Sexual history	Sex education and knowledge; sexual experiences, including victimisation; sexual relationships and sexual satisfaction; sexual attitudes; sexual beliefs and values; sexual interests and preferences; sexual arousal; crossover; sexual blocks and dysfunctions.
3. Sexual fantasies	
4. Cognitive distortions	
5. Denial and responsibility	
6. Victim empathy and awareness	
7. Disinhibitors	Pornography, drugs, alcohol.
8. The current sexual offences (allegations)	
9. The 'cycle of abuse'.	
10. Feedback and outcomes	Feedback session; pro-forma assessment report format.

Figure 7: The components of a comprehensive assessment.

Workers need to ensure that the following process is sustained throughout the assessment. An introductory phase is essential to establish openness, ground rules and trust. We should then move on to address them as an offender before going on to address any issues they may have as victims. To invert this usually results in the offender redirecting any attempts to address their offending behaviour and can create anxiety through delay, and the assessment can be incomplete. The argument for addressing their offending behaviour first rests on the belief that once they begin to understand their deviant arousal patterns and behaviours, other problems such as the lack of social skills or family problems can be addressed (Bengis, 1986; Breer, 1987; Perry and Orchard, 1992). Their own abuse does not constitute an acceptable explanation for their offending. Addressing their offending behaviour first emphasizes their responsibility for their behaviour. We should not be seduced by their victim features, as doing so serves as a justification to them that their behaviour is acceptable. We should tackle the two problems separately, and in the given order. There are issues about balancing the two. The dilemma is that if you challenge the offender, you run the risk of rejecting the victim; whereas if you nurture the victim, you run the risk of condoning and colluding with the offender (Neate, 1990).

Having addressed their own offending, the workers can try and shift the offender to develop victim empathy. This sequence very much represents a traditional approach to the problem. In more recent times in the United States, it is being challenged. Freeman-Longo (1994) argued that this may be a misguided approach since the denial and dissociation shown by some offenders about their behaviour has its roots in the reaction to their own abuse. In such cases, it may only be possible to work by first acknowledging and addressing their own experience of abuse. Kahn and Lafond (1988) found that until offenders are able to effectively discard all self-blame and guilt over their own abuse, they are unable to fully acknowledge responsibility for their offending (p142). By inverting the suggested sequence, a trusting relationship can be developed within which confrontation can be used and may well be effective. Ryan (1994) supports this, arguing that confrontation should only ever occur in the context of a therapeutic relationship in which a degree of trust has been established. We should therefore consider the circumstances of each individual case before ordering the work. It would appear sensible to follow the order outlined unless there are clear contraindications for doing so. Whatever happens, the comfort of the assessors should not determine the order of the work.

1. Social and family history

"Anyone wanting to promote constructive changes in clients must first obtain a comprehensive understanding of the total context in which the behaviours occur" (Lazarus, 1976).

This reinforces the reality that our identity is not exclusively sexual, and we should try and identify social factors, which may have contributed to the development of their sexual offending behaviour. Sex offenders as a group may not be relatively deficient in many aspects of social functioning, but what deficiencies they do have may be functionally related to their offending behaviour. Workers should acknowledge that a social history collected under the guise of a sex offender assessment is fundamentally no different to that elicited in other situations, so we shouldn't be immobilised by the task. What is important is that we recognise that there is likely to be considerable variation among offender's concerning their social histories (Dougher, 1995). This block is a useful starting point as it is typically non-threatening to the offender and provides an opportunity to build a rapport with them. The following information should be sought from the offender and significant others (e.g. partner, previous partners, children, etc.) as part of the process:

(a) The offender's family background and early home life and social support

There are two major reasons for speaking with the offender about his family of origin and social network : to get some sense of what it was like for them growing up as well as wanting to assess the extended family and others as sources of social support.

Many factors related to their upbringing may shed light on the dynamics of sexual abuse and predict prognosis. We need to find out what kind of people his parents were and how he experienced them, particularly if there is a history of little nurturing, significant trauma, and deprivation; physical and/or sexual abuse; a lack of intimacy or attachments; no reference to sex (so they grow up with little sexual knowledge), or paternal modelling of patriarchy, exploitation and/or abuse; as well as social isolation and the absence of social supports—particularly as social isolation can have several functions: it may facilitate, prolong, or be the result of sexual abuse.

Hanson and Scott (1996) researched the social networks of sex offenders and found that there is some evidence that sex offenders are likely to have friends and relatives who are also sex offenders.

Tools

Questions to be asked to collect this information might include:

- The names, date of births and addresses of all immediate and extended family members—

which do they maintain contact with and which do they avoid, and why? The names of past partners can also be helpful as an additional source of information, particularly where they can be traced and are willing to speak to us. They could reveal information about sexual deviancies and domestic violence. The names of children from previous relationships is also helpful as it may uncover information about parallel abuses and other concerns.

- The names, ages and descriptions of all the children in the family, including what pleases/displeases them and what, if anything, they do together? This helps us anticipate any other potential victims. The offender's responses should be assessed, according to: his ability to individualise children in the family so that they are described as separate people with personalities; the affective tone of the relationship with children; the accuracy of the offender's perception and description of the children, based upon the worker's contact with them and the opinions of others, and the presence or absence of inappropriately sexual descriptions of the children. The first two qualities, the ability to individualise and the quality of affect are important in determining whether the offender considers people, particularly children, as objects to be used or manipulated for his interests or needs, or whether he sees them as individuals with their own needs who are valued and loved for themselves. Workers should then look for perceptions of the child as being on either the same level as the offender, or as being described in negative terms or in a manner that suggests that they are to blame for problems associated with the allegation of sexual abuse. Finally, we should be alert to sexual connotations in their descriptions of victims: these may be speculations about the child's future sexual functioning or projections about how other men or boys regard the victim. In other situations, the victim's alleged sexuality provides an excuse to the offender for the abuse (Faller, 1988).
- Aspects of the family history and functioning that may predispose them towards sexually abusive behaviour. In particular, any evidence of sexual or associated abuse—either generally, or perpetrated against the offender themselves, and any demonstrable consequences, extent and duration of such behaviour.
- Any parental convictions for sexual or physical offences (Schedule One status), including any episodes of imprisonment, or a child protection conference finding of harm
- Any intervention for abuse by professional agencies, including domestic violence and any care episodes. (NB. Care should be taken in evaluating the impact of this on the offender.) What success, if any, did they have in addressing the issues of concern?

- The nature and quality of family relationships (siblings, parent–children, etc.) and type and adequacy of role-modelling available.
- The stability and quality of their family life, including substance and alcohol use; separations/bereavements; family activities and interests; allocation of roles and responsibilities; support systems; and any mental illness histories.
- Methods of discipline (how and why), family rules and secrets, and sexual behaviour/attitudes/values.
- Means of resolving disagreements and conflict.
- Establish who they rely on when he or the family needs help. For example, who can they turn to when they have a financial problem? Who can they rely on when they have a problem with one of their children? And who would help out if there was a sickness in their family?
- The details of the offender's personal networks (names, date of births and addresses).

More specifically, workers could ask:

- Where did you live? What kind of work did your mother and father do? How did they feel about their work?
- What is your earliest memory? What are the feelings connected to it?
- What was it like being a small child in your home? Who was special to you, who cared the most about you?
- Give the names and birth dates of other children in the family in which you grew up:
  a. How did you get along with them?
  b. What was your place in the family?
  c. How did the parents treat each of the children?
- How did your family show feelings toward each other?
  a. Anger?
  b. Love?
  c. Closeness?
  d. Fear?
- How did your parents get along with each other? What did they enjoy together? What did they fight about? How did they fight? What effect did their relationship have on you then and now? (Schwartz and Cellini, 1995).

This information should begin to enable us to determine their perceptions of family life, and how they have integrated their experiences into their current make-up. Risk factors would include a history of abuse, substance abuse, criminal family, mental illness history, abandonment, denial of sexual offences, failure to protect children or violence in the home (Carich and Adkerson, 1995).

- Autobiography (Adkins et al., 1985; Long et al., 1989; Schwartz and Cellini, 1995)—which allows the offender to present a summarative history of key issues, patterns or themes in their life which may have influenced their current lifestyle, assumptions, and coping patterns. Offenders are asked to reflect on themselves and their behaviours, thus modelling the reality that they are agents of their own control (Marlatt, 1985). The focus on the broader context of their sexual offending is a useful engagement strategy for workers as they can choose to focus on their strengths and what they see as important, as well as their offending behaviours and difficulties. Quite simply, the offender is asked to write an autobiographical essay which aims to help them, through self-reflection to: learn more about themselves and others; become better able to reflect on their lives, identifying both positive and negative aspects of their experiences; become more aware of their strengths and coping skills; and identify both long-standing as well as more immediate factors that contributed to their offending behaviour. They can be asked to consider beliefs, emotional states, experiences, and behaviours that increase the likelihood of re-offending. The autobiography may be requested either as one piece of work or as several discrete tasks. For those who have problems with reading and writing, they can either ask for help from family or friends, or borrow a tape recorder. Workers can, and should, ask the offender to do further work following analysis and discussion. For example, the offender may initially choose to focus on those risk factors that are the most concrete, external and proximal to the abuse. These are generally circumstances over which they have least control and, therefore, feel the least responsible. Offenders may also accept responsibility for the act itself rather than the preceding planning that accompanies it. Workers can ask the offender to develop a more thorough understanding of risk factors by attending less to situational variables and more to those over which they can gain control, such as substance abuse. They can also identify false beliefs and distortions that need to be addressed (Carnes, 1983). Completed properly, the essay should provide a wealth of information about the beliefs, attitudes, feeling states, and behaviours that play a role in their offending. It can also provide evidence of more pervasive, long-standing personality characteristics as well as revealing features of personality style and any history of being abused themselves (Long et al., 1989).

- Interview format (Groth, 1979).
- Life history questionnaire (Lazarus, 1976).
- Generalised contentment scale (Simmons, 1986)*: A 25 item questionnaire designed to measure the degree of contentment they have with their new life and surroundings.
- Genogram: This is a type of family tree, which

contains additional information about the family. It is helpful to compare genograms completed by different family members. A genogram can show names and ages of all family members, preferably for at least three generations (including those who are no longer alive); exact dates of birth, marriages, separations, divorces, deaths of family members; and details of occupation, places of residence, important life events and any descriptions of the relationships/alliances within the family. When compiling the genogram, workers need to draw out family members on particular topics, e.g. how did the parents meet, how do other family members perceive their relationship, how long has it lasted?

The advantages of a genogram are:
- It provides an overall view of complex family constellations in a very concise form.
- It shows immediately available information but also indicates gaps.
- It highlights patterns and themes in previous and present generations.
- It provides a structure in which the workers and the family can share information whilst at the same time encouraging the expression of feeling about people and events, which in itself is important information.
- It can provide information about a family's lifestyle, cultural and ethnic origin. During the completion of the genogram, the worker will also wish to note key information on the current addresses of mother, father, siblings, grandparents and other significant family members (DoH, 1988).

For a further discussion on how to adapt the genogram for use with families from other cultures, please refer to Calder (1998), and Hardy and Laszloffy (1995).
See Calder (1997) for example of a genogram.

- Eco-mapping: A method of gathering information from the family about their networks: personal and professional. These networks can be organised around the offender to reflect closeness or distance in their relationships or support they offer. It could identify those who are aware of the abuse and those who may need to be protected. See Calder (1997) for an example of an eco-map.
- The family-of-origin scale (Hovestadt et al., 1985)*: Yields 10 scales related to the level of autonomy and intimacy of the family.
- FACES III (Olsen et al., 1992): A 20 item instrument designed to measure two main dimensions of family functioning; cohesion and adaptability. See Calder (1997) for the questionnaire.
- See Calder (1998b) and Gilgun (forthcoming) for a fuller discussion around identifying and

working with the strengths of individuals, without sacrificing the focus on child protection.

(b) Demographic data

Grubin (1992) points out that sexual offending is a culturally-defined phenomenon. Definitions of sexual offences are located within dominant understandings of sexual behaviour and are considered to be serious the more they deviate from these understandings (Cowburn, 1996). Sexual offenders are driven by two interdependent engines, one internal to the offender, the other fuelled by social contingencies. Whilst we know quite a lot about the demographic features and make-up of individuals who sexually offend, much less is known about the extent to which characteristics of particular societies influence the amount and type of sex crimes that occur within them.

Clinical evidence suggests that there may be some variation in type of sexual abuse by subculture. For example, Pierce and Pierce (1984) indicated that, compared with other racial groups, in black families the offender is more likely to be someone other than the biological father and the family is more likely to take decisive action to protect the child. Thus, information regarding ethnicity can assist the workers in understanding the dynamics of the sexual abuse and alert us to any patterns that may be present (Faller, 1988).

The available research does tend to point to an over-representation of black sex offenders in rapist populations (Grubin and Gunn, 1990), whilst Gebhard (1972) did identify some differences between black and white sex offender groups. He found that there was a correlation between the differences and the traits of the black subculture and the greater socio-economic deprivation they experienced. Black sex offenders were more likely to deny the offences, and the only sub-group of blacks with more convictions than their white counterparts related to homosexual offenders.

Any worker involved with a black offender does need to think how to engage them in the work, particularly as they will have additional obstacles to their white counterparts. These are set out in detail by Cowburn (1996) in relation to access to prison group work programmes. There needs to be an understanding of the additional stigma experienced by them, potential language difficulties (see Calder, 1998 for a discussion around the use of interpreters), and the additional identity problems for men of mixed racial background. Hopkinson (1997) noted that workers have to think about how to incorporate anti-discriminatory messages into the work so as to address the black culture of resistance to white oppression, with the latter often creating additional isolation. Cowburn and Modi (1995) set out a useful discussion about the issues and, in particular, the need for every sex offender to receive a full individualised assessment plan.

(c) Educational history

It is important to establish their school performance and academic achievement; classroom behaviour; the presence or absence of problems within the school (relationships with peers and teachers, attendance and any activity whilst truant, isolation, disciplinary, suspension or exclusion, bullying or bullied with staff and/or peers, etc.); interests in school; aptitudes and abilities; special educational needs/ services (ability or behavioural); school changes (including reasons); and any significant events.

Information about the offender's education tells workers a great deal about their overall functioning and is more important in terms of predicting treatment candidacy than sexual recidivism. School performance gives some information about the offender's ability to persist at long-term goals and his self-discipline and self-esteem (Dougher, 1995). The level of academic ability has a bearing on the type of assessment tools which can be used. Their school adjustment may offer some information about the development of peer relationships and their ability to relate to authority figures in a productive manner (Groth, 1979). As schooling is one of our first major life experiences that places demands on us to handle responsibilities, performance can be a useful predictor of subsequent difficulty or success in fulfilling life demands. Anyone who has failed at almost every major task is unlikely to benefit from any ongoing work (McGovern and Peters, 1988). It is important to establish (and access if possible) any records of special educational needs as they contain contributions from the educational psychologist, school, parent and significant others. A number of studies have indicated that paedophiles have IQs that skew to the lower end of normal thus rendering detection more likely. Sex offenders with learning difficulties may have negative attitudes surrounding new learning and direction from authority as well as problems with language-based comprehension. They found that 50 per cent of paedophiles and 85 per cent of aggressive sex offenders had repeated at least one year in school. Risk factors in this block include truancy and drop out, special education placement discipline problems and any sexual offending or harassing (Carich and Adkerson, 1995).

Tools

Questions to ask the offender include:

- How did you feel when you started school? What was good about school? What was bad about it?
- Who were your friends at school? What did you do with them? What games or hobbies did you enjoy with other children?
- How did the teachers treat you?

- Did you enjoy school-work? Was any of it hard for you? What subjects?
- What did your parents want for you in school? Did they want you to do well in sports, school-work, or religion?
- Were there changes in your living arrangements or family during secondary school years? Financial changes? Deaths? Moves?
- Did your feelings about school or achievements in school change in your secondary school years?
- What friends and/or activities were you involved with during your secondary school years?
- What kind of future job dreams or plans did you think about in your secondary school years? What were your goals? (Schwartz and Cellini, 1995).

(d) Occupational history
It is useful to obtain a record of the offender's work history, including types of jobs, job performance, level of responsibility and employment stability, job satisfaction, relationships with colleagues and their ability to support themselves and their family (Dougher, 1995; Groth, 1979). This information can throw light on their persistence, relationships, responsibilities and dependability—all keys to effective professional intervention and the creation of sustained change. Anyone who has been nomadic and created problems in work are unlikely candidates for treatment. Close scrutiny of their work record is essential as we may uncover inappropriate work, e.g. providing access to children. Other risks include excessive work hours, sporadic absenteeism, and frequent job changes (Cumming and Buell, 1997).

(e) Religious beliefs
Religious beliefs should be thoroughly evaluated with this population, particularly any stability/inconsistencies associated with their beliefs. We need to establish the meaning of religion for them, as it can have a role in the dynamics of their offending. Offenders frequently come from religious backgrounds which instill repressive sexual attitudes, fear of adult sexuality, and a lack of accurate sexual knowledge. We need to establish what their religious perspective is on sex and gender issues, plus whether there are there any cult or unusual practices. Other individuals escape from the guilt and responsibility of their offending by suddenly becoming extremely religious. They often state that they no longer need an assessment to understand their behaviour as they have been 'forgiven' for their 'sins'. We need to establish, however, whether their reason for sanctuary in the church is a cover for access to children via church-related activities, particularly as there is not yet a police vetting system for screening volunteers.

Individuals of certain denominations may express religious objections to certain types of assessment or treatment procedures including the viewing of sexually explicit materials or techniques using masturbation (Dougher, 1995).

Risk factors include the use of faith to justify offending (particularly if of their own invention); the use of a fall from faith to justify offending; a frequent shift in beliefs; the religious community supporting their denial or condemning any intervention; and any sexual abuse experiences associated with religion (Carich and Adkerson, 1995).

(f) Financial history
Financial history should include debts and assets. An individual's level of stability may be reflected on how they manage their finances (Cumming and Buell, 1997). Furthermore, Faller (1988) reported that over a quarter of cases of sexual abuse are marked with the onset of unemployment or some other factor has an impact on the offender's self-esteem. It is therefore important to identify any such stresses, which may contribute to the dynamics of child sexual abuse.

(g) Recreational interests
Groth (1979) pointed to the need for a description of the offender's leisure interests and activities, hobbies and clubs (particularly where they involve contact with children, such as football coach or scout leader) as they indicate how the offender amuses himself as well as reflecting their social skills and self-image. Attention should be paid to solitary, high-risk activities such as drinking or an obsession with weapons.

(h) Criminal history
A comprehensive understanding of the offender's criminal history and their attitudes towards their crimes can be useful in understanding the sexual abuse, developing a treatment plan, and in predicting prognosis, particularly if it indicates any other sex crimes. Sometimes the offender will be forthcoming and admit to his past history of criminal activity, but often the workers will have to rely upon a police check or data from other sources for this information (such as child protection conference minutes). We should always endeavour to elicit the circumstances of conviction, as it is not uncommon for 'plea bargains' to conceal the true nature and extent of their offending behaviour. This can be very difficult given the speed at which some agency and court records are destroyed.

Other offences are important indicators, such as arson, physical assaults or cruelty to animals . It is important to establish whether their sexual offending is unique or part of an extended pattern of criminal behaviour.

Once this history has been elicited, workers should explore anything unlawful that they didn't get caught for; any times the police were called to their house; and any arrests that didn't lead to a conviction, with reasons. The aim is for there to be a close match between the official records and the offender self-report. Valuable information can sometimes be elicited from the extended family and friends. It may also be appropriate to explore their experiences of custody—particularly if they have been on rule 43 (or equivalent if served as a young person)—as this may have a bearing on their sexual attitudes and behaviour.

In general, the best predictor of future sexual offences is the number of previous sexual offences (Dreiblatt, 1982). As such, the more sexual offences there are, the less optimistic workers should be regarding the prognosis for successful intervention. If there are previous offences, it is useful to determine whether the modus operandi and antecedent conditions or behaviours are similar, and whether there has been any escalation in frequency and types of sexual deviancy. Chronic recidivists generally begin their deviant sexual behaviour at an early age and may avoid detection for years (see Calder 1997a; 1997b).

For a discussion around the differences between sexual and non-sexual recidivism, the reader is referred to Hanson (in press). For more information on the assessment of general, violent recidivism, see Bonta et al. (1998). This is relevant as some sex offenders (such as rapists) are as likely to recidivate with a non-sexual violent offence as with a sexual offence (Hanson and Brussiere, 1996; 1998).

(i) Psychiatric history

Between 5 per cent and 10 per cent of sex offenders present with some form of identifiable mental illness (cf. Webster et al., 1982). It represents an important, minority factor, which must be addressed before any useful assessment of sexual offending behaviour can be completed. For example, an associated feature of antisocial personality disorder is persistent lying and other forms of deception (American Psychiatric Association, 1987), which have a direct link to the usefulness of self-report questionnaires. Psychiatrists frequently employ the MMP1-2 as a screen for mental illness and for examining a variety of personality traits, or other personality measures developed from it (cf. Langevin et al., 1990 a and b, for a review of these). It is important to know if a mental illness seen in the sex offender explains their sexual offending or is coincidental to it. The presence of an antisocial personality disorder is an important risk factor for acting out and hence re-offending (Langevin and Watson, 1996), largely because they may have weak impulse control and may engage in inappropriate behaviour in exchange for the most fleeting gratification, without regard for the consequences (McGovern and Peters, 1988).

Historically, many offenders may have been referred to mental health services as a direct alternative to pursuing any criminal prosecution, so a detailed trawl of psychiatric records can harnass useful information of relevance. It is for this reason that permission for disclosure may be refused by the offender, and, as such, any refusal should be seen as significant by the workers.

There are three reasons for exploring the offender's history for mental illness:

- Mental problems must be taken into account in assessing overall functioning. The longer the mental illness and the more severe its presentation, the poorer the treatment prognosis.
- Certain kinds of mental illness are indicative of poor object relations, and can affect the offender's ability to relate to children and partners.
- In a few cases, mental illness plays a key role in sexual abuse. For example, a psychotic offender may have specific delusions which justify his sexual abuse. In other circumstances, an assessment may be needed to establish whether it was the cause or the outcome of the sexual abuse, e.g. an offender suffering from depression. Here, the worker might query how long the depression has existed to determine whether it in part precipitated the sexual abuse or whether it is a result of the sexual abuse or its discovery. Furthermore, the offender's illness usually means he has few other positive experiences in life and also has impaired judgement, which may lead to repeated incidences of sexual abuse.

Tools
Questions to be asked include:

- Have they ever been hospitalised, and why? What medication have they taken previously? Or what are they currently taking? Have they ever felt anxious, easily upset or sad—and, if so, how have they managed such feelings? What views do they hold regarding both the victim(s) and the allegations?
- Observations of the offender may be diagnostic: poor responses in interview; information from the earlier education block regarding special educational needs, etc.; evidence of depression, persecutory beliefs, etc. These should be checked with significant professionals, family members or friends as there is often a continuum of mental health, and we need to know where they might have been at the time of the offences and the interviews.
- A psychiatric assessment is often needed and we should ensure the regional forensic psychiatry service are provided with all the relevant background information and concerns to allow them to comment both on their current presentation as well as their history.
- The sex offender lifestyle cognitive—behavioural inventory (Carich and Sterkel, 1992)*: This is

designed to measure an individual's level of thought and behaviour on specific personality categories (i.e. antisocial, narcissistic, borderline, schizoidal, and obsessive-compulsive), which are known to accompany, in whole, or in part, sex offender personality profiles.

- Millon clinical multiaxial inventory—II (Millon, 1987): consists of 175 statements associated with a wide variety of personality and clinical symptoms to which the respondent answers 'true' or 'false'. 22 clinical scales and 3 correction scales are divided into 5 categories: modifier indices, clinical personality pattern types, severe personality pathology scales (schizotypical, borderline, paranoid), clinical syndrome scales and severe clinical syndrome scales (thought disorder, major depression, delusional disorder).

- The Jackson personality inventory (Jackson, 1984), is a 320 item true–false personality inventory consisting of 16 scales, each with 20 statements. The statements include: anxiety, breadth of interest, complexity, conformity, energy level, innovation, interpersonal affect, organisation, responsibility, risk-taking, self-esteem, social adroitness, social participation, tolerance, value orthodoxy, and infrequency.

It is important to assess their attitude to attempted intervention, whether they have been self-referred or coerced with a legal mandate, and any changes post-intervention. Risk factors include a history of resistance to treatment, or any disorder which renders treatment ineffective (Carich and Adkerson, 1995).

(j) Neurological and biological factors

Wherever possible, a neurological examination should be conducted since some disorders manifest as sexually deviant behaviours, whilst some neurological abnormalities can influence their sexual behaviour. For example, damage to the temporal and frontal lobe (involved in sexual behaviours) can lead to sexual offending. Epilepsy and brain damage is significant in the genesis of unusual sexual behaviour, and diabetes can mimic psychosis, with mood fluctuations, poor judgement and confused sexual behaviour (Langevin and Bain, 1992). Diabetics, like sex offenders, are often resistant to the prescribed regime. It is clear, however, that only a few sex offenders present with unusual sex hormone profiles (Langevin, 1988). Workers should look for subtle evidence of neurological disorders such as learning disabilities, difficulties in concentration or memory, psychomotor deficiencies, and/or sensory deficits (Dwyer and Coleman, 1994)—since the relationship between these and offending behaviour is complex, but can influence recidivism risk and treatment outcome. These medical procedures are helpful but will not assist workers dealing with evasive offenders in denial.

Conversely, offenders with learning difficulties may not manage the assessment process despite their motivation to change. Medical treatment can lessen obsession with deviant sexual arousal (cf. Coleman and Cesnit, 1991) and hence reduce the likelihood of recidivism.

Whilst offenders with learning difficulties do present special problems for assessment, they can be engaged in the processes of assessment and change with commitment from the workers (Griffiths et al., 1989).

(k) Interpersonal relationships

Information about relations with significant others can be of benefit in understanding the dynamics and prognosis of sexual abuse. We will restrict our discussion here to relationships other than marital (sexual) as this will be explored in the next block under the notion of intimacy. A careful examination of the full range of sexual offenders personal relationships is not only useful for identifying intimacy deficits, but may also reveal direct social support for sexual offending (e.g. paedophile rings, peer support for rape), (Hanson, in press). In a recent study of sex offenders in the community, Hanson et al. (1997) found that the recidivists were more likely than the non-recidivists to have predominantly negative influences (43 per cent versus 21 per cent respectively).

Interpersonal communication is a dominant human function, and many of our problems stem from our concerns over the way we relate to other people, and the manner in which they respond to us (Lazarus, 1976). It is not surprising, therefore, that interpersonal relations are a central part of dealing with a sex offender, particularly since the offence is an interpersonal act (Groth, 1979). The nature of their problems will vary from case to case and thus need to be isolated if we are to tailor our intervention to the individual.

Weiss (1974) identified six key areas which isolated people miss out on. They are: attachment, provided by close affectional relationships, which give a sense of security and place; social integration, provided by membership of a network of persons having shared interests and values; the opportunity for nurturing others, usually children, which gives some incentive for continuing in the face of adversity; reassurance of personal worth, which promotes self-esteem and comes both from those at home as well as from colleagues; a sense of reliable alliance, which is obtained mainly from kin; and obtaining help and guidance from informal advisors when difficulties have to be resolved. Examples of the items include: at present, do you have someone you can share your most private feelings with (confide in) or not? Who is this mainly? Do you wish you could share more with them, or is it just about right the way it is? Would you like to have someone like this or would you prefer to keep your feelings to yourself?

Research findings

- Segal and Marshall (1986) found that sex offenders lacked confidence about their performance in social interactions. Parker (1984) reported that 31 per cent of the incest cases in his study said they had almost no friends, compared to only 11 per cent of the controls. Quinn (1984) and Strand (1986) found that incestuous fathers have low levels of group activity and participation and Strand found impoverished interpersonal relationships with incestuous fathers. Other studies have corroborated these findings (e.g. Kirkland and Bower, 1982; Panton, 1978).

- Fisher and Howells (1993) reviewed the issue of social relationships in sexual offending and considered the relationship variables in relation to Finkelhor's four factor model. They argued that within the first factor—motivation to offend—there are important issues to embrace. The factor is broken down into three components: emotional congruence, sexual arousal and blockage. Many sex offenders report an affinity for the company of children, finding them attractive in ways other than physical or sexual—that they don't find in adults. This may be related to their preoccupation with the need to dominate. Blockage appears to refer to obstacles in the development of socially acceptable relationships, although the relevance of social isolation and loneliness to sexual offending remains unclear. In the third factor—overcoming external inhibitions—they argue that sexual abuse is inhibited where the child is effectively embedded within a normal context of relationships. Mothers, neighbours, friends, etc., are all potential deterrents or inhibitors of sexual abuse. Where a relationship with any of these is abnormal, then the normal regulatory function performed by such relationships is diminished. Smith (1998) also argued that if you put a sex offender in an environment with vulnerable children, then sexual abuse becomes inevitable. Finally, overcoming the child's resistance also concerns relationships, as the offender often deliberately manipulates their relationship with the child to secure compliance.

- As Groth (1979) points out, *"a careful study and analysis of his relationships to others will reveal his affiliation needs; his social and empathic skills; his mode of relating; the depth, range, and stability of his relationships; his ability to differentiate among others; his perceptions of men and women; what importance he places on such relationships; and his interpersonal effectiveness. The type of person he tends to associate with offers some insight into self-image and value system."*

- Fisher and Howells (1993) argued very cogently that no consideration of the nature of social relationships is complete in the absence of socio-cultural influences. This includes the high tolerance level of sexual aggression in society as a whole and the associated encouragement of victim blaming. They concluded that *"... the quality of social relationships is not simply about the level of social skill the individual possesses, but that social behaviour is likely to be greatly influenced by the attitudes and beliefs perpetrators have about their rights and expectations in sexual relationships, as well as their own perception of their functioning within those relationships."*

Tools

In exploring interpersonal relationships, we need to consider:

- The nature and quality of the offender's relations with peers.
- The nature, quality and duration of the offender's friendships.
- The relative age and gender and number of the offender's friends and the kinds of friends they select as associates. Are they susceptible to the influence of others?
- The nature and extent of social isolation which may possibly indicate a more severe psychopathology.
- Whether the offender is active or passive in social relations e.g. social interests, activities and memberships. Are they self-centred? Excessively controlling and competitive?
- The nature and stability in their relationships. Obtain a relationship history, including the ages and sexes of the ex-partners children (adapted from Dougher, 1995; and Groth, 1979).
- The worker–offender communication dynamic within the assessment should not be disregarded either. These interpersonal communications involve not only overt acts and statements, but also a range of unspoken, non-verbal, covert and connotative elements such as body posture (Lazarus, 1976). There may be reactions from workers, induced by the offender, which highlight a problem in the way in which they relate to others. Conversely, the offender may react aggressively either to a male or female worker and this needs to be understood.
- Supervised contact sessions can provide workers with useful observational information on family relationships, whilst bail hostels, supervising officers or work colleagues can provide useful information about the offender.
- The dyadic adjustment scale (Spanier, 1976): This is particularly valuable for assessing problem areas outside of the sexual domain. It consists of 32 items designed to assess the quality of the relationship as perceived by married or cohabiting couples. It provides a general measure of marital/cohabiting satisfaction.
- The liking people scale (Filsinger, 1981): This is

a 15 item scale designed to measure that aspect of interpersonal orientation. It aims to differentiate between individuals who have high versus low levels of liking people.

- Dating and assertion questionnaire (Levenson and Goltman, 1978)*: This is an 18 item questionnaire designed to find out how the individual is likely to act in certain ways.
- The social skills game (Searle and Streng, 1995) is a therapeutic game to help young people who experience difficulties with relationships (see resource section for further details).
- The interview schedule for social interaction (Henderson et al., 1980): This is designed to assess the availability and perceived adequacy for any individual of a number of facets of social relationships. It explores areas like their personal networks (e.g. the range of their social relationships); the number of persons in different categories of relationship with whom they have contact in their daily life; as well as an assessment of what it is these relationships provide for the offender.
- Parental attitude scale (Simmons, 1986)*: This is a 25 item questionnaire designed to measure the degree of contentment they have in their relationship with their children.
- The revised UCLA loneliness scale (Russell et al., 1980)*: A 20 item report which requires that they indicate how often they see the ways described in each of the statements, designed at capturing the level of satisfaction or dissatisfaction with social relationships.
- Loneliness rating scale (Scalise et al., 1984)*: A 40-item questionnaire describing loneliness, and they are asked to indicate which would most describe how they feel. It can be adapted to include scoring relating to any identified situations by the workers.
- The provisions of social relations scale (Turner et al., 1983): A 23 item questionnaire designed to establish something about their relationships with other people.
- There are some excellent books covering various aspects of interpersonal relationships: Filsinger (1983); McCubbin et al. (1996); Weiss and Margolin (1986). The reader can refer to these for further ideas.

(I) Anger, aggression and assertiveness

1. Anger

Anger is a normal and natural emotion, which we all experience from time to time. Used constructively, it can motivate us to resolve problems. Alternatively, it can hurt us if repressed, as well as others if allowed to be expressed uncontrollably. These options do highlight that there are choices when managing anger (Freeman-Longo et al., 1996) which is like an energy which eventually seeks

release in one form or another. Mayer (1988) viewed anger as a continuum from explosive rage/uncontrollable anger (lack of control) through to mild irritation, annoyance, impatience and resentment (control).

Many sex offenders have serious difficulties with the appropriate expression of anger. It is often a primary source of motivation for sexual offences, and the failure to manage anger does increase the likelihood of displacement through aggression toward others (Green, 1995). For example, many sex offenders lack adaptive coping responses to stress, utilizing their pre-assault cycle as their primary method of stress reduction, e.g fantasy. Others use substances to the same end, or ignore their feelings until it is too late (Dougher, 1995).

Most sexual offenders have a pattern of anger that keeps them going in cycles, just like their sexual abuse cycle. They get hurt and resent the pain. As they let themselves smoulder with resentment, they start thinking about getting even with whoever is around them. They think about how others have wronged them in the past, covering up their insecurity by establishing power as they have a need to control others. They repeat to themselves all the hurtful things anyone has ever said to them until, eventually, they take revenge verbally, physically, emotionally, or financially. In many instances, this can be physical and/or sexual abuse. The longer it goes on, the deeper they sink into the anger cycle (Freeman-Longo et al., 1996).

Many offenders harbour substantial anger, often directed towards women. Many rapists report being angry at a woman at the time of their assault (Rada, 1978), whilst Pareza (1987) found that incestuous fathers were very likely to be angry and abusive. Pithers et al. (1988) determined that in 88 per cent of rapes and 32 per cent of sexual attacks on children, generalised anger was evident in the offender. Anger is a motivator for sexual offences and to a higher degree for rapists.

Many sex offenders do have histories of physical or sexual abuse, conflict or trauma which has resulted in anger that has either been suppressed, repressed, or otherwise redirected. Miller (1983) paints a powerful picture of angry and violent

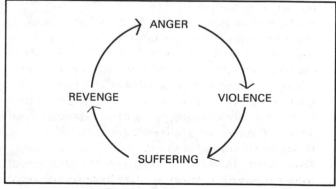

Figure 8: The anger cycle (Freeman-Longo et al, 1996).

behaviour resulting from authoritarian, abusive and neglectful styles of child-rearing. These sources of anger may play a role in the commission of sexual offences. This can be coupled with the physiological similarity between sexual arousal and anger. For those offenders who have unhappy backgrounds, the fusion of sex drives with violent ones can lead to a release in deviant sexual behaviour (Mayer, 1988). It can give the offender the illusion of having power and control. For the sex offender with feelings of inadequacy, it can be a comfortable emotion, providing temporary relief from the more painful feelings of vulnerability, fear and rejection, which lower self-esteem.

For a full discussion of the overt patterns of behaviour resulting from anger, please refer to Mayer (1988).

Tools

- Impulse control checklist (Simmons, 1986)*.
- Multi-dimensional anger inventory (Siegel, 1986)*: This includes 36-items selected to measure certain dimensions of anger; frequency, duration, magnitude, range of anger-arousing situations, mode of expression and hostility outlook.
- An anger diary (Marsh et al., 1988)*.
- Anger and assertiveness test (Marsh et al., 1988)*.
- Anger inventory (Novaco, 1975): This is a useful source of information on arousal-heightening cognitions with adults. It was designed to assess the degree of anger an individual would experience in provocative situations. It comprises 90 statements of provocation incidents for which the individual rates his degree of personal anger or provocation on a 5-point scale ranging from 'not at all' to 'very much'.
- State–Trait anger scale (Spielberger et al., 1983): This is useful as an index of change. State anger refers to an emotional state consisting of subjective feelings of tension, annoyance, irritation, fury and rage, along with concomitant activation or arousal of the automatic nervous system. State anger varies with temporal and situational context. Trait anger refers to individual differences in the frequency that state anger was experienced over time.
- Buss–Durkee hostility index (Buss and Durkee, 1957): Contains 66 true/false items that measure the following 7 aspects of hostility: negativism; resentment; indirect hostility; assault; suspicion; irritability; and verbal hostility.
- Use of "men and anger: A relapse prevention guide to understanding and managing your anger" (Freeman-Longo et al., 1996).
- Hostility towards women scale (Check, 1985): This scale addresses resentment and anger towards women. It comprises 30 agree–disagree items. The items are seen to reflect resentment towards women, e.g. 'I get upset by even slight criticism from a woman'.

2. Aggression

Aggression is a complex behaviour and too narrow an intervention focus runs the risk of missing important information. Each assessment must establish the circumstances for the arousal of aggressiveness and carrying out a violent behaviour should be examined for each person, i.e. whether it occurs in the context of the family, or only under the influence of alcohol, etc. Sexual aggression is often related to the offender's developmental history. For example, the quality of early interpersonal attachments and the experience of sexual abuse as a child can play a significant role in sexual aggression in adulthood (Cerce et al., 1984). Indeed, relationships in the family, and with significant others, during our formative years is crucial. Feelings of abandonment, of aggression, and often alcoholism in the parents are precursors of the adult sex offender of tomorrow.

Research findings

- Mehrabain and Epstein (1972) examined the relationship of empathy to agressiveness in college research volunteers. As expected, low empathy individuals aggressed more readily than high empathy individuals, but results were influenced by immediate availability of victims.
- Aggressiveness has readily been ascribed to rapists and other men who sexually assault adult females, but traditionally men who sexually offend against children have been considered shy, passive, unassertive, and un-aggressive. More recent research has questioned this assumption (cf. Christie et al., 1979; Lang et al., 1988; Langevin et al., 1985) and a segment of child sexual offenders are now recognized to be aggressive in their sexual offences as well as in other contexts. The same reasoning applies with respect to empathy—the more aggressive individuals may show greater deficits in empathy in order to carry out aggressive acts on children. Indeed, Langevin and Watson (1996) found that some 20 per cent of sex offenders engage in gratuitous violence against their sexual abuse victims.

Tools

Whilst few standard assessment measures exist, or are universally accepted, the following tools may be considered:

- The attraction to sexual aggression scale (Malamuth, 1989): A a 14-item scale designed to measure attraction to sexual aggression.
- Aggressive sexual behaviour inventory (Mosher and Anderson, 1986): Assesses a history of coercive and violent sexual behaviour in adult males. It directly asks the frequency with which

the respondent has engaged in various coercive and aggressive sexual acts. Each of the 20 items is rated on a 7 point scale from 'never' to 'extremely frequent'.

- The cumulative violence scale (CVS) (Langevin, 1985): This is a collection of items examining many aggressive behaviours throughout childhood and adulthood but is not considered predictive of future violence (Langevin, 1985). It does provide a fairly comprehensive collection of items that should be examined in an interview dealing with violence. The scale focuses on *actual behaviours* rather than *perceptions* of violent behaviours since violent offenders so often distort what they label as 'aggressive' or 'violent' (see Lang et al., 1988). Scales frequently ask whether the individual *considers himself* to be a violent person so he rates himself as violent or non-violent. Many violent offenders think they are normal or they lie about themselves. However, when asked for objective behaviour, such as, 'How often do you hit your wife?', frequently they provide some number, although it is noteworthy that the more aggressive the crimes, the more frequently they lie about their behaviour patterns (cf. Lang et al., 1988).

- The sexual aggression test (Loss et al., 1988)*: A 40 item scale designed to elicit their views on a range of sexually aggressive situations.

- See Goldstein and Keller (1987) for a detailed discussion of assessing aggression.

- There is an excellent resource from Morran and Wilson (1997) which sets out in detail a group work practice manual for men who are violent to women. It contains nearly 300 pages of materials, which can be readily adapted to work with aggressive sex offenders.

3. Assertiveness

As Beckett et al. (1994) pointed out, assertiveness is a multi-dimensional concept, covering such areas as an individual's ability to generally express feelings, stand up for their rights in public situations, initiate and maintain interaction with others, deal with criticism and pressure, and make requests and appropriate demands. Over-assertiveness/aggression can interfere with constructive problem solving and alienate others both generally and in intimate relationships, whilst a failure to assert can lead to them becoming socially and emotionally isolated, and can contribute to offenders being unable to extricate themselves from situations that may present a risk for further offences. Sub-assertive or passive communication patterns are often found among sex offenders who perceive themselves to be inadequate or inferior either to their peers or to authority figures. Fearful of expressing their thoughts or feelings, they often suppress their emotions, which can then manifest themselves through aggressive behaviour (Beckett et al., 1994; Green, 1995). Individuals who are appropriately assertive are those who have skills in social perception, problem solving and behavioural enactment. Sex offenders can therefore be either under-assertive or over-assertive.

It is important to identify whether the offender exhibits assertive or non-assertive behaviour as a result of their feelings, thoughts and beliefs. This should not be confused with aggressive behaviour, which represents inappropriate ways of expressing thoughts, feelings and beliefs.

Research findings

- Assertiveness deficits have assumed theoretical significance in a number of sexual anomalies (cf. Langevin, 1985). The rapist has been portrayed as unassertive, but aggressive, whilst the paedophile has been considered shy, unassertive, and lacking in masculinity, similar to incest offenders, and other sex offenders (Langevin et al., 1988a).

- The results of the assertiveness research on sex offenders, however, have been mixed. In some cases there are deficits and, in others, there are not (cf. Lang et al., 1988; Langevin et al., 1985; Langevin, 1983). Marshall et al. (1995); Overholsen and Beck (1986); and Segal and Marshall (1986) have all found child molesters to be unassertive. Overholsen and Beck (1986) found child molesters to be less assertive than rapists, non-sex offenders, and community controls, and Stermac and Quinsey (1985) reported less assertiveness in rapists, but only in heterosexual situations. Abel et al. (1985) found that 40.8 per cent of child abusers had deficits in assertiveness and 46.9 per cent of rapists also had problems of under assertion. Inability to be appropriately assertive was implicated as the immediate precursor of sex offences in 42 per cent of rapists and general social skill problems were implicated as immediate precursors of sexual offences in 59 per cent of child abuses and 50 per cent of rapists (Pithers et al., 1987).

- One significant confounding factor has been the prisoner status of the respondent. Segal and Marshall (1985) found that sexually aggressive incarcerated offenders were less assertive than community controls but they did not differ from other incarcerated non-sex offenders. Prisoners may be less willing to express their assertiveness while incarcerated to persuade a favourable parole application.

Tools

- Asserting yourself: A practical guide for positive change (Bower and Bower, 1976).

- The college self-expression scale: A measure of assertiveness (Galassi et al., 1974): A 50-item self-report measure, aimed to measure 3 aspects of assertiveness: positive, negative and self-denial.

- Rathus assertiveness schedule (Rathus, 1973): A 30-item schedule for assessing or encouraging and promoting assertive behaviour.
- Assertion inventory (Gambrill and Richey, 1975): This is a 40 item self-report inventory which permits respondents to note for each item the degree of discomfort, their probability of engaging in the behaviour, and situations they would like to handle more assertively. In order to make maximum use of this inventory, the reader is referred to Morton et al. (1981); and Rakos (1991).
- Bakker assertiveness–aggressiveness inventory (Bakker et al., 1978)*: This 36 item inventory measures assertiveness in terms of two components necessary for social functioning: the ability to refuse unreasonable requests ('assertiveness', AS), and the ability to take the initiative, make requests, or ask for favours ('aggressiveness', AG). Each item is rated on a 5-point scale from 'almost always' to 'almost never' according to how the respondent would behave in a specified manner. Each scale is scored separately. Higher scores indicate that they are less likely to exhibit assertiveness or aggressiveness.
- Interpersonal behaviour survey (Groth, 1979; 1983): This is an inventory designed to measure an individual's interpersonal behaviours, with an emphasis on assertive and aggressive behaviour. It consists of 272 items to which the respondent scores 'true' or 'false'.
- Interpersonal behaviour survey (Mauger and Adkinson, 1987): This is an interesting inventory as it samples features that are considered important to sex offenders: namely defensiveness in 3 scales: denial, infrequency and impression management; aggressiveness in 7 scales: general aggressiveness, hostile stance, expression of anger, disregard for rights, verbal aggressiveness, physical aggressiveness, and passive aggressiveness; and assertiveness in 8 scales: general assertiveness; self-confidence; initiating assertiveness; defending assertiveness; frankness; praise (giving/receiving); requesting help; and refusing demands: and relationships in three scales: conflict avoidance, dependency and shyness.

(m) Self-esteem, sexual esteem and self-concept

Self-esteem is defined as the way in which a person perceives themselves, values themselves and rates themselves in relation to other people (Briggs et al., 1998).

Snell et al. (1989) defined sexual esteem as *"positive regard for, and confidence in, the capacity to experience ones sexuality in a satisfying and enjoyable way."* They argued that the higher the sex offenders sexual esteem, the lower their sexual depression (e.g. the experience of feelings of depression regarding ones sexual life), and the more willing they would be discussing a variety of topics dealing with their sexuality with male workers.

Research findings

- Low self-esteem is a common presenting characteristic of sex offenders, and is believed to be a significant component accounting for both the development and the maintenance of sexual offending (Marshall and Mazzucco, 1995). These suggestions have been provided with some support by the observations of Pithers et al. (1987) who analysed the precursors to the offences of 136 paedophiles and 64 rapists and found that low self-esteem was a precursor for 56 per cent of rapists and 61 per cent of paedophiles, and by Howells (1981) who reported that child molesters find children attractive because, unlike adults, children are seen as submissive and non-threatening.
- Stephen Wolf (1984) has discussed the role of low self-esteem in sexual offenders 'cycle of offending' and described how some offenders with low self-esteem compensate by engaging in fantasies of emotional and sexual gratification with children. Many of these may have been the product of their own victimisation. Doing so contributes to such men then seeking association and sexual contact with children. Having committed a sexual assault, Wolf proposes that sex offenders, knowing that they have done wrong and fearing being apprehended, suffer a further fall in self-esteem, withdraw further from those adults around him and engage in more deviant compensatory fantasy, thus completing the cycle. Offenders with low self-esteem often have problems developing victim empathy (discussed later in this chapter).
- Marshall (1989) and Marshall et al. (1993) have suggested that low self-esteem in sex offenders results primarily from their experiences as children. More precisely, they claimed that if the parental attachments of male children were poor, (particularly if the parents were emotionally neglectful or rejecting), then the boy's self-esteem would suffer and they would be vulnerable to other influences that might lead them to become sexual offenders. These authors anticipated that many sex offenders would report parental rejection and that such rejection would be directly related to their current level of self-esteem. In fact, Marshall and Mazzucco (1995) reported that maternal rather than paternal rejection leads to lower self-esteem, whereas they would have expected the opposite. What remains unknown is how individuals take the next step from low self-esteem to sexual offending.

- Low self-esteem would be an expected characteristic of individuals who are lonely, isolated, under-assertive and stigmatised for example, by the label of sex offender. Low self-esteem may be a consequence of contemporary events, e.g. being apprehended and punished, and for some individuals may be a chronic problem stretching back to childhood or adolescence. Low self-esteem is one of many potential consequences of having been sexually abused (Browne and Finkelhor, 1986) and it is noteworthy that a disproportionate number of sex offenders in general (Araji and Finkelhor, 1986) and 74 per cent of sex offenders assessed by STEP (Beckett et al., 1994) had been sexually abused as children. Marshall and Mazzucco (1995) also found that child molesters had significantly lower self-esteem and a higher rate of childhood sexual abuse than did the non-offenders—supporting the notion that child molesters suffer from a deficit in their self-confidence in social situations. Social anxiety is an aetiological significant precursor of sexual offending, particularly the fear of either being criticised or rejected by others, or being negatively evaluated (Overholsen and Beck, 1986).

- Horley and Quinsey (1995) conducted some research to elicit child molesters' construal of themselves, other adults and children. In terms of self-descriptions, molesters described themselves as dirty more often than the community sample did. They may thus be demonstrating a negative self-image when they describe themselves as repulsive, frigid, sexless, soft and dirty. This also suggests that they lack self-esteem. Such views of themselves may be accurate (i.e. in line with consensus views) in that child molesters have been judged as less attractive physically than non-offenders (Segal, 1983). On the other hand, they might be excusing their behaviour when they describe themselves negatively in terms of present attractiveness. Molesters' 'negative' ideal self-ratings, however, may suggest generally lower personal standards or expectations, in agreement with the lower self-esteem view.

- In addition to negative self-descriptions, the molesters also described women as frigid, and spouses were described as sexless, frigid, repulsive, and ugly. This may be because they only attract women they view as unattractive, or more likely, that they excuse their behaviour on the basis that they are forced to interact sexually with children.

- Horley, Quinsey and Jones (1997) extended their original study to expand some of their earlier findings (e.g. to encompass belief, attitude and value measures). They hypothesized that molesters would see themselves as relatively unattractive, whilst children would be viewed as physically and sexually attractive, trusting and kind. These views should be moderated by victim gender and prior treatment.

- They found that child molesters revealed higher scores in their ratings of women than non-child molesters, indicative of a more supportive, enlightened, or 'positive' view of adult females. However, this does need to be seen in the context that molesters described women and spouses as less sexy and more frigid than did comparisons. Molesters also described themselves as less seductive, less beautiful, less sexy and less erotic—than did non-child molesters, possibly to elicit sympathy and/or support. Molesters also described themselves as kinder, calmer, softer and more pleasant than did non-molesters. Horley et al noted that these are not a general lack of self-esteem, but relate specifically to physical and sexual attractiveness. This may be, in part, related to the negative views of others towards sex offenders, which are then internalized. The authors did acknowledge that these ratings may not reflect poor self-esteem exclusively—also perhaps the result of incarceration and/or overwhelming condemnation by others.

- Ward, McCormack and Hudson (1997) found that child molesters in their sample had a more negative view of themselves than other groups. This was evident in their greater sensitivity to rejection and tendency toward fearful or preoccupied attachment styles, both of which are characterized by a negative view of self. Rapists, by contrast, were more likely to hold a negative view of others, as evidenced by their less positive perceptions of their partners, lower commitment to their relationships, and perceptions of little support from their partners.

- However, workers also need to be cautious regarding high self-esteem, which can also be dangerous as it is often associated with the offender having a distorted sense of their own importance (Pithers, 1994). Both high and low self-esteem is an important variable in considering the likelihood of repeat offending.

- Marshall, Anderson and Champagne (1996) integrated and reviewed the literature in relation to self esteem and sexual offending, finding that people with low self-esteem have many of the same characteristics as sexual offenders and many of these features appear likely to present obstacles to effective therapy with these groups. For example, they are unlikely to commit to change, hesitant to try new behaviours or accept different beliefs, fail to perform the necessary practice to acquire new skills, are easily discouraged in their efforts to change, and readily give up trying because they expect to fail. People with low self-esteem also resist efforts to enhance their confidence, or reinterpret encouraging feedback in order to maintain their present poor self-concept.

- Marshall, Champagne, Sturgeon and Bryce (1997) argued that self-esteem is certainly not a unitary trait manifest across time and situations, but rather as multi-dimensionally manifest within specific domains of functioning. They cite evidence to show that self-esteem fluctuates to varying degrees over time, and it is clear that some individuals are quite confident in some situations or domains of functioning (e.g. in academic pursuits) but not in others (e.g. in social interactions). Indeed, they conceptualize self-esteem as it influences the behaviour of sex offenders as likely to be domain specific, and they continue to work towards developing domain specific measures. Their paper sets out some of the ways and values of enhancing the self-esteem of sexual offenders.

- People with low self-esteem distort available information in self-serving ways, and sexual offenders are characterized by distorted perceptions and cognitions that facilitate offending. Similarly, a lack of empathic concern typifies both low self-esteem subjects and sexual offenders, and they have found that self-esteem and victim empathy are both deficient and significantly correlated among child molesters. Low self-esteem subjects have serious problems in social interactions and in forming relationships with others, and sexual offenders are similarly deficient in intimacy and have other social difficulties. Finally, emotional distress of one sort or another has found to be a significant precursor of sexual offending and subjects who are low in self-esteem typically have similar emotional problems.

Tools

- Autobiography: This can highlight an individual's self-esteem, both in their responses as well as their attitude towards the task itself. Those with low self-esteem often struggle to complete this task. If they do complete it, the workers can assess whether there are any variations in the offender's self-esteem across a variety of situations or roles, e.g. employee, husband, father or friend. Disdain for oneself is rarely fully generalised (Long et al., 1989).
- Interview: In paying careful attention to the offenders verbal and body language.
- Refer to the earlier sections of the social history to assess any influences there may be on the offender's self-esteem such as previous abuse, job and relationship satisfaction, etc.
- Index of self-concept (Simmons, 1986)*: This is a 25 item scale designed to measure how they see themselves.
- Rosenberg self-esteem scale (Rosenberg, 1989): This has 10 scale items dealing with general

feelings about themselves which they have to score from 'strongly agree' to 'strongly disagree' (see Calder, 1997 for this scale).

- Self-esteem questionnaire (Thornton, 1994): A short 8 item questionnaire in which subjects answer true or false to questions regarding how they feel about themselves.

Social self-esteem inventory (Lawson et al., 1979)*: A 30 item inventory, balancing examples of high and low self-esteem and is designed to measure self-confidence in social situations. Each item is responded to on a 6-point scale, resulting in a possible range of scores from 30 to 180, with the higher scores reflecting greater self-esteem.

- The reflected self-esteem and reflected love scales (Turner et al., 1983): A 17 item scale designed to establish how the offender feels they are seen by others. Sample items include: 'Other people think I can change my mind and plans when new information is available to me'; and 'Other people see me as a warm and friendly person'. The offender is asked to respond on a 5 point scale ranging from 'I am very certain that this is true' to 'I am very certain that this is not true'.

- The culture-free self-esteem inventories (Battle, 1992).

- Other than questionnaires, a useful exercise has been designed to look at the offenders' view of themselves. The self-inventory (Loss et al., 1988) is where they split a paper into two columns. In the first, they should list the things they dislike about themselves from the most to the least. In the other, they should list the things they like about themselves from the least to the most. This list should cover characteristics of their personality, behaviour and beliefs. They should put on the list how they see and think about themselves, and not how they think others view them, or what they would like them to change. Positive examples would include 'I enjoy working hard' or 'I'm usually easygoing around others', whilst negative examples would include 'I am often dishonest' or 'Once I lose my temper, I am out of control'.

(n) Social skills and competence

Deficiencies in the offender's social skills are frequently cited as playing a key role in both the origin and then the maintenance of sexual offending by excluding them from access to appropriate sexual partners or preventing them from changing their mode of sexual expression to a more normative one (Marshall et al., 1995). Social skills is a broad term used to describe a wide variety of behaviours and cognitive phenomena presumed necessary for effective functioning in social situations (Conger and Conger, 1986). Sex offenders may present as being quite normal in their social functioning and beliefs, so the following summary needs to be read with this in mind.

Many of the sections to this point will give us a clue as to the offender's social competency (e.g. interpersonal relationships, employment), but it is also important to assess areas such as their ability to manage interpersonal conflict.

Research findings

- Although there have been a number of descriptive studies suggesting a lack of social skills (Lawson et al., 1979), there are only a few studies which have specifically explored the types of deficit found in different groups of sex offenders. For example, exhibitionists have been characterised as having poorer social skills and marital adjustment, poorer heterosexual skills and less heterosexual activity, more difficulty in handling hostility and aggression and are more timid and unassertive than other sex offenders. It would appear that different offence types serve particular functions for the individual, with some being more related to social competence problems than others. Great care has to be taken, therefore, in applying material from one context to another.

- The majority of the research to date in relation to social skill deficits has focused on either child molesters or rapists. Segal and Marshall (1985) compared rapists and child molesters to non-sex offending inmates. They found that lower socio-economic status subjects were less skilled generally and more anxious than higher socio-economic status subjects. The child molesters presented a clearer profile of inadequacy than the rapists and also rated themselves as less skilled and more anxious in heterosexual situations. Gordon et al. (1980) found sex offenders to be more socially anxious, whilst Overholsen and Beck (1986) found child molesters to be less assertive than rapists as well as having an inordinate fear of negative evaluations by others. Marshall et al. (1995) found that child molesters are the most lacking in self-confidence, the most socially anxious and the most unassertive. In addition to this, they as a group held beliefs about social behaviour that were in contrast to the notions generally advanced in the social skills literature about what is appropriate behaviour. They differed starkly from the rapists who were more socially confident, less anxious, less unassertive, and more aggressive. The authors identified the need for workers to concentrate their assessment on the offender's dysfunctional views of assertiveness and their social deficits.

- Other research has found little support for the claim that sexual offenders have significant social problems (Stermac et al., 1990). These results suggest three possibilities: social skill deficits are either a function of being an offender, a function of being incarcerated, or a function of socio-economic class. These need to be considered in each individual case.

- Marshall (1971) argued that if we wanted to help sex offenders change their behaviour, then we needed to equip them with the necessary skills to be successful. He proposed deficits in conversational, assertive and relationship skills needed to be addressed. For example, Lipton et al. (1987) found that rapists miscontrued women's cues on simulated first date situations. In particular, they misread cues from the women as positive and encouraging signs. Segal and Marshall (1986) found that child molesters were poorer than other sex offenders and non-offenders in predicting and evaluating their own performance in conversations with females. Barbaree et al. (1988) reported that although child molesters were as good as non-offenders at recognizing a problem in a social situation and generating alternative solutions, they typically chose poor solutions and appeared not to consider the likely consequences of their choices. Decision-making skills involve being able to generate options, choose the best option and then evaluate the consequences of choosing that option (Fisher and Howells, 1993). These issues are often more profound in offenders with learning disabilities (cf. Murphy et al., 1983). Where the sex offender has learning difficulties, their level of social skills is often very low and this requires that we adapt the materials used as well as prioritising them for social skills training.

- In addition, Segal and Marshall (1986) regarded self-efficacy as crucial since an individual's awareness of performance is essential for skilled behaviour, and they found that child molesters in their sample were lowest and significantly poorer at predicting and evaluating their performance. As Marshall and Eccles (1991) have astutely pointed out, the reason why there is such scant evidence of sex offenders having deficits of social competence is that studies have failed to separate out specific skills for research. This is alarming since many treatment programmes focus on this broad area in quite some detail.

- Stermac and Segal (1989) also found that child molesters saw children's behaviour as more seductive and saw children as more responsible for sexual contacts than did others. However, it remains unclear whether this is because of either a social skill deficit or a cognitive distortion (explored in detail later in this chapter).

- Workers will come across offenders who are socially adept as well as ones who cannot sustain appropriate interactions with others – often alienating them from reinforcing victim creating patterns of behaviour (Becker et al., 1978).

Tools

- The interview itself can provide clues as to the offender's social skills behaviours (verbal and non-verbal). Deficits may be indicated where they look away excessively, fail to listen, interrupt readily, lack social pleasantry, appear socially awkward, jump topics suddenly, become over-familiar with the worker or ask personal questions of the workers which are unrelated to the background relevant to the inquiry (Carich and Adkerson, 1995). However, we need to be mindful of Segal and Marshall's (1985) findings as they reported that the offenders response and presentation within the interview situation may not accord with their behaviour elsewhere. Whilst role-play is advocated to counter this (Dougher, 1995), it is often difficult within individual sessions and maybe more practical in a group setting.
- It is also important to explore the relationship of any social skill deficiencies to their pre-assault cycle. In assessing the offender's perceptions, a number of questions need to be asked: Do they tend to be involved in insular activities? Do they value spending time with others? Has the influence of others been experienced primarily in negative or positive terms? Are there any differences in the way they describe interactions with children, same sex adults, and opposite sex adults?
- The social skill assessment scale (Barlow et al., 1977). This scale consists of the major categories of voice, form of conversation, and affect, with the sub-categories specified. During assessment, subjects are asked to role-play three, 2½-minute scenes with a female. The scenes are designed to increase in intimacy from an initial meeting to a date with someone they have known for a long time. All scenes are videotaped and rated at a later time in 30-second blocks for the presence or absence of the specific behaviours outlined. The tapes are also reviewed for such behaviours as inappropriate touching of the body (i.e. touching the genitals or picking the nose), unusual body mannerisms or facial gestures that make the patient 'appear odd', and inappropriate verbalisations such as asking for a kiss when first meeting someone. We observe these types of gross behavioural deficits more often in the offender with learning difficulties and they must be targeted early in our work if they are to avoid continued social rejection.
- For a comprehensive review of assessment issues, please refer to Conger and Conger (1986) and for further ideas see Squirrel (1998).
- Conflict tactics scale (Strauss, 1979): This was designed to assess three primary modes of dealing with conflict within families: reasoning, verbal aggression and violence.

- The internal control index (Duttweiller, 1984): This is a measure of internal focus of control in adults. It consists of 28 items with response alternatives that fall along a 5 point scale from A (rarely) to E (usually).
- Social avoidance and distress scale (Watson and Friend, 1969): A 28 item true–false questionnaire which measures the degree to which a person avoids social situations due to anxiety, distress and fear, plus assessing individuals levels of personal distress in social interactions.
- Fear of Negative Evaluation (Watson and Friend, 1969): Designed to measure anxiety related to being evaluated by others in interpersonal situations.
- Self-control questionnaire (Rehm, 1977; 1984)*: Contains 40 items that assess attitudes and beliefs about self-control behaviour.
- Adult locus of control scale (Nowicki and Strickland, 1973)*: This was designed to measure the extent to which an individual feels he is in personal control of his life (internal locus of control) versus the extent to which he feels that power resides outside of himself in the form of luck, fate, chance, other people or events (external locus of control).

(o) Health and medical history

It should be routine to request the offender's medical history which can be offset against any self-report questionnaires or interviews. It is important that this includes:

- Pre-natal, delivery and neonatal development, including birth defects.
- Basic information about chronic and acute medical conditions—particularly any side-effects which may affect their sexual drive or performance.
- Illnesses or handicaps.
- Medication use, including conditions necessitating it (past and present), and any non-compliance.
- Surgical history.
- Congenital disorders.
- Hospitalisations (and conditions necessitating this).
- Significant medical problems within the extended family.
- Self-harming behaviours/suicide attempts.
- Any major loss of schooling or periods of employment.
- Sexual diseases.
- Depression or mental illness.
- History of addictions (gambling, eating disorders, etc.). Any substance abuse accompanying medical treatment?
- Crime-related injuries (adapted from Groth, 1979; Wincze and Carey, 1991).

Workers may wish to refer the offender for further medical evaluation, particularly if there are huge gaps in the history or where any outstanding concerns remain. The medical history may produce important clues regarding self-image, impulse management and control and feelings of self-worth and adequacy (Groth, 1979). Offenders may also use their medical conditions as a means of avoiding assessment work.

Tools

- General health questionnaire (Goldberg and Hillier, 1979): Contains 28 items consisting of four sub-scales: somatic symptoms, anxiety and insomnia, social dysfunction and severe depression. It is a self-administered questionnaire designed to detect early psychiatric disorder. See Calder (1997) for sample items.
- The Beck depression inventory (Beck et al., 1961) is a well known measure of depression and is used to assess depressive symptomology by requiring the offender to complete the 21 categories of symptoms and attitudes. Several dimensions of depression often described by survivors, such as self-dislike, guilt, pessimism, sadness, sleep disorders, and social withdrawal are covered. A shorter version of this instrument contains 13 items (Beck and Beck, 1972). Each category consists of 4–5 self-evaluated statements, which are ranked to reflect the range of severity.
- Illness behaviour questionnaire (Pilowsky, 1983)*: Useful for measuring the ways individuals experience and respond to their health status. It is a 62 item questionnaire designed to measure a respondent's attitudes, ideas, affects, and attributions in relation to illness. It comprises seven major sub-scales, each of which has at least 5 items. The 7 scales are general hypochondriasis, disease conviction, psychologic versus somatic perceptions of illness, affective inhibition, affective disturbance, denial and irritability. Details on how to access the scoring manual details are available in the resources section.
- Automatic thoughts questionnaire—revised (Hollon and Kendall, 1980; Kendall et al., 1989)*: A 40 item instrument that measures the frequency of automatic negative statements about the self.
- An excellent source of questionnaires and scales for measuring health is McDowell and Newell (1987).

2. Sexual history

"In the absence of a personal and social history, it is impossible to provide an appraisal of risk" (Becker and Quinsey, 1993).

Few of us are trained in, or feel comfortable with, taking the kind of sexual history necessary in the assessment. We can make this easier if we address this block after we have established a viable working relationship with the offender and if we have formulated a very clear idea of the questions prior to interview (Calder, 1997). In this section, we offer a detailed structure for taking a sexual history, which is useful in establishing what effect, if any, their early experiences have on their attitudes, values, beliefs, knowledge and behaviour.

A number of measures are suggested to generate discussion with the offender (particularly useful if they are in denial). Whilst these are useful in designing future work programmes, their prognostic significance has yet to be established (Becker and Quinsey, 1993).

Sexual histories are useful because:

- It may help in confirming a diagnosis of sexual abuse or understanding the dynamics of sexual abuse.
- It identifies their sexual development, experiences, habits and interests (e.g. sado-masochism), performance, satisfactions, blocks and dysfunctions.
- It identifies their sexual attitudes, values and orientations.
- It charts their sex education (formal or peer).
- It establishes how comfortable they are in discussing sex. N.B. Pay attention to their non-verbal behaviour in addition to the content of their responses to your questions.
- It may offer an opportunity for them to discuss any sexual abuse they have experienced.
- It may highlight distorted family attitudes or practices regarding sex or sexuality.
- It may highlight sexual preferences, via patterns of behaviour.
- It may uncover the presence of other problems which are contributory to their sexual offending.
- It is useful in assessing risk, making treatment recommendations and predicting prognosis and outcomes (adapted from Becker and Quinsey, 1993; Beckett, 1994; Faller, 1988; and Groth, 1979).

Workers should prepare carefully for this component and should select any questionnaires, which they might want to use with the offender. They should clarify the offender's vocabulary and establish whether they feel comfortable with certain words, and if they accurately understand them. The offender should be given time to provide detailed and thoughtful responses to all questions and homework assignments.

There are a number of useful sexual inventories, which can assist us in collecting a detailed sexual history. These include:

- The Thorne sex inventory (Thorne, 1966): This was designed as a clinical screening instrument for the assessment of both identified as well as potential sex offenders. Intended to be used *with* an interview, it comprises 200 true–false questionnaire items, arranged into 9 sub-scales, which includes sex drive and interest, sexual maladjustment and frustration, neurotic conflict associated with sex, sexual fixation and cathexes, repression of sexuality, loss of sex controls, homosexuality, sex role confidence, and promiscuity.

- Scales for rating sexual experience (Thorne, 1966): 10 sex experience scales are described, referring to the dimensions of sex drive, sexual sensuality, physical intimacy, loving emotionality, spiritual union, procreative urgency, orgasmic potency, orgasmic intensity, sex satisfyingness and sex satisfaction.

- The Clarke sex history questionnaire (Paitich et al., 1977): A 225 item sexual history for males that sample a wide range of sexually anomalous as well as conventional heterosexual behaviours. It contains 24 scales which relate to the frequency and type of erotic preferences and behaviour. Samples include heterosexual and homosexual behaviour, cross-dressing, paedophilia, masturbation fantasies, voyeurism, obscene telephone calls, exhibitionism, toucherism and frottage, peeping, masochism, and rape. It also includes questions on animal sex, death, group sex, outdoor masturbation, incest, fire and the current frequency of their sexual outlet. These outlets include dating, kissing and various forms of contact with breasts, mouths, genitals and anus. It is available in full in Langevin (1983). Sample questions include: 'How many girls or women have you kissed on the lips since the age of 16? (a) None (b) 1 only (c) 2–3 (d) 4–5 (e) 6–10 (f) 11–20 (g) 21–40 (h) 41–70 (I) 71–100 (j) over 100.' 'Have you ever wanted to do this?' 'Would this be disgusting to you?' 'How many times have you put your penis into the rear end (rectum) of a girl or woman since the age of 16?' 'Have you ever wanted to do this?' 'Would this be disgusting to you?' 'When you expose yourself to females do you hope that they will get enjoyment out of seeing your penis?' 'Do you ever hope that they will be impressed by the size of your penis?'

- The revised Clarke sex history questionnaire for males (Langevin et al., 1985): This is an 86 item version, with 177 questions in the supplementary SHP scales, which extends the above to embrace further behaviours such as fantasies and the concept of orgasmic preference. In order to sort out behaviours and desires that are sexual curiosities from being lasting erotic preferences, the frequency of orgasm accompanying all behaviours should be ascertained. Those sexual behaviours that do not culminate in orgasm are often, but not always, less important in the individuals pattern of sexual behaviour. Among the sexual behaviours that do involve orgasm,

some are preferred over others and it is these that are of greatest concern (see Russon, 1985 for the sex history questionnaire scoring manual). Sample questions include: 'Has a sex partner ever complained that they were not satisfied after having sex with you?' 'How often have you been unable to get an erection with a sex partner?' Have you ever fantasised about: 'Beating a female partner?' 'Saying obscene things to a girl or woman?' 'A girl or woman humiliating or embarrassing you?'

- The multiphasic sex inventory (Nicols and Molinder, 1984): This test was constructed to assess a range of sexual characteristics of identified sex offenders, including child molesters, rapists, exhibitionists, and other paraphiliacs. The sub-scales assess attributes related to sexual attitudes, sexual history, sexual knowledge, sexual dysfunction, and denial/defensiveness concerning sexual behaviour. It is a 300 item, true–false questionnaire with 14 clinical and validity scales, which takes one and a half hours for the offender to complete. Three of these scales measure sexually offensive behaviour (rape, child molestation, exhibitionism), five measure sexual deviations, four measure sexual dysfunction, one measures sexual knowledge and attitudes, and the scale also provides a measure of the offender's attitude towards treatment. The sub-scales include: *social/sexual desirability*—35 items that aim to assess the offenders denial and/or minimisation of normal sexual interests; *sexual obsession*—20 items intended to assess high levels of sexual fantasy and activity; *child molester lie scales*—13 items intended to assess the extent to which identified child molesters deny/minimise their sexual activities with, and sexual interest in, children; *rape lie scale*—13 items that aim to assess denial/minimisation in identified rapists; *cognitive distortions and immaturity*—21 items are intended to assess the extent to which the offender adopts a 'victim stance' in relation to the present offences; *justification scales*—24 items address various justifications that sex offenders may use to explain their offence; *treatment attitudes scale*—8 items assess the extent to which the offenders consider themselves to have a sexual problem justifying treatment, e.g. 'I need help because I am not able to control any sexual behaviour'; *child molest scale*—39 items are direct questions concerning sexual interest and sexual activity with children. There are 4 additional sub-scales: fantasy, cruising/grooming, sexual assault and aggravated assault. *Rage scale*—28 items that address rape interest and rape behaviour; sado-masochism – 10 items that address sadistic sexual interest and behaviour; *exhibitionism*—19 items that address exhibitionist activity and interest; *paraphilias*—are a collection of sub-scales, related to fetishism, voyeurism, obscene phone calls, bondage and discipline; *sexual dysfunction*—which includes any sexual inadequacies, premature ejaculation, physical disabilities and impotence; *sex knowledge and beliefs*—these 24 items assess their knowledge of sexual anatomy and physiology; *sex history*—including sex deviance development, marriage development, gender identity development, gender orientation development and sexual assault behaviour.

- The Derogatis sexual functioning inventory (Derogatis, 1978): This was designed to provide a broad assessment of individuals presenting with sexual dysfunctions. The scales address sexual attitudes, sexual knowledge, specific sexual problems, and general measures of subjective well-being. It is an inventory with 10 sub-scales: information, experience, drive, attitudes, psychological symptoms, affects, gender role definitions, fantasy, body image, and sexual satisfaction. Each sub-scale has its own items and scoring: *information*—26 items true/false test of basic sexual information; *experience*—list of common sexual acts and asks the respondent if they have engaged in these activities; *sex drive*—attempts to assess sex drive through the frequency of sexual activity; *attitudes*—addresses liberal versus conservative sexual attitudes; *symptoms and affects*—general measures of subjective distress and psychopathology; *gender role*—self-ratings on 30 trait adjectives; *fantasy*—where they are asked to indicate which of the 20 fantasies listed they have had, either as daydreams or asleep. They contain normal and deviant sexual practices; body image and addressing how pleased they are with their physical appearance. The satisfaction scale contains 10 true–false items concerning satisfaction with their sexual life. (Please see the resources section for further information).

- The sex form (Walker et al., 1988): A 324 true–false item form presented to the offender which covers such factors as a tendency towards aggressive sexual deviancy, tendency toward non-aggressive sexual deviancy, sex guilt, receptivity to therapy, conservative values, romanticism, fantasy versus action potential, gender identity confusion, sex drive, impulse control, marital happiness, sexual knowledge, and overall adjustment.

- A sexual autobiography (Bolton et al., 1989): Useful in extending the time available to the workers, although it is often precautionary to provide the offender with detailed guidance and structure before they embark on this task, as 'males often assume, erroneously, that some abuse of sexuality events are unimportant or irrelevant. Also, many males are reluctant to reveal sexual experiences they consider 'unman-

ly' or embarrassing and need encouragement and structure to do so'. The authors provide the following structure:

A. Age segments.

Early childhood	(0 through 5 years)
Middle childhood	(6 through 10 years)
Early adolescence	(11 through 14 years)
Adolescence	(15 through 18 years)
Young adult	(19 through 24 years)
Adult	(25 and beyond)

B. Within this age format, the male is instructed to provide personal information about the following areas:

- First awareness of anything 'sexual', including feelings, observations and experiences.
- The development of feelings about sexual matters.
- Sexual activities, including those related to early childhood curiosity and exploration.
- Masturbation, including age of first experience, fantasies, feelings and frequency.
- Dating experiences, including first dates, feelings, activities, courtship, marriage, infidelity.
- First heterosexual sexual experiences.
- First homosexual sexual experiences.
- Sexual attitudes and behaviour exhibited by family members and other persons important to them.
- Sources for, and type of, information about sexuality.
- Sexual fantasies.
- Sexually transmitted diseases.
- Sexual problems, such as premature ejaculation, impotencies, low or high sexual drive.
- Sexual satisfaction and preference.
- Self-concept as it relates to their sexuality.
- 'Unusual' sexual experiences, either initiated by another or themselves. Include their feelings about the experience.
- Counselling for sex-related matters.
- Standardised sexual history formats do exist and the reader can refer to the following as alternatives to our model, which follows: Carich and Adkerson (1995); Faller (1990); Mayer (1988); Masters and Johnson (1970); Pomeroy et al. (1982).
- Offender scripts (White, 1992): These are designed to complement sexual autobiographies. Scripts are life patterns and behaviours resulting from an incorporation of the behaviour and statements of significant people in the developing personality of the offender, while they were children. Most learning is the result of a constant repetition of messages in various forms over years. For example, a father may say 'don't mess around with women' and the developing child, in what Berne described as 'cop out thinking', decides 'OK, I will mess around with boys'. This can help workers begin to unravel the

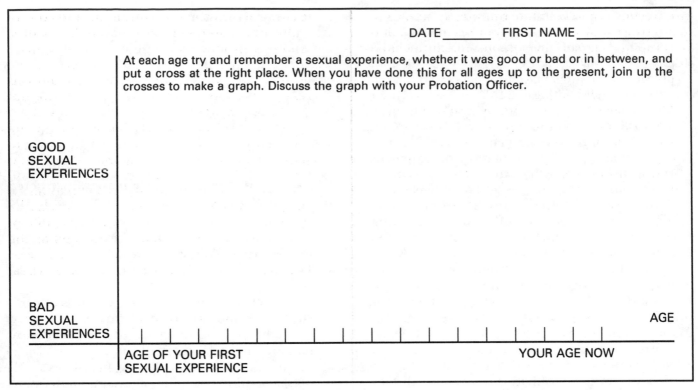

Figure 9: Sexual history life graph.

origins of the offending behaviour, looking at how the early decisions made in a child-like way, without full thinking ability, have been developed. A script questionnaire (a lengthy document asking for much information about parental attitudes and actions) may be useful and should be constructed by the workers referring to the transactional analysis literature. The offender may find that once the process is started much will be remembered—if not, it could be helpful for him to write an autobiography which will not only encourage memory links but may form the basis for much further questioning. This is another area where the workers need to keep their intuition carefully attuned, following up hunches about what is described and what is left unsaid.

• Sexual history life graph: This amounts to a means for the offender to explore and acknowledge the formative sexual experiences, both good and bad, that have helped to shape their sexual attitudes, beliefs and behaviour at the current time. The method is to identify at each selected age, experiences that they can remember, and plot them on a graph. This may for example, reveal at a particular age, or ages, they were a victim of sexual abuse themselves. When completed, it gives an overview of the offender's sexual development. A useful addition to this is to place an A4 sized overhead projector acetate over the sexual history life graph. Then after drawing the vertical and horizontal lines directly over those below, name the vertical axis 'sexual arousal' and the horizontal axis 'age'. The top of

the vertical axis represents 'high sexual arousal' whereas the bottom of the vertical axis 'low sexual arousal'. A further graph is then plotted of the ups and downs of sexual arousal at particular times, and particular experiences. Again this leads to greater awareness and understanding of the offenders arousal patterns. It is the start of them acknowledging the relationship between sexual arousal and the offences they have committed.

Sexual history format

(a) Sex education and knowledge

Coleman (1997) has noted that if we believe that sexuality is intuitive, natural and normal, then it follows that there is no need to educate. However, the consequences of failing to openly discuss sexuality works against any offender who is sexually naïve, often leaving them confused, requiring accurate and even explicit sex education. This confusion is fed by silence from parents about the subject as well as the media portrayal of distorted sex role images and inaccurate information about human sexuality.

Embedded in the media messages is the impression that violence and sexual exploitation are normal parts of interpersonal relationships and are therefore acceptable. Coleman questions whether the media reflects society's views and values, or creates them.

Thornburg (1981) reported that most teenagers received their information about sex from peers, with the media and literature running second. Only about 10% of all children obtain sex information from their parents (Masters, Johnson and Kolodny, 1992).

Furthermore, fathers play a passive role in the sex education of their children.

Most people get their sex education from a variety of sources. Peer groups are usually a major source of information and young people may compare notes, borrow books from a friend, or pool scraps of information. Often the information from peers is inaccurate and facts do need separating from 'old wives' tales. Other children are more isolated and thus may have more problems accessing information, particularly as many parents find it difficult to provide their children with sex education. This maybe because they themselves received inadequate sex education and may be worried about revealing this, or they may simply be too embarrassed to talk openly about sex.

We all need sex education as we are growing up to help us make sense of the physical changes of puberty, such as menstruation and wet dreams, as well as the parallel emotional changes.

Despite the nature of their offences, it is not unusual for sex offenders to have limited sexual education and knowledge. This makes this block a crucial element of any sexual history. Many sex offenders also hold attitudes and myths, which reflect this lack of information. This can contribute to their avoidance of intimate, mutually consenting sexual relationships as well as their treatment of children as objects. The level of experience an offender has had sexually correlates positively with reported degrees of success and satisfaction in sexual relationships. These issues are often more acute in adult sex offenders with learning disabilities: they can be extremely deficient in their knowledge of both the biological and social aspects of sex, and many have extensive misinformation. In addition, many carers have adopted restricting or punitive attitudes towards sex for fear of promiscuity or sexual acting out, but this can lead to them denying their sexuality or experiencing guilt regarding sexual functioning (Murphy et al., 1983). Many sex offenders express concern that they were never able to talk about their sexuality with their parents.

There has been controversy about what should be taught and what should be included in the school curriculum.

The legislation and guidance concerning sex education is complex: we need to refer to both the Education Act (1996) and the circular 'Education Act 1993: Sex education in schools'. These documents provide for sex education in three distinct places: in biology lessons within the National Curriculum for Science (restricted to the purely biological aspects of sexual behaviour, and it is compulsory); the non-biological aspects within the basic curriculum (which remains under the control and discretion of the school governing bodies, coupled with parents having the absolute right to withdraw their children from this aspect of the curriculum); and outside the classroom. From this comes a realization that young people do not receive the necessary information to prepare them for healthy and fulfilling relationships. Young people themselves have argued that their sex and relationship education is 'too little', 'too late' and 'too biological'. It focuses on information and avoids the social and personal skills development and moral dimension of considering and clarifying values and attitudes. It avoids any discussion of relationships, feelings and emotions as well as the more sensitive issues of sexual activity and sexuality, including lesbian and gay issues (Lenderyou, 1998).

Monk (1998) has argued that sex education has two distinct purposes: it is concerned with both the future and the present. Education is clearly aspirational in that one of its functions is to construct future citizens and consequently sex education is concerned with the construction of the sexual citizens of the future and to prepare children for the rights and responsibilities of that role. However, awareness of the fact that children are increasingly sexually active has meant that it also responds to the present. This is a more problematic role for sex education as it confronts dominant social and legal norms which construct children as 'sexual innocents' and non-sexual. The social and cultural ambivalence regarding young people's sexual activity results in a lack of any clear consensus as to the purposes of sex education and reinforces the conflict between preparing children for sexual adulthood and providing practical advice to sexual children.

Research findings

- Swift (1979) explored the hypothesis that many sex offenders are sexually ignorant. She found that there was a marked reduction in sex crimes in Denmark linked to the increased availability of pornographic materials, with some suggestion that this material acted as a source of sex education for men deprived of such information from other sources. She argued that it can thus facilitate their graduation to adult sexual partners. Swift also argued that such deficits often emerge through a lack of discussion of sex in the home, and low parental tolerance towards nudity in the home. Paedophiles more than any other group receive less education about sexual matters during their childhood than any other group.

- Davies (1986) sets out the essential components of a sex education programme, which may need to be actioned after we have identified the level of information held by the offender being assessed. She argued that we need to provide an adequate knowledge of anatomy of the sexual organs, secondary sexual characteristics, male and female reproductive physiology, intercourse, conception, gestation, birth, contraception, sexually transmitted diseases, varieties of sexual behaviour, marriage and parenting. We also need to develop rational and understanding attitudes towards sex in its various manifestations; help people gain an insight into their relationships with members of the both sexes; provide the education and understanding that will enable individuals to use their sexuality effectively and sensitively in any role whether an individual partner or parent; and to help people understand social expectations regarding sexuality and develop a responsible attitude towards their own sexuality and that of others. Where the offender has a physical disability, we also need to provide an adequate knowledge of the effect of their particular disability on sexual function; genetic counselling and its availability; to explore attitudes to masturbation; to help people to come to terms with their disability and develop a positive self-image; and to provide an environment in which people can explore their attitude and feelings towards sexuality in its widest sense, including any (often considerable) fears (see resources for contact details).

- Gilgun and Gordon (1985) summarised the sex education issue for inclusion in a prevention programme for children. They believe that sex education holds the most promise for the prevention of the development of sexually abusive behaviours in the first place. They argued that any such programme should include:

1. **Self-esteem**: There is evidence that the core beliefs of an offender are highly negative and contribute to extreme self-centredness.
2. **Human equality and fostering the well-being of others**: Equality of the sexes, respect for the dignity of all human beings, including children, and equal access to opportunities which foster human growth and development are important considerations in any democracy. The sexual abuse of children blocks their opportunity for growth and development. For some sex offenders, sexual interaction and the fostering of the well-being of others are mutually contradictory. They have learned to associate sexual behaviour with physical aggression, coercion, and manipulation. Sex offenders thus become deeply ashamed of their sexual needs and desires. They need to learn that sex is good, the genitals are good, and sexual desire is good if used to promote one's own well-being and the well-being of others. When anyone's sense of self is violated, sexual behaviour becomes destructive, both to the self and to others.

3. **Caring**: for oneself and others is important, particularly as respect for one's own feelings and wants and those of other people appear to be necessary for the development of the ability to love. Men are often discouraged from expressing feelings of hurt, loss, sadness, as well as from expressing warm and caring feelings toward others. Unfortunately, many sex offenders lose touch with their own feelings and the feelings of others.
4. **Masturbation**: is natural and normal, particularly as a sexual outlet, even where we are involved in a satisfying sexual relationship with another adult. Offenders often do not understand this. Many masturbate while fantasising, but, because it makes them feel even more guilty, it becomes part of the problem.
5. **Sexual thoughts and fantasies**: People fantasise about all kinds of sexual behaviours, including those, which could harm themselves or others. Most adults accept these feelings for what they are and do not become guilt-ridden about them. They have learned that these thoughts, in themselves, are not harmful, unlike the sex offender who obsesses over such feelings.

Tools

Questions to be asked:

- Where, when and how did they learn about sex? (peers, parents, TV, magazines, school, other, etc.).
- What were they taught? Elicit detail.
- What questions do they still have? Write these down and consider whether an education block is needed with the offender (see Calder, 1997 for discussion on this issue).
- Ask them to describe the mechanics of sexual intercourse, masturbation, etc.
- Ask them to describe the developmental changes they experienced in adolescence. How did they feel about them?
- Was sex discussed at home? With siblings? Friends?
- What did their parents tell them about sex and masturbation?
- What was their parents' sexual behaviour like? How did they feel about it?
- Were their parents affectionate with them, their siblings, and each other?
- Understanding of sexual offences' legislation— homosexuality, consent, etc.
- Establish their knowledge of 'safe' sex, contraception, sexual diseases, etc.
- Establish how they would normally make contact with a potential partner in a normal, appropriate, consensual way.
- What is their understanding of consent?
- When did they first realise that they were different sexually? (eg. developing patterns of sexually abusive behaviour?).

- How old were they when their sexual problems began?
- Sexual knowledge and attitude test (SKAT), (Lief and Reed, 1972): This was designed as a means of gathering information about sexual attitudes, knowledge, degree of experience in a variety of sexual behaviours, as well as a means of obtaining a diversity of biographical information. The SKAT has two scorable sections: the knowledge and the attitudes. The attitude section consists of 35 five-alternative, Likert-type items, and responses to these items result in scores on four attitude scales: Heterosexual relations, sexual myths, abortion and auto-eroticism or masturbation. The knowledge section is composed of 71 true–false items, and it yields a single score which reflects the offender's knowledge of biological, psycho-biological, psychological, and social aspects of human sexuality. The biographical information and sexual experience sections of the SKAT are not scored.
- Essential adult sex education curriculum for the mentally retarded (Zelman and Tyster, 1979).
- The Mach tech sex test (Kirby, 1984)*: Designed to assess both their sexual knowledge as their attitudes and values.
- Miller–Fisk sexual knowledge questionnaire—adapted (Gough, 1974): This is a 24 item questionnaire designed to explore family planning, attitudes towards abortion, etc. Sample questions include: 'The single most important factor in achieving pregnancy is: (a) time of exposure in the cycle (b) female's desire or wish to become pregnant (c) frequency of intercourse or (d) female's overall state of health'. 'Menopause is a time of: (a) diminished sexual drive (b) absolute infertility (c) rapid ageing or (d) altered reproductive and menstrual functioning'.

(b) Sexual experiences

The exploration of sexual experiences is important as some offenders will claim that their behaviour is a poor attempt to get some sexual experience. Whilst the history of some offenders will reveal little or no sexual experience, there is ample evidence that this, in itself, is not a sufficient factor to sexually abuse Those men who often feel inadequate sexually, or even overwhelmed by the prospect of a sexual experience with an adult, may fall into, or seek out, sexual relationships with young children.

Research findings

- Groth (1977) produced essential research that uncovered that 86 per cent of his sample had previous interpersonal sexual experiences prior to their sexual offence.
- Becker et al. (1986) also found that the mean age of onset of non-deviant sexual behaviour predated the onset of deviant sexual behaviour.

They found that some 95 per cent reported a prior, non-deviant, non-genital experience, whilst 59 per cent reported a prior, non-deviant, genital experience.

- Longo (1982) found that 86 per cent of those in his sample reported having their first sexual experience before the age of 12.
- Brown et al. (1996) conducted a study to investigate whether or not masturbation is a good idea for sex offenders. They took a sample of sex offenders and asked them to either masturbate at their usual frequency, or cease masturbation for a month. Of 20 out-patient paedophiles, 3 withdrew from the study because they felt that not masturbating increased their risks of re-offending. A further 4 men reported an increased interest in paedophilic activities during the 30 day period of abstention from masturbation. 15 of the 17 men who completed the study (88 per cent) felt it was helpful to masturbate, thus suggesting that abstinence appears to be more dangerous than continuing to masturbate at their habitual frequency. There is some evidence that masturbation, carried to the point of orgasm, usually has the effect of decreasing sexual interest.

Tools

Workers need to be exploring the following with the offender:

- Their history of sexual encounters and the evolution of their sexual learning experiences, e.g. 'normal' sexual experiences—ages of first genital and non-genital experiences; sexual play with other children (playing doctor or 'show me' games; what sex games did they play as a child?; how did they feel about them?).
- The number of sexual partners: get them to list everyone they have dated and/or enjoyed a sexual experience with (male and female), including names, ages of both parties, activity, etc.
- Did they use any contraception? What kind?
- When did they start dating and what were their feelings about it?
- What was their most embarrassing sexual experience and which are they most ashamed about?
- Get them to describe their sexual and emotional relationships in their teenage years. What was their reaction to new physical developments in puberty?
- What was the expected sexual behaviour of men and women during their teenage years?

Workers can then move on to ask questions regarding any deviant sexual experiences, including the offender's own experience of abuse and its consequences, and homosexuality. Questions to ask may include:

- Did they have any sexual contact with other family members? Who? When?
- Did any other upsetting experiences happen to them as a child? Or to their siblings and/or friends?
- Was there ever more than one person abusing them?
- How did these experiences affect their feelings, relationships, behaviour, attitudes? [Note. While the role of childhood sexual abuse in the aetiology of sexual offending is debatable, there is some preliminary evidence that sexually abused sex offenders do often have problems that aren't found in non-abused offenders (Hanson, 1991). Despite this, the seriousness of the abusive behaviour of sex offenders is not mitigated by their having been sexually abused.]
- Was the abuse ever reported? To whom? Was anything ever done about it? If yes, what and when? What was their reaction?
- If they prefer boys, have they ever told anyone?
- Have they ever had any homosexual experiences? When? What were their feelings about that? How fixed are they in their sexuality? And sexual orientation? Are they attracted to both sexes?
- Have they ever sold sex? In what circumstances?
- Have they ever felt guilty or dirty about sex? What sexual outlets do they have (e.g. video, magazines, strip shows, etc?).

Finally, workers should explore the offender's masturbation history and frequency, using such questions as:

- How do they feel about masturbation? And exploring their own body?
- Do they think it is harmful or enjoyable?
- When did they start masturbating?
- How often do they masturbate now?
- To what thoughts and/or fantasies do they usually masturbate to?
- Do they have different kinds of fantasies that they masturbate to? When? Have they changed over time?
- Describe their most common sexual fantasy. Do they reflect their behaviour or self-image?
- When did they have their first wet dream?
- Do they use their sexual experiences as a source of fantasy and masturbation? Or do they prefer pornography?
- What effects, if any, does alcohol, drugs or pornography have on their sexual practices and arousal?

Note. Masturbation activity is important in the assessment of most sex offenders.

Risk factors in this block include the lack of any history of relationships, a failure to initiate relationships, age-inappropriate partner choices, dysfunctional partner choices, lack of depth or stability in relationships, choosing partners with victim-aged children, a high anger level in relation-ships (or violence) or revenge and power themes in relationship interactions, e.g. revenge plans or stalking behaviours (Carich and Adkerson, 1995).

- The sexual experience survey (Koss and Oros, 1982)*: A 12 item questionnaire that assesses past experience with sexual aggression. The questions refer explicitly to sexual intercourse associated with various degrees of coercion, threat and force. It was developed to identify individuals from the 'normal' population with experience with sexual aggression/victimisation.
- Negative attitudes towards masturbation (Abramson and Mosher, 1985)*: This scale measures masturbation guilt and negative attitudes towards masturbation. The 30 items are declarative statements that are rated on a 5 point scale from 'not at all true' to 'strongly true for you', e.g. 'I feel guilty about masturbating'; 'Excessive masturbation leads to mental dullness or fatigue'. Masturbation is a normal, healthy outlet. A factor analysis yields three factors: positive attitude toward masturbation, false beliefs about the harmful nature of masturbation, and personally experienced negative affects associated with masturbation.
- The sexual orientation method (Feldman et al., 1966): Useful in assessing the relative degree of homo and hetero-erotic orientation of men who show homosexual behaviour. It is not designed to detect homosexuality in those who have never exhibited any homosexual characteristics. It has 120 pairs of questions: half covering attitudes to men, and half, attitudes toward women. They are asked to respond with one of six adjectives (interesting, attractive, handsome, hot, pleasurable and exciting) to two concepts: 'men are sexually to me . . .' and 'women are sexually . . .' Five scale positions are used for each adjective, e.g. very attractive, to very unattractive.
- The sexual experience life map (Cook and Taylor, 1991): This is a useful way of mapping out the offender's sexual experiences. The offender is given a life map divided into years up to their present age. The authors set out 25 'experiences', which the offender has to add to the map at the age in which they first experienced it. This can be very useful as a mechanism for generating further discussion, particularly around which they find the most, and least, exciting or frightening.
- Sexual experiences survey (Lisak and Roth, 1988)*: A 29 item scale designed to elicit the range of the respondent's sexual experiences.

(c) Intimacy: sexual relationships and sexual satisfaction

Whilst we still have a long way to go before we are clear about the roles played by intimacy and relationship problems in the development and maintenance of sexual offending, it is clear from the work of Finkelhor (1986) that any blockage to the development of satisfying adult relationships is part of the offender's motivation to sexually offend. Such blocks might include there being little or no communication between the partners; and there being no sexual relationship between the partners or that it is not emotionally gratifying. Such problems in adult relationships may contribute to a gravitation toward children for emotional and sexual gratification (Faller, 1988). On the surface, sexual satisfaction appears quite straightforward: either an individual is or is not satisfied with their sexual relationships. There are, however, a number of distinct, but related facets, relating to sexual satisfaction. These might include: frequency of sex and the degree of variation in sexual activities; communication between sexual partners, about preference, such as foreplay; or broader factors such as the actual interpersonal relationship itself (Derogatis and Melisaratos, 1979). Metts and Lupach (1989) argued that satisfaction in sexual relations is a function of the equitable nature of the relationship, (as well as being facilitated be effective communication about sex); and impeded by various dysfunctional beliefs and expectations, e.g. that simultaneous orgasm must occur if mutual satisfaction is to be secured, or sex is duty. It follows, therefore, that sexual satisfaction is related to levels of satisfaction in the rest of the relationship. It has been reported that men who are dissatisfied with sex in their relationship ask for an increase in the frequency of sex and for more variations and a greater degree of spontaneity (Hite, 1981), whereas women ask for more love, affection and caring during sex. Woman may argue, however, that they just want the men to learn to 'do it' properly.

Interpersonal dyadic relationships can be defined by three relatively independent dimensions: boundary, power and intimacy. Since the development of intimacy is a process, boundary and power cannot be isolated from any definition of intimacy (Waring and Reddon, 1983). A healthy intimate relationship is characterised by the capacity for constructive, respectful expression of positive and negative emotions. These expressions should be mutually acceptable and promote the psychological well-being of the individuals involved; their function is primarily to define boundaries, to communicate concern and commitment, to negotiate roles, and to resolve conflicts (Coleman, 1987). Offenders with a history of being abused themselves have often lacked healthy role models, and boundaries between family members are too weak or too firm. The boundary difficulties resulting from these factors may lead to two distinct problems with intimacy: they may be needy, intrusive, enmeshed, or controlling resulting from a lack of clear boundaries between self and others, or the person may be avoiding and distancing, the outcome of boundaries too tightly drawn.

Intimacy is clearly important in establishing effective emotional and sexual relations with other adults (Brehm, 1992), and those who are able to develop it are seen to be warm and sincere; less aggressive, and better able to resist stress. Their relationships also provide them with a sense of security, emotional comfort, shared experiences, an opportunity to be nurturing plus a sense of self-worth (Marshall, 1993). Intimacy is a universal human characteristic. If thwarted in adult relationships, then sex offenders may seek intimacy in other less appropriate ways. This failure to achieve intimacy leads to the experience of emotional loneliness, which causes considerable frustration. If this frustration is experienced as emotional isolation from effective relations with women, adult females may be seen by these men as the cause of their loneliness (Marshall, 1989). Offenders who report a low sexual satisfaction with their adult partners are clearly more likely to overcome the resistance to sex with children (and therefore inappropriate partners) in their quest for intimacy.

Loneliness is usually split into social and emotional loneliness, with the latter proving the more difficult to endure. Social loneliness is a sense of isolation resulting from few social contacts. Emotional loneliness, the more severe condition, is at the heart of intimacy dysfunction, and arises when there is a lack of intimacy in personal relationships. Marshall et al. (1996) defined emotional loneliness as *"what we feel when we are either separated for a prolonged period from our loved ones, or when a love relationship is terminated"*.

The association of the need for emotional closeness with the drive for sex can also lead to an increase in sexual behaviour as offenders escalate their attempts to achieve intimacy through sexual contact (Ward et al., 1997). This is likely to lead to sexual dissatisfaction, a gnawing sense of emptiness, and emotional isolation. As offenders arguably confuse sexual and intimacy needs, they may use sex as a way of coping with emotional loneliness and feelings of rejection arising from interpersonal difficulties. Sex becomes their way of coping or responding to negative affective states. Many offenders will therefore report feeling sexually dissatisfied when the crucial issue is actually a lack of intimacy. Their sense of loneliness may be aggravated by being processed as a sex offender due to the extensive negative responses by both the general public and other prisoners (Garlick et al., 1996). It is worth noting here, however, that intimacy deficits and loneliness are not the products of incarceration, they were present before and during their offences (Bumby and Hanson, 1997).

Research findings

- Lisak and Ivan (1995) have noted that the reduced need for intimacy with others is the outcome of male gender socialisation in general and, coupled with a lack of empathy, produces a predisposition for sexual aggression. They noted that there are a number of interconnected components in their argument: that sexually aggressive men are more likely than are non-aggressive men to have experienced negative relationships with their fathers; they score higher on measures of 'hostile masculinity', on hostility toward women and the need to dominate women; they score higher on a measure of hyper-masculinity and male gender role stress; and lower on two different measures of feminininity. We should never forget, or underestimate, the difficulties many offenders have in establishing loving and satisfying adult social and sexual relationships.

- Complaints of disturbed marital and sexual relationships are common among incest offenders (Justice and Justice, 1979) and many report that their offences occurred during periods of marital discord (Gebhard et al., 1967). Indeed, Bownes (1993) identified a prevalence of 62 per cent for marital/relationship dysfunction among sex offenders generally who had a current relationship with an adult female partner and a prevalence of 57 per cent for sexual dysfunction among offenders who had experienced heterosexual intercourse with an adult. Faller (1988) reported that for many sex offenders, their interpersonal interactions are sexualised in an attempt to attain intimacy. For example, they may speak of having sex several times a day with their wives, often at awkward times, such as when the children are demanding attention or when the wife is attempting to engage in some other absorbing activity. They may engage in semi-public sex, such as fondling their partners' intimate parts in a bar or having sexual intercourse in a park. They may describe having concurrent affairs with several women and report sexual experimentation such as nudism, mate swapping, or group sex. Many offenders use adult relationships with women as a 'front' (presenting as socially adept and engaged in a number and range of either social or sexual relationships) whilst they are sexually abusing children at the same time (more reflective of the true picture of isolation and a lack of intimate relationships).

- Bownes (1993) found that the greater the number of previous convictions for sexual offences a sex offender has, the more severe the problems he is likely to have with his current relationship. He went on to report that the proportion of men with significant sexual difficulties was highest among the incest offenders (66 per cent), whilst significant proportions of sex offenders were likely to have problems in specific areas of sexual functioning, e.g. difficul-ties with communication on sexual matters (25 per cent) and lack of satisfaction with sexual activity (22 per cent). They are also less likely to see the impact of their actions on others.

- Bumby and Marshall (1994) found that intra-familal offenders were more fearful of intimacy in relationships than were rapists or their non-sex offending control group, and that rapists reported less intimacy in their relationships with males and family members than did the child molesters. However, Seidman et al. (1994) found that neither incest offenders nor exhibitionists appeared to be particularly deficient in intimacy, although they were equally as lonely as were the other sex offenders. This reminds us that we need to assess each case with an open mind, and it also shows how much more research is needed when we uncover similarities of this nature in two very different types of sex offender.

- Marshall (1989) originally pointed to the importance of deficits in the sex offender's capacity for intimacy in relations with adults as one part of our understanding of the problem. He also suggested that the roots lie in poor intimacy relations with adults, producing emotional loneliness which leads to a self-serving lifestyle, an aggressive disposition and a tendency to pursue sex with diverse partners in the hope of finding intimacy through sexuality and through less threatening partners. Emotional loneliness leads to hostile attitudes towards women and children as well as acceptance of violence and interpersonally aggressive behaviour (Diamont and Windholz, 1981). Check et al. (1985) also found that loneliness was significantly related to an acceptance of violence directed at women and anger at rejection by women; whilst others have related it to externalising behaviour problems such as anger and aggression, and internalising problems such as self-doubt, shame, anxiety, depressive feelings and paranoia (Becker-Lausen and Mallon-Kraft, 1997).

- The most acute emotional loneliness comes from poor quality childhood attachments (especially when this involves parental rejection) which subsequently alienates them from others, thus preventing them from forming effective adult relationships which satisfy their need for intimacy.

- Marshall (1989; 1993) has developed a theoretical framework integrating research on attachment theory, intimacy deficits, and sexual offending. He argues that the failure of sex offenders to develop secure attachment bonds in childhood results in a failure to learn the interpersonal skills and self-confidence necessary to achieve intimacy with other adults. Attachment theory is concerned with the bond between children and their care-givers. A child often displays discomfort and anxiety when separated from an attachment figure. If attachment bonds are insecure in childhood, individuals do not acquire the necessary skills to establish close relationships, and may fear, rather than desire, intimacy with another adult.

- Poor attachments also lead to low self-confidence, poor social skills, little understanding of relationship issues and a decided lack of empathy for others (Garlick et al., 1996), as well as deficiencies in adult intimacy and are far more prone to violence than are intimately effective persons (Seidman et al., 1994). Deficiencies in social skills (i.e. problems in accurately perceiving social cues, problems in deciding on appropriate behaviour, and deficiencies in the skills to enact effective behaviour) seriously restrict the opportunity for attaining intimacy. For example, Tingle et al. (1986) found that 74 per cent of the child molesters in their sample had few or no friends when young. These deficits in social and relationship functioning are precisely those shown by sex offenders (Marshall et al., 1995; McFall, 1990), whilst Marshall and Mazzucco (1995) demonstrated that at least some of these features are significantly related to the quality of sexual offender's attachments to their parents.

- Hudson and Ward (1997) developed an attachment-based model that relates four types of attachment to a set of offending styles and related interpersonal goals. This follows on from the comprehensive attachment model of intimacy deficits articulated by Ward et al. (1995). They found that it was more important to consider attachment styles rather than the types of offences committed in considering intimacy difficulties in sex offenders. They suggested that *securely attached individuals (positive self/positive others)* have high levels of self-esteem and view others as generally warm and accepting and, as a result, experience high levels of intimacy in their romantic relationships. *Preoccupied people (negative self/positive others)* see others in positive terms, but their own sense of unworthiness leads them to seek the approval of valued others to an undue level. They typically are sexually preoccupied and prone to sexualising the need for security and affection through sexual interaction (Shaver and Hazan, 1988). Because this style is unlikely to lead to satisfactory relationships for either partner, high levels of loneliness are expected together with low levels of aggression (Bartholomew and Horowitz, 1991). If a preoccupied man crosses the boundaries with a child and begins to fantasise about a sexual relationship, he will begin the grooming process, and may well view the child as a lover, although any sexual involvement will follow the courtship ritual. *Fearful individuals (negative self/negative others)* desire social contact but avoid such interactions because of their distrust and fear of rejection, often keeping their partners at a distance. They are likely to express their aggression indirectly rather than directly (although they may use force to attain their goals), experience loneliness as their relationships will tend to be impersonal and be rather unempathic towards their victims as a result of their negative views of others. They rarely experience any guilt in relation to their offending behaviour. Finally, *dismissing individuals (positive self/negative others)* are sceptical of the value of close relationships and place considerable value on independence and autonomy from others in order to remain invulnerable. Therefore, they are unlikely to report being lonely and are more likely to fear intimacy; whilst others will view them as aloof and cold. They are likely to seek relationships or social contacts that involve minimal levels of emotional or personal disclosure. They also blame others for their lack of intimacy and tend to be angry and overtly hostile towards potential partners. They often exhibit profound empathy deficits and, when they do offend, they do so aggressively, even sadistically as an additional measure of their hostility.

- Workers need to understand the need to get a detailed history of how the offender was parented. The family homes of adult sex offenders are often characterised by violence and repeated disruptions/estrangements (Rada, 1978), and as children these offenders did not identify with their parents (Langevin et al., 1985). Bumby and Hanson (1997) found that 39 per cent of the child molesters in their sample had been physically abused, 45 per cent reported being sexually abused and 42 per cent reported having witnessed domestic violence. Becker-Lausen and Mallon-Croft (1997) argued that the term intimacy conveys a range of experiences that are problematic for survivors of abuse. Their outcomes may be sexual promiscuity (the avoidance of intimacy), teenage pregnancy (an intimacy fantasy often shattered by the realities of parenting demands) and problematic parenting (e.g. intrusive, restrictive, or insensitive care-giving). Offenders who have experienced sexual abuse themselves are more likely to have experienced ineffective parenting and a failure to secure attachment bonds. This can lead to deficiencies in intimacy skills or a rejection of the value of intimacy which will leave them feeling lonely and alienated from others (Marshall et al., 1996).

- Seidman et al. (1994) found that non-familial child molesters did not seem to have been exposed to significant violence in their family of origin. For some sex offenders, emotional issues rather than violence in the home may be a more salient feature of disrupted attachment bonds. For example, Marshall et al. (1991) found that exhibitionists did not report greater violence in their lives as children than do non-offender subjects, but they do indicate far greater degrees of emotional rejection by their parents. This can be most acute when they are making the transition at puberty to peer relationships: making social messages that objectify others, portray people as instruments of sexual pleasure, emphasise power and control over others and deny the need for social skills and compassion for others (Marshall, 1993) all the more attractive. Marshall et al. (1993) reported that young people who, for a variety of reasons, struggle to meet the social task demands of adolescence are more at risk for sexual offending.

- Ward et al. (1997) identified a very important issue in relation to intimacy—its complexity. They identified 12 categories from their research: *relationship commitment, evaluation of the partner, self-disclosure, trust, expression of affection, sexual satisfaction, giving and receiving of support, empathy, conflict resolution, autonomy,* and *sensitivity to rejection.* They found all of these to be significant aspects of sexual offenders' perceptions of their intimate relationships. Interestingly, they did not find any evidence for an independent category of loneliness. One major finding of their study was that sex offenders tended to receive low ratings on the various dimensions associated with the attainment of intimacy—yet were not specific to this group. They called for further investigations into the attitudes, interpersonal goals and the strategies utilised by offenders in their intimate relatinships.

Tools

Whilst we all vary in our motivation for intimacy, many sex offenders do present as isolated loners or as having superficial or unsatisfying relationships. The assessment of intimacy deficits and loneliness may facilitate a more thorough understanding of the factors associated with the initiation and maintenance of sexually deviant cognition and patterns of behaviour.

Questions to be asked in interview include:

- A good way to approach this part of the assessment is to employ questions similar to those asked about children: (1) What is your partner like or what kind of a person is she? (2) What about her pleases you? (3) What displeases you? (4) What kind of things do you do together? Do you enjoy these? (5) Do you ever do things together without the children? (6) Are there things about your partner you would like changed? (7) Do you tell her things you don't tell anyone else? (8) How do you show her when she pleases you or you are happy with her? (9) How does she show you when you please her or she is happy with you? (10) How does she know when you are displeased? (11) How do you know when she is displeased? (12) What do you have arguments about? (13) Have you ever used physical force with each other? If yes, please describe (Faller, 1988).

- The marital relationship needs to be specifically targeted for information, eliciting how they met their partners; how they were attracted to them; how long it lasted (if it has ended, why and when); how many serious relationships they had before they married; why they decided to marry; how their relationship changed after marriage; what were the good and bad parts of the marriage; did they or their wives have other sexual relationships? why?; when?; the number of children and their relationship with them; their attitudes and expectations regarding marriage; any history of rape, domestic violence, etc.; the quality of their relationships, their ability to see their spouse as a separate individual with her own needs, and the extent to which their descriptions correspond with information elicited from other sources. Marriage failures may reflect an inability to form lasting relationships, or to meet someone else's needs.

- How is their sexual relationship with their wife? Can they describe the kinds of sexual activity they engage in and their approximate frequency? How often do they engage in sexual activity? Has this relationship been more or less the same over the years or changing? Who initiates sex?

- Nature and age of partners (girlfriend, wife, child prostitute).

- Level of sexual satisfaction with different partners.

- The importance of sex to them in their relationships.

- The aspects of their sexual relationships they would change, and how.

- Their ability to discuss their sexual likes and dislikes with their partner.

- Their desired sexual competency.

- It is very important to establish what each individual offender understands by intimacy and relationships, any blocks or fears they have in these areas, and whether these are related to one or multiple relationship types (e.g. partner, friends, etc.) how they communicate and we should always point out any examples of inappropriate intimacy, e.g. with children or young people.

- How the offender reacts to the workers (and vice versa) may provide us with vital clues as to their ability to form adult relationships—as should parallel areas such as observations of supervised contact, joint interviews with their partner, etc. Workers do need to be conscious of the likelihood of different responses to the degree of loneliness and/or intimacy experienced by the offender, at the time of their work as compared to the time of their offending.

- Workers need to model, and stress the importance in understanding, the close relationship between emotions, behaviours and intimate relationships. It may identify 'chains' of emotions and behaviours associated with their intimate relationships and can lead to interventions tailored to them, e.g. addressing specific relationship deficits rather than the broader emphasis on social skills training (Ward et al., 1995).
- It is well worth spending some time on this area as, once identified, there is the potential to help the offender make huge changes in the areas of relationships and intimacy deficits (Marshall, 1995).
- Texts covering the issue of loneliness can be found in Peplau and Perlman (1982), Perlman and Peplau (1984) and Weiss (1974). For information on adult attachment refer to Bartholomew and Perlman (1991), and for information on psychometrically sound measures of intimacy please refer to Perlman and Duck (1987). A detailed framework for assessing couples can be found in Fruzzetti and Jacobsen (1992) and Spanier (1979), whilst Nowinski and LoPiccolo (1979) have provided a framework for assessing sexual behaviour in couples. Schiavi et al. (1979) provided a review of the materials for assessing sexual function and marital interaction

(NB. Questionnaires point only to whether problems with intimacy are present or absent, and to what degree.)

- Miller's social intimacy scale (Miller and Lefcourt, 1982)*: This was designed to assess intimacy in a variety of adult relationships (such as friendships, family, spouse). It consists of 17 items asking the respondent to indicate the frequency or intensity with which he engages in activities that reflect intimacy with his current (or most prolonged prior) girlfriend or wife. Higher scores reveal greater intimacy in relationships. The measure consists of 6 items that measure the frequency of intimate contacts and 11 items that assess the intensity of intimate relations. Each of the items are rated on 10 point scales, ranging from 1 (very rarely or not much) to 10 (almost always or a great deal).
- Waring's intimacy scale (Waring, 1984; Waring and Reddon, 1983): Comprises 90 statements about a man's relationship with his wife or partner that the offender must indicate 'true' or 'false' for him. It comprises 8 independent

content scales: conflict resolution, affection, cohesion, sexuality, identity, compatibility, autonomy, and expressiveness. It is useful in those situations where we want to explore broader aspects of close relationships than that covered in Miller's scale.

- Psychosocial intimacy questionnaire (Tesch, 1985): A 60 item self-report measure that assesses the degree of intimacy attained in a romantic relationship. Offenders indicate their degree of agreement with each statement about their relationship using a 6 point scale. Sample questions include: '. . . is physically very affectionate towards me.' 'I discuss my private feelings with . . .' '. . . accepts me as I am, both good and bad.' 'When I'm with . . ., I feel I must act the way s/he expects me to act.'
- Fear of intimacy scale (Descutner and Thelen, 1991)*: A 35 item scale designed to assess individuals anxieties about close, dating relationships. They rate each of the items on a 5 point scale ranging from 1 ('not at all characteristic of me') to 5 ('extremely characteristic of me'). It correlates positively with a loneliness measure; but correlated negatively with self-disclosure, social intimacy and social desirability measures.
- Assessing intimacy: the personal assessment of intimacy in relationships (PAIR) inventory (Schaefer and Olson, 1981): Produces systematic information on 5 types of intimacy: emotional, social, sexual, intellectual and recreational. Individuals, married or unmarried, describe their relationship in terms of how they currently perceive it (perceived) and how they would like it to be (expected). It measures the expected versus realised degree in the 5 identified areas of intimacy. It is easy to administer because of its 36 items. Sample questions include: 'I feel neglected at times by my partner.' 'My partner disapproves of some of my friends.' 'My partner seems disinterested in sex.' 'My partner helps me clarify my thoughts.' 'We seldom find time to do fun things together.' 'I have some needs that are not being met by my relationship.'
- The relationship scales questionnaire (Griffin and Bartholomew, 1994): A 30 item self-report questionnaire that asks offenders to rate themselves on a 5 point scale from 1 ('not at all like me') to 5 ('very much like me') in response to a series of statements about their close relationships (e.g. 'I find it easy to get emotionally close to others'). It provides scores on four separate sub-scales secure, fearful, preoccupied and dismissing types. It can be worded in terms of general orientations to close relationships, romantic relationships, or a specific relationship. Sample questions include: 'I want to be completely emotionally intimate with others.' 'I am uncomfortable being close to others.' 'I worry about being alone.'

- The revised UCLA loneliness scale (Russell et al., 1980)*: A 20 item scale that evaluates the perceived present state of loneliness in relationships with intimates, friends and acquaintances. It comprises 10 positively worded and 10 negatively worded items. Offenders are asked to indicate on a 4 point scale how frequently they experience various feelings or circumstances in their relationships, ranging from 1 (never) to 4 (often).

- The marital intake interview (Haynes et al., 1981): Designed to assess the degree of marital dissatisfaction, degree of commitment to the marital relationship, mediation potential, specific areas of conflict within the marriage, and goals of each spouse; satisfaction with sex, affection and communication within the marriage. It is able to discriminate between satisfied and dissatisfied couples—normally when couples are interviewed separately.

- The Locke–Wallace marital adjustment inventory (Locke and Wallace, 1959; Locke and Williamson, 1958): Can be very useful in uncovering a variety of types of sexual dysfunction that may be present. It provides a measure of marital adjustment covering marital adjustment and satisfaction. It consists of 15 items concerning how husbands and wives perceive or assess their marriage. There is a variety of formats used, some requiring that they choose one from a multiplicity of choices, whilst others ask about the extent of agreement or otherwise on a range of marital issues, such as 'dealing with the in-laws'.

- The sexual interaction inventory (LoPiccolo and Steger, 1974): A paper and pencil self-report inventory for assessing the sexual adjustment and sexual satisfaction of heterosexual couples. It consists of 17 heterosexual behaviours, each of which are rated by both parties along 6 dimensions. The scales assess the degree of satisfaction with the frequency and range of sexual behaviours for the male and female respectively; self-acceptance regarding the pleasure derived from engaging in sexual activities; pleasure obtained from sexual activity; accuracy of knowledge of partner's preferred sexual activities; and degree of acceptance of partner. Thus, the final questionnaire contains 102 questions that measure both satisfaction with, and frequency of, sexual behaviour in heterosexual couples.

- The marital communication inventory (Bienvenu, 1970): A 46 item questionnaire requiring the spouse to describe some aspect of marriage in terms of relative frequency in 4 categories (usually, sometimes, seldom and never). There are separate forms for husbands and wives. It was designed to provide an objective measure of success or failure in marital communication.

Sample questions include: 'Do you and your partner discuss the manner in which the family income should be spent?' 'Is it hard to understand your partners feelings and attitudes?' 'Does your partner complain that you don't understand them?'

- Index of marital satisfaction (Simmons, 1986)*: Includes questions such as: 'I feel my spouse really cares for me'; 'I feel that our marriage is empty'; 'I feel we do not have enough interests in common'; and 'I feel we manage our arguments and disagreements very well' (scored on a scale 1–7). The aim of this questionnaire is to measure the offender's degree of satisfaction with their current partner.

- Index of sexual satisfaction (Simmons, 1986): Includes statements such as: sex is fun for my partner and me; my sex life is monotonous; my partner dwells on sex too much; and my partner does not want sex when I do (scored on a scale 1–7). The aim here is to establish the degree of sexual satisfaction with their current partner.

- Marital comparison level index (Sabatelli, 1984)*: A 32 item instrument designed to measure an individual's perception of the degree to which s or her marital relationship is living up to their expectations. The respondent is asked to score each item on a 7 point Likert scale which should indicate the degree to which their relationship outcomes fall above or below expectations.

(d) Sexual attitudes

Sexual attitudes were defined by Lisak and Roth (1988) as *"predominantly consciously held thoughts or ideas, such as 'the best place for the woman is in the home'"*. It is essential that we understand sexual attitudes as part of our understanding of sexual functioning. Derogatis and Melisaratos (1979) argued that in their 'value expressive' function, an individual's attitudes concerning sexual activities provide us with insight into their socio-cultural background. The mores of a society as a whole, and the significant subcultural units (e.g. family, friends) in which the individual holds membership, are communicated through attitude postures about sexuality. They also reported the role of attitudes acting as a 'gating' function in that they may act to screen selective information that is in conflict with the individual's predominant value orientation. Athanasion (1973) refers to this aspect of attitudes as their 'ego-defensive' function. This function relates attitudes to affects and thus may provide the workers with a window on the conflicted aspects of the offender's sexuality. It is important to have a valid appraisal of their attitudes about sex so that any communications are not presented in a fashion to produce a direct confrontation with value systems.

It is clear that there is a wide range of sexual

attitudes just as there are a wide range of sexual behaviours. These will change over time as the wider culture changes also. Eysenck (1970) also confirmed that different personality types differ profoundly in their attitudes towards sexual issues. Marshall and Eccles (1991) have argued that many offenders hold attitudes, beliefs and distortions, which serve to both justify their offending and dehumanise women. This means that workers not only need to identify the inappropriate attitudes and beliefs but also the thoughts which underpin them if they are to understand their role in the commission of the sexual offences.

Research findings

• The most alarming finding is the lack of detailed research into the area of sexual attitudes in the sexual offending arena. Indeed, workers need to appraise themselves of the material in relation to rapists to try and unpick the issues that may arise in relation to the sexual abuse of children.

• Scott and Tetreault (1987) noted that there are two major theoretical approaches concerning rape: it is either the result of uncontrollable sexual or aggressive impulses in the psychopathology of the rapist, or it is an extension of a culturally sanctioned male dominance of women. Groth (1979) has argued that rapists lack confidence in their masculinity and consequently feel angry towards women who they blame for their low self-confidence and for the lack of power and control they feel over their lives. In attempting to express their anger through rape, they engage in unnecessary aggression during their assaults and they often attempt to humiliate and degrade their victims. Indeed, an offence may have been preceded by an incident where they were angered by a woman and this can heighten their arousal. Scott and Tetreault (1987) found that the rapist group in their research differed significantly in their attitudes towards women from both the non-sex related violent group and the matched control group. They identified oppositional attitudes towards the growing equality of women in the workplace, a focus on restricted freedom and independence for women, and strong support of subservient, stereotypical, passive roles for women in male–female relationships. Collectively the attitudes reflect a need to control women, especially sexually. This does highlight the view that rape is the outcome of sexual stereotyping and conservative attitudes towards women. One hypothesis about this relationship is that negative attitudes towards women may be related to sexually assaultive behaviour in several ways. This includes the belief that sex must be coerced from a woman, that men have the right to request sex from a woman and that if women were more protected and sheltered they would be less vulnerable to rape (Brownmiller, 1975; Clark and Lewis, 1977). Field

(1978) also reported that those who view women in more traditional roles were more likely to see rape as being the woman's fault.

• Many rapists thus have negative views of women, endorse rape myths, condone violence against women, and are hostile toward women (Segal and Stermac, 1990). Feminists argue that sexual offending satisfies power motives, particularly of males over females. Abel at al (1978) claim that rapists display a 'hyperidentifcation with the masculine role', and more recently Muehlenhard and Falcon (1991) have found that males who endorse traditional sex-role attitudes are more likely to have engaged in verbally and physically coercive sexual behaviours.

• In developing their attitudes towards sex, many sex offenders will have struggled to integrate their religious beliefs into their sexuality, e.g. being raised and told to suppress their sexual thoughts or arousal.

Tools

Questions to be asked include:

• What were the attitudes within their family to sex and nudity?
• What are their attitudes towards men, women and children, particularly the division of roles and responsibilities?
• What are their attitudes towards masturbation, intimacy, relationships, prejudice, discrimination, etc.?
• How important is sex to them?

(NB: Questionnaires may be too simplistic for assessing some of the offenders more subtle attitudes towards women.)

• The sexual attitudes survey (Wyre, 1987): Offers 77 statements covering a wide range of situations which they are asked to score on a scale ranging from 1–7 (1 being 'strongly disagree' and 7 being 'strongly agree'). Examples of the kind of questions asked include: 'Men rely on force to maintain their status and position.' 'Women often make up a story that they have been raped to avoid the implications of having had sex with someone.' 'Men are often the victims of female emotional swings.' 'Naked pictures of women in papers and magazines lead some men to sexually assault women.' 'The way some women dress I can understand them getting raped.' 'Women should not be believed by the police when they report sexual assault.' 'Sex offenders are men who are mentally ill.' 'Women's sexual fantasies often include being raped.' 'Women enjoy men using a degree of violence sexually.' 'Being roughed up is stimulating to many women', and 'Most women who say 'no' to sexual advances don't mean it.'

• Sexism scale (Rombough and Ventimiglio, 1981): This is useful in measuring sex-role attitudes. It is divided into two sets of items: internal versus external division of labour, and sex differences. It contains 20 items

- Hypermasculinity (Mosher and Sirkin, 1984): This is intended to assess 'macho' personality characteristics of adult males. It consists of 30 forced choice items designed to measure three components of macho personality: callous sexual attitudes towards women, interpersonal violence as masculine, and risk-taking/danger as exciting.

- Attitudinal survey (Smith and Self, 1981): A 21 item self-report measure of feminist versus traditional sex roles.

- Sexual attitudes questionnaire (Eysenck, 1988)*: This is a 158 item questionnaire designed to test a number of hypotheses regarding the relationship between sexuality and personality. It is also used to predict marital satisfaction, sexual abnormalities, and masculinity–femininity.

- Measuring sexual attitudes (Whalley and McGuire, 1978): Uses 9 measures: sexual satisfaction, heterosexual nervousness, sexual curiosity, hostility, pruriency, sexual repression, heterosexual distaste, and sexual promiscuity.

- Attitude toward rape scale (Field, 1978): This was developed to empirically assess different groups of individuals' attitudes towards rape in society. It comprises 32 positively and negatively worded items on a 6 point Likert scale of agree–disagree.

- Rape attitude scale (Hall et al., 1986): Aims to measure attitudes tolerant of rape in offenders and community populations. It contains 14 statements to which the respondents are asked to rate with agreement–disagreement.

- Heterosexual relationships scale (Hall et al., 1986): Designed to assess sexist attitudes specific to heterosexual relationships (both adults and adolescents). It doesn't aim to provide a global assessment of sexist attitudes, rather male domination specific to heterosexual interactions.

- Attitudes towards offending (Garrison, 1992)*: A series of statements which the offender is asked to respond to as either being 'true' or 'false'.

- Attitudes to child sexuality (Wyre, 1987), includes statements such as: 'The age of consent for boys and girls should be 10 years.' 'It is not against the law for children to have sex in Eastern countries.' 'Having sexual contact with a child is a good way of explaining sex education' and 'A child under 10 is able to say 'yes' to sexual contact.'

- Attitudes towards women scale (Spence and Helmreich, 1978): A 15 item scale focusing on the rights and roles of women. Respondents are asked to respond to each statement on a 4 point scale from 'agree strongly' to 'disagree strongly'. It is designed to measure an individual's attitudes towards the rights and roles of women

in areas such as vocational, educational and intellectual activities, freedom and independence, etiquette, dating, sexual behaviour and marital relationships.

- Burt scales (Burt, 1980; Burt and Katz, 1987)*: A new 44-item scale measuring the acceptance or rejection of myths about rape. It is the equivalent of the cognition scales although it focuses on rape rather than sexual abuse. It also helps assess their attitude towards women and violence.

- Burt rape myth acceptance scale (Burt, 1980)*: A 19-item scale measuring the acceptance or rejection of myths about rape. It has become a widely used measure with the sex offender population.

- Hanson sex attitudes questionnaire (Hanson, 1992)*: A scale designed to assess attitudes associated with sexual offending. The sexual entitlement scale concerns the extent to which the respondent feels compelled and entitled to fulfil his sexual urges. The sexy children scale addresses the perception of children as sexually attractive and sexually motivated.

- The Mach tech sex test (Kirby, 1984)*: Designed to assess both their sexual knowledge as well as their attitudes and values.

- Sexual attitudes for self and others Questionnaire (Story, 1988)*: This is a questionnaire used to allow the respondent to describe their emotional reactions to the idea of themselves or others participating in the 12 categories of sexual behaviour described. They are asked to respond on a scale ranging from (1) 'I feel great about it' to (4) 'I feel repulsed by it'.

- Sex knowledge and attitude test (Lief and Reed, 1972): The attitude section comprises 71 true–false items geared towards establishing the offender's attitudes towards a range of situations.

- Dysfunctional attitude scale (Weissman, 1980)*: A 40 item instrument designed to identify cognitive distortions held by the offender.

- Sex role survey (MacDonald, 1974): A self-report scale measuring the offender's attitudes towards sex roles. It contains 53 items scored on a 9 point scale ranging from 'I agree very much' through to 'I disagree very much'. Scores yield a total score and four factors: equality in business and the professions, sex-role appropriate behaviour, equal involvement in social and domestic work, and power in the home. An example is:' As head of the household, the father should have final authority over children'.

- Attitudes towards homosexuality scale (MacDonald et al., 1973): This is a 28 item scale for measuring the respondents attitudes towards homosexuality regardless of their own sexual orientation. It is scored on a 9 point scale from 'strongly agree' to 'strongly disagree'.

- Semantic differential scales (Marks and Sartorius, 1968): Are recommended for the measurement of attitude change. Changes are measured along 13 scales: 7 sexual ('sexual intercourse', 'women', 'my wife', 'women's panties', 'stockings', etc.) and 13 non-sexual concepts (such as 'Father Christmas', 'men', 'people with the same trouble as me', 'my mother', 'my father', and 'myself as I'd like to be').

(e) Sexual beliefs

All beliefs are ways of making sense of the world, or the sense that is made of the world (Horley, 1991). Ordinary beliefs have been described as 'expectancies' (e.g. Rokeach, 1980) formed to deal with aspects of daily existence. Schiebe (1970), however, characterised expectancy beliefs as only one belief sub-class, and he argued convincingly that many beliefs concern the present or the past only. Ordinary beliefs, then, refer to propositions about the nature of the world (past, present and future). They are typically expressed in the form 'S believes that P', where S (subject) is the believer and P (proposition) is that which is believed.' (Horley, 1991).

Research findings

- Abel et al. (1984) investigated the role that certain beliefs and attitudes play in continued sexual involvement by adults with children. They focused on seven types of beliefs about children and sex they termed 'cognitive distortions'. These distorted beliefs were as follows: If children fail to resist advances, they must want sex; sexual activity with children increases sexual knowledge; if children fail to report sexual activity, they must condone it; in the future, sex between adults and children will be acceptable if not encouraged; if one fondles rather than penetrates, sex with children is acceptable; any children who ask questions about sex really desire it; one can develop a close relationship with a child through sexual contact. According to Abel and his colleagues, the commonality among child molesters who hold these views is that they make no attempt to validate their beliefs against the experience of others. Other writers such as Stermac and Segal (1989) have confirmed this view. They found that child molesters, compared with normals, perceived more benefits for children as a result of adult sexual contact, greater complicity on the child's part, and less responsibility on the adult's part.
- Beliefs supportive of sexually abusive behaviours are multi-dimensional and sexual conflict is often a means of supporting and reinforcing certain beliefs. For example, Briere et al. (1985) found that the absence of serious relationships with members of the other sex is associated with

a belief that victims are responsible for their own rapes and the belief that women enjoy sexual violence. Another example can be found in the tabloid press, where a father reports having a sexual relationship with his 14 year old daughter. He argued that he placed some of the blame squarely at the door of his wife because for the past 4 years she had denied him any sex, which is why he turned to his daughter. In more dubious pornographic magazines there is material which reinforces a sex offenders belief that sex between an adult and a child is acceptable. It is not uncommon for sex offenders to hold exclusively rigid or puritanical attitudes and beliefs about sexuality. We also know that many hold irrational beliefs (about who is responsible for their offences and the impact of their actions on their victims) and these support their offending behaviour, along with cognitive distortions (dealt with in a later component). These irrational beliefs can often be concerned with what it is to be a man ('macho' or low in confidence) and beliefs about women, e.g. 'all' are rejecting. This has to be carefully managed if the workers are female. Some sex offenders believe that children benefit from, and enjoy, their sexual encounters with adult men. This is an area of importance in the assessment, but there is a surprising lack of material specifically about this component in the literature. Authors such as O' Carroll (1980) have provided material, which supports the actions of offenders, challenging the assumption that sex between adults and children is morally problematic.

Ellis (1989) originated the concept of irrational beliefs. He claimed that one's behaviour is influenced by one's beliefs. Irrational beliefs might include:

- The idea that it is an absolute necessity for an adult to be loved by everyone for everything he does. Therefore, if I perceive I am unloved, I have a right to hurt others and seek approval.
  Rational: There is no research that shows that one needs the love or approval of anyone to survive. To be loved by everyone is the impossibility of perfectionism. To be unloved does not give anyone a right to hurt others.
- The idea that certain acts are awful or wicked, and that people who perform such acts should be severely punished is irrational. Therefore criminals may say, 'I have a right to do what I want to people' (distorted view).
  Rational: Nothing is awful: things just are or are not and I added the labels awful, terrible, horrible etc., which don't change reality. There is no evidence that punishment works—there are consequences of behaviour.
- The idea that it is horrible when things are not the way one thinks they should be (high

expectations). Criminals say, 'Therefore I have the right to do what I want. I'm entitled.'

Rational: Horrible is a label, people have little control over life and events and to control everything is an expectation.

- The unrealistic idea that human misery is externally caused and is forced on one by outside people and events. Offenders say, 'Therefore I can't change because . . .'

Rational: The bottom line is that people create their own misery from their perceptions and belief systems or frame of reference of the activating event. This does not give anyone the right to be irresponsible and infringe on other's rights.

- The idea that if something is or may be dangerous or fearsome one should be terribly upset about it. Therapy may be viewed as dangerous and thus too scary to change, for the offender.

Rational: People encounter dangerous events frequently and survive. The meaning that is attached to them depends upon their perception.

- The idea that it is easier to avoid than to face life's difficulties and self-responsibilities.

Rational: Procrastination doesn't resolve the problem. Offenders may use this to avoid change.

- The idea that one needs something other or stronger than oneself to rely on, something or someone outside of one's self. Offenders tend to engage in this belief.

Rational: Everyone is responsible for their own behaviour.

- The idea that one should be thoroughly competent, intelligent, and achieving in all possible respects. Offenders say, 'If I can't be perfect, screw it.'

Rational: Perfectionism is a myth that doesn't exist.

- The idea that because something once strongly affected one's life, it should indefinitely affect it. Offenders state, 'Therefore because this happened I have no other choice but to offend.'

Rational: The past doesn't control one's life unless one consciously or unconsciously chooses to be controlled by the past. People are self-deterministic and make decisions. The past has influences and the individual chooses how to respond to them.

- The idea that one must have certain and perfect control over things and people including one's self. Offenders feel that they should control others.

Rational: Perfectionism is a myth and no excuse to offend. One can't control others, just influence them, and it is up to that person to follow it.

- The idea that human happiness can be achieved by inertia and inaction. Offenders feel that there is magic in treatment.

Rational: There is no magic in life. Procrastination doesn't resolve problems.

- The idea that one has virtually no control over one's emotions and that one cannot help feeling certain feelings. Offenders feel helpless in that they can't control themselves.

Rational: My emotions are the results of my ideas, beliefs and philosophies (Criddle, 1975).

'Disowning behaviours'

- Carich et al. (1992) would argue that these irrational beliefs form a small part of a much broader concept of 'disowning behaviours'. These are any behaviours that enables the Target Dysfunctional Behaviours (TDBs) and enables the individual to evade and avoid responsibility. Disowning behaviours are a combination of coping/defensive structures, cognitive distortions and thinking errors. They play a significant role in the offending process. There appear to be two related components to disowning. These are irresponsibility and enabling factors. The first component refers to the offender not taking or accepting responsibility for his behaviour. The second factor, enabling factors, are any overt/covert behaviours that enable or facilitate the offender's decision to offend. Both are related, as offending behaviours are irresponsible given the devastating consequences to others.

- Carich (1993) set out several assumptions about disowning. Disowning behaviours are choices made by the offender. Disowning serves several purposes, including compensation dynamics, coping strategies, maintaining psychological balance, and enabling target dysfunctional behaviours. Disowning occurs at both conscious and unconscious levels of awareness. It is learned at both levels. Disowning behaviours are integrated into the offender's lifestyle and usually operate automatically at unrecognised levels.

- Carich et al. (1992) set out two basic categories: covert disowning behaviours and overt disowning behaviours. These are discussed in detail in their paper and address the following:

1. Covert disowning behaviours: Consist of any internal response that allows the offender to make choices to engage in offending behaviours and avoid responsibility. The subcategories include:

   a. Cognitive DBs: are a type of cognition or thought process that the offender has to avoid responsibility and engage in offending. The specific subcategories include: cognitive distortions and irrational beliefs, Samenow's (1979) criminal thinking defects, and other criminal thinking defects.

b. Affective/emotional DBs: are any feelings, emotions or moods used to evade responsibility and enable or facilitate offending behaviours. For example, many offenders use anger, loneliness, apathy, boredom, depression etc., to enable them to offend and behave irresponsibly. Offenders use these feelings, accompanied by cognitive distortions to engage in offending.

c. Psychodynamic coping strategies: are specific 'protective' coping responses to stimuli that are usually threatening in nature. They involve elements of cognitive distortions.

2. Overt disowning behaviours: These are any observable activities or behaviours used to evade responsibility and engage in offending. They include:

a. Overt activities: referring to psychomotor behaviours, such as doing something, or engaging in doing some behaviour. They are typically accompanied by feelings and preceded by thoughts, perceptions etc. They include avoiding things, alienating self etc.

b. Social DBs: socialising is a natural behaviour and a necessity for living. The type of peer group or social networking the offender has can either prevent or enable offending. Negative or dysfunctional peer groups tend to encourage distorted beliefs, and thus enable offending. For example, negative peer groups can enhance self-pity, unwarranted entitlements, a victim stance, blurring, rationalisations, etc.

Tools

Questions to be asked include:

- What, or how important was your religious background?
- What are their beliefs about sex? Masturbation? Relationships? Do they believe sex can only be legitimately expressed within marriage?
- Do they know what healthy or constructive beliefs might be?
- Can they identify any beliefs which may have contributed towards their sexual offending?
- Get them to describe themselves as (a) a man and (b) as a sexual person, identifying any differences.

Questionnaires include:

- The parental beliefs questionnaire (Briggs et al., 1998): 14 items or statements which the offender is asked to respond 'true' or 'false' to.
- The 'Is it all right to' questionnaire (Briggs et al., 1998): Describes various behaviours between people which the offender is asked to respond to as either 'acceptable' or 'unacceptable'.
- Negative attitudes towards masturbation inventory (Abramson and Mosher, 1978)*: A 30 item

questionnaire designed to measure the negative attitudes of masturbation, particularly related to masturbation guilt.

(f) Sexual values

To talk of an individual's values is to refer to a system of learned beliefs concerning preferential objects, modes of conduct, and/or existential end states. Values include *"what is wanted, what is best, what is desirable or preferable, what ought to be done"* (Schiebe, 1970). Horley (1991) also noted that another generally accepted aspect of values is that they represent the essence of an individual. People come to see themselves, and others come to see them, by the standards that seem to guide their affairs. This is not to say that people always act according to their (ever changing) standards of behaviour; they often find their own behaviour falling short of their ideals. Rather, their considered or expressed desires to see themselves and others act in a certain manner capture who people are as individuals. Also, people's views on non-human matters, expressed by, say, a set of religious values, seem to make an important statement about essences. Self-knowledge and self-identity can thus be seen in terms of taking stock of values. Rokeach (1973) defined the term moral values as *"those values that have an interpersonal focus, which, when violated, arouse pangs of conscience and feelings of guilt for wrongdoing."* It follows, therefore, that values are a special type of belief.

Prendergast (1991) has developed a five-stage value development schematic to chart the evolution of value formation progression, which is important when we have identified values that need to be challenged. It is set out below:

Five stages of value formation

Stage 1: The prisoner stage (birth to 2 years)

- All values are learned from parents and other adults in the child's home.
- Absolute obedience is necessary for acceptance and love.
- No comparisons are made at this stage.

Stage 2: The neighbourhood stage (from 2 to 5 years)

- Friends, neighbours, relatives and others outside the home introduce new values.
- Comparisons by the developing child begin, and result in confusion and the first negative perceptions of parents and self.
- The first blame and guilt for failures also occurs during this stage.
- Inadequacy as a characteristic most likely begins at this stage.

Stage 3: The societal stage (from 5 years to puberty)

- School, religion and the law introduce additional values.
- Teachers, policemen etc. become new parent symbols and comparison intensifies.

- Value confusion is strong, especially when a behaviour is acceptable at home and is not acceptable in school or vice versa.
- The need to please adults appears strongest in this stage and the child is therefore more vulnerable to seduction by the offender, especially when the home is not fulfilling his or her needs.
- Parent-substitute interaction during this stage is critical to the mature and stable development of the child. Each needs to know what values the other is teaching and which values they are in disagreement with.

Stage 4: The peer stage (from the onset of puberty)

The need to please adults ends and they seek acceptance from their peers. In pursuit of their independence and personal identity, they break away from the protective clutches of the parents and form their own values, behaviours etc. The problems most commonly associated with this stage include:

- Fears, self-doubts, confusion, shifts of loyalty, body-image problems and constant testing of both themselves and others.
- Communication abruptly stops and needs to be fostered regularly.
- Sexuality explodes and becomes a major focus. Indecisiveness and confusion about all aspects of sex dominate this stage. For boys, the need to be strong, macho and heterosexual dominates the male adolescent value system. They are homophobic and thus can't seek out help if abused themselves during this stage.
- Guilt of all types flourishes and imprints.

Stage 5: The 'I' stage

All other stages and values are re-examined and decisions for adult life are made in this stage. Those who have developed distorted, damaging or guilt-provoking values are very difficult to change, e.g. sex = love, or masturbation = dirty. Indeed, one of the most common traits of the repetitive sex offender is their long-term belief that sex equals love. This is the most frequently seen and most destructive of all the distorted values found in sex offenders. Often, when asked why they committed a particular offence, they say that they were only showing their victim 'love', not harming them. The source of this value must be found (using the schematic above) before any change can be effected. This may stem from education from their parents—'we are making love''—or if they have been the victim of sexual abuse themselves—and this was used by the abuser to justify their behaviour.

Tools

Questions to be asked include:

- What are their values? When, where and how did they learn them?

- Do they hold any unhealthy or inaccurate values, or stereotypes that are unhelpful?
- Is there any correspondence between their stated values and actual behaviours?

Questionnaires include:

- Norms and values continuum (Willis, 1993): Sets out 32 situations and the offender can be asked to score their response to these. Examples include: 'Seven year old daughter likes to give father a wet kiss.' 'Father baths his 11 year old child.' 'When making love to his wife, husband fantasises about their daughter.'
- Values questionnaires (1 + 2), (Mayer, 1988): The first value questionnaire sets out 18 questions which the offender is asked to respond to in two or three sentences. It aims to elicit information regarding impulse/anger control, sexuality, problem-solving skills, moral development, use of defences, stress management, and social isolation. The second questionnaire sets out 8 situations designed to focus on moral values and concepts of social deviance. The offender is asked to respond as to whether the situation is right or wrong; harmful to anyone; or meriting legal involvement. They are also asked what advice they would give to a friend if involved in the described situations. Examples include: 'React to the statement that everyone is capable of murder under the right circumstances.' 'React to the statement that all men are penis-centred.' 'List three aspects of your life that you value and describe the reasons why.' 'Is it right or wrong for a man to habitually masturbate in his car while watching attractive women on the street?'

(g) Sexual interests and sexual preferences

The sexual preference hypothesis is that sexual offending is driven by sexual desires for deviant sex (Marshall, 1996). It is criticised on the notion that you cannot always differentiate sex offenders from non-sexual offenders. Sexual preference is believed to be a relatively stable individual trait (Freund, 1981) and it is now considered to be an essential part of the assessment of sex offenders. It is a specialised component that needs the skills and expertise of psychologists, but we will explore the issues briefly here as we need to be clear about them as commissioning agents of the work. It is also important to have some knowledge of the issues as we may supplement any specialist assessment as part of our ongoing work with the offender.

Any assessment attempts to determine whether the offender shows an unusual sexual preference (e.g. for children) as this escalates the likelihood of them engaging in such acts. We will explore in a later block the reality that the offender, whatever the anomalous sexual preference, will fantasise and be driven by their unusual urges (Langevin, 1988). There are repeated observations that sex offenders frequently ruminate over their sexual fantasies involving the types of behaviour in which they engage. The identification of some sexual preferences, such as sadism, is essential, as when aroused, they may want to rape and/or injure someone. There is a need, therefore, to identify the sexual preferences and then explore their relative strength, their duration, their potency for the individual, and if they are orgasmic in nature (Langevin, 1983). We have to remember that the offender may attempt to conceal their preferences either through guilt or fear of consequences such as imprisonment, and we need to acknowledge that the current charges or allegations do not always reflect the total map of their sexual preferences. Indeed, there may be other preferences unrecorded anywhere and there may be overlap between the recorded sexual crimes. The common practice of inferring sexual preferences on the basis of index offences is thus very questionable. We know that many offenders have multiple victims over time: some younger, some older, and their current offence may not accurately reflect their true sexual preferences. Factors such as opportunity, disinhibiting effects of drugs or alcohol, social incompetence, or sexual frustration due to marital discord or dissolution etc., may dispose men to commit a sexual crime with a child that is not sexually ideal in their mind (Langevin and Lang, 1988). It is therefore important to describe an offender's most desired partner (e.g the victim's age and sexual features) and the desired victim response (e.g. admiration, fear or pain) (Frenzel and Lang, 1989).

Determining sexual preferences is important because they imply cognitive and behavioural patterns that are long-lasting and resistant to change. Thus, the male who has a preferential erotic attraction to children over adults may continue to be at risk of sexual offending throughout his life, although other factors such as age can be mitigating (Frenzel and Lang, 1989). The identification of specific sexual preferences is an essential prerequisite for individualised, offender/offence-specific treatment programmes and relapse prevention plans.

It is also important to determine whether the sexual offending is down to either preference or opportunity, particularly as sexual preference patterns differ within the sex offender population; or whether it is the person or the activity they are attracted to. Some men have fixed sexual preferences whilst others are more transient.

Research findings

- There is accumulating evidence that sex offenders are a heterogeneous group in terms of their sexual preference profiles (Frenzel and Lang, 1989). For example, extra-familial offenders are predominantly paedophilic, whereas less than a quarter of intra-familial sex offenders are (Langevin and Watson, 1996).

- Research studies have identified that incest offenders have approximately 'normal' age preferences: that is, greater responding to adults than children (Freund, 1967a and b; Murphy et al., 1986). Quinsey et al. (1979) have argued that incest offenders are likely to be 'situational' offenders, and Quinsey (1977) has hypothesised that they are a particular type of situational offender in that their offences are related to family dynamics and opportunism rather than inappropriate sexual preferences. Quinsey et al. (op. cit.) explored the sexual preference profiles of incestuous and non-incestuous child molesters. They found that the incestuous group showed more appropriate sexual age preferences than non-incestuous offenders and the difference appeared greater in the cases where the incest involved daughter victims. Frenzel and Lang (1989) found that incest offenders tend to choose slightly older victims than other sex offenders, although they do show some apparent sexual preference for the pubescent female (13–15 years) over the adult.

- Despite these findings, Barbaree and Marshall (1989) have found that there are both deviant as well as normal profiles within incest offenders, suggesting population differences.

- With incest offenders, the worker faces a problem in that both single and multiple victim incest offenders have a low recidivism rate, though this group does contain true paedophiles (Frenzel and Lang, 1989).

- Barbaree and Marshall (1989) found that one-third of men who molested boys revealed a preference for males. Homosexual men, both in terms of their offence history and their erotic preferences, preferred pubescent boys (mean age = 12.5 years) and the heterosexual offenders preferred pre-pubescent boys (mean age = 7.5 years). Freund (1967) found that men who offend against boys were more aroused by children than adults. Marshall et al. (1988) examined a large group of men who had molested boys in order that they could describe their preferences for age and gender, as well as their preference for types of sexual acts and their responses to coercive sexual interactions. Their study revealed two important features of men who molest boys. First, their sexual responses to males in general were greater than those displayed by controls, and their arousal to sex with boys was also greater than those of their controls. Whilst they did differ from controls in their arousal to males (adult and child), they did not differ at all in their arousal to females. The second finding was that a homosexual and heterosexual sub-group could be delineated among these offenders. As such, men who abuse boys are not a homogeneous population. Homosexuals were more aroused to male boys over 13 years and were far more aroused by sexual interactions with boys even when those interactions required that the man be forceful. Approximately 30 per cent of men who molest boys have had anal sex with their victims (Langevin et al., 1985). The homosexuals identified the features of the boys that they found most attractive: the early experience of male secondary sexual features, particularly the size of the boys' penises as being important to them and in some cases at least, this appeared to be related to their wish for the boys to penetrate the man's anus.

- The heterosexual group also identified attractive features of their victims: young boys who did not have any body hair and that their bodies were smooth and soft reflecting the finding that they targeted pre-pubescent boys.
- Bisexuals are unique in that they frequently show arousal both to boys and girls (Frenzel and Lang, 1989).
- Exhibitionists show consistently high arousal to thoughts of exposing (Maletzky, 1980), although it has also been suggested that they are aroused to appropriate activities (such as sexual intercourse), but they approach women in the hope of achieving such goals in an inappropriate way.
- Frenzel and Lang (1989) found that heterosexual extra-familial offenders responded most to the adult female, as well as to children in the 9–11 and 13–15 year age range, with little discrimination between less sexually mature girls and adult women. These results thus suggest that they may, under certain conditions, target as surrogate sex partners, female children of any age with whom they come into contact.
- Marshall et al. (1986) explored age and gender preferences among men who molest the female children of other people. They found that they are a heterogeneous group (like the men who molest boys). They found several important observations. Firstly, heterosexual offenders were more aroused by stimuli involving children than were the other two groups, although they were also highly aroused to adult females. Secondly, they found that the greater the number of victims, the more varied their sexual preferences. This may be associated with greater sexual experiences. Thirdly, they found that those men with an IQ under 80 are more likely to display greater arousal to stimuli depicting children than those with higher IQs. This maybe because they have not learned the appropriate constraints against arousal to young girls, or it may be because they are unable to discriminate age satisfactorily.

Tools

Questions to be asked include:
It is important to try and isolate each offender's particular sexual interests and preferences. Get them to write their reactions to each of the following:

- Oral sex
- Anal sex
- Sexual intercourse
- Foreplay
- Sex with animals (bestiality)
- Different sexual positions
- Exhibitionism
- Frottage
- Extra-marital sex
- Pornography
- Prostitution
- Cross-dressing
- Peeping
- Sex with children
- Sex with older people
- Obscene phone calls
- Massage parlours
- Group sex
- Rape
- Sexual fantasies
- Sex in public
- Partner swapping
- Homosexual experiences
- Sado-masochism
- Voyeurism

The worker can add to this list according to the requirements of each presenting case.

- We need to identify the sexual preferences of the offender and then explore their relative strength, their duration, their potency for the individual, and if they are orgasmic in nature (Langevin, 1983).
- What are the current charges and previous allegations/convictions, and what, if anything, do they tell us about their sexual preferences?
- Are their sexual preferences clearly identifiable? Are they fixed, transient, or is there evidence of cross-over? Have they changed over time? If so, in what way?
- What would you expect to identify as their sexual preferences given the charges and the elicited history?
- What evidence of force is there?
- Do you suspect the offence is driven by opportunity or careful selection and grooming?
- What is their most desired partner and victim response?

Questionnaires include:

- Sexual interest questionnaire (Harbison et al., 1974): This is a 140 item questionnaire designed to measure the degree of interest a male (or female) indicates in particular sexual situations, either of a homosexual or heterosexual nature. It measures 5 different concepts of sexual behaviour: kissing, being kissed, touching sexually, being touched sexually and sexual intercourse.

These are then scored along 5 scale positions: very erotic, quite erotic, neither erotic nor frigid, quite frigid and very frigid. It can be used to isolate sexual interests as well as being useful in predicting treatment outcome, plus motivation for treatment. It can also be used to assess any shift in sexual interests from young people to adult partners.

- Abel and Becker sexual interest cardsort (Abel and Becker, 1985)*: This sets out 75 items which are scored to provide a measure of the offender's sexual interests and thus arousal pattern.
- Homosexual erotic preference (Bell et al., 1981): A 175 page interview designed to assess homosexual erotic preference.
- Pedo Admitter and Hebe Admitter scales (Freund, 1981).
- Gender identity and erotic preference scale (Freund and Blanchard, 1988)*.
- Use of any of the standardised sex history questionnaires set out earlier in this chapter.
- See Barbaree and Peacock (1995) for a discussion on the assessment of sexual preferences in cases of alleged child sexual abuse.

(h) Sexual arousal

This is linked closely with sexual preferences. One of the unique traits of the sex offender is the obsessive/compulsive nature of their deviant sexual arousal patterns for masturbation or other sexual excitability needs. When the compulsion is active, they are unable to get aroused to a normal sexual stimulus or fantasy regardless of how hard they try. If they do get erect, and a percentage do to anything that contains nudity or sexual suggestion, they are unable to reach orgasm unless they change the fantasy to include their own subjective deviant stimulus pattern (Prendergast, 1991). Fantasy is a guide to sexual arousal and, as such, their content can help to quantify the likelihood of recidivism. It is crucial to establish in what way arousal (fantasy) contributes to the origins and the maintenance of sexual offending. This is explored later in the chapter.

Rowland (1995) noted that sexual arousal, as well as its end point, sexual behaviour, involves a web of physiological, psychological, and cultural factors. There have been several models put forward for sexual arousal, each becoming progressively more sophisticated. Masters and Johnson (1966) developed a 'sexual response cycle' which attempted to describe the sequence of physiological (mainly genital) events occurring during sexual arousal and orgasm. Thus, the sequential phases of sexual excitement, plateau, orgasm, and resolution corresponded to specific genital changes, beginning with increased blood flow to the genitalia, on to the muscular contractions of orgasm, and finally to the period of deactivation following climax.

Kaplan (1974) offered a different model of sexual response, which incorporated three components: desire, excitement, and orgasm. The addition of desire (a psychological construct closely connected to motivation) was very helpful, building on the description of sexual response as a sequence of ordered events. This model also highlighted the interdependence among the components, e.g. problems with the orgasmic phase could result from insufficient arousal, or problems with arousal might actually be seated in the desire phase. The model also appealed because its components coincided with the types of problems encountered by the clinician. For example, the dysfunctional individual may lack an interest or desire in sex, may not be able to become sexually excited, or may indicate a problem with orgasm.

Byrne and Kelley (1986) added more to the psychological dimension of the problem, by embracing informational, affective and attitudinal factors. Here, both innate and learned stimuli operate on a number of central mediating processes, including those representing memories and images, beliefs and expectations, and emotions and subjective perceptions. These systems guide physiological responses and sexual activity. Barlow (1986) went on to offer a model of male sexual arousal, differentiating the response of sexually functional men from that of dysfunctional men. The chain of events begins with the expectation of sexual performance from the partner, which typically evokes a positive emotional response, directs attention toward erotic cues, and results in automatic arousal and sexual performance. In some circumstances, the expectations of performance may evoke a negative emotional response, which then focuses attention on performance or other non-erotic cues. Automatic sexual arousal under these conditions leads to dysfunctional sexual performance.

Rowland (1995) argues that we need to use each of the models to help ground us with a comprehensive understanding of sexual arousal. He argues that certain preconditions are necessary for sexual response to occur, including the appropriate external stimuli (partner, sexual situation, etc.) and internal conditions (desire, readiness, etc.). These internal conditions are mediated through both psychological and physiological influences and contribute to the ability to experience sexual arousal. Second, a constellation of psychological factors influences and guides sexual response. These include affects, cognitions, attitudes and beliefs. Third, sexual response itself consists of a series of events. Arousal, an important first step, is multifaceted, having both a central component and a peripheral (autonomic) component. The subsequent behavioural response (a sexual act) is maintained through ongoing psychological and peripheral physiological processes, which, through feedback mechanisms, may culminate in orgasm and resolution. Rowlands explores in more detail each of these areas in the chapter.

Research findings

- A major factor predisposing sexually abusive acts of some offenders is a distorted sexual arousal pattern. Indeed, dominance as a motivation for sexual activity can be a significant predictor of high sexual arousal (Malamuth and Check, 1983). Pithers et al. (1987) found that 69 per cent of rapists and 57 per cent of paedophiles exhibited deviant sexual preferences during phallometric evaluation, whilst only 17 per cent of the rapists and 51 per cent of the paedophiles self-reported that they experienced greater sexual interest in abusive sexuality than affectionate sexuality with adults. Neglecting to evaluate an offender's arousal pattern may result in a failure to identify or address a central aetiological factor of that offender's abusive behaviours. If we do identify a disordered arousal pattern, it always indicates a need for specialist and focused treatment rather than it being used to exempt them from treatment (Pithers and Laws, 1995). Indeed, Quinsey (1981) has argued that the best available predictor of long-term treatment success is the reduction of deviant sexual arousal coupled with an adequately high level of appropriate sexual arousal. To date, much more is known about the arousal patterns in rapists than in sex offenders against children or men in the general population.

- By far the greatest amount of sexual pleasure is derived during the period of sexual arousal prior to orgasm (MacCulloch et al., 1983). In their study of sadists, they found several concordant themes with their sexual fantasies: recurrent sadistic fantasies, linked to sexual arousal, which included control over a victim. Their index offences were recognisably part of the fantasy sequence. All the respondents reported sexual arousal and mental pleasure during the offence. Many reported normal, heterosexual fantasies following puberty, with some developing deviant sexual fantasy content such as transvestism, fetishism and exhibitionism. Many reported a clear progression in their sadistic fantasies some 1–7 years after the onset of masturbation.

- Yates et al. (1984) examined the effects of anger arousal on the sexual responses of 'normal' men to rape cues, in order to demonstrate the effects of anger on deviant sexual arousal. They found that anger towards females makes the pattern of sexual arousal of 'normal' males resemble those of rapists, e.g. more responsive to violence and cues of non-consent. This correlates with other work which has found links between highly erotic films and an increase in aggressive behaviour in men who had been previously angered and anger—inducing films that have

been shown to increase overall levels of sexual arousal. It remains unclear what part the availability of hard-core porn and images of sexual violence in the mass media are contributory towards sexual arousal.

- The need to assess deviant sexual arousal is indicated most in those cases where their sexual offending is an expression of their sexual desire (albeit misdirected) and workers need to be clear about what focus there would need to be to subsequent treatment on redirecting sexual desires or inhibiting deviant sexual thoughts.

- The nature and number of an individual's relationships may also give us an indication of their arousal pattern. Many try to present themselves as only having adult relationships, but this is often easy to challenge. We need to see if there is any pattern to the genders or ages of the children they mix with; what lengths they will go to to access their preferred victims. For example, they may go to where children congregate, such as circus', McDonalds etc., join activities with children, such as scouts, swimming or football clubs etc.

- Research has also identified evidence that non-offenders can become aroused to children (Freund et al., 1972) or to rape scenes (Barbaree et al., 1979). Baxter et al. (1986) has also found that college students have shown phallometric responses of 20–40 per cent of full erections to rape scenes, and even higher levels of arousal have been shown for college men with strong sex-role stereotypes (Check and Malamuth, 1983).

- Langevin et al. (1985) found that sadists are sexually aroused by controlling their victim as well as by their fear, humiliation, embarrassment and ultimately by injuring them. Sexually aggressive men are not only aggressive but are lacking in empathy. Rapists get aroused by rape cues, regardless of the discomfort or resistance of their victims.

- Griffiths (1975) found that men with greater sexual experience report more arousal to depictions of those activities they had previously experienced (e.g. fellatio, intercourse) than do men lacking these experiences.

- Finally, deviant sexual arousal is related to sexual recidivism (for a review, see Quinsey et al., 1995).

Tools

Questions to be asked:

- It is important to differentiate arousal to gender (male, female, or both), ages, preferred sexual contact (e.g. anal sex; oral–genital contact, etc.), as well as sexual offences and behaviour type (e.g. frottage, exhibitionism etc.).

- It is important to remember that subjective interviews may not accurately reflect physiological arousal, in that we only usually elicit partial or conservative estimates of their actual arousal.

- Link to the later section on fantasy and the earlier section on relationships for ideas on how to tackle this block.

Questionnaires include:

- Sexual pleasure inventory (Annon, 1976): 130 items with 5 possible responses to each item, from 'not at all' to 'very much'. It is a check-list of people, objects and behaviour that is likely to lead to pleasure. It was developed to assess the relative degree of arousal or other pleasant feelings they may associate with sexually related activities and experiences. A wide range of activities is covered, from the normally expected to the more rare.

- Sexual arousability inventory and the sexual arousability inventory—expanded (Hoon and Chambless, 1988)*: This is made up of 28 items pertaining to sexual activities or stimuli. Each item is rated on a 7 point Likert-type scale ranging from—1 (adversely affects arousal; relaxing; or dissatisfied) to 5 (extremely arousing; extremely anxiety provoking; or extremely satisfied).

- Self-monitoring measures: Offenders can be asked to record basic information every time they are sexually aroused/stimulated, including time, place and people present, accompanying thoughts and feelings, and any action taken to subvert deviant sexual impulses (Hanson et al., 1991).

- Attraction to sexual aggression scale (Malamuth, 1989): Designed to assess the components of male sexual aggression among those who are prone or predisposed to such behaviour. He sets out 5 components that emerge from the ASA: attraction to conventional sex, attraction to bondage, attraction to homosexuality, attraction to unconventional sex (e.g. anal intercourse), and attraction to deviant sex (e.g. paedophilia). The questionnaire comprises 9 questions, with each item having from 13 to 17 items. The aim is to elicit how frequently the offender believes that people engage in a variety of sexual acts; whether they find such acts 'attractive'; whether they find them sexually arousing; what percentage of their male friends have engaged in these acts; and what the likelihood is that they would engage in these acts. Sample questions include: ' How sexually arousing do you think you would find the following sexual activities if you engaged in them (even if you have never engaged in them)? Necking (deep kissing), petting, oral sex, heterosexual intercourse, anal intercourse, male homosexual acts, group sex, bondage, whipping, spanking, rape, forcing a female to do something sexual she didn't want to do, transvestism, or paedophilia (sex with a child)?'

- Sexual arousal patterns (Carich and Adkerson, 1995)*.

- Arousal portfolio and cardsort (Farrenkopf, 1986): Consists of pictorial collages of men, women, and children in booklet form. It is a deck of 36 three-by-five cards each with two or three sentences describing a sexually explicit scene in the second person, three items for each category. The categories include sex with male and female children, adolescents, and adults respectively, as well as descriptions of rape, exhibitionism, voyeurism, frottage, obscene phone calls and fondling women's underwear. Subjects are asked to rate their arousal on each card on the same scale of 0–100 (0=no arousal to 100=very high arousal) and then sort the cards into a designated rating category (0, 10, 20 etc. to 100).

(i) Crossover

Sexual offending can occur within and outside the family; with male and female victims, of varying ages; and there can be a variety of sexually deviant behaviours. They are not always discrete or compartmentalised. Those sex offenders who are caught offending inside the family are potentially a threat to children living outside the family as a preference for that kind of behaviour develops (Wolf, 1984; Abel et al., 1987).

Research findings

- Abel and colleagues found that whilst there are clearly some sex offenders that only abuse inside or outside families, some 65 per cent of intra-familial offenders also abused outside the family.

- Research by Abel et al. (1987, 1988) has significantly influenced our approach to sex offenders, as their work demonstrated that sex offenders have a larger number of victims, acts, and multiple paraphilias than had previously been assumed. Few offenders were found to have a single paraphilia or to have only abused a single child. Indeed, extra-familial offenders were found to have an average of 19.8 victims (for those molesting a girl) and 150 victims (for those molesting a boy). The figures for incest offenders were significantly lower (approximately 2 victims). However, over half or more of incest offenders were noted to have abused outside their families, and 70 to 95 per cent were noted to have engaged in another paraphilia, most commonly rape or exhibitionism.

- Earlier research (Abel et al., 1985) also established that many incest perpetrators who avowed no attraction to same sex children disclosed a history of abusing children of both sexes and 44 per cent of them also revealed an astonishing number of child victims in addition to numerous other paraphilias. Abel and colleagues (1987) reinforced this crossover between different sexually deviant behaviours. Indeed, they revealed that 23.3 per cent offended against both family and non-family members, 20 per cent offended against both sexes whilst 26 per cent offended against both sexes and 26 per cent used touching and non-touching behaviours.

- Freund and Blanchard (1986) also pointed out that sex offenders who have committed more than one type of sexual offence or deviation belonged to the group called 'courtship disorders': exhibitionism, voyeurism, obscene calls, toucherism, and sadistic rape. Freund et al. (1983) found that 45 of the 86 exhibitionists, 11 of the 22 touchers, and 2 of the 7 voyeurs reported co-occurrence of these deviations. Abel et al. (1988) investigated 561 male sex offenders and found that at least 72 per cent of the sex offenders and deviants other than transexuals reported additional deviations.

- Day (1994) reported that mentally handicapped sex offenders are more likely than non-handicapped sex offenders to commit offences against both males and females, against both same age and older victims, and are less likely to know their victims, to commit violence, or to commit penile penetration of the vagina.

- The biggest question for workers is how generalised can such findings be used. McConaghy (1993) did question the conclusions we can draw from these findings, as the studies did not report the frequencies with which the additional deviations were performed, so they might conceivably have been isolated acts. Marshall et al. (1991) reported on their findings from using a different subject selection and interview techniques. In some areas their findings were similar. For example, only slightly fewer subjects were found to report to their sexual interest in children began or was first manifested during adolescence, 10.5 to 41 per cent, compared with 25 to 50 per cent in the Abel studies, both suggesting that a substantial proportion of molesting had an adolescent onset. However, findings differed sharply in terms of victimisation rates and presence of multiple paraphilias. In contrast to Abel et al., only 8 to 14 per cent were found to have an additional paraphilia and mean number of victims were generally far lower (4.7 vs 19.8 for extra-familial girl offenders; 3.3 vs 15 for extra-familial boy molesters; 1.4 vs 1.8 for intra-familial girl molesters). Even where the more chronic or deviant sex offenders were separated from the overall sample, mean numbers of victims and numbers of additional paraphilias did not approach the figures cited by Abel et al. For a detailed exploration of the differences between these two studies, the reader is referred to Chaffin (1994). Thornton (1994) reported on the PPG results of Malcolm et al. with a group of Canadian sex offenders being assessed for suitability for sex offender programmes. They explored gender and age ratios and found that they could accurately predict sexual re-offending through the age preference index. They found that they tended to have responded more strongly to images of children rather than adults. Thornton argues that these findings have implications for the notion of crossover. They show that the majority of sex offenders do often have a preference for victims of a particular age/gender, and there is a limited crossover. He believes that we should always consider the possibility of crossover, but the probability is that it will be unlikely. Few sex offenders represent a risk to everyone.

- The principal implications of crossover relate to the number of children at risk, the possibility of an indiscriminate sexual arousal, as well as the practical difficulties surrounding where they live and whom they see.

Tools

These findings do highlight a number of points for us as assessors:

- Firstly, we must be thorough in our assessment work or commissioning brief to others.
- Secondly, we must err on the side of caution and assess a general risk to all children, not forgetting the need to exclude the likelihood of crossover where it is discounted.
- Finally, it shows us the need for objective measures of sexual interest, arousal and preference if our assessment conclusions are any where near accurate.

Any failure to accurately identify these areas will have potentially serious consequences as the offender may be able to continue some aspects of their sexual offending outside any intervention framework, and their behaviour may continue to change and/or escalate. This means that all children are at risk from the individual and more stringent controls are needed if they are to have opportunities to offend restricted or closed down completely. Whilst it is clearly accepted in the literature that intra-familial and extra-familial child molesters represent two distinct groups of sexual offending, any lack of clarity on the assessment to which group the offender must belong leaves us to assume a generalised risk until revised as the assessment process unfolds.

Penile plethysmograph

Sexual preferences and arousal can be measured in a number of different ways: self-report, interview, standardised sexual history questionnaires or phallometric assessment. Whilst these may seem personal, intrusive and embarrassing to some workers, they are useful to extract crucial assessment information. Sexual arousal itself can also be measured in a number of ways, as there are a number of physiological changes accompanying arousal (such as physical changes in blood pressure or heart rate; or cognitively in terms of fantasy).

The value of penile plethysmography in assessing sexual preference has been widely reported in the United States, but has been more cautiously received in the United Kingdom. Phallometric assessments of sex offenders have long been identified as contributing important information. We are of the view that it can be useful in certain circumstances (e.g. post-conviction, to gauge eligibility for treatment, to measure change, and to provide a baseline on risk and focus), particularly as the more assessments there are, the more accurate the recommendations that flow from them. We are also aware that it can be used to provide information concerning the relative strength of arousal to all of the possible categories of sexual stimulation and then provide a periodic review of any arousal control as the work progresses or any relapses to deviant fantasies. It can indicate the most likely type of victim or preferred sex partner; some information on the possible degree of violence or coercion the offender might use; reduce the denial potential as well as giving insight into the progress or lack of progress in the treatment process (Farrall, 1992).

The assessment of sexual arousal and preference is imperative, and penile erection is the most valid indicator of sexual arousal (Zuckerman, 1971). The PPG offers a psycho-physiological measure of sexual arousal. The PPG assessment involves using a sensor designed to measure changes in a man's penis size in response to a variety of stimuli. The aim is to identify the stimuli to which he is sexually responsive, e.g. complete erection (or unresponsive, e.g. flaccidity). The stimuli can be either slides (to assess age and gender differences), audio tapes (to assess activity preferences), films, or video tapes. Slides are considered the weakest stimuli, whilst videotapes the most arousing. Various sexual stimuli are chosen to represent those categories of behaviour thought to be relevant to the offences. They involve males, females, adults and children. Various themes are presented, including consenting interactions, forced sexual behaviour, and sexual offending against children. Given that most offenders deny arousal to deviant stimuli, we should present them with the widest range of available stimuli. Visual stimuli usually comprise nude or semi-nude male or female adults and children; sexual intercourse; and anomalous acts, such as bondage and beatings. Audiotapes are necessary because many men with unusual sexual preferences will be most aroused to the body shape of adult females but they also desire unconventional sexual behaviours, such as peeping, exposing, etc. It also offers the offender the opportunity to use their

imagination and fantasies, and thus descriptions of rape, intercourse with a child may be presented (Langevin, 1988).

The material is classified as either deviant (e.g. sex with children) or appropriate (e.g. mutually consenting sex between adults) and a ratio representing the man's arousal to these two classes of stimuli are calculated. For example, greater arousal to child stimuli as compared to adult stimuli would seem to indicate that the individual has a sexual preference for children.

There is some evidence that where the offender is provided with a copy of their own arousal patterns, they are more willing to engage in the identified work (McGovern and Peters, 1988) and often see the links between their deviant arousal and inappropriate sexual behaviour. Indeed, Abrams (1991) reported that 71 subjects made 166 admissions before the test; an additional 538 admissions were made during the procedure, and a further 92 admissions were made post-testing. Repeat testing may be useful to ensure they are not holding back on any information. Marshall and Eccles (1991) found that 46 per cent of the men referred to their outpatient clinic denied their accusations, but 54 per cent of these deniers changed their position to admitting their guilt after evaluation. Confronting the offender with the information elicited clearly encourages increased honesty and fosters additional self-disclosure and accepting increased responsibility for their crimes (Pithers and Laws, 1995).

The PPG is probably the most valid and reliable method for determining sexual preference, particularly where offender self-report remains suspect. Its limitations lie in the fact that whilst it is a test for an individual's sexual preference, it cannot determine whether an individual has acted or will act on it. For example, there may well be many individuals with abnormal sexual preferences but who can desist from offending by using their conscience/internal controls. We may also be faced with 'normal' profiles that do not indicate any sexual attraction to children. It should never be used to try and prove guilt or innocence of a particular crime as it may yield more false positives (innocent people wrongly asserted to be guilty) than in guilty people concluded to be innocent. Sexually experienced men may not find the materials arousing, citing them as dull or uninteresting. Older men are not as easily aroused as younger men.

It is a highly technical assessment requiring considerable skill and appropriate facilities, and is often administered either by psychologists or the regional forensic psychiatry services. The assessment tool is only as good as its operator, and can only be valid if the proper questions are asked and phrased correctly.

Ethically, the stimuli themselves may encourage deviant tendencies and arguably degrade women and depict children as sexual objects. This could also be seen as providing us with another sample of their behaviour.

Many argue that the PPG should never be used with men who have not been convicted or admitted the offence, largely because of the intrusiveness of the procedure (Simon and Schouter, 1992).

The procedure can be faked by offenders: either by knowingly or unknowingly suppressing responses, and this is aggravated by fatigue, masturbation, anxiety, discomfort, nervousness, ageing, drugs, and alcohol: all of which may inhibit their reactivity and disrupt their characteristic arousal. To some extent, they can exert control over their arousal (e.g. by creating increased reactions to the appropriate categories, such as consenting sexual intercourse with an adult female), and thus create an appropriate looking record. They may think about something other than that being shown, or turn away as a show of their disinterest. Many offenders do however acknowledge this if confronted post-testing (Dwyer and Coleman, 1995, p341). For a fuller review of the signs of feigning, please refer to Freund et al. (1988).

Whilst there is a critical need for information that can be used to determine whether sexual offences against children have occurred, the PPG is unable to fulfil this task. It is but one component of a comprehensive assessment and it is useful as it can be less susceptible to the distortions and biases that can occur with interviews and questionnaires, particularly where the offender has a huge investment in appearing healthy. As a diagnostic aid, it seems valuable in sorting cases according to sexual preference (Frenzel and Lang, 1989) as it is the window to the offender's 'sexual playground' (Pithers and Laws, 1988).

The debriefing post-procedure can help us to understand the offender's cognitive reaction to erotic stimulation, and they can be asked to subjectively score their arousal and compare these with the objective results. The PPG, like any assessment tool, can be useful if used correctly and interpreted cautiously. Many argue it should always be used as workers need all the help they can get when assessing sex offenders.

For a full review of the PPG the reader is referred to Pithers and Laws (1995); whilst Launey (1994) reviews the professional and research issues in some detail.

(j) Sexual blocks and sexual dysfunction

What exactly is dysfunctional is open to a wide range of interpretations, and has been thoroughly explored elsewhere (e.g. Jehu, 1979; Langevin, 1983). Over the last couple of decades research in this area has witnessed the introduction of numerous terms to describe the negative attitudes and emotions towards sex. For example, Masters and Johnson (1970) have used the terms 'negative sexual value systems' and 'performance fears',

whilst LoPiccolo (1980) has used the term 'performance anxiety'. Other terms include 'sexual conflict' (Eisler, 1968), 'sexual guilt' (Mosher, 1965) and 'sexual avoidant anxiety' (Galbraith, 1968). The problem for workers is that there is no clarification of overlaps and differences to unify their work.

Mosher (1965) defined sex guilt as "*a generalised expectancy for self-mediated punishment (i.e. negative reinforcement) for violating, anticipating the violation of, or failure to attain internalised standards of proper behaviour*". High sex-guilt individuals were found to have less self-reported sexual experience; to have a higher level of religious activity; to orient at a lower stage of moral reasoning; to spend less time viewing sexually explicit material; and to find this type of material more offensive. What is important is that both sexual guilt as well as sexual anxiety has similar effects on behaviour—they both serve to inhibit sexual behaviour. Janda and O'Grady (1980) defined sexual anxiety as "*a generalised expectancy for non-specific external punishment for the violation of, or the anticipation of violating, perceived standards of acceptable sexual behaviour. This generalised expectancy need not be realistic or rational: rather, it reflects the individual's past learning experiences related to sexual issues. As such, the crucial differentiation between the sexually guilty and the sexually anxious is that the sexually guilty individuals are concerned with what they think about themselves, whereas sexually anxious individuals are concerned with what others will think of them.*"

There are a number of theories as to the causes of sexual dysfunction. They may be due to anxiety, and this may be due to the new wave of women's sexual liberation, which has produced problems in the male partners, such as fear of competition or comparison. A second theory is that depression, anger and a loss of libido is contributory: anger and depression may induce impotence, whilst the associated impact on the self-esteem, sleep patterns and appetite may cause a loss of libido. Physical abnormalities, disease and chemicals are a third causal factor, lying in the psychological rather than the physical or the social domains. Some 90 to 95 per cent of sexual dysfunction are thought to lie in this domain (Langevin, 1983). There are a number of conditions that can result in impotence: diabetes, epilepsy, multiple sclerosis, bladder stones, sickle cell anemia and leukemia. Chemicals such as heroin addiction, tranquillisers, and chronic excessive alcohol results in temporary impotence. For a fuller discussion of sexual dysfunction, the reader is referred to Jehu (1979).

Research findings

- The stereotype of the sexual dysfunctional as a group is to be low on joy, contentment, vigour and affection, but higher on anxiety, depression, guilt and hostility (Langevin, 1983).
- Men with normal erotic preferences may experi-

ence difficulties during sexual intercourse. Some are impotent since they either cannot obtain an erection or sustain it once they do have it. Impotence does increase with age; so whilst impotence is not uncommon in men over 50 years of age, this is not accompanied by a reduction in their interest in sex. Another problem is premature ejaculation in which the man climaxes too soon to allow his female partner to attain orgasm as well.

- Research evidence supports the view that a significant proportion of sex offenders against children will probably admit to difficulties with their sexual functioning. Sexual frustration is the result of 'pent-up sexual impulse' (Guttmacher and Weihofen, 1952). This notion is not supported by authors such as Brownmiller (1975) who note that many offenders are either married or have regular sexual partners (Groth, 1979; Rada, 1978). Kanin (1983; 1984; 1985) has put forward supportive data, finding that date rapists are relatively more sexually frustrated than their non-aggressive peers. They are, in fact, more sexually active than their peers, but their expectations are so much higher, that they remain chronically frustrated. Fitch (1962) reported that 40 per cent felt frustrated in their sexual functioning. Bownes (1993) found that 52 per cent of rapists scored significant sexual dysfunction—often at some point in the attack, sometimes leading to increased aggression towards the victim (Bownes and Gorman, 1991). Pithers et al. (1987; 1988) in their study examining precursors to sexual offending, found sexual dysfunction in 11 per cent of both the rapist and paedophile samples. Since most sexually dysfunctional males do not victimise others, dysfunction obviously cannot be considered a causal factor of sexual abuse. However, in conjunction with other factors, inability to engage in affectionate, sexual relationships with peers appears to be related to some offenders' crimes. Gebhard et al. (1965) found that a range of sex offenders reported a range of 31 to 61 per cent incidence of impotence, the highest being incest offenders.

Tools

Questions to be asked:
Any history of sexual dysfunction should be elicited at the outset, particularly as blocks regarding the use of explicit terms such as anal sex can, unless resolved, render the assessment useless. It is important to explore the following areas:

- History of sexual offences and any other relevant, previous offences.
- Sexual deficiencies or abnormalities, such as impotencies, premature ejaculation, pain during sex, venereal disease, etc.
- How do they feel before, during and after sex? If happy, please describe. If not, how do they feel?

- Is there anything that has scared or humiliated them sexually? How? When?
- Why have their relationships ended?
- Do they experience and enjoy other stimuli, such as taste, auditory or visual, tactile pleasures? This is important as sensory sensations are often interlinking.

Questionnaires include:

- The sexual aggression test (Loss et al., 1988)*: A 40 item scale designed to elicit their views on a range of sexual aggression situations.
- Sexual interaction inventory (LoPiccolo and Steger, 1974): Assesses the levels of sexual functioning and satisfaction and was developed to sample sexual dysfunction.
- Derogatis sexual functioning inventory (Derogatis et al., 1976): This is a 247 item self-report inventory that measures 8 areas of sexual functioning: information, experience, drive, attitudes, symptoms, body image, gender role definition, and fantasies; and two global indices: sexual functioning and global sexual satisfaction. It is primarily suited to studying sexual dysfunction.
- Sex anxiety inventory (Janda and O'Grady, 1980): This is a 25 item inventory in which the offender can be asked to answer under three sets of instructions: answer honestly, attempt to create a favourable impression, and attempt to create an unfavourable impression. It aims to distinguish sexual guilt (the result of a violation of internal standards of proper behaviour) and sexual anxiety (an expectancy of external punishment for infractions of external standards of behaviour).
- The sexual anxiety inventory (Chambless and Lifshitz, 1984)*: Uses the same items as the previously cited sexual arousability inventory but uses a different 7 point Likert scale ranging from 'no anxiety' through to 'always causes anxiety/extremely anxiety producing'. Anxiety can, under some circumstances, facilitate sexual arousal, although the effects of anxiety on physiological sexual arousal remain unclear. Anxiety does remain an important area to assess in each individual case. Greater sexual experience is related to increased sexual responsiveness, whereas anxiety is negativity correlated with experience (Kinsey et al., 1953) and a higher frequency of orgasm is associated with lower sexual anxiety and higher arousability (Barbach, 1980).

Risk factors may include offending in response to sexual dysfunction; anger or blame of partner for their dysfunction; use of deviant fantasies to maintain arousal; or where the dysfunction is absent with the victim, but present with an appropriate partner (Carich and Adkerson, 1995).

Summary and conclusions

At the end of the sexual and social history, the worker should be able to generate hypotheses about their sexual behaviours in areas such as:

- Sexual satisfactions, arousal, preferences, and dysfunction.
- Sexual beliefs and values, as well as their origins.
- Their approaches to sex, men, women and children.
- Any discrepancies between their responses and their behaviour.

For a fuller discussion of the role of hypotheses in the assessment process, the reader is referred to the stepwise model outlined in Chapter 5, and Samra-Tibbets and Raines (1998).

It is not uncommon for offenders to be presented with one offence, e.g. indecent assault, but this may not be a true reflection of their sexual make-up or offending pattern. Great care needs to be taken in narrowing the range of risk between intra and extra-familial contexts, as well as between age groups and genders. The sexual history can clearly help identify any overlap of sexual behaviours (Langevin, 1983), e.g. the exhibitionist may also be a sadist. This can be facilitated by meticulous preparation and planning by the workers, who need to systematically cross-check all aspects of offender self-report, (wherever possible), against the reports of others: such as the victims of his offences, family, partners, and other agencies.

Additional information

It is important that workers have the opportunity to add their own materials to this framework, particularly over time as new material and research findings become available. Please add your own suggestions here:

Sex education and knowledge:

Sexual experiences:

Intimacy: sexual relationships and satisfaction:

Sexual attitudes:

Sexual beliefs:

Sexual values:

Sexual interests and sexual preferences:

Sexual arousal:

Sexual blocks and sexual dysfunction:

3. Sexual fantasies

Sexual fantasies are a component of normal sexual activities of most males and females, yet it is also considered important in the aetiology and maintenance of sexual offending.

Fantasy has been defined in a number of different ways. Burgess et al. (1986) defined it as *"an elaborate thought with great preoccupation, anchored with emotion, and having origins in daydream"*, whilst the National Task Force (1993) added that it was also the *"product of creative imagination; mental pictures, images or representations of something not present."* Sexual fantasies have been defined as *"those thoughts and feelings that we have regarding sexual behaviour that we have done or would like to do, or sexual thoughts and feelings that turn us on, that arouse us"* (Heinz et al., 1987). Glen Wilson (1978) has pointed out that *"nearly all of us have sexual fantasies at some time or another. They may occur as fleeting daydreams while at work, bizarre and intricate dreams during sleep, or exciting images accompanying intercourse or masturbation. Often they are things we would like to do in reality. Other times they are physically impossible or things we would have no desire actually to experience. Sometimes they appear in our heads spontaneously. Sometimes they are deliberate plans relating perhaps to the evening's activity. Mostly we enjoy our fantasies, but for some people they are disturbingly repetitive or a constant reminder of some frustration. Frequently they relate to actual events from our past, or things that we have seen or read which were experienced as very exciting at the time, and the memory retains power to arouse us in the present. There are many kinds of sexual fantasy and the distinctions are difficult to draw."*

In the past we tended to keep such thoughts very secret for fear of being seen as perverted. With the new permissiveness there is an increasing realisation that everyone is a little 'kinky' in their own way and if anything, this makes them normal rather than abnormal. Even so, our sexual fantasies remain a very private area of our mental life. Most of us would rather tell a stranger about them than a close friend or lover.

Little research has been published about the common sexual fantasies and daydreams of the general public. It is known that young men engage in more sexual fantasies than older men and that more sexually experienced men engage in more sexual fantasies than less experienced men, regardless of age. Crepault and Couture (1980) addressed more specifically the issue of content. They were surprised by the diversity of fantasies reported. Paedophilic, voyeuristic, and rape fantasies were surprisingly common. Klein (1988) noted that deviant content often produces anxiety in the person who fantasises it and probably results in keeping these fantasies secret.

Sexual fantasies are linked to cognitive, affective and behaviour responses as fantasies can contain factual information, produce emotional reactions, and lead to overt responses (Byrne, 1977). Various functions of fantasy have been postulated: as an escape, as an outlet for anger, or as a means of regulating one's life. The following findings do help us understand how sexual fantasies might be translated into sexual offending behaviour:

Research findings

- The great majority of males fantasise while masturbating, although they may not fantasise on every occasion. Masturbation can reinforce fantasy.

- Broadly speaking, fantasy accords with the individual's overt experiences, but may become highly elaborated. Kirkendall and McBride (1990) found that 50 per cent of their college samples claimed that their childhood fantasies had been influenced by their childhood sexual experiences, with some non-sexual elements of early experience. They also found that some who had unpleasant sexual experiences had their fantasy inhibited. Many described their earliest sexual fantasy remaining their favourite fantasy. Those who have been sexually abused may begin masturbation earlier and use these experiences as the basis of their fantasy (Rhue and Lynn, 1987). Whilst the broad themes of fantasy appear to be laid down early in life, it can also embody a great deal of wish fulfilment that exceeds their actual experience (Gebhard et al., 1965). Many sex offenders generate fantasy through their offences.

- Gold and Clegg (1990) assessed the relationship between sexual fantasies and past coercive sexual attitudes or sexual experiences. They found that subjects with coercive experiences in their background had fewer emotions, greater explicitness in their fantasies, and a greater number of sexual partners. Malamuth (1986) also found that males with more sexual experience were more sexually aggressive. Respondents with a more coercive attitude tended to have more fantasies with the theme of extreme submissiveness, and to rate themselves less happy after their fantasies (Gold and Clegg, 1990). They also found that force in sexual fantasies was associated with more explicit fantasies and less happy feelings after their fantasies. They were also less satisfied with their current sex life and more excited by their fantasies.

- Howitt (1995) found that only a few paedophiles actually reported orgasm as part of their offending, whilst many would masturbate to fantasy, at a later time, arising out of their offending. This differs from Glueck's findings when he found that 70 per cent of males enjoyed masturbation fantasies before their offences (Glueck, 1956). Their sexual fantasies of illegal acts, seems to predispose them to enacting these thoughts—through the associated excitement which also reduces inhibitions and guilt. In some cases, fantasies may become a necessary condition for sexual arousal.

- Whilst there is an assumption that fantasy is a prelude to action, particularly where it features over a period of time, it can also be a *substitute* for offending. Legal and illegal fantasies may co-exist, for example, they may fantasise about sex with a child during sexual intercourse with an adult.

- For offenders who lack social contacts and sexual experience, sexual fantasy becomes their primary (if not their only) source of sexual arousal. They may fantasise about their successful control and dominance of the world and this relieves any sense of failure they feel. It thus becomes easier and more pleasurable for the individual to retreat into their fantasy world (MacCulloch et al., 1983).

- For the habitual abuser, sexual fantasy is something which is activated at times of stress and strong negative (occasionally positive) emotional states. They retreat into their world of sexual fantasising, rather like an alcoholic might return to drink (Briggs, 1994) as a means of minimising their anxieties and ensuring that their stress becomes bearable.

- The relationship between fantasy and offending is unclear. Wolf (1984) argued that sexual fantasy fulfils three roles: it acts as a disinhibitor towards the person being thought about, it reinforces the attraction towards the behaviour, and it reinforces the rationalisations used in fantasy which is the focus for masturbation. In short, these fantasies serve as a cognitive rehearsal for deviant behaviour. The escape to fantasy puts them in control and they can modify their fantasy, giving it more power in terms of efficiency as a source of arousal and pleasure (MacCulloch et al., 1983). They then start to target victims that match their deviant sexual interest. Indeed, if they fix their fantasy on a specific behaviour or individual, it will increase the need for, and attraction to, that behaviour or individual. Fantasy could possibly drive the escalation of their sexual offending behaviour. Cognitively distorting the abuse allows them to overcome their own inhibitions and allows them to minimise and justify the abuse, thus making the unacceptable behaviour 'acceptable'. It is not unusual for guilt and embarrassment to follow (although this is often linked to their fear of getting caught), and this is usually pushed away quickly, reflecting a general inability to take responsibility for themselves. As the process has not been broken, they continue in their pattern of abusive behaviour.

- Howitt (1995) identified that there may also be substantial differences between offending and fantasy. Some men's fantasy includes sexual acts not to be found directly in their offending. A process of active negotiation may occur between fantasy and offending. For example, fantasies of buggery may be very arousing but its physical expression rejected because of the physical pain it might cause. In some cases, fantasy reverses reality. The offender who imagines himself the abused victim is a good example of this. Rather than being a script or plan for offending, fantasy engages with significant aspects of the experience and lifestyle before being expressed in action. In addition, it is often wrong to see offending as the source of sexual relief. Much sexual offending lacks immediate sexual release, and orgasm is not characteristic of all offences. In some cases sexual arousal and not sexual relief appears to be the main motive.

- Barclay (1973) studied male and female sexual fantasies and found that males mentioned visual aspects to their fantasies much more frequently, often reporting details about the appearance of female sexual characteristics such as pubic hair and breast size. He also reported that males tend to be active, impersonal and visually orientated in their fantasies, compared to women, whose fantasy themes are relatively passive.

- Fantasies are more evident with those committing 'courtship-type' offences, such as voyeurism (Awad and Saunders, 1989). Rada (1978) confirmed that as many as 50 per cent of convicted rapists engaged in voyeurism, exhibitionism, fetishism or incest in their early adolescence.

- Prentky et al. (1989) found that the organised sex offender is more likely than the disorganised offender to be characterised by a fantasy life that drives their offences.

- Crepault and Couture (1980) identified three main themes in the male fantasies: confirmation of sexual power, aggressiveness, and masochistic fantasies.

- Wilson and Lang (1981) identified four main types of fantasy: exploration (group sex, promiscuity, homosexuality, mate-swapping); intimacy (oral sex, passionate kissing, outdoor love and masturbating a partner); impersonality (sex with strangers, fetishism, watching others, using objects for stimulation, looking at obscene pictures); and sado-masochism (whipping, being forced to have sex). They found that men were likely to be active in the fantasies and they were likely to be associated with dissatisfaction (frustration?)—possibly explained by difficulties in acting out their desires, and driven by the higher average level of libido. Men reported about twice as much fantasy as women.

Tools

The assessment of masturbation fantasy often remains a taboo topic and workers need to acknowledge this when approaching the issue with the offender, and it can be helpful to be prescriptive when asking questions in order to maximise a likely response. Open-ended questions may lead to short, vague responses. Whichever approach is employed, accessing sexual fantasies, thoughts and masturbation remains difficult. Most offenders distort their perceptions in ways which psychologically justify their abuse. They also prefer to present their offences as momentary lapses, rather than a planned and erotic focus on children. Insistence by the offender that they did not experience any sexual fantasies or feelings denotes denial.

It is important to try and elicit information, which addresses the content of their sexual fantasies. It is important to differentiate between fantasy content. For example, homosexual, sado-masochism, sexual contact with animals, or residual contact such as peeping or exhibitionism (Gebhard et al., 1965). The ages of the subjects should also be established. It is important to establish the number of sexual fantasies within each masturbation episode as well as their frequency and escalation. The role of stimulants such as pornographic magazines, videos, and television should be established, as should any internal states that trigger or intensify them.

- Logging masturbation activities/fantasies over an agreed period, e.g. a week, recording date, time, fantasy, pleasure sought and arousal. For example, did it involve a famous person or pop star? Or a complete stranger? Do they involve intercourse, oral sex, etc.? Does it involve violence or submission? Were any disinhibitors used, such as drink or drugs? Sexual fantasies are not a homogeneous phenomenon, and, as such, need to be addressed on a content basis.
- Fantasy record chart (Briggs et al., 1998).
- Masturbatory pie chart (Briggs, 1994): Where clients are asked to consider the last 100 times they have masturbated and to think about the range of different fantasies that they have used. These are then displayed as a segment of a pie chart to reflect the relative frequency of each fantasy.
- The Wilson sex fantasy questionnaire (Wilson, 1978): Offers 40 situations or actions, which they are asked to score on the following scale: 0 = never, 1 = seldom, 2 = occasionally, 3 = sometimes, 4 = often, and 5 = regularly. Examples of these questions are: 'making love out of doors in a romantic setting e.g. field of flowers, beach at night; intercourse with someone you know but have not had sex with; participating in an orgy; forcing someone to do something; being whipped or spanked; hurting a partner; being tied up; having incestuous sexual relations; having sex with someone much older than yourself; having sex with someone much younger than yourself.'
- Feelings journal: Ask them to write down how they were feeling when they had sexual fantasies, and how they enable them to get what they want.
- Rosebush fantasy exercise (Heinz et al., 1987). On a piece of paper ask them to write a fantasy describing themselves as if they were a rosebush. Ask them to include the following:

  I. 'What you look like (describe your leaves, stems, and flowers).
  II. Describe in detail where you are growing.
  III. If a rosebush could see, what would you see? What sees you?
  IV. Describe the weather today and most other days.
  V. Describe how you get nourished. Who feeds you, your roots, and the soil you are in; and where do you get you water?
  VI. Describe those who care for you, if anyone does.
  VII. Tell us what is going to happen to you next week.'

This exercise is useful in getting the offender to understand the amount of detail that will be required when looking at more intimate fantasies.

- Fantasy questionnaire (adapted from Heinz et al., 1987)*: Consists of 18 items in which they are asked to respond on how often they have the fantasies outlined. Workers can add to this according to the presenting case.
- The 'projective' technique: Where subjects are shown some very vague and unstructured pictures and asked to describe or interpret them. In doing so, they are pressured to project their own fantasies onto the picture (Wilson, 1978).
- Ideal offence fantasy (Carich and Adkerson, 1995)*.
- Paraphilic sexual fantasy questionnaire (O'Donohue et al., 1997): Contains 155 items designed to measure paraphilic and non-paraphilic fantasies. It comprises 7 scales: normal, bondage, sadism, masochism, rape, child, and other paraphilias, and they are broken down into sentences which describe specific sexual acts about which an individual may fantasise. Respondents are asked to rate the frequency at which each item is fantasised. The choices are *never*, *sometimes* (at least once in my life but less than once a week) and *frequently* (at least once a week). Examples include: 'Getting a blow-job from a woman who is enjoying it.' 'Overpowering a man and forcing him to have sex with me.' 'Rubbing a boy's penis.' 'Rubbing myself with a pair of panties until I come.'
- Erotic fantasy during heterosexual activity (Crepault and Couture, 1980): Each subject is provided with a list of 46 erotic fantasies and asked to indicate whether they had used these fantasies during sexual activities with their usual partner, or any other one. Sample questions

include: 'Scene where you relive a previous sexual relationship.' 'Scene from an erotic film that excited you.' 'Scene where you think you are a sexual superman.' 'Scene where the woman that you seduce pretends resisting.' 'Scene where you think you have another body.'

Note. Workers should be cautious when using questionnaires for the assessment of fantasies as:

- They only measure fantasy in a transparent way (Wilson, 1978): As we depend on the quality and accuracy of self-report.
- They are vulnerable to offender denial and the effect of social desirability (Beckett, 1994).
- They are rarely conducive to complete disclosure given the sensitivity of the subject.
- They may need follow-up interview time to allow the offender to debrief or expand on their written project.

4. Cognitive distortions

The role of offenders' excuses in sexual offending is a pivotal assessment area. To date, however, much of the material developed has emerged in the absence of any theoretical framework (such as that now being developed by writers such as Johnston and Ward, 1996; Ward et al., 1997; Ward et al., 1995). Whilst these authors have provided us with a framework for cognitive distortions, the work of Carich (1991; 1993) have provided us with a much broader framework for understanding 'disowning behaviours', of which cognitive distortions is just one component. This framework has been discussed earlier in the section on sexual beliefs.

Most excuses are not simply excuses but are manifestations of underlying cognitive distortions or belief systems which may play a direct role in the initiation or maintenance patterns of sexual offending (Abel et al., 1985). Others, such as Quinsey (1986) believe that they are the consequence rather than the cause of offending. The term 'cognitive' refers to an individual's internal processes, including the justifications, perceptions and judgements used by the sex offender to rationalise his child molesting behaviour. Clinically, a child molester's cognitive distortions appear to allow the offender to justify his ongoing sexual abuse of children without the anxiety, guilt and loss of self-esteem that would usually result from an individual committing behaviours contrary to the norms of society (Abel et al., 1989).

Cognitive distortions related to sexual offending are learned assumptions, sets of beliefs, and self-statements about deviant sexual behaviours such as child molestation and rape which serve to deny, justify, minimise, and rationalise an offender's actions (Bumby, 1996). These beliefs and cognitive distortions function to avoid negative self-evaluation and social disapproval and facilitate

the disengagement of the offender's inhibitions regarding sexual offending (Ward et al., 1995). For example, offenders may attribute responsibility for offending to their marital problems or a child's supposed seductiveness, or exclaim that they are entitled to satisfy their sexual needs no matter what the cost is to others (Hanson et al., 1994).

Cognitive distortions can thus be defined as:

"Thoughts which are based on erroneous perceptions; a misrepresentation of reality" (National Task Force, 1993); or as

"a statement one makes to oneself, which contains distorted information about the reality of the situation, (e.g. an offender who sexually abuses children say 'she seduced me', 'it's an education for the child', or 'it causes no harm')," (Beck, 1976), *"particularly when they are used to deny, minimise, justify or rationalise their behaviour."* (Murphy, 1990).

When these distortions are processed by the offender, they are often represented as thinking errors, defined as *"patterns of thinking which are based on distorted perceptions, therefore seeming rational on the basis of some private logic, but irrational in the light of societal reality"* (National Task Force, 1993). It can be said that this mode of thinking is the means by which the offender is able to translate fantasy into action, and subsequently to maintain their behaviour. Thinking errors become a way of life for sex offenders. They are tempting to the offender as, when these thoughts are used, they feel power and control, a sense of self-worth, and a general satisfaction. Cognitively distorting the offence allows the offender to overcome his own inhibitions and allows the offender to minimise and justify the offence, thus making the unacceptable behaviour 'acceptable'. Put simply, if the offender thought that there was nothing wrong with his behaviour, he would see no reason for stopping it (Jones and Lewis, 1990/1).

Cognitive distortions are arguably a partner for denial and minimisation for the offender. Most sex offenders deny the accusations against them, often despite overwhelming evidence to the contrary. Even in those who admit their guilt initially, there is often an effort to shift the blame from themselves. Related to this are the distorted perceptions related to the act itself. The sex offender typically sees the child as sexually provocative and as eagerly seeking sex with them. Innocent childlike behaviours (e.g. sitting in a manner, which exposes the child's underwear or excessively seeking physical contact) are often construed as indicating sexual intent. Similarly, when the offender is engaging the child in sexual acts, he will typically see passivity on the part of the child as active agreement to participate in the behaviours (Ward et al., 1995).

Sex offenders also engage in covert planning (Laws, 1989; Pithers, 1990) in which they make decisions, which they see as justified and unrelated to any explicit plan to offend. It is as though they are deliberately suppressing full awareness of their intentions to gain access to the victim, by rationalising to themselves that their decisions, at each of the steps, serves a nobler cause and then, when the ultimate opportunity to offend arises, it is an accident rather than plan. Such rationalisations obviously allow circumstances to unfold in a way that facilitates offending, but no doubt, once offending has occurred, serve to avoid any sense of guilt (Ward et al., 1995). Sex offenders frequently suspend self-regulation during their offence chain, failing to consider long-term consequences for short-term needs. As a consequence, they do not experience any emotional incongruity between their behaviour and their self-image, nor do they feel any distress concerning the responses of the victim.

An incredible, extreme example of cognitive distortions appeared in the *Wellington Evening Post* on 13 May 1997. *"I am technically guilty"*, Roger Katz, a 50 year old teacher, told the judge, *"But things are not as they seem, for I was not motivated by lust. I may have broken earthly laws, but that was only because I had to obey the celestial law of Karma . . . Yes, I had an affair with a 14 year old girl student, but this was not the first time we had met. You see, I first penetrated her in Tibet in 640 AD, when I was a teenage monk in a Buddhist monastery, and she was an old woman. She saved my life by taking an arrow out of my chest and sucking out the poison, after I had been attacked by a horseman from a rival religion, so it seemed the decent thing to do. When she turned up in my maths class last semester, I recognised her instantly, and I knew that I had to repay the debt of love and devotion that I had carried with me for 14 centuries. That is why I booked a motel room and invited her over. I have no idea what the snorkel and flippers were doing in the room. They must have been left there by a previous occupant."* (He was sentenced to 5 years imprisonment.)

Research findings
The following points have been gleaned from research and may help guide workers when exploring the issues in interview as well as deciding on their significance for further work:

- Becker and Abel (1985) have argued that cognitive distortions are a necessary prerequisite to the abuse as it allows the offender to translate their fantasies into action. Despite this, Marshall et al. (1991) found that only 21.7 per cent in their sample indicated that fantasies preceded their abuse. There is little clarity on the point at which fantasy of abuse actually occurs. It is clearly variable, and might only follow the abuse.
- Freeman-Longo (1983) found that the average

age at which sex offenders begin to have deviant sexual fantasies was 15. If they entertain them, then they develop a distorted thinking process that further condones the continuation of deviant thoughts, fantasies and behaviours.
- Pennell (1996) found no difference in cognitive distortions between young people who had been abused and those who had not. We can hypothesise that those who have may well have more entrenched cognitive distortions and that these findings hold true for adult sex offenders.
- Stermac and Segal (1989) examined the beliefs or cognitions of child molesters drawn from a treatment population and compared these to those of rapists, mental health clinicians, and lay persons. They found that child molesters perceived more benefits of sexual abuse to the child, attributed more responsibility to the child for the abuse, and attributed less overall responsibility to themselves for the offence than any of the other groups. Child molesters also endorsed more permissive attitudes about adult sexual contact with children than did the other groups. Differences of this sort suggest that the cognitions of men who have had sexual contact with children may play a contributory or facilitative role in such behaviour.
- Anecdotal reports on the content of sex offenders' cognitions do highlight many similarities, and include: ideas that children are informed and consent to, or refuse sex with an adult; that children are under no pressure to have sex with an adult; that children want sexual contact with adults; that sexual contact between adults and children is not harmful unless force is used; and that the prohibition against such activity represents an arbitrary social sanction (Finkelhor, 1984). These cognitions (and belief systems) are often modified by the offender in order to support and justify their deviant behaviour (Abel et al., 1984).
- Abel et al. (1984) hypothesised that as a child molester becomes aware of the discrepancy between sexual behaviour with children and the social mores of his culture, he begins to adjust by developing an idiosyncratic belief system of cognitions. The offenders continued sexual involvement with children is supported by the contribution of two factors: there are often no negative consequences for sexual involvement with children, such as arrest or discovery by peers, family and employers; and the offender never witnesses the negative effects suffered by their victims, since he leaves the site of the sexual involvement with the child.
- Abel et al. (1989) found that cognitive distortions tend to increase as child molestation behaviours continue. The longer the offending goes on, the more cognitive distortions they endorse. They also found that child molesters do

report beliefs and attitudes that are dramatically different from those of non-child molesters, suggesting that the normalisation of these faulty cognitions may be an integral part of the successful treatment of child molesters.

- Hayashino et al. (1995), in a study embracing incestuous offenders, extra-familial offenders, rapists, incarcerated non-sexual offenders and lay persons, found that extra-familial sex offenders have a higher level of cognitive distortion than all other groups, whilst rapists and extra-familial sex offenders have a greater fear of negative evaluation. They may hold negative attitudes towards women that contribute to their maintaining a sexual and emotional interest in children. They were unable to establish whether these distorted beliefs were the cause and effect of their offending, but it did appear that they had a greater need to minimise and justify their behaviour. They also found that the lay persons group endorsed several cognitive distortions. For example, at least a quarter of the lay persons believed that a child who does not resist an adult's sexual advances really wants to have sex with the adult; that a child's flirting with an adult means she or he wants to have sex with the adult; and that if an adult has sex with a young child, it prevents the child from having sexual hang-ups in the future. In addition, 19 per cent of the lay persons reported some likelihood of engaging in sexual contact with a child if assured they would not be punished.

- Marshall and Eccles (1991) have noted that the problematic attitudes of these offenders concern not only their view of sex with children but also their more general views of children. For instance, Howells (1978) showed that child molesters saw children as non-dominant and compliant and viewed adults as dominant and threatening. They also tended to idealise children and to see them as having positive attributes that allowed the offenders both to feel more comfortable with children and to exercise non-sexual mastery over them. Gore (1988) also found that child molesters were more likely than other sex offenders and 'normals' to see children as seductive, as wanting sex with an adult, as able to consent to sex with adults, and as unharmed by such activities. Stermac and Segal (1990) essentially replicated these findings with the added observations that child molesters judged children to be more responsible than the offenders for sexual contacts with an adult and are more likely to benefit from the experience.

- As we have already pointed out earlier, many sexual offenders may also have certain deficiencies or distortion's which impair their ability to manage their lives responsibly or constructively. For example, they may have poor social skills and shyness, leading to avoidance of female or male peers. Feeling alone and perceiving themselves to be isolated from socially appropriate partners, they may seek primary social gratification and acceptance from children. They resort to children for intimacy and to gain a sense of competency and/or adequacy (Green, 1995).

- These points having been noted, most of us experience cognitive distortions, or errors in the way we think, at one time or another. We use them to push our point of view or to defend ourselves. However, when cognitive distortions continue or become extreme, they may poison our ability to function in a healthy manner. Steen (1993) pointed out that there are special kinds of distorted thinking common to most sex offenders. These include: misinterpreting what their victim is thinking, such as believing the person is asking for sex when the person really isn't and doesn't want it; excusing their sexual offences; minimising the harm they have done, and denying responsibility.

- There are always consequences for behaviour that is based on distorted thinking: what you think affects the way you feel and act and everything you do has many effects on yourself and others. Distorted thinking can give you a false sense of being different from, more important than, or more deserving than others. It can lead to a belief that you have a right to do whatever you want (Freeman-Longo et al., 1996).

- Hartley (1998) explored the cognition incest offenders in treatment use to overcome their initial inhibitions against offending and to maintain their offending once begun. The cognitions identified are grouped into four separate categories (with some overlap):

Cognition relating to socio-cultural factors

Cognition related to socio-cultural factors typically involve beliefs based on messages offenders perceive, or misperceive, from society that they use to rationalise their offending behaviour. They include: the weak sanctions against sexual abuse in our society, particularly as few ever face severe consequences for their behaviour; the acceptance that the use of alcohol excuses their behaviour, as society is more tolerant and understanding of crimes committed while intoxicated; or that their behaviour wasn't serious as it doesn't extend to intercourse, based on societal tolerance of sexual interest in children as long as certain lines are not crossed. Knowing that the legal consequences for sexually offending are weak may make it easier for an offender to overcome initial inhibitions against offending.

Cognition used to reduce the fear of disclosure

Cognition used to reduce fear of disclosure typically involved some very real parent–child relationship problems that may have made it difficult for the child to disclose. For example, they may include: a knowledge of conflict in the mother–child relationship, increasing the child's fear of maternal retaliation; fear by the child of hurting their mother; or concern that the child's mother either wouldn't believe a disclosure or they could talk them out of taking action. The offender often uses these problems to his advantage in overcoming his inhibitions against offending. Offenders also used their perceptions that the child was somehow 'interested' in the contact to reduce their fear of disclosure. Interestingly, they found that the majority of offenders did not think about the possibility of disclosure, even though all knew what the possible consequences of their behaviour were, but they were able to set aside any concern and proceed with the offence.

Cognition used to diminish responsibility

Cognition used to diminish responsibility typically involved distortions related to the context in which the contact began. A perception that the contact started accidentally or innocently (i.e. a game), did not involve force or coercion, or that the child reacted 'positively' (or didn't react negatively) to the offender, served to reduce the offender's sense of responsibility for the abuse.

Cognition related to permission seeking

Respondents gave themselves permission to offend both by interpreting the child's reaction as neutral or favourable or by asking the child directly for permission. This does not imply that the child colluded with the contact; instead the offender typically observed and misinterpreted the child's response or reaction as permission to continue. Offenders described asking their daughters if the contact was 'OK' and only doing what she 'let him do'. If the child did not resist, displayed no reaction, or seemed interested, this was permission to ignore inhibitions and continue the abuse.

- The study demonstrates that offenders do not just use these rationalisations to excuse their behaviour after disclosure. Rather, offenders reported using these rationalisations as a way of overcoming their internal inhibitions against offending.
- Ward et al. (1995) have proposed a theory on the role of cognitions in sexual offending that mirrors much of what was found in that study. Their theory suggests that offenders engage in a process of *cognitive deconstruction* related to offence events. According to Ward et al., cognitive deconstruction is a process in which *"people attempt to avoid the negative implications of self-awareness in order to escape from the effects of traumatic or particularly stressful experience."* In a cognitively deconstructed state, self-awareness is suspended or stunted and the person is typically focused on sensations in the here and now. While in this state, a person is not engaged in appropriate self-evaluative processes. This suspension of self-awareness may serve to help people reduce inhibitions and be more likely to violate their usual moral and personal standards. This theory of cognitive deconstruction may explain the offenders' lack of understanding of the child's or other's reactions to the abuse and their lack of fear about disclosure. Many offenders thus suspend their self-awareness of the impact or consequences of their behaviour so that this awareness would not inhibit them both beginning and continuing the abuse.

- There is likely to be a relationship between cognitive factors and the offence chain. Models of the offence chain (e.g. Ward et al., 1995) typically specify the cognitive, behavioural, motivational and contextual factors associated with a sexual offence. These models make explicit the temporal component of offending and suggest that the functional role of cognitive distortions may change over the offence cycle. Some of these cognitive processes change markedly throughout the offending sequence as a result of increased sexual arousal and fluctuating mood states. The ways in which offenders interpret, explain and evaluate both victims' and their own actions can function to precipitate and entrench offending behaviour (Johnston and Ward, 1996).
- Ward et al. (1998) provided us with a descriptive model to clarifying sex offenders' cognition concerning their offending behaviour. They argue that we need to extend our focus from post-offence cognition to all phases of the offending cycle, which consists of four sets of categories: *offence chain*, *cognitive operations*, *cognitive content* and *meta-variables*. Given the detail of their arguments, the reader is advised to refer to the full paper for a detailed discussion of the points raised. The model aims to clarify statements made by the offender rather than to identify underlying distorting schemata. It offers the most advanced and dynamic conceptualisation of cognition.
- Ward et al. (1997) provided us with an excellent review of the available literature on cognitive distortions using a social cognition framework. They argued that the study of cognitive factors in sexual offending has been hampered by the lack of a theoretical framework. They note that there are a number of cognitive variables in addition to distortions (which they define as offence supportive beliefs or attitudes): such as cognitive structures (e.g. schemata), operations (e.g. information processing) and products (e.g. self-statements, attributions) and sex offenders may differ from non-offenders on some, but not

all, of these variables. They argued that we need to assess more of these components if we are to effectively intervene to treat these sex offenders. That being stated, it is clear that specialist assessment is clearly needed in these areas.

- Bumby (1996) found that child molesters are likely to have more cognitive distortions about sexually offending behaviour in general and, thus, may tend to justify numerous forms of sexual deviance rather than exclusively holding distorted beliefs about child molestation.

Tools

The goals of assessing cognitive distortions include:

- To separate superficial distortions of defence from those that are more deeply entrenched, since the latter are commonly associated with a sexual preference for children and indicate an individual at greater risk of re-offending.
- To identify and elicit the origins, history and specific content details of each distortion.
- To identify the triggers that precipitate the offending cycle as the basis of offering alternatives.
- Whether certain moods or situations make such distortions more likely to occur (e.g. drinking).
- How they behave when they occur.
- To isolate the origins of their cognitive distortions, e.g. seeing children as having adult characteristics, which enable them to be sexually provocative and being able to consent; beliefs about women (e.g. demanding); or social skill deficits.
- To list the offenders' excuses for their behaviour and anyone they attribute any culpability to.
- To reinforce to the offender that these distortions feed their offending behaviour and need modifying.
- To determine future risk/relapse.
- To challenge the distortions and empower the offender to move from a passive to an active account of their offending.
- To allow the offender to accept the responsibility for their actions and to consider the harmful effects their behaviour has had on their victims.
- To use the cognitive distortions as an index of change, repeating assessments at various stages of the work.
- To determine treatment viability (adapted from Beckett, 1994; Briggs et al., 1998; Jones and Lewis, 1990/1; Moore, 1991).

For many offenders, the cognitive distortions they exhibit are essentially 'defence mechanisms' constructed during the course of the abuse to cope with guilt and anxiety associated with the abusive behaviour. Because of this, and because the legal system is more likely to increase the severity of punishment for those who fully disclose, workers need to recognise the investment the offender has

in maintaining their defences. For this reason, workers may need to use direct confrontation, in the knowledge that this may not necessarily be productive, since it might serve merely to drive the distortions 'underground', where they are no longer accessible to exploration and change. It is appropriate, however, to be inquisitive and offer hypotheses as part of the work.

Adopting an approach which involves eliciting, rather than immediately confronting cognitive distortions can put considerable demands upon the worker, particularly where offenders are disclosing beliefs and attitudes which provoke anger and outrage in the worker. Moreover, it requires the worker to constantly be aware of the risk of collaborating with the offender in their distorted belief system. Few sex offenders will spontaneously abandon well-practised and emotionally satisfying cognition and actions simply because they have been discovered (Moore, 1991).

Suggested materials to elicit required information include:

- Brainstorm a list of excuses, rationalisations or distortions that they have used to 'justify' their sexually abusive behaviour. We need to cover their pre and post-offence distortions as they may not necessarily be the same.
- Most offenders need to know that they made various types of thinking errors when committing their sexual offences. Their thinking is not based on real facts. They may offer some of the following statements to justify their behaviour:

—They didn't stop me doing it.
—They didn't say no.
—I think they liked it. It gives her as much pleasure as it does me. She must like it, she responds.
—I'll only go so far and then stop.
—Sex can't hurt children.
—I only did it once or twice.
—I only touched them—nothing more.
—It happened on the spur of the moment.
—It happened to me at that age.
—Someone has to teach them about sex.
—It comforts the child.
—I was drunk/ill/mad.
—I was only showing her how to insert a tampon.
—I saw my friend doing it to her too.
—I get a buzz from doing it.
—I did it because I love them.
—When women say no, they really mean yes.
—I deserve whatever I want.
—Rape is just forceful sex; women like being raped.
—Some children know more about sex than adults.
—Children can make me do things against my will.

—I was checking 'it' works.
—Unsatisfactory marital sexual relationships.
—Everyone wants to, but most don't dare.
—Somebody made me.
—I didn't know it was wrong.
—It's only the law that says its wrong.
—It's a good form of punishment.
—It's unlikely to be discovered.
—It's better me than someone else.
—She never told anyone.
—It's an urge no-one can control.
—It's an expression of love (adapted from, Fawcett, 1989; and Willis, 1993).

[For a more extensive catalogue of common cognitive distortions used by sex offenders, the reader is referred to Abel et al. (1984b); Abel et al. (1985); and Willis (1993).]

- The offender can by asked which of the distortions listed above apply to them, and what others they might want to add to the list. Steen (1993) has suggested that they be advised to ask the following questions of themselves if they are unclear about whether they are thinking correctly or incorrectly: Is this something someone might find harmful, embarrassing or unpleasant? Is this something I would feel uncomfortable telling others about, e.g. workmates or friends? Is this something I wouldn't like someone to do to me if I were their age or in this situation? Am I breaking any laws or rules by doing this? Would there be negative consequences if I were caught doing this? If they answer 'no' to all of the above then we might assume that their thinking is correct.
- Thinking error journal (Green, 1995): This is the same as the masturbation log in that the offender is asked to keep a journal to record daily thinking errors. It should be completed daily embracing the thinking errors as well as the situations surrounding them. This is useful for the offender as it provides them with practice in identifying those errors whilst also providing the workers with an opportunity for assessing the offenders motivation and degree of self-awareness. Since many sex offenders are rather concrete in their thought structures, they find structures like this very helpful in effecting change and for holding themselves accountable. Anyone who is unable to recognise thinking errors is unlikely to benefit from further 'treatment' work. Conversely, just because they can recognise their distortions does not equate with them shifting in their beliefs, although it does at least indicate willingness to explore their cognitive process and assumptions (Willis, 1993).
- Alexandria Associates (nd) identified the following examples of thinking errors, which the workers can try to use for each offender to build up their individual profile of cognitive distortions:

—*Excuses*: allow the offender to have a reason for everything other than accept responsibility for what has happened.
—*Blaming*: can be used as an excuse not to solve the problem and can be used to build up resentment toward someone else for 'causing' whatever happened.
—*Pity pot*: is used by the offender to get others to feel sorry for them, often to make them feel better and distance them from feeling in the wrong.
—*Justifying*: is where they find a way of explaining the reason for things as they are.
—*Redefining*: allows them to shift the focus of an issue to avoid solving the problem, or as a power play to get the focus away from the sex offender, or the real issue.
—*Pet me*: is their ploy to receive 'pats on the head' for something. They want to be noticed or applauded, thus feeding their selfishness and their own needs. For example, completing tasks to elicit approval from the workers rather than for the purpose of learning or changing behaviour.
—*Lying*: is done in many ways to confuse, distort, or make fools of other people. This might be making up things that are simply not true; states things that are partially true, but leaves out certain things; and when they behave or act in a way that isn't accurate or suggests something that is not true.
—*Uniqueness*: allows them to think they are special, and thus different from all the other offenders.
—*Making fools of*: other people so they experience power and control, a sense of dependency on them, and then they deliberately fail—making others regret that they counted on them.
—*Assuming*: what others think and feel as they are arrogant and believe that they are that powerful, and that others don't have thoughts, feelings and attitudes.
—*Fact stacking*: where they arrange the facts for their own benefit, so that they feel both powerful and comfortable.
—*Phoniness*: occurs when the offender pretends or projects themselves as being co-operative and helpful, while in fact, a great deal of manipulation is taking place. They might be nice to others, but only as they expect something in return.
—*Minimising*: allows them to believe what they have done is not really important. They can minimise the entire act, thus rendering their actions unimportant, insignificant and not really as bad.

—*Vagueness*: is a tactic used to avoid being pinned down, thus making it difficult to examine the detail or the reality of their actions.

—*Anger*: can be used to manipulate and control others, and can be used to redirect the focus onto their anger or outrage, rather than the offences.

—*Secretiveness*: allows them to avoid examining the reality of the situation. They may do this under the guise of the importance of confidentiality, or to regain power as we as workers want information they hold.

—*Keeping score*: when they feel angry and hostile internally, rather than working on these feelings, they choose to keep track of mistakes others make, rather than express anger in a healthy way. So, when they are criticised by the worker, they deflect back to mistakes the worker or other professional has made.

—*Grandiosity*: to make little things into very important things, with the consequence that the important things get left for the insignificant issues. This may well have its seeds sown over several sessions before being used by the offender.

—*Victim status*: of themselves, to elicit sympathy for themselves in the hope it will lead to their behaviour being overlooked and, if not, they seek rescue from others who they have coaxed to accept their position.

—*Let's fight*: when they set a situation up (e.g. the provision of upsetting information) where the workers fight between themselves or with others and they become an innocent by-stander.

—*Puzzlement*: is where they seem puzzled and confused about the reality of the situation. They present genuine concern about issues, but by feigning confusion, others around them will take it upon themselves to figure out the confusion.

—*Helpless*: occurs when they present themselves as being helpless, incapable, and in need of others, e.g. their inability to write. This can lead to others helping them, thus allowing the offender to maintain their overall control of the situation.

—*You're okay, I'm okay*: where they are extremely positive in order to avoid looking at the reality of the offences. They work hard at being co-operative and supportive of the workers, paying them compliments and only addressing the crime or the victim in a superficial and general way.

—*My way*: their need for power is clear throughout. They want things to be done under their terms and under their conditions. They thus answer the question they want to answer, rather than the one posed.

—*The hop overs*: are where they divert the discussion to something more comfortable, thus keeping the discussion moving about, rather than specific.

- Murphy (1990) has also produced a useful model of cognitive distortions which allows the distortions employed by offenders to be categorised under specific cognitive processes, such as justifying reprehensible conduct ('it was sex education'), mis-perceiving consequences ('the child didn't suffer'), or devaluing or attributing blame to the victim ('she was a very seductive child'). Abel et al. (1989) identified six base categories of cognitive distortion in their sample: 'Child-adult sex helps the child'; 'Children initiate child-adult sex for specific reasons'; 'Adults initiate child-adult sex for specific reason'; 'The child's behaviour shows their desire for child-adult sex'; 'Adults can predict when child-adult sex will damage the child in the future'; 'Child-adult sex is or will be acceptable in society.' Which of these categories is used most by the offender subject to the assessment?

Useful questionnaires include:

- Bumby cognitive distortions scales (Bumby, 1995)*: This is a split scale covering molestation and rape. The 'molest scale' comprises 38 items and the 'rape scale' consists of 36 items.
- Abel and Becker cognition's scale (Abel et al., 1984)*: A 29 item scale that is designed to assess the thoughts, ideas and attitudes men might use to excuse their sexual behaviour with children. It measures cognitive distortions regarding the sexual abuse of children on a 5 point scale, with all items scored in the same direction, i.e. the lower the score, the more deviant the cognition. Investigators using the scale have reported that child molesters endorse significantly more distorted thoughts about child molestation than either rapists or community controls (Abel et al., 1989).
- The sex offender cognitive disowning behavioural distortion scale (Carich and Metzger, 1996)*: This scale measures the degree of cognitive distortions and disowning behaviours that an offender displays globally (everyday lifestyle behaviours) and offence-specific behaviours. The disowning behaviours scores are: denial, lying, justifying, minimising, enticement, power games, depersonalisation/ownership, self-pity, extremes, apathy, fallacy of fairness, dumping and trusting, blaming, alienation and isolation.
- Sex offender information questionnaire (Hogue, 1994)*: A 43 item questionnaire designed to measure offence related denial as well as the sex offenders' cognitive distortions about their offences and victims. The questionnaire was

originally developed on a sample of imprisoned sexual offenders prior to undertaking treatment. The four factor analytically derived sub-scale measure denial of victim harm, denial of sexual motivation, denial of responsibility, and denial of treatment need. These sub-scales have shown to be reliable, and relate to both attitudinal and physiological arousal measures in a consistent manner. The measures have been shown to be a useful measure of clinical change and normative information is available both pre and post-treatment samples.

- Thinking errors/cognitive distortions check-list (Carich and Adkerson, 1995)*: A check-list of thinking errors/cognitive distortions (37 items) and defensive structures (11 items) designed to provide a quick summary of those utilised by the client. It is scored by choosing either that the distortion is global (G), or specific to their offending behaviour (0).

- The multiphasic sex inventory (Nichols and Molinder, 1984): Contains two sub-scales, which can tap cognitive distortions: namely the justifications and the cognitive distortions and immaturity sub-scales. The justification scale is a 24 item scale containing various justifications that sex offenders may use to explain their offences. It includes items labelled 'psychological justifications', such as 'My sexual offence occurred as a result of my wife's lack of understanding of me' and 'My sexual offence occurred because of stresses in my life'. There are also a number of items related to attribution of blame to the victim, such as 'My sexual offence would not have occurred if the victim had not been sexually loose'. The cognitive distortions and immaturity sub-scale are more complex. Some of the items tap cognitive distortions, such as 'My problem is not sexual, it is that I really love children'; thinking errors such as 'I'm often hurt by the behaviour of others' or 'I have suffered more hurt in my life than other people.' The sub-scale consists of 21 items designed to assess the offender's self-accountability for his sexual offences, as well as his propensity to adopt a victim stance.

- The Burt rape myth acceptance scale (Burt, 1980)*: Measures distorted beliefs about the rape of adult women. It includes 11 items related to justification of rape and victim blaming, with each item scored on a 7 point Likert-type scale ranging from 'strongly agree' to 'strongly disagree'. Eight additional items relate to false accusations and the respondent's likelihood to believe various individual's claims of rape (e.g. best friend, black woman, white woman). Research with the scale has revealed that men who sexually aggress against adult women endorse a significantly higher number of distorted beliefs about rape than do non-sexually aggressive community controls and university students (Burt, 1980; 1984).

5. Denial and responsibility

"The single most powerful characteristic in child sex offenders is their capacity for denial. They deny their abuse not only to others but to themselves. They deny the true number of their offences, the number of children they have abused, and the true ages of the children abused (abuse of older children is more socially and legally acceptable). They minimise their offences in a multiplicity of ways. As if it was a one off, a coincidence, an accident; it just happened. They put the responsibility onto the children: she wanted it too; she really seduced me; these three year olds can be really provocative." (Watts, 1989 in Gocke, 1991)

Denial is therefore virulent in sex offenders, presenting itself in various forms. Leberg (1997) has defined denial as *"all communication by the offender in which he insists that he did not commit the crime, gives reasons of 'proofs' intended to persuade others of his innocence, or attempts to minimise or distort the extent of his sexual deviance."*

Chaffin (1994) reminds us to be cautious in distinguishing 'denial' (a psychological defence mechanism) from 'lying' (a social behaviour). Lying is often motivated by fear of consequences, particularly short-term consequences whereas denial might be thought of as motivated by a need to maintain a favourable image of self or important others or by fear of overwhelming aversive emotion.

Denial may be motivated by: anticipation of aversive events if responsibility is accepted, e.g. guilt, social stigma, marital breakdown, abuse, punishment, therapy; modelling (e.g. by other prisoners, group members, workers); reward (e.g. power over the worker); and ignorance.

Most sex offenders are referred for assessment via child protection conferences or the courts, and are therefore rarely co-operative or active participants in the assessment process. Whilst this will inevitably impact on the information provided, it may not extend to all the areas of information required. For example, it maybe easier for them to admit to areas such as social incompetence or having a drink problem, than it is to acknowledge that they have committed sexual offences.

Types of denial

If we are to effectively respond to denial, it is important that we furnish workers with a detailed, yet practical framework, which sets out the offender's distorted representations of reality. Figure 10 sets out 15 different dimensions of offender denial, reflecting the reality that it is a spectrum and not a single state. Workers should find that offenders move between these dimensions as the

```
┌─────────────────────────────────────────────────────────┐
│  Hopeless                                     Denial      │
│                                                           │
│        Complete denial of responsibility                 │
│        Attack                                             │
│        Denial of facts                                    │
│        Denial of awareness                                │
│        Denial of intent                                   │
│        Denial of responsibility                           │
│            Psychological                                  │
│            Behaviour                                      │
│        Denial of impact                                   │
│            Intrusiveness                                  │
│            Harm                                           │
│            Seriousness                                    │
│        Denial of frequency                                │
│        Denial of fantasy or planning/grooming             │
│            oneself and the environment                    │
│        Denial of deviant sexual arousal                   │
│        Admission, with                                    │
│            Justification                                  │
│            Minimisation                                   │
│            Fabrication                                    │
│            Mental Illness                                 │
│        Guilty, but not guilty                             │
│        After conviction                                   │
│        Denial of denial                                   │
│        No denial/ acceptance of responsibility            │
│                                                           │
│  Hopeful                                  Responsibility  │
└─────────────────────────────────────────────────────────┘
```

Figure 10: A multi-dimensional typology of denial (Calder, 1998b).

assessment (and treatment work) unfolds (Salter, 1988). These dimensions are not neat compartments as they *frequently overlap*. Denial is not therefore a 'yes' or 'no' phenomenon, but is rather a continuum. Between the two extremes, offenders vary considerably on the level of responsibility they take for their behaviour. Offenders who can project blame on others and find excuses for their behaviour basically are blocked from truly recognising the impact their behaviour has on victims. The typology we present is **not** a continuum given the real difficulty in grading the dimensions suggested.

A multi-dimensional typology of denial
Complete denial of responsibility

Here, the offender completely denies the behaviour described in the allegation, protests their innocence, and accuses others of fabricating lies about them. This is primary denial, and may include statements such as: 'I didn't do it, (even if I got blamed for it)'; 'I was out of the area at the time'; 'She's lying; she made it up'; and 'I was drunk, I must have blacked out.' This is the first reaction of most offenders: they act shocked, surprised, or even indignant about such an allegation. We should never be thrown by strong initial denial from the offender.

Attack

Some sex offenders can use this approach many times during an investigation or prosecution. This reaction consists of attacking or going on the offensive. The offender may harass, threaten, or bribe victims and witnesses; attack the reputation and personal life of the workers; attack the motives of the police or prosecutors; claim the case is selective prosecution; raise issues such as gay rights (if the child victim is the same gender as the offender); and enlist the support of groups and organisations. Physical violence also has to be considered a very real possibility (Lanning, 1986). These reactions are a severe example of denying the real truth of their abuse emerging and a denial of the process of justice.

Denial of facts

Denial of facts can take different forms. They may rationalise the fact that they have been convicted in a court by saying that they were framed. Alternatively, they may not deny that the sexual abuse occurred, they simply state that they were not the offender. It might occur when there is a denial of events on specific days and will often involve the use of alibis, which are clung to despite overwhelming evidence to the contrary. This denial may be aided by relatives, friends, neighbours and others. They may claim that they did have sexual relations with the victims, but it was not an offence as they consented or did not resist, or because the victims received some emotional benefit from the sexual experience, or because they were tricked into thinking the victims were older. Another scenario is where they admit to the act but then go on to deny that the interaction was sexual in nature (e.g. they were administering cream). Typically, the offender will view himself as the victim and will protest his innocence with righteous indignation. The denial of facts position is often assumed by the family when they act as if the abuse has not happened or they ignore salient facts about the abuse. The offender may own the offence of which he is accused, but may represent this offence as the only deviant act committed.

Denial of awareness

This is a process in which the possibility of offending behaviour is considered, although conscious knowledge of the abuse is denied. This type of denial is demonstrated by an offender claiming lapses in memory or through alleged drug and alcohol induced blackouts. They may claim that they know nothing about it or that they do not remember. They may claim their judgement, as well as their memory, was suspended for periods of time, when they were intoxicated.

Denial of intent

Here, the offender may admit some parts of the offence, but they deny that there was any intent on their part to commit the offence. Examples would include: 'It just happened', or 'I didn't want it to happen, things just got out of control', or ' Is it a crime to hug a child?' Workers challenging this view will need to refer to the concept of pre-offence planning as set out very clearly by Finkelhor (1984), and discussed in more detail by Calder in Chapter 4.

Denial of responsibility

This describes a process of inappropriate displacement of responsibility on to non-offending objects. A range of behaviours, emotions, and cognition in which the offender and significant others blame people, substances, or circumstances other than the perpetrator of the abuse. Offenders displaying this position will often attribute their participation in the offence to seductive behaviour by the victim, problems with the spouse, or benevolent intentions such as educating the child for future sexual encounters (Winn, 1996). This might include:

(a) Psychological

This is a more general form of denial of responsibility. It is where the offender does not focus on the concrete details of the alleged offence, as they maintain they are not the kind of person to commit such acts. This 'nice guy' defence is built on the premise that they are the pillar of the community, a devoted family man, with no prior arrests, and a victim of many personal problems. This tactic can be effective where people retain the belief that most sex offenders are 'strangers' or societal misfits (Lanning, 1986). They may try to discredit the victims by calling the victims liars or vindictive.

(b) Behaviour

This is where external factors and mitigating circumstances are put forward to explain their offending. They may make the child responsible for the abuse saying that the child triggered the abuse by their behaviour, or they may say: 'Yes, I did it, but you can't blame me. If my wife hadn't left me, this wouldn't have happened.'

Denial of impact

This is a form of self-preservation in which the offender and significant members of his family or social network minimise or ignore the emotional, social, or physical ramifications of the offender's abusive behaviour. This process can relate to the offender's victims or to the impact of the crisis on the family as a consequence of disclosure (Winn, 1996). The offender may argue that the victim will fully recover and thus will not suffer any long-term effects, or that they have other sexual experience, thus rendering the abuse of no consequence. It might include:

(a) Intrusiveness

Some offenders will admit some sexual acts and deny others. They may admit masturbating their victims and performing oral sex on them, but will deny actually penetrating them. Examples would include 'I only fondled her' or 'I didn't sodomise him, no matter what he says.' This is often noted when the offender minimises the extent of their previous offensive behaviour, the number of past victims, the frequency of their past offences and the degree of force they may have used.

(b) Harm

This occurs when offenders may admit aspects of the offence, but deny that the victims were harmed. For example, they may say 'I did it, but it didn't hurt him, certainly not as bad as they say'; 'It didn't hurt me when I was abused'; 'When I had sex with my daughter I knew at the time it was my responsibility but I didn't hurt her'; 'She never asked me not to do it'; or 'It was a loving thing'. In this sense, they may portray the child as an active or willing participant in the abuse. They may deny any right of the child to say 'no'. The denial of harm allows the offender to pretend that their victims didn't suffer as well as preventing them from seeing their victims as people with thoughts and feelings about what happened to them. This will result in the offender seeing children simply as objects.

(c) Seriousness

This follows on from where the offender has no concept of the severity of their acts, any long-term harm to their victims, or the difficulties involved in changing their pattern of offending behaviour. They may simply say 'It won't happen again', without accepting the likelihood of further abuse occurring; they may deny any abuse of power; they may deny any previous history of sexually deviant behaviour and/or any ongoing sexual problems. They may even present themselves as non-sexual beings. Offenders in this category are unlikely to want to change.

Denial of frequency

The offenders statement of how many times the abuse occurred may be much less than what the victim says occurred, for example, 'I did it, but only a few times, not the 20 times he says'. It is not unreasonable for the worker to double the frequency of admitted abuse, similar to a GP taking a history of alcohol or tobacco use.

Denial of fantasy or planning/grooming oneself and the environment

Some offenders admit the abuse, but deny any (internal) fantasy or (contextual) planning involved in organising the abuse. Offenders demonstrating this position will deny grooming themselves by fantasising deviant material or justifying the abuse to themselves. Similarly, they will deny any manipulation used in securing a victim. Rather, the abuse will be described as if it came 'out of the blue', with no warning to the offenders; or they may say 'I abused children, but the thought of it disgusts me' or 'I never get turned on when I think about it.' They may cite statements that the offence happened on the spur of the moment, for example: 'Her mother was out, she came downstairs in her night dress with no pants on, to watch her favourite TV programme and ...'. They may state that the offence was an isolated, inexplicable incident, or completely out of character, e.g. 'It's never happened before ... it won't ever happen again ... I don't behave like this, I'm happily married ...'

Denial of deviant sexual arousal and inappropriate sexualisation of non-sexual problems

This describes a form of denial in which the offender and his family ascribe intentions for offending to non-sexual reasons. Instead of acknowledging the offence as sexual in nature, this position describes a range of thoughts, feelings, and behaviours which minimise or ignore the fact that the offender has a problem with paraphilic or inappropriate sexual behaviour (such as arousal, interest, or preferences), (Winn, 1996). Many offenders may deny only the sexual offence and intent and be candid about all the other requested information from the workers.

Admission, with ...

(a) Justification

A sex offender typically attempts to justify his behaviour to the police. This maybe where the commission of the act is admitted, but where the extent and seriousness of the behaviour is often minimised and blame deflected onto life events or the victim. Consequently little guilt or blame is felt. This may involve pretending that the abuse was a normal/educational activity: 'I was teaching him about sex', or 'I was checking her out because she said she hurt down there'. They may outline the offence and argue that it included nothing unlawful (e.g. the child 'consented', or they did not know how old a certain victim was), or say that children often make up stories about being sexually abused. They may justify what they have done, saying 'She was sleeping with her boyfriend as well ...'. They may argue that the victim encouraged them, initiating the process and taking the lead, as well as enjoying the sexual encounter. Many argue that the victim hasn't disclosed until now because of these factors. Even where the offender has been seduced by a victim, and they are promiscuous, a crime has still been committed, and such a justification has no meaning. Others will simply believe they have done nothing at all wrong. The offender might claim that he cares for these children more than their parents do and that what he does is beneficial to the child.

(b) Minimisation

If the evidence against the offender rules out total denial, the offender may attempt to minimise what they have done, both in quantity and quality. Offenders minimise their own responsibility for their offences in three ways: attributing blame to the victim, making external (situational) attribu-

tions (such as stressful circumstances, social pressure or provocation) and making irresponsible internal attributions (such as their deprived childhood, their hormones or sex drive). It is also important to recognise that even seemingly co-operative victims may also minimise the quantity and quality of acts. If a certain act was performed 20 times, the victim might claim it only happened ten, and the offender might claim it only happened once. Victims may also deny particular sexual acts, such as anal intercourse by adolescent males. Limited and highly selective admission is commonplace, with the all important planning and fantasising frequently being denied. Here, whilst the offender admits the offence, they use the device of making it sound much less serious than other evidence shows it to be: e.g., 'I only brushed up against her just the once', 'I only touched her', 'It wasn't a big deal', or 'I only put the tip in'. When minimising the full extent of their behaviour, they frequently say that the child precipitated or collaborated with their own abuse. They may also minimise the full extent of their sexual problems. They may also be knowledgeable about the law and might, therefore, be motivated to admit to those acts that carry lesser consequences.

(c) Fabrication

Some of the cleverest sex offenders come up with ingenious stories to explain their behaviour. For example, doctors saying they are researching male youth prostitution. A teacher claimed that his students had such a desperate need for attention and affection that they practically threw themselves at him and misunderstood his resulting affection for sexual advances. Another offender said that his sado-masochistic photographs of children were part of a child discipline programme. One offender claimed that some children made the sexually explicit videotape without his knowledge and he kept it only to show their parents. Workers clearly need to challenge such explanations and attempt to disprove them (Lanning, 1986).

(d) Mental illness

When all other tactics fail, the offender may feign mental illness. Few do so until they are either arrested or charged. Such a diagnosis simply re-frames the need for treatment and never excuses their behaviour.

Guilty, but not guilty

This is where the offender will try to make a deal in order to avoid a public trial. Whilst this has the advantage of sparing the victim the trauma of giving evidence, it allows the offender to plead, in essence, to 'guilty, but not guilty'. In the UK, this can be plea bargaining to a lesser offence. The offender might also say they are pleading guilty to spare the child, or that they cannot afford to contest the charges, but don't accept their guilt despite their pleas. This can confuse the victims further (Lanning, 1986).

After conviction

Post-conviction, and often incarceration, some offenders ask to speak to law enforcement officials in order to share information about organised abuse, including child sex rings, child pornography, abduction of children etc., as this allows them to contextualise and minimise their abuses in the broader framework. It also allows them to plea for a reduced sentence (Lanning, 1986).

Denial of denial

Is a description of the offender's and the family's behaviour which minimises or disqualifies the fact that denial is a necessary means of psychological protection to cope with the shame generated in the maintenance of abusive behaviour. Accepting this fact often enables the offender to monitor themselves better, as they realise that denial has a purpose and cannot be cured but, rather, observed and managed (Winn, 1996).

No denial

This is where the offender's account of the events is essentially the same as the allegation. Examples include: 'I did it. It's my responsibility'; 'I did everything s/he said I did, and there are things I did that s/he didn't mention'; 'I'm sure I hurt him, though I don't know how badly', and 'Even though I hurt him, sometimes I still get turned on when I think about it.' It is very important that we don't allow offenders who start at this point to avoid some detailed assessment work, as it can be a clever tactic to avoid detailed internal enquiry.

Stages of denial

It is clear from this typology, that denial is a spectrum and never a single state. The worker would expect the offender to move between various positions as the work unfolds. As an excellent accompaniment to this typology, Laflen and Sturm (1994) have looked at denial as a series of stages which the sexual offender will go through cyclically as the work unfolds. This will usually extend beyond the assessment phase into treatment.

The first stage is denial of the behaviour, in which offenders deny categorically that they committed any type of offence. The underlying function of the denial for the offenders is to protect themselves from rejection and to preserve the idealised self-image. The goals in this stage are for the offenders to talk honestly about their behaviours, understand the concept of cycles of behaviour, begin improving their self-image by beginning to take responsibility for themselves, and to begin trusting themselves and the relationship with the workers, by beginning to take small risks of honesty. For the worker, the goals are to provide clear, consistent structure in an honest, nurturing manner regarding the boundaries and expectations of the work.

The second stage is minimisation of the seriousness of the behaviours and is driven by their need to save themselves from the pain of facing the fact that they have a problem and that their behaviour hurts others, as well as from facing further shame. The goal of the second stage of denial is for offenders to realise that they have a serious problem and need help, and for them to realise their behaviours caused serious harm to their victims. An additional goal is for the offenders to begin to challenge the cognitive distortions, which is necessary for them to begin to move forward.

The third stage is denial of responsibility for their behaviours. The function of the denial for the offenders in this stage is to preserve their cognitive distortion that if they didn't plan the offence then they are 'not that bad'. This thinking error is intended to protect them from facing the shame and integrating a more reality-based self-image. The goals of this stage are to work with the offender to continue to identify the cycle of their offence and to accept that through their thoughts, feelings and behaviours they planned and executed their offence, as opposed to their offence having been impulsive and the result of some trauma they may have experienced as a child.

The fourth and final stage of denial is full admission of the behaviours accompanied by an acceptance of responsibility for the behaviours and genuine guilt about them. Upon resolution of this stage, the offender is able to clearly identify the thoughts, feelings, and behaviours in their offence cycle and have begun to develop specific relapse prevention strategies. Offenders who are able to complete and begin to implement a comprehensive relapse prevention plan must necessarily be able to identify the cognitive distortions which allowed them to offend, and must accept responsibility for those distortions in order to be able to plan a healthy response to their reoccurrence. This would suggest that the offender is now able to accept as part of themselves the qualities, which previously had to be denied. They now realise that they can be whole people, faults and all, without losing themselves, their connections to others in the world, and the opportunities to have their needs met. Their denial at this point tends to be centred upon their risk of relapse and is addressed during the process of relapse prevention planning.

This model is exceptionally helpful as it helps the worker conceptualise clearly the process through which the offender will hopefully travel throughout the process of assessment and treatment. It also helps the workers set attainable outcomes as they plan the assessment programme as well as being a useful projection for setting treatment goals. Treatment of denial takes time and is often measured in terms of years, rather than months or weeks.

Research findings

- Research has highlighted specific differences with respect to the type of denial used by offenders. Rapists who deny their offence justified their behaviour by focusing on the victim and her role in the event (Scully and Marola, 1984), whereas rapists who admitted their offence characterised themselves as having substance abuse problems or emotional problems, but otherwise perceived themselves to be 'nice guys'. They focused on more socially acceptable personal difficulties that were of a temporary nature. In contrast, admitting child molesters used denial tactics in an effort to deny the impact of their behaviour (Lanyon and Lutz, 1984).

- Nugent and Kroner (1996) examined the correspondence of denial and level of admittance of offences among child molesters and rapists. They found a difference on both counts between the two groups, with child molesters admitting more frequently to the offence. Child molesters tended to deny the extent of the offence, while rapists denied the degree of force. Child molesters are significantly more concerned about what others think about them. For child molesters, they found that denial and lying about the offence went beyond self-protection to being an ingrained and pervasive response embedded in their lifestyle. More worryingly, many will remain unaware about the presence and extent of their denial. They also found that child molesters have a greater number of victims and commit several offences more repetitively than rapists.

- Barbaree (1991) found that among 114 incarcerated rapists, 59 per cent denied they had committed an offence and a further 41 per cent minimised either their responsibility for the offence, or the harm they had done or the extent of their offending (frequency, forcefulness or degree of sexual intrusiveness). Both groups presented justifications which were intended to support their denial or to minimise responsibility for the offence. For example, among those who denied their offence, 31 per cent reasoned that they had not committed an offence because the victim provoked them by being seductive. About one-third of those who denied their offence and one quarter of those who admitted their offence argued that their victims meant 'yes' even though they said 'no'. Of the deniers, 69 per cent claimed that their victims eventually relaxed and enjoyed the rape. The same argument was put forward by 20 per cent of the admitters. 69 per cent of the deniers and 22 per cent of the admitters alluded to the victims'

unsavoury reputations as excuses for their crimes. 77 per cent of the admitters and 84 per cent of deniers excused their behaviour by attributing it to alcohol intoxication, while 40 per cent of deniers and 33 per cent of admitters explained their crimes by pointing to emotional problems caused by an unhappy childhood or current marital conflict. Treatment reduced the number of deniers who remained in therapy for the full programme, from 22 to 3: but 15 of those deniers who admitted to having offended, were still minimising at the end of treatment. Of the 15 who initially admitted but minimised their offence(s), only 3 gave up all evidence of minimising as a result of treatment.

- Bentovim (1994) reported that from his work in Great Ormond Street, only 9 per cent of offenders accepted full responsibility; 15 per cent some responsibility; with 76 per cent refusing to accept any responsibility for their actions. These figures do highlight the centrality of the management of denial in any assessment or treatment work with sex offenders.

- For a full discussion of the nature of excuses provided by sex offenders, the reader is referred to Pollack and Hashmall (1991); Scully and Marola (1984). Pollack and Hashmall (1991) examined 250 justification statements from the clinical records of 86 child molesters. They identified 21 distinct excuses: victim consented; deprived of conventional sex; intoxication; victim initiated; don't know what's wrong with me; family stress; nothing happened; non-sexual touching; just being affectionate; sex with children is not wrong; victim was lying; fear of adult females; just trying to help the victim; acting out of anger; someone is out to get me; financial stress; childhood trauma; sexual abuse; sexual preference for children, punishing the victims; childhood trauma (physical abuse); and victim's parents were lying. Six thematic categories were identified: mitigating factors (situational) sex with children is not wrong; incident was non-sexual; mitigating factors (psychological) blaming the victim; and denial. They also devised an 'excuse syntax' (fig. 11) to define the structure of the offenders reasoning about their sexual improprieties, arguing that it has the advantage of formalising clinical judgements about the individual's level of clinical and personal responsibility, his degree of defensiveness and the logical consistency of his justifications.

- Our view of this model is that it is too simplistic in that it approaches the assessment as the basis of some level of admission, when we believe that the assessment can be completed using a much broader remit. For example, exploring attitudes to sex, women, children etc. as identified in their checks as a whole.

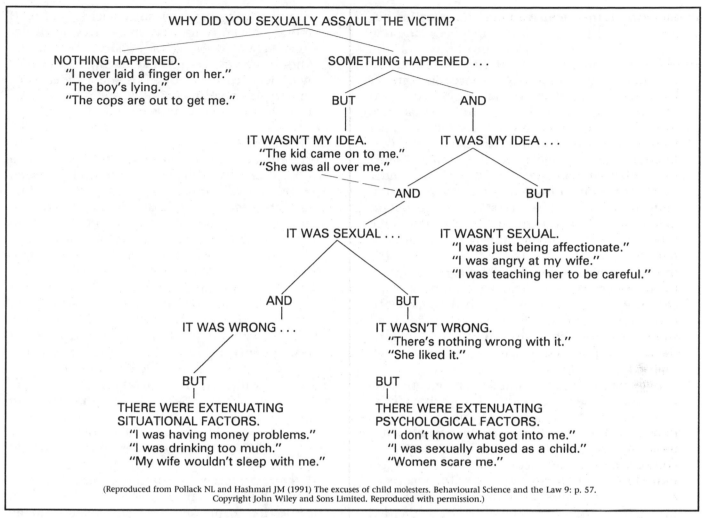

WHY DID YOU SEXUALLY ASSAULT THE VICTIM?

NOTHING HAPPENED.
   "I never laid a finger on her."
   "The boy's lying."
   "The cops are out to get me."

SOMETHING HAPPENED . . .

BUT   AND

IT WASN'T MY IDEA.
   "The kid came on to me."
   "She was all over me."

IT WAS MY IDEA . . .

AND   BUT

IT WAS SEXUAL . . .

IT WASN'T SEXUAL.
   "I was just being affectionate."
   "I was angry at my wife."
   "I was teaching her to be careful."

AND   BUT

IT WAS WRONG . . .

IT WASN'T WRONG.
   "There's nothing wrong with it."
   "She liked it."

BUT   BUT

THERE WERE EXTENUATING SITUATIONAL FACTORS.
   "I was having money problems."
   "I was drinking too much."
   "My wife wouldn't sleep with me."

THERE WERE EXTENUATING PSYCHOLOGICAL FACTORS.
   "I don't know what got into me."
   "I was sexually abused as a child."
   "Women scare me."

(Reproduced from Pollack NL and Hashmari JM (1991) The excuses of child molesters. Behavioural Science and the Law 9: p. 57. Copyright John Wiley and Sons Limited. Reproduced with permission.)

Figure 11. The child molester excuse syntax (Pollack and Hashmari, 1991).

- Excuses are important indicators of remorse, rehabilitation potential and the likelihood of recidivism. We can measure the offender's degree of defensiveness by considering the number of different excuse categories cited. This syntax moves from denial of fact ('nothing happened'); denial of responsibility ('something happened but it wasn't my idea'); denial of sexual intent ('something happened and it was my idea, but it wasn't sexual'); denial of wrongfulness ('something happened and it was my idea, and it was sexual, but it wasn't wrong'); and denial of self-determination ('something happened and it was my idea, and it was sexual and it was wrong, but there were extenuating factors').

- Gocke (1991) found that there is an intractable contradiction when processing sex offenders through the criminal justice system. Whilst adequate assessment and effective treatment are dependent on the offender becoming more open and honest about his offending behaviour, the incentive to minimise the severity of the sentence and to survive the process, may encourage the exact opposite—the entrenchment of denial and rationalisation. Furthermore, the hostility and vindictiveness that appear rife within the system may well result in feelings of victimisation. Far from feeling remorse about the impact of his actions upon his victim, the processed sex offender is likely to feel overwhelmingly sorry for himself. The system would thus appear to work directly against the solution of the problem. The evidence suggests that the process provides conditions that are likely to be conducive to the exacerbation and entrenchment of sex offender denial. Offenders seem forced into a situation where they have to concentrate exclusively on self-survival and consequently defensiveness, manifested in a number of different ways, appears endemic.

- O'Donohue and Letourneau (1993) explored the effectiveness of structured group treatment in reducing the denial of sexual offences in 17 males. Despite an average length of time of denial of nearly 2 years, by post-treatment, the majority of offenders had come out of denial. This supports the process of denial outlined earlier. As indicated by the pre-treatment clinical evaluations of subjects, almost all were in complete denial. One subject was rated as being partial denial (e.g. he claimed to have no memory of the incident due to intoxication but allowed that it could have happened), and one subject fully accepted responsibility for the abuse, but refused treatment. At post-test, 13 (76 per cent) of the subjects were rated as being at least partially out of denial. Given the two subjects who were not in full denial pre-treatment, this indicates that 11 subjects (65 per cent) changed from 'denier' to 'admitter' status. In addition, one subject, (6 per cent) maintained his denial but expressed interest in sex offender treatment in order to change his deviant arousal pattern. Of the 13 subjects who were out of denial at post-treatment, 5 (38 per cent) were rated as only partially admitting their guilt (e.g. admitting to the offence but minimising the impact of their actions of victims; or admitting to an earlier offence while maintaining innocence of the counts upon which they had been convicted). The other 8 subjects fully admitted to the offence they were convicted of (e.g. gave details about the offence). Four subjects remained in denial.

- Langevin (1988) carried out a study of defensiveness in 100 sex offenders, 50 of whom were repeated sex offenders against children, and 50 of whom were sexually aggressive against adult women. He found a comparable degree of admission to the offence in question, whilst less than one-third of the cases admitted both to their offences and their sexually anomalous preferences. Slightly more than a third admitted committing the offences but denied anomalous erotic preferences, and 13 per cent admitted both yet claimed special circumstances such as drunkenness, loneliness, or marital problems, as precipitators of the offences in question. Four men denied committing the offences but did admit to an anomalous sexual preference (i.e. for children or sexual aggression). Fifteen percent denied everything, claiming mistaken identity or being 'framed'. He found that the sex offender differs from other defensive patients in a number of important ways. Most often, he presents a picture of a psychologically normal individual who attempts to minimise any attraction to children, sexual aggression, or other sexually anomalous outlets. He frequently denies the pending legal charges. He may deny a history of anomalous sexual behaviour or may attribute the offence to alcohol and drug abuse. In some cases, a partial denial occurs in which the current problems or substance abuse may be invoked as a contributing factor, even though the offender accepts his responsibility for the criminal behaviour.

- Sex offenders typically deny the true extent of both their sexual problems and offences. This becomes acutely obvious when we consider the full extent of their offending when granted confidentiality pre-disclosure. Abel et al. (1987) found that this usually encourages a greater frequency and range of offences against the known victims, as well as admitting to previously undetected sexual offences and a wider range of paraphilic behaviour, for example, exhibitionism, stealing female underwear and so on.

Assessing denial

Most offenders are referred for assessment on a mandated or coerced basis, and the findings often have very important consequences for sentencing, child protection or custody disputes. Others do not want to give their behaviour up, so they present in a socially desirable way to impress the workers. It is not surprising, therefore, that offenders lie about their offences as a self-protective strategy.

As workers, we can easily become jaded hearing the excuses, minimisations, and denials from sex offenders and soon come to disbelieve every story—mostly with good cause (Maletzky, 1996). Assessing denial is important for two reasons. The degree to which an offender denies or minimises his behaviour will reflect his motivations to participate actively in the work. Secondly, by minimising in some way the significance of their behaviour, we are able to predict a likely recurrence more accurately (Murphy, 1990). If the offender surprises us and starts the work by openly admitting the offences and their responsibility for the crime, then that should not allow them to avoid facing the detailed introspection required to prevent relapse. Many offenders may admit in the hope that we will view the acceptance of responsibility as removing any future risks.

Workers need to understand the offender's motivation for using denial if they are to effectively tackle it in practice. Strategies for interviewing are considered in Chapter 5, yet it is important to look at this in relation to denial. Simplistically, if you believe that denial is a rationalising cognition, then you will be tempted to approach the offender in a confrontational manner in an attempt to separate out the truth from the lies. This approach can lead to denial entrenchment and there is rarely any progress made. If you believe that denial is a natural starting point when looking at the obstacles to accepting responsibility (such as the consequences socially, personally, financially etc.), then you may be inclined to adopt a motivational interviewing approach. This approach views denial as simply a lack of recognition by the offender that they need to change. Schlank and Shaw (1996) set out the use of this approach in a group setting and provided some encouraging results, with some 50 per cent of the offenders modifying the denial to the point that they became eligible for treatment.

Denial is generally assumed to be anti-therapeutic in most cases as each side tries to disprove the other. Hartman and Reynolds (1987) identified five phases of movement with resistant clients: testing worker authenticity; checking the workers' values and experience; movement towards involvement with the workers; committing themselves to the work; and finally, engaging in problem solving with the worker. If workers start by focusing on the sexual offences, then they may not get very far with the proposed work. It is an important area to cover, but if you refer to the details needed in any comprehensive assessment, then you will have many other (non-threatening) places to start, such as social history, fantasy, beliefs and attitudes, etc. Ordering the work is an important consideration when anticipating denial, as workers need to create the right kind of environment in which the offender can think about change. Quite simply, we should encourage the offender to challenge their own denial and thus diminish detail by degrees (Maletzky, 1996) – not only providing the offender with a springboard for change, but also providing the workers with some much needed job satisafaction.

Tools

Questions to be asked:

- The only credible and adequate method of assessing denial is by comparing the acts that offenders self-disclose to the acts recorded by more credible sources (e.g. victim reports, police records).
- What is the source of their denial? Is it overt or covert? What, if any, behavioural manifestations are present, such as body language, clothing or dysfunctional behaviours? Once this information has been elicited, they may be useful for the worker to help the offender bridge resistance with alliance as a foundation for accepting responsibility for their actions.
- Get the offender to draw how they remember the alleged offence situation (or one of the many) and then get them to interpret it as well as offering your interpretation to them for their consideration.
- Ask the offender to list the reasons why they should tell us about what has happened. They might cite being better understood, accessing the right kind of help, removing secrecy, less likelihood of a punitive community and court response etc.
- Ask them to describe the antecedents of their offending and the consequences of it.
- Many sex offenders say that they really didn't believe that they were doing anything wrong, or they didn't hurt the people they sexually abused. One way to test their honesty is to look at whether they told others about what they were doing. If they felt good about their sexual offences, or if they thought there was nothing wrong with what they did, they would have told others about their behaviour. Get

them to list: Who they have told—listing names, relationship, order of who they told, why and when?

- As the offender talks about their offending, try to see the whole picture and how the pieces fit together. Listen for the defensive strategies being used and don't go along with them. He may say that he had been drinking beforehand and so can't recall what happened. Given the nature of the offending it is extremely unlikely that the most important details cannot be recalled, despite how much he had to drink! The motivation for the offending preceded the drinking. The drinking may have, in the words of one sex offender, given 'the courage to do what I really wanted to do'.

Other materials

- Get the offender to construct a number of partial sentences that have a resemblance to their offences and ask them to complete them, for example, 'I use force when ...', 'My attitude towards sex with women/children is ...'
- A continuum of denial (Taylor, 1996)—is very useful in highlighting clearly what changes and shifts need to be made by the offender. Figure 12 offers a visual guide to measure change both for the worker as well as the offender:
- Get them to mark where they think they and each significant member of this family are in this continuum and see if they know where they want to be by the end of the assessment process.
- Workers must consult with victims, appropriate family members and others with access to the offender to cross-check information, but they

---

Hopeless   **Denial**

- Nothing happened.
- Something happened but it wasn't me.
- Something happened but they wanted it to.
- Something happened but not as bad as they said.
- It happened, but at the time I didn't know it was wrong.
- It happened but it was an accident.
- It happened, I don't know what came over me.
- It happened, but it wasn't planned.
- It happened, but it never happened before and I haven't thought about it since.
- It happened, I planned it and I know how it hurt people so it won't happen again.
- It happened, I planned it, it hurt people. I understand now about my thinking so it won't happen again.
- It happened. I planned it. It hurt people. I understand my thinking. I think about it still, but this is my relapse prevention if I feel tempted again.

Hopeful   **Responsibility**

Figure 12. A continuum of denial (Taylor, 1996).

must also acknowledge this may impact on the way they relate to the offender in subsequent assessment sessions. Pay attention to what the offender does as well as what they say and what they say in different contexts, e.g. court, conference, assessment session or home visit. For example, others will make a grand show of remorse during the clinical interview and in front of authority figures such as the judge, their clergyman, or the district attorney; but given the opportunity, they may continue to psychologically, if not sexually, abuse their victim and/or family.

- Why deny it? Coventry NSPCC*.
- Making excuses: Coventry NSPCC*.
- Record of denial. We need to record what is being observed or said, how the attitude has been manifest, to whom, and under what circumstances. See Figure 13.
- Sex offence attitude questionnaire (Proctor, 1994):* This is a 30 item questionnaire with 4 sub-scales: denial of planning, denial of harm (to the victim of the offence), denial of future risk and absolute denial (of having committed an offence).
- Sex offender information questionnaire (Hogue, 1994)*: A 43 item questionnaire designed to measure offence related denial as well as the sex offender's cognitive distortions about their offences and victims. The questionnaire was originally developed on a sample of imprisoned sexual offenders prior to undertaking treatment. The four factor analytically derived sub-scale measure denial of victim harm, denial of sexual motivation, denial of responsibility and denial of treatment need. These sub-scales have shown

to be reliable, and relate to both attitudinal and physiological arousal measures in a consistent manner. The measures have been shown to be a useful measure of clinical change and normative information is available both pre and post-treatment samples.

6. Victim empathy and awareness

Empathy comprises multiple components and processes, which need to be understood as a preface to any work in this area. Empathy has been defined as a cognitive ability to understand and identify with another's perspective (Cronbach, 1955; Taguiri, 1969), an emotional capacity to experience the same feelings as another (Clore and Jeffrey, 1972) or an interplay of cognitive and affective factors (Aronfreed, 1968). Briggs (1994) noted that cognitive empathy is where the offender has an intellectual understanding of the feelings of others without necessarily experiencing any emotional change themself, whilst emotional empathy is where they experience the emotions of others in response to their situations and feelings. Other writers have argued that it should embrace communicative and relational elements. Freeman-Longo et al. (1996) have argued that it is not about being self-centred, harsh, indifferent, resistant, discouraging, unsupportive, impatient, angry, inconsiderate, hostile, irritated, selfish, mean, abusive, cynical.

Sex offenders are thought to suffer from deficits in their capacity to experience empathy—yet the extent is in dispute—and this is considered to be important in the development, and particularly the

Type of denial	Yes/No	How manifested? In what context?
Complete denial		
Complete denial of responsibility		
Attack		
Denial of facts		
Denial of awareness		
Denial of intent		
Denial of responsibility		
Denial of impact		
Denial of frequency		
Denial of fantasy		
Denial of planning or grooming		
Denial of deviant sexual arousal		
Admission with:		
—justification		
—minimisation		
—fabrication		
—mental illness		
Guilty, but not guilty		
After conviction		
Denial of denial		
No denial		

Figure 13: The record of denial (adapted from Briggs, 1994).

maintenance, of their deviant behaviour. The lack of any empathy clearly has a significant impact on the likelihood of repeat and escalatory offending. For example, it is clear that those sex offenders who deny any responsibility for their offences will feel little remorse or shame for what they have done. Indeed, the use of mechanisms such as denial preclude empathic interactions or awareness of the victims' rights, and they also fail to appreciate (or lack) the basic information regarding the consequences of their behaviour—other than for themselves. Far worse than this, many offenders argue that they have helped the child/ren they have abused, e.g. sex is educational and in the 'best interests' of the child. If the offender feels bad after abusing, the child victim, by simply surviving without psychological damage apparent to their offender, gives a covert message of 'its OK'. The offender thus feels better, and this can make it more easy for them to offend again. Victims may subsequently perceive the bad feelings held by the offender and feel responsible, even reassuring him (White, 1992).

Workers always need to consider whether the offender has been sexually abused themselves and how such experiences may affect their thoughts and behaviour. We should also not disregard the possibility that their early life experiences have been characterised by a lack of empathic care, so the workers can model empathy through their relationship with the offender. It is often through recognition of our own pain that empathy is achieved. Whilst this is important, workers can never overlook or excuse their abusive behaviour. The development of empathy for the victim and potential victims is arguably the most important variable to decreasing their potential to re-abuse (DiGeorgio-Miller, 1994).

A model for understanding empathy

Marshall (1993b) argued that empathy involves four processes: recognition of the other person's feelings, the evocation in the observer of those same feelings, the recognition of those states by the observer, and the acceptance of the shared feelings. It is no surprise that our understanding of empathy is often confused given the complexity of the concept. In response to this, Marshall et al. (1995) offered us a multi-component model to help us better understand sex offenders. They argued that empathy is a staged process involving: (1) Emotional recognition; (2) Perspective-taking; (3) Emotion replication; and (4) Response decision.

Stage 1: Emotional recognition—requires that the offender be able to accurately discriminate the emotional state of the victim. The recognition of personal distress seems to be a necessary first step in the unfolding of an empathic response. Any failure to identify such distress prevents the subsequent stages of the empathic response following whilst also allowing a continuation of their sexually abusive behaviour.

In order for someone to 'feel' or experience the emotional state of another, they must first recognise the other person's emotional state.

Stage 2: Perspective-taking—is the ability to put themselves in the victim's place and see the world as they do. In doing so, they are forced to recognise the unpleasantness of their actions, preventing any repetition from occurring. Those offenders who consistently offend against a particular group (e.g. children) or sex (male or female) may see them as quite different from themselves and, therefore, are unable to adopt the victim's perceptions.

Stage 3: Emotion replication—involves the vicarious emotional response that replicates (or nearly replicates) the emotional experience of their victim(s). This requires some emotional repertoire by the offender to allow them to replicate the observed state. It requires that they recognise the emotion (stage 1) and adopt the perspective of that person (stage 2).

Stage 4: Response decision—concerns the offender's decision to act or not to act on the basis of their feelings. They may have worked through the first three stages, yet decide against acting on their feelings.

Empathy in sex offenders: generalised or specific deficits?

(a) Generalised empathy deficits

There is conflicting data on whether sexual offenders have a generalised empathy deficit, as well as whether any identified empathy deficit is significant. Finkelhor and Lewis (1988) suggested that an inability to be empathic toward children in general allows offenders to continue their sexually abusive behaviour. They argue that an 'empathy-with-children' deficiency is one of three aspects of male socialisation that could be associated with sexual abuse of children: along with over-sexualisation of needs and sexualisation of subordination. Marshall and Maric (1996) found clear deficits in generalised empathy among incarcerated sex offenders. Mehrabain and Epstein (1972) found no differences between the various types of sex offenders, although they did find that those who denied their offences reported greater empathy than those who admitted their guilt. This was supported later by Langevin et al. (1988a and b). Marshall et al. (1993) found that sex offenders in the community, and receiving out-patient input, to be the only group to show deficits in empathy, although not so low as to suggest any real problems with empathy. It would appear, therefore, that we should not be employing a generalised approach to our assessment of empathy in sex offenders. Stermac and Segal (1989) found no difference in empathy between a sample of incestuous offenders, extra-familial offenders, rapists, incarcerated non-sexual offenders and lay persons, whilst Beckett et al. (1994) found that convicted child molesters showed more emotional empathy, but less cognitive empathy, than a non-offender comparison group. Thornton et al. (1996) suggest that this finding combines a failure to try to notice how other people are feeling (low score on the perspective-taking scale) with a tendency to show markedly strong emotional reactions when someone else's perspective is noted. Further, although concern for the other person is a part of this emotional reaction, it also involves becoming distressed, freezing and responding with panic, when observing someone else in trouble. They proposed that this combination of empathic reactions is found amongst sex offenders because together they lead to a reduced ability to accurately anticipate when male sexual behaviour will cause distress. They go on to argue that these reactions can lead to increased arousal, which clearly has implications for further work. If the aim of any work is to induce an empathic emotional response from the offender regarding the harm they have caused their victims, then it could disrupt their ability to learn the offender's point of view and learn lessons for the future. We should focus therefore on their cognitive, rather then emotional skills, before reconstructing how sexual abuse is experienced by their victims.

(b) Specific empathy deficits

Abel et al. (1989) have argued that a lack of victim empathy is deliberately adopted—specific to the offender's victim (or all victims). This would imply the potential to dissociate themselves from the distress induced by their offences, thereby suspending any empathic response (stages 1–4 above). It is now necessary to employ person, offence and situation-specific assessment tools/measures, e.g. the rape empathy scale (Deitz et al., 1982) to measure empathy toward victims of rape as well as empathy towards rapists. Workers need to be clear on the deficits each offender has if this needs to be addressed in treatment, e.g. focusing on victim-specific empathy or broader empathy deficits.

Research findings

- It is important that workers identify those offenders who generally lack any empathy response and those who have the capacity for empathy but because of their justifications and cognitive distortions, do not feel it for their own victims and sexual abuse victims in general (Beckett et al., 1994). This distinction is important, as empathy deficits are more person-specific, rather than fixed over time, situations or persons (Marshall et al., 1995). Any failure in empathy disinhibits the offender's constraints against hurting another person and they go on to sexually abuse children (Marshall and Maric, 1996). Owen and Steele (1991) found that a high introversion score at the end of treatment is a clear predictor of future offending, just as sadistic offending is a contraindication to the development of empathy (Fisher and Howells, 1993).

- Empathy normally serves to inhibit aggressive behaviour (Miller and Eisenberg, 1985), presumably as the recognition of distress in another person elicits some compassionate concern for the victim. As such, empathy plays an important part in the successful maintenance of normal social relationships (previous sections have explored the issues and deficits of sex offenders in this area). The hypothesis that successful social functioning is linked to empathy appears highly possible. Being empathic promotes understanding of others, the ability to see others' viewpoints and perhaps a genuine interest in what others have to say.

- Hudson et al. (1993) examined the emotional recognition accuracy of sex offenders and various other groups in two studies. They noted that previous research has identified that adults can accurately identify six categories of emotion: surprise, fear, disgust, anger, happiness, and sadness—and noted that it is an essential prerequisite to being able to respond with empathy to the emotional distress of others. They do note that most sex offenders must thus either suspend their capacity for empathy or they do not have any compassionate concern at all. They hypothesised that in a recognition task, violent and sexual offenders will have greater difficulty, relative to other individuals, in correctly identifying emotions such as fear and anger (as these are the most likely responses from their victims). In their first study, they took 75 male prisoners incarcerated for either violent crimes, sexual crimes, theft, or drug offences. They viewed a series of 36 slides showing people's faces with various expressions and had to accurately identify each. Surprisingly, the violent, non-sexual offenders displayed the greatest sensitivity to the emotional stimuli. The sex offenders displayed the least sensitivity to the emotional stimuli. They frequently interpreted fear as surprise, and confused disgust and anger. In their second study, they explored whether or not the problems of emotional recognition were more specifically related to the offensive behaviours of sex offenders. They had to complete the emotional expression test (i.e. the adult and child sets of stimuli). They found that whilst child molesters were less accurate than controls in identifying emotions in both adults and children, this did highlight that their difficulties are not child specific, but rather there appears to be more general problems in identifying emotional expressions in others. Overall, the results of the two studies do support their view that emotional recognition presents a problem for sex offenders.

- Salter (1988) has described sex offenders as lacking in empathetic response, operating from a self-centred, narcissistic and egocentric orientation. Gilgun (1988) reviewed the research literature in these areas. She defined self-centredness as: *"focus on the self so intense that it precludes consideration of the feelings and choices of others and which at times causes direct emotional and/or physical harm to others."* This self-centredness is supported by: a preoccupation with negative feelings and evaluations about the self; a preoccupation with proving self-worth, which may include a pattern of seeking admiration from others and sometimes exhibitionism; reactions to slights and imagined slights which can be so deeply felt as to cause extreme emotional disequilibrium characterised by severely painful feelings of shame, humiliation, and rage; a drive to re-establish the equilibrium that can be so urgent as not only to block out consideration of the feelings and choices of others but also to bring about the use of manipulation and force, sometimes physical and sometimes psychological, to induce compliance to one's wishes; and the sexual use of smaller, weaker persons to re-establish emotional equilibrium. The self-centredness characterised by this definition is based on the motivation to prove self-worth, to ease pain and feel good, rather than on a primary and deliberate effort to harm or destroy others. The destructiveness of the offender's behaviour may be a consequence of a primary motive to feel good about the self. Self-centredness as experienced by the offender not only can preclude the possibility of experiencing empathy for others during the abusive act but appears to be part of a causal chain leading to behaviours experienced by the victim and the larger society as cruel and exploitative. It appears that for some offenders, having power over others to the point of causing pain, contributes to a temporary sense of well-being.

Assessing victim empathy

An offender's failure to take responsibility for his or her actions or to empathise with the plight of their victims is a primary target both for assessment as well as treatment. It is important to consider the timing of this work, as commencement too early (e.g. when they have a low self-opinion) may lead to an even more acutely reduced level of victim empathy being developed. Victim empathy does not just happen, it must be learned by the offender feeling deeply and paying very close attention to the real feelings of others (Freeman-Longo et al.,

1996). Sex offenders who lack empathy are likely to blame others for their problems, yet we need to continue to emphasise offender responsibility for controlling their feelings, thoughts and behaviours.

Tools

Questions to be asked might include:

- David Briggs (1994) has provided a useful framework for assessing an offender's empathy for their victims. He sets out the following questions that will assist the workers in judging the quality of victim empathy:

  —The physical feelings of their victims before, during and after each offence.
  —The emotional feelings of their victims before, during and after each offence.
  —The thoughts of their victims before, during and after each offence.
  —The physical and emotional state of each of their victims now.
  —The impact of the offences upon the family members of each victim, and
  —The physical and emotional state of those who dealt with the victims, e.g. friends, professionals etc.

- Perry and Orchard (1992) offered several useful indicators of the offender's capacity for empathy which includes: the extent to which he blames the victims, the use of demeaning terms to describe his victims, and a failure to recognise either the short or long-term effects on the victims. We should ensure that the offender personalises the victims by calling them by their names, and this can be modelled most by the workers when exploring the offences (dealt with later in this chapter).

- The offender can be asked to consider the feelings they experienced prior to, during and after each abusive incident. A range of feelings can be written on cards and they put face up those they experienced, whilst they place face down those they did not—at each stage of the problem. They have to justify/articulate their choices. The cards should contain at least the following: planned, ashamed, sexy, in control, angry, confident, proud, turned on, secretive, terrified, macho, loving, determined, 'a buzz', powerful, drunk, satisfied, caring, guilty, worried, out of control, boastful. With the cards that are left, the worker can show the offender that many of the feelings that they experienced were less concerned with the sexual gratification, and more about the feelings about being powerful, in control and able to do what he wanted (Cook and Taylor, 1991). A further set of cards can then be used to look at the abuse from the perspective of the victim; the cards contain both positive and negative feelings, and should be placed face up on the table. The offender is asked to turn face down any cards which they think the abused child did not feel at the time of the abuse. Any unacceptable cards picked up by the offender should be challenged by the worker, and any important cards should be structured to go through each stage of the abuse, with the task of dealing with the victim's feelings at each of the stages. *The victim's feelings on the cards should be*: guilty, in control, sick, confused, dirty, disgusted, powerless, sexy, scared, betrayed, alone, hurt, drunk, playful, threatened, angry, tense, weak, nervous, terrified, ashamed, turned on, unable to tell, out of control, embarrassed and high-spirited. The workers could go on to compare the feelings of the offender and the victim; usually highlighting the powerful–powerless relationship. The offender should be made aware that they have induced these feelings in the victim, which, in turn, may help them in the task of accepting responsibility for their actions.

- On a scale of 0–100 per cent how honest have they been with you regarding the sexual abuse?
- How can they explain their actions to the victim(s)? Why were they picked?
- How do they feel regarding the abuse: themselves, their families, friends as well as the victim(s)?
- The offender can be asked to identify their regrets about the abuse, then place them in order of importance.
- The workers can attempt to assess the offenders empathy in the clinical interview itself, looking at the impact of the abuse on the victim and their family; the consequences (short and long-term; temporary or permanent etc.).
- Empathy can be assessed by analysing answers or observing reactions to reading material. For example, Bray (1997) offers several vivid accounts adaptable into case material; and the workbook on empathy by Freeman-Longo et al. (1996) contains a wealth of useful information. Get the offender to read materials setting out the consequences of their actions. Vizard (1988) has written an excellent paper on the child's experience of sexual abuse and Freeman-Longo et al. (1996) have set out the devastating experiences of being sexually abused: distrust of others and themselves; terror and anxiety; shame, guilt and self-hatred; alienation from their bodies; isolation and withdrawal from people and activities; powerlessness, depression and extreme passivity; anger; obsession with sex or complete aversion to it; questioning their sexuality and gender; drug and alcohol use, abuse and addiction; eating disorders; perfectionism and workism; mental illness and suicide. We should try to establish from the offender how reading about the things that can happen to victims affected them, how they think being sexually abused affects a child's relationship with his/her friends of the same sex and of the opposite sex? Why? Which stories do they identify with?

- Get them to think about things from their victim's perspective. Why did the other person do what s/he did? What role did the offender play in the person's behaviour? What does the offender think the other person really wants (more than getting even)? How can the offender help resolve the other person's problem? (Freeman-Longo et al., 1996).
- Get them to list at least five people (use their first names only and list what their relationship is to them, such as a friend, a sister-in-law, a neighbour) who have problems that are as great or greater than theirs. The people on their list might have severe problems with: mental health, finances, children, parents, spouses, work, basic survival, or being harassed by someone. How do their problems affect their lives? If they did not have these problems, what could they do that they can't do now?
- Get them to list the difficulties they might have as they work on developing empathy. What are the things about them, their feelings and attitudes, their circumstances and life situation right now that might be roadblocks to developing empathy?
- Get them to give examples of ten different times this week they thought of themselves first and either ignored or considered others a distant second. They can only give the same example once.
- Get them to give five examples of times in their life they helped others with no thought of reward or personal advantage, beyond feeling good within themselves for having helped. If they learned to be empathic, how would their family or friends benefit? How could they benefit?
- Jenkins (1990) has offered a series of questions to help the offender unpick the multiple impact dimensions of the sexual abuse on their victims. These include:

—*Confusion*: How would it feel to be innocent and little and to be tricked/forced into something secret you don't understand, by someone whom you love/trust? What would it feel like to have someone doing secret things to you, that you know are wrong but just don't understand? What would it be like to have them say its OK, and giving you stuff for doing bad things?

—*Fear*: What would it feel like if you were forced to do something bad that hurts you? What would it feel like to be always thinking: Is it going to happen tonight? Is he going to hurt me again? If I don't do it/tell, he will hurt me? If I don't do it will he stop loving me?

—*Trapped*: What would it feel like to be the only person that knows about it? What would it feel like to know that you can't hide or resist or stop it because the perpetrator is much bigger, stronger and cleverer than you?

—*Shame/Self-blame/Guilt*: What would it be like to be only . . . years old but treated as though you are old enough to choose to have sex before you even know what sex is? What would it be like to be too young to realise that you have been tricked and too young to know any better? Who would you think is responsible? What would it feel like to know you have accepted favours or things in return for sex? How would this make you feel about yourself?

—*Burden of responsibility*: What would it feel like to carry such a big secret around for so long? What would it feel like to be bribed and threatened not to tell? What would you be up against? What would it feel like to try to bring yourself to tell? What would it feel like to actually tell on your father?

—*Betrayal/Used/Anger*: What would it do to you to be called a liar and be blamed for your father's problem when you finally plucked up the courage to tell?

—*Self-esteem*: If you believed that the abuse was your fault too, how would this make you feel about yourself? How would you start to see yourself? What would it do to your confidence? What message would this give you about yourself? How would you start to think others see you?

—*Future lifestyle*: What would it feel like to realise that you have been robbed of your right to decide on your first sexual experience? What would it feel like to be carrying the secret everywhere you go—at school, with friends—everywhere? What would it be like to be constantly worried whether people will know or can tell? What would it be like trying to make friends?

- If they are known sexual abuse victims themselves, get them to describe how this affected them and if not, ask them to imagine how it might be if their sister, mother or daughter was raped—or if they were raped by inmates in prison. If this induces some degree of upset, they can be reassured that this is empathy.
- Role reversal. Ask the offender to get into the role of the victim and then interview them and see how able and comfortable they are with changing roles. See how they would deal with cases if they were a judge or an investigating police officer.
- In order to reinforce their responsibility, they could be asked to write a letter as if they were writing to the abused child about the abuse,

although they should be clearly told that it will not be sent. Alternatively, they could write a letter from their victim's perspective telling what happened to her or him during and after their assault. Include what their victim(s) thought, felt, and how she or he reacted to their aggression. This is often a very useful mechanism for evaluating the offenders' empathic abilities and can be regularly revisited to act as a measure of change, no movement, or regression.

- Jenkins (1990) has offered a very useful pro forma for the apology letter, which includes 7 key headings: the reason for writing; the statement of apology; the statement of responsibility; a statement of the understanding of impact; a statement setting out what the offender is doing about it; and a statement of future intent.

It is often very illuminating to the workers examining these apology letters. One common finding is that they are self-serving, aimed at feeding their own needs and/or trying to engage the sympathy of their victims (Willis, 1993). Workers should act as teachers, correcting the text to more appropriate contents. For example, changing '. . . as you know I went to prison' to 'I was properly and justly sentenced to . . .'

- Eldridge and Still (1995) identified several themes commonly found in apology letters that feeds information thinking errors implanted by the offender during the abuse. Only those offenders who have developed considerable victim empathy—as opposed to simple victim awareness—manage to avoid them. These themes were:

—*Long-term control: offender belief in the permanently damaged victim*: Sex offending is mostly about power and control, and the notion of the victim's survival or escape from the offender's control is alien to offender thinking.

—*Long-term control: offender pride in his ability to control*: Offenders in the early stages of therapy (and those who do not progress) often take pride in how clever they were to manipulate everyone.

—*Explicit descriptions of the abuse*: Some offenders deliberately do this in order to re-abuse. Others do it because they are at a point in therapy where they are being asked to stop distancing themselves from their offending and to be more explicit. They may not have reached a point where they recognise how this will affect the survivor.

—*Paradoxical statements*: Most offenders say, 'You must feel awful,' 'You must not feel guilty and responsible.' There is an implication that the survivor ought to feel awful and guilty and responsible.

—*Extra burdens*: Many offenders cannot resist laying extra burdens on the survivor. The main burden is, 'Please forgive me.'

—*I'm sorry, **but** ...*: Many apology statements start well and then move into excusing the offender, and minimising and justifying the behaviour. These statements manage to imply that not too much harm was done, really. The offender has suffered much more than the child, and so on.

—*The double message*: This implies that it was the child's fault, really. 'You weren't responsible—but you were.'

—*The textbook approach*: Offenders in therapy who are developing victim awareness become clearer about the possible effects of abuse on children. They put this into an apology. Is it really in the survivor's interests to hear about the possible sequelae of sexual abuse from their offender?

A real apology is usually seen to be an admission by the offender that he was responsible for the abuse and that he regrets his actions. It should be a genuine and explicit statement. It should include a recognition of the preconditions to abuse (Finkelhor, 1984), and the offender should be able to admit his intent and the devious ways in which he overcame external inhibitors, such as other family members, as well as the victim's resistance. The apology should also be genuine and not just an academic exercise.

The apology should be for the survivor's well-being, not just a device to make the offender feel better. Care does need to be taken that there are no hidden messages within it that enable the offender to maintain power and control.

Offenders sometimes do have positive agendas regarding apologies: 'I'll make them feel better'; 'It'll help them see that I was responsible.' However, offenders sometimes have agendas that have nothing to do with genuine apology: 'It'll make it OK.' (And it certainly will not) or 'I'll find a way to show her who's in control. Then maybe she'll keep quiet about the other stuff.' We therefore need to be very guarded against apologies that are further abuse to the victim(s).

- Fisher (1997) introduced the notion of a victim grid for work with non-sadistic sex offenders. This is a diagrammatic exercise that has a powerful impact on offenders as to how they objectified their victims. A diagram of a stick-figure (Figure 14) is introduced in which the offender is asked to describe the victim(s). They are usually brief and respond by detailing their physical attributes such as body build, hair colour, etc. Each contribution is noted and a line is variously drawn across the victim (see Figure 15). They are then asked to add the sexually attractive qualities of their victims (see Figure 16). At the end, they are asked whether they see the victim, the grid? Delay in determining one from the other is the mechanism through which the offender can be made to realise that they have turned their child victims into objects.

Questionnaires

- Developing effective communication skills (Marsh et al., 1988)*: Sets out 10 items which makes the offender look at their body language and the effects of certain kinds of behaviours on others.

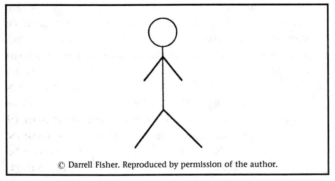

© Darrell Fisher. Reproduced by permission of the author.

Figure 14: The victim grid I.

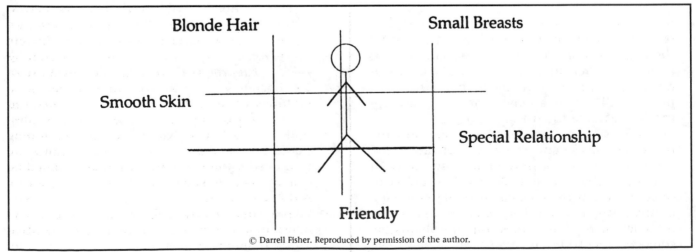

© Darrell Fisher. Reproduced by permission of the author.

Figure 15: The victim grid II.

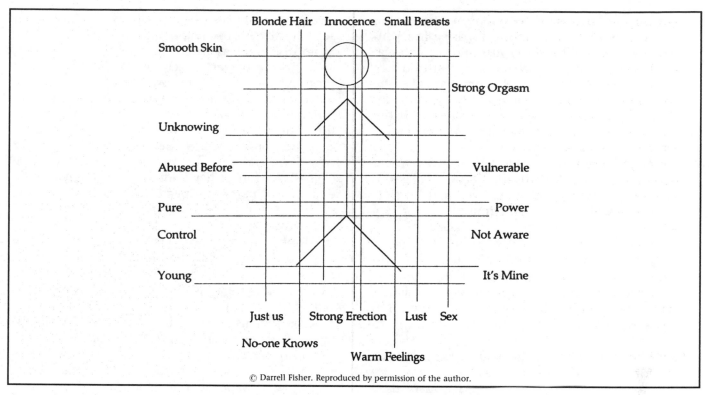

Blonde Hair   Innocence   Small Breasts

Smooth Skin

Strong Orgasm

Unknowing

Abused Before

Vulnerable

Pure

Power

Control

Not Aware

Young

It's Mine

Just us   Strong Erection   Lust   Sex

No-one Knows

Warm Feelings

Figure 16: The victim grid III.

- What is a victim? (MacFarlane and Cunningham, 1988): Sets out a list of reasons, which the offender has to relate to the abusive incident(s)—both those, which they perpetrated and those that they experienced. (Reproduced in Calder, 1997.)
- Carich–Adkerson victim empathy and remorse self-report inventory (Carich and Adkerson, 1995)*: Sets out 25 items aimed at identifying a picture of concern and compassion the offender feels for victims generally. The items are answered on a 4 point scale from 'strongly disagree' to 'strongly agree'.
- The offender as victim (Heinz et al., 1987).
- Interpersonal reactivity index (Davis, 1980; 1983): This is a multi-dimensional measure of the offenders' ability to empathise. It is a 28 item, self-report instrument developed with the objective of discerning various dimensions of empathy previously identified theoretically. Items are answered on a 5 point scale (1=strongly disagree to 5=strongly agree) and comprise 4 components: perspective-taking (measuring cognitive empathy), empathic concern (measuring attentive fantasy), fantasy (the capacity to identify both fictitious characters in movies, plays and books) and personal distress (the extent to which one feels anxious and uncomfortable when witnessing other's anguish). High scores on the perspective-taking scale indicate a greater ability to appreciate other peoples' points of view and high scores on the empathic concern scale indicate a greater ability to feel compassion and concern for others having

negative experiences. Sample questions include: 'I daydream and fantasise, with some regularity, about things that might happen to me.' 'Sometimes I don't feel sorry for other people when they are having problems.' 'I sometimes feel helpless when I am in the middle of a very emotional situation.'
- A measure of emotional empathy (Mehrabain and Epstein, 1972): This is a 33- item scale with inter-correlated sub-scales which measure related aspects of emotional empathy (e.g. susceptibility to emotional contagion; appreciation of the feelings of unfamiliar and distant others; extreme emotional responsiveness; tendency to be moved by others' positive emotional experiences; tendency to be moved by others' negative emotional experiences; sympathetic tendency, and willingness to be in contact with others who have problems. Response to each item is on +4 (very strong agreement) to −4 (very strong disagreement), and the (+) and (−) signing preceding each item indicate the direction of scoring. Emotional empathy is designed as a vicarious emotional response to the perceived emotional experiences of others. Sample questions include: 'It makes me sad to see a lonely stranger in a group.' 'The people around me have a great influence on my moods.' 'I am able to make decisions without being influenced by peoples' feelings.'
- The Hogan empathy scale (Hogan, 1964): Has 64 items that are said to measure the cognitive aspect of empathy. Items are answered as 'true' or 'false'.

- The blame inventory (Gudjonson and Singh, 1989): Has 45 items relating to three independent factors: guilt feeling attribution; external attribution and mental element attribution. Sample items include: 'I feel very ashamed of the crimes I committed.' 'I am entirely to blame for my crimes.' 'I will never forgive myself for the crimes I committed.' 'I feel no remorse or guilt for the crimes I committed.'
- Carich–Adkerson victim empathy and remorse inventory (CAVERI), (Carich and Adkerson, 1997)*: Consists of 40 items which the *worker* rates on a scale (none, sometimes, much or very much).
- Levinson victim empathy scale (Levinson, 1997)*: This is a 37 item measure of victim empathy that comprises 3 sub-scales: empathic response (16 items), interpersonal appreciation (11 items) and interpersonal sensitivity (10 items), rated on a 7 point scale ('always' to 'never').
- Rape empathy scale (Deitz et al., 1982): This is a 20 forced choice item measure of empathy toward rape victims and rapists. It can be used alongside Burt (1980).
- Selfism (Phares and Erskine, 1984)*: This is a 28 item scale which aims to differentiate narcissism from putting others' interests ahead of their own. The more narcissistic they are, the less empathic we can expect them to be.
- Fear of negative evaluation scale (FNE), (Watson and Friend, 1969): This 30 item scale measures sensitivity to negative evaluations by others and avoidance to criticism. High scores (scores range from 0 to 30) indicate greater sensitivity and anxiety in evaluative situations.
- The personality questionnaire (Jackson, 1984): Contains 16 items designed to measure the offender's tendency to portray themselves in a socially desirable manner, by answering 'true' or 'false'.

7. Disinhibitors

It seems clear that disinhibitors are very important in the commission of sexual offences (see Chapter 4). In Finkelhor's model, sex offenders must have some motivation to commit a sexual offence. Whatever their motivation, he argues that they must go on to overcome their internal inhibitions against offending, or they will be unable to act upon that motivation. Such disinhibition explains how the interest, or motivation, to sexually offend becomes translated into actual behaviour. At the individual level, he argues that a number of factors can contribute to offender disinhibition, and include alcohol and drug use, psychosis, impulse disorders, inadequate social skills, and marital problems. We would contend that there are some

offenders who need no such trigger for their sexually abusive behaviour, and that there are many more disinhibitors than those cited by Finkelhor, and include power, anger, sexual frustration and pornography. We will deal with three key areas only in this section: pornography, drugs and alcohol. We do not aim to provide a reflection of the large literature base, which we acknowledge exists in each area. Space dictates that we are selective in our overview, but the reader will be given some suggestions for further reading, should they wish to explore any particular area in detail.

Pornography

It is important that workers evaluate what role, if any, pornography plays in the life of the offender. Sex offenders are known to derive pleasure not only from their offending behaviour but also from fantasy involving the use of erotica/pornographic materials, or using these to stimulate their victims and to model the required acts. Workers need to establish the extent of their 'library'—including magazines, books supporting child sex, photographs, videotapes, diaries, computer images, etc. This may include photographs of their victims, or those they are actively grooming, which they may later use to relive memories of the abuse. Sex offenders are often very territorial about their collections, so they may be uncovered via a police investigation. Others are less discrete and distribute their material to elicit peer acceptance and credibility, and this can lead to networking (McGovern and Peters, 1988). Whenever such information comes to light, it is often very extensive, with lists of up to 80–100 names being the norm.

Recent figures from Scotland Yard illustrate the scale of child pornography in the UK. In 1993, the Obscene Publications Squad uncovered 520 books, 4,822 videos and 6,520 photographs (Cohen, 1995), and the belief is the more we look, the more we will find. This being stated, it is clear that most offenders against children do not rely on child pornography as a sexual stimulant. Many use adult (conventional) pornography which is easily accessible in most newsagents, with more than 70 titles selling millions of copies each month (Baxter, 1990); and via the worldwide internet. Sexually explicit material can also be easily accessed at most local video stores.

Pornography is taken here to be any material used primarily to create sexual excitement and pleasure—regardless of the original intentions (Lang, 1991). At the present time, the links between pornography and sexual offending is unclear. However, the consensus view does appear to be that sex offenders do tend to use erotica in comparable, or even lesser, quantity to non-sex offenders and community volunteers, although this suggests it plays a minor role in sexual offending. Wild (1989) did find, however, that the use of adult and child pornography was linked with organised abuse (sex rings).

There is a view that it is getting harder to avoid pornography in some shape or form, and many sex offenders are thus unmoved by access to it (Gebhard et al., 1965). It has also been found to be used as a release for an impulse to sexually offend (Carter et al., 1987), thus acting as a preventative strategy.

Research findings

- Marshall (1988) in a sample of non-incarcerated sex offenders, found that between 0 per cent (incest offenders) and 39 per cent (homosexual 'paedophilic') used some type of 'hard core' sexual stimuli (defined as being only available in specialised stores and depicting sexually explicit acts with nothing left to the imagination). He found that 13 per cent (incest) and 38 per cent (homosexual offenders against children) admitted to using hard core materials immediately before their offending, and offenders with more than 3 victims were most likely to use erotica to instigate crimes. Marshall also found that exposure to erotica can entrench sexual habits such as preferentially seeking out children for sex.
- The Badgley Commission (1984) found that many victims reported an unwanted exposure to erotica and this frequently preceded the sexual offence. Under the guise of sex education, the child might be shown nude adult females or sexual acts by the offender who would suggest he demonstrates the acts for the child. The recording of the abuse on film or video can then be used to bribe the victim to prevent them disclosing the abuse as well as forming the basis of seducing other children.
- Hunt and Baird (1990) described the effects on children of being photographed in the act of being abused as 'devastating'. The record is then used to reinforce their sense of responsibility for the abuse.
- Lang and Frenzel (1988) found that the material serves as a ploy to attain sexual outlets already desired. There is no link between the type of pornography used and the type of sexual offence. Wyre (1992) has reported that pornography is implicated at most stages for a substantial proportion of offenders: in predisposing men to commit abuse, in legitimising and normalising abuse, in creating and reinforcing false belief systems about victims of abuse, in reducing internal and external inhibitions to abuse and in initiating and carrying out the abuse. It is for this reason that he argues that where there is sexual abuse, we should look for pornography; where there is child pornography, we should assume that sexual abuse of children

is taking place. We have to proceed on the basis that pornography may be instrumental to the sexual offending whilst research into the link between pornography and child sexual abuse is conducted.

- Feminists have argued that male power is the *raison d'être* of pornography: the degradation of the female is the means of achieving this power (Dworkin, 1981).
- It acts as one way of males socially controlling women: reinforcing the socially unequal roles, reinforcing low self-worth in females, whilst instructing men in modes and methods of domination and grants them permission to use these methods. Women are linked with children, thus the link with the sexual abuse of children (both sexes) becomes clearer in terms of motivation and arousal.
- For a more detailed discussion on pornography and sexual abuse/sexual offending, the reader is referred to Kelly (1992) and Wyre (1992).

Tools

Questions to be asked include:

- Do they ever buy pornographic magazines? Which ones? Where from?
- What papers and other magazines do they buy? Or have access to?
- Do they look through catalogue order books for arousal purposes? Which ones? Which sections?
- How often do they buy them?
- Which ones do they prefer?
- How often do they look at the magazines?
- Do they watch pornographic videos? At home, or at the cinema?
- How often do they rent, or watch these?
- What type of movies do they prefer?
- Do they use materials, which contain pictures or images of naked children? Or where adults were having sexual relations with children?
- Do they have access to the internet? What materials have they accessed through it? Or put on it?
- Do they think pornography is harmful or harmless? To whom? Why?
- What effects might pornography have on them? And others? List, e.g. distorts real life relationships? Turns men into rapists? Excites/ arouses them? Exploits women?
- Why do they (and others) use pornography? e.g. to deal with sexual frustration?
- What types of pornography do they find stimulating?
- Did they eroticize non-erotic materials or aspects of their environment?

Drugs

Drug use is important in sexual crimes, but less so than alcohol. The range of drug use is 0 per cent to 58 per cent (Langevin and Lang, 1990), who also found that sex offenders do not generally have a drug dependence problem, despite between 10.7 per cent and 25.9 per cent using some drug at least on a weekly basis.

It is important to take a complete drug history and to access treatment records (if applicable). We should work with specialists in the drug field to access and interpret information. It may also be important to access their medical and psychiatric histories. A common response from the sex offender who admits they have a drug problem is to blame drugs as the sole cause of their sexually abusive behaviour. Drugs do not cause an offender to sexually abuse, although it does reduce inhibitions. At best, it is a catalyst or releasor of sexual or aggressive impulses and social inhibitions in an individual who is already in a frame of mind whereby he is prone to sexually offend. Offenders may not be entirely honest about their drug use (especially illegal) for fear of legal reprisal, and we may not know whether they increased their consumption of drugs at the time of the offence.

Research findings

Langevin and Lang (1990) found that over half of their sample had tried a wide range of street drugs: including minor tranquillisers, amphetamines, barbiturates, cocaine, narcotics, phencyclidene, hallucinogens and solvents. Marijuana was used most, whilst narcotics was used the least. Despite these findings, less than 20 per cent of the sample had a drug abuse problem at the time of examination. Amphetamine use was most associated with paranoia and was associated with hostile feelings.

Tools

Questions to be asked:

- Workers must try and find out the type and quantity of the drugs used, plus the effects on them.
- What is their history and pattern of drug use and abuse?
- What are the cultural and community norms?
- What association with peers is there?
- What is the relationship between their drug use and their sexually abusive behaviour?
- Is there any evidence that drug use or sexual offending precedes or is preceded by anger or hostility?
- Do they think they have a drug problem? Does anyone else?
- How do they fund their habit?
- Where do they access their drugs?
- Do they deal?
- Are they still using? Or abstaining? Are they experiencing any withdrawal symptoms?

Other materials

- The drug abuse screening test (Skinner, 1982): A 20 item questionnaire designed to provide an index in which drug abuse is no problem at all, is a moderate problem, or a severe problem. It asks for their drug use over the last 12 months.
- Get them to submit to random or regular blood or urine testing.
- Refer to appendices information in Calder (1998c).

Alcohol

Alcohol use is commonly associated with a greater incidence of crime, especially violent crimes such as aggravated assault or rape; although the exact relationship between alcohol and sexually abusive behaviour is unknown (see Seto and Barbaree, 1995 for a review).

It is important to take a complete alcohol history and to access treatment records (if applicable), remembering that they will probably be confused historians. Many of the sex offenders are in the younger age bracket, and thus have shorter histories. Medical records may be useful if they highlight conditions such as cirrhosis of the liver. A common response from the sex offender who admits they have a drink problem is to blame drink as the sole cause of their sexually abusive behaviour. Whilst alcoholics usually deny their problems, most would be happier to concede they are an alcoholic rather than a sexual offender against children. Drink does not cause an offender to sexually abuse, although it does reduce inhibitions. Sex offenders do use alcohol to access victims, by inviting young people back to their homes 'for a beer'.

Research findings

- Many sex offenders do drink at the time of their offence (52 per cent—Rada, 1976), but this rarely (if ever) causes impotence. Conversely, it might increase the levels of testosterone, believed to be implicated in sex drive and arousal. Early signs of alcoholism might include blackouts, memory loss or family dysfunction. It is important to get the victim's view on whether they had been drinking before, during or after the offence was committed.
- Evidence suggests that up to 50 per cent of offenders are intoxicated at the time of their offence, although the level of intoxication was unclear (Christie et al., 1979).

  It is also known that sex offenders are 7 to 10 times more likely to be alcoholics than the population at large (Langevin and Watson, 1996). The more violent the crime, the more likely alcohol (or drugs) are involved (Rada, 1976). Rada also found that incest offenders were more often alcoholics than other offenders against children, and they were older and more entrenched in their drinking behaviour. It maybe that alcohol is more important for sub-groups of offenders. It may help some offenders to become assertive and feel powerful; whilst for others, they may need alcohol to allow some sexual release. It has been argued that alcoholics in general manifest sexual problems and engage in unusual sexual behaviour.

Tools

Questions to be asked:

- Workers must consider the local community or culture of the offender to see what role, if any, they may have on their drinking behaviour.
- They must also establish both the level of their alcohol use and whether it is out of control; whether it is used as a vehicle to commit sexual offences, or whether it is part of their overall pattern of anti-social behaviour. Do they mix drinks?
- Do they think they have a drink problem? Does anyone else?
- They must chart their history and type of alcohol use, including their current use of beer, wine and spirits.
- What time of day do they start drinking?
- What is the pattern of drinking after that first drink?
- Do not accept terms such as 'social' drinker, push them for the exact quantities. Do not be drawn into the amount of alcohol used at the time of the offence and what effect this might have had on the individual, as alcohol effect is linked to drink tolerance and the metabolic rate of the alcohol (i.e. was he eating? What is his weight? etc.).
- When did they start drinking?
- Did their parents have a drink problem?
- Anyone else in the family?
- Which periods in their life were they drinking daily?
- When were they drunk?
- How much does it take to get them drunk?
- What is the most you can ever remember drinking?
- Do they ever get hangovers? How long do they last?
- What side-effects have there been—physically (liver) or psychological (e.g. psychotic symptoms)?
- What emotional or behavioural changes have been induced by their drinking behaviour?
- Who else is affected by their drinking? In what ways?
- Do they do things when drunk they might not otherwise do? What?
- Criminal history and degree of drink related causation? (e.g. drink driving.)
- Employment history and drink related problems?
- Was there any violence in the act?
- What is the risk of relapse to sexual abuse if they continue with their alcohol use?

- Are they able to control their behaviour?
- Have they ever tried to stop drinking?
- What is the longest they have abstained from drink for?
- Have they ever been in a detoxification programme? When? Where? With what outcome?
- What is the focus of the intervention (drugs, alcohol, or their sexually abusive behaviour)? Which should be addressed first? Why?
- Do any co-addictive behaviours exist? Such as gambling, eating problems?

For drug and alcohol abuse, the risk factors include increased aggression/anger when under the influence; failure at multiple treatment efforts; use of substances as an excuse of their behaviour; the abuse of multiple substances; they remain abusing substances; or they refuse substance abuse investigations (Carich and Adkerson, 1995).

Questionnaires include:

- The Michigan alcoholism screening test (Selzer, 1971): This is useful as it reveals levels of chronic alcohol use and provides a basis for deciding what degree of intervention, if any, is necessary to address this issue. It is a 25 item self-reported questionnaire that examines the main dimensions of alcoholism, asking the respondent whether they have experienced any physical problems, marital problems or periods of hospitalisation. Sample items include: 'Do you feel you are a normal drinker?' 'Have you ever awakened the morning after some drinking the night before and found that you could not remember a part of the evening?' 'Do you ever feel guilty about your drinking?' 'Are you always able to stop drinking when you want to?' The whole scale is reproduced in Salter (1988).
- For a full review of the assessment of alcohol (and drug) behaviours, please refer to Correa and Sutker (1986).
- The alcohol use inventory (Wanberg et al., 1977): This is a scale based on a set of 147 items measuring 16 primary factors (drink to improve sociability—social benefit; drink to improve mental functioning—mental benefit; gregarious versus solitary drinking; obsessive–compulsive drinking; continuous, sustained drinking; post-drinking worry, fear and guilt; drink to change mood; external support to stop drinking; loss of behaviour control when drinking; social-role maladaption; psychological withdrawal; psycho-physical withdrawal; non-alcoholic drug use; quantity of alcohol used; drinking heavily following marital problems; drinking provoking marital problems; and 4 second-order factors.
- The drinking profile (Marlatt, 1976): Best administered as a structured interview, this extensive questionnaire extracts the majority of the information needed for a full alcohol history. Sample questions include: 'Since drink-

ing first became a real problem for you, what is the longest period of time during which you did not take a drink?' 'Do you have any interests, hobbies, or other pastime activities that take up some of your free time, and that are not connected with your drinking? List.'

8. Exploring the current sexual offences (allegations)

This work should only be undertaken when some kind of worker/client relationship has been developed, and where the workers have collected and digested all the necessary information. The workers need to prepare carefully for this session by obtaining, reading and digesting police statements, social services records, any criminal history and available psychiatric/psychological information. A good foundation of information is essential if we are to be in a position to challenge any denial, distortion, projection and/or rationalisations put forward. The availability of multiple sources of information means we are more likely to get somewhere close to the truth of what has happened. It is highly unlikely that the offender will relay information as though he was bragging about his first consenting sexual experience, and they may have a huge investment in concealing their modus operandi from the assessors. We have to accept that whilst we can use collateral sources to check any information given, it is unlikely this will extend to the sexual interest pattern of the offender. When all the information has been collected, it needs to be organised, e.g. the number of completed sex crimes by category, duration of deviant sexual interests by category, and reported ability to control deviant sexual interests (Becker and Abel, 1985). Even here, we have to accept that we may be unable to identify types of sexual activity as they may be unknown or because we have inconsistent or incomplete accounts of the known offences (Howard, 1993). The offender can be asked to prepare for the sessions by refreshing themselves with the details of their PACE interview.

In some situations, this may be reasonably quick, particularly if requested by the offender themselves. If the assessment is being carried out with someone who intends to plead 'not guilty' to a sexual offence, addressing the offence during the assessment is inappropriate. This should be deferred until after the court has established a finding of guilt.

It is often useful to set aside two sessions for this crucial area of work, whilst also allowing the offender to change their information, based on either encouragement or direct challenge.

The aim of this block is to compare the offender's account with that given by the victims (and others), and any changes that may appear as the process unfolds. It is the offenders account that is more

likely to be distorted. The workers also need to assess how the offender relates to them, as this is an additional and useful piece of information, e.g. open or manipulating, anxious or unconfident? (Zussman, 1989.)

An incremental approach to the work is often useful. Initial discussions are important to establish the offenders level of commitment to the work, the extent to which they are able to discuss their behaviour and others' expectations of it, and ascertaining their understanding of any concerns about their behaviour. It is always worthwhile detailing the allegations or charges against them at the outset. Becker and Kaplan (1988) ask the following questions about the sexual abuse in order to bring about the topic in a non-threatening manner:

1. Do you:

- Agree totally with the police report of these acts?
- Agree with most of the police report of these acts?
- Agree with some of the police reports of these acts?
- Disagree with all of the police reports about these sexual acts?
- Does not apply to me.

2. Concerning the alleged sexual crime you were charged with:

- The alleged victim initiated the involvement.
- Involvement was by mutual consent.
- I initiated the involvement, but the victim went along with it without resistance.
- I initiated and the victim resisted.
- I initiated, the victim resisted, and I had to use force to commit the crime.
- I was not present at the alleged crime.
- None of these apply to me.

3. Concerning the alleged sexual crime you were charged with:

- I was involved just the way it was described in the statements.
- I was involved but wasn't responsible because I was under the influence of alcohol or drugs.
- I was present at the scene but committed no sexual offence.
- I was not present, but knew the victim.
- I was not present, and I did not know the victim.
- Does not apply to me.

It is often useful to get them to complete a questionnaire around their perception of what constitutes a sexual offence. You can set out a number of scenarios similar to those which have been alleged and they have to define which ones they believe constitute a sexual offence. They answer 'no', 'not sure' or 'yes'. The assessors can then explore the answers and can use an answer sheet to open up a discussion /debate. This is likely to be enhanced when they feel the assessor has some interest in them as an individual and in the cause of their sexual problems, and expresses concern to make sure they access the necessary help.

After these initial discussions, we can move into comprehensive discussions of the offending behaviour. This includes reconsidering the full details of the abuse, asking for details about all previous abusive incidents, and considering their thoughts, feelings and actions prior to, during and after the abuse. In approaching the abuse, we need to restrict the discussions to the allegations and not allow them to divert us to any mitigating or aggravating factors, which they will inevitably put forward to try and externalise the blame. Their account rarely provides an accurate picture of their behaviour, although it is often an indication of their current level of denial or distortion. Their account is best measured by reference to the victim statements, which usually contain details of the assailants behaviour, the degree and nature of any coercion, how the child was made vulnerable, the degree of immediate trauma suffered by the victim, and the situational circumstances surrounding the abuse.

We need to get them to describe in detail each of their sexual offences, even if they have not been charged with them as a crime. They should start with the abuse that has led to our current involvement, and which is usually the one we hold most information about. We should ask for a sequential description of everything that happened prior to, during and after the abuse, including their planning. They should be asked about all possible sexual deviations and not simply the presenting one. They should be specific, and we need to keep them on track by seeking clarification and pushing for detail. We should always point out any obvious minimisation and projection of blame onto others. If they are asked general questions, they are likely to respond with general answers, concealing the various behaviours they have participated in. In doing so, we have to be prepared for undisclosed sexual abuse which changes the assessment and the management of the case. We should always advise them that we are happy for them to discuss the abuse in any way they wish to express it, e.g. use of obscene language where the assessor is a female. We need to avoid challenging or interpreting any responses at this stage, other than questions of clarification and seeking elaboration. It is important to hear their spontaneous thinking and feeling, and, by not interpreting, they are less likely to 'clam up' about the abuse. It may also furnish us with essential information about what their perception and rationalisation for the abuse may be, and it should allow the workers to check the similarities and differences in the statement to those held by the police. Our starting point has to be to elicit an overview of the problem before getting down to the specifics. When asking them to tell their story in detail, we should ask them to describe:

- Aspects of preparation, e.g. fantasy/masturbation. Evidence of premeditation.
- Why and how they chose a particular victim (age, gender, race, ability, etc.), or could it have been anyone? Difference in age, physical stature and social status.
- How they created a situation in which they could abuse.
- Level of consent and power relationships.
- Whether drugs, alcohol, or both were a feature of the abuse.
- What they did to the victim. Full details of the nature of the sexual activity.
- What they required the victim to do.
- The response of the victim during and after the incidents.
- The extent to which persuasion, threats or coercion were used to obtain sexual contact, or how they convinced the victims to co-operate.
- Any co-abusers?
- What they did to try to keep from getting caught (e.g. lying)? Level of emotional intimidation.
- How they ensured the victim maintained secrecy?
- How they themselves felt prior to, during and after the abuse.
- Whether they climaxed or later masturbated to climax whilst thinking about the abuse?
- The persistence and frequency of the sexual activity and whether there is any escalation in the nature and frequency of the abuse.
- Why they stopped when they did?
- Their understanding of how they were caught.
- Their feelings on getting caught, and
- The response of their family, friends, victims and others to the disclosure.

Saunders and Awad (1988) caution us to accept that the task of establishing the details of a sexually abusive incident is often quite difficult. DiGeorgio-Miller (1994) has argued that our comfort in discussing the intimate details relies on the comfort level of the assessors and the safe environment created by them. Desensitising ourselves pre-interview is one way of achieving this.

It is frequently useful to split the discussion around the sexual abuse into two sessions. For the offender, this allows them to reflect on what they have said, and allows them to return and provide further information, or clarify that already given. In the interim, they should be asked to go through their version of events to check their honesty outside of the assessment sessions. For the workers, this allows them the necessary space to go through the offenders version of the events and break it down into chronological segments, e.g. prior to the offence, the lead-up to the abuse, the incident itself, post-abuse and subsequent events. They can then work out a series of questions designed to take the offender through the blocks in minute detail, as well as identifying gaps that need to be plugged. Where the offender denies the abuse, the workers need to highlight loopholes and inconsistencies in the story, exposing to them that we believe the version given by the victims. Having stated this, it is often easier said than done. They are often very plausible and convincing in their denials, explanations and excuses, and it is not uncommon for workers to shift towards an acceptance of them, particularly where they are well articulated. The danger of collusion should never be overlooked or underestimated.

Tools

Questions to be asked:

Aspects of preparation, e.g. fantasy/masturbation

- How old were they when they first attempted this kind of behaviour?
- When did they first abuse the victim?
- Where did they get the idea for the offence?
- Did they start to plan it? What did they start to think? What did they start to fantasise about? How did these make them feel? To what extent? Premeditated, victim selected/ premeditated, but no victim selected, or victim not known? How much time did they spend planning it? If not, was it opportunistic? How often did they masturbate around the time of the abuse? More than once a day? Once a week? What were they thinking/imagining?
- When did they start fantasising about the abuse? The victim? The setting? What was the offence like in their mind? What did they hope it would be like?
- Was the sexual abuse the primary intended offence?
- What were their initial warning signs that they might abuse?

Why and how they chose a particular victim

- Did they pick the victim, or could it have been anyone? Was it opportunistic (the victim was in the wrong place at the wrong time)? Was it planned (the victim was known to the offender)? Are they related? Acquaintances? Friends?
- How did they pick the victim? Behaviour they found sexually attractive (e.g. teasing or flirtatious)? Physical attributes such as build, hair colour or style? Vulnerability, such as physical handicap? Clothes, jewellery, make-up? Unlikely to disclose given their ability to communicate? Age? Sex? Male or female only, or evidence of crossover? Emotional attributes? Naivety or innocence?
- How old is the victim? How old were they when they started and then stopped the abuse? Is there a pattern to their age choice, e.g. children, adolescents, or various ages?
- Get them to describe the victim in detail for you – including any crucial selection variables.

How they created a situation in which they could abuse

- Where did the abuse take place? Be specific. Why did they choose this place or setting? Was it randomly selected? Was it isolated or dark? How did they get there? Is the location always the same?
- How did they approach the victim? What did they say? What did the victim say?
- Did they create an opportunity where there was no other adult/supervisor present?
- How did they get there and ensure the victim got there? Did anyone else know? Was anyone else there?
- Did they take them somewhere after they met? Why? How were they feeling? What mood were they in?

Were drugs or alcohol a feature of the abuse?

- If drugs and/or alcohol were used, for what purpose: to entice the victim, to reduce victim resistance/incapacitate them, or to reduce the offender's own inhibitions?
- If yes, what and how much was used? How was the drug taken—orally, intraveneously, nasally?
- Was the victim drunk or high? Did they supply them? To what end? Did it induce compliance?
- Did the victims' presentation add to their sexual arousal?
- Do they think they have a drink or a drug problem?

The offence itself

- Was the offence intra or extra-familial?
- How old was the victim and the offender at the time of the offence?
- What were the specific behaviours acted out, i.e. intercourse (anal, vaginal), simulated intercourse, rape, cunnilingus, fellatio, fondling, exhibitionism, voyeurism, fetishism, forced to watch pornography etc.?
- If the victim was male, did they make them ejaculate? If female, simulate orgasm?
- How long did the abuse last for?
- Was there any evidence of sexual dysfunction during the assault?
- Was the abuse committed under conditions of stress or in a particular psychological state such as depression?
- Was the abuse premeditated or spontaneous/ impulsive? (Note. This is important if we are to identify the offender's cycle of offending and try to isolate the type of offences they may commit in future. For example, we need to know whether to target stress, substances or impulses as a regime for treatment.)
- What was happening in their lives just before the offences? How were they feeling? Happy/ angry/sad/scared/hurt/rejected/lonely/sexually

aroused/a failure? What sort of mood were they in? What was their state of mind at that time? What made them feel that way?

- What was the incident that triggered their sexually abusive behaviour? What antecedents led up to the offence being committed? What did they want from their behaviour?
- What evidence of escalation over time is there? How far did they take things?

Groth (1979) notes that we must view the offence against the background of the offender's developmental history, the social-environmental context of this development, the environmental–situational context of the crime, the current psychological and emotional life of the offender, and the social–environmental features of the life situation that the offender will probably remain in, or return to (post-incarceration).

What they did to the victim

- What did they do and say to the victim? Was it threatening, foul, or instructional language? Before, during and after the abuse?
- How did it make them feel?
- What kind of games did they play with the victim?
- Did they shave the victim? Where?
- Did they kiss them? Where and how?
- Did they touch them? Where and why? How were they feeling at this point?
- Did they use a condom, lubrication, restraint?
- Did they take or use photographs?
- Was anyone watching them? Who and why?
- Did they both undress? Did they make them undress or did they do it for them?
- List all the different types of sexual activity they tried with the victims (e.g. exposing, oral, anal, vaginal sex, digital penetration, etc).
- How many times did they abuse the victims?
- Over what period of time did this happen?
- Did they have an erection? Did they ejaculate? When? How many times?
- On a scale of 0–10, how strong were their sexual feelings during and after the abuse?
- What was the victim's reaction? Did the victim ask them to stop? Was the victim scared, crying, passive, submissive or combative?
- When did they first notice that the victim was distressed by the abuse? How did that make them feel? How did they justify their behaviour to themselves?
- Did the offender stop at anytime because of the victim's reactions? Why? Or did their response arouse the offender further? How did they overcome the resistance?
- Why did you not do that they would have liked to have done?
- What didn't they try these things out? Would they if they saw the victim again?

- Would they try these things with anyone else? Is there someone else they are attracted to now? What would they do if they were left alone with that individual?
- Where they successful in the abuse that they intended? If not, what stopped them from carrying it out?
- How did they feel after the abuse? Have they ever attempted to stop their abusive behaviour? How? Did they hope the victim would stop it, or did they try and stop themselves? Which of them tried the hardest? When? With what outcome?

The use of force in the abuse

It is essential that we assess the offender's history of violence and violence-proneness.

- How did they get the victim to comply/submit? They might deploy verbal threats, enticements, intimidation, trickery, physical abuse, a weapon or a threat to harm people close to the victim?
- What kind of threats did they use or act out?
- How sexually exciting was the use or the threat of using force?
- What instruments did they use, e.g. weapon? Did they show it to the victim?
- What did they say to them, e.g. threaten to kill their pet etc.?
- What prevented them from being more violent?
- What injuries did the victim sustain in the abuse?

Post-abuse considerations

- How did they justify their abuse—initially, later on, and in the face of distress?
- How have they tried to stop people believing the victim?
- What are they doing now to stop their sexually abusive behaviour?
- How are they managing the consequences of disclosure?
- What other kinds of sexual problems might they develop if they don't get any help?
- Who would their next victim be?
- When did they last offend? When did they last plan to offend? How far had they progressed? Fantasy? Masturbation? Use of pornography or photographs?
- Do they accept responsibility for their behaviour, or are they maintaining that they are the victims of circumstances?
- What was the offence itself like?
- What did they say to themselves post-offence?
- What trends can they identify in their offending?

The sessions on the abuse undoubtedly place the workers in a powerful position compared to the offender, particularly where they are well prepared. This can induce considerable anger in the offender,

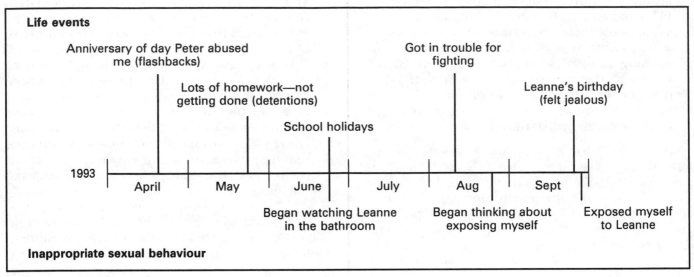

Figure 17: Time-line (Gist et al., 1994).

particularly if they have to change their story a number of times. Their excuses and rationalisations need to be challenged and supplementary questions need to be constructed to add more detail. We should allow them the space and opportunity to ask questions of the workers. They should be allowed breaks where necessary, particularly where they are being challenged to fill in gaps or elaborate on partial information. Expect a distortion of belief and attitude when they are under pressure for a more detailed account. The aim has to be to challenge their distortions and help them move from a passive to an active account of their sexually abusive behaviour. In doing this, we are allowing them to accept the responsibility for, and the effects of, their behaviour. At the end of this block, we need to establish the degree of congruence between the accounts of the offender and the victims. If others are identified in the abuse, then we need to establish the actions or words of the other person in the incident.

Other materials

- Sexual offence information questionnaire (Hogue, 1994)*: Measures their perception of the offence as well as the extent to which they accept responsibility.
- Blame inventory (Gudjonsson and Singh, 1989): Has 45 items relating to three independent factors: (a) guilt feeling attribution—18 items which relates to the extent to which they report feelings of shame and remorse for the crime they committed; (b) external attribution—15 items which reflects the extent to which they blame the victim and society for their behaviour and report certain justifications for their crime; and (c) mental element attribution—9 items which relates to how much mental control they report they had at the time of the crime.
- Cartooning (Gist et al., 1994): Which involves

the offender drawing the abusive incident in pictures rather than using words. It can sometimes enable them to describe their actions when they are finding it difficult to find the right words. It is a freeze-frame showing what happened at a particular point in time.

- Time-line (Gist et al., 1994): Helps us obtain a wider view of the abuse and more clearly observe the spatial relationships between the abusive incidents and other significant events in the offenders life. The time-line should usually start at least one month prior to the first reported incident of inappropriate sexual behaviour. It can be extended backwards to include any new information about earlier reported incidents (fig. 17).
- Second person (Gist et al., 1994): This is where they describe the abuse through the eyes of a second person (e.g. those who have been abused or observed the abuse). This technique can provide them with another perspective on what happened as well as furnishing us with an idea of how they see the views of others.
- Film director (Gist et al., 1994): Here, the offender describes the abuse as though they are a film director, and they are asked to outline their abusive behaviour as a continuous process, moving from one place to another rather than simply giving a snapshot of particular moments in time. This has the advantage of providing more information than might otherwise be the case.
- Anatomically correct dolls (Gist et al., 1994): These are a useful aid to the offender when describing their behaviour, particularly where they are struggling to discuss exactly what happened. It can be useful in visually depicting to the offender how their story may be impossible or not credible. There needs to be some consideration as to the level of possible arousal these may induce in the offender.

- Sexual offence assessment questions (Freeman-Longo, 1985)*.
- Cook and Taylor (1991) found the use of drawings and diagrams valuable as a means of clarifying exactly what happened where, and who had been present. It should include details on house layout with the positioning of beds and other pieces of furniture. An understanding of the mechanics of the abuse usually provides information upon which to challenge the offender. The use of dolls houses or play furniture for the offender to build a representation of the environment, and play figures to represent themselves, the victims and any other appropriate others puts information via the third party which can be less threatening. It may also be useful when working with adults with learning disabilities.
- The offender can be asked to develop their own collages, recreating the events which allow the abuse to occur in picture form, rather than recreating the abuse itself. For example, a picture of a man and a little girl bathing together. This can provide useful information on how the events have been manipulated or planned, what the offender was thinking and feeling, and how he believed he could affect his own behaviour if he was in a similar position in the future. It has the additional potential for tapping into the offender's fantasies.
- Associations: Where the offender associates thinking about young children with going to court. The task of getting the offender to associate consequences to particular feelings, behaviours, and thoughts can help them to learn from their own mistakes, by recognising the danger signals early, planning how they can avoid or escape these dangerous situations by using others they can trust to help them, or by helping themselves.
- Ask them to pretend that they are a judge hearing the details of their sexually abusive behaviour, and ask them to outline what they would do in this case and why. What would they do if they were assuming the role of victim in ruling on the information?
- Ask them to complete a risk continuum to locate themselves on a range from 'very safe' to 'very likely to repeat their behaviour' (Willis, 1993). This can be useful in indicating how much they understand their behaviour.
- Clarke violence scale (Langevin et al., 1985b): This is useful for assessing violence proneness in sex offenders. This 137 item test samples the frequency of varied violent acts from family-of-origin fighting, school behaviour, childhood peer fighting, peer fighting after age 16, marital fighting and child abuse, use and possession of weapons, fire setting, cruelty to animals, employment violence, suicide attempts, interest in violent hobbies, and temper tantrums as a child. A 5 point scale is used for responses.
- Generalised scale of acceptance (Simmons, 1986)*: This is a 49 item self-report questionnaire that can be used to unwrap the offender's current position in relation to accepting responsibility for the offences and future self-control.
- Offence analysis (Calder, 1997)*: A worksheet which can be used by the offender alone, or by the workers, to guide the discussion around the sexual offence.

Van Beek and Mulder (1992) set out the details of the 4 stages of the offence script, each requiring a different approach from the worker, and different sets of expectancy from the offender. In the educational stage, the objectives are motivating and instructing the offender. The worker is both teacher and that of someone who can empathize with the difficulties the offender encounters in outlining his offence script. The worker invites the offender to pose questions and to make critical amends. Workers acknowledge the highly difficult level of the procedure, but stress the enormous benefits in outlining the offence script: more revealing insight in the offence and in himself, higher control of his own behaviour, reduced chance of recidivism, etc. There is no direct pressure for the offender to cooperate (e.g. 'Well, maybe too difficult at this point'). In the 'remedial' stage, it is important for the offender to adapt the procedure and to learn to distinguish between the various components and to work out each one of them. Any lack of skills to outline an offence script are tackled here. Behavioural avoidance might be discusses (such as forgetfulness, no homework, etc.). The offender is asked to remember the last offence. From the actual moment of the offence he has to go back in time six hours. This represents the offence script starting point. He then has to relate all his important feelings, thoughts, actions, and circumstances during the first hour. It is a sort of guided fantasy tour. The worker helps the offender by asking him what-where-how questions and to extemporize. Questions as to the why are avoided at this point. The same process is followed for the second hour, and the worker still doesn't take so-called amnesia very seriously yet. They reassure the offender as the basis of allowing recuperation of memory ('e.g. We'll see how far we get, missing bits might come up somehow or other'). Avoidance of certain topics by the offender may be commented upon by the worker—without direct challenge. For example, 'Are you sure? I don't get it. I can't believe this'. In the confrontational stage, the offence script is further elaborated upon. The aim is to get a complete picture, to fill in any gaps and to reduce resistance as far as possible. The offence script is to become more emotionally charged, and the offender is supposed to be feeling more responsible for his behaviour. Information given by the offender is compared with that from other sources. The offender is shown possible discrepancies and important issues are highlighted. In essence, the offence is dissected and the offender made to feel responsible for his thinking, feeling and acting. Denial is no longer accepted, even though confrontation does raise the possibility of shame, anger or fear for the offender. This leads into the treatment stage, where the worker-offender relationship often becomes more co-operative as mutual targets for change are devised.

The authors argue that the offence script serves several key functions: it provides vital information about the way the offender deals with potential stressful situations, how he handles conflicts within himself and with others, what roles sexuality and aggression play in the offence, and whether a pattern of behaviour in the offences can be determined. It also provides a view of the offender towards their offences. It also allows specific offence-related treatment plans to be formulated.

The script is a tool for the worker and the offender to use, and it is readily adaptable to a wide range of offences, approaches and circumstances. They provide a useful proforma checklist from which to work

Homework assignments may include:

- Describe how their sexually abusive behaviour is a problem and for whom?
- What efforts have they made or would want to make to stop this behaviour? Who can help them?
- Make a list of all the problems they had before they sexually abused.
- How did the sexual abuse affect them, their victims and their families?
- List why the victims would fabricate allegations of sexual abuse against them. What have they to gain from doing so?
- List all the needs (other than sex) that are met for them through their sexual offending.
- Get them to rewrite their statements relating to the offences and then compare this with the original statement to the police. Any movement is a useful indicator of attitude change. It can, and should, be repeated as the work continues.
- Get them to describe a typical day (both before the allegations of sexual abuse, and now), beginning with when they get up in the morning, and including who is in the home, where they go, with whom, who might they meet, etc. What contact might they have with children with some other adults present, or alone? When do people go to bed, and with

whom? Are there atypical days? Do weekdays differ from weekends? This might give us information on their access to victims, their overall functioning, and possible intervention strategies.
- Set out why they feel guilty/remorseful/sorry about their sexually abusive behaviour.

9. The cycle of abuse

The 'cycle of abuse' articulated by Steven Wolf (1984) is a very popular framework for workers when trying to understand offending patterns (see Chapter 4 for a detailed discussion). This is probably because it breaks down the offending pattern into a series of stages: the period leading up to the offence, committing the offence, reconstituting after the offence, leading back to the stage of committing further offences. This has many parallels with the notion of an addictive assault cycle, where the offender becomes more addicted to their behaviour over time. Whilst there are some sex offenders who fit neatly into Wolf's framework, there are many who do not. This being acknowledged, it is always best to proceed on the basis that you can identify a clear pattern of sexually abusive behaviour, as addictions can be very powerful and intractable, with a tenacious grip on behaviour that will persistently frustrate initiatives for change (Carnes, 1983). As the compulsion grows in intensity and severity of consequence, it comes to pervade virtually every aspect of the offender's life, with the result that their day-to-day routines often become organised around the offending (Gocke, 1991).

Some offenders have continuous cycles whilst others have inhibited cycles. Offenders with continuous cycles often have belief systems which legitimise their behaviour to the point where the cycle is only interrupted by their perceived risk of being caught, e.g. a faulty choice of victim. These offenders do strongly believe that they are in the right. For others, they may not be so secure, and their internal inhibitions interject to break their offending cycle. These inhibited offenders frequently question their own behaviour, and the strength of such questioning is directly linked to the length of their breaks. They do offend when they make excuses for their behaviour, such as feeling sorry for themselves and thus entitled to some small comfort. Wyre (1987) has also identified several different types of offending cycles: fixated paedophile, professional paedophile, anger rapist, and indecent assault. Please refer to the text for the detail.

More recently, Ward et al. (1995) have provided us with a descriptive model of the offence chain for sex offenders—which provides an analysis of the offender's thoughts and behaviours preceding the offence. Comprising nine stages, the model incorporates offender type, offence type, and offers a description of the possible interactions between the various stages and factors. This does help to impress on the offender the process and not the spontaneity of their behaviour.

Tools

Questions to be asked include:

- We would suggest that you take the offender through the questions set out in the last block, but being far more specific for each part of the cycle and for each offence they have committed. This should help identify any patterns of offending. It should also help identify which is their primary pattern (e.g. incest) and this can help clarify any degree of secondary patterns ('crossover'). Whilst the broad framework can be used in most cases, the content and details will differ considerably. The frequency in which they complete the cycle is an integral consideration when predicting likelihood of re-offending.
- Give the offender a blank offending cycle chart (see fig. 18 below) to fill in with their own details. Ask them to work backwards from the abuse and to identify any precursors to the abuse. Tell them we are assuming none are 'first time' offenders. Get them to link all the

---

Offender's name:

Full name of victim:

Date of offence:

Date form completed:

Each respondent is asked to complete their particular sexual abuse cycle in detail. This should include their fantasies, masturbation, arousal and offending, and a new cycle should be completed for each different offence.

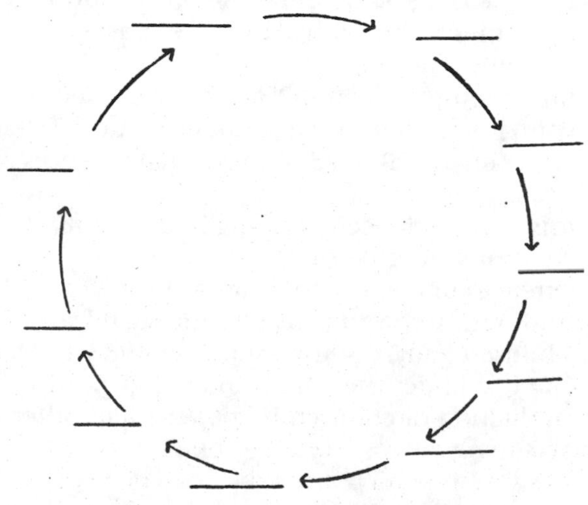

Figure 18: The cycle of offending exercise

---

component factors which have come together to allow the offence to have been committed, such as masturbation, fantasy, visual sexual stimulation and offending. Push for detail. If this is being completed with the workers present, the workers may have completed their idea of what the offenders cycle may look like, and they should get the offender to record the detail as it unfolds, for accuracy.
- Ask them to identify strategies, which might allow them to break out of the cycle that led to their offending.
- Post-assessment, get the offender to agree to masturbate first to a fantasy of some consensual sexual activity before then masturbating to their deviant arousal. This may play some small part in gradually decreasing their arousal to the deviant cues. Get them to identify personal strategies to avoid repeating their abusive behaviour. Whilst this exercise is most likely to be used in the treatment phase, it is potentially useful in the assessment phase with a willing offender.

10. Feedback and outcomes

To ensure the offender does not acquire any aggravated distortion of their cognitions, they need to be debriefed at the end of the assessment. They should be given the opportunity to hear the assessment feedback alone, before their partner is included, if that is what they want. A post-assessment interview should incorporate the information gathered from all the assessments, particularly where they are similar, different, or highlight more questions. The following issues should be covered in the feedback session:

- A report will be written to the commissioning body, although they will have sight of it.
- An appraisal of the assessments should be undertaken, with reference to any shifts in acceptance or attitudes noted, and any remaining concerns.
- The viability of future work, with specific details, time-scale, and any mandate required.
- A treatment agreement could be discussed and some consensus on its content reached.
- The family's response to the abuse is central to child protection planning and placement issues, and thus need to be discussed.

The meeting to feedback often precedes the full assessment report and should always be done before a decision on disposal is made. We would recommend the following framework for the assessment report that addresses:

- Details of the offender and their family.
- Reason for referral—summary of the offence. This should always describe in detail the

behaviour, the location and duration of the offence, and how the offender gained access to the victim.

- Brief background information on the offender (individual and family profile).
- Engagement with the work (number of sessions, commitment and motivation).
- The assessment of their offending behaviour—including statements from the offender in their own words, covering the process of their cycle-in sequence. If they are denying, minimising or projecting blame elsewhere, this should be reported. Draw attention to remaining discrepancies between the offender's statements and those given by the victim and any witnesses.
- Their sexual history.
- Victim awareness.
- Summary and recommendations.
- Involvement of others in the process, including partners.

We need to remember that we have to use the information gleaned from the questionnaires with some caution as many of them are untried and unverified in practice. However, they are very useful in opening up avenues for discussion, and this is important when we know that there is no single or identifying pattern of responses from all groups who perpetrate sexual crimes.

In the next chapter, Calder explores the outcome issues from all the commissioned assessments and provides us with a framework, which explores offender motivation to change; risk and recidivism; offender eligibility for treatment; treatment goals, components, and plans; prognosis for family rehabilitation, and recovery assessments.

Footnote

A Schedule One offender is someone convicted of an offence against a child or young person.

The following list of Schedule One offences leads to this status being applied to sexual offenders:

(a) The murder or manslaughter of a child or young person (including the aiding, abetting, counselling or procuring the suicide of a child or young person.
(b) Infanticide.
(c) Offences under the Offences Against the Person Act 1861:
  S5 Manslaughter of a child or young person
  S27 The abandonment or exposure of a child under two so as to endanger its life or health
  S42 Common assault on a child or young person
  S43 Aggravated assault of a female child with intent to deprive a person having the lawful care or charge of such child or the possession of such child or receiving or harbouring a child with such intent

knowing it to have been so taken away or detained.
(d) Offences under the CYPO Act 1988
  S1 Cruelty to a person under sixteen
  S3 Allowing a person under sixteen to be in a brothel
  S4 Causing or allowing a person under sixteen to be used for begging
  S11 Exposing a child under twelve to risk of burning
  S23 Causing, procuring or allowing a person under sixteen to take part in dangerous performance
(e) Offences under the Sexual Offences Act 1956, against a child or young person: (aged under 17 years)
  S2 Procurement of women by threats
  S3 Procurement of women by false pretences
  S4 Administering drugs to obtain or facilitate intercourse
  S5 Intercourse with a girl under thirteen
  S6 Intercourse with a girl between thirteen and sixteen
  S7 Intercourse with an idiot or imbecile
  S10 Incest by a man
  S11 Incest by a woman
  S12 Buggery
  S13 Indecency between men
  S15 Indecent assault on a man
  S16 Assault with intent to commit buggery
  S19 Abduction of unmarried girl under eighteen from parent or guardian
  S20 Abduction of unmarried girl under sixteen from parent or guardian
  S22 Causing prostitution of women
  S23 Procuration of girl under twenty-two
  S24 Detention of women in brothel or other premises
  S25 Permitting a girl under thirteen to use premises for intercourse
  S26 Permitting a girl between thirteen and sixteen to use premises for intercourse
  S28 Causing or encouraging prostitution of, intercourse with, or indecent assault on a girl under sixteen.
(f) Any attempt to commit against a child or young person an offence under Section 2, 5, 6, 7, 10, 11, 12, 22 or 23 of the Sexual Offences Act 1956.
(g) Any other offence involving bodily injury to a child or young person.
(h) Offences under S1 of the Indecency with Children Act 1960 (except with regard to Children and Young Persons Act 1933, S15).
(j) Offence under the Child Abduction Act 1984 (abduction of children by parents and other persons).

Chapter 8
Outcome measures: separating the wood from the trees

This chapter aims to provide a broad framework for workers involved in looking at the way forward in the child sexual abuse, post-assessment phase. This is important when we consider the volume and complexity of the information given/collected. The arena of treatment for sex offenders is a very complex one, and one which has taken up many books in its own right. As such, the issues addressed in this chapter are both summarative and selective. I do feel it is important to explore issues relating to: the offenders motivation to change; a model of change; offender eligibility for treatment; the aims of treatment; the potential component parts of a treatment package; the risk factors identified within the assessment and the issue of recidivism; the reconstitution of the family; and offender–child/ren contact. A new concept about offender recovery and its association with a clear, objective-driven, treatment plan is explored.

Motivation to change
Morrison (1991) offered us a very useful continuum of motivation (Figure 19), which can help us assess the level of motivation to change within the offender.

Within this framework, the offender who argues that they do not have any problems is unlikely to agree to any of the necessary work on a voluntary basis, and some legal mandate is usually needed to ensure their compliance. Those who argue that they want to change need similar careful assessment to determine their motivation for this stance. Whilst many are genuine and do want to undertake the work necessary to effect change, we need to identify and manage those who adopt this stance in the hope that they circumvent the necessary work.

Tools

Questions to be asked:
We need to carefully assess the offender's motivation to go into very intrusive and protracted treatment work, and the following questions may help us with this:

- Why is it important that I change?
- Do I have the ability to change?
- What does change really mean? What will I have to do that I can't do now? What will I not have to do that I do now?
- Who can help me change, and in what way? and
- What have I tried to change in the past, and why wasn't it successful?

Internal motivators

I want to change.
I don't like things as they are.
I am asking for your help.
I have resources to help solve this.
I think you can help me.
I think things can get better.
I have other support, which I will use to encourage me.
I accept that I am doing something wrong.
I accept what you say needs to change.
I accept that others are right (family, friends, community, agencies).
You defining the problem clearly helps.
I understand what change will involve.
I accept that if I do not change, you will take my children away.
I can change if you do this for me.
I'll do whatever you say.
I agree to do this so the family can be reconstituted.
It's your job to solve my problem.
You are my problem.
I am right and you are wrong.
I don't have any problems.

External motivators

Figure 19: A continuum of motivation (adapted from Morrison, 1991).

Additional tools:

- The dartboard exercise (fig. 20) (Calder, 1997) is where the offender is asked to locate certain scenarios put to them within concentric circles. This can help them identify how change may take place in different areas of their offending behaviour.
- The offender can be asked to list the warning signs that they may show before re-offending or putting themselves into a risky situation where they might easily re-offend. They should include warning signs that happen long before they are in trouble, as well as ones that are present when they are in trouble again. When they have listed all their warning signs, they are asked to rank them on a scale of 0–5 (0=most serious and 5=least serious). They must have a minimum of 5 warning signs and they must be specific (Loss et al., 1988). They could consider whether they would be tempted to re-offend with the victim(s) if the opportunity arose again, or whether there are other children with similar characteristics and vulnerability that may tempt them.
- They need to consider the likely consequences of

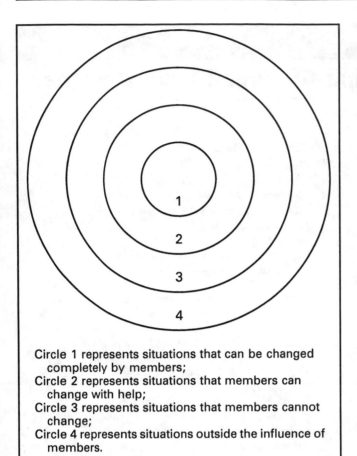

Circle 1 represents situations that can be changed completely by members;
Circle 2 represents situations that members can change with help;
Circle 3 represents situations that members cannot change;
Circle 4 represents situations outside the influence of members.

Figure 20: The dartboard exercise (Calder, 1997)

continuing to sexually offend. Cook and Taylor (1991) use a large piece of paper to draw two pathways to the future, which they are then asked to complete. It should look something like (fig. 21):

Simply put, the offender is asked to set out their hopes for the future on one of the pathways, and the consequences they anticipate if they re-offend on the second pathway. This clearly sets

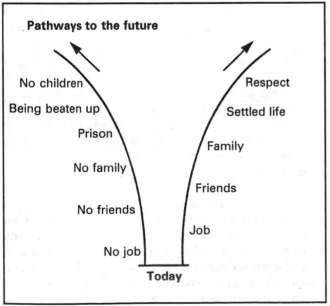

Figure 21: Pathways to the future.

out the two different pathways so they can see the likely shape of their lives depending on their future behaviour. They could be asked where the offences they have already committed puts them in this framework.

- The workers can also use the decision quadrants suggested by Steen and Monnette (1989), which allows the offender to fill in the benefits of changing (not abusing) and what it will cost them to change (not abuse), as well as the benefits of continuing to offend (not changing) and the costs of not changing (continue to abuse).
- Reasons to change (Coventry NSPCC).*
- Stages of change questionnaire (McGonnaughy et al., 1989): Sets out 32 questions which the respondent is asked to answer true or false. Sample items include: 'It might be worthwhile to work on my problem.' 'I wish I had more ideas on how to solve my problem.' 'I would rather cope with my faults than try to change them.' 'I guess I have my faults, but there's nothing that I really need to change.'

A model of change (Prochaska and DiClemente, 1982, 1986)

This model offers a comprehensive model of change, which allows for a range of change methods and skills to be delivered by different professionals according to the needs of individual offenders and their families. It is a very useful model for setting out realistic plans of work at the outset, for setting attainable targets, and for reviewing what progress, if any, has been made. Morrison (1991) originally applied the model to the broader child protection arena, and it is very appropriate to the child sexual abuse field as it originated from work with addicts (see Chapter 4 for a fuller discussion around this issue). The model is set out visually in fig. 22.

Pre-contemplation:
This is where the individual is considering change far less than the professionals, who are often reacting to the presenting situation. Morrison (1995) pointed out that this phase is characterised by blaming others, denying responsibility, or simply being unaware of the need to change, e.g. depression. Whilst in this stage no change is possible. Individuals thus require information and feedback in order that they can raise their awareness of the problem and the possibility of change (Miller and Rollnick, 1991). Pre-contemplation is the point at which the initial assessment takes place in order to ascertain, and hopefully enhance motivation to at least consider and contemplate, the need for change. Whilst the professionals enter the work at the action stage, the offender is probably only in the pre-contemplation change. Such a combination cannot succeed as the two groups are at incongru-

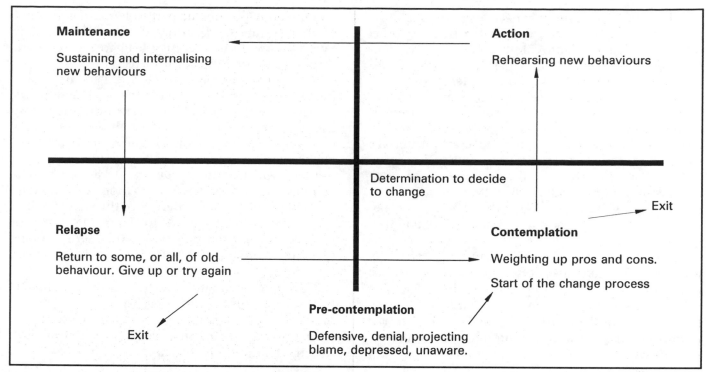

Figure 22: A comprehensive model of change (Prochaska and DiClemente, 1982; 1986)

ent stages of change. There may also be a very different definition of the problem between the two groups. For the offender, they are unlikely to be in a position to meaningfully engage in the proposed assessment work and a legal mandate often has to be sought. Offenders are the prime candidates to be resistant to any change efforts.

DiClemente (1991) identified four categories of pre-contemplation. Reluctant pre-contemplators are those who through lack of knowledge or inertia do not want to consider change. Rebellious pre-contemplators have a heavy investment in the problem behaviour and in making their own decisions. The resigned pre-contemplator has given up on the possibility of change and seems overwhelmed by the problem. The rationalising pre-contemplator has all the answers but have discounted change as they have figured out the odds of personal risk, or they have plenty of reasons why the problem is not a problem or is a problem for others but not for them.

Contemplation:
Offenders in this stage are most open to consciousness-raising interventions, such as observations, confrontations and interpretations (Prochaska and DiClemente, 1986). Through this process, their awareness of the problem increases, and they are then free to reject or adopt to change. The worker's aim is to tip the balance in favour of change (Miller and Rollnick, 1991). Contemplation is often a very paradoxical stage of change. The fact that the client is willing to consider the problem and the possibility of change offers hope for change. However, the fact that ambivalence can make it a

chronic condition can be very frustrating. It is the stage where many of the offenders will be waiting for the one final piece of information that will compel them to change. The hope is that the information makes the decision for them. Failing this, we need to offer them incentives to change by looking at past changes and by accentuating the positives (DiClemente, 1991). It is only after such contemplation that a viable contract for work can be made. There are six steps to the contemplation stage before we can move into the action stage and attempt change. They are:

- I accept that there is a problem
- I have some responsibility for the problem
- I have some discomfort about the problem and my part in it
- I believe that things must change
- I can see that I can be part of the solution
- I can see the first steps towards change

In the determination stage, the offender may now accept that something has to change although they may be unsure how it can be achieved. The task for workers is to remove any barriers to change, and create an environment where change is a realistic possibility.

Change remains a very painful process.

Action:
This is the stage where the offender engages in structured work to bring about a change, in a way that they believe they have determined. Such a tact avoids dependency on the workers. Yet action is a potentially stressful stage of change as they can fail and feel that they have failed or been rejected. We need to plan for relapse and involve the wider

family and the community networks, for it is they who are most likely both to spot the early signs of lapse, and who will provide the most day to day support (Morrison, 1995). This stage is where the individual is seen 'in action', implementing the plan. It is where they feel able to make a public commitment to action; to get some external confirmation of the plan; to seek support; to gain greater self-efficacy; and finally to create artificial, external monitors of their activity (DiClemente, 1991). For the worker, they should focus on successful activity and reaffirm the client's decisions. They should point out that change can be predicted where a person adheres to advice and the plan. The focus should be on learning, exploring and rehearsing ways of relating, thinking, behaving and feeling. All change is essentially a combination of these four basic human processes. This stage may take several months as new behaviour takes time to become established. At the end of the initial planning stage, the aim is to produce a longer-term plan of work.

Maintenance:
This is about sustaining and consolidating change and preventing relapse. This is the real test. It occurs when the new ways of relating and behaving become internalised and generalised across different situations. They do not now depend on the presence of the workers, but become consolidated and owned by the individual/family as part of themselves. It is through this process that the client's sense of self-efficacy has been increased (Morrison, 1995). Successful maintenance builds on each of the processes that has come before, as well as an open assessment of the conditions under which a person is likely to relapse (Prochaska and DiClemente, 1986). Stability and support will be essential to sustaining change, especially with the many families who have such poor experience of problem solving (Morrison, 1991).

Relapse:
The cyclical model of change allows for the reality that few people succeed first time round. Change comes from repeated efforts, re-evaluation, renewing of commitment, and incremental success. Relapse is thus part of, rather than necessarily hostile to, change. Change is a battle between the powerful forces that want us to stay the same, and our wish to be different (Morrison, 1991). It usually occurs gradually after an initial slip (often due to unexpected stress), rather than occurring spontaneously (DiClemente, 1991). It can lead to a loss of all or most of the gains, resulting in a giving-up and a return to pre-contemplation. This can be counteracted by the worker, giving feedback, on how long it takes to accomplish sustained change. They should aim to keep the change effort going rather than becoming disengaged and stuck. Morrison (1995) found that where it is noticed

quickly enough, and help is urgently sought and available from friends, family or professionals, all is by no means lost. This may lead to further work through the contemplation stage.

The assessment of change is a very uncertain process, and is often very fragile where it is achieved. Attitudinal changes are often the most noticeable to the workers, although we should also look for evidence of a willingness to engage and struggle with painful issues; a clearer understanding of their own continued potential for abusiveness; a willingness to share new information; and a clearer grasp of the victims experiences of the abuse (Willis, 1993). Workers do need to help the offender understand that the more they disclose, the more likely reduction, rather, than increase in, the risks they pose.

It is important that we acknowledge that change is very slow and it is often clearer to trust the lack of change as being an indicator of treatment failure than trusting change in a target area as evidence that the treatment is working.

Risk and recidivism

"There are no 'low risk' offenders and, without treatment, recidivism is almost inevitable" (Giarretto, 1982).

Risk factors place the individual at risk to re-offend. They are guidelines only and not absolute predictors. A risk factor is defined as *"any experience, event, environmental influences/parameters, internal/ external behaviour, historical factor, situations, that presents or enhances the offender's chances of re-offence. These may or may not be cycle behaviours and triggering events."* (Carich, 1994).

In determining the risk a sex offender presents, we need to consider the types of offences committed, sexual history, treatment history, and amenability to treatment. The complexity of assessing risk is reflected in the need to consider a range of issues, like the 21 features of risk articulated earlier by McEwan and Sullivan (1996). McGrath (1992) suggests that we focus on a further five factors, in order to look at offender risk: probability of re-offence; degree of harm most likely to result from a re-offence; conditions under which re-offence is most likely to occur; likely victims of a re-offence; and the time-scale within which a re-offence is most likely to occur. These are dealt with below.

1. *Offender risk:* Cannot be exclusively defined by the nature of the problem for which the offender has been referred, when we are aware of potential crossover of acts, the genders and ages of the victims, and the context of the offence, e.g. inside or outside the family. For example, Maletzky (1991) found that offenders who target victims outside the family are eight times more likely to re-offend, whilst those with multiple

victims are five times more likely to re-offend. Abel et al. (1985) also found that 75 per cent of recidivists crossed both age and sex in their choice of victims. The incest offender has the lowest recidivism rates (although they are known to offend against more than one child), whilst untreated exhibitionists have the highest recidivism rates. The younger the incest victim, the higher the risk of re-offence (Williams and Finkelhor, 1992). Offenders who abuse unrelated boys have higher recidivism rates than those who abused unrelated girls (McGrath, 1991); whilst the probability of recidivism rises with each offence. The degrees of force is associated with an increased risk to re-offend, especially those who are sexually aroused by aggression. Deviant sexual arousal is also associated to recidivism. Repeated sexual crimes remain an important predictor of future behaviour. The sexual abuse may well not be the only concern that needs to be resolved before rehabilitation can be effected. Stermac et al. (1990) found that 55 per cent of incest offenders demonstrated non-sexual forms of violence and abuse within their homes. As such, issues of anger, power, and control need to be addressed. An offender's specific beliefs about his own behaviour is likely to be predictive of future behaviour (Marshall and Eccles, 1991), as is their general attitude to sexual aggression (Segal and Stermac, 1990). Serin et al. (1994) found that psychopaths are at higher risk of re-offending than non-psychopaths, they re-offend sooner, and they are likely to become increasingly violent.

2. *Harm from the offence*: Again correlated with the use of weapons or force, and any escalation in the patterns of offending is significant.

3. *Conditions associated with re-offending*: Embraces their response to the assessment, degree of co-operation or compliance with any requests or conditions set down; the opportunity to access victims, either through family, friends or leisure interests, e.g. football coaching; the use of substances; availability of sexually stimulating material; level of mobility, e.g. through work, leisure outlets such as train-spotting; any anger related to job loss or restricted contact with their birth children.

4. *Likely victims*: through preference in previous offences, or as admitted by the offender in the work to date.

5. *When?* Many offenders act when they have opportunity, or they actively create them. The degree of supervision the offender receives from professionals and others, such as the family, will have a bearing on this point (see Hampson, Chapter 6). In broader terms, research does suggest that the risks from sex offenders against children is over a significant length of time and it is a myth that the risk reduces over time (particularly in the absence of treatment).

Assessing risk accurately is difficult when we know that this group lacks any distinct profile, and there is an absence of longitudinal studies post-offence to accurately predict recidivism. The task is compounded further if the offender is selective in the provision of information, or where the information derives solely from a single source.

There are as many different sets of risk factors from different instruments, authors and lists, that workers do not know where to begin. Some argue that there has been too great an emphasis on risk at the expense of rehabilitation, although there is a continuing difficulty in allowing rehabilitation in the absence of acknowledgement (Lusk, 1996).

Research findings

- Recidivism is a difficult issue because of different research definitions, samples and methods. There are several useful reviews of recidivism: Furby et al., 1989; Gendreau et al., 1996; Hanson and Bussiere, 1996, 1998; Hanson and Harris, 1998; and Marshall and Peters, 1994;

- Marshall and Barbaree (1990) indicated that the recidivism rate for child abusers increased from 12.5 per cent after two years to 64.3 per cent after four years if they had not received any treatment, whereas the figures were 5.5 per cent after two years and 25 per cent after four years if they had received treatment. They found that recidivism of untreated offenders was more likely if they were of low intellect, whereas being over forty and the offence being either genital-to-genital/anal contact was more predictive of treated offenders, as was an assault on a female child. They also found that different categories of untreated offender have different re-offence rates, e.g. incest offenders against girls 4–10 per cent, non-familial offenders against children 10–29 per cent (against females) and 13–40 per cent (against males).

- Mayer (1988) argued that there are identifiable factors which, where the offender makes gains in the treatment process, is considered a low risk for recidivist behaviour. These factors include: low stress level; employment stability; lack of denial/rationalisations; victim empathy; social support system; sexual adjustment with age-mates; absence of serious psychopathology; non-violent behaviours; anger management; adequate communication skills (assertiveness); absence of chemical abuse; knowledge of the dynamics of abuse and high-risk situations; ability to express feelings; absence of deviant fantasies; and willingness to receive help. She also pointed out that the likelihood of recidivism decreases with age.

Tools

- MacHovec (1994)* developed a different framework for assessing risk of future dangerousness.

He set out twenty risk factors that are most frequently cited in the literature and asks the offender to score themselves on a relative risk scale (0–1 is low; 2–3 is moderate; and 4–5 is high). The maximum score is 100. High score correlates with increased risk for re-offending. The findings can inform any treatment programme for the individual.

- Brearley (1982)* produced a set of questions for analysing the evidence regarding risk to a child. By considering the possible dangers and then dividing the hazards, i.e. the things that might cause the danger to occur, into two types—predisposing and situational—workers and the family are helped to examine the processes which may lead to a child being harmed, and actions which could cause or prevent situations from becoming dangerous. The model is also useful as it focuses on strengths which can be used to reduce risk and also gaps in information, i.e. what the workers have not been able to find out in the assessment. The model is summarised as an appendix.

- Evaluation of dangerousness for sexual offenders (Bays and Freeman-Longo, 1995)* developed a scale comprising 29 areas and 111 questions. The scale is designed to determine risk of the offender to the community, and preferably offset against other items and the offender's overall personality, given the authors concern that it is un-validated and, in any event, there is no scale which can always accurately predict dangerousness.

- Risk assessment check-list scale (Carich and Metzger, 1996b)*: This is based on both historical (16 factors) and non-historical (20 factors) risk factors. It provides some useful guidelines for assessing risk, based on probabilities, rather than absolutes.

- Risk assessment check-list scale protocol (Carich, Metzger and Cambell, 1996)*: This is a brief interview protocol designed to provide useful guidelines to assess for risk. It is an accompanying sister document to the item above.

- For a review of the variety of risk factors, the reader is referred to Carich (1994a and b) who explores the different risk factors from different instruments, authors, and previous lists.

Eligibility for treatment

A number of factors are key in determining offender suitability for treatment.

Most treatment programmes require that the offender must acknowledge that he committed the sexual abuse and take responsibility for his behaviour. Realistically, many offenders still have a long way to go at the end of the assessment, but they must have shown some commitment and movement in the right direction if they are to benefit further from treatment. We also need to note that some dimensions of denial (such as admission with justification) are less responsive to intervention, often entrenching the denial further. In order to benefit from treatment, the offender must acknowledge that their behaviour has been harmful to the victims; they must consider their offending behaviour a problem that they want to stop, and that they have expressed a desire to change; they must be willing to enter into and participate in treatment, and they must be prepared to comply with any conditions relating to the management of the risks they pose. Simply being in treatment should help reduce the risks.

There will be some offenders who meet the above eligibility criteria, but whose offences are so serious that they need to be incarcerated. In general terms, the offender eligible for community treatment is the individual who has an overall pro-social lifestyle; one who has demonstrated the capacity to follow through on tasks; who has relationships in the community; and who has no history of pronounced physical violence (Wolf et al., 1988).

One of the aims of the assessment is to gate-keep treatment, which is lengthy (12–24 months) and should arguably be reserved for cases where some success is anticipated. Yet we need to target the high-risk groups where the cost of not intervening substantially is ongoing, arguably escalating patterns of offending as they get older. This may not do wonders for the success rates for treatment, but it has to be cost-effective in the community (Breiling, 1994).

My view is that every sex offender has to be considered eligible for treatment as the costs of not offering it to them are evident in the longer-term. If choices have to be made on the basis of resources, we should opt to treat the high-risk groups, whilst using a legal mandate to determine a safe and appropriate placement, and supervised contact with children. However, it is futile to make a treatment recommendation when we are not in a position to offer any input, or where the quality of the treatment programme is questionable. Neither should we duck the need to make a 'no-treatment' recommendation where it is **absolutely necessary**, as inappropriate treatment recommendations are harmful to both the offender and to society. Frances et al. (1984) suggested the following benefits that may follow from a no-treatment decision:

- Avoiding a semblance of treatment when no effective treatment exists.
- Delaying treatment until a more appropriate time.
- Protecting the offender and the workers from wasting time, effort and money.

Mayer (1988) argued that some sex offenders do have a very poor prognosis and remain a high risk, regardless of what the workers might like to try to achieve. She set out numerous factors which contribute to poor-risk candidates for treatment. They included: the use of force or violence during the offences; they have a prior criminal record; they present with bizzare rituals associated with the offences; they chronically use alcohol or drugs; they sexually abused very young children; there is evidence of severe mental health problems; a history of severe childhood abuse; low IQ/capacity for insights; and chronic stressors in the environment.

Tools

- Workers may want to ask the offender to write down any previous treatment they have been involved in, for what kinds of problems, and with what outcome, to assist them in this task. They should also be asked to list at least five goals of treatment if they were accepted.
- The MSI (Nicols and Molinder, 1984) possesses a scale, which measures the sex offenders attitudes towards treatment.
- Workers may well make false positive or false negative errors in determining recidivism, risk as well as eligibility for treatment.

Treating sex offenders in denial: a crucial consideration

The issue of whether to allow sex offenders in denial into treatment is a crucial and contentious issue. Ethically, there is an argument against allowing them access whilst in denial, particularly as this can be misleading to the courts and others. It also appears unfair to allocate some of the precious places in treatment to those who claim they are innocent. If the denier is to remain in the community, we have to consider whether they will be accepted by the community and, if rejected, how this will affect their chances of relapse. The alternative view is that there is such a broad range of denial, with a clear starting point, that we should allow them access to treatment in order to facilitate some positive movement. This group does pose such a high risk for re-offending that they should be offered priority treatment places so they do not cause continued harm to others and themselves. Unfortunately, even where treatment is mandated, there is no guarantee that the offender will be engaged in the process of change.

Given that denial is central to most cases of sexual abuse, we have learned to develop some strategies for confronting these defences and assisting the offender to participate fully in any treatment programme. There needs to be time-limited focus on challenging denial in the first stages of treatment, and the offender can be very responsive to the recognition that they are viewed as 'whole' people and the focus is not simply on their sexual offences in isolation. The reader is referred to Schlank and Shaw (1996; 1997) for discussions of how to treat sex offenders in denial.

Brake and Shannon (1997) explored the concept of using a pre-treatment phase to increase admission in sex offenders. They reminded us that, as denial is neither a static nor a dichotomous concept, a 'snapshot assessment' of denial can be inaccurate. When was it done (at one week, a month etc.)? and by whom (police officers, psychologists, courts etc.)? They argue that a programme for 'deniers' offers the advantage of being able to evaluate the offender over time and deal with the range of their oppositional behaviour as it arises. Such a programme acknowledges that treatment requires a gradual, incremental approach, allowing for a systematic approach from the workers. Their pre-treatment programme aims to lessen denial so the offender can become eligible for the broader treatment regime. The programme consists of six stages: containment (to de-escalate and contain power struggles); symptom relief (which allows the offender to shift from their defence mechanisms which entrench rather than resolve their despair); reframe denial (by exploring with them the protective function served by denial); reframe accountability (so they may become ready to risk abandoning old defensive manoeuvres and accept increasing accountability and pro-social behaviour); enhance empathy (as the offender begins to accept increasing personal responsibility for his behaviour, he can begin to recognise the pain of others and identify it as his own); and successive approximation of confrontation (where they may now be ready to accept gradual confrontation of his behaviour). Using this approach, the authors have found a significant reduction in denial in 58 per cent of offenders.

They argue that an accurate assessment of denial should take into account the full range of the offender' resistance and defensiveness, both conscious and unconscious. Offenders who deny some aspect of the offence or who minimise and justify their behaviour are less amenable to change than other groups of deniers, as they become more entrenched in their resistance.

The aims of treatment

If the assessment of sex offenders is aimed at risk management, then the goal of assessment is to identify the factors related to the risk for sexual offending, and the goal of treatment is to change these risk factors amenable to change (Hanson et al., 1991). Other aims may include:

- Helping them control their actions in a way that avoids, or lessens, the risk of further abuse/ developing relapse prevention skills and establishing supervision conditions.
- Accepting responsibility and modifying cognitive distortions.
- Developing victim empathy.
- Controlling sexual arousal.

- Lengthening the time between the abusive incidents.
- Reducing the seriousness of the abusive incidents.
- Encouraging pro-social interactions by the offender/improving social competence.
- Strengthening the family unit by focussing on healthier, interactional communication patterns.
- Decreasing the pathology by creating healthier family dynamics (adapted from Griggs and Bold, 1995).

Sex offender treatment aims to reduce the possibility of future sex offending from the level it would have maintained without treatment (Perkins, 1987), and each treatment programme is based upon the nature of the offending and the circumstances of the offender.

Giarretto (1982) proposed a comprehensive child sexual abuse treatment programme which included individual counselling (child, father, mother), mother–daughter counselling, marital counselling, father–daughter counselling, family counselling and group counselling. Such a programme is very useful in providing a structure for many different pieces of work as well as providing a pathway towards considering rehabilitation. This is only likely to take place where the children themselves want to work towards a return home of the offender, and the offender is motivated to change.

Treatment components
Whilst each treatment package should be tailored to meet the needs of each individual, the components of an offender treatment package could include:

- Acceptance of responsibility.
- Confronting denial.
- Victim awareness and increased victim empathy.
- Full understanding of their abusive cycle.
- Full understanding of their targeting and grooming behaviours.
- Fantasy work—fully exploring their distorted thought processes.
- Decreasing cognitive distortions.
- Decreasing deviant arousal.
- Sexuality and perception.
- Sex and relationship education.
- Communications skills.
- Personal and social skills/increased social competency.
- Anger management.
- Assertiveness training.
- Reinforcement of internal and external inhibitors.
- Addressing family dynamics.
- Identifying risk factors.
- Where appropriate, addressing their own experiences of being abused.
- Work with the family.

- Identification of a relapse prevention programme.

Any treatment programme, regardless of its theoretical base, can only stand a chance of being successful if it is both flexible as well as being rigorously and properly implemented. Treatment programmes should be individualised, planned, implemented and fully evaluated by fully trained staff, under supervision.

Treatment goals and planning
Treatment outcome and treatment planning are linked: poor and unclear planning and goals correlate with poor and unsafe outcomes. The workers need to translate the aims of treatment into measurable goals and an explicit plan. They must be specific to the individual case, and must include dates for review and revision as new information or changing circumstances present themselves. Carich and Adkerson (1995) set out twelve common sex offender treatment goals:

- Acknowledge and accept personal responsibility for complete sexual assault history.
- Improve understanding of human sexuality, including normal sexual development and functioning, reproduction, and sexual health.
- Develop an understanding of how sexual assault negatively impacts the victim (short and long-term harm/risks) and develop empathy for own victim.
- Develop social and relationship skills to improve ability to meet social/sexual needs through appropriate relationships with age-mates.
- Separate anger, power, and other motivational issues from sexual behaviour. Improve anger management skills and remediate other motivations as needed.
- Clarify sexual arousal patterns and utilise modification techniques as appropriate.
- Clarify personal sexual offence cycle, include thoughts, feelings, behaviours and situations preceding offence. Demonstrate ability to recognise recurring aspcts of the cycle.
- Actively change the distorted thinking and lifestyle supports of the sexual offence behaviour.
- Develop realistic, achievable intervention plans for each step in the sexual assault cycle. Demonstrate ability to intervene in cycle.
- Develop motivation and commitment to recovery and to remaining offence-free.
- Inform significant others completely and honestly about offending problem and seek support in offence abstinence from appropriate sources.
- Explore unresolved issues from personal victimisation, sexual or other, and work toward healing.

MacHovec (1994) argued that two major treatment goals should be included in treatment planning: normalisation and re-socialisation. Normalisation is intra-personal because it involves a thorough understanding of societal, community, and family values, lawful behaviour, and appropriate sexual outlet. It requires exploring and processing what is, and is not, normal behaviour and the self-concept including role identity, sexual preference, and self-esteem to restore personality function and continue normative development. Re-socialisation is interpersonal because it educates the offender in appropriate social and socio-sexual interaction in society, the home and community.

Tools

- MacHovec and Wieckowski (1992)* developed a single comprehensive classification system of ten factors which apply to all sex offenders. Each factor is rated on a scale of 0 (no clinical significance) to 5 (extreme deviation). They produced a graphic profile to assess treatment need and which can be used as a longitudinal measure of treatment progress (or lack of it). The reader is referred to the original paper for the details of how it was formulated.
- MacHovec (1994)* also produced a treatment needs assessment and progress summary checklist, where he suggests 10 factors with a 0 to 5 rating scale. This can be used at various stages of the treatment process and when they change setting (e.g. prison to community) or change workers. He explores the treatment variables further in Calder (forthcoming).
- Carole Metzger and Mark Carich (1997) have developed a very useful 11 point treatment plan in which they set out clear goals and criteria against which these can be judged. Contact the author for more details of this substantial 40 page plan (see resources section for details).

Reconstituting the family?

The following are very useful guides to prognosis speculation and reconstitution of the family. In making a decision about rehabilitating the offender home, we should consider certain factors, which include:

1. That the parents:
- Have accepted responsibility for the abuse.
- Are working for and achieving changes.
- Have demonstrated commitment to rehabilitation.
- Are open and honest with professionals.
- Have willingness and capacity to ask for help if problems occur.
- Have realistic expectations of the child and understand and accept the problems that remain.
2. Relationships within the family are stable and supportive.
3. External stressors are manageable.
4. There is an agreed child protection plan, which

is SMART (specific, measurable, appropriate, realistic, and time-limited).
5. Which is consistent with the child's needs and wishes and feelings.

Evaluating the assessment as a basis for planning

Workers need to consider:

- Whether the circumstances giving rise to the causes for concern are fully understood.
- What patterns of interaction were operating in the family and the family–worker system during the assessment?
- Have changes occurred? Can you produce evidence to back these up?
- Is there a clear capacity for change? Is there evidence for this?
- Do the circumstances, which led to concern, still exist?

A framework for assessing prognosis

Bentovim et al. (1987) set out a useful framework for considering the prognosis of a successful reconstitution of the family:

Hopeful

- The offender accepts responsibility for the abuse, and informs all family members of this. He needs to accept punishment/ treatment, as well as accepting the primary responsibility for monitoring and managing his future behaviour.
- The child is not blamed, and is not scapegoated by any family member.
- The child needs to be heard in the family and allowed to speak for themselves.
- The marital relationship is improved.
- The mother accepts some future responsibility for protecting the child, and is caring and supportive.
- The seriousness for the child has been recognised and accepted.

Doubtful

- Multi-generational culture of abuse is evident.
- There is evidence of a collusive coping pattern.
- There is uncertainty about what ought to happen to the offender or the marital relationship.
- There is conflict between adult and children's needs and they remain unresolved.
- There is a likelihood of the child being scapegoated.
- The child is unsure of themselves and remains tentative, silent and half-frozen.
- Siblings old enough to distance themselves from any risks.
- The offender does not accept any responsibility for the abuse.
- The mother is a 'victim'.
- The relationship between mother and victim is very poor.

Hopeless

- The responsibility is denied by all the adults.
- The child is blamed and rejected outright.
- The mother is unable to protect the child.
- The offender shows no guilt and remains powerful in the family.
- Generational evidence of abuse.
- Parents put their own needs first—above the child.
- Child seen as the initiator.
- Unable or unwilling to accept help.
- Career paedophile.
- Longstanding problems with alcohol, patterns of promiscuity, psychiatric illness etc. (adapted from Bentovim et al., 1987).

Criteria for the reconstitution of the family:

- The father acknowledges responsibility for the sexual (and other) abuse and does not project blame onto the daughter. They must also accept that 'old rules' no longer operate.
- All family members appreciate the seriousness of what has occurred and the need for change.
- The workers and all family members express reasonable assurance that the child is safe from repeated abuse.
- The daughter expresses and demonstrates the ability to seek professional help in the event that she is again approached. The workers must be confident that the child victim is not pressured by other family members, to request, or agree to, the offender's return home. They may be aware of the effects on the family of their disclosure and self-blame, or be scapegoated by the family.
- The mother has demonstrated an ongoing ability to prioritise the protection of the children, and herself, from abuse. Where the offender continues to pose a high risk, then he clearly should not be at home, as it is unfair and unrealistic to expect the mother to assume the primary responsibility for the offender's behaviour.
- The worker and family members are confident that sufficient progress has been made towards the resolution of short and long-term treatment goals. This should include all identified problems, particularly where different forms of abuse co-exist.
- Communication between family members has improved and there is evidence of setting appropriate boundaries and listening/talking to each other.
- The mother–daughter relationship has improved and the mother does not hold the victim accountable for the abuse.
- The relationship boundaries have been strengthened resulting in more appropriate family roles and improved marital relationship (adapted from Server and Janzen, 1982).

For a paper specifically relating to the reconstitution of the incestuous family, the reader is referred to Powell and Ilett (1992).

Reviewing progress: moving towards relapse prevention

Any offender developing a relapse prevention programme should adopt the ACE system: *Avoidance* strategy (if you can't avoid, then control); *Control* strategies (If you can't control, then escape); and *Escape* strategies. A relapse prevention module, in treatment, attempts to accomplish several goals for the offender: dispel any misconception that treatment will eliminate all problems with future sexually deviant behaviour; identify reactions which create a high risk for relapse and the subsequent chain of responses culminating in re-offence; identify cognitive and behavioural skills which will enable the offender to control his behaviour and reduce the likelihood of relapse; as well as being able to demonstrate the use of the relapse prevention strategies (Green, 1995).

Workers may want to periodically re-test offenders with certain tasks and questionnaires to measure any change or regression in the offender, and any other significant family members. The following list highlights areas of concern for the offender should they emerge at any stage in the process of completing the work, and for some time afterwards.

MacHovec (1994) suggests that sex offender treatment should be seen as a 3 stage process:

- Awareness, acknowledgement of the offence, accepting responsibility for it, and amenable to therapy. The major obstacles are denial and minimisation, and the goal is admitting the offence.
- Understanding the underlying factors in the personality, environment, victim selection, trigger situations and offence method. The major obstacles are distancing, discounting, rationalisation, intellectualisation, with the goal being empathy and remorse.
- Change, to know, choose, and practice appropriate socio-sexual and responsible personal behaviours. The major obstacles include arrested development, personality traits or disorder. The goal is to make amends, and restitution where appropriate.

Recovery assessments

Carich has developed materials relating to a recovery assessment, which are very much the wave of the future. He talks about four types of assessment: the initial assessment, a progress assessment (where the offender's progress in treatment is measured), a risk assessment (which addresses the probability that the offender will re-offend), and the recovery assessment. Recovery assessments are evaluations of the offender's capability to maintain abstinence from sexual offending.

Carich (1997b) does accept that the concept of recovery in sex offender treatment is a controversial one. Recovery assessments are similar to, but yet different from risk assessments. Risk assessments generally assess the offender's current risk, or probability of re-offence. Likewise, recovery assessments provide indications of progress, levels of change, along with areas that still need improvement. These include the following important dimensions: motivation to change and recovery; commitment; personal responsibility; social interest; social dimension/relationships; offending cycle; lifestyle behaviours; insight into developmental/ motivational factors; resolution of developmental/ motivational dynamics; sexual identity issues; arousal control; psychopathology; disowning behaviours; relapse intervention; and self-structure (Carich, 1997). These are the typical goals of offender treatment. The variable of treatment adds a different dimension to assessment, and the recovery assessment evaluates the progress of the offender's recovery.

Recovery is a lifelong process and time does not heal sex offenders, although treatment can help the offender to learn to manage their life, including reducing deviant responses and incorporating appropriate responses.

Tools

- Carich (1997) has produced a useful framework for evaluating recovery in which he explores the components of the fifteen elements and then provides us with an interview profile with over eighty questions for the offender (see Appendices).
- He has also provided us with a recovery scale (Carich, 1996)*, a recovery inventory (Carich, 1991b)*, and a recovery risk assessment scale (Carich et al., 1994)*, which correspond with these.
- Finally, the recovering offender may show some of the following characteristics: more honest; less frequency of deviant behaviour; takes responsibility in general; appears less narcissistic consistently; expresses/experiences victim empathy; capable of explaining dynamics of their offending without blaming; knowing their cycle, cues and triggers; uses anger controls and interventions; has a variety of coping strategies; has positive self-esteem; has a stable support system; doesn't keep secrets; or is proud of their accomplishments (Carich, 1997).

Space and the focus of the book dictate against a further exploration of this important emerging concept, but the author details as a future contact point for interested workers is contained in the resources section. Carich and Lampley (forthcoming) considers the implications of these ideas for young people who sexually abuse.

Behaviour changes to be observed in the offender when they return home include:

- Starts to abuse alcohol or drugs.
- Stresses the impossibility of re-offending.
- Interested in pornography.
- Stresses the innocence of his sexual contact with children.
- Begins to minimise the impact of his past offending.
- Keeps leaving the house for no apparent reason.
- Lies in other areas of his life.
- Gets involved in youth activities.
- Wants to be left alone with the children.
- Changes noticeably in his sexual functioning.
- Discusses sexual issues in front of the children.
- Starts to use innuendos.
- Becomes paranoid and stresses the fact that you don't trust him (Wyre, 1987).

Contact issues

Whilst the issue of contact enshrined in the Children Act (1989) expects the local authority to promote contact between children and their parents, this guiding principle needs refining in relation to the circumstances for a child who has been sexually abused. Jones and Parkinson (1995) argued that *"English courts have made extensive use of the option of supervised access as a means of keeping alive the parent-child relationship with the expressed hope that at a later time perhaps when the child is older and better able to protect himself or herself, or when the parents' propensity to sexual abuse has diminished, unsupervised access will be possible."*

They go on to identify the factors which most influence courts in making decisions about contact where sexual abuse is a concern. These are:

- *"The strength of the relationship between the father and the child prior to the discovery."*
- *"The need to have the same contact arrangements for all the children."*
- *"The child desires this contact."*
- *"The view taken by the parent with whom the children are living."*

Significantly, Jones and Parkinson also highlighted that courts are reluctant to pursue contact against the recommendation of the local authority. The perceived view of the courts is often a powerful influencing factor when social workers are making early decisions about contact. The presumption is, that whilst contact is supervised, the child/young person can be protected whilst also facilitating positive parenting and promoting parental responsibility in a climate of partnership. Rose (1998) has argued that, for the child who may have been sexually abused, this is at best an unhelpful starting point.

Understanding the effects of sexual abuse

Rose goes on to argue that one of the strengths that the social services perspective brings to the decision-making process in cases of child sexual abuse, is in having both a broad understanding of the mental process for the offender in offending as well as an understanding of the trauma for the child who becomes the victim. The courts tend to view child sexual abuse as an event, or series of events. They operate on the need to make definite findings of fact. The task for the court in looking at contact, therefore, is seen as ensuring that a further 'event' does not take place. For social workers, the tasks evolve from understanding that child sexual abuse is a planned process over a long period of time, requiring the offender to develop thinking errors, and the capacity to deny all this to themselves and others. Alongside this is the knowledge of the effects of the abuse on the child. This understanding means that at the initial stages of investigation and assessment, the social workers can make assumptions that:

- The development of the relationship between the offender and child is based on a distortion of thinking and action.
- Within the relationship there will be blurred role boundaries.
- There will be long-standing cognitive manipulation of the child.
- The child will lack conviction that what happened was wrong and/or was not their fault.
- The relationship between the child and his/her mother is also likely to have been distorted by the actions of the offender.
- The child will believe in the domination and power of the offender.
- The non-abusing carer will not have had time to unpack the overwhelming and conflicting range of emotions for herself, let alone those of her child.

Importantly, any consideration of the child's own wishes and feelings in relation to contact also needs to be viewed in the context not only of their age and understanding but all of the above.

Decision-making in contact

It is now accepted good practice that following allegations of child sexual abuse, where concerns are high, if possible the alleged offender should be removed from the child's home. The multiple abuses are built-up in hidden and subtle ways often over long periods of time, and for both the offender and child it is a lengthy process for these to begin to be resolved. Physical separation does not change distorted thinking or emotional damage. It is therefore safe to assume that the assumptions made at the initial stages of the investigation and assessment (listed above) will also be true during any initial contact. The implications of this are that, in cases of child sexual abuse, there is a need to suspend contact between the child and the offender in the first instance. A failure to do this leaves the opportunity for the negative messages for the child, listed above, to be further exploited.

It is inevitably at the forefront of the social workers and courts' minds that stopping contact may damage a relationship between a parent and child. However, there are very real risks of longer-term harm to a child in promoting contact where there may have been sexual abuse, is far greater.

The next process is to consider the long-term view, i.e., following assessment, should contact happen in the future and, if so, in which circumstances. Jones and Parkinson (1995) suggest that the key question is, 'Is the contact desirable if it is free of abuse?' Given that the relationship has developed through distortion, it may be difficult to perceive its appropriateness for the child. However, it is necessary to pursue a more thorough assessment before considering this as an option. The process of assessment when considering contact between a child and a sexual offender should be based on four areas of work:

- Individual work with the child. This work should address both the effects of abuse for the child, validate their feelings, and counteract the distortions.
- Individual work with the non-abusing carer.
- Work with the child and non-abusing carer together. This work should promote the strengthening of their relationship.
- Individual work with the offender.

If the renewal of contact is to be healthy, the evaluation of these pieces of work requires, at the very least, a profound change in the behaviour and attitude of the offender. In conjunction with this, the relationship between the child and the non-abusing carer needs to be strengthened and, at the very least, the child needs to have increased self-esteem and a clear understanding of where the responsibility for the abuse lies. This is based on the assumption therefore that where sexual abuse has occurred, continued contact with the offender, without change, presents an unacceptable risk of physical, emotional and/or psychological harm to the child. The task for renewal of contact is to provide evidence that this risk is sufficiently reduced, rather than the assumption that normal parent–child interaction can continue as long as an abusive incident does not occur. The primary onus to provide this evidence must be in the work with the offender. That is, the offender should begin to acknowledge the abuse without minimising it and acknowledge, at an emotional as well as intellectual level, the harm caused to the child. The child and non-abusing carer must have time and opportunity to recover from the trauma at some fundamental levels and the child's wishes and feelings must be placed in the context of our understanding the effects of abuse.

The long-term welfare of the child is dependent upon the recognition that, for a child who has been sexually abused, it is necessary to stop contact with the offender in the first instance and then work towards a position where the inherent risks to the child are sufficiently reduced.

Should contact be reintroduced, then this should be done gradually—outside the home at first, with both the frequency and duration of the contacts increasing over time. Venues outside the home do allow new behaviours to be tested in public before returning to the home. It also allows the supervising officer to look at interactions and the resolution of any emerging problems.

References

ABEL GG and BECKER JV (1985) Sexual Interest Cardsort.

ABRAMS S (1991) The use of polygraphy with sex offenders. Annals of Sex Research 4: 239–263.

ABEL GG, BECKER JV and CUNNINGHAM-RATHNER J (1984) Complications, consent and cognition in sex between children and adults. Interpersonal Journal of Law and Psychiatry 7: 89–103.

ABEL GG, BECKER JV, CUNNINGHAM-RATHNER J, KAPLAN M and REICH J (1984b) The Treatment of Sex Offenders. NY: SBC-TM.

ABEL GG, BECKER JV, CUNNINGHAM-RATHNER J, MITTLEMAN RS and ROULEAU J (1988) Multiple paraphiliac diagnosis among sex offenders. Bulletin of the American Academy of Psychiatry and the Law 16: 153–168.

ABEL GG, BECKER JV, CUNNINGHAM-RATHNER J, ROULEAU J and MURPHY W (1987) Self-reported crimes of non-incarcerated paraphiliacs. Journal of Interpersonal Violence 2: 3–25.

ABEL GG, BECKER JV, MURPHY N and FLANAGAN B (1981) Identifying dangerous child molesters. In Stuart RB (ed.) Violent behaviour: Social learning approaches to prediction, management and treatment. NY: Brunner-Mazel, 116–137.

ABEL GG, BLANCHARD E and BECKER JV (1978) An integrated treatment program for rapists. In Rada R (ed.) Clinical aspects of the rapist. NY: Grune and Stratton, 161–214.

ABEL GG, GORE DK, HOLLAND CL, CAMP N, BECKER JV and RATHNER J (1989) The measurement of cognitive distortions of child molesters. Annals of Sex Research 2: 135–153.

ABEL GG, MITTLEMAN MS and BECKER JV (1985) Sex offenders: Results of assessment and recommendations for treatment. In Ben-Aron MH, Hucker SJ and Webster CD (eds.) Clinical criminology: The assessment and treatment of criminal behaviour. Toronto: M&M graphics, 191–205.

ABEL GG, ROULEAU J and CUNNINGHAM-RATHNER J (1985). Sexual aggressive behaviour. In Curran W, McGarry A and Shah S (eds.) Modern legal psychiatry and psychology. Philadelphea: EA Davis.

ABRAMSON P and MOSHER DL (1985) Development of a measure of negative attitudes towards masturbation. Journal of Consulting and Clinical Psychology 43: 485–490.

ADCOCK M (1995) Assessment. In Wilson K and Jones A (eds.) The child protection handbook. London: Bailliere Tindall, 188–210.

ADKINS BJ, TABER JI and RUSSO AM (1985). The spoken autobiography: A powerful tool in group psychotherapy. Social Work 30: 435–439.

ALEXANDRIA ASSOCIATES Adult sex offender program. Oregon: Alexandria Associates.

ALLEN CM and POTHAST HL (1994) Distinguishing characteristics of male and female child sex abusers. Young Victims, Young Offender. NY: Haworth Press, 78–89.

AMERICAN PSYCHIATRIC ASSOCIATION (1987) Diagnostic and statistical manual of mental disorders (3rd edition). Washington, DC: American Psychiatric Association.

ANDERSON BL and BROFFITT B (1988) Is there a reliable and valid self-report measure of sexual behaviour? Archives of Sexual Behaviour 17(6): 509–525.

ANGUS G and WOODWARD S (1995) Child abuse and neglect in Australia 1993–94. Child Welfare Series, No 13. Canberra: Australian Institute of Health and Welfare.

ANNON JS (1976) The behavioural treatment of sexual problems (Vol 2). Intensive Therapy. Honolulu: Enabling Systems Inc.

ARAJI S and FINKELHOR D (1986) Abusers: A review of the research. In Finkelhor D (ed.) A sourcebook on child sexual abuse. Beverly Hills, Ca.: Sage, 89–118.

ARONFREED J (1968) Conduct and conscience: The socialisation of internalised control over behaviour, NY: Academic Press.

ATHANASION R (1973) A review of public attitudes on sexual issues. In Zubin J and Money J (eds.) Contemporary sexual behaviour: Critical issues in the 1970s. Baltimore: John Hopkins University Press.

ATOLLO JF, GODDARD MA and KEENEY KS (eds.) (1991) A co-ordinated community approach to child sexual abuse: Assessing a model. Huntsville, Alabama: National Research Centre on Child Sexual Abuse.

AWAD GA and SAUNDERS EB (1989) Adolescent child molesters: Clinical observations. Child Psychiatry and Human Development 19(3): 195–206.

BADGLEY R (1984) Sexual offences against children: Report of the committee on sexual offences against children and youths (Vols 1&2). Ottowa, Canada; Ministry of Supplies.

BADGLEY R, ALLARD H, McCORMICK N, PROUDFOOT P, FORTIN D, OGILVIE D, RAE-GRANT Q, GELINAS P, PEPIN L and SUTHERLAND S (1984) Sexual offences against children (Vol. 1). Ottowa: Canada Government Publishing Centre.

BAER PE, COLLINS FH, BOUIANOFF GG and KETCHEL MF (1979) Assessing personality factors in essential hypertension with a brief self-report instrument. Psychosomatic Medicine 4: 321–330.

BAGLEY C (1997) Children, sex and social policies. Aldershot: Avebury.

BAKER AW and DUNCAN SF (1985) Child sexual abuse: A study of prevalence in Great Britain. Child Abuse and Neglect 9: 457–476.

BAKKER CB, BAKKER-RABDAU MK and BREIT S (1978) The measurement of assertiveness and aggressiveness. Journal of Personality Assessment 42: 277–284.

BANCROFT J (1991) The sexuality of sexual offending. Criminal Behaviour and Mental Health 1: 181–192.

BARBAREE HE (1991) Denial and minimisation among sex offenders: Assessment and treatment outcomes. Forum on Corrections Research 3: 30–33.

BARBAREE HE and MARSHALL WL (1989) Erectile responses among heterosexual child molesters, father-daughter incest offenders, and matched non-offenders: Five distinct age preference profiles. Canadian Journal of Behavioural Sciences 21: 70–82.

BARBAREE HE and PEACOCK EJ (1995) The assessment of sexual preferences in cases of alleged child sexual abuse. In Ney T (ed.) True and false allegations of child sexual abuse: Assessment and case management. NY: Brunner/Mazel, 242–259.

BARBAREE HE, MARSHALL WL and CONNOR J (1988) The social problem-solving of child molesters. Unpublished manuscript, Queen's University, Ontario, Canada.

BARBAREE HE, MARSHALL WL and LANTHIER RD (1979) Deviant sexual arousal in rapists. Behaviour Research and Therapy 17: 215–222.

BARCLAY AM (1973) Sexual fantasies in men and women. Medical Aspects of Sexuality 7: 205–216.

BARLOW DH (1986) Causes of sexual dysfunction: The role of anxiety and cognitive interference. Journal of Consulting and Clinical Psychology 54: 140–148.

BARLOW D, ABEL G, BLANCHARD E, BRISTOW A and YOUNG L (1977) A heterosocial skill checklist for males. Behaviour Therapy 8: 229–239.

BARKER M and MORGAN R (1993) Sex offenders: A framework for the evaluation of community-based treatment. London: Home Office.

BARTHOLOMEW K and HOROWITZ LM (1991) Attachment styles among adults: A test of a four-category model. Journal of Personality and Social Psychology 61: 226–224.

BARTHOLOMEW K and PERLMAN D (eds.) (1991) Attachment processes in adulthood. London: Jessica Kingsley.

BATTLE J (1992) Culture-free self-esteem inventories. Austin: Pro-Ed.

BAXTER DJ, BARBAREE HE and MARSHALL WL (1986) Sexual responses to consenting and forced sex in a large sample of rapists and non-rapists. Behaviour Research and Therapy 24: 513–520.

BAXTER M (1990) Flesh and blood: Does pornography lead to sexual violence? New Scientist 5.5.90, 37–41.

BAYS L and FREEMAN-LONGO R (1995) Evaluation of dangerousness for sexual offences. In Carich MS and Adkerson D (eds.) Adult sexual offender assessment packet. Brandon, VT: Safer Society Press.

BECK A and SHIPLEY BE (1989) Recidivism of prisoners released in 1983. Washington: US Department of Justice.

BECK A and WEISHEAR ME (1989) Cognitive therapy. In Corsini A and Wedding D (eds.) Current psychotherapies. Itasca, Il: FE Peacock, 285–320.

BECK AT (1976) Cognitive theory and emotional disorders. NY: Meridian.

BECK AT and BECK RW (1972) Screening depressed patients in family practice – a rapid technique. Postgraduate Medicine 52: 81–85.

BECK AT, WARD CH, MENDELSON M, MOCK J and ERBAUGH J (1961) An inventory for measuring depression. Archives of General Psychiatry 4: 561–571.

BECKER JV and ABEL GG (1985) Methodological and ethical issues in evaluating and treating adolescent sex offenders. In Otey EM and Ryan GD (eds.) Adolescent sex offenders: Issues in research and treatment. Rockville, MD: US Dept. of Health and Human Services, 109–129.

BECKER JV, ABEL G, BLANCHARD E, MURPHY W and COLEMAN E (1978) Evaluating social skills of sexual aggressives. Criminal Justice and Behaviour 5(4): 357–367.

BECKER JV and KAPLAN MS (1988) The assessment and treatment of adolescent sexual offenders. Advances in Behavioural Assessment of Children and Families 4: 97–118.

BECKER JV and KAPLAN MS (1988b) The adolescent sexual interest cardsort.

BECKER JV and QUINSEY VL (1993) Assessing suspected child molesters. Child Abuse and Neglect 17: 169–174.

BECKER JV, CUNNINGHAM-RATHNER J and KAPLAN MS (1986) Adolescent sex offenders, criminal and sexual histories and demographics, and recommendations for reducing future offences. Journal of Interpersonal Violence 1: 431–445.

BECKER-LAUSEN E and MALLON-KRAFT S (1997) Pandemic outcomes: The intimacy variable. In Kanber GK and Jasinski JL (eds.) Out of the darkness: Contemporary perspectives on family violence. Thousand Oaks, Ca.: Sage, 49–57.

BECKETT RC (1994) Assessment of sex offenders. In Morrison T, Erooga M and Beckett RC (eds.) Sexual offending against children: Assessment and treatment of male abusers. London: Routledge, 55–79.

BECKETT RC, BEECH A, FISHER D and FORDHAM AS (1994) Community-based treatment for sex offenders: An evaluation of 7 treatment programmes. London: Home Office.

BECKETT RC, BEECH A, FISHER D and SCOTT-FORDHAM A (1994) Community-based treatment for sex offenders: And evaluation of seven treatment programmes. London: HMSO.

BECK-SANDER A (1995) Childhood abuse in adult offenders: The role of control in perpetrating cycles of abuse. The Journal of Forensic Psychology 6(3): 486–498.

BEEZLEY-MRAZEK PJ, LYNCH MA and BENTOVIM A (1983) Sexual abuse of children in the UK. Child Abuse and Neglect 7: 147–153.

BEITCHMAN JH, ZUCKER KV, HOOD JE and DACOSTA JA (1991) A review of the short-term effects of child sexual abuse. Child Abuse and Neglect 15: 537–556.

BEITCHMAN JH, ZUCKER KV, HOOD JE, DACOSTA JA, ACKERMAN D and CASSAMA E (1992) A review of the long-term effects of child sexual abuse. Child Abuse and Neglect 16: 101–118.

BELL AP, WEINBERG MS and HAMMERSMITH SK (1981) Sexual preference: Its development in men and women. Bloomington Il.: Indiana University Press.

BENGIS SM (1986) A comprehensive service delivery system with a continuum of care for adolescent sexual offenders. Orwell, VT: Safer Society Press.

BENTOVIM A (1994) Is the increasing criminalisation of child abuse an obstacle to working in partnership? Keynote presentation to the 2nd national congress on child abuse and neglect, University of Bristol, 5–8 July 1994.

BENTOVIM A, ELTON A and TRANTER M (1987) Prognosis for rehabilitation after abuse. Adoption and Fostering 11(1): 26–31.

BENTOVIM A, ELTON A, HILDEBRAND J, TRANTER M and VIZARD E (eds.) (1988) Child sexual abuse within the family: Assessment and treatment. London: Wright.

BERNARD J and BERNARD M (1984) The abusive male seeks treatment: Jekyll and Hyde. Family Relations 33: 543–547.

BIENVENU MJ (1970) Measurement of marital communication. Family Co-ordinator 19: 26–31.

BLANCHARD GT (1995) The difficult connection: The therapeutic relationship in sex offender treatment. Brandon, VT: Safer Society Press.

BLISS P (1990) The ABC exercise. Derbyshire Probation Service.

BLUME ES (1986) The walking wounded – post-incest syndrome. Siecus Report 15: 5–7.

BOLTON FG, MORRIS LA and MacEACHRON (1989) Males at risk: The other side of child sexual abuse. Newbury Park, Ca.: Sage.

BONTA J, LAW M and HANSON RK (1998) The prediction of criminal and violent recidivism among mentally disordered offenders: A meta-analysis. Psychological Bulletin 123: 123–142.

BOWER SA and BOWER GH (1976) Asserting yourself: A practical guide for positive change. Reading, Mass.: Addison-Wesley Publishing Co.

BOWNES IT (1993) Sexual and relationship dysfunction in sexual offenders. Sexual and Marital Therapy 8(2): 157–165.

BOWNES IT and GORMAN EC (1991) Assailant's sexual dysfunction during rape reported by their victims. Medicine, Science and the Law 31: 322–328.

BRADFORD JMW (1985) Organic treatments for the male sexual offender. Behavioural Sciences and the Law 3: 355–375.

BRAKE SC and SHANNON D (1997) Using pre-treatment to increase admission in sex offenders. In Schwartz BK and Cellini HR (eds.) The sex offender: New insights, treatment innovations and legal developments. Kingston, NJ: Civic Research Institute.

BRANNON R and DAVID P (1976) The male sex role. In David P and Brannon R (eds.) The 49% majority: The male sex role. NY: Addison-Wesley.

BRAY M (1997) Sexual abuse: The child's voice. Poppies on the rubbish heap. London: Jessica Kingsley.

BREARLEY CP (1982) Risk and social work: Hazards and helping. London: Routledge and Kegan Paul.

BREER W (1987) The adolescent molester. Springfield, Ill.: Charles C Thomas.

BREHM SS (1992) Intimate relationships (2nd edition). NY: McGraw Hill.

BREILING J (1994) Paper presented at the 10th national training conference of the National Adolescent Perpetrator Network. Denver, Colorado, February 1994.

BRIERE J and RUNTZ M (1989) University males sexual interest in children: Predicting potential indices of 'paedophilia' in a non-forensic sample. Child Abuse and Neglect 13: 65–75.

BRIERE J, MALAMUTH N and CHECK JVP (1985) Sexuality and rape supportive beliefs. Interpersonal Journal of Women's Studies 8: 398–403.

BRIGGS D, DOYLE P, GOOCH T and KENNINGTON R (1998) Assessing men who sexually abuse: A practice guide. London: Jessica Kingsley.

BRIGGS DI (1994) Assessment of sex offenders. In McMurran and Hodge JE (eds.) The assessment of criminal behaviours of clients in secure settings. London: Jessica Kingsley, 53–67.

BRIGGS DI (1994b) The management of sex offenders in institutions. In Morrison T, Erooga M and Beckett RC (eds.) Sexual offending against children: Assessment and treatment of male abusers. London: Routledge, 55–79.

BRIGGS DI (1998) Men as victims of sexual abuse, men as abusers. In Bear Z (ed.) Good practice in counselling people who have been abused. London: Jessica Kingsley, 106–116.

BROWN CM, TRAVERSO G and FEDEROFF JP (1996) Masturbation prohibition in sex offenders: A crossover study. Archives of Sexual Behaviour 25: 397–408.

BROWNE A and FINKELHOR D (1986) Impact of child sexual abuse: A review of the research. Psychology Bulletin 99(1): 66–77.

BROWNMILLER S (1975) Against our will: Men, women and rape. London: Penguin.

BUCHANAN A (1996) Cycles of child maltreatment: Facts, fallacies and interventions. Chichester: John Wiley and Sons.

BUDIN LE and JOHNSON CF (1989) Sex abuse prevention programs: Offenders' attitudes about their efficacy. Child Abuse and Neglect 13(1): 77–87.

BUIKHUSEN W, van der PLAS-KORENHOFF C and BONTEKUE HM (1985) Parental home deviance. International Journal of Offender Therapy and Comparative Criminology 29: 201–210.

BUMBY KM (1995) Bumby cognitive distortions scales. In Carich MS and Adkerson DL (eds.) Adult sexual offender assessment packet. Brandon, VT: Safer Society Press, 77–80.

BUMBY KM (1996) Assessing the cognitive distortions of child molesters and rapists: Development and validation of the molest and rape scales. Sexual Abuse: A Journal of Research and Treatment 8(1): 37–54.

BUMBY KM and HANSON DJ (1997) Intimacy deficits, fear of intimacy and loneliness among sex offenders. Criminal Justice and Behaviour 24(3): 315–331.

BUMBY KM and MARSHALL WL (1994) Loneliness and intimacy deficits among incarcerated rapists and child molesters. Paper presented to the 13th annual conference of the association for the treatment of sexual abusers. San Fransisco, Ca., October 1994.

BURBACH L (1980) Women discover orgasm. NY: Free Press.

BURGESS AW, HARTMAN CR, RESSLER RK, DOUGLAS JE and MacCORMACK A (1986) Sexual homicide: A motivational model. Journal of Interpersonal Violence 1: 251–272.

BURKHARDT SA and ROTATORI AF (1995) Treatment and prevention of child sexual abuse: A child-generated model. Washington, DC: Taylor and Francis.

BURNHAM D et al. (1990) Offending and masculinity: Working with males. Probation Journal, September 1990, 106–111.

BURNS DD (1981) Feeling good: The new mood therapy. NY: American Library.

BURT MR (1980) Cultural myths and supports for rape. Journal of Personality and Social Psychology 38(2): 217–230.

BURT MR and KATZ BC (1987) Dimensions of recovery from rape: Focus on growth outcomes. Journal of Interpersonal Violence 2(1): 57–81.

BUSS AH and DURKEE A (1957) An inventory for assessing different kinds of hostility. Journal of Clinical Psychology 21: 343–349.

BYRNE D (1977) Social psychology and the study of sexual behaviour. Personality and Social Psychology Bulletin 3: 3–30.

BYRNE D and KELLEY K (eds.) (1986) Alternative approaches to the study of sexual behaviour. Hillside, NJ: Erlbaum.

CALDER MC (1989) 'Child abuse is the portion of harm to children that results from human action that is prescribed, proximate and preventable'. Is this a sufficiently useful definition of child abuse?

Unpublished paper. University of Lancaster: PQ Diploma in Child Protection.

CALDER MC (1992) Towards an ecological formulation of system maltreatment. Unpublished MA dissertation, University of Lancaster.

CALDER MC (1994) Assessing adult sex offenders: A framework. Unpublished manuscript.

CALDER MC (1994a) Risk assessment of sex offenders: Punishment or partnership? Part 1. Panel News 7(1): 10–23.

CALDER MC (1994b) Risk assessment of sex offenders: Punishment or partnership? Part 2. Panel News 7(2): 8–18.

CALDER MC (1994c) Risk assessment of sex offenders: Punishment or partnership? Part 3. Panel News 7(3): 13–25.

CALDER MC (1995) Child Protection: Balancing partnership and paternalism. British Journal of Social Work 25(6): 749–766.

CALDER MC (1996) Partnership and protection: An integrated framework for practice. Presentation to the 11th ISPCAN conference on child abuse and neglect, Dublin, Ireland, 18–21 August 1996.

CALDER MC (1997) Juveniles and children who sexually abuse. A guide to risk assessment. Dorset: Russell House Publishing.

CALDER MC (1997b) Young people who sexually abuse: Towards International Consensus? Social Work in Europe 4(1): 36–39.

CALDER MC (1997c) Offence analysis. Unpublished text.

CALDER MC (1998) Towards anti-oppressive practice with ethnic minorities. In Calder MC and Horwath J (eds.) Working for children on the child protection register: An inter-agency practice guide. Aldershot: Arena.

CALDER MC (1998b) Presentation to Salford SSD staff on working with adult male sex offenders. Summer 1998.

CALDER MC (1998c) Pre-birth risk assessment protocol: A report to Salford ACPC. July 1998.

CALDER MC (1999) Managing allegations of child abuse against foster carers. In Wheal A (ed.) The companion to foster care. Dorset: Russell House Publishing.

CALDER MC (ed.) (forthcoming) Working with young people who sexually abuse. New pieces of the jigsaw. Dorset: Russell House Publishing.

CALDER MC and HORWATH J (1998) Policies and procedures: Developing a framework for working together. In Calder MC and Horwath J (eds.) Working for children on the child protection register: An inter-agency practice guide. Aldershot: Arena.

CALDER MC and HORWATH J (1998) Working for children on the Child Protection Register: An inter-agency practical guide. Aldershot, Arena.

CANTWELL HB (1988) Child sexual abuse: Very young perpetrators. Child Abuse and Neglect 12: 579–582.

CAREN A and FAY J (1981) No more sercrets: Protecting your children from sexual assault. Impact Publishers.

CAREY MP, FLASHER LV, MAISTO SV and TURKAT ID (1984) The 'a priori' approach to psychological assessment. Professional Psychology: Research and Practice 15: 515–527.

CARICH MS (1991) Evaluating and detecting the phoniness of clients. INMAS Newsletter 4(2): 13–14.

CARICH MS (1991) The sex offender recovery inventory. INMAS Newsletter 4(4): 13–17.

CARICH MS (1993) A list of disowning behaviours. INMAS Newsletter 6(1): 9–11.

CARICH MS (1994) A review of different risk factors. INMAS Newsletter 7(4): 3–10.

CARICH MS (1994) List of risk factors used in risk assessment. INMAS Newsletter 7(2), p9.

CARICH MS (1996) 15–factor sex offender recovery scale. Unpublished manuscript.

CARICH MS (1997) Evaluating sex offender recovery: A booklet for professionals. Unpublished manuscript.

CARICH MS (1997b) Towards a concept of recovery in sex offenders. The Forum 9(2), 10–11.

CARICH MS and LAMPLEY M (forthcoming) Recovery assessments with young people who sexually abuse.

CARICH MS and ADKERSON DL (1995) Adult sexual offender assessment packet. Brandon, VT: Safer Society Press.

CARICH MS and METZGER C (1996b) Risk assessment checklist scale. Unpublished manuscript.

CARICH MS and METZGER C (1996) The sex offender cognitive disowning behavioural distortion scale. Unpublished manuscript.

CARICH MS and STERKEL SR (1992) Sex offender lifestyle cognitive-behavioural inventory. Adler School of Professional Psychology. Unpublished manuscript.

CARICH MS, FISCHER S and CAMBELL TD (1994) Recovery risk assessment scale for sex offenders. Unpublished paper.

CARICH MS, METZGER C and CAMBELL T (1996) Risk assessment checklist scale protocol. Unpublished manuscript.

CARICH MS, MICHAEL DM and STONE M (1992) Categories of disowning behaviours. INMAS Newsletter 5(4): 2–13.

CARNES PJ (1983) Out of the shadows: Understanding sexual addiction. Minneapolis: Compcare Publications.

CARNES PJ (1990) Sexual addiction. In Horton A (ed.) The incest perpetrator. Beverly Hills, Ca.: Sage, 126–143.

CARNES PJ (1991) Don't call it love. Deerfield park, Fl.: Health Communicators Inc.

CARTER DE, PRENTKY R, KNIGHT RA, VANDERVEER PL and BOUCHER RS (1987) Use of pornography on the criminal and developmental histories of sexual offenders. Journal of Interpersonal Violence 2: 196–211.

CERCE D, DAY SR, PRENTKY RA and KNIGHT RA (1984) The correlative relationship between family instability in childhood and sexually aggressive behaviour in adulthood. Paper at the 2nd national conference for family violence researchers, Durham: University of New Hampshire.

Chartered Institute of Housing (1998) Rehousing sex offenders: A summary of the legal and operational issues.

CHAFFIN M (1992) Factors associated with treatment completion and progress among intra-familial child molesters. Child Abuse and Neglect 16: 251–264.

CHAFFIN M (1994) Research in action: Assessment and treatment of child sexual abusers. Journal of Interpersonal Violence 9(2): 224–237.

CHAMBLESS DL and LIFSHITZ JL (1984) Self-reported sexual anxiety and arousal: the expanded Sexual Arousability Inventory. The Journal of Sex Research 20: 241–254.

CHECK JVP (1985) The hostility towards women scale. Dissertation Abstracts International 45(12).

CHECK JVP and MALAMUTH MN (1983) Sex role stereotyping and reactions to depictions of stranger versus acquaintance rape. Journal of Personality and Social Psychology 45: 344–356.

CHECK JVP, PERLMAN D and MALAMUTH MN (1985) Loneliness and aggressive behaviour. J. Soc. Person. Relations 2: 243–252.

CHRISTIE M, MARSHALL WL and LANTHIER R (1979) A descriptive study of incarcerated rapists and paedophiles. Report of the Solicitor General of Canada. Ottowa: Canada.

CLARE ICH (1993) Issues in the assessment and treatment of male sex offenders with mild learning disabilities. Sexual and Marital Therapy 8(2): 167–180.

CLARE ICH and GUDJONSSON GH (1993) Interrogative suggestibility, confabulation, and acquiescence in people with mild learning disabilities. British Journal of Clinical Psychology 32.

CLARK K and LEWIS D (1977) Rape: The price of coercive sexuality. Toronto: The Women's Press.

CLARK NK (1993) Sex offenders: An overview. In Clark NK and Stephenson TM (eds.) Sexual offenders: Context, assessment, and treatment. Leicester: British Psychological Services.

CLORE GL and JEFFREY KM (1972) A descriptive study of incarcerated rapists and paedophiles. Report of the Solicitor General of Canada. Ottowa. Canada.

COHEN M, SEGHORN T and CALMAS W (1969) Sociometric study of the sex offender. Journal of Abnormal Psychology 74: 249–255.

COHEN P (1995) Sex, lies and videotapes. Community Care 12–18/11/95, 14–15.

COLEMAN E (1987) Chemical dependency and intimacy dysfunction: Inextricably bound. Journal of Chemical Dependency 1(1): 13–26.

COLEMAN E and CESNIK J (1991) Use of serotonergic medications in the treatment of non-paraphilic and paraphilic compulsive sexual behaviour. Paper presented at the second international conference on the treatment of sex offenders. Minneapolis.

COLEMAN E, DWYER SM and PALLONE NJ (1997) Sex offender treatment: Biological dysfunction, intra-psychic conflict and interpersonal violence. NY: Haworth Press.

COLEMAN H (1997) Gaps and silences: The culture and adolescent sex offenders. Journal of Child and Youth Care 11(1): 1–13.

CONGER JC and CONGER AJ (1986) Assessment of social skills. In Ciminero AR et al. (eds.) Handbook of behavioural assessment. NY: John Wiley and Sons, 526–560.

CONTE JR (1983) Development and use of self-report techniques for assessing sexual functioning: A review and critique. Archives of Sexual Behaviour 12(6): 555–575.

CONTE JR (1985) Clinical dimensions of adult sexual abuse of children. Law and Psychiatry 3: 341–354.

CONTE JR (1991) Child sexual abuse: Looking backward and forward. In Patton MQ (ed.) Family sexual abuse: Frontline research and evaluation. Newbury Park, Ca.: Sage, 3–22.

CONTE JR, WOLF S and SMITH T (1989) What sexual offenders tell us about prevention. Child Abuse and Neglect 13: 293–301.

COOK S and TAYLOR J (1991) Working with young sex offenders. Liverpool SSD/Barnardo's North-West.

CORCORAN K and FISCHER J (1987) Measures for clinical practice: A sourcebook. NY: The Free Press.

CORREA EL and SUTKER PB (1986) Assessment of alcohol and drug behaviours. In Ciminero AR, Calhoun KS and Adams HE (eds.) Handbook of behavioural assessment (2nd edition). NY: John Wiley, 446–495.

COWBURN M (1996) The black male sex offender in prison: Images and issue. Journal of Sexual Aggression 2(2): 122–142.

COWBURN M and MODI P (1995) Justice in an unjust context: Implications for working with adult male sex offenders. In Ward D and Lacey M (eds.) Probation: Working for justice. London: Whiting and Birch, 185–207.

CRAFT A (1992) Remedies for difficulties. Inside Supplement. 25.6.92, iii-iv.

CREPAULT C and COUTURE M (1980) Men's erotic fantasies. Archives of Sexual Behaviour 9: 565–581.

CREWDSON J (1988) By silence betrayed. Boston: Little, Brown and Co.

CRIDDLE W (1975) Guidelines for challenging irrational beliefs. Rational Living 9(1): 8–13.

CRONBACH LJ (1955) Processes affecting scores on 'understanding of others' and 'assumed similarity'. Psychological Bulletin 52(3): 177–193.

CUMMING G and BUELL M (1997) Supervision of the sex offender. Brandon, VT: Safer Society Press.

DAVIES M (1986) Sex education for young disabled people. Adoption and Fostering 10(1): 38–9.

DAVIES N (1998) The epidemic in our midst that went unnoticed. The Guardian, 2 June, 1998, 4–5.

DAVIS CM, YARBER YL, BAUSERMAN R, SCHEER G and DAVIS SL (1998) Handbook of sexuality-related measures. Thousand Oaks, Ca.: Sage.

DAVIS M (1980) A multi-dimensional approach to individual differences in empathy. JSAS Catalog of Selected Documents in Psychology 10,85.

DAVIS M (1983) Measuring individual differences in empathy: Evidence for a multi-dimensional approach. Journal of Personality and Social Psychology 44: 113–126.

DAY K (1993) Crime and mental retardation: A review. In Howells K and Hollin CR (eds.) Clinical approaches to the mentally disordered offender. Chichester: John Wiley and Sons.

DAY K (1994) Male mentally handicapped sex offenders. British Journal of Psychiatry 165: 630–639.

DEITZ PE (1983) Sex offences: Behavioural aspects. In Kadish SH (ed.) Encyclopaedia of crime and justice. NY: Free Press.

DEITZ SR, TIEMANN-BLACKWELL K, DALEY PC and BENTLEY BJ (1982) Measurement of empathy towards rape victims and rapists. Journal of Personality and Social Psychology 43: 372–384.

DEPARTMENT OF HEALTH (1988) Protecting children: A guide for social workers undertaking a comprehensive assessment. London: HMSO.

DEROGATIS L (1978) The Derogatis sexual functioning inventory. Baltimore, Md.: Derogatis Publishers.

DEROGATIS LR (1980) Psychological assessment of

psychosexual functioning. Psychiat. Clin. N. Aner. 3: 113–131.

DEROGATIS LR and MELISARATOS N (1979) The DSFI: A multi-dimensional measure of sexual functioning. Journal of Sex and Marital Therapy 5: 244–281.

DEROGATIS LR, MEYER JD and DUPKIN CN (1976) Discrimination of organic versus psychological impotence with the DSFI. Journal of Sex and Marital Therapy 2: 229–240.

DESCUTNER CJ and THELEN MH (1991) Development and validation of a fear-of-intimacy scale. Psychological Assessment 3(2): 218–225.

DIAMONT L and WINDHOLZ G (1981) Loneliness in college students: Some theoretical, empirical and therapeutic considerations. Journal of College Students' Personality 22: 515–522.

DiCLEMENTE C (1991) Motivational interviewing and the stages of change. In Miller W and Rollnick S (eds.) Motivational interviewing. London: Guilford Press.

DiGEORGIO-MILLER (1994) Clinical techniques in the treatment of juvenile sex offenders. Young Victims, Young Offenders 21(1/2): 117–126.

DOMINELLI L (1989) Betrayal of trust: A feminist analysis of power relationships in incest abuse and its relevance for social work practice. British Journal of Social Work 19: 291–307.

DOUECK HJ, ENGLISH DJ, DEPANFILIS D and MOORE GT (1993) Decision-making in child protective services: A comparison of selected risk assessment systems. Child Welfare 72: 441–452.

DOUGHER MJ (1995) Clinical assessment of sex offenders. In Schwartz BK and Cellini HR (eds.) The sex offender: Corrections, treatment and legal practice. Kingston, NJ: Civic Research Institute, Inc.

DOWNS A (1972) Up and down with ecology and the 'issue-attention' cycle. Public Interest 32: 38–50.

DRAUCKE CB (1992) Counselling survivors of childhood sexual abuse. Newbury Park, Ca.: Sage.

DREIBLATT IS (1982) Issues in the evaluation of the sex offender. Paper presented at the annual meeting of the Western Psychological Association, Seattle, Washington.

DUTTWEILER PC (1984) The internal control index: A newly developed measure of locus and control. Educational and Psychological Measurement 44: 209–221.

DWORKIN A (1981) Pornography: Men possessing women. NY: Perrigee.

DWYER SM and COLEMAN E (1994) Assessment of the adult alleged offender. In Krivacska JJ and Money J (eds.) The handbook of forensic sexology. NY: Prometheus Books.

EARLE RH and EARLE MR (1995) Sex addiction: Case studies and management. NY: Brunner/Mazel.

EARLS CM (1992) Clinical issues in the psychological assessment of child molesters. In O'Donohue W and Geer JH (eds.) The sexual abuse of children (Vol 2) Clinical Issues. NJ: Lawrence Erlbaum, 232–255.

EDWARDS AL (1966) Edwards personality inventory. Chicago: Science Research Association.

EDWARDS SSM and SOETENHORST J (1994) The impact of 'moral panic' on professional behaviour in cases of child sexual abuse: An international perspective. Journal of Child Sexual Abuse 3(1): 103–126.

EISLER RM (1968) Thematic expression of sexual conflict under varying stimulus conditions. Journal of Consulting and Clinical Psychology 32: 216–220.

ELDRIDGE H and STILL J (1995) Apologies and forgiveness in the context of the cycles of adult male sex offenders who abuse children. In Salter AC (ed.) Transforming trauma. Thousand Oaks, Ca.: Sage, 131–158.

ELLIOTT M (1986) Keeping safe: A practice guide to talking to children. London: NVCO/Bedford press.

ELLIOTT M (1993) Female sexual abuse of children: The ultimate taboo. London: Longman.

ELLIOTT M, BROWNE K and KILCOYNE J (1995) Child sexual abuse prevention: What offenders tell us. Child Abuse and Neglect 19(5): 579–594.

ELLIS A (1989) Rational emotional therapy. In Corsini A and Wedding D (eds.) Current psychotherapies: Itasca, Il.: FE Peacock 197–238.

EPPS KJ (1993) A survey of experience, training and working practices among staff working with adolescent sex offenders in secure units. In Clark NK and Stephenson GM (eds.) Sexual offenders: Context, assessment and treatment. Leicester: British Psychological Society.

EPPS KJ (1996) Sex offenders. In Hollin CR (ed.) Working with offenders: Psychological practice in offender rehabilitation. Chichester: John Wiley and Sons, 150–187.

EPPS KJ (forthcoming) Casual explanations: Filling the theoretical reservoir. In Calder MC (ed.) Working with young people who sexually abuse. New pieces of the jigsaw. Dorset: Russell House publishing.

EROOGA M (1994) Where the professional meets the personal. In Morrison T, Erooga M and Beckett RC (eds.) Sexual offending against children: Assessment and treatment of male abusers. London: Routledge, 203–224.

ETHERINGTON K (1995) Adult male survivors of childhood sexual abuse. London: Pitman Publishing.

EYSENCK HJ (1970) Personality and attitudes to sex: A factorial study. Personality 1: 355–376.

EYSENCK HJ (1988) The Eysenck inventory of attitudes to sex. In Davis CM, Yarber WL and Davis SL (1988) Sexuality-related measures: A compendium. Iowa: Graphic Publishing Co., 28–34.

FALLER KC (1988) Child sexual abuse: An inter-disciplinary manual for diagnosis, case management, and treatment. London: MacMillan.

FALLER KC (1990) Understanding sexual maltreatment. Newbury Park, Ca.: Sage.

FARGASON CA, BARNES D, SCHEIDER D and GALLOWAY BW (1994) Enhancing multi-agency collaboration of child sexual abuse. Child Abuse and Neglect 18(10): 859–869.

FARRALL WR (1992) Instrumentation and methodological issues in the assessment of sexual aroused. In O'Donohue and Geer JH (eds.) The sexual abuse of children (Vol 2) Hillsdale, NJ: Lawrence Erlbaum Associates, 188–231.

FARRENKOPF T (1986) Comprehensive arousal pattern assessment. In 'Treating the juvenile sexual abuse perpetrator'. Minneapolis: University of Minnesota.

FARRENKOPF T (1992) What happens to therapists who work with sex offenders? Journal of Offender Rehabilitation 18(3/4): 217–223.

FAWCETT J (1989) Breaking the habit: The need for a comprehensive long-term treatment strategy for sexually abusing families. NSPCC Occasional Paper 7. London: NSPCC.

FEATHERSTONE B and LANCASTER E (1996) Contemplating the unthinkable: Men who sexually abuse children. Critical Social Policy 17(4): 51–71.

FEDEROFF JP and MORAN B (1997) Myths and misconceptions about sex offenders. The Canadian Journal of Human Sexuality 6(4): 263–276.

FEDEROFF JP and PINKUS S (1996) The genesis of paedophilia: Testing the 'abuse–to–abuser' hypothesis. Journal of Offender Rehabilitation 23: 85–101.

FELDMAN MP, MacCULLOCH, MELLOR V and PINSCHOF JM (1966) The application of anticipatory avoidance learning to the treatment of homosexuality. The sexual orientation method. Behav. Res. Ther. 4: 289.

FIELD H (1978) Attitudes towards rape: A comparative analysis of police, rapists, crisis counsellors and citizens. Journal of Personality and Social Psychology 36: 156–179.

FILSINGER EE (1981) A measure of interpersonal orientation – The liking people scale. Journal of Personality Assessment 45: 295–300.

FILSINGER EE (ed.) (1983) Marriage and family assessment: A sourcebook for family therapy. Beverly Hills, Ca.: Sage.

FINKELHOR D (1979) Sexually victimised children. NY: The Free Press.

FINKELHOR D (1979b) What's wrong with sex between adults and children? American Journal of Orthopsychiatry 49(4): 692–697.

FINKELHOR D (1982) Sexual abuse: A sociological perspective. Child Abuse and Neglect 6: 95–102.

FINKELHOR D (1984) Child sexual abuse: Theory and research. NY: The Free Press.

FINKELHOR D (1985) Sexual abuse and physical abuse: Some critical differences. In Newberger EH and Bourne R (eds.) Unhappy families. Littleton, Mass.: PSG.

FINKELHOR D and BROWNE A (1986) Sexual abuse: Initial and long-term effects: A conceptual framework. In Finkelhor D (ed.) A sourcebook on child sexual abuse. Beverly Hills, Ca.: Sage.

FINKELHOR D and LEWIS IA (1988) An epidemiological approach to the study of child molestation. In Prentky RA and Quinsey VL (eds.) Human sexual aggression. NY: New York Academy of Sciences.

FINKELHOR D and REDFIELD D (1984) How the public defines sexual abuse. In Finkelhor D (op. cit.) 107–133.

FISHER D (1994) Adult sex offenders: Who are they? Why and how do they do it? In Morrison T, Erooga M and Beckett RC (eds.) Sexual offending against children: Assessment and treatment of male abusers. London: Routledge, 1–24.

FISHER D (1997) The victim grid. NOTA News 24: 38–41.

FISHER D and HOWELLS K (1993) Social relationships in sexual offenders. Sexual and Marital Therapy 8(2): 123–136.

FITCH JH (1962) Men convicted of sexual offences against children: A descriptive follow-up study. British Journal of Criminology 3: 18–37.

FRANCES A, CLARKIN J and PERRY S (1984) Differential therapeutics in psychiatry. NY: Brunner/Mazel.

FRASER BG (1981) Sexual child abuse: The legislation and the law in the United States. In Mrazek PB and Kempe CH (eds.) Sexually abused children and their families. Oxford: Pergamon, 55–73.

FREEMAN-LONGO RE, BAYS L and BEAR E (1996) Empathy and compassionate action: Issues and exercises. A guided workbook for clients and treatment. Brandon, VT: Safer Society Press.

FREEMAN-LONGO RE (1983) Developmental histories in sexual offences. Unpublished study.

FREEMAN-LONGO RE (1985) The adolescent sex offender: background and research perspectives. In Otey EM and Ryan GD (eds.) Adolescent sex offenders: Issues in research and treatment. Rockville, MD: DHHS Publications.

FREEMAN-LONGO RE (1994) Paper presented to the 10th national conference of the National Adolescent Perpetrator Network, Denver, Colorado, February 1994.

FRENZEL RR and LANG RA (1989) Identifying sexual preferences in intra-familial and extra-familial child sexual abuse. Annals of Sex Research 2: 255–275.

FREUD S (1901) Psychopathology of everyday life. London: Hogarth.

FREUD S (1905) Three essays on the theory of sexuality. NY: Basic Books.

FREUND K (1967) Diagnosing homo or heterosexuality and erotic age-preference by means of a psycho-physiological test. Behaviour Research and Therapy 5: 209–228.

FREUND K (1967b) Erotic preference in paedophilia. Behaviour Research and Therapy 5: 339–348.

FREUND K (1981) Assessment of paedophiles. In Cook M and Howells K (eds.) Adult sexual interest in children. NY: Academic Press, 139–179.

FREUND K and BLANCHARD R (1986) The concept of courtship disorder. Journal of Sex and Marital Therapy 12: 79–92.

FREUND K and BLANCHARD R (1988) Gender identity and erotic preference in males. In Davis CM, Yarber WL and Davis SL (eds.) Sexuality-related measures: A compendium. Iowa: Graphic Publishing Co.

FREUND K, McKNIGHT CK, LANGEVIN R and CIBIRI S (1972) The female child as a surrogate object. Archives of Sexual Behaviour 2: 119–133.

FREUND K, SCHER H and HUCKER S (1983) The courtship disorder. Archives of Sexual Behaviour 12: 369–379.

FREUND K, WATSON R and RIENZO D (1988) The value of self-report in the study of voyeurism and exhibitionism. Annals of Sex Research 1: 243–262.

FRIEDMAN M and ROSENMAN RH (1974) Type A behaviour and your heart. NY: Knopf.

FRUDE N (1982) The sexual nature of sexual abuse: A review of the literature. Child Abuse and Neglect 6: 211–223.

FRUZZETTI AE and JACOBSEN WS (1992) Assessment of couples. In Rosen JC and McReynolds P (eds.) Advances in psychological assessment (Vol 8). NY: Plenum Press, 201–224.

FURBY L, WEINROTT MR and BLACKSHAW L (1989) Sex offender recidivism: A review. Psychological Bulletin 105: 3–30.

FURNISS T (1990) Dealing with denial. In Oates RK (ed.) Understanding and managing child sexual abuse. Marrickeville: Harcourt Brace Jovanovich, 242–257.

FURNISS T (1991) The multi-professional handbook of child sexual abuse. London: Routledge.

GALASSI JP, DELO JS, GALASSI MD and BASTIEN S (1974) The college self-expression scale: A measure of assertiveness. Behaviour Therapy 5: 165–171.

GALBRAITH GG (1968) Effects of sexual arousal and guilt upon free associative sexual responses. Journal of Consulting and Clinical Psychology 32: 707–711.

GAMBRILL ED and RICHEY CA (1975) An assertion inventory for use in assessment and research. Behaviour Therapy 6: 550–561.

GARLAND RJ and DOUGHER AJ (1996) The abused/abuser hypothesis of child sexual abuse: A critical review of theory and research. In Feierman JR (ed.) Paedophilia: Biosocial dimensions. NY: Springer–Verlag, 488–509.

GARLICK Y, MARSHALL WL and THORNTON D (1996) Intimacy deficits and attribution of blame among sexual offenders. Legal and Criminological Psychology 1: 251–258.

GARRISON K (1992) Working with sex offenders: A practice guide. Social Work Monograph 112. Norwich: UEA.

GEBHARD PH (1972) A comparison of white-black offender groups. In Resnick ALP and Wolfgang ME (eds.) Sexual behaviours: Social, clinical and legal aspects. Boston: Little, Group and Co.

GEBHARD PH, GAGNON JH, POMEROY WB and CHRISTERSON CV (1965) Sex offenders. NY: Harper and Row.

GEBHARD PH, GAGNON JH, POMEROY WB et al. (1967) Sex offenders. NY: Bantam Books.

GENDREAU P, GOGGIN C and LITTLE T (1996) Predicting adult offender recidivism: What works! Canada: Public Works and Government Services.

GIARRETTO H (1982) Integrated treatment of child sexual abuse. Palo Alto: Ca., Science and Behaviour.

GILGUN JF (1988) Self-centredness and the adult male perpetrator of child sexual abuse. Contemporary Family Therapy 10(4): 216–234.

GILGUN JF (1991) Resilience and intergenerational transmission of child sexual abuse. In Patton MQ (ed.) Family sexual abuse: Frontline research and evaluation. Newbury, Park: Ca, Sage, 93–105.

GILGUN JF (1994) Avengers, conquerors, playmates and lovers. Roles played by child sexual abuse perpetrators. Families in Society 75(8): 467–479.

GILGUN JF (Forthcoming) CASPARS: Clinical assessment instruments that measure strengths and risks in children and families. In Calder MC (ed.) Working with young people who sexually abuse: New Pieces of the jigsaw. Lyme Regis, Dorset: Russell House Publishing.

GILGUN JF and CONNOR TM (1989) How perpetrators view child sexual abuse. Social Work 34: 249–251.

GILGUN JF and GORDON S (1985) Sex education and the prevention of child sexual abuse. Journal of Sex Education and Therapy 11(1): 46–52.

GILLHAM B (1996) Child sexual abuse: Myth and reality. In Gillham B and Thomson JA (eds.) Child safety: Problem and prevention from pre-school to adolescence. London: Routledge, 113–127.

GIST R, TAYLOR J and FISHER D (1994) Assessment programme: Assessment of young people who display inappropriate sexual behaviour. Coventry NSPCC.

GLUECK B (1956) Final report of the research project for the study of persons convicted of crimes involving sexual aberrations. June 1952 to June 1955. NY: State Department of Hygiene.

GOCKE B (1991) Tackling denial in sex offenders. Probation Monograph 98. Norwich: UEA.

GOLD SR and CLEGG CL (1990) Sexual fantasies of college students with coercive experiences and coercive attitudes. Journal of Interpersonal Violence 5(4): 464–473.

GOLDBERG DP and HILLIER VF (1979) A scaled version of the general health questionnaire. Psychological Medicine 9:139–145.

GOLSTEIN AP and KELLER HR (1987) Aggressive behaviour: Assessment and intervention. NY: Pergamon Press.

GOMES-SCHWARTZ B, HOROWITZ JM and CARDARELLI AP (1990) Child sexual abuse: The initial effects. Newbury Park, Ca.: Sage.

GOODMAN GS (ed.) (1984) The child witness. Journal of Social Issues 40(2), Summer 1984.

GOODWIN J, CORMIER L and OWEN J (1983) Grandfather-granddaughter incest: A tri-generational view. Child Abuse and Neglect 7: 163–170.

GORDON A, WEISMAN RG and MARSHALL WL (1980) The effects of flooding with response freedom on social anxiety. Paper at the 14th annual convention of the Association for the Advancement of Behaviour Therapy. New York.

GORE DK (1988) Measuring the cognitive distortions of child molesters. Unpublished doctoral thesis. Atlanta, GA: Georgia State University.

GOUGH HG (1974) A 24 item version of the Miller-Fisk sexual knowledge questionnaire. Journal of Psychology 87:183–192.

GRAY AS and WALLACE R (1992) Adolescent sexual offender assessment packet. Orwell, VT: Safer Society Press.

GREEN R (1995) Psycho-educational modules. In Schwartz BK and Cellini HR (eds.) The sex offender: Correction, treatment and legal practice. Kingston, NJ: Civic Research Institute, Inc.

GRIFFIN DW and BARTHOLOMEW K (1994) The metaphysisis of measurement: The case of adult attachment. In Bartholomew K and Perlman D (eds.) Attachment processes in adulthood. London: Jessica Kingsley, 17–52.

GRIFFITHS W (1975) Sexual experience and sexual responsiveness. Archives of Sexual Behaviour 4: 529–540.

GRIFFITHS DM, QUINSEY VL and HINGSBURGER D (1989) Changing inappropriate sexual behaviour: A community-based approach for persons with developmental disabilities. Baltimore: Paul H. Brookes.

GRIGGS DR and BOLD A (1995) Parallel treatment of parents of abuse-reactive children. In Hunter M (ed.) Child survivors and perpetrators of sexual abuse: Treatment innovations. Thousand Oaks, Ca.: Sage, 147–165.

GROTH AN (1977) The adolescent sex offender and his prey. Journal of Offender Therapy and Comparative Criminology 25: 265–275.

GROTH AN (1979) Men who rape: The psychology of the offender. NY: Plenum.

GROTH AN (1983) Treatment of sexual offences in a

correctional institution. In Greer J and Stuart I (eds.). The sexual aggressor: Current perspectives on treatment. NY: Van Nostrand Reinhold.

GROTH AN and BURGESS AW (1977) Motivational intent in the sexual assault of children. Criminal Justice and Behaviour 4: 253–271.

GROTH AN and OLIVERI FJ (1989) Understanding sexual abuse offence behaviour and differentiating among sexual abusers: Basic conceptual issues. In Sgroi SM (ed.) Vulnerable populations (Vol 2). Lexington: DC Health, 309–327.

GROTH AN, HOBSON WF and GARY TS (1982) The child molester: Clinical observations. Social Work and Human Sexuality 1: 129–144.

GRUBIN D (1992) Sexual offending: A cross-cultural comparison. Annual Review of Sex Research 3: 201–217.

GRUBIN D and GUNN J (1990) The imprisoned rapist and rape. London: Institute of Psychiatry.

GRUBIN D and MATHEWS R (1997) Medical models of sexual deviance. In Laws DR and O'Donohue W (eds.) Sexual deviance: Theory, assessment and treatment. NY: The Guilford Press, 434–448.

GUDJONSSON GH and SINGH KK (1989) The revised Gudjonsson blame attribution inventory. Person Individ. Diff 10(1): 67–70.

GUTTMACHER MS and WEIHOFEN H (1952) Psychiatry and the law. NY: Norton.

HAAVEN J, LITTLE R and PETRE-MILLER D (1984) Treating intellectually disabled sex offenders: A model residential program. Orwell, VT: Safer Society Press.

HACKETT S (1993) Women's place. Community Care, 26.8.93, p11.

HALL ER, HOWARD JE and BOEZIO SL (1986) Tolerance of rape: A sexist or antisocial attitude. Psychology of Women Quarterly 10: 101–118.

HALL GCN and HIRSCHMAN R (1992) Sexual aggression against children: A conceptual perspective of etiology. Criminal Justice and Behaviour 19(1): 8–23.

HANSON RK (1991) Characteristics of sex offenders who were sexually abused as children. In Langevin R (ed.) Sex offenders and their victims: New research findings. Toronto: Juniper Press, 77–85.

HANSON RK (1992) Hanson sex attitudes questionnaire. In Carich MS and Adkerson DL (eds.) Adult sexual offender assessment packet. Brandon, VT: Safer Society Press, 75–6.

HANSON RK (in press) Sex offender risk assessment. In HOLLIN CR (ed.) Handbook of offender assessment and treatment. Chichester: John Wiley and Sons.

HANSON RK and BUSSIERE MT (1996) Predictors of sexual recidivism: A meta-analysis. Ontario: Deapartment of the Solicitor General.

HANSON RK and BUSSIERE MT (1998) Predicting recidivism: A meta-analysis of sexual offender recidivism studies. Journal of Consulting and Clinical Psychology 66(2): 348–362.

HANSON RK and HARRIS A (1998) Dynamic predictors of sexual recidivism. Ontario: Department of the Solicitor General.

HANSON RK and SCOTT H (1996) Social networks of sex offenders. Psychology, Crime and Law 2: 249–258.

HANSON RK and SLATER S (1988) Sexual victimisation in the history of child sexual abusers: A review. Annals of Sex Research 1: 485–499.

HANSON RK, COX B and WOSZCSYNA C (1991) Sexuality, personality and attitude questionnaires for sex offenders: A review. Cat no JS4–1/1991–13. Ottowa: Supply and Services, Canada.

HANSON RK, GIZZARRELLI R and SCOTT H (1994) The attitudes of incest offenders: Sexual enticement and acceptance of sex with children. Criminal Justice and Behaviour 21(2): 187–220.

HANSON RK, HARRIS AJR, FOURUZAN A, McWHINNIE AJ and OSWEILER MC (1997) Dynamic predictors of sexual reoffence project 1997. Presentation at the 16th annual research and treatment conference of the Association for the Treatment of Sexual Offenders, Arlington, VA.

HARBISON JJM, GRAHAM PJ, QUINN JT, McALLISTER H and WOODWARD R (1974) A questionnaire measure of sexual interest. Archives of Sexual Behaviour 3: 357.

HARBURG E, ERFURT JC, HAUENSTEIN LS, CHAPE C, SCHULL WJ and SCHORK MA (1973) Socio- ecological stress, suppressed hostility, skin color, and black-white male blood pressure. Psychosomatic Medicine 35: 276–296.

HARDY KV and LASZLOFFY TA (1995) The cultural genogram: Key to training culturally competent family therapists. Journal of Marital and Family Therapy 21(3): 227–237.

HARTLEY CC (1998) How incest offenders overcome internal inhibitions through the use of cognitions and cognitive distortions. Journal of Interpersonal Violence 13(1): 25–39.

HARTMAN C and REYNOLDS D (1987) Resistant clients: Confrontation, interpretation and alliance. Social Casework, April 1987: 205–213.

HAUGAARD JJ and REPPUCCI ND (1988) The sexual abuse of children. San Fransisco, Ca.: Jossey-Bass.

HAYASHINO DS, WURTELE SK and KLEBE KJ (1995) Child Molesters: An examination of cognitive factors. Journal of Interpersonal Violence 10(1): 105–116.

HAYNES SN, JENSEN BJ, WISE E and SHERMAN D (1981) The marital intake interview: A multi-method criterion validity assessment. Journal of Consulting and Clinical Psychology 49(3): 379–387.

HEBENTON B and THOMAS T (1997) Keeping track? Observations on sex offender registers in the US. Home Office Police Research Group, Crime Detection and Prevention Series Paper 83. Home Office.

HECHLER D (1988) The battle and the backlash: The child sexual abuse war. Lexington, Mass.: Lexington Books.

HEDDERMAN C and SUGG D (1996) Does treating sex offenders reduce sex offending? Home Office Research and Statistics Directorate, Research Findings No. 45, October 1996.

HEIM N and HURSCH CJ (1979) Castration for sex offenders: Treatment or punishment? Archives of Sexual Behaviour 8: 281–304.

HEINZ JW, GARGARO S and KELLY KG (1987) A model residential juvenile sex offender treatment program: The Hennepin County Home School. Orwell, VT: Safer Society Press.

HENDERSON S, DUNCAN JONES P, BYRNE DG and SCOTT R (1980) Measuring social relationships. Psychol. Med. 10: 723–734.

HILTON NZ, JENNINGS KT, DRUGGE J and STEPHENS J

(1995) Childhood sexual abuse among clinicians working with sex offenders. Journal of Interpersonal Violence 10(4): 525–532.

HITE S (1981) The Hite report on male sexuality. NY: Knoff.

HMP RISLEY (1994) Presentation on their sex offenders core programme, 8 April.

HO T (1997) Mentally retarded sex offenders: Criminality and retardation. Journal of Contemporary Criminal Justice 13(3): 251–263.

HOBBS CJ, HANKS HGI and WYNNE JM (1993) Child abuse and neglect: A clinician handbook. London: Churchill–Livingstone.

HOGAN R (1964) Development of an empathy scale. Journal of Consulting and Clinical Psychology 33: 307–316.

HOGUE TE (1993) Attitudes towards prisoners and sexual offenders. Issues in Criminological and Legal Psychology 19: 27–32.

HOGUE TE (1994) Sexual offence information questionnaire: Assessment of sexual offenders' perceptions of responsibility, empathy and control. In Clark NC and Stephenson G (eds.) Rights and risks: The application of forensic psychology. Leicester: British Psychological Society.

HOLLON SD and KENDALL PC (1980) Cognitive self-statements in depression: Development of an automatic thoughts questionnaire. Cognitive Therapy and Research 4: 383–395.

HOME OFFICE Circular 39/1997 Sex Offenders Act 1997.

HOME OFFICE Circular 38/1998 Crime and Disorder Act 1998.

HOME OFFICE/DOH (1992) Memorandum of good practice on video recorded interviews with child witnesses for criminal prosecution. London: HMSO.

HOME OFFICE/HM INSPECTOR OF PROBATION (1998) Exercising constant vigilance: The role of the probation service in protecting the public from sex offenders. London: Home Office.

HOON EF and CHAMBLESS D (1988) Sexual arousability inventory and sexual arousability inventory—expanded. In Davis CM, Yarber WL and Davis S (eds.) Sexuality-related measures: A compendium. Iowa: Graphic Publishing Co.

HOOPER CA (1989) If women do it too. Community Care, 16.11.89, p26–27.

HOPKINSON J (1997) Some thoughts on working with sex offenders and racial difference. NOTA News 13: 18–22.

HORLEY J (1991) Values and beliefs as personal constructs. Construct Psychology 4: 1–14.

HORLEY J and QUINSEY VL (1995) Child molesters' construal of themselves, other adults and children. Journal of Constructivist Psychology 8: 193–211.

HORLEY J, QUINSEY VL and JONES S (1997) Incarcerated child molesters' perceptions of themselves and others. Sexual Abuse: A Journal of Research and Treatment 9(1): 43–55.

HORTON A (ed.) (1990) The incest perpetrator. Beverley Hills, Ca.: Sage.

HOVESTADT AS, ANDERSON WT, PIERCY FP, COCHRAN SW and FINE M (1985) A family-of-origin scale. Journal of Marital and Family Therapy 11(3): 287–297.

HOWARD A (1993) Victims and perpetrators of sexual abuse. In Dwivedi KN (ed.) Groupwork with children and adolescents: A handbook. London: Jessica Kingsley, 220–232.

HOWELLS K (1978) Some meanings of children for paedophiles. In Cook M and Wilson ET (eds.) Love and attraction. Elmsford, NY: Pergammon, 57–82.

HOWELLS K (1981) Adult sexual interest in children: Considerations relevant to theories of aetiology. In Cook M and Howells K (eds.) Adult sexual interest in children. London: Academic Press, 55–94.

HOWITT D (1995) Paedophiles and sexual offences against children. Chichester: John Wiley and Sons.

HUDSON A (1992) The child sexual abuse 'industry' and gender relations in social work. In Langan and Daly (eds.) Women, oppression and social work. London: Routledge, 129–148.

HUDSON SM and WARD T (1997) Future directions. In Laws DR and O'Donohue W (eds.) Sexual deviance: Theory, assessment and treatment. NY: Guilford Press, 481–500.

HUDSON SM and WARD T (1997) Intimacy, loneliness and attachment styles in sex offenders. Journal of Interpersonal Violence 12(3): 323–339.

HUDSON SM, MARSHALL WL, WALES D, McDONALD E, BAKKER L and McLEAN A (1993) Emotional recognition skills of sex offenders. Annals of Sex Research 199–211.

HUGHES B and PARKER H (1994) Save the children. Community Care 3.3.94, p24–5.

HUNT P and BAIRD M (1990) Children of sex rings. Child Welfare LX1X(3): May-June.

INGERSOLL SL and PATTON SO (1990) Treating perpetrators of sexual abuse. Lexington, Mass.: Lexington Books.

INGHAM R (1994) Some speculations on the concept of rationality. In Albrecht G (ed.) Advances in medical sociology (Vol 10). Greenwich, Conneticut: JAI Press.

ITZIN C (1992) Pornography and the social construction of sexual integrity. In Itzin C (ed.) Pornography: Women, violence and civil liberties. NY: Oxford University Press, 57–75.

ITZIN C (ed.) (1992) Pornography, violence and civil liberties. Oxford: Oxford University Press.

JACKSON DN (1984) Personality research forum manual (3rd edition). Port Huron, M1: Research Psychologist Press.

JANDA LH and O'GRADY KE (1980) Development of a sex anxiety inventory. Journal of Consulting and Clinical Psychology 48: 169–175.

JEHU D (1979) Sexual dysfunction: A behavioural approach and causation, assessment and treatment. Chichester: John Wiley and Sons.

JENKINS A (1990) Invitations to responsibility: The therapeutic engagement of men who are violent and abusive. Australia: Dulwich Centre publications.

JOHNSTON L and WARD T (1996) Social cognition and sexual offending: A theoretical framework. Sexual Abuse A Journal of Research and Treatment 8(1): 55–80.

JONES C and LEWIS J (1990/1) A pilot prison treatment group for sex offenders at HMP Norwich. Prison Service Journal 81: 44–46.

JONES D (1985) False reports of sexual abuse: Do children lie? Paper presented at the 7th national conference on child abuse and neglect. Chicago: November 1985.

JONES E and PARKINSON P (1995) Child sexual abuse, access and the wishes of children. International Journal of Law and the Family 9: 54–85.

JUSTICE B and JUSTICE R (1979) The broken taboo. NY: Human Sciences Press.

KAHN HA and LAFOND M(1986) Treatment of the adolescent sex offender. Child and Adolescent Social Work Journal 5: 135–148.

KAHN HA, MEDALIE JH, NEUFELD HN, RISS E and GOLDBOURT U (1972) The incidence of hypertension and associated factors. American Heart Journal 84: 171–182.

KANIN EJ (1983) Rape as a function of relative sexual frustration. Psychological Reports 52: 133–134.

KANIN EJ (1984) Date rape: Unofficial criminals and victims. Victimology 9: 95–108.

KANIN EJ (1985) Date rapists: Differential sexual socialisation and relative deprivation. Archives of Sexual Behaviour 14: 219–231.

KAPLAN HS (1974) The new sex therapy. NY: Brunner/Mazel.

KAUFMAN KL (1995) Comparing female and male perpetrators' modus operandi: Victims' reports of sexual abuse. Journal of Interpersonal Violence 10(3): 322–333.

KEAR-COLWELL J and POLLOCK P (1997) Motivation or confrontation: Which approach to the child sex offender? Criminal Justice and Behaviour 24(1): 20–33.

KELLY L (1988) Surviving sexual violence. Cambridge: Polity Press.

KELLY L (1992) Pornography and child sexual abuse. In Itzin C (ed.) op. cit., 113–123.

KELLY L (1996) Weasel words: Paedophiles and the cycle of abuse. Trouble and Strife 33, Summer 1996.

KELLY L and RADFORD J (1990/1) 'Nothing really happened'! The validations of women's experiences of sexual violence. Critical Social Policy 30: 39–53.

KELLY L, REGAN L and BURTON S (1991) An exploratory study of the prevalence of sexual abuse in a sample of 16–21 year olds. London: Child Abuse Studies Unit.

KELLY L, WINGFIELD R, BURTON R and DEFAN L (1995) Splintered lives: Sexual exploitation of children in the context of children's rights and protection. Ilford, Essex: Barnardo's.

KENDALL PC, HOWARD BL and HAYS RC (1989) Self-referrant speech and psychopathology: The balance of positive and negative thinking. Cognitive Therapy and Research 13(6): 583–598.

KIDD E and PRINGLE K (1988) The politics of child sexual abuse. Social Work Today, 15.9.88.

KILPATRICK AC (1992) Long range effects of child and adolescent sexual abuse experiences. Hillsdale, NJ: Lawrence Erlbaum.

KINSEY AC, POMEROY WB, MARTIN CE and GEBHARD CE (1953) Sexual behaviour in the human female. Philadelphia: Saunders.

KIRBY D (1984) Sexuality education of programs and their effects. Santa Cruz, Ca.: Network Publications.

KIRKENDALL LA and McBRIDE LG (1990) Pre-adolescent and adolescent imagery and sexual fantasies: Beliefs and experiences. In Perry ME (ed.) Handbook of sexology. Vol 7: Childhood and adolescent sexology. Amsterdam: Elsevier, 263–286.

KIRKLAND and BOWER C (1982) MMPI traits of incestuous fathers. Journal of Criminal Psychology 38: 645–649.

KLEIN M (1988) Your sexual secrets: When to keep them, when and how to tell. NY: EP Dutton.

KNIGHT RA and PRENTKY RA (1990) Classifying sexual offenders: The development and corroboration of taxonomic models. In Marshall WL, Laws DL and Barbaree HE (eds.) Handbook of sexual assault: Issues, theories and treatment of the offender. NY: Plenum, 23–54.

KNOPP FH (1984) Retraining adult sex offenders: Methods and models. Orwell, VT: Safer Society Press.

KOESTER-SCOTT L (1994) Sex offenders: Prevalence, trends, model programs and costs. In Roberts AR (ed.) Critical issues in crime and justice. Thousand Oaks, Ca.: Sage, 51–76.

KOSS MP and OROS CJ (1982) Sexual experiences survey: A research instrument for investigating sexual aggression and victimisation. Journal of Consulting and Clinical Psychology 50(3): 455–457.

LAFLEN and STURM WR (1994) Understanding and working with denial in sex offenders. Journal of Sexual Abuse 3(4): 19–36.

LANCASTER E (1996) Working with men who sexually abuse children: The experience of the probation service. In Fawcett B, Featherstone B, Hearn J and Toft C (eds.) Violence and gender relations: Theory and interventions. London: Sage, 130–146.

LANE S (1986) Potential emotional hazards of working with sex offenders. Interchange, Jan 1986. Denver, Co.: Kempe Centre.

LANG RA (1991) Child sexual abusers who use pornography. In Langevin R (ed.) Sex offenders and their victims. Oakville, Ontario: Juniper Press, 53–75.

LANG RA and FRENZEL RR (1988) How sex offenders lure children. Annals of Sex Research 1: 303–317.

LANG RA, BLACK EL, FRENZEL RR and CHECKLEY KL (1988) Aggression and erotic attraction toward children in incestuous and paedophilic men. Annals of Sex Research 1: 417–441.

LANGEVIN R (1983) Sexual strands: Understanding and treating sexual anomolies in men. Hillsdale, NJ: Lawrence Erlbaum Associates.

LANGEVIN R (1988) Defensiveness in sex offenders. In Rogers R (ed.) Clinical assessment of malingering and deception. NY: Guilford Press, 269–290.

LANGEVIN R (ed.) (1985) Erotic preference, gender identity and aggression in men: New research studies. Hillsdale, NJ: Lawrence Erlbaum Associates.

LANGEVIN R (ed.) (1991) Sex offenders and their victims: New research findings. Toronto: Juniper Press.

LANGEVIN R and BAIN J (1992) Diabetes in sex offenders. Annals of Sex Research 5: 99–118.

LANGEVIN R and LANG RA (1988) Incest offenders: A practical guide to assessment and treatment. Toronto: Juniper Press.

LANGEVIN R and LANG RA (1990) Substance abuse among sex offenders. Annals of Sex Research 3: 397–424.

LANGEVIN R and WATSON RJ (1996) Major factors in the assessment of paraphiliacs and sex offenders. Journal of Offender Rehabilitation 23: 33–70.

LANGEVIN R, BAIN J, BEN-ARON MH, COULTHARD R, DAY D, HARDY L, HEASMAN G, HUCKER SJ, PUSINS

JE, ROPER V, RUSSON A, WEBSTER CD and WORTZMAN G (1985) Sexual aggression: Constructing a predictive equation: A controlled pilot study. In Langevin R (ed.) Erotic preference, gender identity and aggression in men: New research studies. Hillsdale, NJ: Lawrence Erlbaum Associates.

LANGEVIN R, HANDY L, PAITICH D and RUSSON AE (1985b) Appendix A. A new version of the Clarke sex history questionnaire for males. In Langevin R (ed.) Erotic preference, gender identity and aggression in men: New research studies. Hillsdale, NJ: Lawrence Erlbaum Associates.

LANGEVIN R, HUCKER SJ, BEN-ARON MH, PURINS JE and HOOK HJ (1985c) Why are paedophiles attracted to children? Further studies of erotic preference in heterosexual paedophilia. In Langevin R (ed.) Erotic preference, gender identity and aggression in men: New research studies. Hillsdale, HJ: Lawrence Erlbaum Associates, 181–210.

LANGEVIN R, PAITICH D and RUSSON AE (1985d) Are rapists sexually anomalous, aggressive or both? In Langevin R (ed.) Erotic preference, gender identity and aggression in men: New research studies. Hillsdale NJ, Lawrence Erlbaum Associates, 13–38.

LANGEVIN R, WRIGHT P and HANDY L (1988) Empathy, assertiveness, aggressiveness and dangerousness among sex offenders. Annals of Sex Research 1: 533–547.

LANGEVIN R, WRIGHT P and HANDY L (1988b) What treatment do sex offenders want? Annals of Sex Research 1: 363–385.

LANGEVIN R, WRIGHT P and HANDY L (1990) Use of the MMPI and its derived scales with sex offenders, 1: Reliability and validity studies. Annals of Sex Research 3: 245–291.

LANGEVIN R, WRIGHT P and HANDY L (1990b) Use of the MMPI and its derived scales with sex offenders, II: Reliability and criterion validity. Annals of Sex Research 3: 453–486.

LANNING KV (1986) Child molesters: A behavioural analysis. Washington DC: National Centre for Missing and Exploited Children.

LANYON RI (1991) Theories of sexual offending. In Hollin CR and Howells K (eds.) Clinical approaches to sex offenders and their victims. Chichester: John Wiley and Sons, 35–54.

LANYON RI and LUTZ RW (1984) MMPI discrimination of defensive and non-defensive felony sex offenders. Journal of Consulting and Clinical Psychology 52: 841–843.

LAUNEY G (1994) The phallometric assessment of sex offenders: Some professional and research issues. Criminal Behaviour and Mental Health 4: 48–70.

LAWS DR (ed.) (1989) Relapse prevention with sex offenders. NY: Guilford Press.

LAWS DR and O'DONOHUE W (eds.) (1997) Sexual deviance: Theory, assessment and treatment. NY: Guilford Press.

LAWSON JS, MARSHALL WL and McGRATH P (1979) The social self-esteem inventory. Educational and Psychological Measurement 39: 803–811.

LAZARUS AA (1976) Multi-modal behaviour therapy. NY: Springer Publishing Company.

LEBERG E (1997) Understanding child molesters: Taking charge. Thousand Oaks, Ca.: Sage.

LENDERYOU G (1998) Entitlement to sex and relationship education. Children and Society 12: 315–317.

LEVENSON RW and GOLTMAN JM (1978) Toward the assessment of social competence. Journal of Consulting and Clinical Psychology 46: 453–462.

LEVINSON BS (1997) Levinson victim empathy scale. In Prentky R and Edmunds SB (eds.) Assessing sexual abuse: A resource guide for practitioners. Brandon, VT: Safer Society Press.

LEWIS-HERMAN J (1990) Sex offenders: A feminist perspective. In Marshall WL, Laws DR and Barbaree HE (eds.) Handbook of sexual assault. NY: Plenum Press, 177–93.

LI CK, WEST DJ and WOODHOUSE TP (1990) Children's sexual encounters with adults. London: Duckworth.

LIDDLE AM (1993) Gender, desire and child sexual abuse: Accounting for the male majority. Theory, Culture and Society 10: 103–126.

LIEF H and REED D (1972) Sexual knowledge and attitude test. University of Pennsylvania: Department of Psychiatry.

LILLY R, CUMMINGS JL, BENSON DF and FRANKEL M (1983) The human Kluver-Bucy syndrome. Neurology 33: 1141.

LIPTON, McDONEL EC and McFALL RM (1987) Heterosocial perception in rapists. Journal of Consulting and Clinical Psychology 55:17–21.

LISAK D and IVAN C (1995) Deficits in intimacy and empathy in sexually aggressive men. Journal of Interpersonal Violence 10(3): 296–308.

LISAK D and ROTH S (1988) Motivational factors in non-incarcerated aggressive men. Journal of Personality and Social Psychology 55(5): 795–802.

LOCKE HJ and WALLACE KM (1959) Short marital adjustment and prediction tests: Their reliability and validity. Marr. Fam. Living 21: 251.

LOCKE HJ and WILLIAMSON RC (1958) Marital adjustment: A factor analysis study. Am. Soc. Rev. 23:

LONG JD, WUESTHOFF A and PITHERS WD (1989) Use of autobiographies in the assessment and treatment of sex offenders. In Laws DR (ed.) Relapse prevention with sex offenders. NY: Guilford Press, 88–95.

LONGO RE (1982) Sexual learning and experience among adolescent sexual offenders. International Journal of Offender Therapy and Comparative Criminology 26(3): 235–241.

LoPICCOLO J and STEGER J (1974) The sexual interaction inventory: A new instrument for assessment of sexual dysfunction. Archives of Sexual Behaviour 3: 585–595.

LoPICCOLO J (1978) Direct treatment of sexual dysfunction. In LoPiccolo J and LoPiccolo L (eds.) Handbook of sex therapy. NY: Plenum Press.

LOSS P, ROSS JE and RICHARDSON J (1988) Psycho-educational curriculum for adolescent sex offenders. New London; CT: Loss and Ross.

LLOYD C, MAIR G and HOUGH M (1994) Explaining reconviction rates: A critical analysis. London: HMSO.

LLOYD C and WALMSLEY R (1989) Changes in rape offences and sentencing. Home Office Research Study No. 105 London: HMSO.

LUSK A (1996) Rehabilitation without acknowledgement. Family Law 26: 742–745.

MacCULLOCH MJ, SNOWDEN PR, WOOD PJW and

MILLS HE (1983) Sadistic fantasy, sadistic behaviour and offences. British Journal of Psychiatry 143: 20–29.

MacDONALD AP (1974) Identification and measurement of multi-dimensional attitudes toward equality between the sexes. J. Homosex 1: 165.

MacDONALD AP, HUGGINS J, YOUNG S and SWANSON RA (1973) Attitudes toward homosexuality: Preservation of sex morality or the double standard? Journal of Consulting and Clinical Psychology 40: 161.

MacFARLANE K and CUNNINGHAM C (1988) Steps to healthy touching. Mount Dora, Fl.: Kidsrights.

MacHOVEC F (1994) A systemic approach to sex offender therapy: Diagnosis, treatment and risk assessment. Psychotherapy in Private Practice 13(2): 93–108.

MacHOVEC F (forthcoming) The case for paraphilic personality disorder: Detection, diagnosis and treatment. In Calder MC (ed.) Working with young people who sexually abuse: New pieces of the jigsaw. Dorset: Russell House Publishing.

MacHOVEC FC (1993) Treatment and rehabilitation of sex offenders. Treating Abuse Today 3(2): 5–12.

MacHOVEC FJ and WIECKOWSKI E (1992) The 10 FC – Ten factor continua of classification and treatment criteria for male and female sex offenders. Medical Psychotherapy 5: 53–63.

MacLEOD M and SARAGA M (1988) Challenging the orthodoxy: Towards a feminist theory of practice. Feminist Review 28: 16–55.

MacLEOD M and SARAGA E (1991) Clearing a path through the undergrowth: A feminist reading of recent literature on child sexual abuse. In Carter P, Jeffs T and Smith MK (eds.) Social work and social welfare. Milton Keynes: Open University Press, 30–45.

MADGE N (1998) Abuse and survival: A fact file. London: The Prince's Trust.

MALAMUTH NM (1986) Predictors of naturalistic sexual aggressor. Journal of Personality and Social Psychology 56: 953–962.

MALAMUTH NM (1989) The attraction to sexual aggression scale: Part 1. Journal of Sex Research 26(1) 26–49.

MALAMUTH NM (1989b) The attraction to sexual aggression scale: Part 2. Journal of Sex Research 26(3) 324–354.

MALAMUTH NM and CHECK JVP (1983) Sexual arousal to safe depictions: Individual differences. Journal of Abnormal Psychology 92(1): 55–67.

MALATESTA VJ and ADAMS AE (1986) Assessment of sexual behaviour. In Piminero AR, Calhoun KS and Adams CH (eds.) Handbook of behavioural assessment (2nd edition) NY: John Wiley, 496–525.

MALETZKY BM (1980) Assisted covert sensitization. In Cox DJ and Daitzman RJ (eds.) Exhibitionism: Description, assessment and treatment. NY: Garland, 187–252.

MALETZKY BM (1996) Denial of treatment or treatment of denial? Sexual Abuse, A Journal of Research and Treatment 8(1): 1–5.

MANN R (ed.) (1996) Motivational interviewing with sex offenders: A practice manual. Hull: Bluemoon Corporate Services.

MANN R and ROLLNICK S (1996) Motivational inteviewing with a sex offender who believed he was innocent. Behavioural and Cognitive Psychotherapy 24(2): 127–134.

MAPLE FF (1998) Goal focussed interviewing. Thousand Oaks, Ca.: Sage.

MARGETTS T (1998) Establishing multi-agency working with sex offenders: Setting up to succeed. NOTA news 25: 27–38.

MARGOLIN L (1992) Sexual abuse by grandparents. Child Abuse and Neglect 16: 735–741.

MARK P (1992) Training staff to work with sex offenders. Probation Journal 39(1): 1–13.

MARKS IM and SARTORIUS N (1968) A contribution to the measurement of sexual attitude. Journal of Nervous and Mental Disease 145: 441–451.

MARLATT GA (1976) The drinking profile: A questionnaire for the behavioural assessment of alcoholism. In Marsh EJ and Terdal CG (eds.) Behaviour therapy assessment: Design and evaluation. NY: Springer Publishing Co. 121–137.

MARLATT GA (1985) Relapse prevention: Theoretical rationale and overview of the model. In Marlatt GA and Gordon JR (eds.) Relapse prevention: Maintenance strategies in the treatment of addictive behaviours. NY: Guilford Press 3–70.

MARLATT GA and GORDON J (1985) Relapse prevention: Maintenance strategies in the treatment of addictive behaviours. NY: Guilford Press.

MARSH LF, CONNELL P and OLSEN E (1988) Breaking the cycle: Adolescent sexual treatment manual. Beaverton, Oregon: St Mary's Home for Boys.

MARSHALL P (1994) The prevalence of conviction for sexual offending in England and Wales. London: Home Office Research and Statistics Directorate.

MARSHALL WL (1971) A combined treatment method for certain sexual deviations. Behaviour Research and Therapy 9: 292–294.

MARSHALL WL (1988) The use of sexually explicit stimuli by rapists, child molesters and non-offenders. Journal of Sex Research 25: 267–288.

MARSHALL WL (1989) Intimacy, loneliness and sexual offenders. Behavioural Research and Therapy 27: 491–503.

MARSHALL WL (1993) The role of attachment, intimacy, and loneliness in the aetiology and maintenance of sexual offending. Sexual and Marital Therapy 8: 109–121.

MARSHALL WL (1993b) A revised approach to the treatment of men who sexually assault females. In Nagayana-Hall GE, Hirschman R, Graham JR and Zaragoza MS (eds.) Sexual aggression: Issues in aetiology, assessment and treatment. Washington, DC: Taylor and Francis, 143–165.

MARSHALL WL (1996) Assessment, treatment and theorizing about sex offenders. Criminal Justice and Behaviour 23: 162–199.

MARSHALL WL (1996) Psychological evaluation in sexual offence cases. Queen's Law Journal 21: 499–514.

MARSHALL WL, ANDERSON D and CHAMPAGNE F (1996) Self-esteem and its relationship to sexual offending. Psychology, Crime and Law 3: 81–106.

MARSHALL WL and BARBAREE HE (1990) An integrated theory of the aetiology of sexual offending. In Marshall WL, Laws DR and Barbaree HE (eds.) Handbook of sexual assault: Issues theories and treatment of the offender. NY: Plenum, 257–275.

MARSHALL WL and BARBAREE HE (1990) Outcome of

cognitive-behavioural treatment. In Marshall WL et al. (eds.) op. cit., 363–385.

MARSHALL WL and ECCLES A (1991) Issues in clinical practice with sex offenders. Journal of Interpersonal Violence 6: 68–93.

MARSHALL WL and MARIC A (1996) Cognitive and emotional components of generalised empathy deficits in child molesters. Journal of Child Sexual Abuse 5(2): 101–110.

MARSHALL WL and MAZZUCCO M (1995) Self-esteem and parental attachment in child molesters. Sexual Abuse: A Journal of Research and Treatment 7(4): 279–285.

MARSHALL WL and PETERS W (1994) A reconsideration of treatment outcome into sex offenders. Criminal Justice and Behaviour 21: 6–27.

MARSHALL WL, BARBAREE HE and BUTT J (1988) Sexual offenders against male children: Sexual preferences. Behav. Res. Ther. 26(5): 383–391.

MARSHALL WL, BARBAREE HE and CHRISTOPHE D (1986) Sex offenders against female children: Sexual preferences. Canadian Journal of Behavioural Science 18(4): 424–439.

MARSHALL WL, BARBAREE HE and ECCLES A (1991) Early onset and deviant sexuality in child molesters. Journal of Interpersonal Violence 6(3): 323–336.

MARSHALL WL, BARBAREE HE and FERNANDEZ YM (1995) Some aspects of social incompetence in sex offenders. Sexual Abuse: A Journal of Research and Treatment 7: 113–127.

MARSHALL WL, BRYCE P, HUDSON SM, WARD T and MOTT B (1996) The enhancement of intimacy and the reduction of loneliness among child molesters. Journal of Family Violence 11(3): 219–235.

MARSHALL WL, CHAMPAGNE F, STURGEON C and BRYCE P (1997) Increasing the self-esteem of child molesters. Sexual Abuse: A Journal of Research and Treatment 9(4): 321–333.

MARSHALL WL, HUDSON SM and HODKINSON S (1993) The importance of attachment bonds in the development of juvenile sex offending. In Barbaree HE, Marshall WL and Hudson SM (eds.) The juvenile sex offender. NY: Guilford Press, 164–181.

MARSHALL WL, HUDSON SM, JONES R and FERNANDEZ YM (1995) Empathy in sex offenders. Clinical Psychology Review 15(2): 99–113.

MARSHALL WL, JONES R, HUDSON SM and McDONALD E (1993) Generalised empathy in child molesters. Journal of Child Sexual Abuse 2: 61–68.

MARSHALL WL, PAYNE K, BARBAREE HE and ECCLES A (1991) Exhibitionists: Sexual preferences for exposing. Behaviour Research and Therapy 29: 37–40.

MARX SP (1996) Victim recantation in child sexual abuse cases. Child Welfare 75(3): 219–233.

MASTERS WH and JOHNSON VE (1970) Human sexual inadequacy. Boston: Little Brown.

MASTERS WH and JOHNSON VE (1966) Human sexual response. Boston: Little Brown.

MASTERS W, JOHNSON V and KOLODNY R (1992) Human sexuality. NY: Harper Collins.

MATTHEWS R, MATTHEWS J and SPEITZ K (1989) Female sex offenders. Orwell, VT: Safer Society Press.

MAUGER PA and ADKINSON DR (1987) Interpersonal behaviour survey manual. Los Angeles, Ca.: Western Psychological Services.

MAYER A (1988) Sex offenders: Approaches to understanding and management. Holmes beach, FI.: Learning Publications, Inc.

MAYERS GM, CURRIE EF, MacLEOD L, GILIES JB and WARDEN DA (1992) Child sexual abuse: A review of literature and educational materials. Edinburgh: Scottish Academic Press.

McCONAGHY N (1993) Sexual behaviour: Problems and management. NY: Plenum Press.

McCUBBIN HI, THOMPSON A and McCUBBIN MA (1996) Family assessment: Resilience, coping and adaptation – inventories for research and practice. Madison: University of Wisconsin.

McDOWELL I and NEWELL C (1987) Measuring health: A guide to rating scales and questionnaires. NY: Oxford University Press.

McEWAN S and SULLIVAN J (1996) Sex offender risk assessment. In Kemshall H and Pritchard J (eds.) Good practice in risk assessment and risk management. London: Jessica Kingsley, 146–158.

McFALL RM (1990) The enhancement of social skills: An information – processing analysis. In Marshall WL, Laws DR and Barbaree AE (eds.) Handbook of sexual assault. NY: Plenum, 311–330.

McGONNAUGHY EA, DICLEMENTE CC, PROCHASKA JA and VELICER WF (1989) Stages of change in psychotherapy: A follow-up report. Psychotherapy 26(4): 494–503.

McGOVERN K and PETERS J (1988) Guidelines for assessing sex offenders. In Walker LE (ed.) Handbook of sexual abuse of children: Assessment and treatment issues. NY: Springer, 216–246.

McGRATH RJ (1990) Assessment of sexual aggressors: Practical clinical interviewing strategies. Journal of Interpersonal Violence 5(4): 507–519.

McGRATH RJ (1991) Sex offender risk assessment and disposition of planning: A review of empirical and clinical findings. Interpersonal Journal of Offender Therapy and Comparative Criminology 35(4): 328–350.

McGRATH RJ (1992) Assessing sex offender risk. American Probation and Parole Association Perspectives 16(3): 6–9.

McGUIRE RJ, CARLISLE JM and YOUNG BG (1965) Sexual deviations as conditioned behaviour: A hypothesis. Behaviour Research and Therapy 2: 185–190.

McMILLAN C, ZARAVIN S and RIDEOUT G (1995) Perceived benefit from child sexual abuse: A Journal of Consulting and Clinical Psychology 63(6): 1037–1043.

MEHRABAIN A and EPSTEIN N (1972) A measure of emotional empathy. Journal of Personality 40: 525–543.

METTS S and LUPACH WR (1989) The role of communication in human sexuality. In McKinney K and Sprecher S (eds.) Human sexuality: The societal and interpersonal context. NJ: Ablex Norwood, 139–161.

METZGER C and CARICH MS (1997) Eleven point comprehensive sex offender treatment plan. Unpublished manuscript.

MILLAR B, CRUTE V and HARGIE D (1992) Professional Interviewing. London: Routledge.

MILLER BL, CUMMING JL, McINTYRE H, EBERS G and GRODE M (1986) Hypersexuality or altered sexual preference following brain injury. Journal of Neurology, Neurosurgery and Psychiatry 49: 867.

MILLER J (1978) Recidivism among sexual assault victims. Journal of Social Issues 39(2): 139–152.

MILLER M, CUMMINGS M, McINTYRE M, EBERS M and GOODE M (1986), as quoted in Whetshell-Mitchell, 1995, p 42.

MILLER PA and EISENBERG W (1985) The relation of empathy to aggressive and externalising/antisocial behaviour. Psychological Bulletin 103: 324–344.

MILLER RS and LEFCOURT HM (1982) The assessment of social intimacy. Journal of Personality Assessment 46: 514–518.

MILLER W and ROLLNICK S (1991) Motivational interviewing: Preparing people to change addictive behaviour. NY: Guilford Press.

MILLON T (1987) Millon clinical multiaxal inventory II. Minneapolis, MN: National Computer Systems.

MONEY J (1965) Influence of hormones on sexual behaviour. Annual Review of Medicine 16: 67–82.

MONEY J (1986) Lovemaps: Clinical concepts of sexual health and pathology paraphilia and gender transpostition in childhood, adolescence and maturity. NY: Irvington Publishers.

MONEY J (1989) Vandalised lovemaps. Buffalo: Prometheus.

MONK D (1998) Sex education and HIV/AIDS: Political conflict and legal resolution. Children and Society 12: 295–305.

MOORE B (1996) Risk assessment: A practitioners guide to predicting harmful behaviour. London: Whiting and Birch Ltd.

MOORE J (1990) Confronting the perpetrator. Community Care 12.4.90, 20–1.

MOORE J (1991) Winds of change. Community Care 11.7.91, p23–4.

MORRAN D and WILSON M (1997) Men who are violent to women: A groupwork practice manual. Dorset: Russell House Publishing.

MORRISON T (1989) Treating the untreatable? Groupwork with intra-familial sex offenders. In NSPCC Occasional Paper 2, 'The treatment of child sexual abuse.' London NSPCC, 6–13.

MORRISON T (1991) Change, control and the legal framework. In Adcock M, White R and Hollows A (eds.) Significant harm: Its management and outcome. Croydon: Significant Publications, 85–100.

MORRISON T (1992) Managing sex offenders: The challenge for managers. Probation Journal 39(3): 122–128.

MORRISON T (19930 Staff supervision in social care. London: Longman.

MORRISON T (1994) Context, constraints and considerations for practice. In Morrison T, Erooga M and Beckett RC (eds.) Sexual offending against children. London, Routledge, 25–54.

MORRISON T (1994b) Learning together to manage sexual abuse. Rhetoric or reality? Journal of Sexual Aggression 1(1): 29–44.

MORRISON T (1995) Core groups: A catalyst for change? Presentation to the national conference on core groups. Manchester Town Hall, 14.7.95.

MORRISON T (1997) Managing risk: Learning our lessons. Keynote presentation to NOTA conference, September 1997.

MORRISON T and PRINT B (1995) Adolescent sexual abusers: An overview. Hull: Bluemoon Corporate Services.

MORTON JC, RICHEY CA and KELLETT M (1981) Building assertive skills: A practical guide to professional development for allied dental health providers. St Louis: Mosby.

MOSHER DL (1965) Interaction of fear and guilt in inhibiting unaccepatable sexual behaviour. Journal of Consulting Psychology 29: 161–167.

MOSHER DL and ANDERSON RD (1986) Macho personality, sexual aggression and reactions to guided imagery. Journal of Research in Personality 20: 77–94.

MOSHER DL and SIRKIN M (1984) Measuring a macho personality constellation. Journal of Research in Personality 18: 150–163.

MUEHLENHARD CL and FALCON PL (1991) Men's heterosocial skills and attitudes towards women as predictors of verbal sexual coercion and forceful rape. Sex Roles 17.

MURPHY-BRESSAM V (1994) A conceptual framework for thinking about risk assessment and case management in child protective services. Child Abuse and Neglect 18: 193–201.

MURPHY WD, COLEMAN E and HAYNES M (1983) Treatment and evaluation issues with the mentally retarded sex offender. In Greer J and Struart I (eds.) The sexual aggressor: Current perspectives in treatment. NY: Van Nostrand Reinhold Co.

MURPHY WD (1990) Assessment and modification of cognitive distortions. In Marshall WL, Laws DR and Barbaree HE (eds.) Handbook of sexual assault. NY: Plenum Press.

MURPHY WD and SMITH JA (1996) Sex offenders against children: Empirical and clinical issues. In Briere J, Berliner L, Bulkley JA, Jenny C and Reid J (eds.) The APSAC handbook in child maltreatment. Thousand Oaks, Ca.: Sage, 175–191.

MURPHY WD, HAYNES MR, STALGALTIS SJ and FLANAGAN B (1986) Differential sexual responding amongst four groups of sexual offenders against children. Journal of Psychotherapy and Behavioural Assessment 8: 339–353.

NATIONAL CHILDREN'S HOMES (1992) Report of the committee of enquiry into children and young people who sexually abuse other children. London: NCH.

NATIONAL TASK FORCE (1993) The revised report from the National Task Force on juvenile sexual offending. Juvenile and Family Court Journal 44(4): 1–121.

NEATE P (1990) The unknown quantity. Community Care 8.11.90, 17–19.

NELSON S (1998) Time to break professional silences. Child Abuse Review 7(3): 144–153.

NICOLS HR and MOLINDER L (1984) The multiphasic sex inventory. Tocoma, WA: Self-published.

NOELLY D, MUCCIGROSSO L and ZIGMAN E (1996) Treatment successes with mentally retarded sex offenders. In COLEMAN E, DWYER SM and PALLONE NJ (eds.) Sex offender treatment: biological dysfunction, intrapsychic conflict, interpersonal violence. NY: Haworth Press.

NOVACO RW (1975) Anger control: The development and evaluation of an experimental treatment. Lexington, Mass.: DC Heath and Co.

NOWICKI S and STRICKLAND B (1973) A locus of control

scale. Journal of Consulting and Clinical Psychology 40: 148–154.

NOWINSKI JK and LoPICCOLO J (1979) Assessing sexual behaviour in couples. Journal of Sex and Marital Therapy 5(3): 225–243.

NUGENT PM and KRONER DG (1996) Denial, response styles and maintenance of offences among child molesters and rapists. Journal of Interpersonal Violence 11(4): 475–486.

O'CALLAGHAN D (forthcoming) Young abusers with learning difficulties: Understanding and responding. In Calder MC (ed.) Working with young people who sexually abuse. New pieces of the jigsaw. Dorset: Russell House Publishing.

O'CARROLL T (1980) The 'molester' and his 'victim'. In O'Carroll T (ed.) Paedophilia: The radical case. London: Peter Owen Ltd.

O'CONNELL MA, LEBERG E and DONALDSON CR (1990) Working with sex offenders: Guidelines for therapist selection. Beverly Hills, Ca.: Sage.

O'DONOHUE W and LETOURNEAU EJ (1993) A brief group treatment for the modification of denial in child sexual abusers: outcome and follow-up. Child Abuse and Neglect 17: 299–304.

O'DONOHUE W, LETOURNEAU EJ and DOWLING H (1997) Development and preliminary validation of a paraphilic sexual fantasy questionnaire. Sexual Abuse: A Journal of Research and Treatment 9(3): 167–178.

O'HAGAN K (1989) Working with child sexual abuse. Milton Keynes: Open University Press.

OATES RK (ed.) (1990) Understanding and managing child sexual abuse. Marrickville: Harcourt. Brace Jovanovich.

OKAMI P (1991) Self-reports of 'positive' childhood and adolescent sexual contacts with older persons: An exploratory study. Archives of Sexual Behaviour 20: 437–452.

OLAFSON E, CORWIN DL and SUMMITT RC (1993) Modern history of sexual abuse awareness: Cycles of discovery and suppression. Child Abuse and Neglect 17: 7–24.

OLIVER JE and TAYLOR A (1971) Five generations of ill-treated children in one family pedigree. British Journal of Psychiatry 119: 473–480.

OLSEN DH, McCUBBIN HI, BARNES H, LARSEN A, MUXEN M and WILSON M (1992) The families inventories manual. Family Social Science: University of Minnesota.

OVERHOLSEN JC and BECK S (1986) Multi-method assessment of rapists, child molesters, and three control groups on behavioural and psychological measures. Journal of Consulting and Clinical Psychology 54: 682–687.

OWEN G and STEEL NM (1991) Incest offenders after treatment. In Patton MQ (ed.) Family sexual abuse: Frontline research and evaluation. Newbury Park, Ca.: Sage, 178–198.

PAITICH D, LANGEVIN R, FREEMAN R, MANN K and HANDY L (1977) The Clarke SHQ: A clinical sex history questionnaire for males. Archives of Sexual Behaviour 6(5): 421–436.

PALMER J (1995) Young people who sexually abuse. Report to Cleveland ACPC, 11.5.95.

PANTON J (1978) Personality differences appearing between rapists of adults, rapists of children, and non-violent sexual molesters of children. Research Communications in Psychology, Psychiatry and Behaviour 3(4): 385–393.

PAREZA G (1987) Risk factors in father-daughter child sexual abuse: Findings from a case-control study. Paper presented at the 3rd national family violence research conference, Family Research Institutions. Durham, NH.

PARKER H (1984) Intra-familial child sexual abuse: A study of the abusive father. Dissertation Abstracts International 45(12).

PEARCE G (1991) Child sexual abuse: Professional and personal perspectives. Part 2: Inter-professional collaboration. Cheadle: Boys and Girls' Welfare Society.

PENDERGAST WE (1991) Treating sex offenders in correctional institutions and outpatient clinics: A guide to clinical practice. NY: Haworth Press.

PENNELL A (1996) The link between child maltreatment and sexual offending. Paper presented to the 11th ISPCAN congress on child abuse and neglect, Dublin, Ireland, 18–21 August 1996.

PEPLAU LA and PERLMAN D (1982) Loneliness: A sourcebook of current theory, research and therapy. NY: John Wiley and Sons.

PERKINS D (1987) Working with sex offenders. In Horobin G (ed.) Sex, gender and care work. London: Jessica Kingsley, 130–147.

PERLMAN D and DUCK S (1987) Intimate relationships: Development, dynamics and deterioration. Newbury Park, Ca.: Sage.

PERLMAN D and PEPLAU LA (1984) Loneliness research: A survey of empirical findings. In Peplau LA and Goldston SE (eds.) Preventing the harmful consequences of severe and persistent loneliness. Washington, DC: US Government Printing Office.

PERRY GP and ORCHARD J (1992) Assessment and treatment of adolescent sex offenders. Sarasota, Fl.: Professional Resource Press.

PERSON (1991) As quoted in Gocke B, op. cit.

PETERS SQ, WYATT GE and FINKELHOR D (1986) Prevalence. In Finkelhor D (ed.) A sourcebook on child sexual abuse. Beverly Hills, Ca.: Sage.

PHARES EJ and ERSKINE N (1984) The measurement of selfism. Educational and Psychological Measurement 44: 597–608.

PIERCE R and PIERCE L (1984) Race as a factor in child sexual abuse. Paper given at the national conference for family violence researchers, Durham, New Hampshire.

PILOWSKY I (1983) Manual for the Illness Behaviour Questionnaire. University of Adelaide: Department of Psychiatry.

PITHERS W, KASHIMA K, CUMMING GF, BEAL LS and BUELL M (1988) Relapse prevention of sexual aggression. Annals of the New York Academy of Sciences 528: 244–260.

PITHERS WD (1990) Relapse prevention with sexual aggressors: A method for maintaining therapeutic gain and enhancing external supervision. In Marshall WL, Laws DR and Barbaree HE (eds.) Handbook of sexual assault: Issues, theories and treatment of the offender. New York: Plenum.

PITHERS WD (1994) Process evaluation of a group therapy component designed to enhance sex offenders' empathy for sexual abuse survivors. Behavioural Res Ther 32(5): 565–570.

PITHERS WD and LAWS DR (1988) The penile plethysnograph. In Schwartz BK (ed.) A practitioner's guide to treating the incarcerated male sex offender. Washington, DC: Author, 85–94.

PITHERS WD and LAWS DR (1995) Phallometric assessments. In Schwartz BK and Cellini HR (eds.) The sex offender. Kingston, NJ: Civic Research Institute, Inc.

PITHERS WD, BEAL LS, ARMSTRONG J and PETTY J (1989) The identification of risk factors through clinical interviews and analysis of records. In Laws DR (ed.), op. cit., 1–31.

PITHERS WD, BUELL MM, KASHIMA KM, CUMMING GF and BEAL LS (1987) Precursor to sexual offences. Proceedings of the 1st annual meeting of the association for the behavioural treatment of sexual aggressors. Newport, Oregon.

POLLACK N and HASHMARL JM (1991) The excuses of child molesters. Behavioural Sciences and the Law 9, 53–59.

POLSON M and McCULLOCH E (1995) Therapist caring in the treatment of sexual abuse offenders. Journal of Child Sexual Abuse 4(1): 21–43.

POMEROY C, FLAX C and WHEELER C (1982) Taking a sex history. NY: The Free Press.

POWELL MB and ILETT MJ (1992) Assessing the incestuous family's readiness for reconstitution. Family in Society 73(7): 417–423.

PRENDERGAST WE (1991) Treating sex offenders in correctional institutions and outpatient clinics: A guide to clinical practice. NY: Haworth Press.

PRENTKY RA and EDMUNDS SB (1997) Assessing sexual abuse: A resource guide for practitioners. Brandon, VT: Safer Society Press.

PRENTKY RA and BURGESS AW (1991) Hypothetical biological substrates of a fantasy-based drive mechanism for negative sexual aggression. In Burgess AW (ed.) Rape and sexual assault III: NY: Garland, 235–256.

PRENTKY RA, BURGESS AW, ROKOUS F, LEE A, HARTMAN C, RESSLER R and DOUGLAS J (1989) The presumptive role of fantasy in sexual homicide. American Journal of Psychiatry 146: 887–891.

PRINGLE K (1993) Gender politics. Community Care, 4.3.93, 16–17.

PROCHASKA JO and DiCLEMENTE CC (1982) Transtheoretical therapy: Toward a more integrative model of change. Psychotherapy, Theory, Research and Practice 19: 276–288.

PROCHASKA JO and DiCLEMENTE CC (1986) Towards a comprehensive model of change. In Miller WN and Heather N (eds.) Treating addictive behaviours: Processes of change. NY: Plenum Press, 3–27.

PROCTOR E (1994) The sex offence attitude questionnaire. Oxford: Oxford Probation Service.

PROCTOR E (1996) Community based interventions with sex offenders organised by the probation service—a survey of current practice. Association of Chief Officers of Probation (ACOP).

QUINN JM (1984) Father-daughter incest: An ecological model. Dissertation Abstracts International 45(2): 3957B.

QUINSEY VL (1977) The assessment and treatment of child molesters: A review. Canadian Psychological Review 18: 204–220.

QUINSEY VL (1981) Prediction of recidivism and the evaluation of treatment programs for sex offenders. Paper at sexual aggression and the law: A symposium. Vancouver, Canada.

QUINSEY VL (1984) sexual aggression: Studies of offenders against women. In Weisstub DN (ed.) Law and mental health: International perspectives (Vol 1) NY: Pergammon Press.

QUINSEY VL (1986) Men who have sex with children. In Weisstub DN (ed.) Law and mental health: International perspectives (Vol 2) NY: Pergamon Press, 140–172.

QUINSEY VL, CHAPLIN TC and CARRIGAN WF (1979) Sexual preferences among incestuous and non-incestuous child molesters. Behavioural Therapy 10: 562–565.

QUINSEY VL, LALUMIERE M, RICE M and HARRIS G (1995) Predicting sexual offences. In Cambell J (ed.) Assessing dangerousness: Violence by sexual offenders, batterers and child abusers. Thousand Oaks, Ca.: Sage.

RADA RT (1976) Alcoholism and the child molester. Annals of the New York Academy of Justice 273: 492–6.

RADA RT (ed.) (1978) Clinical aspects of the rapist. NY: Grune and Stratton.

RADZINOWICZ L (1967) Sexual offences: A report of the Cambridge department of criminal science. London: MacMillan and Co, Ltd.

RAKOS RF (1991) Assertive behaviour: Theory, research and training. London: Routledge.

RASKIN DC and YUILLE JC (1989) Problems in evaluating interviews of children in sexual abuse cases. In Ceci SJ, Ross DF and Toglia MP (eds.) Perspectives on children's testimony. NY: Springer–Verlag.

RATHUS RA (1973) A 30 item schedule for assessing assertive behaviour. Behaviour Therapy 4: 398–406.

REISER M (1991) Recantation in child sexual abuse cases. Child Welfare 90: 611–621.

REHM LP (1977) A self-control model of depression. Behaviour Therapy 28: 787–804.

REHM LP (1984) Self-management therapy for depression. Advances in Behaviour Research and Therapy 6: 83–98.

RENVOIZE J (1993) Innocence destroyed: A study of child sexual abuse. London: Routledge.

REPPUCCI ND and HAUGAARD JJ (1993) Problems with child sexual abuse prevention programs. In Gelles RJ and Loseke DR (eds.) Current controversies in family violence. Newbury Park, Ca.: Sage.

RHUE TW and LYNN SJ (1987) Fantasy proneness: Developmental antecedents. Journal of Personality 55(1): 121–137.

ROBERTS W and STRAYER J (1996) Empathy, emotional expressiveness, and pro-social behaviour. Child Development 67: 449–470.

ROKEACH M (1973) The nature of human values. NY: Free Press.

ROKEACH M (1980) Some unresolved issues in theories of beliefs, attitudes, and values. In Page MM (ed.) Nebraska symposium on motivation 1979. Lincoln: University of Nebraska Press.

ROMANO E and De LUCA RV (1997) Exploring the relationship between childhood sexual abuse and adult sexual perpetration. Journal of Family Violence 12(1): 85–98.

ROMBOUGH S and VENTIMIGLIO JC (1981) Sexism: A tri-dimensional phenomenon. 7: 747–755.

ROSE K (1998) The issue of contact in relation to child sexual abuse. Salford ACPC. Unpublished paper.

ROSENBURG M (1989) Society and the adolescent self-image. Middletown, CT: Weslyan University Press.

ROSS J (1989) Group treatment approaches. Paper presented at the advanced training for treatment of adolescent sex offenders. Toronto: Canadian Welfare Association.

ROWLANDS DL (1995) The psychobiology of sexual arousal and behaviour. In Diamont L and McAnulty RD (eds.) The psychology of sexual orientation, behaviour and identity: A hanbook. Westport, Conneticut: Greenwood Press, 19–42.

RUSSELL D, PEPLOU LA and CUTRONA CE (1980) The revised UCLA loneliness scale: Concurrent and discriminatory validity evidence. Journal of Personality and Social Psychology 39: 472–480.

RUSSELL DEH (1983) The incidence and prevalence of intra-familial and extra-familial sexual abuse of female children. Child Abuse and Neglect 7: 133–146.

RUSSELL DEH (1984) Sexual exploitation: Rape, child sexual abuse and workplace harassment. Beverly Hills, Ca.: Sage.

RUSSELL DEH (1988) The incidence and prevalence of intra-familial sexual abuse of female children. In Walker LE (ed.) Handbook on sexual abuse of children: Assessment and treatment issues. NY: Springer Publishing Co, 19–36.

RUSSON AE (1985) Sex history questionnaires scoring manual. In Langevin R (ed.), op. cit.

RYAN G, LANE SR and ISAAC CB (1987) Juvenile sex offenders; Development and correction. Child Abuse and Neglect 2: 385–395.

RYAN GD (1994) Presentation to the 10th national training conference of the National Adolescent Perpetrator Network. Denver, Colorado, February 1994.

RYAN GD, METZNER JC and KRUGMAN RD (1990) When the abuser is a child. In Oates RK (ed.), op. cit., 258–273.

SABATELLI RM (1984) The marital comparison level index: A measure for assessing outcomes relative to expectations. Journal of Marriage and the Family 46: 651–662.

SAHD D (1980) Psychological assessment of sexually abusing families and treatment implications. In Holder W (ed.) Sexual abuse of children: Implications for treatment. Englewood, Co: American Humane Association.

SALTER AC (1988) Treating child sex offenders and victims? Assessment and treatment of child sex offenders: A practice guide. Beverly Hills, Ca.: Sage.

SALTER AC (1995) Transforming trauma: A guide to understanding and treating adult survivors of child sexual abuse. Thousand Oaks, Ca.: Sage.

SAMENOW D (1995) Errors in thinking. Unpublished handout.

SAMRA-TIBBETS C and RAYNES B (1998) Assessment and planning. In Calder MC and Horwath J (eds.) Working for children on the child protection register, an inter-agency practice guide. Aldershot: Arena.

SANDERSON C (1990) Counselling adult survivors of child sexual abuse. London: Jessica Kingsley.

SARADJAN J and HANKS H (1996) Women who sexually abuse children: From research to clinical practice. Chichester: John Wiley and Sons.

SAUNDERS EB and AWAD GA (1988) Assessment, management and treatment planning for male adolescent sex offenders. American Journal of Orthopsychiatry 58(4): 571–579.

SCALISE JJ, GINTER EJ and GERSTEIN LH (1984) A multidimensional loneliness measure: The loneliness rating scale. Journal of Personality Assessment 48: 525–530.

SCHAEFER M and OLSON D (1981) Assessing intimacy: The PAIR inventory. Journal of Marital and Family Therapy 7: 47–60.

SCHECHTER MD and ROBERGE L (1976) Sexual exploration. In Helfer RE and Kempe CH (eds.) Child abuse and neglect: The family and the community. Cambridge, Mass.: Ballinger, p129.

SCHIAVI RC, DEROGATIS LR, KURIANSKY J and O'CONNOR D (1979) The assessment of sexual function and marital interaction. Journal of Sex and Marital Therapy 5(3): 169–224.

SCHIEBE KE (1970) Beliefs and values. NY: Holt, Rinehart and Winston.

SCHLANK AM and SHAW T (1996) Treating sexual offenders who deny their guilt: A pilot study. Sexual Abuse: A Journal of Research and Treatment 8(1): 17–23.

SCHLANK AM and SHAW T (1997) Treating sexual offenders who deny: A review. In Schwartz BK and Cellini HR (eds.) The sex offender: New insights, treatment innovations and legal developments. Kingston, NJ: Civic Research Institute.

SCHWARTZ BF (1995) Theories of sexual offenders. In Schwartz BK and Cellini HR (eds.) The sex offender: Corrections, treatment and legal practice. Kingston, NJ: Civic Research Institute, Inc.

SCHWARTZ BK and CELLINI HR (eds.) (1995) The sex offender: Corrections, treatment and legal practice. Kingston, NJ: Civic Research Institute, Inc.

SCHWARTZ MF (1985) Treatment of paraphiliacs, paedophiles and incest families. In Burgess AW (ed.) Rape and sexual assault: A research handbook. NY: Garland Publishing Inc, 350–364.

SCOTT RL and TETREAULT LA (1987) Attitudes of rapists and other violent offenders towards women. The Journal of Social Psychology 127(4): 375–380.

SCULLY D and MAROLA J (1984) Convicted rapists' vocabulary of motives, excuses and justifications. Social Problems 31: 530–544.

SEARLE Y and STRENG I (1995) The social skills game. London: Jessica Kingsley.

SEGAL LE and STERMAC L (1990) The role of cognition in sexual assault. In Marshall WL, Laws DR and Barbaree HE (eds.) Handbook of sexual assault. NY: Plenum, 161–176.

SEGAL ZV (1983) Heterosexual social skills in a population of rapists and child molesters. Unpublished doctoral dissertation, Queens University, Kingston, Ontario, Canada.

SEGAL ZV and MARSHALL WL (1985) Heterosexual social skills in a population of rapists and child molesters. Journal of Consulting and Clinical Psychology 53: 55–63.

SEGAL ZV and MARSHALL WL (1985) Discrepancies

between self-efficacy predictions and actual performance in a population of rapists and child molesters. Cognitive Therapy and Research 10(3): 363–376.

SEGAL ZV and MARSHALL WL (1985b) Self-report and behavioural assertion in groups of sexual offenders. Journal of Behaviour Therapy and Experimental Psychiatry 16: 223–229.

SEGAL ZV and MARSHALL WL (1986) Discrepancies between self-efficiency predictions and actual performance in a population of rapists and child molesters. Cognitive Therapy and Research 10: 363–376.

SEIDMAN BT, MARSHALL WL, HUDSON SM and ROBERTSON PJ (1994) An examination of intimacy and loneliness in sex offenders. Journal of Interpersonal Violence 9(4): 518–534.

SELZER M (1971) The Michigan alcoholism screening test: The quest for a new diagnostic instrument. Journal of Psychiatry 127: 1653–1658.

SERIN RC, MALCOLM PB, KHANNA A and BARBAREE HE (1994) Psychopathy and deviant sexual arousal in incarcerated sex offenders. Journal of Interpersonal Violence 9(1): 3–11.

SERVER JC and JANZEN C (1982) Contradictions to the reconstitution of sexually abusive families. Child Welfare 61: 279–288.

SETO MC and BARBAREE HE (1995) The role of alcohol in sexual aggression. Clinical Psychology review 15(6): 545–566.

SGROI SM (1989) Evaluation and treatment of sexual offence behaviours in persons with mental retardation. In Sgroi SM (ed.) Vulnerable populations: Sexual abuse treatment for children, adult survivors, and persons with mental retardation. Lexington, Mass.: Lexington Books. 245–283.

SGROI SM (ed.) (1982) Handbook of clinical intervention in child sexual abuse. Lexington, Mass.: Lexington Books.

SGROI SM (ed.) (1989) Vulnerable populations: Sexual abuse treatment for children, adult survivors, and persons with mental retardation. Lexington, Mass.: Lexington Books.

SHAVER PR and HAZAN C (1988) A biased overview of the study of love. Journal of Social and Personal Relationships 5: 473–501.

SHEATH M (1990) Confrontive work with sex offenders: Legitimised nonce bashing? Probation Journal 37(4).

SIEGEL JM (1986) The multi-dimensional anger inventory. Journal of Personality and Social Psychology 51(1): 191–200.

SIMMONS J (1986) Child sexual abuse: An assessment process. London: NSPCC.

SIMON WT and SCHOUTER PGW (1992) Problems in sexual preference testing in child sexual abuse cases: A legal and community perspective. Journal of Interpersonal Violence 7(4): 503–516.

SINASON V (1996) From abused to abuser. In Cordess C and Cox M (eds.) Forensic psychotherapy (Vol 2) Mainly practice. London: Jessica Kingsley, 371–382.

SKINNER HA (1982) The drug abuse screening test. Addictive Behaviour 7: 363–371.

SMITH G (1986) Child sexual abuse: The power of intrusion. Adoption and Fostering 10(3): 13–18.

SMITH G (1998) Reassessing protectiveness: Engaging the silent minority. Keynote presentation to the NOTA conference, University of Glasgow, 16–18 September, 1998.

SMITH MD and SELF GD (1981) Feminists – traditionalists. Sex Roles 7: 183–188.

SNELL WE, BELK SS, PAPINI DR and CLARK S (1989) Development and validation of the sexual self-disclosure scale. Annals of Sex Research 2: 307–334.

SOBSEY D and MANSELL S (1994) Sexual abuse patterns of children with disabilities. The International Journal of Children's Rights 2: 96–100.

SOCIAL WORK SERVICES INSPECTORATE FOR SCOTLAND. A commitment to protect. Supervising sex offenders: Proposals for more effective practice. The Scottish Office, 1997.

SPANIER GB (1976) Measuring dyadic adjustment: New scales for assessing the quality of marriage and similar dyads. Journal of Marriage and the Family 38: 15–28.

SPANIER GB (1979) The measurement of marital quality. Journal of Sex and Marital Therapy 5(3): 288–300.

SPENCE JT and HELMREICH RL (1978) Masculinity and femininity: Their psychological dimensions, correlates and antecedents. Texas: University of Texas Press.

SPIELBERGER CD (1988) State-trait anger expression inventory: Professional manual. Odessa, Fl.: Psychological Assessment.

SPIELBERGER CD, JACOBS G, RUSSELL S and CRANE RS (1983) Assessment of anger: The state-trait Anger Scale. In Butcher JN and Spielberger CD (eds.) Advances in personality assessment (Vol 2). Hillsdale, NJ: Lawrence Erlbaum Associates, 159–187.

SQUIRREL G (1998) Developing social skills. Dorset: Russell House Publishing.

STAINTON-ROGERS W (1989) The social construction of childhood. In Stainton-Rogers W, Hevey D and Ash E (eds.) Child abuse and neglect. London: Open University Press.

STEEN C (1993) The relapse prevention workbook for youth in treatment. Brandon, VT: Safer Society Press.

STEEN C and MONETTE B (1989) Treating adolescent sex offenders in the community. Springfield, Ill.: Charles C Thomas.

STERMAC L, DAVIDSON A and SHERIDAN M (1995) Incidence of non-sexual violence in incest offenders. International Journal of Offender Therapy and Comparative Criminology 39(2).

STERMAC LE and QUINSEY VL (1985) Social competence among rapists. Behavioural Assessment 8: 171–185.

STERMAC LE and SEGAL ZV (1989) Adult sexual contact with children: An examination of cognitive factors. Behaviour Therapy 20: 573–584.

STERMAC LE and SEGAL ZV (1991) Clinicians' cognitions about sexual contact with children: A reply to Murphy. Behaviour Therapy 22: 125–127.

STERMAC LE, SEGAL ZV and GILLIS R (1990) Social and cultural issues in sexual assault. In Marshall WL, Laws DR and Barbaree HE (eds.) Handbook of sexual assault: Issues, theories and treatment of the offender. NY: Plenum, 143–159.

STEWART WF and YOUNG R (1992) The rehabilitation of the child sexual abuse syndrome in trail courts in Kentucky. Journal of Child Sexual Abuse 1(4): 133–141.

STOLLER R (1975) Perversion: The erotic form of hatred. NY: pantheon.

STORY MD (1988) Sexual attitudes for self and others

questionnaire. In Davis CM, Yarber WL and Davis SL (eds.) Sexuality-related measures: A compendium. Iowa: Graphic Publishing Co.

STRAND V (1986) Parents in incest families: A study of the differences. Dissertation Abstracts International 47(8), 3191A.

STRAUS MA (1979) Measuring intra-family conflict and violence: The conflict tactics scale. Journal of Marriage and the Family 4: 75–88.

SUMMIT RC (1983) The child sexual abuse accommodation syndrome. Child Abuse and Neglect 7: 177–193.

SUMMIT RC (1990) The specific vulnerability of children. In Oates RK (ed.) Understanding and managing child sexual abuse. Marrickville: Harcourt Brace Jovanovich, 59–74.

SWIFT C (1979) The prevention of child sexual abuse: Focus on the perpetrator. Journal of Clinical Child Psychology 8: 133–136.

TAGUIRI R (1969) Person perception. In Lindzey G and Aronson E (eds.) The handbook of social psychology (Vol 3). Reading, Mass.: Addison-Wesley, 395–449.

TAYLOR G (1996) Working with denial. Workshop at the Barnardo's conference, 'Learning to change', Liverpool Town Hall, 14 March, 1996.

TAYLOR R (1972) The significance and interpretation of motivational questions: The case of sex offenders. Sociology 6: 23–39.

TAYLOR-BROWNE J 91997) Obfuscating child sexual abuse 1. The identification of social problems. Child Abuse Review 6: 4–10.

TEMPLEMAN TL and STINNETT RD (1991) Patterns of sexual arousal and history in a 'normal' sample of young men. Archives of Sexual Behaviour 20(2).

TESCH SA (1985) The psycho-social intimacy questionnaire. Journal of Social and Personal Relationships 2: 471–488.

THORNBURG H (1981) Adolescent sources of information on sex. Journal of School Health 51: 274–281.

THORNE F (1966) The sex inventory. Journal of Clinical Psychology 22: 367–374.

THORNTON D (1994) Self-esteem questionnaire. In Beckett RC et al., op. cit.

THORNTON S, TODD B and THORNTON D (1996) Empathy and the recognition of abuse. Legal and Criminology Psychology 1: 147–153.

TIMNICK L (1985) 22% in survey were child abuse victims. Los Angeles Times, 25.8.85.

TIMNICK L (1985b) Children's abuse reports reliable, most believable. Los Angeles Times, 26.8.85.

TINGLE D, BARNARD GW, ROBBIN L, NEWMAN G and HUTCHINSON D (1986) Childhood and adolescent characteristics of paedophiles and rapists. International Journal of Law and Psychiatry 9: 103–116.

TOMISON AM (1995) Update on child sexual abuse. Melbourne, Australia: Australian Institute of Family Studies.

TONKIN B (1988) Pockets of resistance. Community Care, 18.8.88, p27.

TOWER CC (1989) Understanding child abuse and neglect. Boston: Allyn and Bacon.

TROWELL J (1991) Teaching about child sexual abuse. In Pietroni M (ed.) Right or privilege? Post-qualifying training for social workers, with special reference to child care. London: CCETSW.

TURNER AJ, FRANKS BG and LEVIN DM (1983) Social support: Conceptualisation, measurement and implications for mental health. Research in Community and Mental Health 3: 67–111.

VAN BEEK DJ and MULDER JR (1992) The offence script: A motivational tool and treatment method for sex offenders in a Dutch forensic clinic. International Journal of Offender Therapy and Comparative Criminology 36: 155–167.

VIZARD E (1988) Child sexual abuse—The child's experience. British Journal of Psychotherapy 5(1): 77–91.

WALKER CE, BONNER BL and KAUFMAN KC (1988) The physically and sexually abused child: Evaluation and treatment. NY: Pergammon Press.

WANBERG KW, HORN JL and FOSTER FM (1977) A differential assessment model for alcoholism: The scales of the alcohol use inventory. Journal of Studies on Alcohol 38(3): 512–543.

WARD T and HUDSON SM (1998) The construction and development of theory in the sexual offending area: A meta-theoretical framework. Sexual Abuse: A Journal of Research and Treatment 10(1): 47–63.

WARD T, CONNOLLY M, McCORMACK J and HUDSON SM (1996) Social workers' attributions for sexual offending against children. Journal of Child Sexual Abuse 5(3): 39–55.

WARD T, FON C, HUDSON SM and McCORMACK J (1998) A descriptive model of dysfunctional cognitions in child molesters. Journal of Interpersonal Violence 13(1): 129–155.

WARD T, HUDSON SM and FRANCE KG (1993) Self-reported reasons for offending behaviour in child molesters. Annals of Sex Research 6: 139–148.

WARD T, HUDSON SM and MARSHALL WL (1995) Cognitive distortions and affective deficits in sex offenders: A cognitive deconstructionist interpretation. Sexual Abuse: A Journal of Research and Treatment 7: 67–83.

WARD T, HUDSON SM, JOHNSON L and MARSHALL WL (1997) Cognitive distortions in sex offenders: An integrative review. Clinical Psychology Review 17(5): 479–507.

WARD T, HUDSON SM, MARSHALL WL and SIEGERT R (1995) Attachment style and intimacy deficits in sexual offenders: A theoretical framework. Sexual Abuse: A Journal of Research and Treatment 7(4): 317–335.

WARD T, LONDEN K, HUDSON SM and MARSHALL WL (1995) A descriptive model of the offence claim for child models. Journal of Interpersonal Violence 10: 452–472.

WARD T, McCORMACK J and HUDSON SM (1997) Sexual offender's perceptions of their intimate relationships. Sexual Abuse: A Journal of Research and Treatment 9(1): 57–74.

WARING EM (1984) The measurement of marital intimacy. Journal of Marital and Family Therapy 10: 185–192.

WARING EM and REDDON JR (1983) The measurement of intimacy in marriage. Journal of Clinical Psychology 39: 53–57.

WARWICK L (1991) Probation work with sex offenders. Probation Monograph 104. Norwich: UEA.

WATERHOUSE L and CARNIE J (1992) Assessing child protection risk. British Journal of Social Work 22: 47–60.

WATERHOUSE L, CARNIE J and DOBASH R (1993) The abuser under the microscope. Community Care, 24.6.93, 24–25.

WATERHOUSE L, DOBASH R and CARNIE J (1994) Child sexual abusers. The Scottish Office Edinburgh.

WATKINS B and BENTOVIM A (1992) The sexual abuse of male children and adolescents: A review of current research. Journal of Child Psychiatry 33(1): 197–248.

WATSON D and FRIEND R (1969) Measurement of social-evaluative anxiety. Journal of Consulting and Clinical Psychology 33(4): 448–457.

WATTAM C, HUGHES JA and BLAGG H (eds.) (1989) Child sexual abuse: Listening, hearing and validating the experiences of children. London: Longman.

WATTS (1989) quoted in Gocke B (1991) Tackling denial in sex offenders. Probation Monograph 98. Norwich: UEA.

WEBSTER CD, MENZES R and JACKSON MA (1982) Clinical assessment before trail: Legal issues and mental disorders. Toronto: Butterworths.

WEINROTT MR and SAYLOR M (1991) Self-report of crimes committed by sex offenders. Journal of Interpersonal Violence 6(3): 286–300.

WEISSMAN AN (1980) Assessing depressogenic attitudes: A validation Study. Paper presented at the 51st Annual Meeting of the Eastern Psychological Association, Hartford, Conneticut.

WEISS R and MARGOLIN L (1986) Assessment of marital conflict and accord. In Ciminero AR, Calhoun KS and Adams HE (eds.) Handbook of behavioural assessment (2nd edition). NY: John Wiley and Sons, 561–600.

WEISS RS (1974) The provisions of social relationships. In Rubin Z (ed.) Doing unto others. Englewood, Cliffs, NJ: Prentice-Hall.

WELLDON EV (1996) Contrasts in male and female sexual perversions. In Cordess C and Cox M (eds.) Forensic psychotherapy (Vol 2) Mainly practice. London: Jessica Kingsley, 273–289.

WEST DJ (1986) The victim's contribution to sexual offences. In Hopkins J (ed.) Perspectives on rape and sexual assault. London: Harper and Row, 1–14.

WHALLEY LJ and McGUIRE RJ (1978) Measuring sexual attitudes. Acta Psychiatric Scandinavia 58: 299–314.

WHETSHELL-MITCHELL J (1995) Rape of the innocent: Understanding and preventing child sexual abuse. London: Taylor and Francis.

WHITE C (1992) A TA approach to child sex abusers. Probation Journal 39(1): 36–41.

WIDOM CS (1989) The Intergenerational transmission of violence. In Weiner NA and Wolfgang ME (eds.) Pathways to criminal violence. Newbury Park, Ca.: Sage, 137–201.

WILD N (1989) Prevalence of child sex rings. British Medical Journal 293: 183–185.

WILLIAMS L and FINKELHOR D (1992) The characteristics of incestuous fathers. Unpublished manuscript: University of New Hampshire Research Laboratory.

WILLIAMS RB, HANEY T, LEE KL, KONG Y, BLUMENTHAL JA and WHALEN RE (1980) Type A behaviour, hostility, and coronary atherosclerosis. Psychosomatic Medicine 42: 539–550.

WILLIS GC (1993) Unspeakable crimes: Prevention work with perpetrators of child sexual abuse. London: Children's Society.

WILSON BD and LANG RJ (1981) Sex differences in sexual fantasy patterns. Personality and Individual Differences 2: 343–346.

WILSON E (1990) Immoral panics. New Statesman and Society, 31.8.90, 18–19.

WILSON G (1978) The secrets of sexual fantasy. London: Jim Pert and Sons.

WINCZE JP and CAREY MP (1991) Sexual dysfunction: A guide for assessment and treatment. NY: Guilford Press.

WINN ME (1996) The strategic and systemic management of denial in the cognitive/behavioural treatment of sex offenders. Sexual Abuse: A Journal of Research and Treatment 8(1): 25–36.

WOLF S (1984) A multi-factor model of deviant sexuality. Paper at 3rd international conference on victimology. Lisbon, Portugal, November, 1984.

WOLF SC, CONTE JR and ENGEL-MEINIG M (1988) Assessment and treatment of sex offenders in a community setting. In Walker IEA (ed.) Handbook of sexual abuse of children. NY: Springer, 365–383.

WRIGHT S (1991) Family effects of offender removal from home. In Patton MQ (ed.) Family sexual abuse: Frontline research and evaluation. Newbury Park, Ca.: Sage, 135–146.

WYATT GE and POWELL PJ (eds.) (1988) Lasting effects of child sexual abuse. Newbury Park, Ca.: Sage.

WYRE R (1987) Working with sex abuse. Oxford: Perry Publications.

WYRE R (1989) Workshop for post-qualifying diploma in child protection. University of Lancaster.

WYRE R (1990) Working with sexual abuse. Presentation to conference on working with the sex offender. London: Regents College, 29.3.90.

WYRE R (1990b) Sex abuse 'addictive'. Social Work Today, 29.3.90, p9.

WYRE R (1991) Options must be kept open. Community Care, 28.3.91, p15.

WYRE R (1992) Pornography and sexual violence: Working with sex offenders. In Itzin C (ed.) Pornography: Women, violence and civil liberties. Oxford: Oxford University Press.

WYRE R (1994) The men who destroy children. British Airways Magazine, summer 1994, 40–45.

YATES E, BARBAREE HE and MARSHALL WL (1984) Anger and deviant sexual arousal. Behaviour Therapy 15: 287–294.

ZELMAN DB and TYSLER KM (1979) Essential adult sex education for the mentally retarded. Madison, Wisconsin: The Madison Opportunity Center.

ZUCKERMAN M (1971) Physiological measures of sexual arousal in the human. Psychological Bulletin 75: 297–329.

ZUSSMAN (1989) Forensic evaluation of the adolescent sex offender. Forensic Reports 2: 25–45.

Resources

1. The multiphasic sex inventory (Nichols and Molinder, 1984) is available from:
   437 Bowes Drive
   Tacoma
   WA 98466-7047
   Tel: 206 565 4539
   Fax: 206 565 0164.

2. The Derogatis sexual functioning inventory (Derogatis, 1978) is available from:
   Clinical Psychometric Research Inc.
   100 West Pennsylvania Avenue
   Towson
   MD 21204, USA
   Tel: 410 321 6165
   Fax: 410 321 6341
   or Leonard R Derogatis
   1228 Winespring Lane
   Baltimore
   MN 21204.

3. Mark S. Carich, Ph.D can be contacted at:
   State of Illinois Department of Corrections
   PO Box 1000
   State Route 37
   Illinois 62846-1000.

4. The stepwise model of assessment was devised by RECONSTRUCT Consultancy, who can be contacted at:
   93 Otterfield Road
   West Drayton
   Middlesex
   UB7 8PF
   Tel: 01895 443632
   Fax: 01895 431696.

5. The Jackson personality inventory (1984) is available from:
   Research Psychologicts Press
   Goshen
   NY 10924, USA.

6. The sex offence information scale scoring and further information is available from Todd E. Hogue, Ph.D., Chartered Forensic Psychologist,
   Psychological Assessment, Treatment and Training
   PO Box 447
   Lincoln
   LN2 3YR, UK
   Tel: 01673 863326.

7. The address of RK Hanson is:
   Corrections Research
   Solicitor General of Canada
   340 Laurier Avenue West
   Ottawa
   Ontario
   Canada K1A 0P8
   Tel: (613) 991 2840
   Fax: (613) 990 8295.

8. Helpful organisations on sex education materials for those with disabilities include:
   The Association to Aid the Sexual and Personal Relationships of People with a Disability (SPOD)
   286 Camden Road
   London N7 0BJ;
   and the Association for Spina Bifida and Hydrocephalus
   22 Woburn Place
   London
   WC1H 0EP.

9. The social skills game is available from:
   Jessica Kingsley Publishers, Ltd.
   116 Pentonville Road
   London
   N1 9JB
   Tel: 0171 833 2307
   Fax: 0171 837 2917.

10. The manual for the illness behaviour questionnaire is available from Professor I Pilowsky at:
    University of Adelaide
    Department of Psychiatry
    Adelaide
    Southern Australia 5000
    Tel: (08) 224 5151
    Fax: (08) 232 3298.
    He has also written a book: Pilowsky I (1997) Abnormal Illness Behaviour. Chichester: John Wiley and Sons, Ltd. ISBN 0471965731 (pbk), at a cost of £27.50. Orders can be taken by phoning the publishers on 01243 770216 or by fax on 01243 770432.

11. Joseph Scalise can be contacted regarding his loneliness rating scale at:
    PO Box 1096
    Watkinsville
    GA 30677, USA.

12. The handbook of sexuality-related measures (Davis, Yarber, Bauserman, Scheer and Davis) is now available from Sage Publications Limited at a cost of £45 (for over 920 pages and 200 instruments.
    Tel: 0171 374 0645
    Fax: 0171 374 8741.
    Full address: 6 Bonhill Street
    London EC2A 4PU.

13. Peter Loss is contactable at:
    PO Box 397
    East Lyme
    Conneticut
    CT 06333, USA
    Tel/fax: (01) 860 739 8877.

14. The general health questionnaire (Goldberg and Hillier, 1979) and the users guide is available from:
    NFER Nelson Publishing Company
    Tel: 01753 858961
    Fax: 01753 856830.

15. NOTA information can be elicited by contacting Carolyn Martinson at:
    POB 508 Hull
    HU5 4YW
    Tel: 01482 343625
    Fax: 01482 472161.

16. For information on working with adult males with learning disabilities, contact:
    NAPSAC
    Floor E
    South Block
    University Hospital
    Queen's Medical centre
    Nottingham
    NG7 2UH.

17. The publication Marsh et al. (1988) 'Breaking the cycle: Adolescent sexual treatment manual' can be purchased from:
    St Mary's Home for Boys
    16535 SW Tualaton Valley Highway
    Beaverton
    Oregon
    97006-5143, USA.

18. Other books available from Martin C. Calder include:
    - Calder MC (1997) Juveniles and children who sexually abuse: A guide to risk assessment. Lyme Regis, Dorset: Russell House Publishing. ISBN 1898924066. £29.95
    - Calder MC and Horwath J (eds.) (1998) Working for children on the child protection register: An inter-agency practice guide. Aldershot, Hampshire: Arena. ISBN 1857423674. £25. Available from Lorna Gordon, Ashgate Publishing Direct Sales, Bookpoint Ltd., 39 Milton Park, Abingdon, Oxon OX14 4TD. Tel: 01235 827730. Fax: 01235 400454.
    - Calder MC (ed) (1999) Working with young people who sexually abuse: New pieces of the jigsaw. Lyme Regis, Dorset: Russell House Publishing. Easter 1999.

Any comments or additional material not cited in this book can be sent to the author c/o Salford Child Protection Unit, Avon House, Avon Close, Little Hulton, Worsley, Greater Manchester, M38 0LA. Tel: 0161 790 6332; Fax: 0161 790 4892.

Appendices

FAMILY-OF-ORIGIN SCALE

Directions: The family of origin is the family with which you spent most or all of your childhood years.
This scale is designed to help you recall how your family of origin functioned.
Each family is unique and has its own ways of doing things. Thus, there are *no right or wrong choices in this scale.* What is important is that you respond as honestly as you can.
In reading the following statements, apply them to your family of origin, *as you remember it.* Using the following scale, circle the appropriate number. Please respond to each statement.

Key:

5 (SA)	=	Strongly agree that it describes my family of origin.
4 (A)	=	Agree that it describes my family of origin.
3 (N)	=	Neutral.
2 (D)	=	Disagree that it describes my family of origin.
1 (SD)	=	Strongly disagree that it describes my family of origin.

		SA	A	N	D	SD
1.	In my family, it was normal to show both positive and negative feelings.	5	4	3	2	1
2.	The atmosphere in my family usually was unpleasant.	5	4	3	2	1
3.	In my family, we encouraged one another to develop new friendships.	5	4	3	2	1
4.	Differences of opinion in my family were discouraged.	5	4	3	2	1
5.	People in my family often made excuses for their mistakes.	5	4	3	2	1
6.	My parents encouraged family members to listen to one another.	5	4	3	2	1
7.	Conflicts in my family never got resolved.	5	4	3	2	1
8.	My family taught me that people were basically good.	5	4	3	2	1
9.	I found it difficult to understand what other family members said and how they felt.	5	4	3	2	1
10.	We talked about our sadness when a relative or family friend die.	5	4	3	2	1
11.	My parents openly admitted it when they were wrong.	5	4	3	2	1
12.	In my family, I expressed just about any feeling I had.	5	4	3	2	1
13.	Resolving conflicts in my family was a very stressful experience.	5	4	3	2	1
14.	My family was receptive to the different ways various family members viewed life.	5	4	3	2	1
15.	My parents encouraged me to express my views openly.	5	4	3	2	1
16.	I often had to guess at what other family members thought or how they felt.	5	4	3	2	1
17.	My attitudes and my feelings frequently were ignored or criticized in my family.	5	4	3	2	1
18.	My family members rarely expressed responsibility for their actions.	5	4	3	2	1

GENERALIZED CONTENTMENT SCALE (GCS)

Name _____ Today's date _____

This questionnaire is designed to measure the degree of contentment that you feel about your life and surroundings. It is not a test, so there are no right or wrong answers. Answer each item as carefully and as accurately as you can by placing a number beside each one as follows:

1. *Rarely or none of the time.*
2. *A little of the time.*
3. *Sometimes.*
4. *Good part of the time.*
5. *Most or all of the time.*

Please begin.

1. I feel powerless to do anything about my life. ____
2. I feel blue. ____
3. I'm restless and can't keep still. ____
4. I have crying spells. ____
5. It is easy for me to relax. ____
6. I have a hard time getting started on things that I need to do ____
7. I do not sleep well at night ____
8. When things get tough, I feel there is always someone I can turn to. ____
9. I feel that the future looks bright for me. ____
10. I feel downhearted. ____
11. I feel that I am needed. ____
12. I feel that I am appreciated by others. ____
13. I enjoy being active and busy. ____
14. I feel that others would be better off without me. ____
15. I enjoy being with other people. ____
16. I feel it is easy for me to make decisions. ____
17. I feel downtrodden. ____
18. I am irritable. ____
19. I get upset easily. ____
20. I feel that I don't deserve to have a good time. ____
21. I have a full life. ____
22. I feel that people really care about me. ____
23. I have a great deal of fun. ____
24. I feel great in the morning. ____
25. I feel that my situation is hopeless. ____

Items to reverse score: 5, 8, 9, 11, 12, 13, 15, 16, 21, 22, 23, 24.

Source: Simmons T (1986) Child Sexual Abuse: An assessment process.

SEX OFFENDER *LIFESTYLE* Cognitive–Behavioral Inventory

©Carich MS and Steckel S (1992). Reproduced with the permission of Mark S Carich.

Application and Utility

This inventory is designed to measure an individual's level of thought and behavior on specific personality categories (i.e., antisocial, narcissistic, borderline, schizoidal, and obsessive–compulsive) which are known to accompany, in whole or in part, sex offender personality profiles. Each category contains a number of dimensions which comprise, but do not necessarily define, each personality category. The specific purpose of this instrument is not necessarily the broad measurement of personality, although this adds much to the understanding of the individual sex offender. Rather, the ultimate utility of this inventory is that the numerous dimensions of each personality category provide a very specified and individualized sex offender profile—that is, the sex offender's *lifestyle*.[1]

Evaluation, Scoring, and Interpretation

Evaluation. Whilst a history of offending and/or behaviors related to the individual's illness is a necessity, it is not the sole basis for this evaluation. Furthermore, the degree to which the entire clinical history is a factor in this assessment is based solely on the goal of the clinician (e.g., assessments for forensic purposes would require a greater reliance on the clinical history than evaluations which have treatment as their goal.)

Scoring. Each dimension within a category has a rating scale which allows for scores ① through ⑥ (see Table 1).

Table 1 *Scoring Guidelines for the Sex Offender Lifestyle Cognitive–Behavioral Inventory*

The individual receives a score of—

(1) if thinking and/or acting in this manner does not characterize the individual in whole or in part.
(2) if he/she thinks and/or acts in this manner infrequently (i.e., rarely).
(3) if he/she thinks and/or acts in this manner periodically (i.e., once in a while).
(4) if he/she thinks and/or acts in this manner consistently (i.e., most of the time).
(5) if he/she thinks and/or acts in this manner persistently (i.e., with few exceptions).
(6) if thinking and/or acting in this manner is a modus operandi for this individual (i.e., this is a fundamental/defining characteristic of the individual's personality).

In general, *the evaluator should assign the score which best describes the individual's thinking and/or behavior* with a given time frame as a context. However, given that the individual's history is a core source for evaluation, for the purpose of an intake and/or forensic evaluation, the evaluator should assign the score which best describes the individual's thinking and/or behavior *based upon all their available history*.

In each category, certain dimensions have been identified with an asterisk (*). Although additional commentary on dimensions are generally encouraged, these specified dimensions require further commentary to clarify specific ways in which the individual manifests the behavior or thought in question. In some cases this clarification requires simple examples, while in other instances frequency and/or historical information is indicated (space for this, and other commentary, is provided at the end of each category). The latter specifications have, in the authors experience, facilitated increased understanding about, and specificity of, the offender's profile. The *total score* in each category is the sum of all dimension scores within a category, while the *average score* in each category is the total score divided by the number of applicable dimensions. The *overall rating* is a general assessment of the client on the category in question (using the same scale as is used for each dimension—① through ⑥). This rating takes into

	SA	A	N	D	SD
19. In my family, I felt free to express my own opinions.	5	4	3	2	1
20. We never talked about our grief when a relative or family friend died.	5	4	3	2	1
21. Sometimes in my family, I did not have to say anything, but I felt understood.	5	4	3	2	1
22. The atmosphere in my family was cold and negative	5	4	3	2	1
23. The members of my family were not very receptive to one another's views.	5	4	3	2	1
24. I found it easy to understand what other family members said and how they felt.	5	4	3	2	1
25. If a family friend moved away, we never discussed our feelings of sadness.	5	4	3	2	1
26. In my family, I learned to be suspicious of others.	5	4	3	2	1
27. In my family, I felt that I could talk things out and settle conflicts.	5	4	3	2	1
28. I felt it difficult to express my own opinions in my family.	5	4	3	2	1
29. Mealtimes in my home usually were friendly and pleasant.	5	4	3	2	1
30. In my family, no one cared about the feelings of other family members.	5	4	3	2	1
31. We usually were able to work out our conflicts in my family.	5	4	3	2	1
32. In my family, certain feelings were not allowed to be expressed.	5	4	3	2	1
33. My family believed that people usually took advantage of you.	5	4	3	2	1
34. I found it easy in my family to express what I thought and how I felt.	5	4	3	2	1
35. My family members usually were sensitive to one another's feelings.	5	4	3	2	1
36. When someone important to us moved away, our family discussed our feelings of loss.	5	4	3	2	1
37. My parents discouraged us from expressing views different from theirs.	5	4	3	2	1
38. In my family, people took responsibility for what they did.	5	4	3	2	1
39. My family had an unwritten rule: Don't express your feelings.	5	4	3	2	1
40. I remember my family as being warm and supportive.	5	4	3	2	1

Reproduced with the permission of the author. Source © Hovestadt AJ, Anderson WT, Piercy FP and Cochran SW (1985). A Family-of-Origin Scale. Journal of Mental and Family Therapy 11(3): 287-297.

SEX OFFENDER *LIFESTYLE* Cognitive–Behavioral Inventory

Client Name _____ ID Number _____ Date _____

Marital Status (Married, Divorced, Separated, Widow(er), Single) _____

Sex (M/F/H) _____ Selected Gender Affiliation _____

Chosen Sexual Activity Orientation (Homosexual, Heterosexual, Bisexual, Other) _____

Purpose for Assessment: Forensic Evaluation _____ Current Assessment _____

Intake Assessment _____ Mid-treatment Assessment _____ Termination _____

Evaluation _____ Outcome Assessment _____ Other _____

I Antisocial Thought and Behavior

		Low				High
(1)	Exploitative (i.e., takes advantage of others)	①	②	③	④	⑤
(2)	Cheats (i.e., the use of trickery, acts dishonestly, etc.)	①	②	③	④	⑤
(3)	Lies (i.e., purposeful and wholly untruthful statements)	①	②	③	④	⑤
(4)	Deceives others (i.e., deliberately concealing/hiding the truth; to obfuscate for the purpose of being misleading)	①	②	③	④	⑤
(5)	Distorts information (i.e., the misrepresentation of facts either by omitting, adding to, or embellishing on information.)	①	②	③	④	⑤
(6)	Secrecy	①	②	③	④	⑤
(7)	Slyness/Slick	①	②	③	④	⑤
(8)	History of conning	①	②	③	④	⑤
(9)	Operates on hidden agendas/motives	①	②	③	④	⑤
(10)	Displays phoniness*	①	②	③	④	⑤
(11)	Disowns behavior* (i.e., irresponsibility which tends to lead to the enabling of the self or which allows others to adopt enabling roles)	①	②	③	④	⑤
(12)	History of cruelty towards others* (mental and physical acts)	①	②	③	④	⑤
(13)	Displays cruelty	①	②	③	④	⑤
(14)	History of sadistic behavior* (mental and physical acts)	①	②	③	④	⑤
(15)	Displays sadistic behavior*	①	②	③	④	⑤
(16)	Destructive	①	②	③	④	⑤
(17)	Reports impulsive behaviors*	①	②	③	④	⑤
(18)	Recklessness	①	②	③	④	⑤
(19)	Victimizes	①	②	③	④	⑤
(20)	Lacks remorse for victims	①	②	③	④	⑤
(21)	Lacks victim empathy	①	②	③	④	⑤
(22)	Unstable work history*	①	②	③	④	⑤
(23)	Nonconforming, breaks rules, and/or laws*	①	②	③	④	⑤
(24)	Lacks *social interest*[1]	①	②	③	④	⑤
(25)	Difficulty maintaining loyalty in relationships	①	②	③	④	⑤
(26)	Lacks guilt (i.e., the acknowledgment of having wrong based on the painful affliction of one's conscience.)	①	②	③	④	⑤
(27)	Lacks remorse (i.e., a painful regret leading to restitution behaviors; the *activity* of attempting to rectify one's wrong doing)	①	②	③	④	⑤
(28)	In terms of relationships with others, he/she has few, if any, close friends. Those friends with whom they do associate are either manipulated actively (i.e., controlled via domination) or enable the antisocial thinking and/or behavior.*	①	②	③	④	⑤

account the average score within the category, the possibility that one or more dimensions may skew the average score in a positive or negative direction, and the intuitive knowledge of the client by the practitioner. Given the latter, this rating should be completed following a review of the category's individual scores *and the comments section* (the *overall rating* is purposefully located at the base of the *comments section*). Once all of the foregoing scoring is completed and transferred to the scoring summary (see last page of the inventory), then the determination of the *general assessment rating* can be initiated. Principally, the determination of this score is based on the average of the overall rating scores throughout the inventory. However, this rating must take into account (a) the possibility that one or more of the overall ratings may skew this rating in a positive or negative direction, and (b) the intuitive knowledge of the client by the practitioner.

Interpretation.[2] When the scoring summary is completed the results yield a general assessment for the entire inventory, an overall rating for each category, a specified average score for each category, and the specific and/or operative level of intensity of each dimension within each category (i.e., a measurement of the degree to which each applicable dimension effects the category as a whole). In terms of an intake assessment, the aforementioned provides (a) a general assessment of the degree of severity/magnitude of the target problem and/or disorder, (b) a general assessment of the degree of severity represented by a category, (c) the baseline data necessary for deciding which general category(s) may need attention, and/or (d) the dimension(s) which need particular focus. Factors such as commentary on specific dimensions or categories, the type and dosage of medication(s), magnitude of the illness, age of the subject, physical capacity, gender, ethnicity, socioeconomics, religion, etc., must be considered.

1. For the purposes of this instrument, the term *lifestyle* is defined as "... a singular pattern of thinking, feeling, and acting that [is] unique to that individual and [represents] the context (Zusammenhang) in which all specific manifestations [have] to be considered" Shulman, B. H. & Mosak, H. H. (1988). *Manual for lifestyle assessment.* p 1. Muncie, IN: Accelerated Development.

2. In reference to the interpretive validity of this inventory, the investigation of internal and external validity is currently in progress. Given that the authors have assessed this population successfully for quite some time along less systematized, yet clinical, lines (which were the fundamental basis for the development of this inventory), they feel that this *infers clinical utility*; therefore, it was concluded that the instrument warranted immediate presentation as a *clinical tool.* Despite this, the authors strongly suggest that the analysis, interpretation, and/or (continued) conclusions made on the basis of this instrument, should be elucidated, described, and/or asserted in terms which clarify the current reliability and validity of this inventory.

(29) Justifies his/her antisocial thought and behavior by projecting blame or responsibility toward the victim. (1)(2)(3)(4)(5)(6)

(30) He/she uses religiosity as a cover-up for their true, and often opposite, disposition ("a wolf in sheep's clothing"). (1)(2)(3)(4)(5)(6)

Total Score (Score of #1+#2 ... +#30) _____
Average Score (Total Score ÷30)

1. For the purpose of this instrument the term social interest is defined as "... 'identification with humanity', a "feeling of community', or 'belonging to life'" (Manister & Corsini, 1982, p. 13), or, the cohesive bond which develops between human beings (i.e., sense of brotherhood) when individuals acknowledge and empathize with the mutual life-struggles that each human being must contend with.
Source of reference: Manister, G. J. & Corsini, R. J. (1982). *Individual psychology*. Itasca, IL: F. E. Peacock.
Copyright ©, 1992

Specific examples, information, and/or commentary on the identified (*) components: (10, 11, 12, 14, 15, 17, 22, 23, 28)
_____
_____

Additional commentary on components:
_____

II Narcissistic Thought and Behavior   Overall Rating _____

	Low					High

(1) Grandiose fantasies* (1)(2)(3)(4)(5)(6)
(2) Me first attitude* (Thinking which expresses/infers that the following is a core belief: "I am first and the rest of you can fight for the scraps".) (1)(2)(3)(4)(5)(6)
(3) Attitude of superiority (1)(2)(3)(4)(5)(6)
(4) Brags and exaggerates about abilities or accomplishments (1)(2)(3)(4)(5)(6)
(5) Egotistical (inflated sense of self-worth) (1)(2)(3)(4)(5)(6)
(6) Stuck-up (snobbish) (1)(2)(3)(4)(5)(6)
(7) Exaggerated sense of self-importance (1)(2)(3)(4)(5)(6)
(8) Me only attitude* (i.e., he/she is solely "out to get for themselves") (1)(2)(3)(4)(5)(6)
(9) Distorted sense of entitlement (Thinking and/or behavior which expresses/infers that the following is a core belief: "I see it. I like it. I want it; therefore, it should be mine!) (1)(2)(3)(4)(5)(6)
(10) Unrealistic expectations* (1)(2)(3)(4)(5)(6)
(11) Displays self-pity* (i.e. poor me attitude) (1)(2)(3)(4)(5)(6)
(12) Is overtly concerned by, and overly reactive to, criticism. (1)(2)(3)(4)(5)(6)
(13) Inconsiderate of others (1)(2)(3)(4)(5)(6)
(14) Self-centeredness (1)(2)(3)(4)(5)(6)
(15) Grandiose behaviors* (1)(2)(3)(4)(5)(6)
(16) Me first behavior (Behavior which demonstrates that he/she considers themselves first and others are merely considered coincidentally.) (1)(2)(3)(4)(5)(6)
(17) Strives for control through power (1)(2)(3)(4)(5)(6)

(18) Pleasure seeking behaviors (1)(2)(3)(4)(5)(6)
(19) Me only behavior* (Behavior which demonstrates that he/she considers themselves to the exclusion of all others regardless of the context.) (1)(2)(3)(4)(5)(6)
(20) Envious (1)(2)(3)(4)(5)(6)
(21) Demanding (1)(2)(3)(4)(5)(6)
(22) Fears situations wherein his/her deficiencies will become known and result in humiliation.* (1)(2)(3)(4)(5)(6)
(23) He/she uses religiosity to enhance a "good person image". (1)(2)(3)(4)(5)(6)

Total Score (Score of #1+#2 ... +#23) _____
Average Score (Total Score ÷23)

Specific examples, information, and/or commentary on the identified (*) components: (1, 2, 8, 10, 15, 22)
_____
_____

Additional commentary on components:
_____

III Borderline Thought and Behavior   Overall Rating _____

	Low					High

(1) Unstable life-style* (i.e., manner in which he/she lives) (1)(2)(3)(4)(5)(6)
(2) Seeks immediate gratification (1)(2)(3)(4)(5)(6)
(3) Poor impulse control particularly, but not exclusively, in sexual behavior and substance abuse.* (1)(2)(3)(4)(5)(6)
(4) Repeated suicidal ideations* (1)(2)(3)(4)(5)(6)
(5) Repeated suicidal threats* (1)(2)(3)(4)(5)(6)
(6) Repeated suicide gestures* (1)(2)(3)(4)(5)(6)
(7) Repeated suicide attempts* (1)(2)(3)(4)(5)(6)
(8) Unstable, inconsistent, and/or intense relationships (1)(2)(3)(4)(5)(6)
(9) Marked intense moodiness characterized by shifts* (1)(2)(3)(4)(5)(6)
(10) Emotionally unstable* (1)(2)(3)(4)(5)(6)
(11) Dependency (1)(2)(3)(4)(5)(6)
(12) Over-attachment to others (1)(2)(3)(4)(5)(6)
(13) Enmeshed relationships (highly symbiotic) (1)(2)(3)(4)(5)(6)
(14) Vacillates between over-idealizing and devaluating others (1)(2)(3)(4)(5)(6)
(15) Possessiveness (1)(2)(3)(4)(5)(6)
(16) Jealousy (1)(2)(3)(4)(5)(6)
(17) Unstable/vacillating self-image (1)(2)(3)(4)(5)(6)
(18) Unstable/vacillating identity (1)(2)(3)(4)(5)(6)
(19) Sensitivity to, or fear of, real or imagined abandonment (1)(2)(3)(4)(5)(6)
(22) Fears situations wherein his/her thinking and behavior will become known and result in shame.* (1)(2)(3)(4)(5)(6)

Total Score (Score of #1+#2 ... +#22) _____
Average Score (Total Score ÷22)

Specific examples, information, and/or commentary on the identified (*) components: (1, 3, 4, 5, 6, 7, 9, 22)

Additional commentary on components:

Overall Rating _____

IV Schizoidal Thought and Behavior

	Low				High	
(1) Displays flat/restricted affect*	①	②	③	④	⑤	⑥
(2) Avoids people	①	②	③	④	⑤	⑥
(3) Develops superficial relationships	①	②	③	④	⑤	⑥
(4) Isolates self*	①	②	③	④	⑤	⑥
(5) Alienates/distances others	①	②	③	④	⑤	⑥
(6) Emotionally withdrawn	①	②	③	④	⑤	⑥
(7) Unaware of feelings	①	②	③	④	⑤	⑥
(8) Lacks social skills*	①	②	③	④	⑤	⑥
(9) A tendency to enjoy solitary activities*	①	②	③	④	⑤	⑥
(10) Strong emotions are experienced covertly*	①	②	③	④	⑤	⑥
(11) Indifferent to praise	①	②	③	④	⑤	⑥
(12) Is covertly concerned by, and overly reactive to, criticism	①	②	③	④	⑤	⑥
(13) Difficulties with reciprocating non-verbal emotional expression.*	①	②	③	④	⑤	⑥
(14) Few, if any, close friends	①	②	③	④	⑤	⑥

Total Score (Score of #1+#2 ... +#14) _____
Average Score (Total Score ÷ 14) _____

Specific examples, information, and/or commentary on the identified (*) components: (1, 4, 8, 9, 10, 13)

Additional commentary on components:

Overall Rating _____

V Obsessive Thought and Compulsive Behavior

	Low				High	
(1) Controls passively by feigned capitulation, dependency, or inadequacy	①	②	③	④	⑤	⑥
(2) Controls actively: uses perfectionism as an obstacle to evade completing egodystonic tasks (e.g., required tasks)	①	②	③	④	⑤	⑥
(3) Insistent and persistent about his/her rituals*	①	②	③	④	⑤	⑥
(4) Overly fastidious	①	②	③	④	⑤	⑥
(5) Ruminates on matters which are discomforting*	①	②	③	④	⑤	⑥
(6) Obsessively engages in fantasies*	①	②	③	④	⑤	⑥
(7) Avoids mistakes by perseverating and/or being indecisive	①	②	③	④	⑤	⑥
(8) Ambivalent towards the feelings of others	①	②	③	④	⑤	⑥

(9) Antithetical thinking (i.e., The individual has a "all or none", "either or", "neither nor" attitude. He/she has an affinity toward purest/literal interpretations and protestations; they appear pathologically concrete in terms of thinking.) ① ② ③ ④ ⑤ ⑥

(10) Feels that any loss of control of self/situations will result in either embarrassment or a foolish appearance.

(11) Behavior(s) are often used as a means of procrastination* ① ② ③ ④ ⑤ ⑥

(12) Inherent conflicts between goals and methods used for their attainment. ① ② ③ ④ ⑤ ⑥

(13) Is coverly defiant, vindictive, and spiteful toward others (particularly those in authority) who attempt to interrupt obsessive thinking or compulsive behaviors.

(14) Reacts poorly to constructive criticism ① ② ③ ④ ⑤ ⑥

(15) Repeatedly, and at times uncontrollably, has engaged in appetitive/addictive behaviors which have resulted in decrements of personal and social functioning, victimization of others, and has persisted with these behaviors despite the apparent negative consequences.* ① ② ③ ④ ⑤ ⑥

(16) He/she uses religiosity as a means of self-absolution. ① ② ③ ④ ⑤ ⑥

Total Score (Score of #1+#2 ... +#16) _____
Average Score (Total Score ÷ 16) _____

Specific examples, information, and/or commentary on the identified (*) components: (3, 5, 6, 11, 15)

Additional commentary on components:

General commentary on the evaluation:

Scoring Summary

I Antisocial Thought and Behavior

(1) ___	(11) ___	(21) ___
(2) ___	(12) ___	(22) ___
(3) ___	(13) ___	(23) ___
(4) ___	(14) ___	(24) ___
(5) ___	(15) ___	(25) ___
(6) ___	(16) ___	(26) ___
(7) ___	(17) ___	(27) ___
(8) ___	(18) ___	(28) ___
(9) ___	(19) ___	(29) ___
(10) ___	(20) ___	(30) ___

Total score _____ Average score _____
Overall Rating _____

II Narcissistic Thought and Behavior

(1) ___	(11) ___	(21) ___
(2) ___	(12) ___	(22) ___
(3) ___	(13) ___	(23) ___
(4) ___	(14) ___	
(5) ___	(15) ___	
(6) ___	(16) ___	
(7) ___	(17) ___	
(8) ___	(18) ___	
(9) ___	(19) ___	
(10) ___	(20) ___	

Total score _____ Average score _____
Overall Rating _____

DATING AND ASSERTION QUESTIONNAIRE (DAQ)

DESCRIPTION: The 18-item DAQ was designed to measure social competence in two social situations: dating and assertion; the focus is on social skills. Nine items measure the general social skills of dating and nine measure assertion. The measures are sensitive to change resulting from social skills training and therefore, are clinically useful. The Dating items and Assertion items form two separate measures. One limitation of the DAT is that two, and possibly three, of the items pertain to social situations for college students and would not be relevant to other clients.

SCORING: Half of the items are rated on a 1 to 4 scale of how frequently the respondent performs the specified behavior. The other half are rated on a 1 to 5 scale according to how comfortable the respondent would feel in the specified situation. Separate scores are computed for the dating and assertion subscales, noted by an "A" or a "D" beside the items. To compute the assertion subscale score add the responses to items 1, 3, 4 and 6, then divide by 4; next add the responses to items 10, 12, 15, 16 and 18, then divide that product by 5; add these two products together for a dating subscale score. To compute the dating subscale score add the responses to items 2, 5, 7, 8 and 9 and then divide the product by 5; next add the response to items 11, 13, 14 and 17, and then divide by 4. Add these two products together for an assertion subscale score. These scoring procedures are summarized as: Assertion subscale score = [(items 1 + 3 + 4 + 6) ÷ 4] + [(items 10 + 12 + 15 + 16 + 18) ÷ 5]. Dating subscale score = [(items 2 + 5 + 7 + 8 + 9) ÷ 5] + [(items 11 + 13 + 14 + 17) ÷ 4]. Both subscale scores range from one to nine.

We are interested in finding out something about the likelihood of your acting in certain ways. Below you will find a list of specific behaviors you may or may not exhibit. Use the following rating scale:

1 = I never do this
2 = I sometimes do this
3 = I often do this
4 = I do this almost always

Now next to each of the items on the following list, place the number which best indicates the likelihood of your behaving in that way. Be as objective as possible.

_____ 1. Stand up for your rights (A)
_____ 2. Maintain a long conversation with a member of the opposite sex (D)
_____ 3. Be confident in your ability to succeed in a situation in which you have to demonstrate your competence (A)
_____ 4. Say "no" when you feel like it (A)
_____ 5. Get a second date with someone you have dated once (D)
_____ 6. Assume a role of leadership (A)
_____ 7. Be able to accurately sense how a member of the opposite sex feels about you (D)
_____ 8. Have an intimate emotional relationship with a member of the opposite sex (D)
_____ 9. Have an intimate physical relationship with a member of the opposite sex (D)

The following questions describe a variety of social situations that you might encounter. In each situation you may feel "put on the spot." Some situations may be familiar to you, and others may not. We'd like you to read each situation and try to imagine yourself actually in the situation. The more vividly you get a mental picture and place yourself into the situation, the better.

After each situation circle one of the numbers from 1 to 5 which best describes you using the following scale:

1 = I would be so uncomfortable and so unable to handle this situation that I would avoid it if possible.
2 = I would feel very uncomfortable and would have a lot of difficulty handling this situation.
3 = I would feel somewhat uncomfortable and would have some difficulty in handling this situation.

III Borderline Thought and Behavior

(1) _____   (11) _____   (21) _____
(2) _____   (12) _____   (22) _____
(3) _____   (13) _____
(4) _____   (14) _____
(5) _____   (15) _____
(6) _____   (16) _____
(7) _____   (17) _____
(8) _____   (18) _____
(9) _____   (19) _____
(10) _____ (20) _____

Total score _____   **Average score** _____
Overall Rating _____

IV Schizoidal Thought and Behavior

(1) _____   (11) _____
(2) _____   (12) _____
(3) _____   (13) _____
(4) _____   (14) _____
(5) _____
(6) _____
(7) _____
(8) _____
(9) _____
(10) _____

Total score _____   **Average score** _____
Overall Rating _____

V Obsessive Thought and Compulsive Behavior

(1) _____   (11) _____
(2) _____   (12) _____
(3) _____   (13) _____
(4) _____   (14) _____
(5) _____   (15) _____
(6) _____   (16) _____
(7) _____
(8) _____
(9) _____
(10) _____

Total score _____   **Average score** _____   **Overall Rating** _____

General Assessment Rating:

First, add the *Overall rating* of category I + II + III + IV + V = _____. Second, divide the above result by five = _____. Third, consider those factors which were identified under this topic in the *scoring section*. Now, assign the rating which best describes the individual *at this time* _____.

PARENTAL ATTITUDE SCALE (PAS)

Name _____   Today's date _____

This questionnaire is designed to measure the degree of contentment you have in your relationship with your children. It is not a test, so there are no right or wrong answers. Answer each item as carefully and as accurately as you can by placing a number beside each one as follows:

1. *Rarely or none of the time.*
2. *A little of the time.*
3. *Sometimes.*
4. *A good part of the time.*
5. *Most or all of the time.*

Please begin.

1. My children get on my nerves.
2. I get along well with my children.
3. I feel that I can really trust my children.
4. I dislike my children.
5. My children are well behaved.
6. My children are too demanding.
7. I wish I did not have any children.
8. I really enjoy my children.
9. I have a hard time controlling my children.
10. My children interfere with my activities.
11. I resent my children.
12. I think my children are terrific.
13. I hate my children.
14. I am very patient with my children.
15. I really like my children.
16. I like being with my children.
17. I feel like I do not love my children.
18. My children are irritating.
19. I feel very angry toward my children.
20. I feel violent toward my children.
21. I feel very proud of my children.
22. I wish my children were more like others I know.
23. I just do not understand my children.
24. My children are a real joy for me.
25. I feel ashamed of my children.

Items to reverse score: 2, 3, 5, 8, 12, 14, 15, 16, 21, 24.

Source: Simmons T (1986) Child Sexual Abuse: An assessment process.
© London: NSPCC. Reproduced with permission.

---

4 = I would feel quite comfortable and would be able to handle this situation fairly well.

5 = I would feel very comfortable and be able to handle this situation very well.

10. You're waiting patiently in line at the checkout when a couple of people cut right in front of you. You feel really annoyed and want to tell them to wait their turn at the back of the line. One of them says, "Look, you don't mind do you? But we're in a terrible hurry." (A)

11. You have enjoyed this date and would like to see your date again. The evening is coming to a close and you decide to say something. (D)

12. You are talking to a professor about dropping a class. You explain your situation, which you fabricate slightly for effect. Looking at his grade book the professor comments that you are pretty far behind. You go into greater detail about why you are behind and why you'd like to be allowed to withdraw from his class. He then says, "'I'm sorry, but it's against university policy to let you withdraw this late in the semester." (A)

13. You meet someone you don't know very well but are attracted to. You want to ask him/her out for a date. (D)

14. You meet someone of the opposite sex at lunch and have a very enjoyable conversation. You'd like to get together again and decide to say something. (D)

15. Your roommate has several obnoxious traits that upset you very much. So far, you have mentioned them once or twice, but no noticeable changes have occurred. You still have 3 months left to live together. You decide to say something. (A)

16. You're with a small group of people who you don't know too well. Most of them are expressing a point of view that you disagree with. You'd like to state your opinion even if it means you'll probably be in the minority. (A)

17. You go to a party where you don't know many people. Someone of the opposite sex approaches you and introduces themself. You want to start a conversation and get to know him/her. (D)

18. You are trying to make an appointment with the dean. You are talking to his secretary face-to-face. She asks you what division you are in and when you tell her, she starts asking you questions about the nature of your problem. You inquire as to why she is asking all these questions and she replies very snobbishly that she is the person who decides if your problem is important enough to warrant an audience with the dean. You decide to say something. (A)

REFERENCE: Levenson, R. W. and Gottman, J. M. (1978). Toward the assessment of social competence, *Journal of Consulting and Clinical Psychology* 46, 453–462. Instrument reproduced with permission of Robert W. Levenson and the American Psychological Association.

LONELINESS RATING SCALE (LRS)

DESCRIPTION: The LRS is a 40-item instrument in two parts: Part A measures the frequency of certain affects and Part B measures the intensity or impact of the affective experience. The LRS is composed of four factors derived from factor analysis: depletion (a loss of vigor, exhaustion), isolation (an interpersonal segregation), agitation (restlessness, frustration, antagonism), and dejection (a feeling of discouragement or despondency). The original items for the LRS were based on a list of words solicited from students about how they felt when they were lonely, plus review of the loneliness literature. The LRS thus allows measurement of how often a respondent experiences each of the four dimensions of the measure, and of the impact the experience of those feelings has.

SCORING: Eight separate scores are derived from the LRS — four frequency scores and four intensity scores. Scores for each factor are obtained by simply adding up the numbers circled for the items that make up a factor (depletion: 4, 9, 11, 14, 18, 21, 22, 25, 26, 37; isolation: 6, 7, 20, 23, 28, 29, 31, 35, 39, 40; agitation: 3, 8, 12, 13, 15, 17, 24, 32, 33, 34; dejection: 1, 25, 10, 16, 19, 27, 30, 36, 38). If a person circles "never" for frequency, the corresponding intensity (Part B) portion should not be completed. Scores for the frequency dimensions should range from 0 to 30 and scores for intensity from 0 to 50.

PRIMARY REFERENCE: Scalise, J. J., Ginter, E. J. and Gerstein, L. H. (1984). A multidimensional loneliness measure: The Loneliness Rating Scale (LRS), *Journal of Personality Assessment* 48, 525–530. Instrument reproduced with permission of J. J. Scalise.

This is not a test. We are only interested in finding out how you feel when you experience loneliness.

There are 40 two-part questions. In the first part of the question, several words are used to describe loneliness. Indicate which word most describes how you feel by placing the appropriate number of the following scale to the left of each statement.

0 = Never
1 = Occasionally
2 = Frequently
3 = Always

In the second part, you are asked to indicate on a scale of 1 to 5 how much this feeling affects you by writing the appropriate number on the right hand side of the statement.

1	2	3	4	5
bothersome				overwhelming

If your answer to the first part of the statement is "never," skip the second part of the statement.

_____ 1. When I experience loneliness, I feel *low*.
          The feeling of being *low* is: _____

_____ 2. When I experience loneliness, I feel *sad*.
          The feeling of being *sad* is: _____

_____ 3. When I experience loneliness, I feel *angry*.
          The feeling of being *angry* is: _____

_____ 4. When I experience loneliness, I feel *depressed*.
          The feeling of being *depressed* is: _____

_____ 5. When I experience loneliness, I feel *drained*.
          The feeling of being *drained* is: _____

_____ 6. When I experience loneliness, I feel *unloved*.
          The feeling of being *unloved* is: _____

THE REVISED U.C.L.A. LONELINESS SCALE

The Revised UCLA Loneliness Scale

Directions: Indicate how often you feel the way described in each of the following statements. Circle one number for each.

Statement	Never	Rarely	Sometimes	Often
1. I feel in tune with people around me	1	2	3	4
2. I lack companionship	1	2	3	4
3. There is no one I can turn to	1	2	3	4
4. I do not feel alone	1	2	3	4
5. I feel part of a group of friends[a]	1	2	3	4
6. I have a lot in common with the people around me	1	2	3	4
7. I am no longer close to anyone	1	2	3	4
8. My interests and ideas are not shared by those around me	1	2	3	4
9. I am an outgoing person[a]	1	2	3	4
10. There are people I feel close to[a]	1	2	3	4
11. I feel left out	1	2	3	4
12. My social relationships are superficial	1	2	3	4
13. No one really knows me well	1	2	3	4
14. I feel isolated from others	1	2	3	4
15. I can find companionship when I want it[a]	1	2	3	4
16. There are people who really understand me[a]	1	2	3	4
17. I am unhappy being so withdrawn	1	2	3	4
18. People are around me but not with me	1	2	3	4
19. There are people I can talk to[a]	1	2	3	4
20. There are people I can turn to[a]	1	2	3	4

Note. The total score is the sum of all 20 items. [a] Item should be reversed (i.e. 1 = 4, 2 = 3, 3 = 2, 4 = 1) before scoring.

Reproduced with the permission of D. Russell. Source: Russell, D, Peplov L and Cutrona C (1980). The revised UCLA loneliness scale: Concurrent and discriminant validity evidence. Journal of Personality and Social Psychology 39: 472–480.

7. When I experience loneliness, I feel *worthless*.
The feeling of being *worthless* is: ___
8. When I experience loneliness, I feel *nervous*.
The feeling of being *nervous* is: ___
9. When I experience loneliness, I feel *empty*.
The feeling of being *empty* is: ___
10. When I experience loneliness, I feel *blue*.
The feeling of being *blue* is: ___
11. When I experience loneliness, I feel *hollow*.
The feeling of being *hollow* is: ___
12. When I experience loneliness, I feel *humiliated*.
The feeling of being *humiliated* is: ___
13. When I experience loneliness, I feel *guilty*.
The feeling of being *guilty* is: ___
14. When I experience loneliness, I feel *secluded*.
The feeling of being *secluded* is: ___
15. When I experience loneliness, I feel *tormented*.
The feeling of being *tormented* is: ___
16. When I experience loneliness, I feel *self-pity*.
The feeling of being *self-pity* is: ___
17. When I experience loneliness, I feel *aggressive*.
The feeling of being *aggressive* is: ___
18. When I experience loneliness, I feel *alienated*.
The feeling of being *alienated* is: ___
19. When I experience loneliness, I feel *hurt*.
The feeling of being *hurt* is: ___
20. When I experience loneliness, I feel *hopeless*.
The feeling of being *hopeless* is: ___
21. When I experience loneliness, I feel *broken*.
The feeling of being *broken* is: ___
22. When I experience loneliness, I feel *withdrawn*.
The feeling of being *withdrawn* is: ___
23. When I experience loneliness, I feel *disliked*.
The feeling of being *disliked* is: ___
24. When I experience loneliness, I feel *hostile*.
The feeling of being *hostile* is: ___
25. When I experience loneliness, I feel *numb*.
The feeling of being *numb* is: ___
26. When I experience loneliness, I feel *passive*.
The feeling of being *passive* is: ___
27. When I experience loneliness, I feel *confused*.
The feeling of being *confused* is: ___
28. When I experience loneliness, I feel *abandoned*.
The feeling of being *abandoned* is: ___
29. When I experience loneliness, I feel *unacceptable*.
The feeling of being *unacceptable* is: ___

30. When I experience loneliness, I feel *discouraged*.
The feeling of being *discouraged* is: ___
31. When I experience loneliness, I feel *faceless*.
The feeling of being *faceless* is: ___
32. When I experience loneliness, I feel *sick*.
The feeling of being *sick* is: ___
33. When I experience loneliness, I feel *scared*.
The feeling of being *scared* is: ___
34. When I experience loneliness, I feel *tense*.
The feeling of being *tense* is: ___
35. When I experience loneliness, I feel *deserted*.
The feeling of being *deserted* is: ___
36. When I experience loneliness, I feel *miserable*.
The feeling of being *miserable* is: ___
37. When I experience loneliness, I feel *detached*.
The feeling of being *detached* is: ___
38. When I experience loneliness, I feel *unhappy*.
The feeling of being *unhappy* is: ___
39. When I experience loneliness, I feel *excluded*.
The feeling of being *excluded* is: ___
40. When I experience loneliness, I feel *useless*.
The feeling of being *useless* is: ___

MULTIDIMENSIONAL ANGER INVENTORY

Instructions, Anger Dimension, and Source for Multidimensional Anger Inventory Items

Instructions: Everybody gets angry from time to time. A number of statements that people have used to describe the times that they get angry are included below. Read each statement and circle the number to the right of the statement that best describes you. There are no right or wrong answers.

If the statement is completely undescriptive of you, circle a 1.

If the statement is mostly undescriptive of you, circle a 2.

If the statement is partly undescriptive and partly descriptive of you, circle a 3.

If the statement is mostly descriptive of you, circle a 4.

If the statement is completely descriptive of you, circle a 5.

Please answer every item.

Item pool dimension	Item		Source
Frequency	1.	I tend to get angry more frequently than most people.	1 2 3 4 5	Edwards (1966)
	6.	It is easy to make me angry.	1 2 3 4 5	Edwards (1966)
	9.	Something makes me angry almost every day.	1 2 3 4 5	
	14.	I am surprised at how often I feel angry.	1 2 3 4 5	
	17.	At times, I feel angry for no specific reason.	1 2 3 4 5	
Duration	22.	When I get angry, I stay angry for hours.	1 2 3 4 5	
	25.	When I get angry, I calm down faster than most people.*	1 2 3 4 5	Baer, Collins, Bourianoff, & Ketchel (1979)
Magnitude	2.	Other people seem to get angrier than I do in similar circumstances.*	1 2 3 4 5	Baer et al. (1979)
	10.	I often feel angrier than I think I should.	1 2 3 4 5	
	18.	I can make myself angry about something in the past just by thinking about it.	1 2 3 4 5	
Magnitude	26.	I get so angry, I feel like I might lose control.	1 2 3 4 5	Buss & Durkee (1957)
Mode of expression				
Anger-in	3.	I harbor grudges that I don't tell anyone about.	1 2 3 4 5	Baer et al. (1979)
	20.	When I hide my anger from others, I think about it for a long time.	1 2 3 4 5	Kahn, Medalie, Neufeld, Riss, & Goldbourt (1972)
	23.	When I hide my anger from others, I forget about it pretty quickly.*	1 2 3 4 5	
	24.	I try to talk over problems with people without letting them know I'm angry.*	1 2 3 4 5	Harburg, Blakelock, & Roeper (1979)
	27.	If I let people see the way I feel, I'd be considered a hard person to get along with.	1 2 3 4 5	Buss & Durkee (1957)
	29.	It's difficult for me to let people know I'm angry.	1 2 3 4 5	
Anger-out	4.	I try to get even when I'm angry with someone	1 2 3 4 5	Baer et al. (1979)
	7.	When I am angry with someone, I let that person know	1 2 3 4 5	Harburg et al. (1979)
	12.	When I am angry with someone, I take it out on whoever is around.	1 2 3 4 5	
	15.	Once I let people know I'm angry, I can put it out of my mind.	1 2 3 4 5	
	19.	Even after I have expressed my anger, I have trouble forgetting about it.	1 2 3 4 5	

Impulse Control Checklist

Has the Offender?

1. A history of sexual assaults against *children*.
2. A history of sexual assaults against *women*.
3. A history of being sexually assaulted themselves.
4. 'Unusual' sexual interests.
5. 'Unusual' attitudes towards the victims of child sexual abuse (eg 'She asked for it').
6. Singled out victims of decreasing age.
7. A history of extra-marital sexual relationships.
8. An explosive temper.
9. A tendency towards an escalation of force over time.
10. Used weapons.
11. Have a violent family background.
12. Attempted suicide.
13. Suffered disruption in family unity (death, divorce, abandonment).
14. Been placed outside the home.
15. A history of running away from home.
16. A history of 'behavioural problems' (violent sibling rivalry, chronic rebelliousness, etc).
17. A history of encopresis or enuresis into adolescence.
18. A history of school refusal.
19. A problem with alcohol.
20. Been convicted/involved in TDA or reckless driving.
21. Free and easy spending habits.
22. Left jobs on a moment's notice.
23. Been unable to support himself financially.
24. A history of probation breaches.
25. A history of parole violations if imprisoned.
26. A pattern of recidivism.

Source: Simmons T (1986) Child Sexual Abuse: An assessment process.

AN ANGER DIARY

For the next two weeks, keep a diary describing in detail each situation that makes you feel angry.

1. Describe when you are angry. Explain the situation; describe the people involved and the setting.
2. Write about why you are angry.
3. Explain what your exact behavior was when you were angry.
4. Tell whether your anger was expressed appropriately or inappropriately.
5. Tell whether your anger was justified.
6. Below is a list of questions. Answer the ones that apply to the anger situation you have described.

Did your anger last too long?

Was it too intense?

Did you intentionally escalate it?

Did it lead to aggression?

Was it one of many recent outbursts?

Did it cause problems in school, at home, or with someone you care about?

Reproduced with the permission of the authors, Marsh L.F., Connell, P. and Olsen E. (1986), Breaking the Cycle: Adolescent Sexual Treatment Manual. ©Beaverton, Oregon: St. Mary's Home for Boys. See the resource section for purchase details.

Guilt	11.	I feel guilty about expressing my anger.	1 2 3 4 5	Harburg et al. (1979)
	29.	It's difficult for me to let people know I'm angry.	1 2 3 4 5	
Mode of expression				
Brood	15.	Once I let people know I'm angry, I can put it out of my mind.*	1 2 3 4 5	
	19.	Even after I have expressed my anger, I have trouble forgetting about it.	1 2 3 4 5	Kahn et al. (1972)
	20.	When I hide my anger from others, I think about it for a long time.	1 2 3 4 5	
	23.	When I hide my anger from others, I forget about it pretty quickly.*	1 2 3 4 5	
Anger-discuss	24.	I try to talk over problems with people without letting them know I'm angry.*	1 2 3 4 5	Harburg et al. (1979)
Hostile outlook	5.	I am secretly quite critical of others.	1 2 3 4 5	Baer et al. (1979)
	8.	I have met many people who are supposed to be experts who are no better than I.	1 2 3 4 5	Williams et al. (1980)
	13.	Some of my friends have habits that annoy and bother me very much.	1 2 3 4 5	Williams et al. (1980)
	16.	People talk about me behind my back.	1 2 3 4 5	Buss & Durkee (1957)
	21.	People can bother me just by being around.	1 2 3 4 5	Buss & Durkee (1957)
	28.	I am on my guard with people who are friendlier than I expected.	1 2 3 4 5	Buss & Durkee (1957)
Range of anger-eliciting situations	30.	I get angry when:		
	a.	someone lets me down.	1 2 3 4 5	
	b.	people are unfair.	1 2 3 4 5	
	c.	something blocks my plans.	1 2 3 4 5	Edwards (1966)
	d.	I am delayed.	1 2 3 4 5	Friedman & Roseman (1974)
	e.	someone embarrasses me.	1 2 3 4 5	Buss & Durkee (1957)
	f.	I have to take orders from someone less capable than I.	1 2 3 4 5	Williams et al. (1980)
	g.	I have to work with incompetent people.	1 2 3 4 5	Friedman & Roseman (1974)
	h.	I do something stupid.	1 2 3 4 5	
	i.	I am not given credit for something I have done.	1 2 3 4 5	Novaco (1975)

* Indicates that the item is reverse scored.

TEST

Name: _____   Pre: _____

Date: _____   Post: _____

True or False

1. _____ Anger is the result of events that happen, what we think and feel about those things, and how we behave when they happen.

2. _____ Anger is caused by only external events.

3. _____ The internal factors that help to cause anger are our thoughts, expectations, and the things we say to ourselves.

4. _____ We have two internal factors that deal with anger: our thoughts and our emotions.

5. _____ Our behavior results when an external event happens and we think or feel a certain way about it.

6. _____ It is not important to solve our anger problems.

7. _____ It is best to avoid getting angry by withdrawing and not communicating.

8. _____ Self instructions or statements to ourselves can help us get composed.

9. _____ Anger is linked with tension. You can't be angry and relaxed at the same time.

10. _____ If you are angry you shouldn't care what the other person is feeling.

List three ways to resolve anger problems:

11. _____

12. _____

13. _____

ANGER MANAGEMENT AND ASSERTIVENESS SKILLS

Name: _____   Pre: _____

Date: _____   Post: _____

List five ways to tell that anger has become a problem.

1. _____

2. _____

3. _____

4. _____

5. _____

True or False

6. _____ Anger always has a negative function.

7. _____ Anger can disrupt our thoughts or actions

8. _____ When you are angry it is harder to think clearly.

9. _____ Anger always leads to aggression.

10. _____ Some people start the anger cycle all over again and increase it by their own thoughts.

SEXUAL AGGRESSION TEST

1. Most sexual assaults occur as the result of an uncomfortable urge.
   True or false

2. Most sexual assaults involve women and young females who wear no bras, short skirts, tight pants and a lot of make-up.
   True or false

3. Most sexual assaults occur:
   a. Outside discos and bars
   b. In wooded or secluded areas
   c. At night
   d. None of the above

4. Most women are raped by someone of a different race, most likely by a black or an Hispanic.
   True or false

5. The majority of sexual offenders serve prison sentences following their first offence.
   True or false

6. Anybody is capable of committing a sexual offence against another person.
   True or false

7. The average age when an offender begins to exhibit signs of sexual aggression is:
   a. 12-15 years old
   b. 16-21 years old
   c. Over 25 years old
   d. None of these

8. For the most part, the sexual preference of most sexual offenders is:
   a. Heterosexual (prefer someone of the opposite sex)
   b. Homosexual (prefer someone of the same sex)
   c. Bisexual (prefer people of both sexes)
   d. All of the above
   e. None of the above

9. Sexual aggression is a problem primarily influenced by:
   a. Drugs and alcohol
   b. Sexual performance
   c. Availability of sex
   d. All of the above
   e. None of the above

10. Sexual aggression may occur in part as a response to ongoing or past victimisation by adults.
    True or false

11. It is unusual for sexual offenders to have been sexually victimised themselves.
    True or false

12. Which of the following issues contribute to sexual acting-out:
    a. Power & control
    b. Anger
    c. Poor self-esteem
    d. Abuse & neglect
    e. Identification with children
    f. All of the above
    g. None of the above

13. Which of the following behaviors are commonly found in a sexual offender's history:
    a. Fire setting
    b. Obscene phone calling
    c. Exposing oneself
    d. Peeping into windows
    e. All of the above
    f. None of the above

14. During their younger years, many sexual offenders:
    a. Fantasised about violence and destruction
    b. Set fires
    c. Experienced school difficulties
    d. Exhibited difficulties with stealing, shoplifting, B&E
    e. All of the above

15. The vast majority of sexual offenders are considered to be:
    a. Emotionally disturbed
    b. Psychotic
    c. Schizophrenic
    d. All of the above
    e. None of the above

16. Making obscene phone calls and exposing oneself are activities considered to be bizarre and unusual and not typically found in a sexual offender's profile.
    True or false

17. Women often fantasise about rape and eventually want men to force them into sexual situations against their will.
    True or false

18. A person who does nothing to resist is not really being sexually assaulted.
    True or false

19. Half of all reported rape victims are younger than 18 and half that number are younger than age 12.
    True or false

20. Infants, young boys and men are usually never sexually assaulted.
    True or false

21. In the majority of sexual assaults (75-80%), the offender is not a stranger but rather someone known to the victim and family as well.
    True or false

22. The long-term emotional and psychological effects on the victim are minimal when compared to the physical threats and pain inflicted on the victim by the offender.
    True or false

23. Young children who have been victims of sexual assaults always:
    a. Hate their assailant
    b. Are better off if they do not talk about it
    c. Forget about it after a while
    d. All of the above
    e. None of the above

24. Children who have been sexually assaulted:
    a. Always tell someone about their problem
    b. Are not really being molested if they continue contact with the offender
    c. Usually lie about the details of the molestation
    d. All of the above
    e. None of the above

25. Sexual abuse does not always have negative effects on people and most of the time is usually forgotten about in a short period of time, especially if it doesn't happen over and over.
    True or false

26. It is a normal part of adolescent development to have sexual fantasies about:
    a. Intercourse
    b. Consenting sex with peers
    c. Sex with children
    d. A and B only
    e. All of the above

27. Persistent deviant sexual fantasies (fantasies about rape and child molesting) indicate an offender is more serious than originally thought and probably indicates he is not taking his treatment seriously.
    True or false.

28. Most sexual offenders have persistent fantasies and thoughts about sexual assault dating back to the time they were teenagers and carry on to adulthood.
    True or false

29. Learning to control deviant sexual fantasies is an essential aspect of sex offender treatment.
    True or false

Questions

30. As long as a young person consents to a sexual experience, then there is no sexual abuse taking place.

    True or false

31. It is appropriate for me to demand sex from:

    a. A wife   b. A girlfriend
    c. All of the above d. A homosexual
    e. All of the above f. None of the above

32. With the proper specialised sexual offender treatment, the offender:

    a. Can learn to manage and control his sexual acting-out
    b. Can be cured of his illness and prevent this from happening ever again
    c. All of the above
    d. None of the above

33. Specialised sexual offender treatment must involve other areas of the offender's life, such as responsibility to family work and marriage, if it is to be effective.

    True or false

34. Maintaining a strict policy of no contact with one's victim is a crucial component at the onset of evaluation and treatment.

    True or false

35. Mandatory sexual offender treatment through the courts only hampers an offender's treatment because he feels threatened.

    True or false

36. Typically, if an offender is to benefit from treatment, a good programme lasting three months of specialised therapy is usually sufficient to bring about sufficient change.

    True or false

37. The use of a formal treatment agreement is not necessary once an offender has owned up to at least his offences of record.

    True or false

38. Reporting prior offences to the authorities serves no useful purpose to the offender once in treatment since it fails to create a sense of trust between offender and therapist.

    True or false

39. As long as an offender is in prison and receiving treatment, he does not need to concern himself with safeguards since he has no access to potential victims.

    True or false

40. Being incarcerated may prevent an offender from gaining access to his potential victims, but it serves no therapeutic function other than punishment.

    True or false

ANSWER SHEET

#	Answer	#	Answer
1.	False	21.	True
2.	False	22.	False
3.	D	23.	E
4.	False	24.	E
5.	False	25.	False
6.	True	26.	D
7.	A	27.	False
8.	A	28.	True
9.	E	29.	True
10.	True	30.	False
11.	False	31.	F
12.	F	32.	A
13.	E	33.	True
14.	E	34.	True
15.	E	35.	False
16.	False	36.	False
17.	False	37.	False
18.	False	38.	False
19.	True	39.	False
20.	False	40.	False

Reproduced with the permission of Peter Loss. Source: © Loss, P, Ross JE and Richardson J (1988) Psychoeducational curriculum for adolescent sex offenders, New London, Connecticut: Loss and Ross. (See Resource Section for further details)

BAKKER ASSERTIVENESS—AGGRESSIVENESS INVENTORY (AS—AGI)

DESCRIPTION: This 36-item inventory measures assertiveness in terms of two components necessary for social functioning: the ability to refuse unreasonable requests ("assertiveness" AS), and the ability to take the initiative, make requests, or ask for favors ("aggressiveness" AGI). Aggressiveness is different from hostility. It tends to relate more to being responsible and taking the initiative in social situations. The two instruments can also be used separately as 18-item measures.

SCORING: Each item is rated on a 5-point scale from "almost always" to "almost never" according to the likelihood the respondent would behave in the specified manner. Each scale is scored separately. Those items with a plus sign before the alternative are reverse-scored as follows: 1 becomes 5, 2 becomes 4, 4 becomes 2, and 5 becomes 1. The item responses for each scale are summed with a range from 18 to 90. Higher scores indicate that the individual is less likely to exhibit assertiveness or aggressiveness.

Below are several different situations. Each is followed by one way of responding. Your task is to read each question and indicate how likely you are to respond in that way, according to the following scale:

1=Almost always
2=Frequently
3=Occasionally
4=Sometimes
5=Almost never

Record your answers in the space to the left of each item.

AS Items

1. You have set aside the evening to get some necessary work done. Just as you get started some friends drop over for a social visit.
   –You welcome them in and postpone what you had planned to do.

2. You are standing in line when someone pushes ahead of you.
   +You tell the person to get back in line behind you.

3. A friend or relative asks to borrow your car or other valuable property but you would prefer not to lend it to them.
   –You lend it to them anyway.

4. A person who has kept you waiting before is late again for an appointment.
   –You ignore it and act as if nothing has happened.

5. Someone has, in your opinion, treated you unfairly or incorrectly.
   +You confront the person directly concerning this.

6. Friends or neighbors fail to return some items they have borrowed from you.
   +You keep after them until they return them.

7. Others put pressure on you to drink, smoke pot, take drugs, or eat too much.
   +You refuse to yield to their pressure.

8. Another person interrupts you while you are speaking.
   –You wait until the other is finished speaking before you go on with your story.

9. You are asked to carry out a task that you do not feel like doing.
   +You tell the other that you don't want to do it.

10. Your sexual partner has done something that you do not like.
    –You act as if nothing bothersome has happened.

11. A salesperson has spent a great deal of time showing you merchandise but none of it is exactly what you want.
    –You buy something anyway.

12. You are invited to a party or other social event, which you would rather not attend.
    –You accept the invitation.

13. In a concert or a movie theater a couple next to you distracts you with their conversation.
    +You ask them to be quiet or move somewhere else.

14. In a restaurant you receive food that is poorly prepared.
    +You ask the waiter or waitress to replace it.

15. You receive incorrect or damaged merchandise from a store.
    +You return the merchandise.

16. A person who seems a lot worse off than you asks you for something you could easily do without but you don't like to.
    –You give the person what he/she asks for.

17. Someone gives you—unasked for—a negative appraisal of your behavior.
    +You tell the other you are not interested.

18. Friends or parents try to get information from you that you consider personal.
    –You give them the information they want.

19. You have been appointed to a newly formed committee.
    +You take a leadership role.

20. You are in a bus or plane sitting next to a person you have never met.
    +You strike up a conversation.

21. You are a guest in a home of a new acquaintance. The dinner was so good you would like a second helping.
    +You go ahead and take a second helping.

22. You are being interviewed for a job you really want to get.
    –You undersell yourself.

23. You are meeting or greeting several people.
    +You make physical contact with each other in turn either by hugging, putting an arm around their shoulders, or slapping their backs.

24. You have observed that someone has done an excellent job at something.
    –You don't tell that person about it.

25. In a store or restaurant the personnel are very busy and many customers seem to be waiting a long time for service.
    +You manage to get service ahead of other customers.

26. You observe someone behave in a suspicious manner.
    –You don't do anything because it is none of your business.

27. You have parked your car but notice that you do not have the correct change for the parking meter.
    +You ask a passer-by for the change.

28. Someone has done or said something that arouses your curiosity.
    –You refrain from asking questions.

REFERENCE: Bakker, C. B., Bakker-Radbau, M. K. and Breit, S. (1978). The measurement of assertiveness and aggressiveness. *Journal of Personality Assessment* 42, 277–284. Reprinted by permission of C. B. Bakker.

SOCIAL SELF-ESTEEM INVENTORY

NAME _____

Please place a number in the space provided beside each of the statements below according to the following scale:

COMPLETELY UNLIKE ME 1 2 3 4 5 6 EXACTLY LIKE ME

Thus, for example, if you felt that a statement described you exactly, you would place a '6' beside that item. If the statement was completely UNlike you, then you would place '1' against the item. The numbers '2' through '5' represent varying degrees of the concept "like you". Please choose the number that appropriately reflects your similarity to the position expressed in the statement.

1.* ___ I find it hard to talk to strangers.
2.* ___ I lack confidence with people.
3. ___ I am socially effective.
4. ___ I feel confident in social situations.
5. ___ I am easy to like.
6. ___ I get along well with other people.
7. ___ I make friends easily.
8. ___ I am lively and witty in social situations.
9.* ___ When I am with other people I lose self-confidence.
10.* ___ I find it difficult to make friends.
11.* ___ I am no good at all from a social standpoint.
12. ___ I am a reasonably good conversationalist.
13. ___ I am popular with people my own age.
14.* ___ I am afraid of large parties.
15. ___ I truly enjoy myself at social functions.
16.* ___ I usually say the wrong thing when I talk with people.
17. ___ I am confident at parties.
18.* ___ I am usually unable to think of anything interesting to say to people.
19.* ___ I am a bore with most people.
20.* ___ People do not find me interesting.
21.* ___ I am nervous with people who are not close friends.
22. ___ I am quite good at making people feel at ease with me.
23.* ___ I am more shy than most people.
24. ___ I am a friendly person.
25. ___ I can hold people's interest easily.
26.* ___ I don't have much "personality."
27. ___ I am a lot of fun to be with.
28. ___ I am quite content with myself as a person.
29.* ___ I am quite awkward in social situations.
30.* ___ I do not feel at ease with other people.

*These items are negatively phrased, and they are scored by subtracting the number placed against them from 7.

REFERENCE: Lawson, J. R., Marshall, W. L. and McGrath, P. (1979). The social self-esteem inventory. *Educational and Psychological Measurement* 39, 803–807. Reproduced by permission of W. L. Marshall.

INDEX OF SELF-CONCEPT (ICS)

Name _____ Today's date _____

This questionnaire is designed to measure how you see yourself. *It is not a test, so there are no right or wrong answers. Please answer each item as carefully and as accurately as you can by placing a number beside each one as follows:*

1. *Rarely or none of the time.*
2. *A little of the time.*
3. *Sometimes.*
4. *A good part of the time.*
5. *Most or all of the time.*   *Please begin.*

1. I feel that people would not like me if they really knew me well.
2. I feel that others get along much better than I do.
3. I feel that I am a beautiful person.
4. When I am with other people, I feel they are glad I am with them.
5. I feel that people really like to talk with me.
6. I feel that I am a very competent person.
7. I think I make a good impression on others.
8. I feel that I need more self-confidence.
9. When I am with strangers, I am very nervous.
10. I think that I am a dull person.
11. I feel ugly.
12. I feel that others have more fun than I do.
13. I feel that I bore people.
14. I think my friends find me interesting.
15. I think I have a good sense of humour.
16. I feel very self-conscious when I am with strangers.
17. I feel that if I could be more like other people I would have it made.
18. I feel that people have a good time when they are with me.
19. I feel like a wallflower when I go out.
20. I feel I get pushed around more than others.
21. I think I am a rather nice person.
22. I feel that people really like me very much.
23. I feel that I am a likable person.
24. I am afraid I will appear foolish to others.
25. My friends think very highly of me.

Items to reverse score: 3, 4, 5, 6, 7, 14, 15, 18, 21, 22, 23, 25

Source: Simmons T (1986) Child Sexual Abuse: An Assessment Process. © London: NSPCC. Reproduced with permission.

SELF-CONTROL QUESTIONNAIRE

INSTRUCTIONS: Please read each of the following statements and indicate on your answer sheet just how characteristic or descriptive of you the statement is by using the letters of the code given below:

4 0 A=Very characteristic of me, extremely descriptive
3 1 B=Rather characteristic of me, quite descriptive
2 2 C=Somewhat characteristic of me, slightly undescriptive
1 3 D=Rather uncharacteristic of me, quite undescriptive
0 4 E=Very uncharacteristic of me, extremely undescriptive

E 1. Rewarding myself for progress toward a goal is unnecessary and may actually spoil me.

A 2. Concentrating on the final goals as well as the immediate results of my efforts can help me feel better about my work.

E 3. When things are going well, I often feel that something bad is just around the corner and there's nothing I can do about it.

A 4. I am aware of my accomplishments each day.

A 5. Thinking about how well I'm doing so far is what keeps me trying.

A 6. When I do something right, I take time to enjoy the feeling.

A 7. It usually works best for me to save my special treats until after I carry out what I intended to accomplish.

A 8. What is most important is how I feel about my actions, not what others think.

E 9. There is nothing I can do to change things that are upsetting me.

A 10. The way to achieve my goals is to reward myself along the way, in order to keep up my own efforts.

E 11. Punishing myself for only making partial gains toward a goal is the smart way to keep pressure on and get the job done.

A 12. I get myself through hard things largely by planning on enjoying myself afterwards.

E 13. I depend heavily on other people's opinions to evaluate objectively what I do.

E 14. When I don't feel like doing anything, sometimes it helps if I take time out to do something I really enjoy.

E 15. I always seem to remember the bad things that happen to me more than the good.

A 16. It's success at the little thing that encourages me to go on trying.

A 17. To get good results, I have to observe what I'm actually doing in order to decide what I need to do next.

E 18. The things in life that are most important depend on chance more than anything I can do.

A 19. Planning each step of what I have to do helps me to get things done well.

E 20. It's no use trying to change most of the things that make me miserable.

E 21. My mood is unrelated to my behavior.

E 22. There isn't anything to do when I want something important other than be patient and hope for good luck.

E 23. Activities which fail to lead to something immediately should be dropped in favor of those that do so.

A 24. My goals seem distant and unreachable.

E 25. I think talking about what you've done right or well is just boastful and tooting your own horn.

E 26. Unless I set and reach very high goals, my efforts are likely to be wasted.

E 27. When I feel blue, the best thing to do is focus on all the negative things happening to me.

A 28. Judging what I've done realistically is necessary for me to feel good about myself.

E 29. How I feel about myself has a lot to do with what I'm accomplishing.

E 30. I shouldn't dwell on things I've done well in hopes of feeling good about myself.

A 31. When there is some goal I'd like to reach, I find it best to list specifically what I have to do to get there.

A 32. My mood changes in relation to what I'm doing.

A 33. It's just as important to think about what will happen later as a result of my actions, as it is to watch for immediate effects.

E 34. I'd just be fooling myself if I tried to judge my reactions myself.

E 35. Keeping watch on what I do wrong is more helpful than watching what I do correctly.

E 36. Criticizing myself is often the best way to help me get through a difficult task.

A 37. Not only what goes on around us, but also the things we say and do to ourselves determine how we feel from day to day.

A 38. I encourage myself to improve by treating myself to something special whenever I make progress.

E 39. It's more helpful to receive criticism than praise for my actions.

A 40. I'd be unlikely to change for the better if I didn't silently praise myself or feel good for every step in the right direction.

© Reprinted by permission of L. P. Rehm.

LOCUS OF CONTROL SCALE (N-SLCS)

AUTHORS: Stephen Nowicki, Jr. and Bonni R. Strickland

PURPOSE: To measure locus of control

DESCRIPTION: This is a 40-item yes/no questionnaire that measures the extent to which individuals feels that events are contingent on *their* behavior and the extent to which they feel events are controlled externally.

We are trying to find out what men and women your age think about certain things. We want you to answer the following questions the way *you* feel. There are no right or wrong answers. Don't take too much time answering any one question, but do try to answer them all.

One of your concerns during the test may be, "What should I do if I can answer both yes and no to a question?" It's not unusual for that to happen. If it does, think about whether your answer is just a little more one way than the other. For example, if you'd assign a weighting of 51 percent to "yes" and assign 49 percent to "no," mark the answer "yes." Try to pick one or the other response for all questions and not leave any blanks.

Circle yes or no next to each item. Be sure to put your name and the date on your answr sheet.

Thank you.

THE LOCUS OF CONTROL SCALE

Item

1. Do you believe that most problems will solve themselves if you just don't fool with them? (Yes)[a,b]
2. Do you believe that you can stop yourself from catching a cold? (No)
3. Are some kids just born lucky? (No)
4. Most of the time do you feel that getting good grades means a great deal to you? (No)
5. Are you often blamed for things that just aren't your fault? (Yes)[b]
6. Do you believe that if somebody studies hard enough he or she can pass any subject? (No)
7. Do you feel that most of the time it doesn't pay to try hard because things never turn out right anyway? (Yes)[a,b].
8. Do you feel that if things start out well in the morning that it's going to be a good day no matter what you do? (Yes)
9. Do you feel that most of the time parents listen to what their children have to say? (No) [a,b]
10. Do you believe that wishing can make good things happen? (Yes)[a]
11. When you get punished does it usually seem its for no good reason at all? (Yes)[b]
12. Most of the time do you find it hard to change a friend's (mind) opinion? (Yes)[b]
13. Do you think that cheering more than luck helps a team to win? (No)
14. Do you feel that it's nearly impossible to change your parent's mind about anything? (Yes) [a,b]
15. Do you believe that your parents should allow you to make most of your own decisions? (No)
16. Do you feel that when you do something wrong there's very little you can do to make it right? (Yes)[a,b]
17. Do you believe that most kids are just born good at sports? (Yes)[a,b]
18. Are most of the other kids your age stronger than you are? (Yes)[a]
19. Do you feel that one of the best ways to handle most problems is just not to think about them? (Yes)[a,b]
20. Do you feel that you have a lot of choice in deciding who your friends are? (No)
21. If you find a four leaf clover do you believe that it might bring you good luck? (Yes)
22. Do you often feel that whether you do your homework has much to do with what kind of grades you get? (No)
23. Do you feel that when a kid your age decides to hit you, there's little you can do to stop him or her? (Yes)[a,b]
24. Have you ever had a good luck charm? (Yes)
25. Do you believe that whether or not people like you depends on how you act? (No)
26. Will your parents usually help you if you ask them to? (No)
27. Have you felt that when people were mean to you it was usually for no reason at all? (No)
28. Most of the time, do you feel that you can change what might happen tomorrow by what you do "today" (No)[b]
29. Do you believe that when bad things are going to happen they just are going to happen no matter what you try to do to stop them? (Yes)[a,b]
30. Do you think that kids can get their own way if they just keep trying? (No)
31. Most of the time do you find it useless to try to get your own way at home? (Yes)[a,b]
32. Do you feel that when good things happen they happen because of hard work? (No)
33. Do you feel that when somebody your age wants to be your enemy there's little you can do to change matters? (Yes)[a,b]
34. Do you feel that it's easy to get friends to do what you want them to? (No)
35. Do you usually feel that you have little to say about what you get to eat at home? (Yes)[a,b]
36. Do you feel that when someone doesn't like you there's little you can do about it? (Yes)[a,b]
37. Do you usually feel that it's almost useless to try in school because most other children are just plain smarter than you are? (Yes)[a,b]
38. Are you the kind of person who believes that planning ahead makes things turn out better? (Yes)[a,b]
39. Most of the time, do you feel that you have little to say about what your family decides to do? (Yes)[a,b]
40. Do you think it's better to be smart than to be lucky? (No)

Reproduced with the permission of Stephen Nowicki; Source: ©Nowicki S and Strickland B (1973). A locus of control scale for children. Journal of Consulting and Clinical Psychology 40:148-154. Updated reference lists and research findings can be obtained by writing to Stephen Nowicki Jr. at the Department of Psychology, Emory University, Atlanta, Georgia 30322, U.S.A.

SCORING
Scoring is done by assigning one point for every answer that matches the following answer key:

1. Y	11. Y	21. Y	31. Y
2. N	12. Y	22. Y	32. N
3. Y	13. N	23. Y	33. Y
4. N	14. Y	24. Y	34. N
5. Y	15. N	25. N	35. Y
6. N	16. Y	26. Y	36. Y
7. Y	17. Y	27. Y	37. Y
8. Y	18. Y	28. N	38. N
9. N	19. Y	29. Y	39. Y
10. Y	20. N	30. N	40. N

ILLNESS BEHAVIOR QUESTIONNAIRE (IBQ)

PURPOSE: To measure the ways individuals experience and respond to their health status.

DESCRIPTION: The IBQ is a 62-item instrument designed to measure a respondent's attitudes, ideas, affects, and attributions in relation to illness. The IBQ consists of seven major subscales derived through factor analysis, each of which has at least 5 items. The seven scales of the IBQ are general hypochondriasis (GH), disease conviction (DC), psychologic versus somatic perceptions of illness (P/S), affective inhibition (AI), affective disturbance (AD), denial (D), and irritability (I). The IBQ also generates scores on the Whiteley Index of Hypochondriasis (WH) and two other minor factors. The IBQ is written in easily understood language, is easily scored, and translations in several languages are available. Some of the scales have cut-off points for the detection of abnormality. The IBQ is useful for examining illness behavior in general and for identifying physical complaints that are manifestations of a psychiatric disorder.

SCORING: The IBQ is very easily hand scored by using the scoring key available in the manual. The scoring key on the questionnaire describes which items on the IBQ belong to which subscale and the meaning of a "yes" or "no" on each item. The "correct" answers and the items for each subscale are shown in the right-hand column of the questionnaire. These items are summed to obtain the subscale scores. For the Whiteley Index of Hypochondriasis; a "yes" answer to items 1, 2, 9, 10, 16, 21, 24, 33, 34, 38, 39, and 41 and a "no" answer to item 8 are the "correct" scores.

SCORING KEY

Key	Answer options	#	Question
Yes	Yes No	1.	Do you worry a lot about your health?
Yes	Yes No	2.	Do you think there is something seriously wrong with your body?
Yes	Yes No	3.	Does your illness interfere with your life a great deal?
No	Yes No	4.	Are you easy to get on with when you are ill?
Yes	Yes No	5.	Does your family have a history of illness?
Yes	Yes No	6.	Do you think you are more liable to illness than other people?
No	Yes No	7.	If the doctor told you that he could find nothing wrong with you would you believe him?
Yes	Yes No	8.	Is it easy for you to forget about yourself and think about all sorts of other things?
Yes	Yes No	9.	If you feel ill and someone tells you that you are looking better, do you become annoyed?
Yes	Yes No	10.	Do you find that you are often aware of various things happening in your body?
Yes	Yes No	11.	Do you ever think of your illness as a punishment for something you have done wrong in the past?
Yes	Yes No	12.	Do you have trouble with your nerves?
Yes	Yes No	13.	If you feel ill or worried, can you be easily cheered up by the doctor?
No	Yes No	14.	Do you think that other people realize what it's like to be sick?
Yes	Yes No	15.	Does it upset you to talk to the doctor about your illness?
No	Yes No	16.	Are you bothered by many pains and aches?
Yes	Yes No	17.	Does your illness affect the way you get on with your family or friends a great deal?
Yes	Yes No	18.	Do you find that you get anxious easily?
Yes	Yes No	19.	Do you know anybody who has had the same illness as you
Yes	Yes No	20.	Are you more sensitive to pain than other people?
No	Yes No	21.	Are you afraid of illness?
Yes	Yes No	22.	Can you express your personal feelings easily to other people?
No	Yes No	23.	Do people feel sorry for you when you are ill?
Yes	Yes No	24.	Do you think that you worry about your health more than most people?
Yes	Yes No	25.	Do you find that your illness affects your sexual relations?
Yes	Yes No	26.	Do you experience a lot of pain with your illness?
No	Yes No	27.	Except for your illness, do you have any problems in your life?
Yes	Yes No	28.	Do you care whether or not people realize you are sick?
Yes	Yes No	29.	Do you find that you get jealous of other people's good health?
GH-Yes	Yes No	30.	Do you ever have silly thoughts about your health which you can't get out of your mind, no matter how hard you try?
D-No	Yes No	31.	Do you have any financial problems?
GH-Yes	Yes No	32.	Are you upset by the way people take your illness?
DC-No	Yes No	33.	Is it hard for you to believe the doctor when he tells you there is nothing for you to worry about?
AI-Yes	Yes No	34.	Do you often worry about the possibility that you have got a serious illness?
GH-Yes	Yes No	35.	Are you sleeping well?
GH-Yes	Yes No	36.	When you are angry, do you tend to bottle up your feelings?
	Yes No	37.	Do you often think that you might suddenly fall ill?
	Yes No	38.	If a disease is brought to your attention (through the radio, television, newspapers, or someone you know) do you worry about getting it yourself?
DC-Yes	Yes No	39.	Do you get the feeling that people are not taking your illness seriously enough?
	Yes No	40.	Are you upset by the appearance of your face or body?
	Yes No	41.	Do you find that you are bothered by many different symptoms?
	Yes No	42.	Do you frequently try to explain to others how you are feeling?
D-No	Yes No	43.	Do you have any family problems?
P/S-Yes	Yes No	44.	Do you think there is something the matter with your mind?
	Yes No	45.	Are you eating well?
P/S-No	Yes No	46.	Is your bad health the biggest difficulty of your life?
AD-Yes	Yes No	47.	Do you find that you get sad easily?
	Yes No	48.	Do you worry or fuss over small details that seem unimportant to others?
	Yes No	49.	Are you always a cooperative paitent?
	Yes No	50.	Do you often have the symptoms of a very serious disease?
	Yes No	51.	Do you find that you get angry easily?
	Yes No	52.	Do you have any work problems?
AI-Yes	Yes No	53.	Do you prefer to keep your feelings to yourself?
Ad-Yes	Yes No	54.	Do you often find that you get depressed?
D-Yes	Yes No	55.	Would all your worries be over if you were physically healthy?
I-Yes	Yes No	56.	Are you more irritable towards other people?
P/S-Yes	Yes No	57.	Do you think that your symptoms may be caused by worry?
AI-Yes	Yes No	58.	Is it easy for you to let people know when you are cross with them?
AD-Yes	Yes No	59.	Is it hard for you to relax?
D-No	Yes No	60.	Do you have personal worries which are not caused by physical illness?
I-Yes	Yes No	61.	Do you often find that you lose patience with other people?
AI-Yes	Yes No	62.	Is it hard for you to show people your personal feelings?

REFERENCE: Pilowsky, I. (1983). Manual for the Illness Behaviour Questionnaire. University of Adelaide, Department of Psychiatry. Reproduced by permission of the author.

AUTOMATIC THOUGHTS QUESTIONNAIRE—REVISED

DESCRIPTION: The ATQ is a 40-item instrument that measures the frequency of automatic negative statements about the self. The ATQ taps four aspects of these negative thoughts: personal adjustment and desire for change; negative self-concepts and negative expectations; low self-esteem; and helplessness. Items are rated on the frequency of occurrence from 'not at all' to 'all the time'. Total scores are the summation of all 40 items.

REFERENCE: The original ATQ appeared in Hollon S. D. and Kendall P. C. (1980). Cognitive self-statements about depression: development of an automatic thoughts questionnaire. *Cognitive Therapy and Research* 4, 383–395. The revised ATQ is reproduced here with the permission of Philip C. Kendall. It is discussed in more detail in Kendall, P. C., Howard, B. L. and Hays, R. C. (1989). Self-referent speech and psychopathology: the balance of positive and negative thinking. *Cognitive Therapy and Research* 13(6), 583–598.

Instructions

Listed below are a variety of thoughts that pop into people's heads. Please read each thought and indicate how frequently, if at all, the thought occurred to you *over the last week*. Please read each item carefully and circle the appropriate answers on the answer sheet in the following fashion 0 = "not at all", 1 = "sometimes", 2 = "moderately often", 3 = "often", and 4 = "all the time").

Responses	*Thoughts*
0 1 2 3 4	1. I feel like I'm up against the world.
0 1 2 3 4	2. I'm no good.
0 1 2 3 4	3. I'm proud of myself.
0 1 2 3 4	4. Why can't I ever succeed?

Remember, each sentence that you read is a *thought* that you may have had often, less frequently, or not at all. Tell us how often *over the last week* you have had each of the thoughts.

0 1 2 3 4	5. No one understands me.
0 1 2 3 4	6. I've let people down.
0 1 2 3 4	7. I feel fine.
0 1 2 3 4	8. I don't think I can go on.
0 1 2 3 4	9. I wish I were a better person.
0 1 2 3 4	10. No matter what happens, I know I'll make it.
0 1 2 3 4	11. I'm so weak.
0 1 2 3 4	12. My life's not going the way I want it to.
0 1 2 3 4	13. I can accomplish anything.
0 1 2 3 4	14. I'm so disappointed in myself.
0 1 2 3 4	15. Nothing feels good anymore.
0 1 2 3 4	16. I feel good.
0 1 2 3 4	17. I can't stand this anymore.
0 1 2 3 4	18. I can't get started.
0 1 2 3 4	19. What's wrong with me?
0 1 2 3 4	20. I'm warm and comfortable.
0 1 2 3 4	21. I wish I were somewhere else.
0 1 2 3 4	22. I can't get things together.
0 1 2 3 4	23. I hate myself.
0 1 2 3 4	24. I feel confident I can do anything I set my mind to.

Remember, each sentence that you read is a *thought* that you may have had often, less frequently, or not at all. Tell us how often *over the last week* you have had each of the thoughts.

0 1 2 3 4	25. I'm worthless.
0 1 2 3 4	26. Wish I could just disappear.
0 1 2 3 4	27. What's the matter with me?
0 1 2 3 4	28. I feel very happy.
0 1 2 3 4	29. I'm a loser.
0 1 2 3 4	30. My life is a mess.
0 1 2 3 4	31. I'm a failure.
0 1 2 3 4	32. This is super!
0 1 2 3 4	33. I'll never make it.
0 1 2 3 4	34. I feel so helpless.
0 1 2 3 4	35. Something has to change.
0 1 2 3 4	36. There must be something wrong with me.
0 1 2 3 4	37. I'm luckier than most people.
0 1 2 3 4	38. My future is bleak.
0 1 2 3 4	39. It's just not worth it.
0 1 2 3 4	40. I can't finish anything.

THE MACH TECH SEX TEST (KIRBY, 1984)

ATTITUDE AND VALUE INVENTORY

This is NOT a knowledge test. There are no right or wrong answers. Your answer is correct if it accurately describes you.

The items on the ATTITUDE AND VALUE INVENTORY are a list of statements. Please rate each item on a 1 to 5 scale according to how much you agree or disagree with the statement.

Circle
1 if you **strongly disagree** with the statement
2 if you **disagree** with the statement
3 if you feel **neutral** about the statement
4 if you **agree** with the statement
5 if you **strongly agree** with the statement

	strongly disagree	disagree	neutral	agree	strongly agree
1. I am very happy with my friendships.	1	2	3	4	5
2. Unmarried people should not have sex.	1	2	3	4	5
3. Overall, I am satisfied with myself.	1	2	3	4	5
4. Two people having sex should use some form of birth control, if they aren't ready for a child.	1	2	3	4	5
5. I'm confused about my personal sexual values and beliefs.	1	2	3	4	5
6. I often find myself acting in ways I don't understand.	1	2	3	4	5
7. I am not happy with my sex life.	1	2	3	4	5
8. Men should not hold jobs traditionally held by women.	1	2	3	4	5
9. People should never take "no" for an answer when they want to have sex.	1	2	3	4	5
10. I don't know what I want out of life.	1	2	3	4	5
11. Families do very little for their children.	1	2	3	4	5
12. Sexual relationships create more problems than they're worth.	1	2	3	4	5
13. I'm confused about what I should and should not do sexually.	1	2	3	4	5
14. I know what I want and need emotionally.	1	2	3	4	5
15. A person should not pressure someone into sexual activity.	1	2	3	4	5
16. Birth control is not very important.	1	2	3	4	5
17. I know what I need to be happy.	1	2	3	4	5
18. I am not satisfied with my sexual behavior.	1	2	3	4	5
19. I usually understand the way I act.	1	2	3	4	5
20. People should not have sex before marriage.	1	2	3	4	5
21. I do not know much about my own physical and emotional sexual response.	1	2	3	4	5
22. It is all right for two people to have sex before marriage if they are in love.	1	2	3	4	5
23. I have a good idea of where I'm headed in the future.	1	2	3	4	5
24. Family relationships are not important.	1	2	3	4	5
25. I have trouble knowing what my beliefs and values are regarding my personal sexual behavior.	1	2	3	4	5
26. I feel I do not have much to be proud of.	1	2	3	4	5
27. I understand how I behave around others.	1	2	3	4	5
28. Women should behave differently from men most of the time.	1	2	3	4	5
29. People should have sex only if they are married.	1	2	3	4	5
30. I know what I want out of life.	1	2	3	4	5
31. I have a good understanding of my own sexual feelings and reactions.	1	2	3	4	5
32. I don't have enough friends.	1	2	3	4	5
33. I'm happy with my sexual behavior now.	1	2	3	4	5
34. I don't understand why I behave with my friends as I do.	1	2	3	4	5
35. At times I think I'm no good at all.	1	2	3	4	5
36. I know how I react in different sexual situations.	1	2	3	4	5
37. I have a clear picture of what I'd like to be doing in the future.	1	2	3	4	5
38. My friendships are not as good as I would like them to be.	1	2	3	4	5
39. Sexually, I feel like a failure.	1	2	3	4	5
40. More people should be aware of the importance of birth control.	1	2	3	4	5
41. At work and at home, women should not have to behave differently than men, when they are equally capable.	1	2	3	4	5
42. Sexual relationships make life too difficult.	1	2	3	4	5
43. I wish my friendships were better.	1	2	3	4	5
44. I feel that I have many good personal qualities.	1	2	3	4	5
45. I am confused about my reactions in sexual situations.	1	2	3	4	5
46. It is all right to pressure someone into sexual activity.	1	2	3	4	5
47. People should not pressure others to have sex with them.	1	2	3	4	5
48. Most of the time my emotional feelings are clear to me.	1	2	3	4	5
49. I have my own set of rules to guide my sexual behavior.	1	2	3	4	5
50. Women and men should be able to have the same jobs, when they are equally capable.	1	2	3	4	5
51. I don't know what my long-range goals are.	1	2	3	4	5
52. When I'm in a sexual situation, I get confused about my feelings.	1	2	3	4	5
53. Families are very important.	1	2	3	4	5

BEHAVIOR INVENTORY

This questionnaire includes personal questions about your social and sexual behavior. It is written for many different groups of young people. Some of these young people have had more sexual experience and others have had less. In order to make this questionnaire fit almost everyone, we have included some items that do not apply to everybody. Whenever a question does not apply to you, please check the response, "Does Not Apply." You should NOT conclude from the questions that you should have had all the experiences mentioned in this questionnaire.

Part 1. The questions below ask how often you have done some things.

Circle:
1 if you do it "Almost never" which means about 5% of the time or less.
2 if you do it "Sometimes" which means about 25% of the time.
3 if you do it "Half the time" which means about 50% of the time.
4 if you do it "Usually" which means about 75% of the time.
5 if you do it "Almost always" which means about 95% of the time.
DNA if the question "Does Not Apply" to you.

	almost never	sometimes	half the time	usually	almost always	does not apply
1. When things you've done turn out poorly, how often do you take responsibility for your behavior and its consequences?	1	2	3	4	5	DNA
2. When things you've done turn out poorly, how often do you blame others?	1	2	3	4	5	DNA
3. When you are faced with a decision, how often do you take responsibility for making a decision about it?	1	2	3	4	5	DNA
4. When you have to make a decision, how often do you think hard about the consequences of each possible choice?	1	2	3	4	5	DNA
5. When you have to make a decision, how often do you get as much information as you can before making a decision?	1	2	3	4	5	DNA
6. When you have to make a decision, how often do you first discuss it with others?	1	2	3	4	5	DNA
7. When you have to make a decision about your sexual behavior (for example, going out on a date, holding hands, kissing, petting, or having sex), how often do you take responsibility for the consequences?	1	2	3	4	5	DNA
8. When you have to make a decision about your sexual behavior, how often do you think hard about the consequences of each possible choice?	1	2	3	4	5	DNA
9. When you have to make a decision about your sexual behavior, how often do you first get as much information as you can?	1	2	3	4	5	DNA
10. When you have to make a decision about your sexual behavior, how often do you first discuss it with others?	1	2	3	4	5	DNA
11. When you have to make a decision about your sexual behavior, how often do you make it on the spot without worrying about the consequences?	1	2	3	4	5	DNA

	strongly disagree	disagree	neutral	agree	strongly agree
54. It is all right to demand sex from a girlfriend or boyfriend.	1	2	3	4	5
55. A sexual relationship is one of the best things a person can have.	1	2	3	4	5
56. Most of the time I have a clear understanding of my feelings and emotions.	1	2	3	4	5
57. I am very satisfied with my sexual activities just the way they are.	1	2	3	4	5
58. Sexual relationships only bring trouble to people.	1	2	3	4	5
59. Birth control is not as important as some people say.	1	2	3	4	5
60. Family relationships cause more trouble than they're worth.	1	2	3	4	5
61. If two people have sex and aren't ready to have a child, it is very important that they use birth control.	1	2	3	4	5
62. I'm confused about what I need emotionally.	1	2	3	4	5
63. It is all right for two people to have sex before marriage.	1	2	3	4	5
64. Sexual relationships provide an important and fulfilling part of life.	1	2	3	4	5
65. People should not be expected to behave in certain ways just because they are male or female.	1	2	3	4	5
66. Most of the time I know why I behave the way I do.	1	2	3	4	5
67. I feel good having as many friends as I have.	1	2	3	4	5
68. I wish I had more respect for myself.	1	2	3	4	5
69. Family relationships can be very valuable.	1	2	3	4	5
70. I know for sure what is right and wrong sexually for me.	1	2	3	4	5

Top section (Items 25–44)

	comfortable	a little uncomfortable	somewhat uncomfortable	very uncomfortable	does not apply
25. Getting together with a group of friends of the opposite sex.	1	2	3	4	DNA
26. Going to a party.	1	2	3	4	DNA
27. Talking with teenagers of the opposite sex.	1	2	3	4	DNA
28. Going out on a date.	1	2	3	4	DNA
29. Talking with friends about sex.	1	2	3	4	DNA
30. Talking with a date or boy/girlfriend about sex.	1	2	3	4	DNA
31. Talking with parents about sex.	1	2	3	4	DNA
32. Talking with friends about birth control.	1	2	3	4	DNA
33. Talking with a date or boy/girlfriend about birth control.	1	2	3	4	DNA
34. Talking with parents about birth control.	1	2	3	4	DNA
35. Expressing concern and caring for others.	1	2	3	4	DNA
36. Telling a date or boy/girlfriend what you want to do and do not want to do sexually.	1	2	3	4	DNA
37. Saying "no" to a sexual come-on.	1	2	3	4	DNA
38. Having your current sex life, what ever it may be (it may be doing nothing, kissing, petting, or having intercourse).	1	2	3	4	DNA

If you are not having sexual intercourse, circle "DNA" in the four questions below.

	comfortable	a little uncomfortable	somewhat uncomfortable	very uncomfortable	does not apply
39. Insisting on using some form of birth control, if you are having sex.	1	2	3	4	DNA
40. Buying contraceptives at a drug store, if you are having sex.	1	2	3	4	DNA
41. Going to a doctor or clinic for contraception, if you are having sex.	1	2	3	4	DNA
42. Using some form of birth control, if you are having sex.	1	2	3	4	DNA

Part 3: Circle the correct answer to the following two questions.

43. Have you ever had sexual intercourse?   Yes   No

44. Have you had sexual intercourse during the last month?   Yes   No

Part 4: The following questions ask about activities during the last month. Put a number in the right hand space which shows the number of times you engaged in that activity. Put a "O" in that space if you did not engage in that activity during the last month.

Think CAREFULLY about the times that you have had sex during the last month. Think also about the number of times you did not use birth control and the number of times you used different types of birth control.

Bottom section (Items 12–24)

	almost never	sometimes	half the time	usually	almost always	does not apply
12. When a friend wants to talk with you, how often are you able to clear your mind and really listen to what your friend has to say?	1	2	3	4	5	DNA
13. When a friend is talking with you, how often do you ask questions if you don't understand what your friend is saying?	1	2	3	4	5	DNA
14. When a friend is talking with you, how often do you nod your head and say "yes" or something else to show that you are interested?	1	2	3	4	5	DNA
15. When you want to talk with a friend, how often are you able to get your friend to really listen to you?	1	2	3	4	5	DNA
16. When you talk with a friend, how often do you ask for your friend's reactions to what you've said?	1	2	3	4	5	DNA
17. When you talk with a friend, how often do you let your feelings show?	1	2	3	4	5	DNA
18. When you are with a friend you care about, how often do you let that friend know how you care?	1	2	3	4	5	DNA
19. When you talk with a friend, how often do you include statements like "my feelings are...", "the way I think is...", or "it seems like ... to me"?	1	2	3	4	5	DNA
20. When you are alone with a date or boy/girlfriend, how often can you tell him/her your feelings about what you want to do and do not want to do sexually? ("boy/girlfriend" means "boyfriend" if you are a girl, and it means "girlfriend" if you are a boy.)	1	2	3	4	5	DNA
21. If a boy/girl puts pressure on you to be involved sexually and you don't want to be involved, how often do you say "no"? ("boy/girl" means "boy" if you are a girl, and it means "girl" if you are a boy.)	1	2	3	4	5	DNA
22. If a boy/girl puts pressure on you to be involved sexually and you don't want to be involved, how often do you succeed in stopping it?	1	2	3	4	5	DNA
23. If you have sexual intercourse with your boy/girlfriend, how often can you talk with him/her about birth control?	1	2	3	4	5	DNA
24. If you have sexual intercourse and want to use birth control, how often do you insist on using birth control?	1	2	3	4	5	DNA

Part 2. In this section, we want to know how uncomfortable you are doing different things. Being "uncomfortable" means that it is difficult for you and it makes you nervous and up-tight. Indicate how uncomfortable you are with the following activities by circling one of the four numbers after each item. Whenever a question does not apply to you, please circle the response, "DNA," which means "Does Not Apply".

Circle:
1   if you are comfortable
2   if you are a little uncomfortable
3   if you are somewhat uncomfortable
4   if you are very comfortable
DNA   if the question Does Not Apply to you

SEXUAL EXPERIENCES SURVEY

DESCRIPTION: This self-report instrument is designed to provide an assessment of unidentified victims of rape and unidentified perpetrators of rape. The survey is now a 13-item report instrument that is also designed to reflect various degrees of sexual aggression and victimisation.

Each respondent is asked to answer 'yes' or 'no' to the following questions:

Item

Have you ever:

1. Had sexual intercourse with a man (woman) when you both wanted to?
2. Had a man (woman) misinterpret the level of sexual intimacy you desired?
3. Been in a situation where a man (you) became so sexually aroused that you felt it was useless to stop him even though you did not want to have sexual intercourse? (could not stop yourself even though the woman didn't want to?)
4. Had sexual intercourse with a man (woman) even though you (she) didn't really want to because he (you) threatened to end your relationship otherwise?
5. Had sexual intercourse with a man (woman) when you (she) didn't really want to because you (she) felt pressured by his (your) continual arguments?
6. Found out that a man had obtained sexual intercourse with you by saying things he didn't really mean? (Obtained sexual intercourse by saying things you didn't really mean?
7. Been in a situation where a man (you) used some degree of physical force (twisting your [her] arm, holding you [her] down, etc.) to try to make you (a woman) engage in kissing or petting when you (she) didn't want to?
8. Been in a situation where a man (you) tried to get sexual intercourse with you (a woman) when you (she) didn't want to by threatening to use physical force (twisting your [her] arm, holding you [her] down, etc.) if you (she) didn't cooperate, but for various reasons sexual intercourse did not occur?
9. Been in a situation where a man (you) used some degree of physical force (twisting your [her] arm, holding you [her] down, etc.) to try to get you (a woman) to have sexual intercourse with him (you) when you (she) didn't want to, but for various reasons sexual intercourse did not occur?
10. Had sexual intercourse with a man (woman) when you (she) didn't want to because he (you) threatened to use physical force (twisting your [her] arm, holding you [her] down, etc.) if you (she) didn't cooperate?
11. Had sexual intercourse with a man (woman) when you (she) didn't want to because he (you) used some degree of physical force (twisting your [her] arm, holding you [her] down, etc.)?
12. Been in a situation where a man (you) obtained sexual acts with you (a woman) such as anal or oral intercourse when you (she) didn't want to by using threats or physical force (twisting your [her] arm, holding you [her] down, etc.)?
13. Have you ever been raped? (women only)

PRIMARY REFERENCE: Koss. M. P. and Oros, C. J. (1982). Sexual Experiences Survey: A research instrument. *Journal of Consulting and Clinical Psychology* 50, 455–457. ©American Psychological Association. Reproduced with the permission of APA and Dr Mary Koss.
OTHER REFERENCES: Koss, M. P. and Gidycz, C. A. (1985) Sexual Experiences Survey: Reliability and validity. *Journal of Consulting and Clinical Psychology* 53, 422–423. Koss, M. P., Gidycz, C. A. and Wisniewski, N. (1987). The scope of rape: Incidence and prevalence of sexual aggression and victimisation in a national sample of higher education students. *Journal of Consulting and Clinical Psychology* 55(2), 162–170.

---

45. Last month, how many times did you have sexual intercourse? ____ Times in the last month

46. Last month, how many times did you have sex when you or your partner did not use any form of birth control? ____ Times in the last month

47. Last month, how many times did you have sex when you or your partner used a diaphragm, withdrawal (pulling out before releasing fluid), rhythm (not having sex on fertile days), or foam without condoms? ____ Times in the last month

48. Last month, how many times did you have sex when you or your partner used the pill, condoms (rubbers), or an IUD? ____ Times in the last month

(If you add your answers to questions #46 plus #48, it should equal your answer to #45. If it does not, please correct your answers.)

49. During the last month, how many times have you had a conversation or discussion about sex with your parents? ____ Times in the last month

50. During the last month, how many times have you had a conversation or discussion about sex with your friends? ____ Times in the last month

51. During the last month, how many times have you had a conversation or discussion about sex with a date or boy/girlfriend? ____ Times in the last month

52. During the last month, how many times have you had a conversation or discussion about birth control with your parents? ____ Times in the last month

53. During the last month, how many times have you had a conversation or discussion about birth control with your friends. ____ Times in the last month

54. During the last month, how many times have you had a conversation or discussion about birth control with a date or boy/girlfriend? ____ Times in the last month

NEGATIVE ATTITUDES TOWARD MASTURBATION INVENTORY (NAMI)

DESCRIPTION: This 30-item instrument measures negative attitudes toward masturbation. Negative attitudes can emerge from a lack of information or from inadequate information about sexuality; additionally, negative attitudes may develop from conditioned emotional reactions. Negative attitudes tend to be related to a lower frequency of masturbation and to sexual inexperience. Negative attitudes are considered evidence of guilt over masturbation. Knowledge of negative attitudes toward masturbation can assist in therapeutic work on sexuality and the treatment of some orgasmic disorders. The scores on the NAMI were not influenced by gender.

SCORING: Each item is rated on a 5-point Likert scale by recording a number from (1) strongly disagree to (5) strongly agree in the space to the left of the item. Items 3, 5, 8, 11, 13, 14–17, 22, 27, 29, are reverse-scored. Total scores are then the sum of all items and range from 30 to 150 with higher scores indicating more negative attitudes.

PRIMARY REFERENCE: Abramson, P. R. and Mosher, D. L. (1975). Development of a measure of negative attitudes toward masturbation, *Journal of Consulting and Clinical Psychology*, 43, 485–490. Instrument reproduced with permission of Dr Paul R. Abramson.

Below are thirty statements regarding masturbation. Please indicate the degree to which you agree with each by placing the appropriate number to the left of the statement. The numbers are based on the following scale:

1 = Strongly disagree
2 = Disagree
3 = Neither agree nor disagree
4 = Agree
5 = Strongly agree

1. People masturbate to escape from feelings of tension and anxiety.
2. People who masturbate will not enjoy sexual intercourse as much as those who refrain from masturbation.
3. Masturbation is a private matter which neither harms nor concerns anyone else.
4. Masturbation is a sin against yourself.
5. Masturbation in childhood can help a person develop a natural, healthy attitude toward sex.
6. Masturbation in an adult is juvenile and immature.
7. Masturbation can lead to homosexuality.
8. Excessive masturbation is physically impossible, as it is a needless worry.
9. If you enjoy masturbating too much, you may never learn to relate to the opposite sex.
10. After masturbating, a person feels degraded.
11. Experience with masturbation can potentially help a woman become orgastic in sexual intercourse.
12. I feel guilty about masturbating.
13. Masturbation can be a "friend in need" when there is no "friend in deed."
14. Masturbation can provide an outlet for sex fantasies without harming anyone else or endangering oneself.
15. Excessive masturbation can lead to problems of impotence in men and frigidity in women.
16. Masturbation is an escape mechanism which prevents a person from developing a mature sexual outlook.
17. Masturbation can provide harmless relief from sexual tensions.
18. Playing with your own genitals is disgusting.
19. Excessive masturbation is associated with neurosis, depression, and behavioral problems.
20. Any masturbation is too much.
21. Masturbation is a compulsive, additive habit which once begun is almost impossible to stop.
22. Masturbation is fun.
23. When I masturbate, I am disgusted with myself.
24. A pattern of frequent masturbation is associated with introversion and withdrawal from social contacts.
25. I would be ashamed to admit publicly that I have masturbated.
26. Excessive masturbation leads to mental dullness and fatigue.
27. Masturbation is a normal sexual outlet.
28. Masturbation is caused by an excessive preoccupation with thoughts about sex.
29. Masturbation can teach you to enjoy the sensuousness of your own body.
30. After I masturbate, I am disgusted with myself for losing control of my body.

MILLER SOCIAL INTIMACY SCALE (MSIS)

DESCRIPTION: The MSIS is a 17-item instrument designed to measure closeness with others. It is based on the findings of several studies that show intimacy to be an important predictor of healthy psychological and physical functioning, especially in regard to marriage, relationships with others, bereavement, and response to stress. The initial item pool of 30 was generated by intensive interviews with university undergraduates; subsequent tests produced the current 17 items, 6 of which are frequency items and 11 of which measure intensity. The MSIS is structured to permit an assessment of intimacy in the context of friendship or marriage.

SCORING: The original instrument, scored on a 10-point scale, has been revised to the 5-point scale reproduced here. Items 1, 2, 3, 21, and 22 are not scored. Items 5 and 17 are reverse-scored, then the individual items are summed (A=1, E=5) to produce an overall score for the MSIS, with higher scores indicating greater amounts of social intimacy.

PRIMARY REFERENCE: Miller, R. S. and Lefcourt, H. M. (1982). The assessment of social intimacy. *Journal of Personality Assessment* 46(5), 514–518. Instrument reproduced with permission of Herbert M. Lefcourt.

A number of phrases are listed below that describe the kind of relationships people have with others. Indicate, by filling in the appropriate letters in the answer field, how you would describe your current relationship with your closest friend. This friend can be of either sex and should be someone whom you consider to be your closest friend at this time. While it is not necessary to specify the name of this friend, please indicate his/her sex in question 1.

Remember that you are to indicate the kind of relationship you have now with your *closest friend*.

1. Sex of your closest friend: M _____ F _____
2. Your marital status: single _____ married _____ common-law _____ separated or divorced _____ widowed _____
3. Is the friend you describe your spouse? Yes _____ No _____

	Very rarely	Some of the time	Almost always
4. When you have leisure time how often do you choose to spend it with him/her alone?	A	B C	D E
5. How often do you keep very personal information to yourself and do not share it with him/her?	A	B C	D E
6. How often do you show him/her affection?	A	B C	D E
7. How often do you confide very personal information to him/her?	A	B C	D E
8. How often are you able to understand his/her feelings?	A	B C	D E
9. How often do you feel close to him/her?	A	B C	D E
	Not much	A little	A great deal
10. How much do you like to spend time alone with him/her?	A	B C	D E
11. How much do you feel like being encouraging and supportive to him/her when he/she is unhappy?	A	B C	D E
12. How close do you feel to him/her most of the time?	A	B C	D E
13. How important is it to you to listen to his/her personal disclosures?	A	B C	D E
14. How satisfying is your relationship with him/her?	A	B C	D E
15. How affectionate do you feel towards him/her?	A	B C	D E
16. How important is it to you that he/she understand your feelings?	A	B C	D E
17. How much damage is caused by a typical disagreement in your relationship with him/her?	A	B C	D E
18. How important is it to you that he/she be encouraging and supportive to you when you are unhappy?	A	B C	D E

SEXUAL EXPERIENCES QUESTIONNAIRE (Lisak and Roth, 1988)

1. Have you ever had sexual intercourse with a woman?
2. Do you discuss your sexual experiences with your male friends?
3. Do you feel pressured by your male friends to be more sexually active than you are?
4. Do you feel that you aren't having sex as often as you "should" be?
5. Have you ever felt while on a date that you had consumed enough alcohol or drugs that you weren't really in control of your actions?
6. Do you ever act on the spur of the moment without even stopping to think?
7. Do you sometimes do whatever makes you feel cheerful—"right now"—even at the cost of some more distant goal?
8. Do you sometimes feel that society's "rules of conduct" are more for show than for any real purpose?
9. Have you ever felt inadequate because you felt a woman was comparing the way you kiss, or your "performance," with other men?
10. Have you ever felt that women sometimes like to act and talk like they were your mother?
11. Do you sometimes feel subtly "put down" by women—criticized or ridiculed in a way that makes it hard to defend yourself or respond?
12. Have you ever felt the urge to assert yourself with a woman because she was getting a little too "pushy," a little too domineering?
13. Have you ever felt that women sometimes try to make you feel "small," like a little boy?
14. Have you ever felt that, despite their claims to the contrary, women secretly feel superior to men?
15. Do you feel that women deliberately act seductively toward you—tease you:
    (a) Even when they aren't really interested in you sexually?
    (b) As a way of trying to show their power over you?
16. Have you ever felt that a woman was taking advantage of you by implying in subtle ways that she would have sex with you in order to get you to pay for various things (drinks, entertainment, etc.), but then later refused?
17. Have you ever been deceived by a woman?
18. Have you ever been betrayed by a woman?
19. Have you ever been manipulated by a woman?
20. Have you ever had sexual intercourse with a woman when she didn't want to because you threatened to end your relationship with her otherwise?
21. Have you ever had sexual intercourse with a woman when she didn't want to because she felt pressured by your continual arguments?
22. Have you ever obtained sexual intercourse with a woman by making her think that you cared for her more than you really did?
23. Have you ever obtained sexual intercourse with a woman by deliberately getting her too drunk to resist?
24. Have you ever persisted in having sexual intercourse with a woman, without using force, even though she verbally tried to stop you? If yes, please rate yourself on the following feelings which you may have experienced at the time. Anger . . . Need to assert yourself . . . Sexual frustration.
25. Have you ever been in a situation where you used or threatened to use physical force (twisting her arm, holding her down) to make a woman engage in kissing or petting when she didn't want to? If yes, please rate . . .
26. Have you ever been in a situation where you *tried, but for various reasons did not succeed,* in having sexual intercourse with a woman by *using or threatening to use* physical force (twisting her arm, holding her down, etc.) if she didn't cooperate? If yes, please rate . . .
27. Have you ever *had* sexual intercourse with a woman when she didn't want to because you *used or threatened to use* physical force (twisting her arm, holding her down, etc.) if she didn't cooperate? If yes, please rate . . .
28. Have you ever had oral sex with a woman when she didn't want to because you *used or threatened to use* physical force (twisting her arm, holding her down, etc.) if she didn't cooperate? If yes, please rate . . .
29. Have you ever felt the urge to physically force a woman to have sexual intercourse with you even though you did not act on the urge? If yes, please rate . . .

In Lisak, D. and Roth, S. (1988). Motivational factors in non-incarcerated sexually aggressive men. *Journal of Personality and Social Psychology,* 55(5), 795–802. © American Psychological Association. Reproduced with the permission of APA and D. Lisak.

FEAR-OF-INTIMACY SCALE

DESCRIPTION: This 35-item scale is designed to assess individual's anxieties about close, dating relationships. The respondent rates each of the items on a 5-point scale ranging from 1—'not at all characteristic of me' to 5—'extremely characteristic of me.'

REFERENCE: Descutner, C. J. and Thelen, M. H. (1991) Development and validation of a fear-of-intimacy scale. *Psychological Assessment*, 3(2), 218–225. Reproduced with the permission of Mark Thelen.

Fear-of-Intimacy Scale

Part A Instructions: Imagine you are in a *close, dating* relationship. Respond to the following statements as you would *if you were in that close relationship*. Rate how characteristic each statement is of you on a scale of 1 to 5 as described below, and put your responses on the answer sheet.

1	2	3	4	5
not at all characteristic of me	slightly characteristic of me	moderately characteristic of me	very characteristic of me	extremely characteristic of me

Note. In each statement "O" refers to the person who would be in the close relationship with you.

1. I would feel uncomfortable telling O about things in the past that I have felt ashamed of.
2. I would feel uneasy talking with O about something that has hurt me deeply.
X3. I would feel comfortable expressing my true feelings to O.
4. If O were upset I would sometimes be afraid of showing that I care.
5. I might be afraid to confide my innermost feelings to O.
X6. I would feel at ease telling O that I care about him/her.
X7. I would have a feeling of complete togetherness with O.
X8. I would be comfortable discussing significant problems with O.
9. A part of me would be afraid to make a long-term commitment to O.
X10. I would feel comfortable telling my experiences, even sad ones, to O.
11. I would probably feel nervous showing O strong feelings of affection.
12. I would find it difficult being open with O about my personal thoughts.
13. I would feel uneasy with O depending on me for emotional support.
X14. I would not be afraid to share with O what I dislike about myself.
15. I would be afraid to take the risk of being hurt in order to establish a closer relationship with O.
16. I would feel comfortable keeping very personal information to myself.
X17. I would not be nervous about being spontaneous with O.
X18. I would feel comfortable telling O things that I do not tell other people.
X19. I would feel comfortable truting O with my deepest thoughts and feelings.
20. I would sometimes feel uneasy if O told me about very personal matters.
X21. I would be comfortable revealing to O what I feel are my shortcomings and handicaps.
X22. I would be comfortable with having a close emotional tie between us.
23. I would be afraid of sharing my private thoughts with O.
24. I would be afraid that I might not always feel close to O.
X25. I would be comfortable telling O what my needs are.
26. I would be afraid that O would be more invested in the relationship than I would be.
X27. I would feel comfortable about having open and honest communications with O.
28. I would sometimes feel uncomfortable listening to O's personal problems.
X29. I would feel at ease to completely be myself around O.
X30. I would feel relaxed being together and talking about our personal goals.

Part B Instructions: Respond to the following statements as they apply to your past relationships. Rate how characteristic each statement is of you on a scale of 1 to 5 as described in the instructions for Part A.

31. I have shied away from opportunities to be close to someone.
32. I have held back my feeling in previous relationships.
33. There are people who think that I am afraid to get close to them.
34. There are people who think that I am not an easy person to get to know.
35. I have done things in previous relationships to keep me from developing closeness.

Note. X denotes items reversed for scoring.

---

19. How important is it to you that he/she show you affection?   A   B   C   D   E
20. How important is your relationship with him/her in your life?   A   B   C   D   E
21. You have just described the relationship you have now with your closest friend. We are interested in knowing *how long* this person has been your closest friend. Please check the appropriate category:

    less than a month _____   1–4 months _____   5–8 months _____   9–12 months _____
    over a year _____

22. Recall your *previous* closest friend. Are you less close _____ just as close _____
    or closer _____ with the current friend you described on this scale?

225

INDEX OF SEXUAL SATISFACTION (ISS)

Name _____ Today's date _____

This questionnaire is designed to measure the degree of satisfaction you have in the sexual relationship with your partner. It is not a test, so there are no right or wrong answers. Answer each item as carefully and as accurately as you can by placing a number beside each one as follows:

1. Rarely or none of the time.
2. A little of the time.
3. Sometimes.
4. Good part of the time.
5. Most or all of the time.

Please begin.

1. I feel that my partner enjoys our sex life. ___
2. My sex life is very exciting. ___
3. Sex is fun for my partner and me. ___
4. I feel that my partner sees little in me except for the sex I can give. ___
5. I feel that sex is dirty and disgusting. ___
6. My sex life is monotonous. ___
7. When we have sex, it is too rushed and hurriedly completed. ___
8. I feel that my sex life is lacking in quality. ___
9. My partner is sexually very exciting. ___
10. I enjoy the sex techniques that my partner likes or uses. ___
11. I feel that my partner wants too much sex from me. ___
12. I think sex is wonderful. ___
13. My partner dwells on sex too much. ___
14. I feel that sex is something that has to be endured in our relationship. ___
15. My partner is too rough or brutal when we have sex. ___
16. My partner observes good personal hygiene. ___
17. I feel that sex is a normal function to our relationship. ___
18. My partner does not want sex when I do. ___
19. I feel that our sex life really adds a lot of our relationship. ___
20. I would like to have sexual contact with someone other than my partner. ___
21. It is easy for me to get sexually excited by my partner. ___
22. I feel that my partner is sexually pleased with me. ___
23. My partner is very sensitive to my sexual needs and desires. ___
24. I feel that I should have sex more often. ___
25. I feel that my sex life is boring. ___

Items to reverse score: 1, 2, 3, 9, 10, 12, 16, 17, 19, 21, 22, 23.

Source: Simmons, T (1986). Child Sexual Abuse: An assessment process. © London: NSPCC. Reproduced with permission.

INDEX OF MARITAL SATISFACTION (IMS)

Name _____ Today's date _____

This questionnaire is designed to measure the degree of satisfaction you have with your present marriage. It is not a test, so there are no right or wrong answers. Answer each item as carefully and as accurately as you can by placing a number beside each one as follows:

1. Rarely or none of the time.
2. A little of the time.
3. Sometimes.
4. Good part of the time.
5. Most or all of the time.

Please begin.

1. I feel that my spouse is affectionate enough. ___
2. I feel that my spouse treats me badly. ___
3. I feel that my spouse really cares for me. ___
4. I feel that I would not marry the same person if I had to do it over ___
5. I feel that I can trust my spouse. ___
6. I feel that our marriage is breaking up. ___
7. I feel that my spouse doesn't understand me. ___
8. I feel that our marriage is a good one. ___
9. I feel that ours is a very happy marriage. ___
10. I feel that our life together is dull. ___
11. I feel that we have a lot of fun together. ___
12. I feel that my spouse doesn't confide in me. ___
13. I feel that ours is a very close relationship. ___
14. I feel that I cannot rely on my spouse. ___
15. I feel that we do not have enough interests in common. ___
16. I feel that we manage arguments and disagreements very well. ___
17. I feel that we do a good job of managing our finances. ___
18. I feel that I should never have married my spouse. ___
19. I feel that my spouse and I get along very well together. ___
20. I feel that our marriage is very stable. ___
21. I feel that my spouse is pleased with me as a sex partner. ___
22. I feel that we should do more things together. ___
23. I feel that the future looks bright for our marriage. ___
24. I feel that our marriage is empty. ___
25. I feel there is no excitement in our marriage. ___

Items to reverse score: 1, 2, 5, 8, 9, 11, 13, 16, 17, 19, 20, 21, 23.

Source: Simmons, T (1986). Child Sexual Abuse: An assessment process. © London: NSPCC. Reproduced with permission.

226

MARITAL COMPARISON LEVEL INDEX (MCLI)

DESCRIPTION: The MCLI is a 32-item instrument designed to measure an individual's perception of the degree to which his or her marital relationship is living up to his or her expectations. The MCLI can be viewed as a global assessment of the respondent's complaints about his or her marital relationship. It is based on the notion that one complains about some aspect of the marriage only when that aspect fails to meet one's expectations. The items were initially generated from theory based on comprehensive review of the marital satisfaction/adjustment literature. Through factor analysis, with the elimination of four items, the MCLI was found to be unidimensional. In order to assess marital outcomes relative to expectations, each item was scored on a 7-point scale with the midpoint on the scale reflecting the respondent's expectation level. This allows respondents to indicate the degree to which their relationship outcomes fall above or below expectations.

SCORING: The MCLI is scored by assigning 1 point to an answer of −3, 4 points when a person circled "0" (the midpoint), and 7 when a person circled +3. The individual item scores are then summed with higher scores indicating more favorable evaluation of outcomes relative to expectations.

PRIMARY REFERENCE: Sabatelli, R. M. (1984). The Marital Comparison Level Index: A measure for assessing outcomes relative to expectations, *Journal of Marriage and the Family*, 46, 651–662. Instrument reproduced with permission of Ronald M. Sabatelli.

Indicate by circling the appropriate number how your current experiences compare to your expectations.

	Worse than I expect			About what I expect			Better than I expect	
	−3	−2	−1	0	+1	+2	+3

1. The amount of companionship you experience   −3 −2 −1 0 +1 +2 +3
2. The amount your partner is trusting of you   −3 −2 −1 0 +1 +2 +3
3. The amount of sexual activity that you experience   −3 −2 −1 0 +1 +2 +3
4. The amount of confiding that occurs between you and your spouse   −3 −2 −1 0 +1 +2 +3
5. The amount of conflict over daily decisions that exists   −3 −2 −1 0 +1 +2 +3
6. The amount of time you spend together   −3 −2 −1 0 +1 +2 +3
7. The amount of affection your partner displays   −3 −2 −1 0 +1 +2 +3
8. The amount of the responsibility for household tasks is shared   −3 −2 −1 0 +1 +2 +3
9. The amount your partner is willing to listen to you   −3 −2 −1 0 +1 +2 +3
10. The amount of relationship equality you experience   −3 −2 −1 0 +1 +2 +3
11. The amount of conflict over money you experience   −3 −2 −1 0 +1 +2 +3
12. The amount of compatibility that you experience   −3 −2 −1 0 +1 +2 +3
13. The amount of conflict over the use of leisure time that you experience   −3 −2 −1 0 +1 +2 +3
14. The amount of disagreement over friends that you experience   −3 −2 −1 0 +1 +2 +3
15. The amount of interest in sex your partner expresses   −3 −2 −1 0 +1 +2 +3
16. The fairness with which money is spent   −3 −2 −1 0 +1 +2 +3
17. The amount of criticism your partner expresses   −3 −2 −1 0 +1 +2 +3
18. The amount of mutual respect you experience   −3 −2 −1 0 +1 +2 +3
19. The degree to which your interpersonal communications are effective   −3 −2 −1 0 +1 +2 +3
20. The amount of love you experience   −3 −2 −1 0 +1 +2 +3
21. The degree to which your needs are met   −3 −2 −1 0 +1 +2 +3
22. The amount of freedom you experience in pursuing other friendships   −3 −2 −1 0 +1 +2 +3
23. The amount of responsibility your partner accepts for household chores   −3 −2 −1 0 +1 +2 +3
24. The amount that you and your partner discuss sex   −3 −2 −1 0 +1 +2 +3
25. The amount of privacy you experience   −3 −2 −1 0 +1 +2 +3
26. The amount to which your spouse supports your choice of an occupation   −3 −2 −1 0 +1 +2 +3
27. The amount to which you and your spouse agree on your life-style   −3 −2 −1 0 +1 +2 +3
28. The amount to which you and your spouse agree on the number of children to have   −3 −2 −1 0 +1 +2 +3
29. The degree of physical attractiveness of your partner   −3 −2 −1 0 +1 +2 +3
30. The amount of arguing over petty issues that you experience   −3 −2 −1 0 +1 +2 +3
31. The amount of jealousy your partner expresses   −3 −2 −1 0 +1 +2 +3
32. The amount of commitment you experience from your spouse   −3 −2 −1 0 +1 +2 +3

Eysenck Inventory of Attitudes to Sex

Age: _____ Sex: _____
Married/Single/Some Form of Permanent or Semi-Permanent Union (underline correct response)

This questionnaire is anonymous, to encourage truthful answers.

Read each statement carefully, then underline or circle the 'yes' or 'no' answer, depending on your views. If you cannot decide, under the '?' reply. Please answer every question. There are no right or wrong answers. Don't think too long over each question; try to give an immediate answer which represents your feeling on each issue. Some questions are similar to others; there are good reasons for getting at the same attitude in slightly different ways.

No.	Statement		?		M[a]	F
1	The opposite sex will respect you more if you are not too familiar with them	Yes	?	No	45	48
2	Sex without love ('impersonal sex') is highly satisfactory	Agree	?	Disagree	43	6
3	Conditions have to be just right to get me excited sexually	Yes	?	No	15	42
4	All in all I am satisfied with my sex life	Yes	?	No	64	70
5	Virginity is a girl's most valuable possession	Yes	?	No	8	12
6	I think only rarely of sex	Agree	?	Disagree	5	12
7	Sometimes it has been a problem to control my sex feelings	Yes	?	No	50	38
8	Masturbation is unhealthy	Yes	?	No	4	4
9	If I love a person I could do anything with them	Yes	?	No	69	61
10	I get pleasant feelings from touching my sexual parts	Yes	?	No	81	66
11	I have been deprived sexually	Yes	?	No	22	15
12	It is disgusting to see animals having sex relations in the street	Yes	?	No	5	6
13	(M) I do not need to respect a woman, or love her, in order to enjoy petting and/or intercourse with her (F) I do not need to respect a man, in order to enjoy petting and/or intercourse with him	Yes	?	No	43	26
14	I am sexually rather unattractive	Yes	?	No	10	6
15	Frankly, I prefer people of my own sex	Yes	?	No	4	3
16	Sex contacts have never been a problem to me	True	?	False	32	49
17	It is disturbing to see necking in public	Yes	?	No	12	13
18	Sexual feelings are sometimes unpleasant to me	True	?	False	6	11
19	Something is lacking in my sex life	True	?	False	35	30
20	My sex behavior has never caused me any problems	Yes	?	No	54	57
21	My love life has been disappointing	Yes	?	No	24	20
22	I never had many dates	True	?	False	45	25
23	I consciously try to keep sex thoughts out of my mind	Yes	?	No	3	4
24	I have felt guilty about sex experiences	Yes	?	No	34	36
25	It wouldn't bother me if the person I married were not a virgin	True	?	False	78	83
26	At times I have been afraid of myself for what I might do sexually	Yes	?	No	16	17
27	I have had conflicts about my sex feelings towards a person of my own sex	Yes	?	No	20	14
28	I have many friends of the opposite sex	Yes	?	No	56	68
29	I have strong sex feelings but when I get a chance I can't seem to express myself	Yes	?	No	17	19
30	It doesn't take much to get me excited sexually	True	?	False	75	44
31	My parents' influence has inhibited me sexually	Yes	?	No	29	35
32	Thoughts about sex disturb me more than they should	True	?	False	9	5
33	People of my own sex frequently attract me	Yes	?	No	5	10
34	There are some things I would not want to do with anyone	True	?	No		61
35	Children should be taught about sex	True	?	False	50	53
36	I understand homosexuals	Yes	?	No	96	97
37	I think about sex almost everyday	Yes	?	No	57	53
38	One should not experiment with sex before marriage	Agree	?	Disagree	7	8
39	I get excited sexually very easily	Yes	?	No	68	40
40	The thought of a sex orgy is disgusting to me	True	?	False	15	40
41	It is better not to have sex relations until you are married	True	?	False	10	12
42	I find the thought of a colored sex partner particularly exciting	Yes	?	No	32	11
43	I like to look at sexy pictures	Yes	?	No	80	45
44	My conscience bothers me too much	Yes	?	No	13	20
45	My religious beliefs are against sex	Yes	?	No	1	4
46	Sometimes sexual feelings overpower me	Yes	?	No	25	27
47	I feel nervous with the opposite sex	Yes	?	No	20	11
48	Sex thoughts drive me almost crazy	Yes	?	No	7	3
49	When I get excited I can think of nothing else but satisfaction	Yes	?	No	24	31
50	I feel ill at ease with people of the opposite sex	True	?	No	76	83
51	I don't like to be kissed	False	?		3	5
52	It is hard to talk with people of the opposite sex	No	?		8	6
53	I didn't learn the facts of life until I was quite old	True	?	False	31	35
54	I feel more comfortable when I am with my own sex	Yes	?	No	14	10
55	I enjoy petting	Yes	?	No	95	88
56	I worry a lot about sex	Yes	?	No	7	10
57	The Pill should be universally available	Yes	?	No	85	81
58	Seeing a person nude doesn't interest me	True	?	False	6	28
59	Sometimes thinking about sex makes me very nervous	Yes	?	No	11	11
60	I am embarrassed to talk about sex	Yes	?	No	24	15
61	Perverted thoughts have sometimes bothered me	Yes	?	No	6	6
62	Young people should learn about sex through their own experience	Yes	?	No	39	31
63	Sometimes the woman should be sexually aggressive	Yes	?	No	95	88
64	Sex jokes disgust me	Yes	?	No	7	10
65	I believe in taking my pleasures where I find them	Yes	?	No	34	19
66	A person should learn about sex gradually by experimenting with it	Yes	?	No	58	59
67	Young people should be allowed out at night without being too closely checked	Yes	?	No	69	54
68	I have sometimes felt like humiliating my sex partner	Yes	?	No	22	16
69	I would particularly protect my children from contacts with sex	Yes	?	No	6	12
70	Self-relief is not dangerous as long as it is done in a healthy way	Yes	?	No	84	80
71	(M) I get very excited when touching a woman's breast (F) I get very excited when men touch my breasts	Yes	?	No	74	60
72	I have been involved with more than one sex affair at the same time	Yes	?	No	42	33
73	Homosexuality is normal for some people	Yes	?	No	87	87
74	It is all right to seduce a person who is old enough to know what they are doing	Yes	?	No	67	58
75	I have sometimes felt hostile to my sex partner	Yes	?	No	54	59
76	I like to look at pictures of nudes	Yes	?	No	84	44
77	If I had a chance to see people making love, without being seen, I would take it	Yes	?	No	67	37
78	Pornographic writings should be more freely allowed to be published	Yes	?	No	74	55
79	Prostitution should be legally permitted	Yes	?	No	82	63
80	Decisions about abortion should be the concern of no one but the woman concerned	Yes	?	No	56	68
81	There are too many immoral plays on T.V.	Yes	?	No	9	11
82	The dual standard of morality, allowing men greater freedom, is natural, and should be continued	Yes	?	No	19	14
83	We should do away with marriage entirely	Yes	?	No	8	8
84	I had some bad experiences when I was young	Yes	?	No	13	20
85	There should be no censorship, on sexual grounds, of plays and films	Agree	?	Disagree	73	53
86	Sex is far and away my greatest pleasure	Yes	?	No	35	26
87	Sexual permissiveness threatens to undermine the entire foundation of civilized society	Yes	?	No	9	14
88	Sex should be used for the purpose of reproduction, not for personal pleasure	True	?	False	0	1
89	Absolute faithfulness to one partner throughout life is nearly as silly as celibacy	Yes	?	No	41	28

No.	Statement				M	F
90	I prefer to have intercourse under the bedcovers and with the lights off	Yes	?	No	7	13
91	The present preoccupation with sex in our society has been largely created by films, newspapers, television and advertising	True	?	False	45	54
92	I would enjoy watching my usual partner having intercourse with someone else.	Yes	?	No	18	6
93	Sex play among young children is quite harmless	Yes	?	No	78	74
94	Females do not have such strong sexual desire as males	True	?	False	17	22
95	I would vote for a law that permitted polygamy	Yes	?	No	31	11
96	Even though one is having regular intercourse, masturbation is good for a change	Yes	?	No	55	39
97	I would prefer to have a new sex partner every night	Yes	?	No	7	2
98	I only get sexually aroused at night; never in the daytime	Yes	?	No	1	3
99	I prefer partners who are several years older than myself	Yes	?	No	6	25
100	My sexual fancies often involve flogging	Yes	?	No	9	6
101	I make lots of vocal noises during intercourse	Yes	?	No	26	53
102	Sex is more exciting with a stranger	Yes	?	No	21	7
103	I could never discuss sex with my parents	True	?	False	64	60
104	There are some things I only do to please my sex partner	True	?	False	45	47
105	I don't always know for sure when I have had an orgasm	True	?	False	3	23
106	To me few things are more important than sex	True	?	False	44	26
107	I am very keen on babies	Yes	?	No	29	45
108	My sex partner satisfies all my physical needs completely	Yes	?	No	44	57
109	Sex is not all that important to me	Yes	?	False	11	19
110	Most men are sex-mad	True	?	False	12	16
111	Being good in bed is terribly important to my marriage	True	?	No	57	60
112	I enjoy very lengthy precoital love play	Yes	?	No	69	70
113	(M) I find it easy to tell my sex partner what I like or don't like about her love-making	Yes	?	No	65	66
	(F) I find it easy to tell my sex partner what I like, or don't like about his love-making					
114	I would like my sex partner to be more expert and experienced	Yes	?	No	39	29
115	To me, psychological factors in my sex partner are more important than physical ones	Yes	?	No	55	63
116	I sometimes feel like scratching and biting my partner during intercourse	Yes	?	No	53	67
117	No one has ever been able to satisfy me sexually	True	?	False	5	7
118	I feel sexually less competent than my friends	Yes	?	No	11	11
119	Group sex appeals to me	Yes	?	No	33	10
120	The thought of an illicit relationship excites me	Yes	?	No	52	32
121	I usually feel aggressive with my sexual partner	Yes	?	No	24	18
122	I believe my sexual activities are average	Yes	?	No	66	72
123	It disturbs me to look at sexy photographs	Yes	?	No	8	10
124	I am afraid of sexual relationships	Yes	?	No	6	7
125	(M) I often wish that women would be more forthcoming sexually	Yes	?	No	69	14
	(F) I often wish that men would be less demanding sexually					
126	I can't stand people touching me	Yes	?	No	6	7
127	Physical sex is the most important part of marriage	True	?	False	21	20
128	I prefer my partner to dictate the rules of the sexual game	Yes	?	No	9	37
129	I find 'straight sex' unsatisfactory	True	?	False	19	21
130	I always make love in the nude	Yes	?	No	38	38

No.	Statement				M	F
131	Physical attraction is extremely important to me	Yes	?	No	63	56
132	In a sexual union, tenderness is the most important quality	Yes	?	No	53	58
133	(M) Female genitals are aesthetically unpleasing	Agree	?	Disagree	13	17
134	I object to four-letter swear words being used in mixed company	Yes	?	No	41	41
135	The idea of 'wife swapping' is extremely distasteful to me	True	?	False	37	63
136	Romantic love is just puerile illusion	Yes	?	No	16	15
137	The need for birth control upsets my love-making because it makes everything so cold-blooded and planned	Yes	?	No	16	13
138	I love physical contact with members of the opposite sex	Yes	?	No	83	58
139	(M) I cannot discuss sexual matters with my wife (or habitual sex partner)	True	?	False	3	5
	(F) I cannot discuss sexual matters with my husband (or habitual sex partner)					
140	People who attend 'strip-tease' shows are sexually abnormal	Yes	?	No	5	8
141	The naked human body is a pleasing sight	Yes	?	No	90	81
142	I can take sex and I can leave it alone	True	?	False	41	55
143	I think taking the 'Pill' for any length of time is dangerous to a woman's health	Yes	?	No	26	44
144	(M) It would not disturb me overmuch if my sex partner had sexual relations with someone else, as long as she returned to me	Yes	?	No	36	32
	(F) It would not disturb me overmuch if my sex partner had sexual relations with someone else, as long as he returned to me					
145	(M) Men are more selfish in their love-making than women	True	?	False	55	39
	(F) Women are more selfish in their love-making than men					
146	Some forms of love-making are disgusting to me	Yes	?	No	15	30
147	It is right that man should be the dominant partner in a sex relationship	Yes	?	No	29	43
148	Women often use sex to gain all sorts of advantages	Yes	?	No	59	68
149	The reading of 'girlie' magazines suggests failure to achieve adult attitudes to sex	Yes	?	No	22	29
150	In matters of sex, women always seem to come off second-best	Yes	?	No	20	20

Please underline the correct answer

No.	Statement	M	F
151	If you were invited to see a 'blue' film would you: (a) Accept (b) Refuse	85	72
152	If you were offered a highly pornography book, would you: (a) Accept it (b) Reject it	86	72
153	If you were invited to take part in an orgy, would you: (a) Take part (b) Refuse	48	17
154	Ideally, would you prefer to have intercourse: (a) Never (b) Once a month (c) Once a week (d) Twice a week (e) 3-5 times a week (f) Every day (g) More than once a day	3-5[b]	
155a	(M) Have you ever suffered from impotence: (a) Never (b) Once or twice (c) Several times (d) Often (e) More often than not (f) Always	1-2[b]	
155a	(F) Have you ever suffered from frigidity: (a) Never (b) Once or twice (c) Several times (d) Often (e) More often than not (f) Always		1-2[b]
155b	(M) Have you ever suffered from ejaculatio praecox (premature ejaculation)? (a) Very often (b) Often (c) Middling (d) Not very often (e) Hardly ever (f) Always	d[b]	

ATTITUDES TO OFFENDING

The purpose is to chart changes in attitude and it is based upon statements and assumptions made about sex offenders in relevant theory. It gives an impressionistic view of beliefs and values held by the offender and enables those to be examined in subsequent exercises. The offender is asked to read a list of statements and indicate strong agreement, agreement, uncertainty, disagreement or strong disagreement with each. Each statement is explained and the supervisor may answer questions of clarification. Statements are as follows:

Sex offenders abuse their power

Sex offences do not happen by accident

Sex offences are not committed on the spur of the moment

Victims are in no way responsible for what happens to them

Sex offenders have distorted fantasies and thoughts

Sex offenders have distorted views of gender and sexuality

Sex offenders believe that circumstances are partly to blame for their behaviour

Sex offenders believe that factors beyond their control are partly to blame for their behaviour

Sex offenders believe the victim is partly to blame for their behaviour

Sex offenders commit more offences than they admit to

Sex offenders convince themselves that what they have done is all right

Sex offenders deny the full extent of their offending

Sex offenders make excuses for their offending

Sex offenders lie about their offending

Sex offenders justify their offending

Sex offenders minimise their offending

Sex offenders feel they suffer as much as the victim

Sex offenders rehearse and plan offences

Sex offenders often progress to more serious offences

When caught, sex offenders believe they will never offend again

Sex offenders do not believe that they do much harm

Sex offenders believe they can stop offending whenever they choose

Sex offenders enjoy offending

Sex offenders do not want to stop offending

Sex offenders do not consider stopping if they are not caught

Reproduced with the permission of the author. Source: Garrison K (1992) Working with sex offenders: A practice guide. Social work monographs 112: Norwich: UAE. © Keith Garrison.

		M	F
155b	(F) Do you usually have orgasm during intercourse:		
	(a) Very often		
	(b) Often		
	(c) Middling		
	(d) Not very often		
	(e) Hardly ever		
	(f) Never		
156	At what age did you have your first intercourse (if virgin, leave blank)	19.84	19.52
157	Rate the habitual strength of your sexual desire from 10 (absolutely overwhelming and all embracing) to 1 (very weak and almost nonexistent). Rating _____	7.33	6.82
158	Rate the strength of the influences that inhibit you sexually (moral, aesthetic, religious, etc.) from 10 (terribly strong, completely inhibiting) to 1 (very weak, and almost non-existent). Rating: _____	2.58	2.95

The following eight items are included in the short form of the scale:

1. It is all right for children to see their parents naked.
2. It wouldn't bother me if the person I married were not a virgin.
3. I had some bad experiences when I was young.
4. Perverted thoughts have sometimes bothered me.
5. I could get sexually excited at any time of the day or night.
6. Women who get raped are partly responsible themselves.
7. Buttocks excite me.
8. Men marry to have intercourse; women have intercourse for the sake of marriage.

[a] Percentage of males and females in the Eysenck (1976) sample who answered yes to each item.
[b] The most common answer.

DESCRIPTION: The lengthy version consists of 158 questions, devised to test a number of hypotheses concerning the relation between sexuality and personality—including marital satisfaction, sexual abnormalities and masculinity-femininity.

Most of the questions are of the *yes no* variety, but some have to be answered by endorsing *agree* or *disagree*, or *true or false*, or in other ways. The instrument is applicable to all types of population, as the wording is simple, and should be intelligible to anyone who can read. It takes from 20 minutes to an hour to complete the instrument, depending on intelligence, reading speed, etc.

SCORING: The details can be located in Eysenck, H. J. (1976). Sex and personality. London: Open Books.

REFERENCE: Reprinted from Davis, C. M., Yarber, W. I. and Davis, S. L. (1988). Sexuality-related measures: a compendium. Iowa: Graphic Publishing Company, pp. 28–34—with the permission of the author.

BURT RAPE SCALES

For the statements which follow, please circle the number that best indicates your opinion - what you believe:

Scale: 1 = STRONGLY DISAGREE, 2 = DISAGREE SOMEWHAT, 3 = DISAGREE SLIGHTLY, 4 = NEUTRAL, 5 = AGREE SLIGHTLY, 6 = AGREE SOMEWHAT, 7 = AGREE STRONGLY

Sex role satisfaction

How satisfied are you with:

Statement	1	2	3	4	5	6	7
your sympathy and understanding for others	1	2	3	4	5	6	7
your competence and skilfulness	1	2	3	4	5	6	7
the amount of socialising you do	1	2	3	4	5	6	7
the amount of money you earn	1	2	3	4	5	6	7
your independence and ability to make decisions by yourself	1	2	3	4	5	6	7
your participation in sports and athletic activities	1	2	3	4	5	6	7
your ability to express you emotions	1	2	3	4	5	6	7
your initiative or "get-up-and-go"	1	2	3	4	5	6	7
your dependability in times of crisis	1	2	3	4	5	6	7
your attractiveness to the opposite sex	1	2	3	4	5	6	7

Sex role stereotyping

Statement	1	2	3	4	5	6	7
A man should fight when the woman he's with is insulted by another man.	1	2	3	4	5	6	7
It is acceptable for the woman to pay for the date. R	1	2	3	4	5	6	7
A woman should be a virgin when she marries.	1	2	3	4	5	6	7
There is something wrong with a woman who doesn't want to marry and raise a family.	1	2	3	4	5	6	7
A wife should never contradict her husband in public.	1	2	3	4	5	6	7

Statement	1	2	3	4	5	6	7
It is better for a woman to use her feminine charm to get what she wants rather than ask for it outright.	1	2	3	4	5	6	7
It is acceptable for a woman to have a career, but marriage and family should come first.	1	2	3	4	5	6	7
It looks worse for a woman to be drunk than for a man to be drunk.	1	2	3	4	5	6	7
There is nothing wrong with a woman going to a bar alone. R	1	2	3	4	5	6	7

Adversarial sexual beliefs

Statement	1	2	3	4	5	6	7
A woman will only respect a man who will lay down the law to her.	1	2	3	4	5	6	7
Many women are so demanding sexually that a man just can't satisfy them.	1	2	3	4	5	6	7
A man's got to show the woman who's boss right from the start or he'll end up henpecked.	1	2	3	4	5	6	7
Women are usually sweet until they've caught a man, but then they let their true self show.	1	2	3	4	5	6	7
A lot of men talk big, but when it comes down to it, they can't perform well sexually.	1	2	3	4	5	6	7
In a dating relationship a woman is largely out to take advantage of a man.	1	2	3	4	5	6	7
Men are out for only one thing.	1	2	3	4	5	6	7
Most women are sly and manipulating when they are out to attract a man.	1	2	3	4	5	6	7
A lot of women seem to get pleasure in putting men down.	1	2	3	4	5	6	7

Sexual conversation

Statement	1	2	3	4	5	6	7
A woman who initiates a sexual encounter will probably have sex with anybody.	1	2	3	4	5	6	7
A woman shouldn't give in sexually to a man too easily or he'll think she's loose.	1	2	3	4	5	6	7

BURT RAPE MYTH ACCEPTANCE SCALE

DESCRIPTION: This is a 19-item scale measuring the acceptance or rejection of myths about rape. This scale is the equivalent of Abel and Becker's Cognitions Scale; the difference is that the Cognition Scale measures cognitive distortions around child molestation, while the Burt measures cognitive distortions around rape.

SCORING: Items 1—11 are scored on a 7-point scale from "strongly disagree" to "strongly agree." Numbers 12 and 13 are scored on a 7-point scale ranging from "almost none" to "almost all." Items 14 through 19 are scored on a 7-point scale from "never" to "always." The scoring is reversed on item 2 and on items 14—19.

For the statements which follow, please circle the number that best indicates your opinion—what you believe. If you strongly disagree you would answer "1"; if you strongly agree you would answer "7"; if you feel neutral you would answer "4"; and so on.

	Disagree strongly	Disagree Some-what	Disagree slightly	Neutral	Agree slightly	Agree Some-what	Agree strongly
1. A woman who goes to the home or apartment of a man on their first date implies that she is willing to have sex.	1	2	3	4	5	6	7
2. Any female can get raped.	1	2	3	4	5	6	7
3. One reason that women falsely report a rape is that they frequently have a need to call attention to themselves.	1	2	3	4	5	6	7
4. Any healthy woman can successfully resist a rapist if she really wants to.	1	2	3	4	5	6	7
5. When women go around braless or wearing short skirts or tight tops, they are just asking for trouble.	1	2	3	4	5	6	7
6. Women who get raped while hitchhiking get what they deserve.	1	2	3	4	5	6	7
7. A woman who is stuck-up and thinks she is too good to talk to guys on the street deserves to be taught a lesson.	1	2	3	4	5	6	7
8. Many women have an *unconscious* wish to be raped, and may then *unconsciously* set up a situation in which they are likely to be attacked.	1	2	3	4	5	6	7
9. If a woman gets drunk at a party and has intercourse with a man she's just met there, she should be considered "fair game" to other males at the party who wants to have sex with her too, whether she wants to or not.	1	2	3	4	5	6	7
10. In the majority of rapes, the victim is promiscuous or has a bad reputation.	1	2	3	4	5	6	7
11. If a girl engages in necking or petting and she lets things get out of hand and it is her own fault if her partner forces sex on her.	1	2	3	4	5	6	7

	STRONGLY DISAGREE	DISAGREE SOMEWHAT	DISAGREE SLIGHTLY	NEUTRAL	AGREE SLIGHTLY	AGREE SOMEWHAT	AGREE STRONGLY
Men have a biologically stronger sex drive than women.	1	2	3	4	5	6	7
A nice woman will be offended or embarrassed by dirty jokes.	1	2	3	4	5	6	7
Masturbation is a normal sexual activity. **R**	1	2	3	4	5	6	7
People should not have oral sex.	1	2	3	4	5	6	7
I would have no respect for a woman who engages in sexual relationships without any emotional involvement.	1	2	3	4	5	6	7
Having sex during the menstrual period is unpleasant.	1	2	3	4	5	6	7
The primary goal of sexual intercourse should be to have children.	1	2	3	4	5	6	7
Women have the same needs for a sexual outlet as men. **R**	1	2	3	4	5	6	7

Acceptance of interpersonal violence

	STRONGLY DISAGREE	DISAGREE SOMEWHAT	DISAGREE SLIGHTLY	NEUTRAL	AGREE SLIGHTLY	AGREE SOMEWHAT	AGREE STRONGLY
People today should not use "an eye for an eye and a tooth for a tooth" as a rule for living.	1	2	3	4	5	6	7
Being roughed up is sexually stimulating to many women. **R**	1	2	3	4	5	6	7
Many times a woman will pretend she doesn't want to have intercourse because she doesn't want to seem loose, but she's really hoping the man will force her.	1	2	3	4	5	6	7
A wife should move out of the house if her husband hits her. **R**	1	2	3	4	5	6	7
Sometimes the only way a man can get a cold woman turned on is to use force.	1	2	3	4	5	6	7
A man is never justified in hitting his wife. **R**	1	2	3	4	5	6	7

R = reverse before scoring.

Reproduced with permission of Martha Burt. This scale was used in the study described by Burt and Katz (1987) but was not reported in that article. The original item (Burt, 1980) does give these scale items.

HANSON SEX ATTITUDES QUESTIONNAIRES*

Read each statement carefully and circle the answer which best represents your feelings about the statement.

If you completely agree	Circle 5
If you somewhat agree	Circle 4
If you neither agree or disagree	Circle 3
If you somewhat agree	Circle 2
If you completely disagree	Circle 1

Sexual Entitlement

1. A person should have sex when ever it is needed.   1 2 3 4 5
2. Women should oblige men's sexual needs.   1 2 3 4 5
3. Everyone is entitled to sex.   1 2 3 4 5
*4. Sex must be enjoyed by both parties.   1 2 3 4 5
5. Men need sex more than women do.   1 2 3 4 5
6. I have a higher sex drive than most people.   1 2 3 4 5
7. I am often bothered by thoughts of having sex.   1 2 3 4 5
*8. I have no trouble going without sex if my partner is not interested.   1 2 3 4 5
9. A man who is denied sex suffers more than a woman who has sex when she does not want it.   1 2 3 4 5

*Reversed items: i.e., 1=5   2=4   3=3   4=2   5=1

Sexy Children

1. Some children are mature enough to enjoy sex with adults.   1 2 3 4 5
2. An eight year old child can enjoy sex.   1 2 3 4 5
3. Some children like to sexually tease.   1 2 3 4 5
4. Some children are so willing to have sex that it is difficult to stay away from them.   1 2 3 4 5
5. Young boys want sex as much as adult men do.   1 2 3 4 5
6. Young girls want sex as much as adult women do.   1 2 3 4 5
7. Children are often able to understand an adult's needs better than other adults can.   1 2 3 4 5
8. The innocent look of young girls makes them attractive.   1 2 3 4 5
9. The lack of hair makes children's bodies attractive.   1 2 3 4 5
10. Children don't tell others about sexual activity because they do not want it to stop.   1 2 3 4 5
11. A child who does not resist sexual touching really feels OK about being touched.   1 2 3 4 5
12. If a child does not say "no", it means the child wants sex.   1 2 3 4 5

Note: The items should be administered in a random order, preferably mixed with other items. They are shown here as discrete scales for display purposes only.

Hanson RK, Gizzarelli R and Scott S (1994). The attitudes of incest offenders: sexual entitlement and acceptance of sex with children. Criminal Justice and Behaviour 21 (2): 187-202. © 1994 by Sage Publications, Inc. Reprinted by permission of Sage Publications and Ric Hanson.

Please use the following key to answer the next two questions.

	Almost None	A few	Some	About Half	Many	A lot	Almost all

Circle the number that shows what fraction you believe to be true.

12. What percentage of women who report a rape would you say are lying because they are angry and want to get back at the man they accuse?   1   2   3   4   5   6   7

13. What percentage of reported rapes would you guess were merely invented by women who discovered they were pregnant and wanted to protect their own reputation?   1   2   3   4   5   6   7

14. A person comes to you and claims they were raped. How likely would you be to believe their statement if the person were:
15. Your best friend?   1   2   3   4   5   6   7
16. An Indian woman?   1   2   3   4   5   6   7
    A neighborhood woman?   1   2   3   4   5   6   7
17. A young boy?   1   2   3   4   5   6   7
18. A black woman?   1   2   3   4   5   6   7
19. A white woman?   1   2   3   4   5   6   7

SOURCE: Burt, M. R. (1980). Cultural Myths and Supports for Rape. Journal of Personality and Social Psychology, 38(2), 217–230. Copyright © 1980, American Psychological Association. Reprinted with permission.

HANSON SEX ATTITUDES QUESTIONNAIRES*

Read each statement carefully and circle the answer which best represents your feelings about the statement.

If you completely agree	Circle 5
If you somewhat agree	Circle 4
If you neither agree or disagree	Circle 3
If you somewhat agree	Circle 2
If you completely disagree	Circle 1

Sexual Entitlement

1. A person should have sex when ever it is needed.   1 2 3 4 5
2. Women should oblige men's sexual needs.   1 2 3 4 5
3. Everyone is entitled to sex.   1 2 3 4 5
*4. Sex must be enjoyed by both parties.   1 2 3 4 5
5. Men need sex more than women do.   1 2 3 4 5
6. I have a higher sex drive than most people.   1 2 3 4 5
7. I am often bothered by thoughts of having sex.   1 2 3 4 5
*8. I have no trouble going without sex if my partner is not interested.   1 2 3 4 5
9. A man who is denied sex suffers more than a woman who has sex when she does not want it.   1 2 3 4 5

*Reversed items: i.e., 1 = 5   2 = 4   3 = 3   4 = 2   5 = 1

Sexy Children

1. Some children are mature enough to enjoy sex with adults.   1 2 3 4 5
2. An eight year old child can enjoy sex.   1 2 3 4 5
3. Some children like to sexually tease.   1 2 3 4 5
4. Some children are so willing to have sex that it is difficult to stay away from them.   1 2 3 4 5
5. Young boys want sex as much as adult men do.   1 2 3 4 5
6. Young girls want sex as much as adult women do.   1 2 3 4 5
7. Children are often able to understand an adult's needs better than other adults can.   1 2 3 4 5
8. The innocent look of young girls makes them attractive.   1 2 3 4 5
9. The lack of hair makes children's bodies attractive.   1 2 3 4 5
10. Children don't tell others about sexual activity because they do not want it to stop.   1 2 3 4 5
11. A child who does not resist sexual touching really feels OK about being touched.   1 2 3 4 5
12. If a child does not say "no", it means the child wants sex.   1 2 3 4 5

Note. *The items should be administered in a random order, preferably mixed with other items. They are shown here as discrete scales for display purposes only.*

Hanson RK, Gizzarelli R and Scott S (1994). The attitudes of incest offenders: sexual entitlement and acceptance of sex with children. Criminal Justice and Behaviour 21 (2): 187-202. © 1994 by Sage Publications, Inc. Reprinted by permission of Sage Publications and Ric Hanson.

Hanson Sex Attitudes Questionnaires – Scoring Information

Sexual Entitlement

Group	Number	Mean	Standard Deviation
Incest Offenders	50	20.7	8.8
Family Violence	25	16.2	4.6
Non-offenders	25	16.2	5.6

ANOVA $F = 3.9$, df $= 2, 97$, $p < .03$

Proposed interpretation: 9-21 normal range; 22-26 some problems in this area; 27-45 severe problems

Sexy Children

Group	Number	Mean	Standard Deviation
Incest Offenders	50	22.8	11.0
Family Violence	25	18.0	5.0
Non-offenders	25	16.8	9.4

ANOVA $F = 4.7$, df $= 2, 97$, $p < .02$

Proposed interpretation: 12-24 normal range; 25-31 some problems in this area; 32-60 severe problems.

Although the average scores are more reliable than the responses to individual items, the responses to each individual item should also be examined. Agreement with any of the items (except the reversed items) could indicate problematic sexual attitudes.

The results presented above are from Gizzarelli (1993).

Hanson Sex Attitudes Questionnaires – Scales

The Hanson Sex Attitudes Questionnaires were developed to assess attitudes associated with child molesting. The scales were designed to be used with adult or late adolescent males. The *Sexual Entitlement* scale concerns the extent to which the respondent feels compelled and entitled to fulfil his sexual urges. The *Sexy Children* scale addresses the perception of children as sexually attractive and sexually motivated. Gizzarelli (1993) found that incest offenders reported more deviant attitudes on the above scales than did comparison groups of male batterers or community controls. The scales were not significantly correlated with the Marlowe-Crowne Social Desirability Scale (Crowne & Marlowe, 1960), and were internally consistent. Cronbach's alpha was .81 for *Sexual Entitlement* and .92 for *Sexy Children.*

Research on the scale is continuing. For further information about this research contact R. Karl Hanson, Corrections Branch, Ministry Secretariat, Solicitor General Canada, 340 Laurier Avenue West, Ottawa, Canada, K1A 0P8. Telephone: (613) 991 2840.

References

Gizzarelli, R. (1993). *A comparison of male incest offenders with men who present no sexual deviancy and men who are involved with domestic assault.* Unpublished master's thesis, Department of Social Work, York University, Toronto, Ontario, Canada.

Crowne, D.P., & Marlowe, D. (1960). A new scale of social desirability independent of psychopathology. *Journal of Consulting Psychology,* 24, 349-354.

SEXUAL ATTITUDES FOR SELF AND OTHERS QUESTIONNAIRE

DESCRIPTION: The questionnaire allows the respondents to describe their emotional reactions to the idea of themselves or others participating in certain categories of sexual behaviours. Twelve categories of sexual behaviours are explored and the respondent is asked to respond on a scale ranging from 'I feel great about it' to 'I feel repulsed by it.' The questionnaire should take less than 15 minutes to complete.

REFERENCE: Reprinted from Sexuality-related measures: a compendium of C. M. Davis, W. L. Yarber and S. L. Davis, editors and publishers. Reprinted with the permission of Dr Marilyn Story.

Sexual Attitudes for Self and Others Questionnaire

Sexual Attitude Scale

Instructions: Please indicate your feelings about these specific activites, using the following alternative responses.

1—I feel *great* about it
2—I feel *comfortable* about it
3—I feel *neutral* about it
4—I feel *repulsed* about it

Mark the number of the response you prefer in each case on the answer sheet provided. Please also write your sex and the date on the answer sheet. Do not put your name on the answer sheet but write some identification code you will remember in the name space so you may later claim your paper.

I. Using masturbation as a form of sexual outlet:
1) 1 2 3 4 5   for yourself[a]
2) 1 2 3 4 5   for others

II. Mutual masturbation with someone of the opposite sex (An affectionate and tender relationship between the partners is assumed. It is also assumed that there is no danger of venereal disease.):

III. Mutual masturbation with someone of the same sex (An affectionate and tender relationship between the partners is assumed. It is also assumed that there is no danger of venereal disease.):

IV. Sexual intercourse with someone of the opposite sex (An affectionate and tender relationship between the partners is assumed. It is also assumed that there is no danger of venereal disease.):

V. Oral-genital stimulation with someone of the opposite sex (An affectionate and tender relationship between the partners is assumed. It is also assumed that there is no danger of venereal disease.):

VI. Oral-genital stimulation with someone of the same sex (An affectionate and tender relationship between the partners is assumed. It is also assumed that there is no danger of venereal disease.):

VII. Engaging in sex with your partner in the presence of others:

VIII. Three or more people engaging in intercourse and other sexual activity together:

IX. Maintaining more than one sexual relationship at a given time:

X. The woman in a heterosexual relationship being the more aggressive partner at times:

XI. Using erotica (erotic literature, pictures, films, live sex shows) to stimulate sexual arousal:

XII. Intercourse during the menstrual flow:

25. Abortion is an acceptable means of terminating an unwanted pregnancy.
agree–disagree—Mark number one on the answer sheet for *agree* or mark number two for *disagree*.

[a]These options are repeated for Items II–XII.

Hanson Sex Attitudes Questionnaires – Scoring Information

Sexual Entitlement

Group	Number	Mean	Standard Deviation
Incest Offenders	50	20.7	8.8
Family Violence	25	16.2	4.6
Non-offenders	25	16.2	5.6

ANOVA F = 3.9, df = 2, 97, p < .03

Proposed interpretation: 9-21 normal range; 22-26 some problems in this area; 27-45 severe problems

Sexy Children

Group	Number	Mean	Standard Deviation
Incest Offenders	50	22.8	11.0
Family Violence	25	18.0	5.0
Non-offenders	25	16.8	9.4

ANOVA F = 4.7, df = 2, 97, p < .02

Proposed interpretation: 12-24 normal range; 25-31 some problems in this area; 32-60 severe problems.

Although the average scores are more reliable than the responses to individual items, the responses to each individual item should also be examined. Agreement with any of the items (except the reversed items) could indicate problematic sexual attitudes.

The results presented above are from Gizzarelli (1993).

Hanson Sex Attitudes Questionnaires – Scales

The Hanson Sex Attitudes Questionnaires were developed to assess attitudes associated with child molesting. The scales were designed to be used with adult or late adolescent males. The *Sexual Entitlement* scale concerns the extent to which the respondent feels compelled and entitled to fulfil his sexual urges. The *Sexy Children* scale addresses the perception of children as sexually attractive and sexually motivated. Gizzarelli (1993) found that incest offenders reported more deviant attitudes on the above scales than did comparison groups of male batterers or community controls. The scales were not significantly correlated with the Marlowe-Crowne Social Desirability Scale (Crowne & Marlowe, 1960), and were internally consistent. Cronbach's alpha was .81 for *Sexual Entitlement* and .92 for *Sexy Children*.

Research on the scale is continuing. For further information about this research contact R. Karl Hanson, Corrections Branch, Ministry Secretariat, Solicitor General Canada, 340 Laurier Avenue West, Ottawa, Canada, K1A 0P8. Telephone: (613) 991 2840.

References

Gizzarelli, R. (1993). *A comparison of male incest offenders with men who present no sexual deviancy and men who are involved with domestic assault.* Unpublished master's thesis, Department of Social Work, York University, Toronto, Ontario, Canada.

Crowne, D.P., & Marlowe, D. (1960). A new scale of social desirability independent of psychopathology. *Journal of Consulting Psychology.* 24. 349-354.

DYSFUNCTIONAL ATTITUDE SCALE (DAS)

DESCRIPTION: The DAS is a 40-item instrument designed to identify cognitive distortions—particularly the distortions that may underlie or cause depression. Based on the cognitive theory model of Aaron Beck, the items on the DAS were constructed so as to represent seven major value systems: approval, love, achievement, perfectionism, entitlement, omnipotence, and autonomy. Two 40-item parallel forms of the DAS which are highly correlated and have roughly the same psychometric properties, were derived from an original pool of 100 items. Although the overall score on the DAS is considered the key measure, practitioners can also examine areas where the respondent is emotionally vulnerable or strong by analyzing responses to specific items. Clinical work can then be directed at correcting the distortions underlying the depression, rather than only at the depressive symptoms per se.

SCORING: The DAS is easily scored by using zeros for items omitted, assigning a score of 1 (on a 7-point scale) to the adaptive end of the scale, and simply summing up the scores on all items. With no items omitted, scores on the DAS range from 40 to 280 with lower scores equaling moe adaptive beliefs (few cognitive distortions).

PRIMARY REFERENCE: Weissman, A. N. (1980). Assessing depressogenic attitudes: A validation study. Paper presented at the 51st Annual Meeting of the Eastern Psychological Association, Hartford, Connecticut. Instrument reproduced with permission of Arlene N. Weissman.

This questionnaire lists different attitudes or beliefs which people sometimes hold. Read *each* statement carefully and decide how much you agree or disagree with the statement.

For each of the attitudes, indicate to the left of the item the number that *best describes how you think*. Be sure to choose only one answer for each attitude. Because people are different, there is no right answer or wrong answer to these statements. Your answers are confidential, so please do not put your name on this sheet.

To decide whether a given attitude is typical of your way of looking at things, simply keep in mind what you are like *most of the time.*

1 = Totally agree
2 = Agree very much
3 = Agree slightly
4 = Neutral
5 = Disagree slightly
6 = Disagree very much
7 = Totally disagree

1. It is difficult to be happy unless one is good looking, intelligent, rich, and creative.
2. Happiness is more a matter of my attitude towards myself than the way other people feel about me.
3. People will probably think less of me if I make a mistake.
4. If I do not do well all the time, people will not respect me.
5. Taking even a small risk is foolish because the loss is likely to be a disaster.
6. It is possible to gain another person's respect without being especially talented at anything.
7. I cannot be happy unless most people I know admire me.
8. If a person asks for help, it is a sign of weakness.
9. If I do not do as well as other people, it means I am a weak person.
10. If I fail at my work, then I am a failure as a person.
11. If you cannot do something well, there is little point in doing it at all.
12. Making mistakes is fine because I can learn from them.
13. If someone disagrees with me, it probably indicates he does not like me.
14. If I fail partly, it is as bad as being a complete failure.
15. If other people know what you are really like, they will think less of you.
16. I am nothing if a person I love doesn't love me.
17. One can get pleasure from an activity regardless of the end result.
18. People should have a chance to succeed before doing anything.
19. My value as a person depends greatly on what others think of me.
20. If I don't set the highest standards for myself, I am likely to end up a second-rate person.
21. If I am to be a worthwhile person, I must be the best in at least one way.
22. People who have good ideas are better than those who do not.
23. I should be upset if I make a mistake.

Background Information Sheet

Instructions: Please complete the following information as it applies to you at the present time by marking the number of the correct response in each case on the answer sheet provided. Do not put your name on the answer sheet but write the same identification code in the name space that you wrote on the Sexual Attitude Scale answer sheet.

1. College Classification
   1. freshman
   2. sophomore
   3. junior
   4. senior

2. Marital Status
   1. single and never married
   2. married
   3. divorced
   4. widowed

3. Political Affiliation
   1. democrat
   2. republican
   3. independent
   4. other

4. Religious Affiliation
   1. catholic
   2. protestant
   3. other
   4. none

5. Sex
   1. male
   2. female

6. Social Nudity Behavior
   1. Practice social nudity at nudist clubs and/or free beaches as well as at home
   2. Practice at-home nudity only, being generally nude with my family at home
   3. Practice neither social or at-home nudity

7. Age _____

8. Cumulative Grade Point Average _____

ABEL AND BECKER SEXUAL INTEREST CARD SORT (SICS)

DESCRIPTION: The Sics is a self-report measure of sexual preference or sexual interest. There are 75 items with 5 questions relating to 15 different categories, which include: adult homosexual, adult heterosexual, voyeurism, exhibitionism, frottage, female paedophilia, male paedophilia, female incest, male incest, rape, sadism, masochism, sexual identity female, sexual identity male, and transvestism. The cardsort can also double as a questionnaire, as both have the same system. If used as a cardsort, each item should be typed on a separate index card with the statement on the front and an abbreviation for the category (e.g. HO for adult homosexual) plus a number from 1–5 on the back to facilitate scoring. The top card should contain instructions whereby the respondent reads the item cards and places them on 7 index cards which represent a continuum: ranging from 'highly repulsive', 'slightly repulsive', 'moderately repulsive', 'slightly repulsive', 'neutral', 'slightly arousing', 'moderately arousing', through to 'highly arousing'.

SCORING: After the respondent has completed the task, the cards are scored by placing a number from −3 (highly repulsive) to +3 (highly arousing) in the appropriate box on the scoring form. Each category is then averaged presenting the offender's report of his sexual arousal pattern.

REFERENCE: © 1985 Gene Abel and Judith Becker. Reproduced by permission of both authors.

Instructions: Please *circle the number beside each statement* which best describes how you feel about the statement.

−3 = extremely sexually repulsive	+1 = slightly sexually arousing
−2 = moderately sexually repulsive	+2 = moderately sexually arousing
−1 = slightly sexually repulsive	+3 = extremely sexually arousing
0 = neutral (neither sexually arousing nor sexually repulsive)	

1. A 25 year old man and I are lying side by side touching each other all over.   −3 −2 −1 0 +1 +2 +3

2. I'm peering through a girl's window. She's an attractive brunette with a great figure; she's taking a shower.   −3 −2 −1 0 +1 +2 +3

3. I have an erection. My penis is between an 8 year old girl's legs.   −3 −2 −1 0 +1 +2 +3

4. I'm looking through the partially drawn window shades. I'm watching a woman sleeping. The covers have fallen off her nude body.   −3 −2 −1 0 +1 +2 +3

5. A beautiful woman is stroking my dick and balls as she lays beside me. We are both getting excited.   −3 −2 −1 0 +1 +2 +3

6. I'm standing over a woman I've just beaten up. She's bruised and bleeding. She can't move any more.   −3 −2 −1 0 +1 +2 +3

7. I'm lying on top of my son. I feel his hot body beneath mine as I kiss his back and feel his skin.   −3 −2 −1 0 +1 +2 +3

8. A 10 year old girl and I are lying on the couch. I'm rubbing her soft skin, all over her body. I'm feeling her breasts.   −3 −2 −1 0 +1 +2 +3

9. The subway train is extremely packed. I've really got a stiff hard-on. I'm face to face with a young woman, pushing my dick right up against her. She's trying to move away but she can't.   −3 −2 −1 0 +1 +2 +3

10. I'm pleading with a tall woman to stop hitting me with her belt. The pain is tremendous.   −3 −2 −1 0 +1 +2 +3

11. I'm lying back naked on the bed with my daughter sitting on top of me. I'm stroking her naked body with my hands and pushing my fingers into her cunt.   −3 −2 −1 0 +1 +2 +3

12. I'm pinching a 25 year old woman's breasts with pliers. She's beginning to bleed. She's crying.   −3 −2 −1 0 +1 +2 +3

13. I see two good looking 22 year old girls walking down the street. I drive slowly by with no clothes on, rubbing my penis. I get excited as they look at me with disbelief.   −3 −2 −1 0 +1 +2 +3

14. I followed a 20 year old blonde girl into the parking lot at the public library. I take my dick out and begin to beat it as she sees me and looks tense.   −3 −2 −1 0 +1 +2 +3

---

24. My own opinions of myself are more important than others' opinions of me.
25. To be a good, moral, worthwhile person I must help everyone who needs it.
26. If I ask a question, it makes me look stupid.
27. It is awful to be put down by people important to you.
28. If you don't have other people to lean on, you are going to be sad.
29. I can reach important goals without pushing myself.
30. It is possible for a person to be scolded and not get upset.
31. I cannot trust other people because they might be cruel to me.
32. If others dislike you, you cannot be happy.
33. It is best to give up your own interests in order to please other people.
34. My happiness depends more on other people than it does on me.
35. I do not need the approval of other people in order to be happy.
36. If a person avoids problems, the problems tend to go away.
37. I can be happy even if I miss out on many of the good things in life.
38. What other people think about me is very important.
39. Being alone leads to unhappiness.
40. I can find happiness without being loved by another person.

15. I'm holding a burning cigarette butt against the big tits of a 30 year old brunette. She's screaming for me to stop.   −3 −2 −1 0 +1 +2 +3

16. It's packed in the train and I've pinned a woman up against the people in front of her. I'm rubbing her ass with my hands. She tells me to stop. She can't get away from me. I just keep rubbing her.   −3 −2 −1 0 +1 +2 +3

17. It's very crowded in the subway train. I'm facing a beautiful girl. I'm rubbing her tits and her crotch. She has a blank expression on her face.   −3 −2 −1 0 +1 +2 +3

18. I'm unbuttoning my daughter's blouse. I'm feeling her small tits. She likes it.   −3 −2 −1 0 +1 +2 +3

19. I've pulled an attractive woman to the ground. I've pulled her panties off. I'm forcing my penis in her. She is screaming.   −3 −2 −1 0 +1 +2 +3

20. I'm kneeling beside my son, holding him close to me. I'm kissing his forehead and getting an erection.   −3 −2 −1 0 +1 +2 +3

21. I'm pulling down my little daughter's shorts and underwear. I'm going to fingerfuck her.   −3 −2 −1 0 +1 +2 +3

22. I've forced my way into an apartment. I've forced a brunette to take off her clothes. I'm raping her.   −3 −2 −1 0 +1 +2 +3

23. I'm lying on a deserted beach with a real handsome guy. He has wrapped his arms and legs around me. He really enjoys making love with me.   −3 −2 −1 0 +1 +2 +3

24. I have a hard on. My dick is between the legs of a young boy.   −3 −2 −1 0 +1 +2 +3

25. I would like to be a wife.   −3 −2 −1 0 +1 +2 +3

26. We're in the 69 position with me on top. I'm sucking a young guy's dick as he sucks mine. I'm starting to come.   −3 −2 −1 0 +1 +2 +3

27. A 12 year old girl is sucking my cock. I'm about to come.   −3 −2 −1 0 +1 +2 +3

28. I'm thinking about putting on some sheer nylon tights with no crotch. I'm feeling them in my hands.   −3 −2 −1 0 +1 +2 +3

29. I would like to have a good physique.   −3 −2 −1 0 +1 +2 +3

30. I have a woman spread eagled on the floor. I'm torturing her, burning her fingertips.   −3 −2 −1 0 +1 +2 +3

31. An attractive woman looks surprised as I tell her I'm going to rape her. I make her undress and put my dick between her legs as I hold her down.   −3 −2 −1 0 +1 +2 +3

32. I would like to be a mother.   −3 −2 −1 0 +1 +2 +3

33. I can feel myself getting turned on as my daughter hugs me.   −3 −2 −1 0 +1 +2 +3

34. I would like to be a husband.   −3 −2 −1 0 +1 +2 +3

35. I've broken into a house. No one is home. I've found some women's underclothes and I'm pulling on some cotton panties.   −3 −2 −1 0 +1 +2 +3

36. I would like to wear beautiful, feminine clothes.   −3 −2 −1 0 +1 +2 +3

37. I go by the girls' gym at college and look through the dressing room window. I can see several girls there, all partly undressed.   −3 −2 −1 0 +1 +2 +3

38. I have a hard-on. My dick is between my daughter's legs as I'm ejaculating.   −3 −2 −1 0 +1 +2 +3

39. I feel my partner on top of me, with her knees holding my hips. She is moving up and down on my dick.   −3 −2 −1 0 +1 +2 +3

40. My son is curled up beside me in bed. I'm gently rubbing his small penis; he is getting an erection.   −3 −2 −1 0 +1 +2 +3

41. I've fucked a 25 year old woman. She has come again and again. She is thinking that I'm really great in bed.   −3 −2 −1 0 +1 +2 +3

42. I've gotten my son to rub my cock. I'm getting hard.   −3 −2 −1 0 +1 +2 +3

43. A beautiful woman is pinching my skin with pliers. I'm afraid she's going to pinch my balls with it, too.   −3 −2 −1 0 +1 +2 +3

44. I'm in my sister's bedroom alone. I'm pulling on a pair of beige nylon panties.   −3 −2 −1 0 +1 +2 +3

45. I'm forcing a well-stacked girl to hold still as I push my dick into her. She cries out as I rape her.   −3 −2 −1 0 +1 +2 +3

46. My hands and legs are tied up. The ropes are biting into my skin. A woman in high heeled black boots is coming towards me, snapping a whip in her hand.   −3 −2 −1 0 +1 +2 +3

47. I would like to be a woman.   −3 −2 −1 0 +1 +2 +3

48. I would like to have male genitals.   −3 −2 −1 0 +1 +2 +3

49. A 12 year old boy is sucking my cock. I'm about to come.   −3 −2 −1 0 +1 +2 +3

50. I'm following a woman off the subway train. I move in right hind her as she waits for the next train. The crowd moves forward onto the next train. I start to rub her ass from behind.   −3 −2 −1 0 +1 +2 +3

51. I'm chained to a wall. A woman in tall, black boots is holding a burning cigarette butt close to my nipples. She smiles as she brings the cigarette closer.   −3 −2 −1 0 +1 +2 +3

52. I'm lying face down on the ground. An attractive woman is sitting on my ass, slashing my back with a razor blade. I'm pleading with her to stop. The blood is gushing out.   −3 −2 −1 0 +1 +2 +3

53. A good-looking man is pressing against me as we kiss very tenderly. We hold each other close.   −3 −2 −1 0 +1 +2 +3

54. I am following a nicely built blond, 18 year old girl down the stairs at school. I take my dick out, holding my books in front of it and begin to beat it. As I follow her, I feel it get hard.   −3 −2 −1 0 +1 +2 +3

55. A handsome man is lying on top of me in bed. He has his tongue in my ear and his hand on my dick. I'm really excited.   −3 −2 −1 0 +1 +2 +3

56. I'm wearing a matching bra, panties and slip, all lacy. I'm touching and feeling the underclothes against my body.   −3 −2 −1 0 +1 +2 +3

57. I'm standing naked beside the car. A 20 year old girl in a bikini is coming from the swimming pool. I feel my hard penis in my hand as she sees me and looks shocked.   −3 −2 −1 0 +1 +2 +3

58. I've gotten a young boy to rub my cock. I feel it getting hard.   −3 −2 −1 0 +1 +2 +3

59. I'm sucking my son's small dick. He seems to like it.   −3 −2 −1 0 +1 +2 +3

60. A lovely little boy is curled up beside me in bed. I'm gently rubbing his small penis.   −3 −2 −1 0 +1 +2 +3

61. I've lured a 9 year old girl into the house. She's really good looking. I'm pulling her shorts and underwear down.   −3 −2 −1 0 +1 +2 +3

62. I'm lying on top of my partner. She is digging her hands into my back, lifting her ass up. She is really excited.   −3 −2 −1 0 +1 +2 +3

63. I would like to rape her.   −3 −2 −1 0 +1 +2 +3

64. I would like to have female genitals.   −3 −2 −1 0 +1 +2 +3

65. A 10 year old girl with long blond hair is holding my dick. She seems to be fascinated by it.   −3 −2 −1 0 +1 +2 +3

66. I've got a young woman tied down in the woods. I'm sticking needles into her vagina. She is screaming with terror.   −3 −2 −1 0 +1 +2 +3

67. A girl in the women's bathroom has taken her clothes off. I've pinned her down. I'm starting to rape her.   −3 −2 −1 0 +1 +2 +3

68. I'm lying on a couch, wearing only my feminine underclothes, bright red panties, large-cupped bra, sheer hose, and a see-through slip.   −3 −2 −1 0 +1 +2 +3

69. At an apartment complex a 25 year old girl is just dressed in her panties. I'm looking at her through the window.   −3 −2 −1 0 +1 +2 +3

70. I'm looking from my upstairs window down into the apartment across the way. I can see a woman with big tits reading with a see-through negligee on.   −3 −2 −1 0 +1 +2 +3

71. I've walked out of the field house shower so a young girl can see me. The 13 year old girl is surprised as she looks at my penis.   −3 −2 −1 0 +1 +2 +3

238

72. My partner and I are in the bath tub. She is sitting between
my legs, leaning back against me. I'm playing with her tits.   −3 −2 −1   0 +1 +2 +3
73. I would like to be a man.   −3 −2 −1   0 +1 +2 +3
74. There are very few people on the suburban train. I sit down
next to an attractive woman and let my hand fall down into
her crotch. I start to rub her.   −3 −2 −1   0 +1 +2 +3
75. A 10 year old boy with soft dark hair is holding my dick. He
seems to be fascinated by it.   −3 −2 −1   0 +1 +2 +3

SCORING

After the subject has completed the task, the cards are turned over and scored by placing a number from −3 ("highly repulsive") to +3 ("highly arousing") in the appropriate box on the scoring form. (See attached scoring form.) Each category score is then averaged presenting the offender's report of his sexual arousal pattern. (See attached scoring summary.)

Name _____
Date _____

Means

Columns: Ho He V E F Hol Hel HoP HeP T S M R MSI FSI

Graph rows:
Sexually Arousing +3
+2
+1
Neutral 0
−1
−2
Sexually Repulsive −3

Categories (graph): Adult Homosexual, Adult Heterosexual, Voyeurism, Exhibitionism, Frottage, Homosexual Incest, Heterosexual Incest, Homosexual Pedophilia, Heterosexual Pedophilia, Transvestism, Sadism, Masochism, Rape, Male Sexual Identity, Female Sexual Identity

ABEL Card Sort Graph Scoring Summary

Name _____
Date _____

CARDS

CATEGORIES

CATEGORIES	1	2	3	4	5	X̄
Adult Homosexual (Ho)						
Adult Heterosexual (He)						
Voyeurism (V)						
Exhibitionism (E)						
Frottage (F)						
Homosexual Incest (Hol)						
Heterosexual Incest (Hel)						
Homosexual Pedophilia (HoP)						
Heterosexual Pedophilia (HeP)						
Transvestism (T)						
Sadism (S)						
Masochism (M)						
Rape (R)						
Male Sexual Identity (MSI)						
Female Sexual Identity (FSI)						

Card Sort Raw Data Scoring Form

GENDER IDENTITY AND EROTIC PREFERENCE IN MALES

KURT FREUND AND RAY BLANCHARD

DESCRIPTION: This questionnaire contains 7 scales: 6 are concerned with the assessment of erotic preference and erotic anomalies, 1 is concerned with the assessment of gender identity. Most of the scales are a mixture of dichotomous and multiple-choice questions.

SCORING: Subjects check one and only one response option for each item. The shortest scale takes only a few minutes to complete; the longest (the full =FGIS) takes about 15 minutes. Subjects are permitted to ask for clarification on any item whose meaning they do not understand. Scoring weights for each response option of each item follow that option in parentheses in the Exhibits. The total scores for each scale (and for the three subscales of the FGIS) are obtained by totalling the subject's scores for each item in that scale (or subscale). For all scales, high scores indicate that the relevant attribute (e.g., sadism, feminine gender identity) is strongly present, and low scores indicate that it is absent.

REFERENCE: © Reprinted from Sexuality-related measures: A compendium of C. M. Davis, W. L. Yarber and S. L. Davis, editors and publishers—with the permission of Ray Blanchard and Clive Davis.

Exhibit 1

Feminine Gender Identity Scale for Males

Part A

1. Between the age of 6 and 12, did you prefer
   a. to play with boys (0)
   b. to play with girls (2)
   c. didn't make any difference (1)
   d. not to play with other children (1)
   e. don't remember

2. Between the ages of 6 and 12, did you
   a. prefer boy's games and toys (soldiers, football, etc.) (0)
   b. prefer girl's games and toys (dolls, cooking, sewing, etc.) (2)
   c. like or dislike both about equally (1)
   d. had no opportunity to play games or with toys (1)

3. In childhood, were you very interested in the work of a garage mechanic? Was this
   a. prior to age 6 (0)
   b. between ages 6 and 12 (0)
   c. probably in both periods (0)
   d. do not remember that I was very interested in the work of a garage mechanic (1)

4. Between the ages of 6 and 14, which did you like more, romantic stories or adventure stories?
   a. liked romantic stories more (2)
   b. liked adventure stories more (0)
   c. it did not make any difference (1)

5. Between the ages of 6 and 12, did you like to do jobs or chores which are usually done by women?
   a. yes (2)
   b. no (0)
   c. don't remember (1)

6. Between the ages of 13 and 16, did you like to do jobs or chores which are usually done by women?
   a. yes (2)
   b. no (0)
   c. don't remember (1)

7. Between the ages of 6 and 12, were you a leader in boys' games or other activities
   a. more often than other boys (0)
   b. less often than other boys (1)
   c. about the same, or don't know (0)
   d. did not partake in children's games and/or other activities (1)

8. Between the ages of 6 and 12, when you read a story did you imagine that you were
   a. the male in the story (cowboy, detective, soldier, explorer, etc.) (0)
   b. the female in the story (the girl being saved, etc.) (2)
   c. the male sometimes and the female other times (1)
   d. neither the male nor the female (1)
   e. did not read stories (1)

9. In childhood or at puberty, did you like mechanics magazines?
   a. between ages 6 and 12 (0)
   b. between ages 12 and 14 (0)
   c. probably in both periods (0)
   d. do not remember that I liked mechanics magazines (1)

10. Between the ages of 6 and 12, did you wish you had been born a girl instead of a boy
    a. often (2)
    b. occasionally (1)
    c. never (0)

11. Between the ages of 13 and 16, did you wish you had been born a girl instead of a boy
    a. often (2)
    b. occasionally (1)
    c. never (0)

12. Since the age of 17, have you wished you had been born a girl instead of a boy
    a. often (2)
    b. occasionally (1)
    c. never (0)

13. Do you think your appearance is
    a. very masculine (0)
    b. masculine (0)
    c. a little feminine (1)
    d. quite feminine (2)

14. In childhood, did you sometimes imagine yourself a well-known sports figure, or did you wish you would become one? Was this
    a. prior to age 6 (0)
    b. between ages 6 and 12 (0)
    c. probably in both periods (0)
    d. do not remember such fantasies (1)

15. In childhood fantasies did you sometimes wish you could go hunting big game? Was this
    a. prior to age 6 (0)
    b. between ages 6 and 12 (0)
    c. probably in both periods (0)
    d. do not remember such fantasies (1)

16. In childhood fantasies did you sometimes imagine yourself as being a policeman or soldier? Was this
    a. prior to age 6 (0)
    b. between ages 6 and 12 (0)
    c. probably in both periods (0)
    d. do not remember that I had such a fantasy (1)

17. In childhood was there ever a period in which you wished you would, when adult, become a dressmaker or dress designer? Was this
    a. prior to age 6 (1)
    b. between ages 6 and 12 (1)
    c. probably in both periods (1)
    d. do not remember having this desire (0)

18. In childhood fantasies did you sometimes imagine yourself driving a racing car? Was this
    a. prior to age 6 (0)
    b. between ages 6 and 12 (0)
    c. probably in both periods (0)
    d. do not remember having this fantasy (1)

19. In childhood did you ever wish to become a dancer? Was this
    a. prior to age 6 (1)
    b. between ages 6 and 12 (1)
    c. probably in both periods (1)
    d. do not remember having this desire (0)

Part B

20. What kind of sexual contact with a male would you have preferred on the whole, even though you may not have done it?
    a. inserting your privates between your partner's upper legs (thighs) (0)
    b. putting your privates into your partner's rear end (0)
    c. you would have preferred one of those two modes but you cannot decide which one (0)
    d. your partner putting his privates between your upper legs (thighs) (1)
    e. your partner putting his privates into your rear end (2)
    f. you would have preferred one of those two latter modes but you cannot decide which one (1)
    g. you would have liked all four modes equally well (1)
    h. you would have preferred some other mode of sexual contact (1)
    i. had no desire for physical contact with males (exclude subject)

Exhibit 2
Androphilia Scale

1. About how old were you when you first made quite strong efforts to see males who were undressed or scantily dressed?
   a. younger than 12 (1)
   b. between 12 and 16 (1)
   c. older than 16 (1)
   d. never (0)

2. About how old were you when you first felt sexually attracted to males?
   a. younger than 6 (1)
   b. between 6 and 11 (1)
   c. between 12 and 16 (1)
   d. older than 16 (1)
   e. never (0)

3. Since what age have you been sexually attracted to males only?
   a. younger than 6 (1)
   b. between 6 and 11 (1)
   c. between 12 and 16 (1)
   d. older than 16 (1)
   e. never (0)

4. Since the age of 16, have you ever fallen in love with a person of the male sex?
   a. yes (1)
   b. no (0)

5. How old were you when you first kissed a male because you felt sexually attracted to him?
   a. younger than 12 (1)
   b. between 12 and 16 (1)
   c. older than 16 (1)
   d. never (0)

6. Since age 12, how old were you when you first touched the privates of a male to whom you felt sexually attracted?
   a. between 12 and 16 (1)
   b. older than 16 (1)
   c. never (0)

7. What kind of sexual contact with a male would you have preferred on the whole, even though you may not have done it?
   a. inserting your privates between your partner's upper legs (thighs) (1)
   b. putting your privates into your partner's rear end (1)
   c. you would have preferred one of those two modes but you cannot decide which one (1)
   d. your partner putting his privates between your upper legs (thighs) (1)
   e. your partner putting his privates into your rear end (1)
   f. you would have preferred one of those two latter modes but you cannot decide which one (1)
   g. you would have liked all four modes equally well (1)
   h. you would have preferred some other mode of sexual contact (1)
   i. had no desire for physical contact with males (0)

8. What qualities did you like in males to whom you were sexually attracted?
   a. strong masculine behavior (1)
   b. slightly masculine behavior (1)
   c. rather feminine behavior (1)
   d. did not feel sexually attracted to males (0)

9. Would you have preferred
   a. male homosexual partners (1)
   b. male partners who were not homosexual (1)
   c. had no preference (1)
   d. did not feel sexually attracted to males (0)

10. Since age 18, how old was the oldest male to whom you could have felt sexually attracted?
    a. younger than 6 (1)
    b. between 6 and 11 (1)
    c. between 12 and 16 (1)
    d. between 17 and 19 (1)
    e. between 20 and 30 (1)
    f. between 31 and 40 (1)
    g. between 41 and 50 (1)
    h. older than 50 (1)
    i. did not feel sexually attracted to males (0)

21. What qualities did you like in males to whom you are sexually attracted?
    a. strong masculine behavior (2)
    b. slightly masculine behavior (1)
    c. rather feminine behavior (0)
    d. did not feel sexually attracted to males (exclude subject)

22. Would you have preferred a partner
    a. who was willing to have you lead him (0)
    b. who was willing to lead you (2)
    c. you didn't care (1)
    d. did not feel sexually attracted to males (exclude subject)

Part C

23. Between the ages of 6 and 12, did you put on women's underwear or clothing
    a. once a month or more, for about a year or more (2)
    b. (less often, but) several times a year for about 3 years or more (1)
    c. very seldom did this during this period (0)
    d. never did this during this period (0)
    e. don't remember (0)

24. Between the ages of 13 and 16, did you put on women's underwear or clothing
    a. once a month or more, for at least a year (2)
    b. (less often, but) several times a year for at least 2 years (1)
    c. very seldom did this during this period (0)
    d. never did this during this period (0)

25. Since the age of 17, did you put on women's underwear or clothing
    a. once a month or more, for at least a year (2)
    b. (less often, but) several times a year for at least 2 years (1)
    c. very seldom did this during this period (0)
    d. never did this during this period (0)

26. Have you ever wanted to have an operation to change you physically into a woman?
    a. yes (2)
    b. no (0)
    c. unsure (1)

27. If you have ever wished to have a female body rather than a male one, was this
    a. mainly to please men but also for your own satisfaction (2)
    b. mainly for your own satisfaction but also to please men (2)
    c. entirely for your own satisfaction (2)
    d. entirely to please men (1)
    e. about equally to please men and for your own satisfaction (2)
    f. have never wanted to have a female body (0)

28. Have you ever felt like a woman
    a. only if you were wearing at least one piece of female underwear or clothing (1)
    b. while wearing at least one piece of female underwear or clothing and only occasionally at other times also (1)
    c. at all times and for at least 1 year (female clothing or not) (2)
    d. never felt like a woman (0)

29. When completely dressed in male clothing (underwear, etc.) would you
    a. have a feeling of anxiety because of this (2)
    b. have no feeling of anxiety but have another kind of unpleasant feeling because of this (2)
    c. have no unpleasant feelings to do with above (0)

Exhibit 4
Heterosexual Experience Scale

1. Since age 13, how old were you when you first kissed a female age 13–40 who seemed to be interested in you sexually?
   a. between the ages 13–16 (1)
   b. between the ages 17–25 (1)
   c. 26 or older (1)
   d. never after age 12 (0)

2. Since age 13, how old were you when you first petted (beyond kissing) with a female age 13–40 who seemed to be interested in you sexually?
   a. between the ages 13–16 (1)
   b. between the ages 17–25 (1)
   c. 26 or older (1)
   d. never after age 12 (0)

3. Have you ever attempted sexual intercourse with a female age 17–40?
   a. yes (1)
   b. no, and you are older than 25 (0)
   c. no, and you are 25 or younger (0)

4. When did you first have sexual intercourse with a female age 17–40?
   a. before age 16 (1)
   b. between 16 and 25 (1)
   c. 26 or older (1)
   d. never, and you are older than 25 (0)
   e. never, and you are 25 or younger (0)

5. When did you first get married or begin living common-law?
   a. before 30 (1)
   b. between 30–40 (1)
   c. age 41 or older (1)
   d. never married or had common-law relations, and you are older than 30 (0)
   e. never, and you are 30 or younger (0)

6. Was there any period of 14 days or less when you had sexual intercourse with a female age 17–40 more than 5 times?
   a. yes (1)
   b. no, and you are older than 25 (0)
   c. no, and you are 25 or younger (0)

Exhibit 5
Fetishism Scale

1. Do you think that certain inanimate objects (velvet, silk, leather, rubber, shoes, female underwear, etc.) have a stronger sexual attraction for you than for most other people?
   a. yes (1)
   b. no (0)

2. Has the sexual attractiveness of an inanimate (not alive) thing ever increased if it had been worn by, or had been otherwise in contact with
   a. a female (1)
   b. a male (1)
   c. preferably a female but also when in contact or having been in contact with a male (1)
   d. preferably a male but also when in contact or having been in contact with a female (1)
   e. a female or male person equally (1)
   f. contact between a person and a thing never increased its sexual attractiveness (1)
   g. do not feel sexually attracted to any inanimate thing (0)

3. Did the sexual attractiveness to you of such a thing ever increase if you wore it or were otherwise in contact with it yourself?
   a. yes (1)
   b. no (1)
   c. have never been sexually attracted to inanimate things (0)

4. Were you ever more strongly sexually attracted by inanimate things than by females or males?
   a. yes (1)
   b. no (0)

---

11. Would you have preferred a partner
    a. who was willing to have you lead him (1)
    b. who was willing to lead you (1)
    c. you didn't care (1)
    d. did not feel sexually attracted to males (0)

12. Since age 16 and up to age 25 (or younger if you are less than 25) how did the preferred age of male partners change as you got older?
    a. became gradually younger (1)
    b. became gradually older (1)
    c. remained about the same (1)
    d. never felt attracted to males (0)

13. Since age 16, have you ever been equally, or more, attracted sexually by a male age 17 and over than by females age 17–40?
    a. yes (1)
    b. no (0)

Exhibit 3
Gynephilia Scale

1. Since the age of 17 when you went dancing, was this to
   a. mainly meet girls at the dance (1)
   b. mainly meet male friends at the dance (0)
   c. mainly because you liked dancing itself (0)
   d. never went dancing since age 17 (0)

2. How old were you when you first tried (on your own) to see females 13 or older naked or dressing or undressing (including strip-tease, movies or pictures)?
   a. younger than 12 (1)
   b. between 12 and 16 (1)
   c. older than 16 (1)
   d. never (0)

3. Since age 13, have you ever fallen in love with or had a crush on a female who was between the ages of 13–40?
   a. yes (1)
   b. no (0)

4. Have you ever desired sexual intercourse with a female age 17–40?
   a. yes (1)
   b. no (0)

5. How do you prefer females age 17–40 to react when you try to come into sexual contact (not necessarily intercourse) with them?
   a. cooperation on the part of the female (1)
   b. indifference (1)
   c. a little resistance (1)
   d. considerable resistance (1)
   e. you don't care (0)
   f. do not try to come into sexual contact with females age 17–40 (0)

6. Do you prefer females of age 17–40
   a. who have no sexual experience (1)
   b. who have had a little experience (1)
   c. who have had considerable experience (1)
   d. you don't care how much experience (1)
   e. not enough interest in females age 17–40 to know (0)

7. Between 13 and 16, when you first saw females 13 or over in the nude (or dressing or undressing) including strip-tease, movies or pictures, did you feel sexually aroused?
   a. very much (1)
   b. mildly (1)
   c. not at all (0)
   d. never saw females 13 or over in the nude, dressing or undressing (including strip-tease, movies or pictures) (0)

8. When you have a wet dream (reach climax while dreaming), do you always, or almost always, dream of a female age 17–40?
   a. yes (1)
   b. no (0)
   c. don't remember any wet dreams (0)

9. In your sexual fantasies, are females age 17–40 always, or almost always involved?
   a. yes (1)
   b. no (0)
   c. haven't had such fantasies (0)

10. Has imagining that you were being threatened with a knife or other sharp instrument ever excited you sexually?
   a. yes (1)   b. no (0)

11. Has imagining that you were being tied up by somebody ever excited you sexually?
   a. yes (1)   b. no (0)

Exhibit 7
Sadism Scale

1. Did you ever like to read stories about or descriptions of torture?
   a. yes (1)   b. no (0)

2. Did you usually re-read a description of torture several times?
   a. yes (1)   c. don't remember (0)
   b. no (0)

3. Were you
   a. very interested in descriptions of torture (1)   c. not at all interested (0)
   b. a little interested (0)   d. never read such descriptions (0)

4. Between the ages of 13 and 16, did you find the sight of blood
   a. exciting (1)   c. unpleasant (0)
   b. only pleasant (1)   d. did not affect you in any way (0)

5. Has beating somebody or imagining that you are doing so ever excited you sexually?
   a. yes (1)   b. no (0)

6. Have you ever tried to tie the hands or legs of a person who attracted you sexually?
   a. yes (1)   b. no (0)

7. Has cutting or imagining to cut someone's hair ever excited you sexually?
   a. yes (1)   b. no (0)

8. Has imagining that you saw someone bleeding ever excited you sexually?
   a. yes (1)   b. no (0)

9. Has imagining someone being choked by yourself or somebody else ever excited you sexually?
   a. yes (1)   b. no (0)

10. Has imagining yourself or someone else imposing heavy physical labor or strain on somebody ever excited you sexually?
   a. yes (1)   b. no (0)

11. Has imagining that someone was being ill-treated in some way by yourself or somebody else ever excited you sexually?
   a. yes (1)   b. no (0)

12. Has imagining that you or someone else were causing pain to somebody ever excited you sexually?
   a. yes (1)   b. no (0)

13. Has imagining that you or somebody else were threatening someone's life ever excited you sexually?
   a. yes (1)   b. no (0)

14. Has imagining that someone other than yourself was crying painfully ever excited you sexually?
   a. yes (1)   b. no (0)

15. Has imagining that someone other than yourself was dying ever excited you sexually?
   a. yes (1)   b. no (0)

---

5. What was the age of persons who most increased the sexual attractiveness for you of a certain inanimate object by their contact with it?
   a. 3 years or younger (1)   g. over 60 years (1)
   b. between 4 and 6 years (1)   h. contact between a person and a thing never increased its sexual attractiveness (1)
   c. between 6 and 11 years (1)   i. have never been sexually attracted to inanimate things (0)
   d. between 12 and 13 years (1)
   e. between 14 and 16 years (1)
   f. between 17 and 40 years (1)

6. Is there more than one kind of inanimate thing which arouses you sexually?
   a. yes (1)   c. have never been sexually attracted to inanimate things (0)
   b. no (1)

7. Through which of these senses did the thing act most strongly?
   a. through the sense of smell (1)   e. through the sense of hearing (1)
   b. through the sense of taste (1)   f. have never been sexually attracted to inanimate objects (0)
   c. through the sense of sight (1)
   d. through the sense of touch (1)

8. At about what age do you remember first having a special interest in an inanimate thing which later aroused you sexually?
   a. younger than 2 (1)   e. between 11 and 13 (1)
   b. between 2 and 4 (1)   g. older than 13 (1)
   c. between 5 and 7 (1)   h. have never been sexually attracted to inanimate objects (0)
   d. between 8 and 10 (1)

Exhibit 6
Masochism Scale

1. If you were insulted or humiliated by a person to whom you felt sexually attracted, did this ever increase their attractiveness?
   a. yes (1)   c. unsure (0)
   b. no (0)

2. Has imagining that you were being humiliated or poorly treated by someone ever excited you sexually?
   a. yes (1)   b. no (0)

3. Has imagining that you had been injured by somone to the point of bleeding ever excited you sexually?
   a. yes (1)   b. no (0)

4. Has imagining that someone was causing you pain ever aroused you sexually?
   a. yes (1)   b. no (0)

5. Has imagining that someone was choking you ever excited you sexually?
   a. yes (1)   b. no (0)

6. Has imagining that you have become dirty or soiled ever excited you sexually?
   a. yes (1)   b. no (0)

7. Has imagining that your life was being threatened ever excited you sexually?
   a. yes (1)   b. no (0)

8. Has imagining that someone was imposing on you heavy physical labor or strain ever excited you sexually?
   a. yes (1)   b. no (0)

9. Has imagining a situation in which you were having trouble breathing ever excited you sexually?
   a. yes (1)   b. no (0)

SEXUAL AROUSABILITY INVENTORY

DESCRIPTION: The SAI is a 28-item instrument designed to measure perceived arousability to a variety of sexual experiences. This instrument was originally designed for use with females. The SAI-E is the same instrument, rated by the respondent on both arousability and anxiety dimensions. This instrument has been used with males and females. The arousability and anxiety dimensions are reported to provide independent information. Both instruments are reproduced here. The SAI has been found to discriminate between a "normal" population and individuals seeking help for sexual functioning and also to be sensitive to therapeutic changes. The SAI-E also can be valuable to helping determine if a client has an arousal or anxiety problem related to sexual dysfunctions. Items 1, 2, 5, 6, 9–12, 14–16, 18, 19, 26 can be used as one short-form version of the SAI, and the remaining items can be used as another short form.

SCORING: Both scales are scored by summing the scores on the individual items and subtracting any —1's.

PRIMARY REFERENCE: Hoon, E. F. and Chambless, D. (1986). Sexual Arousability Inventory (SAI) and Sexual Arousability Inventory—Expanded (SAI-E). In C. M. Davis and W. L. Yarber (eds.), Sexuality-Related Measures: A Compendium, Syracuse: Graphic Publishing Co. Instrument reproduced with permission of Emily Franck Hoon.

Sexual Arousability Inventory

Instructions: The experiences in this inventory may or may not be sexually arousing to you. There are no right or wrong answers. Read each item carefully, and then circle the number which indicates how sexually aroused you feel when you have the described experience, or how sexually aroused you think you would feel if you actually experienced it. *Be sure to answer every item.* If you aren't certain about an item, circle the number that seems about right. Rate feelings of arousal according to the scale below.

—1 adversely affects arousal; unthinkable, repulsive, distracting
0 doesn't affect sexual arousal
1 possibly causes sexual arousal
2 sometimes causes sexual arousal; slightly arousing
3 usually causes sexual arousal; moderately arousing
4 almost always sexually arousing; very arousing
5 always causes sexual arousal; extremely arousing

How you feel or think you would feel if you were actually involved in this experience

1. When a loved one stimulates your genitals with mouth and tongue	—1	0	1	2	3	4	5
2. When a loved one fondles your breasts with his/her hands	—1	0	1	2	3	4	5
3. When you see a loved one nude	—1	0	1	2	3	4	5
4. When a loved one caresses you with his/her finger	—1	0	1	2	3	4	5
5. When a loved one stimulates your genitals with his/her finger	—1	0	1	2	3	4	5
6. When you are touched or kissed on the inner thighs by a loved one	—1	0	1	2	3	4	5
7. When you caress a loved one's genitals with your fingers	—1	0	1	2	3	4	5
8. When you read a pornographic or "dirty" story	—1	0	1	2	3	4	5
9. When a loved one undresses you	—1	0	1	2	3	4	5
10. When you dance with a loved one	—1	0	1	2	3	4	5
11. When you have intercourse with a loved one	—1	0	1	2	3	4	5
12. When a loved one touches or kisses your nipples	—1	0	1	2	3	4	5
13. When you caress a loved one (other than genitals)	—1	0	1	2	3	4	5
14. When you see pornographic pictures or slides	—1	0	1	2	3	4	5
15. When you lie in bed with a loved one	—1	0	1	2	3	4	5
16. When a loved one kisses you passionately	—1	0	1	2	3	4	5

16. Has imagining that you or someone else were making it difficult for somebody to breathe ever excited you sexually?
   a. yes (1)   b. no (0)

17. Has imagining that you or someone else were tying up somebody ever excited you sexually?
   a. yes (1)   b. no (0)

18. Has imagining that you or somebody else were threatening someone with a knife or other sharp instrument ever excited you sexually?
   a. yes (1)   b. no (0)

19. Has imagining that someone was unconscious or unable to move ever excited you sexually?
   a. yes (1)   b. no (0)

20. Has imagining that someone had a very pale and still face ever excited you sexually?
   a. yes (1)   b. no (0)

Sexual Arousal Patterns

Check each area of expressed sexual interest. Note gender(s) included in target area of interest and age range included, if a partner/victim is applicable for the sexual interest.

Check under **R** if interest information was obtained from records or collateral reports; **P** if found by phallometric assessment, and under **S** if by verbal or written self-report.

R	P	S	Sexual Interest	Male	Female	Age Range
__	__	__	exhibitionism w/ masturbation	__	__	__
__	__	__	exhibitionism w/o masturbation	__	__	__
__	__	__	voyeurism	__	__	__
__	__	__	obscene calling	__	__	__
__	__	__	frotteurism	__	__	__
__	__	__	kissing	__	__	__
__	__	__	breast fondling	__	__	__
__	__	__	genital fondling	__	__	__
__	__	__	own genitals fondled	__	__	__
__	__	__	dry intercourse	__	__	__
__	__	__	perform oral sex	__	__	__
__	__	__	receive oral sex	__	__	__
__	__	__	perform vaginal intercourse	__	__	__
__	__	__	receive vaginal intercourse	__	__	__
__	__	__	perform anal intercourse	__	__	__
__	__	__	receive anal intercourse	__	__	__
__	__	__	penetration w/ object	__	__	__
__	__	__	penetration by object	__	__	__
__	__	__	urination	__	__	__
__	__	__	defecation	__	__	__
__	__	__	being bound	__	__	__

---

17. When you hear sounds of pleasure during sex	-1	0	1	2	3	4	5
18. When a loved one kisses you with an exploring tongue	-1	0	1	2	3	4	5
19. When you read suggestive or pornographic poetry	-1	0	1	2	3	4	5
20. When you see a strip show	-1	0	1	2	3	4	5
21. When you stimulate your partner's genitals with your mouth and tongue	-1	0	1	2	3	4	5
22. When a loved one caresses you (other than genitals)	-1	0	1	2	3	4	5
23. When you see a pornographic movie (stag film)	-1	0	1	2	3	4	5
24. When you undress a loved one	-1	0	1	2	3	4	5
25. When a loved one fondles your breasts with mouth and tongue	-1	0	1	2	3	4	5
26. When you make love in a new or unusual place	-1	0	1	2	3	4	5
27. When you masturbate	-1	0	1	2	3	4	5
28. When your partner has an orgasm	-1	0	1	2	3	4	5

SEX ANXIETY INVENTORY

DESCRIPTION: The SAI assesses feelings of anxiety that are related to sexual thoughts, ideas or behaviours. The Inventory consists of 25 forced-choice-items—all comprising an 'anxious' response and a 'non-anxious' response.

REFERENCE: Janda, L. H. and O'Grady, K. E. (1980). Development of a sex anxiety inventory. *Journal of Consulting and Clinical Psychology*, 48, 169–175. Reproduced by permission of Louis Janda.

	Item
1. Extramarital sex	
a. is OK if everyone agrees	b. can break up families
2. Sex	
a. can cause as much anxiety as pleasure	b. on the whole is good and enjoyable
3. Masturbation	
a. causes me to worry	b. can be a useful substitute
4. After having sexual thoughts	
a. I feel aroused	b. I feel jittery
5. When I engage in petting	
a. I feel scared at first	b. I thoroughly enjoy it
6. Initiating sexual relationships	
a. is a very stressful experience	b. causes me no problem at all
7. Oral sex	
a. would arouse me	b. would terrify me
8. I feel nervous	
a. about initiating sexual relations	b. about nothing when it comes to members of the opposite sex
9. When I meet someone I'm attracted to	
a. I get to know him or her	b. I feel nervous
10. When I was younger	
a. I was looking forward to having sex	b. I felt nervous
11. When others flirt with me	
a. I don't know what to do	b. I flirt back
12. Group sex	
a. would scare me to death	b. might be interesting
13. If in the future I committed adultery	
a. I would probably get caught	b. I wouldn't feel bad about it

---

R	P	S	Sexual Interest	Male	Female	Age Range
			binding partner			
			inflict physical pain			
			receive physical pain			
			mutilation of partner			
			mutilation of self			
			sexual homicide			
			necrophilia			
			stalking			
			acquaintance rape			
			stranger rape			
			bestiality			
			private masturbation			
			cross-dressing			
			photographing others			
			being photographed			
			pornography use			
			shoe fetish			
			foot fetish			
			clothing fetish			
			other (specify):			
			_____			
			_____			
			_____			
			_____			

Reference. Carich, M. S. and Adkerson, D. L. (1995). Adult sexual offender packet. Brandon, V. T: Safer Society Press. Reproduced by permission of Mark S. Carich.

SEXUAL ANXIETY INVENTORY

Now rate each of the items according to how anxious you feel when you have the described experience. The meaning of anxiety is extreme uneasiness distress. Rate feelings of anxiety according to the scale below:

−1 = relaxing, calming
0 = no anxiety
1 = possibly causes some anxiety
2 = sometimes causes anxiety; slightly anxiety producing
3 = usually causes anxiety; moderately anxiety producing
4 = almost always causes anxiety; very anxiety producing
5 = always causes anxiety; extremely anxiety producing

How you feel or think you would feel if you were actually involved in this experience

When a loved one stimulates your genitals with mouth and tongue	−1	0	1	2	3	4	5
When a loved one fondles your breasts with his/her hands	−1	0	1	2	3	4	5
When you see a loved one nude	−1	0	1	2	3	4	5
When a loved one caresses you with his/her eyes	−1	0	1	2	3	4	5
When a loved one stimulates your genitals with his/her finger	−1	0	1	2	3	4	5
When you are touched or kissed on the inner thighs by a loved one	−1	0	1	2	3	4	5
When you caress a loved one's genitals with your fingers	−1	0	1	2	3	4	5
When you read a pornographic or "dirty" story	−1	0	1	2	3	4	5
When a loved one undresses you	−1	0	1	2	3	4	5
When you dance with a loved one	−1	0	1	2	3	4	5
When you have intercourse with a loved one	−1	0	1	2	3	4	5
When a loved one touches or kisses your nipples	−1	0	1	2	3	4	5
When you caress a loved one (other than genitals)	−1	0	1	2	3	4	5
When you see pornographic pictures or slides	−1	0	1	2	3	4	5
When you lie in bed with a loved one	−1	0	1	2	3	4	5
When a loved one kisses you passionately	−1	0	1	2	3	4	5
When you hear sounds of pleasure during sex	−1	0	1	2	3	4	5
When a loved one kisses you with an exploring tongue	−1	0	1	2	3	4	5
When you read suggestive or pornographic poetry	−1	0	1	2	3	4	5
When you see a strip show	−1	0	1	2	3	4	5
When you stimulate your partner's genitals with your mouth and tongue	−1	0	1	2	3	4	5
When a loved one caresses you (other than genitals)	−1	0	1	2	3	4	5
When you see a pornographic movie (stag film)	−1	0	1	2	3	4	5
When you undress a loved one	−1	0	1	2	3	4	5
When a loved one fondles your breasts with mouth and tongue	−1	0	1	2	3	4	5
When you make love in a new or unusual place	−1	0	1	2	3	4	5
When you masturbate	−1	0	1	2	3	4	5
When your partner has an orgasm	−1	0	1	2	3	4	5

Reproduced with the permission of Emily Franck Hoon, Licensed Clinical Psychologist.

---

14. I would
a. feel too nervous to tell a dirty joke in mixed company
b. tell a dirty joke if it were funny

15. Dirty jokes
a. make me feel uncomfortable
b. often make me laugh

16. When I awake from sexual dreams
a. I feel pleasant and relaxed
b. I feel tense

17. When I have sexual desires
a. I worry about what I should do
b. I do something to satisfy them

18. If in the future I committed adultery
a. It would be nobody's business but my own
b. I would worry about my spouse's finding out.

19. Buying a pornographic book
a. wouldn't bother me
b. would make me nervous

20. Casual sex
a. is better than no sex at all
b. can hurt many people

21. Extramarital sex
a. is sometimes necessary
b. can damage one's career

22. Sexual advances
a. leave me feeling tense
b. are welcomed

23. When I have sexual relations
a. I feel satisfied
b. I worry about being discovered

24. When talking about sex in mixed company
a. I feel nervous
b. I sometimes get excited

25. If I were to flirt with someone
a. I would worry about his or her reactions
b. I would enjoy it

IDEAL OFFENCE FANTASY

Offenders typically have an idealized fantasy of the perfect sexual offence, designed to create the highest arousal value and most ego-syntonic scenario. This may be considerably different from the referral offence.

Ideal victim profile:

Age range _____ Gender _____ Race _____

Physical features:

Height and weight _____

Dress and grooming _____

Hair and facial features _____

Genitalia and breast development _____

Legs, feet, other features _____

Mannerisms _____

Personality traits _____

Environmental conditions:

Location _____

Presence/absence of others _____

Special conditions (filming/photography; props; etc.) _____

Interpersonal aspects:

Relationship to victim _____

Victim's thoughts and feelings about offender _____

Offender's thoughts and feelings about victim _____

Offence scenario:

How opportunity arises/is set up _____

Methods of manipulation/coercion employed _____

FANTASY QUESTIONNAIRE (ADAPTED FROM HEINZ ET AL, 1987)

Consists of 18 items in which they are asked to respond on how often they have the following fantasies (Please tick):

	ALWAYS	SOMETIMES	RARELY	NEVER
1 Sex with someone in the family - peer age				
2 Sex with someone in the family - younger				
3 Sex with someone in the family - older				
4 Sex with a friend or acquaintance - same age				
5 Sex with a friend or acquaintance - 2 years younger or more				
6 Sex with a friend or acquaintance - older				
7 Sex with someone famous (eg. pop singer, TV presenter, sportsperson)				
8 Sex with anyone				
9 Sex with anyone with particular characteristics or age				
10 Sex with anyone you do not know				
11 Sex with another male				
12 Sex with a female only				
13 Sex with more than one abuser				
14 Sex with more than one victim				
15 Sex involving pain for you				
16 Sex involving pain for the victim				
17 Sex involving animals				
18 Sex involving someone you could never have (eg. teacher, neighbour)				

BUMBY COGNITIVE DISTORTION SCALES

Please read each statement below carefully and circle the number that indicates how you feel about it. This is about what YOU truly believe, so DO NOT try to answer in a way that you think others will want you to answer.

1 = strongly disagree
2 = disagree
3 = agree
4 = strongly agree

The MOLEST Scale

	Strongly Disagree			Strongly Agree
1. I believe that sex with children can make the child feel closer to adults.	1	2	3	4
2. Since some victims tell the offender it feels good when the offender touches them, the child probably enjoys it and it probably won't affect the child much.	1	2	3	4
3. Many children who are sexually assaulted do not experience any major problems because of the assaults.	1	2	3	4
4. Sometimes, touching a child sexually is a way to show love and affection.	1	2	3	4
5. Sometimes children don't say no to sexual activity because they are curious about sex or enjoy it.	1	2	3	4
6. When kids don't tell that they were involved in sexual activity with an adult it is probably because they liked it or weren't bothered by it.	1	2	3	4
7. Having sexual thoughts and fantasies about a child isn't all that bad because at least it is not really hurting the child.	1	2	3	4
8. If a person does not use force to have sexual activity with a child, it will not harm the child as much.	1	2	3	4
9. Some people are not "true" child molesters – they are just out of control and made a mistake.	1	2	3	4
10. Just fondling a child is not as bad as penetrating a child and will probably not affect the child as much.	1	2	3	4
11. Some sexual relations with children are a lot like adult sexual relationships.	1	2	3	4
12. Sexual activity with children can help the child learn about sex.	1	2	3	4
13. I think child molesters often get longer sentences than they really should.	1	2	3	4
14. Kids who get molested by more than one person probably are doing something to attract adults to them.	1	2	3	4
15. Society makes a much bigger deal out of sexual activity with children than it really is.	1	2	3	4
16. Sometimes molesters suffer the most, lose the most, or are hurt the most as a result of a sexual assault on a child more than a child suffers or is hurt.	1	2	3	4
17. It is better to have sex with one's child than to cheat on one's wife.	1	2	3	4

In Carich, M. S. and Adkerson, D. L. (1995). Adult sex offender assessment packet. Brandon, V. T: Safer Society Press. Reproduced by permission of Mark S. Carich.

Detail of sexual behaviors/contacts _____

Victim's thoughts/feelings during offence _____

Victim's sexual/physical responses _____

Offender's thoughts/feelings during offence _____

Desired outcome post-offence _____

Please read each statement below carefully and circle the number that indicates how you feel about it. This is about what YOU truly believe, so DO NOT try to answer in a way that you think others will want you to answer.

1 = strongly disagree
2 = disagree
3 = agree
4 = strongly agree

The RAPE Scale

	Strongly Disagree			Strongly Agree
1. Men who commit rape are probably responding to a lot of stress in their lives, and raping helps to reduce that stress.	1	2	3	4
2. Women who get raped probably deserve it.	1	2	3	4
3. Women usually want sex no matter how they can get it.	1	2	3	4
4. Since prostitutes sell their bodies for sexual purposes anyway, it is not as bad if someone forces them into sex.	1	2	3	4
5. If a woman does not resist strongly to sexual advances, she is probably willing to have sex.	1	2	3	4
6. Women often falsely accuse men of rape.	1	2	3	4
7. A lot of women who get raped had "bad reputations" in the first place.	1	2	3	4
8. If women did not sleep around so much, they would be less likely to get raped.	1	2	3	4
9. If a woman gets drunk at a party, it is really her own fault if someone takes advantage of her sexually.	1	2	3	4
10. When women wear tight clothes, short skirts, and no bra or underwear, they are just asking for sex.	1	2	3	4
11. A lot of women claim they were raped just because they want attention.	1	2	3	4
12. Victims of rape are usually a little bit to blame for what happens.	1	2	3	4
13. If a man had had sex with a woman before, then he should be able to have sex with her any time he wants.	1	2	3	4
14. Just fantasizing about forcing someone to have sex isn't all that bad since no one is really being hurt.	1	2	3	4
15. Women who go to bars a lot are mainly looking to have sex.	1	2	3	4
16. A lot of times when women say "no", they are just playing hard to get and really mean "yes."	1	2	3	4
17. Part of a wife's duty is to satisfy her husband sexually whenever he wants it, whether or not she is in the mood.	1	2	3	4
18. Often a woman reports rape long after the fact because she gets mad at the man she had sex with and is just trying to get back at him.	1	2	3	4
19. As long as a man does not slap or punch a woman in the process, forcing her to have sex is not as bad.	1	2	3	4
20. When a woman gets raped more than once, she is probably doing something to cause it.	1	2	3	4

	Strongly Disagree			Strongly Agree
18. There is no real manipulation or threat used in a lot of sexual assaults on children.	1	2	3	4
19. Some kids like sex with adults because it makes them feel wanted and loved.	1	2	3	4
20. Some men sexually assaulted children because they really thought the children would enjoy how it felt.	1	2	3	4
21. Some children are willing and eager to have sexual activity with adults.	1	2	3	4
22. During sexual assaults on children, some men ask their victims if they like it because they really want to please the child and make them feel good.	1	2	3	4
23. Children who have been involved in sexual activity with an adult will eventually get over it and go on with their lives.	1	2	3	4
24. Some children can act very seductively.	1	2	3	4
25. Trying to stay away from children is probably enough to prevent a molester from molesting again.	1	2	3	4
26. A lot of times, sexual assaults on children are not planned ...they just happen.	1	2	3	4
27. Many men sexually assaulted children because of stress, and molesting helped to relieve that stress.	1	2	3	4
28. A lot of times, kids make up stories about people molesting them because they want to get attention.	1	2	3	4
29. If a person tells himself that he will never molest again, then he probably won't.	1	2	3	4
30. If a child looks at an adult's genitals, the child is probably interested in sex.	1	2	3	4
31. Sometimes victims initiate sexual activity.	1	2	3	4
32. Some people turn to children for sex because they were deprived of sex from adult women.	1	2	3	4
33. Some young children are much more adult-like than other children.	1	2	3	4
34. Children who come into the bathroom when an adult is getting undressed or going to the bathroom are probably just trying to see the adult's genitals.	1	2	3	4
35. Children can give adults more acceptance and love than other adults.	1	2	3	4
36. Some men who molest children really don't like molesting children.	1	2	3	4
37. I think the main thing wrong with sexual activity with children is that it is against the law.	1	2	3	4
38. If most child molesters hadn't been sexually abused as children, then THEY probably never would have molested a child.	1	2	3	4

ABEL & BECKER COGNITIONS SCALE

DESCRIPTION
This is a 29-item scale that measures cognitive distortions regarding the sexual molestation of children.

SCORING
Respondents mark each item on a scale from 1 ("strongly agree") to 5 ("strongly disagree"). The items are noted clinically rather than scored quantitatively. Each item represents statements that have been made by sex offenders to justify their behavior.

INTERPRETATION
Agreement with any of the items represents an example of distorted cognitions to be addressed in therapy.

Read each of the statements below carefully, and then circle the number that indicates your agreement with it.

1. Strongly agree
2. Agree
3. Neutral (neither agree or disagree)
4. Disagree
5. Strongly disagree

1. (4) If a young child stares at my genitals it means the child likes what she (he) sees and is enjoying watching my genitals.   1 2 3 4 5
2. (2) A man (or woman) is justified in having sex with his (her) children or step-children, if his wife (husband) doesn't like sex.   1 2 3 4 5
3. (3) A child 13 or younger can make her (his) own decision as to whether she (he) wants to have sex with an adult or not.   1 2 3 4 5
4. (4) A child who doesn't physically resist an adult's sexual advances, really wants to have sex with the adult.   1 2 3 4 5
5. (4) If a 13 year old (or younger) child flirts with an adult, it means he (she) wants to have sex with the adult.   1 2 3 4 5
6. (1) Sex between a 13 year old (or younger child) and an adult causes the child no emotional problems.   1 2 3 4 5
7. (6) Having sex with a child is a good way for an adult to teach the child about sex.   1 2 3 4 5
8. (2) If I tell my young child (step-child or close relative) what to do sexually and they do it, that means they will always do it because they really want to.   1 2 3 4 5
9. (2) When a young child has sex with an adult, it helps the child learn to relate to adults in the future.   1 2 3 4 5
10. (4) Most children 13 (or younger) would enjoy having sex with an adult, and it wouldn't harm the child in the future.   1 2 3 4 5
11. (2) Children don't tell others about having sex with a parent (or other adult) because they like it and want to continue.   1 2 3 4 5
12. (6) Sometime in the future, our society will realize that sex between a child and an adult is all right.   1 2 3 4 5
13. (5) A adult can tell if having sex with a a young child will emotionally damage the child in the future.   1 2 3 4 5
14. (6) An adult just feeling a child's body all over without touching her (his) genitals is not really being sexual with the child.   1 2 3 4 5

	Strongly Disagree			Strongly Agree
21. Women who get raped will eventually forget about it and get on with their lives.	1	2	3	4
22. On a date, when a man spends a lot of money on a woman, the woman ought to at least give the man something in return sexually.	1	2	3	4
23. I believe that if a woman lets a man kiss her and touch her sexually, she should be willing to go all the way.	1	2	3	4
24. When women act like they are too good for men, most men probably think about raping the women to put them in their place.	1	2	3	4
25. I believe that society and the courts are too tough on rapists.	1	2	3	4
26. Most women are sluts and get what they deserve.	1	2	3	4
27. Before the police investigate a woman's claim for rape, it is a good idea to find out what she was wearing, if she had been drinking, and what kind of person she is.	1	2	3	4
28. Generally, rape is not planned - a lot of times it just happens.	1	2	3	4
29. If a person tells himself that he will never rape again, he probably won't.	1	2	3	4
30. A lot of men who rape do so because they are deprived of sex.	1	2	3	4
31. The reason a lot of women say "no" to sex is because they don't want to seem loose.	1	2	3	4
32. If a woman goes to the home of a man on the first date, she probably wants to have sex with him.	1	2	3	4
33. Many women have a secret desire to be forced into having sex.	1	2	3	4
34. Most of the men who rape have stronger sexual urges than other men.	1	2	3	4
35. I believe that any woman can prevent herself from being raped if she really wants to.	1	2	3	4
36. Most of the time, the only reason a man commits rape is because he was sexually assaulted as a child.	1	2	3	4

Reproduced with permission of the author. It should be linked to BUMBY KM (1996) Assessing the Cognitive distortions of child molesters and rapists: Development and validation of the MOLEST and RAPE scales. Sexual Abuse: A Journal of Research and Treatment 8 (1):37-54. © Kurt Bumby.

THE SEX OFFENDER COGNITIVE DISOWNING BEHAVIORAL DISTORTION SCALE

MARK S. CARICH, Ph.D./CAROLE METZGER, MSW
November, 1996

ADMINISTRATION OF SO-CDBD SCALE

NAME _____ NUMBER _____ DATE _____
EVALUATOR _____ AGENCY _____
AGENCY _____
ADDRESS _____

This scale measures the degree of cognitive distortions and disowning behaviors that an offender displays globally (everyday lifestyle behaviors) and offense specific behaviors.

DISOWNING BEHAVIOR refers to any way (activity, thought, etc.) that one does to evade/avoid responsibility and/or enable one to offend. This encompass any type of cognitive or thought process and activity. (This includes beliefs, defense, emotional patterns, and activities.)

DISTORTED THINKING and BEHAVING are inappropriate/dysfunctional patterns of thinking and/or behavior that enable one to offend. This is the root of offending.

DIRECTIONS:

Circle to indicate the Frequency of Occurrence.
0—N/A, this doesn't apply.
1—Rarely—Low, once per week.
2—Occasionally—Moderate, couple (3) times per week.
3—Frequently—High, everyday occurrence.
4—Always-very High Level, uses more than once per day.

Reproduced with the permission of the author Mark S. Carich.

EXAMPLES OF EACH DISOWNING BEHAVIOR

1. DENIAL—is omitting or not admitting specific information;
   Examples
   (1) Holding out on giving information.
   (2) It never happened.
   (3) I would never hurt anyone.
   (4) I love children, what do you mean, did I molest a child.
   (5) I'm not a violent person.
   (6) There was no nudity in the video, so it was not pornography (while he filmed a girl using the stool).

2. LYING—any type of deliberate distorting, twisting, and not telling the truth;
   Examples
   (1) Generating or making up stories.
   (2) Deliberate giving misinformation.
   (3) I hate the idea of someone forcing sex on any other person.
   (4) I never gave a child a gift expecting anything in return, especially sex.

15.	(3)	I show my love and affection to a child by having sex with her (him).	1	2	3	4	5
16.	(3)	It's better to have sex with your child (or someone else's child) than to have an affair.	1	2	3	4	5
17.	(1)	An adult fondling a young child or having the child fondle the adult will not cause the child any harm.	1	2	3	4	5
18.	(4)	A child will never have sex with an adult unless the child really wants to.	1	2	3	4	5
19.	(NA)	My daughter (son) or other young child knows that I will still love her (him) even if she (he) refuses to be sexual with me.	1	2	3	4	5
20.	(2)	When a young child asks an adult about sex, it means that she (he) wants to see the adults sex organs or have sex with the adult.	1	2	3	4	5
21.	(2)	If an adult has sex with a young child it prevents the child from having sexual hang-ups in the future.	1	2	3	4	5
22.	(2)	When a young child walks in front of me with no or only a few clothes on, she (he) is trying to arouse me.	1	2	3	4	5
23.	(1)	My relationship with my daughter (sor) or other child is strengthened by the fact that we have sex together.	1	2	3	4	5
24.	(1)	If a child has sex with an adult, the child will look back at the experience as an adult and see it as a positive experience.	1	2	3	4	5
25.	(1)	The only way I could do harm to a child when having sex with her (him) would be to use physical force to get her (him) to have sex with me.	1	2	3	4	5
26.	(1)	When children watch an adult masturbate, it helps the child learn about sex.	1	2	3	4	5
27.	(5)	An adult can know just how much sex between him (her) and a child will hurt the child later on.	1	2	3	4	5
28.	(NA)	If a person is attracted to sex with children, he (she) should solve that problem themselves and not talk to professionals.	1	2	3	4	5

Note: each item number is followed by its Factor Base Scale category in parentheses.

Reproduced with permission of J.V. Becker and Gene Abel who retain the ©. Reference: Abel G, Becker JV, Cunningham-Rathner J, Rottleau J, Kaplan M and Reich J (1984) The treatment of child molesters (Available from SBC-TM, 722 West 168th Street, PO Box 17, NY, NY 10032, U.S.A.)

3 JUSTIFYING—making bad deviant behaviors okay;

Examples
(1) I deserve it.
(2) I didn't use no force.
(3) I didn't hurt them.
(4) I only touched the little boy/girl because I love children.
(5) I would not rape that woman if she had not asked for it by wearing those shorts.
(6) She's a bitch and deserved it.

4 MINIMIZE—any form of making less significant or less important;

Examples
(1) My molesting is private and personal.
(2) My molesting is infrequent, immodest, and convenient.
(3) I only rubbed up against the woman.
(4) It was a phone call, no one was touched.

5 ENTITLEMENT—unwarranted, unrealistic, inappropriate requests, expectations, wants, demands placed on self or another;

Examples
(1) I want it now!!
(2) I deserve it.
(3) He, she, and/or they shouldn't have.
(4) I want that right now, give it here!!
(5) Give me your milk.

6 POWER GAMES—tendencies to control, manipulate and play power games, attempts to be superior/one up, putting another down.

Examples
(1) Any type of passive-aggression behavior.
(2) Any type of defying authority.
(3) Putting another person down.
(4) I am as dumb as John Doe.
(5) I will not talk in group, because I don't want to.

7 DEPERSONALIZE/OWNERSHIP—viewing and treating people as objects (i.e., property, pieces of meat, furniture) as if one owned them;

Examples
(1) She's my woman and she only does what I tell her to do.
(2) I sure would like some of that.
(3) He has a cute butt.
(4) Would you look at that set of hooters.

8 SELF PITY—generating dysfunctional (crippling) sympathy, unwarranted sorrow, etc., for self.

Examples
(1) Taking the victim stance and/or role.
(2) Pity pot = I don't need anyone to care about me.
(3) No one cares about me.
(4) I'm working hard in treatment and no one cares.

9 EXTREMES—it is either/or type or thinking, absolutes, perfectionism, etc., all of which implies rigidly held views of life, self and others.

Examples
(1) Things are black or white, this or that way with no gray or middle area.
(2) I always do everything right.
(3) I never do anything right.
(4) I never get to talk in class/groups.
(5) Why do I always get in trouble and no one else ever does.

10 APATHY—lack of care or concern, giving up.

Examples
(1) "Who cares" attitude.
(2) Giving up attitude.
(3) Who cares if I continue to offend.
(4) What's the difference if I rape/molest or not.
(5) Yeah, I did it, so what?

11 FALLACY OR FAIRNESS—you feel resentful because you think you know what's fair but other people won't agree with you.

Examples
(1) This isn't fair.
(2) He got to go to gym and I didn't.
(3) Why did I get the SPD law or 30 years in prison and he got two years. (It's not fair).
(4) Life ain't fair.

12 DUMPING AND TRASHING—engaging in verbal and/or physical rages, in which, someone or something gets trashed or dumped on.

Examples
(1) I hate this place, it's awful, how can you stand it here.
(2) That conselor is awful, she's driving me crazy, she picks on everyone. Thanks, Joe, I feel better.

13 BLAMING—placing the burden of one's responsibility onto another.

Examples
(1) Pointing fingers.
(2) It's your, his, her, or their fault.
(3) My mother beat me, that's why I molested.
(4) It's his responsibility we're at the bar.

14 ALIENATION AND ISOLATION—this implies two things, social withdrawal and emotional withdrawal. Social withdrawal involves physical isolation. Emotional withdrawal involves numbing one's feelings, feeling cold, avoiding feelings, etc.

Examples
(1) Avoiding people.
(2) Not communicating with others.
(3) Get anger so people will stay away from you by saying things like, "I hate you, you're a moron."

THE SEX OFFENDER COGNITIVE DISOWNING BEHAVIORAL DISTORTION SCALE

Score Sheet Analysis

Name _____ Number _____ Date _____

Instructions:

Scale: NA; (L) Low (rare); (M) Moderate (occasionally); (H) High (frequently); (VH) Very High (always).

Circle the appropriate rating from the scale.

	Global	Offense Specific
1. Denial	NA/L/M/H/VH	NA/L/M/H/VH
2. Lying	NA/L/M/H/VH	NA/L/M/H/VH
3. Justifying	NA/L/M/H/VH	NA/L/M/H/VH
4. Minimize	NA/L/M/H/VH	NA/L/M/H/VH
5. Entitlement	NA/L/M/H/VH	NA/L/M/H/VH
6. Power Games	NA/L/M/H/VH	NA/L/M/H/VH
7. Depersonalizing/Ownership	NA/L/M/H/VH	NA/L/M/H/VH
8. Self-Pity	NA/L/M/H/VH	NA/L/M/H/VH
9. Extremes	NA/L/M/H/VH	NA/L/M/H/VH
10. Apathy	NA/L/M/H/VH	NA/L/M/H/VH
11. Fallacy of Fairness	NA/L/M/H/VH	NA/L/M/H/VH
12. Deumping and Trashing	NA/L/M/H/VH	NA/L/M/H/VH
13. Blaming	NA/L/M/H/VH	NA/L/M/H/VH
14. Alienation/Isolation	NA/L/M/H/VH	NA/L/M/H/VH

SEX OFFENDER COGNITIVE DISOWNING BEHAVIORAL DISTORTION SCALE

*These distorted CD's were selected from a list taken from CARICH (1993) and CARICH and STONE (1995).

DISTORTIONS	GLOBAL	OFFENSE SPECIFIC
1. **Denial**—Omitting or not admitting to information, including leaving out the details of the offense; secrets; holding out information; not telling.	0 1 2 3 4	0 1 2 3 4
2. **Lying**—Any type of deliberate distorting of information; leaving out information; not telling the truth; twisting information to fit ones needs.	0 1 2 3 4	0 1 2 3 4
3. **Justifying**—Making bad deviant behaviors "ckay"; making it alright, making excuses	0 1 2 3 4	0 1 2 3 4
4. **Minimize**—To make smaller or less important; reduce the significance	0 1 2 3 4	0 1 2 3 4
5. **Entitlement**—unwarranted inappropriate requests, expectations, and an attitude of "I want what I want when I want it and I want it right NOW! and I'm going to get it any way I can	0 1 2 3 4	0 1 2 3 4
6. **Plays Power Games**—Being superior, dominant, controlling, bossy, defying authority. . . . (my way, no way).	0 1 2 3 4	0 1 2 3 4
7. **Depersonalizing and Ownership**—Not seeing people as people, but as objects or as your property to be manipulated, such as "meat" or as someone else, objectifying	0 1 2 3 4	0 1 2 3 4
8. **Self pity**—poor me or pity pot, and sympathy for self; feeling sorry for self.	0 1 2 3 4	0 1 2 3 4
9. **Extremes**—Rigidly held views, absolutes, perfectionism, either all or none type of thinking.	0 1 2 3 4	0 1 2 3 4
10. **Apathy**—Doesn't care; lack of concern; giving up.	0 1 2 3 4	0 1 2 3 4
11. **Fallacy of fairness**—Expectations that life should be fair, life better be fair, and when it doesn't one feels crushed anc takes the victim stance, in which sets up the victim/perpetrator cycle.	0 1 2 3 4	0 1 2 3 4
12. **Dumping and Trashing**—Engaging in rape, in which one tears up stuff, verbally trashes others, and spews anger all over.	0 1 2 3 4	0 1 2 3 4
13. **Blaming**—Placing one's responsibility onto others, i.e., pointing fingers, etc.	0 1 2 3 4	0 1 2 3 4
14. **Alienation and Isolation**—Avoidance and distancing socially and/or emotionally by using physical distance and coldness to withdraw.	0 1 2 3 4	0 1 2 3 4

0—N/A
1—Low–Rarely
2—Moderate–Occasionally
3—High–Frequently
4—Very High Level–Always

SOIQ-r

Name: _____

Today's Date: _____

Location: _____

Date of Birth: _____

Referral Reason: _____

Problem Behaviour: _____

The following are a series of statements relating to how you think about yourself and your offending behaviour. There are no right or wrong answers. Please agree or disagree with each of the statements by circling the word that shows how you feel at **this point in time.**

The questions are worded so that they apply to a wide range of individuals and their offences. When the question refers to 'he/she' please read this as the person who is considered to be the "victim" in your offence. If possible, please make a 'best guess' at the answer to all of the questions.

Indicate how you feel by circling the statement as follows;

Strongly Agree   (Agree)   Neutral   Disagree   Strongly Disagree

1. What I did was not an assault because (s)he got something out of it too.
   Strongly Agree — Agree — Neutral — Disagree — Strongly Disagree

2. This offence occurred because I have an uncontrollable sex drive.
   Strongly Agree — Agree — Neutral — Disagree — Strongly Disagree

3. I came on to him/her.
   Strongly Agree — Agree — Neutral — Disagree — Strongly Disagree

4. I had an urge or desire which I simply could not control.
   Strongly Agree — Agree — Neutral — Disagree — Strongly Disagree

5. I was sexually abused as a child and that made me a sexual abuser.
   Strongly Agree — Agree — Neutral — Disagree — Strongly Disagree

6. This is an exceptional incident so it should not be taken too seriously.
   Strongly Agree — Agree — Neutral — Disagree — Strongly Disagree

7. The experience must have been painful for him/her.
   Strongly Agree — Agree — Neutral — Disagree — Strongly Disagree

8. It is definitely wrong to do what I did.
   Strongly Agree — Agree — Neutral — Disagree — Strongly Disagree

9. It happened because I was not having 'appropriate' sexual relations often enough.
   Strongly Agree — Agree — Neutral — Disagree — Strongly Disagree

10. (S)he led me on.
    Strongly Agree — Agree — Neutral — Disagree — Strongly Disagree

11. What I did was not abuse because (s)he did not resist.
    Strongly Agree — Agree — Neutral — Disagree — Strongly Disagree

12. The incident happened because I was anxious or depressed.
    Strongly Agree — Agree — Neutral — Disagree — Strongly Disagree

13. (S)he got me so sexually aroused, I couldn't help what happened.
    Strongly Agree — Agree — Neutral — Disagree — Strongly Disagree

14. What happened will not cause any long lasting harm to him/her.
    Strongly Agree — Agree — Neutral — Disagree — Strongly Disagree

15. I did it because I was under too much stress at the time.
    Strongly Agree — Agree — Neutral — Disagree — Strongly Disagree

16. Compared to most offences, this one was really quite minor.
    Strongly Agree — Agree — Neutral — Disagree — Strongly Disagree

---

SEX OFFENDER COGNITIVE DISOWNING BEHAVIORAL SCALE GRAPH

MARK S. CARICH, Ph.D./CAROLE METZGER, MSW 11/96

OFFENSE SPECIFIC GRAPH

Instructions: Plot the score of each item on the graph by marking the circle in the appropriate column.

Frequency of occurrences (scale scores)	Denial (1)	Lying (2)	Justification (3)	Minimize (4)	Entitlement (5)	Power Games (6)	Depersonalize/Repersonalize (7)	Self-Pity (8)	Extremes (9)	Apathy (10)	Fallacy of Fairness (11)	Dumping & Trashing (12)	Blaming (13)	Alienation/Isolation (14)
Always Score of 4	O	O	O	O	O	O	O	O	O	O	O	O	O	O
High (Score of 3)	O	O	O	O	O	O	O	O	O	O	O	O	O	O
Moderate (Score of 1)	O	O	O	O	O	O	O	O	O	O	O	O	O	O
Low (Score of 1)	O	O	O	O	O	O	O	O	O	O	O	O	O	O
Zero Level (N/A Score)	O	O	O	O	O	O	O	O	O	O	O	O	O	O

GLOBAL GRAPH

Instructions: Plot the score of each item on the graph by marking the circle in the appropriate column.

Frequency of occurrences (scale scores)	Denial (1)	Lying (2)	Justification (3)	Minimize (4)	Entitlement (5)	Power Games (6)	Depersonalize/Repersonalize (7)	Self-Pity (8)	Extremes (9)	Apathy (10)	Fallacy of Fairness (11)	Dumping & Trashing (12)	Blaming (13)	Alienation/Isolation (14)
Always Score of 4	O	O	O	O	O	O	O	O	O	O	O	O	O	O
High (Score of 3)	O	O	O	O	O	O	O	O	O	O	O	O	O	O
Moderate (Score of 1)	O	O	O	O	O	O	O	O	O	O	O	O	O	O
Low (Score of 1)	O	O	O	O	O	O	O	O	O	O	O	O	O	O
Zero Level (N/A Score)	O	O	O	O	O	O	O	O	O	O	O	O	O	O

Thinking Errors/Cognitive Distortions

This checklist is to provide a quick summary of the types of thinking errors or cognitive distortions typically utilized by the client. Place a check mark in one or both of the categories to denote if the distortion is global (G) in the client's thinking or specific to offending behavior (O).

G	O	Thinking Error/Cognitive Distortion
___	___	minimizing
___	___	denial
___	___	exaggeration
___	___	over-generalizing
___	___	justifying (giving excuses or reasons to suggest the behavior is okay)
___	___	projecting blame/placing responsibility on others
___	___	polarized (either/or) thinking
___	___	selective memory (remembering only what he/she wants to remember)
___	___	displacing
___	___	doing the opposite (i.e., becoming outwardly religious while actively offending)
___	___	attitude of ownership (i.e., viewing others as personal property)
___	___	intellectualizing
___	___	supressing or holding in feelings
___	___	anger/aggression to control
___	___	plays dumb
___	___	fabrication
___	___	omission
___	___	distortion
___	___	"me first" attitude
___	___	good guy syndrome
___	___	objectifying
___	___	"poor me" attitude
___	___	undoing (making up for)
___	___	excessive pride
___	___	uniqueness (rules don't apply)

---

17. The offence happened just like (s)he said it did. — Strongly Agree / Agree / Neutral / Disagree / Strongly Disagree
18. (S)he was not looking for sexual contact at all. — Strongly Agree / Agree / Neutral / Disagree / Strongly Disagree
19. Although what I did was wrong, I never hurt him/her. — Strongly Agree / Agree / Neutral / Disagree / Strongly Disagree
20. I often thought about sexual offending prior to my offence(s). — Strongly Agree / Agree / Neutral / Disagree / Strongly Disagree
21. (S)he enjoyed themselves at the time of the offence. — Strongly Agree / Agree / Neutral / Disagree / Strongly Disagree
22. The victim(s) of my offences are also to blame for the offences happening. — Strongly Agree / Agree / Neutral / Disagree / Strongly Disagree
23. I feel able to discuss how my sexual behaviour got me into trouble. — Strongly Agree / Agree / Neutral / Disagree / Strongly Disagree
24. I have been manipulative in my approach to sexual relationships. — Strongly Agree / Agree / Neutral / Disagree / Strongly Disagree
25. I feel able to talk about my offences to others. — Strongly Agree / Agree / Neutral / Disagree / Strongly Disagree
26. I was treated too harshly by the court. — Strongly Agree / Agree / Neutral / Disagree / Strongly Disagree
27. If I have inappropriate sexual fantasies I am able to discuss these as a way of getting help. — Strongly Agree / Agree / Neutral / Disagree / Strongly Disagree
28. Upon release, I will be able to seek help, should I need to, regarding my offending behaviour. — Strongly Agree / Agree / Neutral / Disagree / Strongly Disagree
29. I feel sorry for the victim(s) of my offence(s). — Strongly Agree / Agree / Neutral / Disagree / Strongly Disagree
30. The victims of my offences haven't suffered as much as I have. — Strongly Agree / Agree / Neutral / Disagree / Strongly Disagree
31. I will have to work at not committing similar offences in the future. — Strongly Agree / Agree / Neutral / Disagree / Strongly Disagree
32. Before this sentence I knew I needed to seek help with my offending behaviour. — Strongly Agree / Agree / Neutral / Disagree / Strongly Disagree
33. I am powerless to control/change my sexual offending behaviour. — Strongly Agree / Agree / Neutral / Disagree / Strongly Disagree
34. There are some situations which I must avoid if I am to stop sexual offending. — Strongly Agree / Agree / Neutral / Disagree / Strongly Disagree
35. My offending behaviour is a serious problem for me. — Strongly Agree / Agree / Neutral / Disagree / Strongly Disagree
36. No matter what the situation, it will be easy to control my offending behaviour. — Strongly Agree / Agree / Neutral / Disagree / Strongly Disagree
37. The victim(s) of my offence(s) will get over the experience easily. — Strongly Agree / Agree / Neutral / Disagree / Strongly Disagree
38. I understand why I committed my sexual offence(s). — Strongly Agree / Agree / Neutral / Disagree / Strongly Disagree
39. I have felt excited when I think about my sexual offence(s). — Strongly Agree / Agree / Neutral / Disagree / Strongly Disagree
40. I could not control myself at the time of my offence(s). — Strongly Agree / Agree / Neutral / Disagree / Strongly Disagree
41. It is likely that I will be tempted to commit similar offence(s) in the future. — Strongly Agree / Agree / Neutral / Disagree / Strongly Disagree
42. At the time I had a sexual urge that I could not control. — Strongly Agree / Agree / Neutral / Disagree / Strongly Disagree
43. Had I tried harder I could have stopped myself committing my offence(s). — Strongly Agree / Agree / Neutral / Disagree / Strongly Disagree

Thinking Error/Cognitive Distortion

G   O

- "trash city" (everything is bad; why bother)
- victim role/portrays self as victim
- being superficial
- phoney fawning ("kissing up")
- procrastination (putting off)
- "who cares" attitude/apathetic
- passive aggressive
- "know-it-all"
- paranoia as evasion
- unrealistic expectations
- personalization (inappropriately takes things personally)
- entitlement (I deserve to get all I want when I want it)
- _____
- _____
- _____

Comments: _____

Defensive Structures

G   O

- repression (unconscious elimination or "forgetting" information)
- suppression (conscious elimination or "forgetting" information)
- rationalizations (using reasons to justify one's position)
- projections (placing own blame/feelings onto someone else)
- reaction formation (engaging in opposite behavior)
- denial (not admitting to)
- displacement (discharging energy onto others)
- emotional isolation/insulation (withdrawal, alienating self from others)
- intellectualization (splitting off cognitive)
- self-pity
- detachment or dissociation—specify circumstances: _____

Comments: _____

In Carich, M. S. and Adkerson, D. L. (1995). Adult sex offender assessment packet. Brandon, V. T: Safer Society Press. Reproduced by permission of Mark S. Carich.

Making Excuses

Put a circle around the excuses that you made.

I didn't do it.

I always get blamed.

She/He is lying.

She/He asked for it.

I was drunk

I wasn't there.

She/He started it.

I can't remember.

Someone else did it.

It was someone who looked like me.

We were just playing a game.

She/He led me on.

He/She loved it.

She/He has done it before.

It didn't hurt her.

The whole family is like it.

I only ....

I am being fitted up.

My mates have done it.

She didn't say no.

It's a big fuss over nothing.

I didn't intend it to happen.

I was just teaching.........

I got carried away.

It was done to me.

It won't happen again

What other excuses did you make ? Write them here :

Why Deny It ?

There are lots of reasons why people deny all or part of their sexual behaviour. What were your reasons ?

My parents won't love me.

I might have to leave home.

I might be sent to prison.

I might have to leave school.

People will want to hurt me.

Nobody will trust me again.

People will think I'm a pervert.

I will lose my friends.

I won't be allowed to go out.

I hate myself when I think about it.

Everyone will get to hear about it.

Maybe I'll get away with it.

I might have to admit other things.

Who would want to employ me.

I will lose my job.

I feel sad/depressed/ when I think about it.

It would bring shame on my family.

What other reasons did you have ? Write them here :

258

SEXUAL OFFENCE ATTITUDES QUESTIONNAIRE

DESCRIPTION: The Sex Offence Attitude Questionnaire (SOAQ) is designed to measure the attitudes that sexual offenders have to their offending. It aims to chart the progress of the offender in treatment and to provide an outcome measure for the effectiveness of programmes in restructuring distorted cognitions.

The SOAQ is best conceptualised as a "Criterion Reference" test, given that the prime objective of the measure is to provide quantitative information about how distorted the cognitions of sexual offenders are. In other words, the SOAQ aims to distinguish those sex offenders who have distorted attitudes from those who do not.

The SOAQ consists of 30 items which are randomly ordered to disguise any pattern so the respondent is not able to work out what the questionnaire is seeking to measure in anything other than a general sense. Each item is rated on a 5-point Likert scale which ranges from 1 ('completely true') to 5 ('completely untrue'). The 30 items produce 5 scales of distorted thinking: cognitive distortion, denial, victim empathy, perception of risk, and planning.

The **COGNITIVE DISTORTION** scale contains all 30 items. This measures the extent to which a sexual offender justifies, minimises and denies the nature of his offending and the risk and harm that he poses to victims.

The **DENIAL** scale consists of 4 items which measure the extent to which an offender believes he has done nothing wrong and has been unjustly convicted.

"I still believe I am innocent and did not commit the sexual offences I have been charged with"

"I have never committed a sexual offence in my life"

"I accept that I committed a sexual offence"

"I know that I acted illegally"

The **PERCEPTION OF RISK** scale contains 9 items, which measure the perception that a sexual offender has of himself in terms of his risk, dangerousness and seriousness.

"I think that I am at risk of committing further sexual offences"

"I have committed other sexual offences for which I have not been caught"

"I do not consider myself to have a serious sex offending problem"

"Anyone close to me knows that I could never commit a sexual offence"

"I think I am in need of long term treatment to stop me from committing further sexual offences"

"This was a one off offence"

"The pleasure I get from sex offending helps to fill other gaps in my life"

"I am certain I will never commit further sexual offences"

"I do not need anybody to help me control my sexual behaviour"

The **PLANNING** scale contains 7 items, which measure the offenders' attitude to his role in grooming the environment to permit the commission of a sexual offence.

"This offence was an unfortunate accident"

"I often made arrangements to make sure I was alone with my victim"

"I would deliberately set up situations to make it easier for me to offend"

"I made sure that my victim kept the behaviour a secret for as long as possible"

"In the period leading up to my offence, I fantasised about my victim sexually"

"This offence happened completely out of the blue"

"I gained some sexual satisfaction from the behaviour"

The **VICTIM EMPATHY** scale contains 6 items which measure the offenders' awareness of the consequences of his offence for the victim.

"The consequences of this offence has caused me as much grief and pain as my victim"

"It is likely that my victim has overcome most of the distress I caused him/her by now"

"My victim is likely to have become withdrawn and depressed because of my actions"

"I enjoyed having power over my victim"

"I think the harm I caused to my victim will be fairly short lived"

"My victim is bound to have problems forming loving relationships in the future"

The questionnaire is designed to be self completed. Instructions for respondents are contained within the questionnaire itself. Notes are also included to help practitioners to administer the SOAQ effectively.

The SOAQ is scored using a specially designed scoring sheet. This should be used in conjunction with the instructions given below.

SCORING

1. Go through the completed SOAQ, copying the score that has been marked (i.e., a number between 1 and 5) into the boxes. Half of the items (usually every other item) need to be recorded by subtracting the original score from 6 before being entered into the boxes.

2. Once all the boxes been filled in, the five scales can be produced.

3. For the "Perception of risk" scale add all the nine boxes marked with an 'R' together and enter the sum into the box marked S1. The minimum score is 9 and the maximum score is 45.

4. For the "Victim empathy" scale add all the six boxes marked with a 'V' together and enter the sum into the box marked S2. The minimum score is 6 and the maximum score is 30.

5. For the "Denial" scale add all the four boxes marked with a 'D' together and enter the sum into the box marked S3. The minimum score is 4 and the maximum score is 16.

6. For the "Planning" scale add all the seven boxes marked with a 'P' together and enter the sum into the box marked S4. The minimum score is 7 and the maximum score is 35.

7. For the "Cognitive Distortion" scale, add all the boxes together. As a short cut, add the four scale scores which have been calculated so far together (these are marked by boxes S1, S2, S3 and S4) along with the four squares and circles marked with a C. The minimum score is 30 and the maximum score is 150.

NB. If any item has been missed, score a 3. If more than 1 item in each scale has been missed, send the SOAQ back to the respondent. If this is not possible record as a "nil response".

PRINCIPAL REFERENCE: Procter, E. (1994). Sexual offence attitude questionnaire: a guide to the objectives and purpose, construction, administration, scoring, validity, and interpretation of results. Oxfordshire Probation Service: Research and Information Unit. © Reproduced by permission of Oxfordshire Probation Service. 42 Park End Street, Oxford OX1 1JN.

SEX OFFENCE ATTITUDES QUESTIONNAIRE (PROCTER, 1994)

Please indicate how true or untrue you believe the following statements to be about the sexual offence(s) you have most recently been convicted of. Put a circle around the appropriate number:

1 = Completely true
2 = Mainly true
3 = Half true/half *untrue*
4 = Mainly *untrue*
5 = Completely *untrue*

	TRUE				UNTRUE
1. I offended because I have a preference for illegal sexual behaviours	1	2	3	4	5
2. The consequences of this offence has caused me as much grief and pain as my victim	1	2	3	4	5
3. It is likely that my victim has overcome most of the distress I caused her/him by now	1	2	3	4	5
4. I think that I am at risk of committing further sexual offences	1	2	3	4	5
5. I still believe that I am innocent and did not commit the sexual offence(s) I have been charged with	1	2	3	4	5
6. I have committed other sexual offences for which I have not been caught	1	2	3	4	5
7. This offence was an unfortunate accident	1	2	3	4	5
8. I do *not* consider myself to have a serious sex offending problem	1	2	3	4	5
9. I often made arrangements to ensure that I was alone with my victim	1	2	3	4	5
10. Anyone close to me knows that I could never commit a sexual offence	1	2	3	4	5
11. I think that I am in need of long term treatment to stop me from committing further sexual offences	1	2	3	4	5
12. I would deliberately set up situations to make it easier for me to offend	1	2	3	4	5
13. This was a one off offence	1	2	3	4	5
14. My victim is likely to have become withdrawn and depressed because of my actions	1	2	3	4	5
15. I enjoyed having power over my victim	1	2	3	4	5
16. I have never committed a sexual offence in my life	1	2	3	4	5
17. The pleasure I get from sex offending helps to fill other gaps in my life	1	2	3	4	5
18. I am certain that the stress I was under at the time led me to offend	1	2	3	4	5
19. We have to share some of the blame because my victim knew how to sexually seduce me	1	2	3	4	5
20. I made sure that my victim kept the behaviour a secret for as long as possible	1	2	3	4	5
21. In the period leading up to the offence I fantasised about my victim sexually	1	2	3	4	5
22. I think that the harm I caused to my victim will be fairly short lived	1	2	3	4	5
23. I accept that I committed a sexual offence	1	2	3	4	5
24. I am certain I will never commit further sexual offences	1	2	3	4	5
25. My victim is bound to have problems forming loving relationships in the future	1	2	3	4	5
26. This offence happened completely out of the blue	1	2	3	4	5
27. I know that I acted illegally	1	2	3	4	5
28. I would not have offended if it had not been for alcohol	1	2	3	4	5
29. I gained some sexual satisfaction from the behaviour	1	2	3	4	5
30. I do not need anybody to help me control my sexual behaviour	1	2	3	4	5

Please complete the following details about your offence and your victim:

1. Your Age [   ]

2. Your Sex [   ]

3. Most recent sexual offence(s)
[ ] Indecent Assault child
[ ] Gross Indecency with child
[ ] Incest
[ ] Buggery of a child
[ ] USI under 13
[ ] USI under 16
[ ] Indecent Exposure
[ ] Rape
[ ] Indecent assault adult
[ ] Other

4. Relationship to victim(s)
[ ] Natural parent
[ ] Step parent
[ ] Other blood relative
[ ] Responsible adult
(ie. teacher, baby sitter, youth leader etc.)
[ ] Spouse/Co-habitee
[ ] Friend
[ ] Stranger
[ ] No identifiable victim
[ ] Other

(please write in)

5. Age of victim(s)
(when offence started)
[ ] Under 5 years
[ ] 6–10 years old
[ ] 11–14 years old
[ ] 15–16 years old
[ ] 16 years +
[ ] No identifiable victim

(please write in)

6. Sex of victim(s)
[ ] Female
[ ] Male
[ ] Both sexes

SOAQ SCORING SHEET

Q1. score	=	C1	Q16. 6-score	=	D2
Q2. 6-score	=	V1	Q17. score	=	R7
Q3. 6-score	=	V2	Q18. 6-score	=	C2
Q4. score	=	R1	Q19. 6-score	=	C3
Q5. 6-score	=	D1	Q20. score	=	P4
Q6. score	=	R2	Q21. score	=	P5
Q7. 6-score	=	P1	Q22. 6-score	=	V5
Q8. 6-score	=	R3	Q23. score	=	D3
Q9. score	=	P2	Q24. 6-score	=	R8
Q10. 6-score	=	R4	Q25. score	=	V6
Q11. score	=	R5	Q26. 6-score	=	P6
Q12. score	=	P3	Q27. score	=	D4
Q13. 6-score	=	R6	Q27. 6-score	=	C4
Q14. score	=	V3	Q29. score	=	P7
Q15. score	=	V4	Q30. 6-score	=	R9

		Range
Scale scores		
	S1	(9–45)
	S2	(6–30)
	S3	(4–20)
	S4	(7–35)
		(30–150)

Perception of risk scale:	Add all 9 items marked with an 'R'
Victim empathy scale:	Add all 6 items marked with a 'V'
Denial scale:	Add all 4 items marked with a 'D'
Planning scale:	Add all 7 items marked with a 'P'
Cognitive distortion scale:	Add all 4 scale scores marked with an 'S', to all 4 items marked with a 'C'

Reference Number:

OFFENCE QUESTIONNAIRE—PRACTITIONER NOTES

For research purposes it is very important that the questionnaire is administered in a consistent way. This should involve the following:

- The respondent should be told that the questionnaire is being used to collect standardised information about the explanations he or she gives for offending. It should be emphasised that although the questionnaire is not completely anonymous, it will only be used for research purposes, and will not be passed on to any other agency or organisation.
- The respondent should only be given help if he or she is genuinely unable to understand a question. Ideally, he or she should be allowed to complete the questionnaire in private.
- On completion of the questionnaire the respondent should be asked to check that he or she has not missed out a question.
- It is particularly important that the final factual section is completed accurately. It is suggested that the practitioner either completes this final page with the respondent or at least checks to see that the information is correct.

CARICH-ADKERSON VICTIM EMPATHY AND REMORSE
Self Report Inventory

Name: _____ Age: _____ Sex: _____

Agency: _____ ID#: _____

I have been accused of these sexual offenses: _____

_____

_____

Instructions – After completing the items above, read each statement below. Circle the letter that shows how much you agree or disagree with each statement according to this scale:

A = Strongly Disagree
B = Disagree
C = Agree
D = Strongly Agree

1.	I hurt my victim(s).	A	B	C	D
2.	I sexually exploited another person.	A	B	C	D
3.	In reality, no one was really hurt.	A	B	C	D
4.	The victim actually enjoyed it.	A	B	C	D
5.	It was the victim's fault it happened.	A	B	C	D
6.	The victim actually wanted sex.	A	B	C	D
7.	The victim really deserved it.	A	B	C	D
8.	The victim had it coming.	A	B	C	D
9.	Honestly, I can say that I cried for my victims.	A	B	C	D
10.	I can honestly say that I feel sorry for myself because I lost my job, family, home, or freedom, and my life is ruined.	A	B	C	D
11.	In reality, I was only educating my victim.	A	B	C	D
12.	I masturbate to fantasies about my victims.	A	B	C	D
13.	I feel guilty for what I did to my victims.	A	B	C	D
14.	I have no need to somehow make up for the offenses.	A	B	C	D
15.	I really get off on controlling others.	A	B	C	D
16.	I will never have a need to make up for the offenses.	A	B	C	D
17.	I feel so guilty sometimes that I can't function.	A	B	C	D
18.	I seem to cry in counseling (or in front of others) over my victims, but not when I'm alone.	A	B	C	D
19.	I really understand the damage I did to my victims.	A	B	C	D
20.	I seem to spontaneously cry over my victims.	A	B	C	D
21.	I don't deserve what has happened to me.	A	B	C	D
22.	It wasn't my fault.	A	B	C	D
23.	There were really no bad consequences to the victim.	A	B	C	D
24.	I usually felt terrible and upset after the offenses.	A	B	C	D
25.	I enjoy sexually hurting people.	A	B	C	D

DEVELOPING EFFECTIVE COMMUNICATION SKILLS

Name: _____ Pre: _____

Date: _____ Post: _____

Answer the following with True (T) or False (F)

1. _____ It is important to be aware of the type of message our body language sends to others.

2. _____ Observing someone's body language is a good way to get an idea of how they are feeling or reacting.

3. _____ A person's body language always reflects exactly how they are feeling or reacting.

4. _____ Some people use their body language in a negative way; they use body language to intimidate someone to get their own way.

5. _____ You should never point out to a person what kind of a message he's sending.

6. _____ Observing someone else's response to your body language is a good way to become aware of the type of message you're sending.

7. _____ When giving a person feedback on the message he's sending, it's okay to label his behavior as "right" or "wrong".

8. _____ You should let others decide if they want to change their behavior. This means not demanding that others change (Freedom of choice). Example of freedom of choice: "When you raise your voice it makes me nervous."

Example of demanding: "Don't raise your voice."

9. _____ It's okay to delay feedback. Example: "I was really hurt yesterday when you ignored me."

10. _____ You should own your own feelings. This means describing how you feel in the first person.

Example of owning feelings: "I like you very much."

Example of avoiding your own feelings: "You are a likable person."

Carich-Adkerson Victim Empathy and Remorse Inventory

Name: _____ I.D. Number: _____ Date: _____

Evaluator: _____ Agency: _____

Guidelines:

1. This instrument is best used with a clinical interview.

2. Although this assessment is not yet statistically valid, it provides guidelines to help assess the level of victim empathy.

3. Many of the items presented in the assessment are based on the following: history; current behavior during interview, personality characteristics, etc. Evaluate the offender accordingly.

4. Rate the offender by placing a check mark on the most appropriate response.

Definitions: Victim empathy is the intellectual and emotional understanding of the victim. It encompasses remorse (painfully regretting) and guilt (feeling bad for violation others).

Instructions: Select the most accurate response.

	0 = None	1 = Sometimes	2 = Much	3 = Very Much
1. The offender demonstrates empathy (compassion for one's victims) spontaneously.	(0)	(1)	(2)	(3)
2. The offender understands that he/she hurt the victim emotionally.	(0)	(1)	(2)	(3)
3. The offender demonstrates remorse (painfully regrets) violating the one's victim(s).	(0)	(1)	(2)	(3)
4. The offender demonstrates remorse spontaneously.	(0)	(1)	(2)	(3)
5. The offender verbalizes empathy for the victims.	(0)	(1)	(2)	(3)
6. The offender verbalizes remorse for victims.	(0)	(1)	(2)	(3)
7. The offender's verbal/nonverbal behaviors are congruent.	(0)	(1)	(2)	(3)
8. The offender intellectually (i.e. verbalizes awareness) expresses empathy.	(0)	(1)	(2)	(3)
9. The offender emotionally (i.e. tears, sad affect, head down, change in voice tone, etc.) expresses empathy.	(0)	(1)	(2)	(3)
10. The offender intellectually expresses remorse based on consequences only.	(0)	(1)	(2)	(3)
11. The offender emotionally expresses remorse.	(0)	(1)	(2)	(3)
12. The offender manufactures empathy/remorse via tears for secondary gain.	(0)	(1)	(2)	(3)
13. The offender cries on "cue."	(0)	(1)	(2)	(3)
14. The offender demonstrates care and concern for others outside sexual offending.	(0)	(1)	(2)	(3)
15. The offender comes across phoney, as presenting a façade.	(0)	(1)	(2)	(3)

CARICH-ADKERSON VICTIM EMPATHY AND REMORSE
Self Report Inventory Scoring Form

Instructions:
For each item EXCEPT # 1, 2, 9, 13, 15, 17, 19, 20, and 24, add the following:

    3 points for each A
    2 points for each B
    1 point for each C
    0 points for each D

Items # 1, 2, 9, 13, 15, 17, 19, 20, and 24 are scored in reverse.

Raw Score Points:

    56-75 = a high level of victim empathy and remorse
    38-55 = a moderate level of victim empathy and remorse
    19-37 = a minimal level of victim empathy and remorse
    0-18 = a lack of victim empathy and remorse

This instrument has not been statistically validated and should be used only to assist in clinical interpretation. High victim scores on this instrument which contrast with clinical impression and client behavior likely suggest an overt attempt to falsely portray a picture of concern and compassion for the victim.

To assist in the validation process, please send a copy of results to Dr Mark S. Carich, 2153 Pontoon Rd., Granite City, IL 62040.

Score Sheet

Scoring Guidelines

1. Record the score on the item analysis score sheet.
2. Subtotal the responses.
3. Record the subtotals on the subtotal score sheet.
4. Total the subtotals.
5. Divide total score by 40 to get the average score.
6. In order to establish a data base for validity, Please send a copy of the results to: Mark S. Carich, Ph.D, 2153 Pontoon, Granite City, IL 62040.

Item Analysis Score sheet

1. _____	11. _____
2. _____	12. _____
3. _____	13. _____
4. _____	14. _____
5. _____	15. _____
6. _____	16. _____
7. _____	17. _____
8. _____	18. _____
9. _____	19. _____
10. _____	20. _____
Subtotal A. _____	Subtotal B. _____
21. _____	31. _____
22. _____	32. _____
23. _____	33. _____
24. _____	34. _____
25. _____	35. _____
26. _____	36. _____
27. _____	37. _____
28. _____	38. _____
29. _____	39. _____
30. _____	40. _____
Subtotal C. _____	Subtotal D. _____

---

0 = None   1 = Sometimes   2 = Much   3 = Very Much

16. The offender expresses self-pity. (0) (1) (2) (3)
17. The offender tends to victimize or exploit others apart from sexual exploitation. (0) (1) (2) (3)
18. The offender seems very concerned with incarceration. (0) (1) (2) (3)
19. The offender takes responsibility for the offense behavior. (0) (1) (2) (3)
20. The offender masturbates to fantasies of their offense. (0) (1) (2) (3)
21. The offender feels guilty for harming victims. (0) (1) (2) (3)
22. The offender is inconsistent in feeling guilty or feels guilty only from being caught. (0) (1) (2) (3)
23. Offender perceives self as suffering more than the victim(s). (0) (1) (2) (3)
24. The offender justifies the offending behavior. (0) (1) (2) (3)
25. The offender minimizes ("makes little") the offenses. (0) (1) (2) (3)
26. The offender believes the victim is at fault or brought on the offense. (0) (1) (2) (3)
27. The offender believes the victims enjoyed/desired the offense(s). (0) (1) (2) (3)
28. The offender believes the victim deserved it or that the victim had it coming. (0) (1) (2) (3)
29. The offender intellectually expresses remorse based on harm to the victim. (0) (1) (2) (3)
30. The offender denies offense in spite of obvious evidence. (0) (1) (2) (3)
31. The offender believes that the "victim was hurt." (0) (1) (2) (3)
32. The offender believes the victim was being educated. (0) (1) (2) (3)
33. The offender believes that all females or males are "bitches" or "bastards." (0) (1) (2) (3)
34. The offender enjoys exploiting others. (0) (1) (2) (3)
35. The offender made appropriate restitution for offenses. (0) (1) (2) (3)
36. The offender tried to make appropriate restitution for offenses. (0) (1) (2) (3)
37. The offender has an extensive history of sadism (aroused to or pleasure from violence). (0) (1) (2) (3)
38. The offender currently displays or demonstrates features of sadism (enjoy physically hurting others), although it may not be acknowledged. (0) (1) (2) (3)
39. The offender currently verbally/nonverbally admits enjoying hurting others (i.e., torturing). (0) (1) (2) (3)
40. The offender understands that he/she hurt the victim physically. (0) (1) (2) (3)

LEVINSON VICTIM EMPATHY SCALE

DESCRIPTION: the L-VES is a 37-item summated rating scale measuring the degree of empathy sex offenders have towards their victims. The L-VES has 3 sub-scales: empathic response (16 items), interpersonal appreciation (11 items) and interpersonal sensitivity (10 items).

SCORING: The scale describes the procedure, which uses a 7-point Likert Scale for responses, with 7 being 'always' and 1 'never'.

REFERENCE: © Levinson, BS. (1994). Doctoral dissertation. Reproduced by permission of the author.

L-VES SCALE

This statement DESCRIBES ME
7 = always, 6 = very frequently, 5 = frequently, 4 = occasionally, 3 = rarely, 2 = very rarely, 1 = never

DIRECTIONS:
Circle the number that describes you for each statement

	Always						Never
Example: I like to take tests	7	6	5	4	3	2	1
1—It makes me feel good when I see someone stop crying	7	6	5	4	3	2	1
2—When I think about a person being a victim of rape, I want to get revenge	7	6	5	4	3	2	1
3—When I think about a child being victimized, I want to soothe and comfort him or her	7	6	5	4	3	2	1
4—I believe victims make too much of their abuse	7	6	5	4	3	2	1
5—It makes me angry to hear victims' stories	7	6	5	4	3	2	1
6—When I see a T.V. show on incest, I feel bad for the offender	7	6	5	4	3	2	1
7—I think the media makes too much of victim pain	7	6	5	4	3	2	1
8—I understand why a step-father might molest his step-daughter	7	6	5	4	3	2	1

This statement DESCRIBES ME
7 = always, 6 = very frequently, 5 = frequently, 4 = occasionally, 3 = rarely, 2 = very rarely, 1 = never

	Always						Never
9—I think a child being shown the private parts of a man is not an actual victim	7	6	5	4	3	2	1
10—I would not be able to comfort a woman when she has been a victim	7	6	5	4	3	2	1
11—I cannot feel anyone else's pain right now	7	6	5	4	3	2	1
12—I have been the one who has suffered the most in my current situation	7	6	5	4	3	2	1
13—When I see a T.V. Program about sexual abuse I think of what it would be like to be the offender	7	6	5	4	3	2	1
14—It makes me feel good when I can make someone stop crying	7	6	5	4	3	2	1
15—When I watch a T.V. program about sexual abuse I think of how the victim might feel	7	6	5	4	3	2	1
16—People make too much of children's sensitivity	7	6	5	4	3	2	1
17—When I see someone in trouble, I want to help	7	6	5	4	3	2	1
18—I am uncomfortable when I see other people arguing	7	6	5	4	3	2	1

This statement DESCRIBES ME
7 = always, 6 = very frequently, 5 = frequently, 4 = occasionally, 3 = rarely, 2 = very rarely, 1 = never

	Always						Never
19—I can see other people's point of view even if it is different from mine	7	6	5	4	3	2	1
20—I can sense what other people are feeling in emotional situations	7	6	5	4	3	2	1
21—When I see a mother spank her child, it makes me angry	7	6	5	4	3	2	1
22—I often wonder what it would be like to be the person I was accused of offending	7	6	5	4	3	2	1
23—It's hard for me to understand why someone else gets upset	7	6	5	4	3	2	1
24—I don't feel upset when I see someone who is sad	7	6	5	4	3	2	1
25—I can understand when other men cry	7	6	5	4	3	2	1
26—I am able to put myself in someone else's shoes and understand how he/she feels	7	6	5	4	3	2	1
27—When I see someone being hurt I feel protective toward him/her	7	6	5	4	3	2	1
28—I can remain unaffected when I see someone being hurt	7	6	5	4	3	2	1

Scoresheet Basic Bio-Data

Age _____ Sex _____ Date _____
Offense _____ Offense documented _____ Offense not documented _____

SUBTOTAL SCORE SHEET
RAW SCORES

Subtotal A. _____
Subtotal B. _____
Subtotal C. _____
Subtotal D. _____
Total _____ (Total Raw Scores)

Average Score: _____
Total Divided by 40: _____

Scale
Score:
3 pts.—Indicates overall A High level of Empathy
2 pts.—Indicates overall A Moderate level of Empathy
1 pts.—Indicates overall A Minimal level of Empathy
0 pts.—Indicates overall A Lacks Empathy

Total Scores:
90–120 pts.—Indicates A High level of Empathy & Remorse for Victims
60–89 pts.—Moderate level of Empathy & Remorse for Victims
30–59 pts.—Low level of Empathy & Remorse for Victims
0–29 pts.—Lacks Empathy & Remorse for Victims

Raw Score _____ Individual has _____ level of Empathy.
Average Score _____

© Carich and Adkerson. Reproduced with permission of Mark Carich.

265

LEVINSON—VICTIM EMPATHY SCALE Scoring Sheet

EMPATHIC	RESPONSE	INTERP.	APPRECIATION	INTERP.	SENSITIVITY
1		(–) 4		(–) 9	
2		(–) 5		(–)10	
3		(–) 6		(–)11	
14		(–) 7		(–)13	
15		(–) 8		(–)24	
17		(–)12		(–)28	
18		(–)16		(–)31	
19		(–)23		(–)32	
20		(–)30		(–)34	
21		(–)35		(–)37	
22		(–)36		IS Total	
25		IA Total			
26					
27					
29					
33					
ER Total					
Total LVES					

Total Mean: 112; ER Mean: 80; IS Mean: 28.4; IA Mean: 38.8; Highest score achievable 259

This statement DESCRIBES ME
7=always, 6=very frequently, 5=frequently, 4=occasionally, 3=rarely, 2=very rarely, 1=never

29—I try to imagine how I would feel when someone tells me how he/she was hurt 7 6 5 4 3 2 1
30—I find it hard to pay attention when I am with other people 7 6 5 4 3 2 1
31—I can't understand what I have cone wrong 7 6 5 4 3 2 1
32—I don't think I have every hurt anyone too badly 7 6 5 4 3 2 1
33—I feel bad when people I love argue 7 6 5 4 3 2 1
34—I think no victim of sexual abuse I have heard about has been badly hurt 7 6 5 4 3 2 1
35—It is hard for me to understand how I have hurt anybody 7 6 5 4 3 2 1
36—If the victim wasn't badly hurt, I feel angry at him/her when the offender has to go to jail 7 6 5 4 3 2 1
37—When I see a victim tell his or her story, it has nothing to do with me 7 6 5 4 3 2 1

SELFISM (NS)

DESCRIPTION: The NS is a 28-item scale designed to measure narcissism, referred to by developers of this instrument as selfism. Selfism is viewed as an orientation, belief, or set affecting how one construes a whole range of situations that deal with the satisfaction of needs. A person who scores high on the NS views a large number of situations in a selfish or egocentric fashion. At the opposite end of the continuum are individuals who submerge their own satisfaction in favor of others. The NS samples beliefs across a broad range of situations and is not targeted toward a specific need area. Based on a review of the literature, impressionistic sources, and the work of cultural observers, the original 100 items were narrowed down to 28 based on low correlations with the Marlowe-Crowne Social Desirability Scale, high correlations with NS total scores, and a reasonable spread over the five response categories.

SCORING: The NS is scored by summing the individual item scores, each of which is on a 5-point Likert scale, to produce a range of 28 to 140. The following are filler items, included to disguise the purpose of the scale, and are not scored: 1, 6, 8, 12, 15, 19, 23, 26, 30, 34, 38, 39.

PRIMARY REFERENCE: Phares, E. J. and Erskine, N. (1984). The measurement of selfism, *Educational and Psychological Measurement* **44**, 597–608. Instrument reproduced with permission of E. Jerry Phares.

Listed below are 40 statements that deal with personal attitudes and feelings about a variety of things. Obviously, there are *no* right or wrong answers—only opinions. Read each item and then decide how *you personally* feel. Mark your answers according to the following scheme:

5 = Strongly agree
4 = Mildly agree
3 = Agree and disagree equally
2 = Mildly disagree
1 = Strongly disagree

_____ 1. The widespread interest in professional sports is just another example of escapism.
_____ 2. In times of shortages it is sometimes necessary for one to engage in a little hoarding.
_____ 3. Thinking of yourself first is no sin in this world today.
_____ 4. The prospect of becoming very close to another person worries me a good bit.
_____ 5. The really significant contributions in the world have very frequently been made by people who were preoccupied with themselves.
_____ 6. Every older American deserves a guaranteed income to live in dignity.
_____ 7. It is more important to live for yourself rather than for other people, parents, or for posterity.
_____ 8. Organized religious groups are too concerned with raising funds these days.
_____ 9. I regard myself as someone who looks after his/her personal interests.
_____ 10. The trouble with getting too close to people is that they start making emotional demands on you.
_____ 11. Having children keeps you from engaging in a lot of self-fulfilling activities.
_____ 12. Many of our production problems in this country are due to the fact that workers no longer take pride in their jobs.
_____ 13. It's best to live for the present and not to worry about tomorrow.
_____ 14. Call it selfishness if you will, but in this world today we all have to look out for ourselves first.
_____ 15. Education is too job oriented these days; there is not enough emphasis on basic education.
_____ 16. It seems impossible to imagine the world without me in it.
_____ 17. You can hardly overestimate the importance of selling yourself in getting ahead.
_____ 18. The difficulty with marriage is that it locks you into a relationship.
_____ 19. Movies emphasize sex and violence too much.
_____ 20. If it feels right, it is right.
_____ 21. Breaks in life are nonsense. The real story is pursuing your self-interests aggressively.
_____ 22. An individual's worth will often pass unrecognized unless that person thinks of himself or herself first.
_____ 23. Consumers need a stronger voice in governmental affairs.
_____ 24. Getting ahead in life depends mainly on thinking of yourself first.
_____ 25. In general, couples should seek a divorce when they find the marriage is not a fulfilling one.

Levinson Victim Empathy Scale Scoring Guidelines

Empathic Response	Interpersonal Appreciation	Interpersonal Sensitivity
01	(–) 4	(–) 9
02	(–) 5	(–)10
03	(–) 6	(–)11
14	(–) 7	(–)13
15	(–) 8	(–)24
17	(–)12	(–)28
18	(–)16	(–)31
19	(–)23	(–)32
20	(–)30	(–)34
21	(–)35	(–)37
22	(–)36	
25		
26		
27		
29		
33		

*(–) indicates items to be reversed scored

267

SEXUAL OFFENSE ASSESSMENT QUESTIONS

1. Where did you get the idea to do it?
2. What were you thinking (or fantasizing) about when you decided to sexually abuse her/him?
3. How did you pick the victim?
4. Do you think the victim wanted to do it? How do you know?
5. Who else would you have picked if she/he wasn't there?
6. How many times, when did it start, where did it take place?
7. Did the victim cry or ask you to stop? Did that surprise you?
8. What did you do when she/he cried or asked you to stop? How did you stop? Why didn't you do more with the victim?
9. Why didn't you do it more often?
10. What do you think is wrong with this behavior?
11. What do other people think is wrong with this behavior?
12. Why are there laws against it?
13. How did the victim feel? How do you know? What did the victim enjoy about the sex abuse?
14. What did you do to the victim?
15. Did you have an erection? Ejaculation?
16. What part did you enjoy?
17. How did you make sure the victim would not tell?
18. Who else did you abuse?
19. How often do you masturbate? How old were you when you started?
20. What kind of fantasies do you have when you masturbate?
21. What kind of fantasies do you have when you are just daydreaming?

Sexual Offense Assessment Issues

1. How is the reality of the offense being dealt with, i.e., court, CPS?
2. What is the age difference between the victim and offender?
3. What is their social/power relationship?
4. What type of sexual activity is exhibited? Does it reflect knowledge that is advanced for the age of the sex offender?
5. Does the sexual activity have any symbolic meaning?
6. Determine degree of denial or minimization.
7. Evaluate for evidence of a developing pattern of deviant sexual behavior, i.e., repetitive nature of offense, fantasies, number of offenses, number of victims.
8. Level of control sex offender has of his/her sex offense behavior.
9. Determine absence or presence of predatory behavior.
10. Evaluate for evidence of increased aggression or victim involvement.

(Freeman-Longo, 1985)

---

26. Too often, voting means choosing between the lesser of two evils.
27. In striving to reach one's true potential, it is sometimes necessary to worry less about other people.
28. When choosing clothes I generally consider style before matters such as comfort or durability.
29. I believe people have the right to live any damn way they please.
30. Too many people have given up reading to passively watch TV.
31. Owing money is not so bad if it's the only way one can live without depriving yourself of the good life.
32. Not enough people live for the present.
33. I don't see anything wrong with people spending a lot of time and effort on their personal appearance.
34. Physical punishment is necessary to raise children properly.
35. The Peace Corps would be a good idea if it did not delay one's getting started along the road to a personal career.
36. It simply does not pay to become sad or upset about friends, loved ones, or events that don't turn out well.
37. A definite advantage of birth control devices is that they permit sexual pleasure without the emotional responsibilities that might otherwise result.
38. Doctors seem to have forgotten that medicine involves human relations and not just prescriptions.
39. I believe that some unidentified flying objects have actually been sent from outer space to observe our culture here on earth.
40. In this world one has to look out for oneself first because nobody else will look out for you.

268

GENERALISED SCALE OF ACCEPTANCE (GSA)

1. Acceptance of responsibility.
2. Relief that the sexual abuse has ended as opposed to attempts at deflecting treatment by blackmailing the worker on the basis that the therapeutic process is imposing an intolerable, added, strain.
3. Acceptance of the victim's account of the events added the victim's perception of them.
4. Acceptance of the need for separation possibly including the need for care proceedings in respect of the child.
5. Acceptance of the authority of the worker.
6. An acceptance of the need to engage in a treatment programme.
7. *Public* acceptance of sole and full responsibility by the perpetrator.
8. Commitment not to engage in dangerous behaviour towards self or others to be made by both perpetrator and the silent-partner.
9. A commitment to avoid the use of self-destruction as a manipulative manoeuvre.
10. Acceptance of the application of written instruments.
11. Acceptance of the use of action techniques (including role play/journal maintenance/use of anatomically correct dolls etc).
12. Acceptance of the need for a positive attitude.
13. Acceptance of the use of 'the negotiating guidelines'.
14. Acceptance of the need for office-based therapy.
15. Acceptance of the workers' right to demand the attendance of whichever family members they see fit.
16. Acceptance that techniques of 'disinhibition' *were* used and that they must be outlined.
17. Acceptance that 'loss of memory' at any point will lead to termination.
18. Acceptance that intoxication is insufficient excuse.
19. Acceptance of need for specialised assessment/treatment.
20. Acceptance of high levels of personal exploration, including:
    (i) Aggression.
    (ii) Sexuality.
21. Acceptance of the need to begin to formulate a formal statement of apology to the victim.
22. A commitment to engage in any 'homework' the therapy team sets.
23. A commitment to participate in a perpetrators' group which should be single-sex.
24. Acceptance of part responsibility by the single-partner.
25. Acceptance that 'avoidance' strategies were used in the marital, sexual relationship.
26. Acceptance of the need to attend a silent-partner's group.
27. Acceptance *and* verbalisation of the failure to protect.
28. Acceptance of the failure to provide adequate emotional care.
29. Acceptance that the victim was not responsible.
30. A commitment to protect the victim from all such abuse in future.
31. Acceptance of repeated application of the CAM/F scale.
32. Acceptance that individual and dyadic material may be taken into family sessions.
33. Acceptance of the use of the 'index of sexual satisfaction' (ISS).
34. Acceptance of the use of the 'index of marital satisfaction' (IMS).
35. Acceptance of the 'guidelines for problem discussion'.
36. Acceptance that all aspects of the couple's sex life be open to exploration.
37. Acceptance of the need for expert sexual counselling for the perpetrator and the silent-partner.
38. Acceptance that the lack of sexual activity between the perpetrator and the silent-partner (whatever its aetiology) facilitated the abuse.
39. Acceptance that the perpetrator used this to triangulate the victim into an inappropriate sexual role.
40. Acceptance of the repeated application of the 'index of marital satisfaction' (IMS).
41. Acceptance that each person is solely responsible for themselves only.
42. Acceptance of the use of the 'Guidelines for Negotiation'.
43. Acceptance that previous methods of problem resolution were inadequate and facilitated the abuse.
44. Acceptance of the fact that in varying degrees the parenting process had failed and the parents have to accept the responsibility for that.
45. Willingness by the victim to participate in the reconstruction aspect of the work.

46. Acceptance of the need to visit after two weeks to re-apply in the family setting all the written instruments used in the course of therapy for comparison.
47. Acceptance that this should be done in the office setting.
48. Acceptance of the need to formulate a post-treatment 'overview system' through the medium of the case-conference.
49. Acceptance that at the two week meeting a programme of family/therapy team meetings will need to be arranged at reducing frequency rates over the next two years.

Source: Simmons, T. (1986). Child Sexual Abuse: An assessment process.
© London: NSPCC. Reproduced with permission.

REASONS TO CHANGE

Why might you want to change your behaviour?

- To get people off my back
- To get rid of social workers
- To avoid going to court

- I don't want to be locked up
- To be accepted by family/ friends
- To be seen as 'normal' not in spotlight

- I want to be seen as ordinary
- I want to go home
- I want to be with my family

- I want family to approve of me
- I want to please others

- I want to feel better about myself
- I don't want to feel so guilty

- I want to feel comfortable with myself
- I don't want to repeat the behaviour

- I want to be more in control
- To get new friends/new prospects
- I want to stop abusing

- I want to stop being abused
- To improve my job chances
- I want to be allowed more freedom

© Coventry NSPCC. Reproduced with permission of Richard Gist.

OFFENCE ANALYSIS (CALDER, 1997)

Offender's Name: _____
Victim's Name: _____
Family Member?   YES/NO   Age: _____
Date of Conviction: _____
Date of Offence: _____

TASK: TO PROVIDE A DETAILED DESCRIPTION OF YOUR SEXUAL OFFENCE
Please complete a separate worksheet for each individual victim.

1. Antecedents.
- What were you feeling before the offence?
- What worrying signs were there?
- What else was going on in your life just before you offended?
- What led up to the offence being committed?
- How and when did you prepare and plan for the opportunity to offend?
- How did you select the victim?

2. Describe the Offence itself.
- What were you thinking and feeling, as well as doing?
- What did you do?
- What did you say to make them co-operate/to keep quiet?
- What did you ask/threaten the victim to do?
- Where and how many times did you abuse them? How frequently?
- What had you planned that did not happen?

3. Post-Offence Issues.
- Have you felt guilty or satisfaction by your behaviour?
- Do you use the abuse as fuel for fantasy and masturbation?
- What would you plan to do next, given the opportunity?
- What consequences (if any) have you experienced since the abuse came to light?

A model for Risk Assessment

For each stage of the analysis, try to answer the question WHY?

1. List the dangers in this case.
   A 'danger' is something you want to avoid so what possible events would you fear in these circumstances? Rank these danger in order of their significance. Consider not only the "effect" of the danger if it occurs but the "chance" of it happening.

2. List the hazards in the case.
   A 'hazard', in this context, is something which might result in a danger being realised—something that helps to bring about the circumstances you want to avoid.

3. Divide the list of hazards into two:
   (a) predisposing hazards
   (b) situational hazards
   A 'predisposing hazard' makes the danger more likely. It is something that creates vulnerability, though it may need to be activated by something else, perhaps a situational hazard.
   A 'situational hazard' is something that happens, and which has an immediate effect directly related to the danger.

4. List what you consider to be the strengths in this case.
   Strengths are those factors whose effects counteract the danger, and make it less likely to become a reality.

5. Identify the additional information which you believe to be necessary.
   Evaluating the information you already have may indicate that there are some important gaps in your knowledge, gaps which should be filled before a final assessment is arrived at.

6. Indicate the decisions you feel should be taken.

Taken from Brearley, CP. (1982) Risk and Social Work. London: Routledge.

RISK ASSESSMENT RATING SCALE

Therapists treating sex offenders are expected to estimate future dangerousness. Criteria to assess risk for other crimes apply also to sex offenders and twenty factors are most frequently cited in clinical and research literature.

The same basic rating scale as that for classifying and assessing treatment need and progress can be used to assess risk:

RISK FACTOR	LOW		RELATIVE RISK MODERATE		HIGH	
	0	1	2	3	4	5
1. *History of violence.* The best predictor of future violence is past violence	__	__	__	__	__	__
2. *Progressive offense pattern.* Problem sexual behavior is repeated, reinforced, and becomes entrenched	__	__	__	__	__	__
3. *Precipitating events.* Trigger stimuli, provocative situations	__	__	__	__	__	__
4. *Environmental controls.* Structured situations deter excess (school, job rules, public scrutiny)	__	__	__	__	__	__
5. *Offender demographics.* Sex offender base rates: Norton (1988) found highest risk to be males. Mean age 35, IQ 84, 3+ assaults, family dysfunction, juvenile crime, job/personal loss	__	__	__	__	__	__
6. *Stress "noise" level.* High stress and high anxiety disinhibit, impulsivity increases	__	__	__	__	__	__
7. *Cognitive distortion.* Muddled/muddled illogical thinking, preconceived notions, myths	__	__	__	__	__	__
8. *Affect management.* Insufficient control of anger and frustration	__	__	__	__	__	__
9. *Drive state.* High, unvented sex drive with anger-power	__	__	__	__	__	__
10. *Adaptive coping.* History of difficulties	__	__	__	__	__	__
11. *Mental state/personality dynamics.* Underlying mental or personality disorders; paranoid schizophrenia common (Norton, 1988)	__	__	__	__	__	__
12. *Opportunity/victim access.* Available victim plus opportunity and impulse	__	__	__	__	__	__
13. *Method, means.* Secluded place, vehicle, situation, etc	__	__	__	__	__	__
14. *Personal responsibility.* Lack of "social conscience" to behave appropriately	__	__	__	__	__	__
15. *Remorse-empathy.* Compassion, sympathy, guilt, after doing wrong	__	__	__	__	__	__
16. *Baseline motivation.* Day-to-day adaptation to societal values	__	__	__	__	__	__
17. *Socialization.* Appropriate social skills	__	__	__	__	__	__
18. *Substance abuse.* Disinhibits	__	__	__	__	__	__
19. *Psychopathy.* No conscience	__	__	__	__	__	__
20. *Self concept.* Stable, healthy, self esteem, spirituality	__	__	__	__	__	__

Maximum score is 100. High score correlates with increased risk for re-offending reported as mild, moderate, or highly likely. Using such a quantified system provides a standard for assessing risk, a guideline for therapists for treatment planning, and a useful measure for program development, and followup studies of treatment effectiveness.

REFERENCE: MacHovec, F. (1994). A systematic approach to sex offender therapy: diagnosis, treatment, and risk assessment. Psychotherapy in Private Practice 13 (2): 93–108. Reproduced by permission of the author.

Bays & Freeman-Longo
Evaluation of Dangerousness for Sexual Offenders

This scale may be reproduced without permission.

Instructions: For each of the following items, check only one (1) of the selections offered.

A. Sexual offense history:

___ [1] First reported offense. The client has never before been accused of a sexual abuse/assault.
___ [3] The client has two or more accusations or one previous conviction on record for sexual abuse/assault.
___ [5] The client has been accused or convicted of multiple instances of sexual abuse.

B. Criminal history

___ [0] The client has no previous arrests or convictions for a non-sexual felony.
___ [3] The client has one or more arrests or convictions for non-sexual felonies in the last five years without incarceration.
___ [5] The client has one or more incarcerations for a non-sexual felony.

C. Violence in crimes

___ [0] The client has no previous history of violence in crimes.
___ [3] The client has used some violence or threats of violence but without weapons in any offense.
___ [5] The client has used violence or threats of violence with weapons in past or present offense(s).
___ [7] The client has used extreme violence or sadism, with or without weapons in present or past offense(s).

D. Anger

___ [0] The client has no anger associated with or in the offense.
___ [1] The client has minimal anger associated with or in the offense.
___ [3] The client has had consistent problems with anger.
___ [7] The client has anger or revenge as a motivating factor in the offense.

E. Aggression in general

___ [0] The client has no history of interpersonal aggression.
___ [3] The client has a history of mild interpersonal aggression or moderate aggression within the past ten years.
___ [5] The client has a recent history of extreme or consistent interpersonal aggression.

F. Victim Interaction since crime

___ [0] The client has deliberately not had any contact with the victim(s) since the crime was reported.
___ [3] The client has deliberately been in contact with the victim(s) since the crime was reported.
___ [7] The client has made threats to the victim(s) since the offense was reported.

G. Discussion of the offense

___ [0] The client is open and willing to discuss all aspects of the offense.
___ [1] The client avoids the discussion of some parts of the offense.
___ [5] The client refuses to discuss the offense.

H. Responsibility for the offense

___ [0] The client has fully accepted personal responsibility for all aspects of the offense.
___ [1] The client minimizes personal responsibility for the offense.
___ [5] The client minimizes personal responsibility and partially blames the victim, others, or his/her circumstances for the offense.
___ [7] The client denies the offense and/or related responsibility.

I. Remorse about the offense

___ [0] The client expresses great remorse about the offense.
___ [1] The client expresses minimal remorse or is neutral about the offense.
___ [5] The client expresses no remorse for his offense(s).
___ [7] The client defends the offense or expresses interest in activities similar to the offense.

J. Impulsive or compulsive behaviors

___ [0] The client shows little evidence of impulsive or compulsive behaviors.
___ [3] The client has a history of occasional impulsive behaviors that are related to the crime.
___ [5] The client has a history of compulsive behaviors that are related to the offense.
___ [7] The client has a documented history of impulsive and compulsive behaviors that are directly related to offending behavior.

K. Deviant sexual interest/arousal

___ [1] The client has a predominant interest in appropriate sexual themes and/or low deviant sexual arousal with high appropriate sexual arousal.
___ [3] The client has equal interest/arousal to both deviant and appropriate sexual themes.
___ [5] The client has a predominant interest in deviant sexual themes and/or high deviant and low appropriate sexual arousal.

L. Deviant sexual thoughts, urges, and fantasies

___ [0] The client's deviant sexual thoughts, urges, and/or fantasies are spoken of openly and as a problem.
___ [3] The client's deviant sexual thoughts, urges, and/or fantasies are minimized and hidden.
___ [5] The client denies having deviant sexual thoughts, urges, and/or fantasies.

M. Paraphilia

___ [1] The client has a single paraphilia and is involved with only one sex.
___ [3] The client has a single paraphilia and is involved with both sexes.
___ [5] The client has two paraphilias and is involved with one sex.
___ [7] The client has two paraphilias and is involved with both sexes.
___ [5] The client has three or more paraphilias and is involved with one sex.
___ [7] The client has three or more paraphilias and is involved with both sexes.

N. Victims

—— [1] The client has had one or two victims.
—— [3] The client has had three to five victims.
—— [5] The client has had six or more victims.
—— [7] The client has multiple victims with a serial pattern of offending.

O. Location of crime

—— [1] The client has a history of offenses that took place in one type of location that access to is not easily restricted, i.e. family home.
—— [3] The client has a history of offenses that took place in several locations that access to is not easily restricted, i.e. public parks, family home, etc.
—— [5] The client has a history of offenses that have taken place in a particular location that it is easy to restrict access to, i.e. a car in a remote area.
—— [7] The client has a history of offenses that have taken place in many locations, and it is easy to restrict access to these places.

P. History/time of offending behavior

—— [1] The client has a history of sexually offending behavior that took place over a specific period of time that is less than 6 months.
—— [3] The client has a history of sexually offending behavior that has taken place over a period of time less than two years.
—— [5] The client has a history of sexual offending behavior that has taken place over a period of time greater than two years.

Q. Age of the offender

—— [1] Offender is less than thirteen (13) years old.
—— [3] Offender is between fourteen (14) and twenty-one (21) years old.
—— [5] Offender is between twenty-two (22) and forty-five (45) years old.
—— [7] Offender is over forty-five (45) years old.

R. Alcohol and drug use

—— [0] The client has no history of alcohol and or drug use.
—— [1] The client has minimal use of alcohol and/or drugs. Use of alcohol and drugs is UNRELATED to offending behavior.
—— [3] The client has consistent use of alcohol or drugs. Use of alcohol and/or drugs is UNRELATED to offending behavior.
—— [5] The client has a history of alcohol and/or drug use or abuse. Use of alcohol and/or drugs is RELATED to offending behavior.
—— [7] The client has a history of alcohol and/or drug addiction.

S. Social support system

—— [0] The client has non-criminal significant others that he loves and can rely upon for support.
—— [1] The client has non-criminal significant others that will offer him limited support but generally leave him alone.
—— [5] The client has no non-criminal significant others and/or an environment that enable behavior that have contributed to sexual deviance.
—— [7] The client in involved/invested in a criminal support group or criminal sub-culture.

T. Motivation for treatment

—— [0] The client has an active desire to fully participate in treatment.
—— [3] The client has an indifferent motivation for treatment.
—— [5] The client does not want to participate in treatment.
—— [7] The client is hostile towards treatment.

U. Empathy for victim

—— [0] The client verbalizes and demonstrates empathy for victim(s).
—— [3] The client is indifferent to victim(s), never refers to victim's feelings.
—— [5] Client blames victim(s).
—— [7] Client is hostile towards victim(s) and/or threatens victim(s).

V. Self-esteem

—— [0] The client has evidence of self-esteem while able to acknowledge faults, knows of some positive personality characteristics, and feels some hope for the future.
—— [3] The client has low self-esteem, and can think of few positive characteristics about himself. May or may not feel some hope for the future.
—— [5] The client's presentation of self is colored with unrealistic expectations and grandiose ideas about himself.
—— [7] The client displays either very low OR a false image of high self-esteem. He/she presents as either hating him/her self and sees no possibility for improvement in the future, or is overconfident and is filled with unrealistic optimism and expectations about the future.

W. Work/school adjustment

—— [0] The client has a stable work or school history and is able to continue with it.
—— [3] The client has an unstable work or school history and is unable to continue with his current involvements.
—— [5] The client has a chronic and extremely unstable school and/or work history.

X. Depression

—— [0] The client has no evidence of clinical depression.
—— [1] The client is clinically depressed but is able to function in daily living activities.
—— [3] The client has a history of chronic depression but is generally able to function in daily living activities.
—— [5] The client has a history of chronic depression and is not able to presently function in daily living activities.

Scoring and interpretation

This risk assessment scale is not validated. The scale is designed to assist the clinician in determining risk of the offender to the community and providing guidelines for a detailed evaluation of the client, in conjunction with other measures. Therefore, each item must be weighed and considered in respect to the other items and the offender's overall personal history. To the best of the authors' knowledge there exists no validated method or scale of accurately predicting dangerousness.

Instructions

After marking the appropriate selection for each of the above items, add up the point value in front of each selection for a final score and compare with the following scale:

7 — 35	Low Risk	Probable appropriateness for probation.
36 — 69	Moderate Risk	May be appropriate for probation with strict conditions and intensive supervision. Appropriate for work release.
70 — 110	High Risk	Appropriate for incarceration.
Above 111	Very High Risk	Appropriate for incarceration.

Reference: In Carich MS and Adkerson DL (1995) Adult sex offender assement packet. Brandon, VT: Safer Society Press, where it is stated it can be reproduced without permission.

Y. Suicide history

___ [0] The client has no thoughts of suicide and no history of attempts.
___ [3] The client has thoughts of suicide but no history of attempts.
___ [5] The client has thoughts of suicide and a history of attempts.
___ [7] The client has a history of suicide attempts and a present plan.

Z. Mental status

___ [0] The client does not have a history of psychiatric disorders and does not show evidence of any psychiatric disorder.
___ [3] The client has a history of a psychiatric disorder.
___ [5] The client has a major psychiatric disorder.
___ [7] The client has evidence of a major psychiatric disorder with paranoid or psychotic features.

AA. Personal history of abuse (sexual, physical, emotional, or neglect)

___ [0] The client has no history of abuse as a child.
___ [1] The client has a history of mild or occasional neglect as a child.
___ [3] The client has a history of mild or occasional abuse as a child.
___ [5] The client has a history of abuse/neglect as a child.
___ [7] The client has a history of abuse over a long period of time.

BB. Social adjustment

___ [0] The client is well adjusted socially with adequate social skills.
___ [3] The client has poor social adjustment with inadequate social skills.
___ [5] The client has very poor social skills, with a history of avoiding others and isolating himself.

CC. Cooperation during interview

___ [0] Client was cooperative during the interview and readily answered questions.
___ [1] Client was cooperative during interview but needed to be pushed to answer questions completely/thoroughly.
___ [3] Client was somewhat cooperative but resistant to answering questions openly and honestly.
___ [5] Client was uncooperative during interview and reluctant to or resisted answering questions.
___ [7] Client refused to participate in interview.

Instructions

1. Use the interview protocol to obtain the data.
2. Complete the basic data for offender type.
3. Place an "X" or a check mark on any of the factors that apply to the offender.
4. Subtotal the number of X's marked on Section I & II.
5. Total both sections.
6. Take the raw score and locate the level of risk according to the scale.
7. You may use the scoring grid on Page 5 to assist in the addition (if needed).

Risk Assessment Checklist Scale

Section I - Historical Risk Factors

1. ___ Multiple victims (2 or more victims).
2. ___ Extensive history of offending per victim (more than three months).
3. ___ Extensive history of repeated offending (more than two assaults).
4. ___ Extensive legal history of offending and/or other criminal offensives (more than one incarceration and/or previous charges including juvenile).
5. ___ Multiple paraphilia (sexual deviation - more than one).
6. ___ Multiple victim-types by history (more than one).
7. ___ Victim-types are of both genders.
8. ___ History of violent/sadistic crimes.
9. ___ History of killing and/or attempting to kill victims.
10. ___ Drug and/or alcohol history (using alcohol beyond social situations and/or using drugs more than several times).
11. ___ Extensive history of rage and anger (explosive , verbally assaultive, destroys property, physically assaultive, etc.).
12. ___ History of a victim including any of the following: under six years old, elderly, mentally/physically disabled.

Risk Assessment Checklist Scale
© Mark S. Carich, PhD & Carole Metzger, MSW
Terry Campbell, MS
November 1996*

Type of Offender:

___ Adult Rapist   ___ Paraphilia NOS

___ Pedophilia Male   ___ Pedophilia Female

___ Adult Peeping Male   ___ Adult Peeping Female

___ Child Peeping Male   ___ Child Peeping Female

___ Adult Exhibitionist Male   ___ Adult Exhibitionist Female

___ Child Exhibitionist Male   ___ Child Exhibitionist Female

Name _____ Social Security/ID Number _____

Date _____ Agency _____ Interviewer _____

Risk Level _____ Score _____

Assessments: ___ Initial, ___ 2nd, ___ 3rd, ___ 4th

Introduction:

This risk assessment instrument is based on both historical (past history) and non-historical (current behaviors, within 1-2 years) risk factors.

There are sixteen historical items and twenty non-historical items. Items range from:

Personality characteristics, substance use, victimology, mental health, assaultive behaviors.

A brief interview protocol is required to establish guidelines on how to obtain data for this instrument. Data collection can be acquired from any type of clinical historical documents, current/past observations, interviews, police reports. etc.

A risk factor is any overt/covert behaviors, places or situations that enhance the offender to become closer to reoffending.

The scale is not yet validated, however, may provide useful guidelines to assess for risk. The scale is based on probabilities not absolutes, given the risk factors.

275

12. Admits to a high level of masturbation to deviant fantasies.

13. Appears to exhibit high levels of narcissistic behaviors (continuous patterns) by demonstrating any of the following: self-centeredness (the world revolves around self), self-pity, entitlement (I want what I want and I deserve it), acts superior or has a better than thou attitude).

14. Maintains an extensive justification system concerning offenses (i.e., minimization, excuses, blames, denial, religiosity and projection).

15. Appears to be withdrawn, alienated and/or isolated.

16. Engages in dysfunctional (inappropriate, enabling, conflictual, unhealthy, inappropriate sexual connotations, etc.) relationships (i.e., negative volatile partner, dysfunctional friendships, etc.).

17. Appears to be "needy", dependant, overly attached, enmeshed boundaries.

18. Appears to be jealous, overly protective, possessive (ownership of others).

19. Engages in self-destructive behaviors.

20. Appears to enjoy others pain and suffering.

Total Number of Items Checked.

---

13. Preferred victim-type gender is male.

14. Extensive personal history of victimization (family chaos/discord, neglect, sexual, physical, verbal, and mental abuse over a two year period of time).

15. Appears to have a history of self-destructive and social behavior (i.e., gestures, attempts and self-mutilation).

16. Extensive history of anti-social behavior (i.e.. failure to conform to society's rules, lies, impulsiveness, aggressiveness, victimizes, lacks empathy/remorse, sadistic, cruelty, crooked behavior, cheats, etc.)

Total number of item checks.

Section II: Non-Historical Risk Factors

Non-Historical or current behaviors denote consistent patterns or demonstrations of behaviors for less than 6 months to 2 years.

1. Displays dishonesty in any form (i.e., lies, maintains secrets, withholds information, contorts and/or distorts information, etc.).

2. Uncooperative with any type of staff (i.e., argumentive, resistant, misses sessions, disobeys rules/plans, etc.).

3. Appears to avoid taking responsibility for offenses and/ or globally (life in general) in any way (i.e., denial avoidance, minimization, justification, fallacy of fairness, and power games, etc.).

4. Lacks coping skills as demonstrated in dealing with risk factors.

5. Maintains denial (i.e., responsibility, intent, impact of victim fantasy, etc.).

6. Lacks insight into and application of intervention skills in the assault cycle.

7. Appears to continue patterns of antisocial behavior (i.e., anyone consistently exhibiting any of the following: crookedness, sneakiness, lacks empathy/remorse, continuously victimizes, lies and cheats, etc.).

8. Lacks empathy in general, victim empathy (emotional understanding of the victim) and remorse (the painful regret of hurting others).

9. Displays violent and assaultive behaviors.

10. Associates with victim-types and/or substitute victim-types.

11. Admits to a high-level of deviant sexual fantasies (once per day).

Interpretation on four point scale:

1. Low risk - At this time, the offender appears to be at low degree of risk to reoffend. Offender may or may not be in early stages of cycle. Moderate levels of supervision are recommended.

2. Moderate Risk - At this time, the offender appears to be mediocre degree of risk to reoffend. Offender appears to be in cycle frequently. Needs help to defuse cycle. Moderate levels of supervision are recommended.

3. High Risk - The offender appears to be at above average probability to reoffend. Appears to be in close to or is in acting out stage of cycle. There are no predicted time frames of actual offending. High levels of supervision are recommended.

4. Extreme High Risk - The offender seems to be at very high probability to reoffend. The offender appears to be in and stays deep into his/her assault cycle close to or is reoffending. Although there can be no definite time frames reoffending could happen fairly quickly (within six months or less).

See a list of cycle behaviors and in particular risk factor behaviors for clues to indicate offenders actions.

Reproduced with the permission of Mark Carich.

SCALE

Section I. Subtotal _____ + Section II. Subtotal _____ = Grand Total _____

If needed use the scale grid for help to score.

4 point scale

L - low risk	0-4
M - moderate risk	5-8
H - high risk	9-11
EH - extreme high risk	12-36

Offender appears to be - _____ based on a 4 point scale.

Scale scoring grid

Instruction score sheet:

I. Place an "X" on the grid for every checked item.

II. Give one point for each "X".

III. Total each section of the sub-total columns.

IV. Add sub-totals for grand total.

V. Scales are based on raw scores which are indicated by the 4 point scale

SCORING GRID

Section I: Historical Risk Factors

1. ___	5. ___	9. ___	13. ___
2. ___	6. ___	10. ___	14. ___
3. ___	7. ___	11. ___	15. ___
4. ___	8. ___	12. ___	16. ___

Total:

___ + ___ + ___ + ___ = ___

Section I: ___ + Section II: ___ = ___ Grand Total

Section II: Non-Historical risk factors.

1. ___	6. ___	11. ___	16. ___
2. ___	7. ___	12. ___	17. ___
3. ___	8. ___	13. ___	18. ___
4. ___	9. ___	14. ___	19. ___
5. ___	10. ___	15. ___	20. ___

Total:

___ + ___ + ___ + ___ = ___ Grand Total

RISK ASSESSMENT CHECKLIST SCALE PROTOCOL

© Mark S. Carich, PhD & Carole Metzger, MSW
Terry Campbell, MS
September 1996

This brief interview protocol is required to establish guidelines on how to obtain data for this instrument. Data collection can be acquired from any type of clinical historical documents, current/past observations, interviews, police reports, etc.

The scale is not yet validated, however, may provide useful guidelines to assess for risk. The scale is based on probabilities not absolutes, given the risk factors.

This interview will consist of a social history, a checklist of sexual arousal patterns, and brief victimology information.

1. Biographical Data

A. Age: D.O.B. _____ Current Age _____ Years

B. Relationships:
Current Marital Status: _____ single _____ separated _____ married (_____ yrs.)
_____ divorced _____ common-law relationship _____ other _____ engaged

Explanation: _____

C. All protocol questions correspond with scale risk factors.

All "Yes" responses to the protocol questions indicate an item needing checked on the scale.

	Yes	No
1. Was there more than one victim?		
2. Is the offending history more than 3 months?		
3. Was there more than 2 assaults?		
4. Are there other criminal offenses?		
5. Does the offender have more than one sexual deviant behavior?		
6. Is there more than one type of victim (age, gender, build, etc.)?		
7. Are victim types both genders?		
8. Is the offender physically violent and/or sadistic (cruel)?		
9. Did the offender kill and/or attempt to kill the victim?		
10. Has the offender used drugs at all and/or alcohol beyond socially?		
11. Is there a history of anger and explosiveness?		
12. Are any victims disabled, elderly or under age 6?		
13. Was any victim and/or victim type male?		
14. Was the offender abused for a period of 3 years?		
15. Is there a history of self-destruction?		
16. Is there a history of crookedness, antisocial (psychopathic tendencies) behaviors?		

D. Current Behaviors

Questions correspond with scale items.
Does offender exhibit any of the following behaviors?

	Yes	No
1. Any form of dishonesty.		
2. Uncooperativeness.		
3. Avoids responsibility.		
4. Lacks coping skills.		
5. In denial (any form).		
6. Lacks cycle intervention skills.		
7. Appears crooked, manipulative, deviant, etc.		
8. Lacks empathy for victims or in general.		
9. Displays violent behaviors.		
10. Associates with victims types.		
11. Deviant fantasies (one per day).		
12. Masturbates to deviant fantasies.		
13. Narcissistic (acts superior, self-centered, entitled).		

	Yes	No
14. Justifies offenses.		
15. Appears withdrawn.		
16. Dysfunctional relationships.		
17. Appears needy, clingy, dependant.		
18. Appears jealous.		
19. Self-destructive behavior.		
20. Enjoys others pain.		

2. Sexual Arousal Patterns

Check each area of expressed sexual interest. Note gender(s) included in target area of interest. Note age range included, if a partner/victim is applicable for the sexual interest.

Check under **R** if interest information was obtained from records or collateral reports; **P** if found by phallometric assessment; and under **S** if by verbal or written self report.

R	P	S	SEXUAL INTEREST	Male	Female	Age Range
			exhibitionism w/masturbation			
			voyeurism (peeping)			
			obscene calling			
			sexual homicide			
			perform/receive oral sex			
			perform/receive vaginal intercourse			
			perform/receive anal intercourse			
			penetration w/object			
			frotteurism (fondling)			

BRIEF VICTIMOLOGY

**NOTE: If the offender does not know, he/she may estimate.

3. Contact Victims (physical contact)

A. Number of total victims _____ Male _____ Female _____

B. Age range of male victims (children/adolescents/adult) _____ years.

C. Age range of female victims (children/adolescents/adult) _____ years.

D. Number of years or period of time you were offending _____

E. Your age at your first contact sexual assault. _____ years old.

F. Your age at your last contact sexual assault. _____ years old.

G. Indicate if you were sexually victimized:

1. Contact:
   _____ Yes _____ No
   _____ Male _____ Female
   _____ Stranger _____ Non-stranger _____ Family

2. Non-contact:
   _____ Yes _____ No
   _____ Male _____ Female
   _____ Stranger _____ Non-stranger _____ Family

H. Estimated number of contact assaults on males. _____

I. Estimated number of contact assaults on females. _____

J. The amount of time of your longest victimization per victim. _____

4. Non-Contact Victims

A. _____ Flashing

1. Number of male victims _____ /age range _____

2. Number of female victims _____ /age range _____

10 FC PROFILE

DEVIANCE FROM SOCIOSEXUAL NORMS

THERAPY FACTORS	MILD		MODERATE		SEVERE	
	0	1	2	3	4	5
1. Physical aggression						
2. Sexual aggression						
3. Asocialization						
4. Fantasy						
5. Sexual arousal						
6. Offense cycle						
7. Cognitive distortion						
8. Denial-minimization						
9. Remorse-empathy						
10. Prognosis/progress						

Sex offense(s): _____ Victim Sex: _____
Victim age(s): _____

MacHovec and Wieckowski (1992) developed a single comprehensive classification system of ten factors that apply to all sex offenders, male and female, juvenile and adult. Each factor is rated on a scale from 0 (no clinical significance) to 5 (extreme deviation):

1. *Physical aggression*, the offender's history of non-sexual violence, ranging from 0 (none) to 5 (extremely violent, severe injury, torture, or death even after victim submits, cannot vent rage appropriately).

2. *Sexual aggression*, aggression specific to sex offense, rated 0 (totally consensual) to 5 (extremely violent sexual attack event after victim submits, severe injury, torture, or death).

3. *Asocialization*, ability to conform to socio-sexual norms, 0 (socially appropriate in all situations) to 5 (poor socialization in all situations).

4. *Fantasy*, fantasy about deviant sexual behavior, 0 (none) to 5 (fantasy-dominated to delusional extreme).

5. *Sexual arousal*, deviation in what is sexually arousing, 0 (conforms to societal standards, no clinical significance) to 5 (aroused only by inappropriate or deviant sexual stimuli or fantasy).

6. *Offense cycle*, awareness of and ability to interrupt the cycle and pattern of sex offending, thoughts, feelings and events before, during, and after offense, his/her own victimization, family dysfunction, substance abuse if significant, 0 (fully aware, understands, likely to stop cycle every time), to 5 (no awareness or understanding, not likely to stop cycle any time).

7. *Cognitive distortion*, recognizing cognitive distortions or unrealistic expectations, thinking that distorts reality, blocks responsibility for offending behavior, knowledge of sex and sexuality, aware of knowledge and skills deficits that contribute to offenses, relapse prevention, rated 0 (none) to 5 (severe distortion).

8. *Denial-minimization*, offender's use of denial and minimization and conversely self-disclosure, 0 (no denial, accepts full responsibility) to 5 (total denial; "it didn't happen").

9. *Remorse-empathy*, social sensitivity, adaptive and coping skills, 0 (heavily affect-laden verbally and nonverbally) to 5 (no remorse, victims are objects, targets, prey).

10. *Prognosis*, readiness and potential for therapy, therapy, 0 (excellent) to 5 (poor).

REFERENCES: (a) MacHovec, F. (1994). A systematic approach to sex offender therapy. *Psychotherapy in Private Practice*, **13**(2): 93–108.
(b) For a fuller discussion around the 10FC, the reader is referred to MacHovec, F. and Wieckowski, E. (1992). The 10 FC: Ten-factor continua of classification and treatment criteria for male and female sex offenders. *Medical Psychotherapy*, **5**: 53–63.
© Frank MacHovec. Reproduced with his permission.

B.   Peeping
   1. Number of male victims _____ /age range _____
   2. Number of female victims _____ /age range _____

C.   Obscene Phone Calling
   1. Number of male victims _____ /age range _____
   2. Number of female victims _____ /age range _____

D.   Stalking
   1. Number of male victims _____ /age range _____
   2. Number of female victims _____ /age range _____

E.   Verbal Sexual Harassment
   1. Number of male victims _____ /age range _____
   2. Number of female victims _____ /age range _____

F.   Pornography exposure (any type, including filming others)
   1. Number of male victims _____ /age range _____
   2. Number of female victims _____ /age range _____

G.   Total number of victims _____ Male _____ Female

H.   Age range of victims _____ Male _____ Female

I.   Your age at your first non-contact sexual assault. _____ years.

J.   Your age at your last non-contact sexual assault. _____ years.

K.   Estimated number of assaults _____ male _____ female

L.   Longest amount of time of your longest victimization. _____

5. Summary of Contact and Non-Contact Victims

A.   Total Number of Victims _____ Male _____ Female

B.   Age range of Victims _____ Male _____ Female

C.   Total number of years, or amount of time, you were offending. _____

D.   Age of your first assault _____ years
   Age of your last assault _____ years

E.   Total number of estimated assaults on males _____
   Total number of estimated assaults on females _____

F.   Number of male victims by age group _____
   children (pre-puberty) _____
   adolescents (up to 18 years) _____
   adults _____

G.   Number of female victims by age group _____
   children (pre puberty) _____
   adolescents (up to 18 years) _____
   adults _____

H.   Indicate if you were sexually victimized
   1. Contact _____ Yes _____ No
     by _____ Male _____ Female
     by _____ Stranger _____ non-stranger/family
   2. Non-Contact _____ Yes _____ No
     by _____ Male _____ Female
     by _____ Stranger _____ non-stranger/family

Reproduced by permission of Mark S. Carich.

SEX OFFENDER TREATMENT NEEDS ASSESSMENT AND PROGRESS SUMMARY

TREATMENT FACTOR	NONE 0	POOR 1	LOW AVG. 2	AVG. 3	GOOD 4	VERY GOOD 5
1. *Responsibility/readiness*, without denial, minimization or blaming; amerable to therapy		___	___	___	___	___
2. *Cognitive distortion*, overcomes denial, fantasy, and avoidance		___	___	___	___	___
3. *Deviant fantasy*, knows and able to modify to socially appropriate level		___	___	___	___	___
4. *Processes own victimization*, loss, rejection, abandonment, or family dysfunction		___	___	___	___	___
5. *Offense cycle* understood, how to interrupt/control it; sexual arousal pattern, how and when to get help	___	___	___	___	___	___
6. *Impulse control*: anger, power need, frustration, helplessness; improved coping skills; meeting affective needs appropriately; role of substance abuse	___	___	___	___	___	___
7. *Remorse/empathy* for victim, the victim's family, offender's family, friends, society; restitution (victim, community)	___	___	___	___	___	___
8. *Resocialization*: Appropriate life, social, and interpersonal skills, verbal and nonverbal, public and private; building trust; family issues	___	___	___	___	___	___
9. *Normalization*: Understands what appropriate sexual outlets, what is and is NOT considered normal, lawful behavior; consequences	___	___	___	___	___	___
10. *Self concept*, sex role, identity, and preference; appropriate arousal and outlet; stability and spirituality	___	___	___	___	___	___

REFERENCE: MacHovec, F. (1994). A systematic approach to sex offender therapy: diagnosis, treatment, and risk assessment. *Psychotherapy in Private Practice*, **13**(2): 93–108. Reproduced by permission of the author.

EVOLUTION OF RECOVERY: 15 COMMON FACTORS OR ELEMENTS (Carich, 1997).

The concept of recovery is defined as a continuum of progress towards maintaining abstinence. A recovery evaluation is an evaluation of a sex offender's progress in maintaining abstinence. It is assumed that the offender is in some type of treatment program at the time of the assessment or else he/she is in related behaviors to a large amount of change, including a reduction of deviant responses. The rate of recovery at that time can correlate the risk of progress of progress are more apt to re-offend. Those not in treatment should be reflected as not recovered by this criteria. This concept of recovery doesn't mean a magical "cure." This concept of recovery is based on the notion that there is no cure for offenders. The term cure refers to a permanent abstinence or absence of the problem (i.e., deviant responses). Deviant behavior is a choice and often a series of complex choices at both conscious and unconscious levels. It is an ingrained voluntary/involuntary behavior. **Each decision is a choice whether deliberate or automatic.** The potential of relapse is always present. Thus, "treatment" or some form of behavior. Again, it is generally recognized and accepted that there is no "cure" for sex offenders. It is also recognized that recovery is an ongoing lifelong process. In an effort to determine when offenders have recovered to a point where they could be released, the following 15 elements of criteria are established below along with brief definitions. These are typical goals in treatment.

The first element is motivation towards recovery. This is related to one's commitment towards change. It is the internal drive to succeed to recover. Motivation is the determination and amount of energy aimed towards recovery. It is the amount of drive and desire to recover. It is the determination and amount of energy aimed to maintain abstinence. The overall motivation towards recovery can be evaluated by the following elements:

a. Internal motivation towards recovery vs. release
b. Program attendance
c. Program participation
d. Complete task assignments
e. Type of participation in group therapy

The second element is a commitment towards change and recovery. In order to maintain a successful non-offending lifestyle outside the institution one has to be highly committed towards change. Commitment is the pledge, agreement, and compliance towards goals. It is the obligation of engaging in treatment. The offender has to be emotionally impelled to complete treatment goals. Commitment is the actualization of engaging in the change process. As there is no cure for sex offending and thus the offender has to rely on his own self along with external supervision sources in order to maintain a non-offending lifestyle. Specific criteria include:

a. Understand that change requires a commitment towards managing one's behavior
b. Program attendance
c. Participation
d. Level of openness and honesty
e. Completion of task assigments

The third element is personal responsibility. Personal responsibility refers to several things. It is defined as the placement of control of one's behavior. For example, does the individual take and assume full responsibility and accountability for his behavior or does he disown responsibility by using various justifications, rationalizations, and various defenses in order to evade or avoid responsibility. Another element is the admission versus the denial of information, offenses, and offense history. Defensive structures are rooted in cognitive distortions (blame, minimizing, justifying, rationalizing, denial, etc.). This factors into the amount of responsibility the individual is going to take for his life. This also includes accepting the full consequences of one's offending behavior onto his victims. This is referred to as victim impact issues. An outline of elements include:

a. Placement of control or locus of control (self vs. others)
b. Admission vs. denial of offenses and offense history
c. Defensive structures (minimizing, justifying, rationalizing, blaming, etc.)
d. Taking responsibility for one's behavior in general
e. Accepting the consequences of one's offending behavior

The fourth element is social interest. Social interest is the general care and concern for other individuals. This includes compassion and empathy. In terms of sex offenders, it refers to the level of victim empathy and remorse for one's victims. Victim empathy occurs at both intellectual and emotional levels. Empathy is simply the compassion for another individual. In other words, the offender is able to put himself into the victim's position and be able to experience those feelings and respond accordingly. Remorse is the painful regret of violating another individual. Remorse implies a conscience or a sense of authentic guilt which is feeling bad for violating another individual. The bad feeling are those of guilt or pain. Thus the offender experiences victim impact issues. Victim empathy can also be expressed for one's own victims or for victims in general. Specific criteria include:

a. Victim empathy (compassion, intellectual and emotional understanding of the victims situation)
b. Sense of guilt (appropriate guilt)

The fifth element is social dimension. This is the development of social relationships and social skills. More specifically, this category of behaviors includes: level of social skills, number of functional relationships, quality of those relationships, level of superficial behavior within relationships, possessiveness, exploitation, issues within authority figures, power and control issues, intimacy without sexual connotations, an entangled or enmeshed relationship boundary, and emotional alienation and isolation. The social dimension involves behaviors, processes, skills, issues, etc. within the interpersonal relationships. Specific criteria include:

a. Level of social skills ("I" messages, initiating/maintaining/terminating conversations, assertiveness, respect, eye contact, active listening, empathy) confrontation, deferring attention, behavioral description and prescription, summarizing, requesting, direct expression.
b. Number of relationships
c. Quality of those relationships
d. Level of superficial behavior within relationships
e. Relationship dynamics (i.e., possessiveness, jealousy, dependency, over attachment, enmeshed boundaries, etc.)
f. Exploitation
g. Power and control issues
h. Intimacy without sexual connotations
i. Enmeshed relationships boundaries
j. Withdrawal, emotional/behavioral avoidance, and isolation of others
k. Appropriate expression of emotions/feelings

The sixth element is insight into one's offending cycle. The offending cycle is the specific patterns of one's offending behavior or sexually assaultive behavior. There are several types of assault cycles including the unstructured cycle, Laren Bays and Robert Freeman-Longo (1990) four stage cycle (build-up, acting out, justification, and pretend normal), and the six stage model (initial stage, encountering a trigger, pre-search, search, set-up, assault, and aftermath or post-experimental stage) (Carich, 1996). This is the relapse process and/or offending process. No matter what model is used, there are 3 primary components: Pre-assault, assault, and aftermath. It is critical for offenders to identify their offending cycles. This is a primary tool which will enable one to identify when one is in an offending mode and then take specific steps of action in order to defuse the offending response or interrupt the relapse process. In terms of the cycles the following assumptions apply: There are no time frames; individuals may have multiple cycles and sub-cycles; offenders may skip stages, be fixated or regressed and stages may occur at the same time (Carich, 1996).

a. Understanding the concept of the cycle
b. Understanding different models of types of cycles
c. Understanding the offending cycle dynamic processes
d. Insight into one's offending cycle
e. Applying and utilizing the cycle to one self

The seventh element is lifestyle behaviors. Lifestyle behaviors refers to adaptation of the DSM-III-R and the DSM-IV Mental health Diagnostic Manual of personality disorders found on the Axis II diagnosis. (Carich & Adkerson, 1995) Lifestyle behaviors refers to the specific and general tendencies or chronic patterns of behavior. These patterns of behavior consist of automatic thoughts, feelings, tendencies, belief systems, perceptual world views, actual behaviors and activities, etc. They have been formulated as personality disorders in accordance to psychiatric mental disorders. These include: **antisocial, narcissistic, borderline, passive-aggressive and schizoidal.** The degree of intensity and frequency or level that offenders have these behaviors varies. Not all offenders are antisocial and narcissistic or have all of the other characteristics listed below. The act of sexual assault implies antisocial and narcissistic behavior. Some offenders have these characteristics only when offending while others have them chronically ingrained in their lifestyles. Most sex offenders can be analyzed in terms of specific lifestyle behaviors in five categories including:

a. **Antisocial:** lacks remorse and empathy, tends to victimize, tends to exploit, violates rules, sadistic tendencies and behaviors, exhibits phoniness or a facade, lies or distorts information, cheats, exhibits crooked thinking, tends to be over controlling, deviantly manipulates, etc.
b. **Narcissistic behaviors:** self-centeredness, entitlement, superior attitude, egocentric, dramatic, grandiose, demanding, stuck on self, "me only" attitude, overly exaggerated self-importance, out for self at other's expense, etc.
c. **Borderline:** poor impulse control, dependency, marked moodiness, over attachment, over idealization at times, jealousy, possessiveness, enmeshed relationships, history of self-destructiveness, unstable relationships, unstable in general, over attachment towards others, etc.
d. **Passive-aggressive:** expressing anger and hostility inappropriately sideways or indirectly, reacts negatively to criticism, etc.
e. **Schizoidal:** emotional isolation and alienation, lacks social skills, exhibits flat effect, and withdrawn.

The eighth element insight into one's developmental/motivational factors and dynamics. This includes insight into one's perceptions or experiences of one's developmental history known as "developmental perceptions". These are the contributing factors to the various motivational dynamics involved in the offending. These developmental perceptions and experiences formulate the various problematic issues that are considered to be motivational factors or dynamics. Developmental experiences are the various etiological or developmental experiences that feeds the offending. These are fused with and transformed into various motivational factors. Motivational factors are the teleological factors or purposes of the offending behavior. These motivational dynamics center around the purposes of offending. These are the reasons why the offender engages in sexual offending behavior. These are also specific issues in which the offender compensates through sexual aggression. Offenders are urged to develop an intellectual and emotional understanding at their level of functioning. The criteria includes:

a. Cognitive insight into one's significant developmental experience events, processes and dynamics.
b. Emotional insight into one's key motivational factor
c. Cognitive insight into one's significant developmental events.

The ninth element is resolution of various development/motivational dynamics. If the issues above are to be resolved, they remain laden with emotional content. This would put the offender at higher risk to re-offend. Although the memories cannot be totally erased, one's perceptions and feelings about those memories can be alte d. This is the goal in resolving these issues to a lesser degree. Thus, the offender doesn't get the same satisfactions from offending. Specific criteria include:

a. Resolution to a lesser degree of intensity, various etiological factors or significant developmental experiences, based upon perceptions.
b. Resolution to a lesser degree of various motivational dynamics involved in offending.

The tenth element is sexual identity issues and problems. Sexual identity issues are those issues involved in identifying specific sexual roles and preferences that they are going to project onto themselves and society. Sexual identity issues are any issues involving sexual role confusion, issues and/or traumas associated with sexual preference and selection. By definition, sex offenders have sexual identity issues by the selection of (inappropriate) sexual partners (and for methods of sex) and their sexual attraction. The decisions that led up to one's sexual identity need to be reviewed and any hidden difficulties or traumas need to be worked through. Criteria:

a. By definition, sex offenders have sexual identity issues. These issues need to be identified, explored and resolved.
b. Resolving sexual identity issues involves understanding one's sexual preference (heterosexual or homosexual) and feeling comfortable with it.

The eleventh element is control of deviant behaviors refers to the overall management of deviant responses. Thus, arousal control is the level and management of one's deviant behavior. Control of deviant behaviors refers to the level of deviant fantasies, level of violent fantasies, sexual interests and arousal patterns, the level of normal fantasies, and the level of masturbation to deviant, normal and sadistic fantasies. Elements include:

a. Level of frequency of deviant fantasies.
b. Level of violent fantasies
c. Level of normal fantasies
d. Sexual interests/arousal
e. Level of masturbation towards deviant fantasies
f. Level of masturbation towards normal fantasies
g. Level of masturbation towards sadistic fantasies

Methods of Evaluation:

a. Observation
b. Self Report (Self Tracking or Monitoring)
c. Polygraph Assessment
d. Phallometric Assessment
e. Paper pencil inventories
f. Interview process

The twelfth element is the type of psycho pathology. This refers to the level of and type of mental health problems and/or functioning. Specific elements include:

a. Axis I—Degree and type of pathology (mental disorders)
b. Axis II—Degree and type of pathology (personality and mental retardation disorders)
c. Axis III—Medical pathology

Basic criteria for evaluation

a. Orientation and alertness in time, person, and place
b. Overall moodiness, affect or emotional states presented
c. Speech patterns and other indications of psychosis (i.e., delusions, hallucinations ...)
d. Level of organicity
e. Behavioral observation

The thirteenth element is level of disowning behaviors. Disowning behaviors refers to any behavior that enables offending and/or evades or avoids responsibility for one's behavior. These are referred to as common defense mechanisms, thinking errors and/or cognitive distortions. This factor correlates with the 3rd element.

Specific elements include:

a. Defensive structures (i.e., denial, rationalizing, displacement, projections, etc.)
b. Cognitive Distortions (i.e., justification, entitlement, extremes, minimizing, blames, excuses, apathy, fallacy of fairness, victim stancing, etc.)
c. Dysfunctional coping strategies
d. Evaluate the above in terms of offense specific or global patterns.

The fourteenth element is relapse intervention skills. Relapse intervention skills refers to a specific set of skills in which the more motivated offenders learn in order to defuse or interrupt their offending cycles. More specifically, the relapse intervention skills are a set of skills in which offenders learn to identify triggers, cues, cycles, disowning behaviors, deviant cycle behaviors, etc. Offenders learn to neutralize disowning behaviors, as well as, defuse and interrupt relapse cycle responses. They are able to identify and avoid and/or defuse various risk factors anc situations. They have developed various coping skills, or interventions to defuse offending behaviors. Specific elements include:

a. Understanding of the various developmental motivational dynamics as related to sex offending and relapse processes
b. Can identify specific deviant cycles and patterns of offending
c. Can identify triggers (risk factors and situations) or those events that facilitate, initiate and stimulate offending behaviors
d. Identify relapse cues or indicators of offending responses
e. Identify and defuse various disowning behaviors
f. Develop relapse intervention skills that occur at a spontaneous and unconscious levels as automatic responses
g. Understands various risks, factors, and/or situations, along with a level of competence in order to evade and/or defuse offending situations.

The fifteenth element is self-structure in general. Self-structure in general refers to one's internal core beliefs and feelings about one's self. These are referred to as self-esteem issues, self-confidence, self-image, self-worth, loneliness, and various inferiorities.

a. Internal core beliefs/feelings about self (self-concept, self-image)
b. Self-esteem
c. Self-confidence
d. Areas of inferiority (compensated by superiority)
e. Self-image

STANDARD PROTOCOL FOR CONDUCTING RECOVERY EVALUATION

INTERVIEW PROFILE

A. BASIC GOALS:

1. Since there is not an acceptable "cure" or magical permanent absence of offending behavior/responses/problems, the overall goal includes: (1) No more victims!; (2) management of deviant behaviors; (3) lowering of deviant arousal.
2. Recovery evaluations measures progress in treatment and the levels of change, and the degree of the offenders non-offending life cycle.
3. Recovery is an ongoing process and perhaps evaluation needs to be ongoing, referred to as "progress assessments".

AREAS TO FOCUS ON:

1. Victimology
2. Victimizations
3. What they have learned
4. What they have yet to achieve
5. Do they think they are "cured"
6. Type of program attendance (check records)
7. Type of participation (check records)
8. Cruelty to others
9. Type of motivations or why they offended
10. Offense history and extensive review
11. Developmental history

SPECIFIC QUESTIONS:

1. MOTIVATION TOWARDS RECOVERY:
—Review records of attendance and participation;
—Review records of task assignment completion/goal completion;
—Ask the offender:
What are some of the things that you learned?
What areas do you need to work on?
What areas are you sensitive to, or seem problematic?
What are your goals in life?
Why do you want to quit offending?
For those offenders who are not in treatment, check out denial level, and ask how they plan to stop offending?

2. COMMITMENT TOWARDS TREATMENT:
—Review records of attendance and participation;
—Review records of task assignment completion/goal completion;
—Questions to ask the offender:
Where do you think you are in recovery?
What are you willing to give up, in terms of recovery?
Do you think you have any more problems?

3. PERSONAL RESPONSIBILITY:
—Review attendance/participation/ task completion
—Questions may revolve around offense history, work history, family history, etc.;
—Ask the offender to review victimizations and evaluate the responses;
—Questions to ask the offender;
Who was at fault? What was your fault? Was the victim at fault?
Can the offender's responses be evaluated in terms of minimization, denial, blame, justification ... other distortions and defenses, etc.?

4. SOCIAL INTEREST:
Analysis of general care and concern, victim empathy (empathy for specific victims/victims in general), remorse; compassion; respect for others;
—Ask offender to review cases and discuss the short and long term consequences to the victim. Look for cognitive distortions, defenses (i.e., justification, blame, denial, etc.). Other behaviors include: "I" messages, self-centeredness, entitlements, eyes shifting, non spontaneous responses, self-pity, spontaneous and care/sadness vs. phoniness, consistency in responses ...

10. SEXUAL IDENTITY ISSUES:
—Items to look at include: sexual orientation/preferences, sexual interests, "hangups", traumas, past victimizations, etc.;
—Questions to ask:
What experiences lead up to your preferences?
Are you comfortable with your decisions?

11. CONTROL OF DEVIANT RESPONSES:
Control or management of deviant responses. Things to look at include: masturbation patterns and frequency, stimulus sets, level of deviancy, deviant fantasy frequency, type and frequency of normal fantasies and sexual interests.
—Questions to ask:
How often do you masturbate? and to what?
How do you reduce your deviant responses?
How do you control fantasies, urges, etc.?
What is/was your ideal deviant fantasies?
how do you reduce your deviancy?
How often do you fantasize? What are your fantasies?

12. TYPE OF PSYCHOPATHOLOGY:
Psychopathology is the degree of dysfunction and disorders.
—Areas to look at include: abnormalities, dysfunction, disorders, suicidal history; speech patterns; reality testing; mental health exam, etc.
—Questions include:
Have you ever been psychotic? Hallucinations? Delusions? (If so explain)
How many suicide attempts, ideation, do/did you have?
How many times do you hurt yourself?
How often do you get depressed?
Have you ever been hospitalized?

13. LEVEL OF DISOWNING BEHAVIORS:
Disowning behaviors are any behaviors involving any way one behaves irresponsibly and/or enables the offending.
—Focus on earlier questions centering around victim empathy/remorse, past victimizations, etc. Look for: justifications, denial, rationalization, minimizations; etc.
—Questions to ask:
How do you deal with stress? Problems?
How many DB's have you identified in your cycle, lifestyle, etc.?
How do you neutralize them (cognitive restructuring them)?
What are your global DB's (i.e., distortions, defenses, etc.)?

14. RELAPSE PREVENTION/INTERVENTION SKILLS:
These are cognitive-behavioral strategies used to defuse offending cycles.
—Things to look for include: understanding of various models, applications to self, demonstration applying RP/RI concepts, demonstration of using interventions;
—Use futuristic situational competency tests or present futuristic scenarios and obtain both verbal/nonverbal responses.
—Questions to ask:
What is Relapse Prevention/Intervention?
What are the purposes?
What are risk factors? Relapse cues? AVE's (abstinence violational effect)?
PIG's (problem of immediate gratification)? Lapses? Relapses? Triggers?
Disowning behaviors? Cycles? High risk vs. low risk or SIDS (seemingly insignificant decisions)?
What are your risk factors or triggers?
What are your relapse cues? Early warning signals?
Last minute destructive warnings or warning line (DeW Line)?
What are relapse interventions?
What relapse interventions do you use and how? What are some examples?

—Specific questions:
What are the consequences of offending (the victim impact)? Of your offenses?
What are the consequences of your offending to the victim?
Short term? Long term? How do you know?
How much guilt did you feel during the offense? After the offense?

5. SOCIAL DIMENSIONS:
Analysis of relationships, relationship history, social skills, comparison of functional/dysfunctional relationships;
—Look for: enablers, possessiveness, jealousy, over attachment, enmeshed boundaries, power and control, exploitation, the number of relationships, avoidance/isolation, withdrawal, level of social skills, dependency, etc.
—Questions to ask:
What have you learned about relationships?
What type of relationships did you have in the past?
What type of relationships do you have now?
What are the differences of relationships of the past and now?
Do you express your feelings appropriately, give some examples?
What social skills do you have?

6. OFFENDING CYCLE:
The offending or assault cycle are behavioral precursors and cursors to the assault during the assault and the aftermath;
—Questions to ask:
Do you think you have a cycle?
What is the definition of the deviant cycle?
What are the different stages and models?
What is your cycle?
What are the purposes of learning your deviant cycle?
What are your risk factors?
What are your enables? Disinhibitors?

7. LIFESTYLE BEHAVIORS:
—Look for supporting (1) antisocial behavior (crooked, victimizing, cruelty, lying, distorting information); (2) narcissistic behaviors (self-centeredness, entitlement, exaggerated self-importance, me only attitude); (3) schizoidal behaviors (withdrawn, alienation/isolation, flat affect, etc.); and (4) borderline behaviors (instability, marked moodiness, self-destructiveness, dependency, jealousy, possessiveness, over attachment . . .) throughout the interview and the treatment process.
—Questions may center around specific behaviors.

8. INSIGHT INTO DEVELOPMENTAL/MOTIVATIONAL DYNAMICS:
This refers to the offender's perceptions of developmental events that fed into the decisions to offend. With these perceptions, offenders create problems, issues, etc. that form the purposes of offending;
—Points to look at: logical connections, degree of understanding, level of accountability (offenders are held 100% accountable for their behavior, as one's own abusive events are not excuses), distortions, etc.
—Questions to ask:
What developmental events occurred and how does your perceptions feed into your decisions to offend?
What motivations propel your decisions to offend? Or, Why do you offend?
What do you get out of your offending?
How does your life history apply to your offending?

9. RESOLUTION OF DEVELOPMENTAL/MOTIVATIONAL DYNAMICS:
Developmental perceptions and motivational dynamics are resolved to a lower degree of intensity. Look for the same stuff as in #2;
—Questions to ask:
What type of satisfactions are gained?
Do you have any problems? Issues?
What are the differences between now and before treatment?
What type of struggles?
What learning has occurred?
How do you now deal with those significant past relationships and how do you intend to deal with them in the future?

15 FACTOR SEX OFFENDER RECOVERY SCALE
MARK S. CARICH, Ph.D.

NAME: _____ DATE: _____

EVALUATOR: _____ I.D. NUMBER: _____ TYPE OF
                AGENCY: _____ OFFENDER: _____

*Rate the degree of recovery or progress as indicated by each statement.
*Lower scale values indicates major problems, whereas 6 indicates a lack of problems.

1. **Motivation Towards Recover** ---------- Mean Subtotal Score [ ]

   a. Program Attendance   1 2 3 4 5 6
   b. Spontaneous Program Participation   1 2 3 4 5 6
   c. Task Completion   1 2 3 4 5 6
   d. Seems Motivated to Recovery   1 2 3 4 5 6
   e. Appears to Initiate Issues in Treatment   1 2 3 4 5 6

   *Raw Score _____ Divide/5 = _____ (Mean subtotal score/Insert in Box)

2. **Commitment to Change/Treatment** -------- Mean Subtotal Score [ ]

   a. Completion of Program Goals   1 2 3 4 5 6
   b. Adherence to Program Rules   1 2 3 4 5 6
   c. Completes Task Assignment   1 2 3 4 5 6
   d. Degree of Minimization of Offenses   1 2 3 4 5 6
   e. Degree of Denial of Offenses   1 2 3 4 5 6

   *Raw Score _____ Divide/5 = _____ (Mean subtotal score/Insert in Box)

3. **Personal Responsibility** ---------- Mean Subtotal Score [ ]

   a. Doesn't minimize accountability in offenses   1 2 3 4 5 6
   b. Doesn't blame the victim   1 2 3 4 5 6
   c. Doesn't express cognitive distortions   1 2 3 4 5 6
   d. Doesn't deny offenses   1 2 3 4 5 6
   e. Appears sincerely honest concerning offenses 1 2 3 4 5 6

---

15. SELF-STRUCTURE:

This includes: self-concept/self-perception, inner strength, worth, security, image, self-esteem, inferiorities, etc.;

—Look for major inferiorities, self-image, confidence, compensation, over-exaggeration, worth, superiority;

—This data may be obtained from the above interview questions;

—Questions to ask:

How do you feel about yourself?

Ask about deviant/normal fantasies and feelings about self?

How did you feel about yourself and why?

*Raw Score _____ Divide/5 = _____ (Mean subtotal score/Insert in Box)

4. Social Interest ----------- Mean Subtotal Score |___|

a. Expresses care & concern for others   1 2 3 4 5 6
b. Degree of empathy demonstrated for one's victims   1 2 3 4 5 6
c. Demonstrates remorse (painful regret)   1 2 3 4 5 6
d. Demonstrates empathy at emotional levels   1 2 3 4 5 6
e. Demonstrates empathy for victims in general   1 2 3 4 5 6

*Raw Score _____ Divide/5 = _____ (Mean subtotal score/Insert in Box)

5. Social Dimension ------------ Mean Subtotal Score |___|

a. Level of social skills   1 2 3 4 5 6
b. Develops & maintains quality of relationships   1 2 3 4 5 6
c. Doesn't have active power/control issues   1 2 3 4 5 6
d. Doesn't have issues of dependency/possessiveness/jealousy   1 2 3 4 5 6
e. Expresses feelings appropriately   1 2 3 4 5 6

*Raw Score _____ Divide/5 = _____ (Mean subtotal score/Insert in Box)

6. Assault Cycle ----------- Mean Subtotal Score |___|

a. Intellectually understands cycle concepts   1 2 3 4 5 6
b. Demonstrates application of cycle to self   1 2 3 4 5 6
c. Demonstrates understanding of own cycle   1 2 3 4 5 6
d. Is able to identify cycle   1 2 3 4 5 6
e. Is able to interrupt cycle   1 2 3 4 5 6

*Raw Score _____ Divide/5 = _____ Total Mean Score |___|

7. Lifestyle Behaviors ----------- Subtotal Mean Score |___|

A. Antisocial Behaviors

a. Doesn't appear cruel & sadistic   1 2 3 4 5 6
b. Appears honest   1 2 3 4 5 6
c. Doesn't seem to exploit others   1 2 3 4 5 6
d. Level of guilt   1 2 3 4 5 6
e. Doesn't maintain dirty little secrets   1 2 3 4 5 6

*Sub Raw Score _____ Divide/5 = _____ (Mean Subtotal Score) |___|

B. Narcissistic Behaviors --------- Subtotal Mean Score |___|

a. Doesn't seem to be self-centered   1 2 3 4 5 6
b. Doesn't display entitlement   1 2 3 4 5 6
c. Doesn't appear demanding   1 2 3 4 5 6
d. Is not grandiose   1 2 3 4 5 6
e. Doesn't over exaggerate self-importance   1 2 3 4 5 6

*Sub Raw Score _____ Divide/5 = _____ (Mean Subtotal Score) |___|

C. Borderline Behaviors ---------- Subtotal Mean Score |___|

a. Doesn't display dependency   1 2 3 4 5 6
b. Doesn't display possessiveness   1 2 3 4 5 6
c. Isn't unstable in general   1 2 3 4 5 6
d. Doesn't display marked moodiness   1 2 3 4 5 6
e. Doesn't engage in non self-destructive behavior   1 2 3 4 5 6

*Sub Raw Score _____ Divide/5 = _____ (Mean Subtotal Score) |___|

D. Schizoidal Behaviors ----------- Subtotal Mean Score |___|

a. Has appropriate support network   1 2 3 4 5 6
b. Doesn't isolate/alienate self from others   1 2 3 4 5 6
c. Level of social skills   1 2 3 4 5 6
d. Doesn't seem to socially withdraw or avoid others   1 2 3 4 5 6
e. Expresses feelings appropriately   1 2 3 4 5 6

*Sub Raw Score _____ Divide/5 = _____ (Mean Subtotal Score) |___|

Total of 4 categories: A _____ + B _____ + C _____ + D _____ = _____ Divide/4 = _____ (Category Mean Score)

fantasies
c. Low frequency of deviant urges & cravings 1 2 3 4 5 6
d. Ability to defuse deviant responses 1 2 3 4 5 6
e. Level of normal fantasies 1 2 3 4 5 6
*Raw Score _____ Divide/5 = _____ (Mean subtotal score/Insert in Box)

12. Psychopathology ----------- Mean Subtotal Score |___|
a. Fewer paraphilia 1 2 3 4 5 6
b. Paraphilias are decreased 1 2 3 4 5 6
c. Doesn't exhibit psychotic behavior 1 2 3 4 5 6
d. Doesn't exhibit depressive behavior 1 2 3 4 5 6
e. Doesn't exhibit suicidal behavior 1 2 3 4 5 6
*Raw Score _____ Divide/5 = _____ (Mean subtotal score/Insert in Box)

13. Disowning Behaviors ----------- Mean Subtotal Score |___|
a. Lacks defensive behaviors 1 2 3 4 5 6
b. Doesn't exhibit cognitive distortions 1 2 3 4 5 6
c. Doesn't exhibit criminal thinking errors 1 2 3 4 5 6
d. Level of responsibility assumed 1 2 3 4 5 6
e. Has high level of coping skills 1 2 3 4 5 6
*Raw Score _____ Divide/5 = _____ (Mean subtotal score/Insert in Box)

14. Relapse Interventions Skills ----------- Mean Subtotal Score |___|
a. Identifies cycle behaviors 1 2 3 4 5 6
b. Identifies triggering events/risk factors 1 2 3 4 5 6
c. Identifies relapse cues 1 2 3 4 5 6
d. Actively defuses risk factors 1 2 3 4 5 6
e. Learned & uses relapse intervention (coping) skills 1 2 3 4 5 6
*Raw Score _____ Divide/5 = _____ (Mean subtotal score/Insert in Box)

---

8. Insight Into Motivational/Developmental Dynamics - Mean Score |___|
a. Identifies developmental factors 1 2 3 4 5 6
b. Understands developmental factors in decisions to offend 1 2 3 4 5 6
c. Understands motivational factors (purposes) in decisions to offend 1 2 3 4 5 6
d. Understands why he/she made decisions to offend 1 2 3 4 5 6
e. Doesn't blame offending on developmental factors 1 2 3 4 5 6
*Raw Score _____ Divide/5 = _____ (Mean subtotal score/Insert in Box)

9. Resolution of Motivational/Developmental Dynamics - Mean Score |___|
a. Developmental factors/issues resolved to lesser degree 1 2 3 4 5 6
b. Motivational factors (purposes of offense) resolved 1 2 3 4 5 6
c. Specific problems/issues are resolved 1 2 3 4 5 6
d. Specific traumas resolved to lesser degrees 1 2 3 4 5 6
e. Does not have motivational factors/issues interfere with daily living 1 2 3 4 5 6
*Raw Score _____ Divide/5 = _____ (Mean subtotal score/Insert in Box)

10. Sexual Identity ----------- Mean Subtotal Score |___|
a. Sexual roles seem to be confused 1 2 3 4 5 6
b. Secure with one's own masculinity: penis size 1 2 3 4 5 6
c. Resolution of sexual traumas involved in sexual orientation and/or confusion 1 2 3 4 5 6
d. Sexually responds to a variety of stimuli 1 2 3 4 5 6
e. Lacks sexual dysfunction 1 2 3 4 5 6
*Raw Score _____ Divide/5 = _____ (Mean subtotal score/Insert in Box)

11. Control of Deviant Responses ----------- Mean Subtotal Score |___|
*Note: For a,b,c - 6 represents a lack of deviancy.
a. Low frequency of deviant fantasies 1 2 3 4 5 6
b. Low frequency of masturbation to deviant 1 2 3 4 5 6

7C. _____ Score
a. _____
b. _____
c. _____
d. _____
e. _____
Total_____ Div/5=_____ Score Total_____

8. _____ Score
a. _____
b. _____
c. _____
d. _____
e. _____

9. _____ Score
a. _____
b. _____
c. _____
d. _____
e. _____

10. _____ Score
a. _____
b. _____
c. _____
d. _____
e. _____
Total_____ Div/5=_____ Score Total_____

11. _____ Score
a. _____
b. _____
c. _____
d. _____
e. _____

12. _____ Score
a. _____
b. _____
c. _____
d. _____
e. _____

13. _____ Score
a. _____
b. _____
c. _____
d. _____
e. _____
Total_____ Div/5=_____ Score Total_____

14. _____ Score
a. _____
b. _____
c. _____
d. _____
e. _____
Total_____ Div/5=_____ Score Total_____

15. _____ Score
a. _____
b. _____
c. _____
d. _____
e. _____

*Place the final scores on the Summary Score Sheet.

---

15. Self-Structure -------- Mean Subtotal Score |_____|

a. Level of self-worth	1	2	3	4	5	6
b. Lacks inferiority	1	2	3	4	5	6
c. Level of self-esteem	1	2	3	4	5	6
d. Positive self-concept	1	2	3	4	5	6
e. Doesn't compensate via exploitation	1	2	3	4	5	6

*Raw Score _____ Divide/5 = _____ (Mean subtotal score/Insert in Box)

SCORE SHEET

*Place each raw score in the corresponding numbers and letters. Total the column and divide/5. Place your score by the number.

1. _____ Score
a. _____
b. _____
c. _____
d. _____
e. _____
Total_____ Div/5=_____ Score Total_____

2. _____ Score
a. _____
b. _____
c. _____
d. _____
e. _____

3. _____ Score
a. _____
b. _____
c. _____
d. _____
e. _____

4. _____ Score
a. _____
b. _____
c. _____
d. _____
e. _____
Total_____ Div/5=_____ Score Total_____

5. _____ Score
a. _____
b. _____
c. _____
d. _____
e. _____

6. _____ Score
a. _____
b. _____
c. _____
d. _____
e. _____

7. _____ Score
a. _____
b. _____
c. _____
d. _____
e. _____
Total_____ Div/4=_____ Score Total_____

7A. _____ Score
a. _____
b. _____
c. _____
d. _____
e. _____
Total_____ Div/5=_____ Score Total_____

7B. _____ Score
a. _____
b. _____
c. _____
d. _____
e. _____
Total_____ Div/5=_____ Score Total_____

The Sex Offender Recovery Inventory
Mark S. Carich, Ph.D.

Offender: _____ Date: _____
Evaluator: _____

Instructions: Place a (√) for the appropriate response.

1. Level of Motivation to change: ___ High, ___ Medium, ___ Low
   A. Level of commitment to change (as indicated by program attendance, task assignments completed).
      (a) Program attendance. ___ Adequate, ___ Partially, ___ Inadequate
      (b) Completion of therapeutic assignments. ___ Adequate, ___ Partially, ___ Inadequate
      (c) Completion of program phases; Phase ___. ___ Complete, ___ Partially, ___ Incomplete
      (d) Completion of program goals. ___ Complete, ___ Partially, ___ Incomplete
   B. Level of Responsibility (offender acknowledges, assumes and accepts responsibility for behavior). ___ High, ___ Medium, ___ Low
   Comments _____

2. Social Interest/Victim Empathy:
   A. Social Interest (real care and concern, empathy for others). ___ Problem, ___ Partial, ___ No Problem
   B. Remorse (feeling bad, guilt for wronging others). ___ Problem, ___ Partial, ___ No Problem
   C. Conscience (knowing and feeling guilty when one engages in wronging others). ___ Problem, ___ Partial, ___ No Problem
   D. Victim empathy for specific victims (empathy or intellectually/emotionally understanding for one's victims). ___ Problem, ___ Partial, ___ No Problem
   E. Victim empathy for victims in general. ___ Problem, ___ Partial, ___ No Problem
   Comments _____

3. Integrated (both cognitive and emotional) insight into offending problems:
   A. Patterns of offending (understanding specific cognitions, emotions, behaviors, etc. linked together). ___ Insight, ___ Partial, ___ No Insight, ___ Intellectual Only, ___ N/A
   B. Etiology of offending (developmental learnings involved in the foundations of offending). ___ Insight, ___ Partial, ___ No Insight, ___ Intellectual Only, ___ N/A
   C. Teleology of offending (purposes and motivations of offending). ___ Insight, ___ Partial, ___ No Insight, ___ Intellectual Only, ___ N/A
   D. Dynamics of offending (understanding the interplay between the different elements involved in offending). ___ Insight, ___ Partial, ___ No Insight, ___ Intellectual Only, ___ N/A
   E. Insight into sexual identity and role confusion. ___ Insight, ___ Partial, ___ No Insight, ___ Intellectual Only, ___ N/A
   Comments _____

SUMMARY SHEET

NAME: _____ DATE: _____
EVALUATOR: _____ ID# _____ AGENCY: _____

RECOVERY ITEMS   MEAN SCORES

1. Motivation to Recovery............................ ____
2. Commitment to Treatment........................... ____
3. Personal Responsibility........................... ____
4. Social Interest.................................. ____
5. Social Dimension/Relationships................... ____
6. Offending Cycle.................................. ____
7. Lifestyle Characteristics Subtotal: ____ Div/4= ____
   a. Antisocial................................... ____
   b. Narcissistic................................ ____
   c. Borderline.................................. ____
   d. Schizoidal.................................. ____
                          Lifestyle Subtotal: ____
8. Insight into Motivational/Developmental Dynamics.. ____
9. Resolution Motivational/Developmental Dynamics.... ____
10. Sexual Identity................................. ____
11. Control of Deviant Responses................... ____
12. Type of Psychopathology......................... ____
13. Disowning Behaviors............................. ____
14. Relapse Intervention Skills.................... ____
15. Self-Structure................................. ____

TOTAL SCORE ____ Divide/15 = [____]

*Overall Progress of Recovery Score [____]

Scale: Degrees of Sexually Dangerous

1 = Highly Sexually Dangerous
2 = Sexually Dangerous
3 = Moderately Sexually Dangerous
4 = Somewhat Sexually Dangerous
5 = Appears to be Slightly Sexually Dangerous
6 = Currently Appears Nonsexually Dangerous & Recovering Well

4. Resolution (less intense degree) of problems in the offending process:
   A. Resolution of critical/crucial problems and issues involved in offending. ___ Adequate, ___ Partially, ___ Inadequate
   B. Resolution of critical and significant developmental issues. ___ Adequate, ___ Partially, ___ Inadequate
   C. Resolution of Psychodynamics involved in offending. ___ Adequate, ___ Partially, ___ Inadequate
   D. Resolution of identity and role confusion problems. ___ Adequate, ___ Partially, ___ Inadequate
   Comments _____

5. Control of Deviant Urges:
   A. Controls inappropriate acting out sexually. ___ Adequate, ___ Partially, ___ Inadequate
   B. Frequency of deviant sexual fantasies. (#per day ___, #per week ___, #per month ___). ___ Adequate, ___ Partially, ___ Inadequate
   C. Frequency of normal sexual fantasies. (#per day ___, #per week ___, #per month ___). ___ Adequate, ___ Partially, ___ Inadequate
   D. Frequency of masturbation to deviant fantasies. (#per day ___, #per week ___, #per month ___) ___ Adequate, ___ Partially, ___ Inadequate
   E. Frequency of masturbation to deviant urges. (#per day ___, #per week ___, #per month ___) ___ Adequate, ___ Partially, ___ Inadequate
   F. Responses to deviant stimuli. (#per day ___, #per week ___, #per month ___). ___ Adequate, ___ Partially, ___ Inadequate
   Comments _____

6. Lifestyle Transformation:
   A. Offending lifestyle changed to a non offending lifestyle overall, based on the following lifestyle behavior. ___ Change, ___ No Change, ___ Partial
   B. Lifestyle behaviors in general:
   Scale: Rate the level of behaviors exhibited N/A, (N)one, (L)ow, (M)oderate, (H)igh

   1. Antisocial Behaviors in General:
      a. Victimizes — N/A, ___ N, ___ L, ___ M, ___ H
      b. Lacks remorse — N/A, ___ N, ___ L, ___ M, ___ H
      c. Exploits — N/A, ___ N, ___ L, ___ M, ___ H
      d. Controls/dominates — N/A, ___ N, ___ L, ___ M, ___ H
      e. Maintains — N/A, ___ N, ___ L, ___ M, ___ H
      f. Sadistic tendencies — N/A, ___ N, ___ L, ___ M, ___ H
      g. Deviantly manipulates — N/A, ___ N, ___ L, ___ M, ___ H
      h. Engages in crooked/antisocial/criminal harboring — N/A, ___ N, ___ L, ___ M, ___ H
      i. Guarded — N/A, ___ N, ___ L, ___ M, ___ H
      j. Lies/deliberately distorts information — N/A, ___ N, ___ L, ___ M, ___ H
      k. Superficial & phoney — N/A, ___ N, ___ L, ___ M, ___ H

   2. Narcissistic Behaviors:
      a. Grandiose — N/A, ___ N, ___ L, ___ M, ___ H
      b. Self-centered (me only/me first attitude) — N/A, ___ N, ___ L, ___ M, ___ H
      c. Entitlement — N/A, ___ N, ___ L, ___ M, ___ H
      d. Superficial — N/A, ___ N, ___ L, ___ M, ___ H
      e. Hedonistic — N/A, ___ N, ___ L, ___ M, ___ H
      f. Demanding — N/A, ___ N, ___ L, ___ M, ___ H

   3. Borderline Behaviors:
      a. Possessiveness — N/A, ___ N, ___ L, ___ M, ___ H
      b. Jealousy — N/A, ___ N, ___ L, ___ M, ___ H
      c. Dependency — N/A, ___ N, ___ L, ___ M, ___ H
      d. Impulsive — N/A, ___ N, ___ L, ___ M, ___ H
      e. Gets overly attached — N/A, ___ N, ___ L, ___ M, ___ H
      f. Seeks immediate gratification — N/A, ___ N, ___ L, ___ M, ___ H

   4. Schizoidal Behaviors:
      a. Avoids people — N/A, ___ N, ___ L, ___ M, ___ H
      b. Isolates/alienates self — N/A, ___ N, ___ L, ___ M, ___ H
      c. Expresses flat affect — N/A, ___ N, ___ L, ___ M, ___ H
      d. Withdrawn — N/A, ___ N, ___ L, ___ M, ___ H

   5. Others:
      a. Histrionic — N/A, ___ N, ___ L, ___ M, ___ H
      b. Passive-aggressive — N/A, ___ N, ___ L, ___ M, ___ H
   Comments _____

7. Social Dimensions:
   A. Social skills — ___ Adequate, ___ Partially, ___ Inadequate
   B. Uses social skills — ___ Adequate, ___ Partially, ___ Inadequate
   C. Develops functional quality relationships — ___ Adequate, ___ Partially, ___ Inadequate
   D. Socializes with others appropriately — ___ Adequate, ___ Partially, ___ Inadequate
   E. Cooperative in relationships — ___ Adequate, ___ Partially, ___ Inadequate
   Comments _____

8. Relapse Prevention/Intervention:
   A. Insight into offending/relapse processes — ___ Insight, ___ Partial, ___ None, ___ N/A
   B. Insight into specific offending/relapse patterns — ___ Insight, ___ Partial, ___ None, ___ N/A
   C. Insight into triggering events:
      (a) Major/high risk situations and factors — ___ Applicable, ___ N/A
      (b) Minor/low risk situations and factors — ___ Insight, ___ Partial, ___ None, ___ N/A
      (c) Stressors — ___ Insight, ___ Partial, ___ None, ___ N/A
   D. Relapse interventions learned — ___ Developed, ___ Partially, ___ None
   E. Understanding insight into disowning behaviors — ___ Insight, ___ Partial, ___ None
   F. Disowning behaviors neutralized — ___ Adequate, ___ Partial, ___ Inadequate
   Comments _____

9. Psycho-Physiological Measures:
   A. Polygraph assessments — ___ Non deviant, ___ Partial, ___ Deviant
   B. Plethysmograph assessments — ___ Non deviant, ___ Partial, ___ Deviant
   Comments _____

10. Defensiveness/Disowning Behavior: ___ High, ___ Medium, ___ Low
    Comments & types of defenses (examples: suppression, cognitive distortions, isolating self, distancing, justification, denial, rationalization, etc.)
    _____

RECOVERY RISK ASSESSMENT SCALE

MARK S. CARICH, PhD./STEVEN FISCHER, LCSW/TERRY CAMPBELL, M.A. OCTOBER, 1994

INTRODUCTION

This assessment instrument is to be used with the sex offenders who have received treatment or who have "graduated" from institutional treatment programs. It is a non historical risk assessment. Treatment, is often neglected in traditional risk assessments. It is considered a variable. This is not for use as a recovery or treatment evaluation assessment. This instrument is not yet statistically valid. Each item is considered self-explanatory.

INSTRUCTIONS

1. Rate the offender with the number that best applies to him. The higher the number, the more evident the behavior. The lower the number, the less obvious the behavior or trait.

2. Items can be scored instantly or by using the scoring system page. The key process involves: rating each item, subtotalling each category, dividing the subtotal by 5 to get the category risk score. This data is entered onto the summary page and divided by number to get risk score.

3. At least a 2 hour client interview, consultation with a primary supervisory and treatment staff, previous interview data, and a review of records on current behaviors/activities will provide adequate data for completing this inventory. The client interview may consist of a review to test knowledge to relapse interventions/skills, coping responses to risk factors, review of cases to elicit empathy/remorse.

Summary of Progress:

1. _____
2. _____
3. _____
4. _____
5. _____
6. _____
7. _____
8. _____
9. _____
10. _____

Comments: _____
_____

CONCLUSIONS

REFERENCE: Carich, MS. (1991). The Sex Offender Recovery Inventory. INMAS Newsletter **4**(4): 13–17.
© Mark S Carich. Reproduced with the permission of the author.

RECOVERY RISK ASSESSMENT SCALE

MARK S. CARICH, PhD./STEVEN FISCHER, LCSW/TERRY CAMPBELL, M.A. OCTOBER, 1994

NAME _____ I.D. NUMBER _____ AGENCY _____ DATE _____
EVALUATOR _____ RATING _____
RESULTS: RISK SCORE _____

RATING

ITEMS

A. PERSONAL RESPONSIBILITY
1. Lacks openness — 1 2 3 4 5 6
2. Lacks honesty — 1 2 3 4 5 6
3. Denies behavior — 1 2 3 4 5 6
4. Withholds information — 1 2 3 4 5 6
5. Misses therapy sessions — 1 2 3 4 5 6

Subtotal ☐
(Raw Subscore) _____ Divide by 5 = (_____) Risk Score ☐

B. LOCUS OF CONTROL
1. Blames the victim — 1 2 3 4 5 6
2. Distorts (twists) information — 1 2 3 4 5 6
3. Justifies, rationalizes, etc. — 1 2 3 4 5 6
4. Blames others for one's behavior — 1 2 3 4 5 6
5. Minimizes behavior — 1 2 3 4 5 6

Subtotal ☐
(Raw Subscore) _____ Divide by 5 = (_____) Risk Score ☐

C. LEVEL OF COOPERATION
1. Isn't cooperative with aftercare personnel — 1 2 3 4 5 6
2. Interrupts treatment sessions — 1 2 3 4 5 6
3. Disrupts supervision sessions — 1 2 3 4 5 6
4. Misses supervision interviews — 1 2 3 4 5 6
5. Holds back information and/or redirects to avoid disclosing information — 1 2 3 4 5 6

Subtotal ☐
(Raw Subscore) _____ Divide by 5 = (_____) Risk Score ☐

D. CURRENT ANTISOCIAL BEHAVIORAL LEVEL
1. Comes across as phoney — 1 2 3 4 5 6
2. Engages in minor criminal activities — 1 2 3 4 5 6
3. Tends to exhibit dishonesty — 1 2 3 4 5 6
4. Appears sneaky — 1 2 3 4 5 6
5. Appears dishonest — 1 2 3 4 5 6

Subtotal ☐
(Raw Subscore) _____ Divide by 5 = (_____) Risk Score ☐

E. CURRENT NARCISSISTIC BEHAVIORAL LEVEL
1. Appears self centered — 1 2 3 4 5 6
2. Exhibits unwarranted entitlement — 1 2 3 4 5 6
3. Over exaggerated self importance — 1 2 3 4 5 6
4. Overly demanding — 1 2 3 4 5 6
5. Appears arrogant — 1 2 3 4 5 6

Subtotal ☐
(Raw Subscore) _____ Divide by 5 = (_____) Risk Score ☐

F. CURRENT LEVEL OF SCHIZOIDAL BEHAVIOR
1. Tends to alienate — 1 2 3 4 5 6
2. Tends to isolate — 1 2 3 4 5 6
3. Expresses flat affect — 1 2 3 4 5 6
4. Tends to withdraw — 1 2 3 4 5 6
5. Doesn't have many relationships — 1 2 3 4 5 6

Subtotal ☐
(Raw Subscore) _____ Divide by 5 = (_____) Risk Score ☐

G. CURRENT RELATIONSHIP SKILLS & DYNAMICS
1. Doesn't use social skills — 1 2 3 4 5 6
2. Tends to be possessive — 1 2 3 4 5 6
3. Tends to be overcontrolling — 1 2 3 4 5 6
4. Tends to be overly dependent — 1 2 3 4 5 6

Subtotal ☐
(Raw Subscore) _____ Divide by 5 = (_____) Risk Score ☐

H. CURRENT LEVEL OF SOCIAL INTEREST
1. Lacks victim empathy for victims — 1 2 3 4 5 6
2. Lacks empathy in general — 1 2 3 4 5 6
3. Appears to lack remorse — 1 2 3 4 5 6
4. Lacks compassion in general — 1 2 3 4 5 6
5. Tends to victimize others — 1 2 3 4 5 6

Subtotal ☐
(Raw Subscore) _____ Divide by 5 = (_____) Risk Score ☐

I. CURRENT USE OF SUBSTANCES
1. Associates with substance users — 1 2 3 4 5 6
2. Engages in substance abuse — 1 2 3 4 5 6
3. Has high levels of craving for substances — 1 2 3 4 5 6
4. Frequents lounges — 1 2 3 4 5 6
5. Lives with substance user — 1 2 3 4 5 6

Subtotal ☐
(Raw Subscore) _____ Divide by 5 = (_____) Risk Score ☐

J. USES RELAPSE INTERVENTION/PREVENTION SKILLS
1. Doesn't acknowledge lapses — 1 2 3 4 5 6
2. Doesn't use interventions — 1 2 3 4 5 6
3. Doesn't interrupt cycle — 1 2 3 4 5 6
4. Doesn't know deviant cycle — 1 2 3 4 5 6
5. Has dysfunctional coping skills — 1 2 3 4 5 6

Subtotal ☐
(Raw Subscore) _____ Divide by 5 = (_____) Risk Score ☐

K. MANAGES DEVIANCY/AROUSAL CONTROL
1. High level of deviant fantasies — 1 2 3 4 5 6
2. High level of masturbation — 1 2 3 4 5 6
3. Tends to over indulge in other areas of life — 1 2 3 4 5 6
4. Tends to over indulge in sex — 1 2 3 4 5 6
5. High frequency of masturbation to deviant responses — 1 2 3 4 5 6

Subtotal ☐
(Raw Subscore) _____ Divide by 5 = (_____) Risk Score ☐

L. INSTABILITY IN GENERAL
1. Relocates residence — 1 2 3 4 5 6
2. Unstable in relationships — 1 2 3 4 5 6
3. Appears self destructive — 1 2 3 4 5 6
4. Poor anger controls — 1 2 3 4 5 6
5. Appears to lack "Impulse" control — 1 2 3 4 5 6

Subtotal ☐
(Raw Subscore) _____ Divide by 5 = (_____) Risk Score ☐

M. DISINHIBITORS
1. Seems to lack internal inhibitors — 1 2 3 4 5 6
2. Exhibits defenses (denial, rationalization) — 1 2 3 4 5 6
3. Exhibits cognitive distortion and/or thinking errors — 1 2 3 4 5 6
4. Uses substances — 1 2 3 4 5 6
5. Associates with negative peer group — 1 2 3 4 5 6

Subtotal ☐
(Raw Subscore) _____ Divide by 5 = (_____) Risk Score ☐

SCORE SHEET

NAME _____ I.D. NUMBER _____ DATE _____
EVALUATOR _____ AGENCY _____
TYPE OF OFFENDER _____

A. PERSONAL RESPONSIBILITY _____
B. LOCUS OF CONTROL _____
C. LEVEL OF COOPERATION _____
D. CURRENT ANTISOCIAL BEHAVIORAL LEVEL _____
E. CURRENT NARCISSISTIC BEHAVIORAL LEVEL _____
F. CURRENT LEVEL OF SCHIZOIDAL BEHAVIOR _____
G. CURRENT RELATIONSHIP SKILLS & DYNAMICS _____
H. CURRENT LEVEL OF SOCIAL INTEREST _____
I. CURRENT USE OF SUBSTANCES _____
J. USES RELAPSE INTERVENTION/PREVENTION SKILLS _____
K. MANAGES DEVIANCY _____
L. INSTABILITY IN GENERAL _____
M. DISINHIBITORS _____
N. PSYCHOPATHOLOGY _____

TOTAL _____

TOTAL _____ DIVIDED BY 14 [____] RISK SCORE _____

1–2→LOW RISK (SCORING GUIDE)
3–4→MODERATE RISK
5→HIGH RISK
6→EXTREMELY HIGH

COMMENTS: _____

© Carich, Fischer and Campbell, 1994. Reproduced by permission of Mark S. Carich.

N. PSYCHOPATHOLOGY

	1	2	3	4	5	6
1. Seems psychotic (out of touch with reality)	1	2	3	4	5	6
2. Expressed Suicidal ideation and/or behavior	1	2	3	4	5	6
3. Tends to be self destructive	1	2	3	4	5	6
4. Tends to be manicky (hyper for long periods of time)	1	2	3	4	5	6
5. Tends to be depressed	1	2	3	4	5	6

Subtotal _____
(Raw Subscore) _____ Divide by 5 = (_____) Risk Score [____]

SCORING SYSTEM PAGE

INSTRUCTIONS:
(1) Enter each raw score into the appropriate lettered numbered line coordinated with the response.
(2) Subtotal (ST) each column and divide by 5.
(3) Place the score in the appropriate place on the score sheet, total and divide by 14, enter in the risk score of the items.
(4) Each subtotal and risk score will match the scoring system page.

A. 1. _____ B. 1. _____ C. 1. _____ D. 1. _____ E. 1. _____
   2. _____   2. _____   2. _____   2. _____   2. _____
   3. _____   3. _____   3. _____   3. _____   3. _____
   4. _____   4. _____   4. _____   4. _____   4. _____
   5. _____   5. _____   5. _____   5. _____   5. _____
   (ST) _____ (ST) _____ (ST) _____ (ST) _____ (ST) _____
   ST(5) = _____ ST(5) = _____ ST(5) = _____ ST(5) = _____ ST(5) = _____

F. 1. _____ G. 1. _____ H. 1. _____ I. 1. _____ J. 1. _____
   2. _____   2. _____   2. _____   2. _____   2. _____
   3. _____   3. _____   3. _____   3. _____   3. _____
   4. _____   4. _____   4. _____   4. _____   4. _____
   5. _____   5. _____   5. _____   5. _____   5. _____
   (ST) _____ (ST) _____ (ST) _____ (ST) _____ (ST) _____
   ST(5) = _____ ST(5) = _____ ST(5) = _____ ST(5) = _____ ST(5) = _____

K. 1. _____ L. 1. _____ M. 1. _____ N. 1. _____ O. 1. _____
   2. _____   2. _____   2. _____   2. _____   2. _____
   3. _____   3. _____   3. _____   3. _____   3. _____
   4. _____   4. _____   4. _____   4. _____   4. _____
   5. _____   5. _____   5. _____   5. _____   5. _____
   (ST) _____ (ST) _____ (ST) _____ (ST) _____ (ST) _____
   ST(5) = _____ ST(5) = _____ ST(5) = _____ ST(5) = _____ ST(5) = _____

AN OVERVIEW OF THE ELEVEN POINT TREATMENT PLAN

© Metzger C and Carich M. S., 1997

1. **Goal:** Attitude and motivational level toward recovery. .... Pg. 2
   *This goal pertains to recovery factors #1, 2, and 3.

   1) Motivation towards recovery.
   2) Commitment towards change/treatment.
   3) Personal responsibility.

2. **Goal:** Offender shows social interest in general care, concern, victim empathy, and remorse. .... Pg. 4
   *This goal pertains to recovery factor #4.

   4) Social Interest.

3. **Goal:** Offender develops appropriate social relationships and skills. .... Pg. 5
   *This goal pertains to recovery factor #5.

   5) Social dimension or developing relationships, including social skills.

4. **Goal:** Offender understands concept of his assault cycle and identifies his assault cycle. .... Pg. 8
   *This goal pertains to recovery factor #6.

   6) Insight into one's offending cycle.

5. **Goal:** Offender displays changes in lifestyle characteristics. .... Pg. 9
   *This goal pertains to recovery factor #7.

   7) Change in lifestyle behavior.

6. **Goal:** Offender displays insight into developmental/motivational dynamics, including sexual identity issues. .... Pg. 20
   *This goal pertains to recovery factors #8, 9, and 10.

   8) Insight into one's developmental and motivational factors.
   9) Resolution of developmental and motivational dynamics.
   10) Sexual identity issues.

7. **Goal:** Offender will control his deviant behavior. .... Pg. 22
   *This goal pertains to recovery factor #11.

   11) Arousal control.

8. **Goal:** Reduce and manage offender's psycho-pathology. .... Pg. 24
   *This goal pertains to recovery factor #12.

   12) Type of psycho-pathology.

9. **Goal:** To change offender's offense specific/global disowning behaviors. Disowning behaviors relate to any ways the offender uses to enable and/or avoid responsibility for his behaviors. .... Pg. 26
   *This goal pertains to recovery factor #13.

   13) Level of disowning behaviors.

10. **Goal:** Offender will develop and understand relapse intervention model, process, and skills. .... Pg. 30
    *This goal pertains to recovery factor #14.

    14) Relapse intervention skills.

11. **Goal:** Offender will develop appropriate self-structure, self-esteem, self-image, self-confidence, self-worth, and self-concept based on non-deviant behavior. .... Pg. 32
    *This goal pertains to recovery factor #15.

    15) Self-structure in general.

GLOSSARY OF THE TREATMENT PLAN STRUCTURE

A. Goals - Global or General
   * Fifteen (15) Recovery Factors blended with the overall goals.

B. Objectives - Specific Goals

C. Interventions - Plans and/or steps to achieve goals and objectives

D. Outcome - Desired results, achievement or effect

E. Initiated Date - Date started

F. Targeted Date - Projected date of completion in the Goal, Objectives and Interventions sections.

G. Targeted Date - Date expected to be completed in the Outcomes Section.

H. Completion Date - Date done

I. Keywords to be used with the date on A through H

   1. Completed = Com.
   2. Review = Re.
   3. Continue = Con't.
   4. Developed = Dev.

THE ELEVEN POINT TREATMENT PLAN FOR SEX OFFENDER PROGRAMS

Name: _____

1. **GOAL: Attitude and motivational level toward recovery**
   This goal pertains to recovery factors #1, 2 & 3.

INITIATED DATE		TARGETED DATE
___ ___		___ ___

MOTIVATION TOWARD RECOVERY
Motivation is the internal drive to succeed or "recover", incentive, determination, and amount of energy aimed towards recovery.

COMMITMENT TOWARDS CHANGE/TREATMENT
Commitment is the pledge, agreement, and compliance towards treatment with the goals of change. This definition includes an obligation in which offenders are emotionally compelled to change through treatment.

PERSONAL RESPONSIBILITY
Personal responsibility revolves around the locus of control one places on their behavior.

OBJECTIVES:

___ ___	A.	To develop internal motivation toward recovery.
___ ___	B.	To develop a commitment toward treatment.
___ ___	C.	Complete task assignments as assigned.
___ ___	D.	Initiate and maintain journal or log.
___ ___	E.	Initiate life history and/or autobiography.
___ ___	F.	Complete life history and/or autobiography.
___ ___	G.	To accept responsibility for offenses.
___ ___	H.	To develop responsibility in general for one's behaviors.
___ ___	I.	To participate in group.
___ ___	J.	Group attendance.

2

THE ELEVEN POINT TREATMENT PLAN FOR SEX OFFENDER PROGRAMS

NAME: _____ NUMBER: _____ DATE: _____

PHASE: _____

EVALUATOR(S): _____

VICTIM TYPE(S): _____

INSTRUCTIONS:

1. Select treatment goals for the offender.

2. Write the date in the designated column for "Initiated Date" located on the left-hand side of the selected goals.

3. Write in the accompanying date in the "Target Date" column, on the right-hand side, for the expected date for the goal to be accomplished. This provides the specific time frame.

4. Under the specific objectives and intervention sections, the treatment team will place the date of each selected objective and interventions on the left-hand column for the "Initiated Date".

5. Place expected date of completion of the item on the right-hand column in the "Targeted Date" column.

6. In the outcome section, on the targeted date for outcome will be initiated by each item that expected by that "Targeted Date".

7. On the right-hand column of the outcome section, during the semi-annual treatment plan review, when objectives are completed, the date will be place under "Completion Date" column.

NOTES:

1. This is a 3 year treatment plan that will be reviewed semi-annually.

2. It will be accompanied by the semi-annual evaluation.

3. The treatment staff and the offender will review the evaluation together at this time.

4. If the objective is not completed upon the second review, write "Reviewed and Continued" with the date. The target is changed.

1

THE ELEVEN POINT TREATMENT PLAN FOR SEX OFFENDER PROGRAMS

Name: _____

2   GOAL: Offender shows social interest in general care, concern, victim empathy and remorse.
*This goal pertains to recovery factor #4.

		INITIATED DATE	TARGETED DATES

SOCIAL INTEREST
Social interest is the care and concern for other individuals. This includes compassion, empathy, and remorse.

OBJECTIVES:

A. To develop a general care and concern for others.

B. To empathize in general.

C. To develop a list in empathy at intellectual levels (general).

D. To develop victim empathy for one's specific victims at an intellectual level.

E. To develop victim empathy for one's specific victims at emotional levels.

F. To develop remorse.

G. To express empathy.

INTERVENTIONS:

A. Attend group therapy.

B. Attend victim empathy group.

C. Completion of assignments.

D. Taking responsibility for impact on victims.

E. Holding oneself 100% accountable for offenses.

F. Allowing oneself to be vulnerable and feel emotions for others.

G. Disputes cognitive distortions and defenses (i.e. denial, rationalization, blame, projection, intellectualization, justification, minimization, etc.).

4

THE ELEVEN POINT TREATMENT PLAN FOR SEX OFFENDER PROGRAMS

Name: _____

INTERVENTIONS:

	INITIATED DATES	TARGETED DATES

A. Group attendance.

B. Complete task assignments (i.e. life history, maintain journal, complete or work on cycle packets, etc.).

C. Peer group attendance.

D. Doesn't deny, minimize, justify, intellectualize, lie, or distort information by using cognitive restructuring techniques.

E. Participates in other program activities such as one-on-one's and social events.

F. Completes extra assignments in a timely manner.

G. Participates, cooperates and complies with therapeutic milieu (treatment environment).

H. Identify cognitive distortions that enables one to disown responsibility.

I. Challenge the above cognitive distortions.

J. Replace cognitive distortions with functional beliefs.

K. Engage in keeping journal.

L. Initiate life history.

OUTCOMES:

	TARGETED DATE	COMPLETION DATE

A. Make commitment to treatment.

B. Honest and full disclosure.

C. Regular attendance to the above indicated groups.

D. High quality completion of assigned tasks.

E. Takes full responsibility for actions, including offenses.

F. Is fully accountable for actions, including offenses.

3

THE ELEVEN POINT TREATMENT PLAN FOR SEX OFFENDER PROGRAMS

Name: _____

OBJECTIVES:

		INITIATED DATE	TARGETED DATES
A.	Learn specific social skills:		
	1. Respect (doesn't discount).		
	2. "I" messages.		
	3. Eye contact.		
	4. Active listening.		
	5. Confrontation.		
	6. Initiating conversations.		
	7. Maintain conversations.		
	8. Terminating conversations.		
	9. Conflict resolution/compromising skills.		
	10. Appropriate expression of feelings.		
	11. Paraphrasing skills.		
	12. Summarizing skills.		
	13. Other _____		
B.	To identify specific interpersonal issues:		
	1. Power/control.		
	2. Possessiveness.		
	3. Jealousy.		
	4. Enmeshed boundaries.		
	5. Isolation/alienation		
	6. Rejection.		
	7. Dependency.		
	8. Other _____		
C.	To develop appropriate close intimate relationships without sexual connotations.		

6

THE ELEVEN POINT TREATMENT PLAN FOR SEX OFFENDER PROGRAMS

Name: _____

INTERVENTIONS: (cont)

		INITIATED DATE	TARGETED DATES
H.	Participates, cooperates and complies with therapeutic milieu (treatment environment).		
I.	Write victim letters.		
J.	Imagery interventions: 1) images of victims pain and impact; 2) lowering walls; 3) victim empathy journey.		
K.	Role play.		
L.	Victim silhouettes.		
M.	Write out offenses and impact statements.		
N.	Utilize nine (9) elements of victim empathy educational process.		
O.	Attend Victim/Offender Group.		

OUTCOMES:

		TARGETED DATE	COMPLETION DATE
A.	Demonstrates victim empathy at intellectual levels.		
B.	Demonstrates victim empathy at emotional levels.		
C.	Demonstrates remorse (painful regret and guilt).		
D.	Demonstrates empathy for victims in general.		

3. **GOAL: Offender develops appropriate social relationships and skills.**
*This goal pertains to recovery factor #5.

SOCIAL DIMENSION OR DEVELOPING RELATIONSHIPS INCLUDING SOCIAL SKILLS
The social dimension refers to the following: skills in developing and maintaining relationships.

INITIATED DATE	TARGETED DATE

5

THE ELEVEN POINT TREATMENT PLAN FOR SEX OFFENDER PROGRAMS

Name: _____

4. GOAL: Offender understands concept of his assault cycle and identifies his assault cycle. This goal pertains to recovery factor #6.

INITIATED DATES | | TARGETED DATES

INSIGHT INTO ONE'S OFFENDING CYCLE
The offending cycle is the offender's assaultive mode. This cycle consists of recurring patterns that are involved in the assault.

OBJECTIVES:

A. Offender understands the assault cycle concept.

B. Offender applies the concept to self.

C. Offender identifies his assault cycle.

D. Offender identifies and understands Primary 3 Stage Cycle.

E. Offender identifies and understands 4 Stage Cycle.

F. Offender understands the dynamics of offending.

INTERVENTIONS:

A. Learns the general precursors to offense and aftermath.

B. Able to learn his pattern of offending.

C. Learns open-ended cycle.

D. Learns 4 Stage Cycle.

E. Learns 6 Stage Cycle.

F. Learns any other appropriate stage models.

G. Learns dynamic of the cycle.

H. Learns specific cycle behavior and applies them to his daily life.

I. Participates, cooperates and complies with therapeutic milieu (treatment environment).

8

THE ELEVEN POINT TREATMENT PLAN FOR SEX OFFENDER PROGRAMS

Name: _____

INTERVENTIONS:

INITIATED DATES | | TARGETED DATES

A. Learn communication and assertiveness training skills (i.e. "I" messages, active listening, starting conversations, maintaining and terminating conversations, giving and receiving communication.).

B. Understanding and developing appropriate boundaries.

C. Overcoming dependency issues, possessiveness, jealousy, power and control issues.

D. Learn daily living skills (i.e. personal hygiene, appropriate manners, etc.).

E. Learn appropriate expression of feelings to others.

F. Increase number of relationships.

G. Learn how to stop enabling others by recognizing and changing dysfunctional/deviant/inappropriate behaviors.

H. Learn to overcome fears of others.

I. Learn conflict resolution.

J. Learn to have quality relationships without sexual connotations.

K. Participates, cooperates and complies with therapeutic milieu (treatment environment).

L. Work through interpersonal issues by identifying, challenging, and changing related distorted beliefs and developing appropriate base of worth, security, etc.

M. Anger management group.

N. Stress management group.

O. Social skills group.

OUTCOMES:

TARGETED DATE | | COMPLETION DATE

A. Demonstrates social skills.

B. Demonstrates appropriate boundaries.

C. Demonstrates appropriate relationships.

D. Demonstrates appropriate affect.

E. Demonstrates management of interpersonal relationship issues.

F. Demonstrates conflict resolution skills.

7

THE ELEVEN POINT TREATMENT PLAN FOR SEX OFFENDER PROGRAMS

Name: _____

OBJECTIVES:

INITIATED DATES		TARGETED DATES

A. Antisocial behavioral characteristics that need to be addressed and changed to appropriate behaviors.

1. Exploitation (takes advantage of others).
2. Cheats (uses trickery, acts dishonestly).
3. Lies (purposefully and wholly untruthful statements).
4. Deceives others (deliberate concealing/hiding the truth; intentionally misleading).
5. Distorts information (through omission, adding facts, or embellishment).
6. Secrecy.
7. Slyness/slick.
8. Operates on hidden agendas/motives.
9. History of conning.
10. Displays phoniness.
11. Disowns behavior.
12. History of cruelty toward others.
13. Currently displays cruelty.
14. History of sadistic behavior.
15. Current display of sadistic behavior.
16. Destructive.
17. Impulsive behavior.
18. Recklessness.
19. Victimizes others.
20. Lacks remorse for victims.
21. Lacks victim empathy.
22. Unstable work history.
23. Nonconforming, breaks rules and/or laws.
24. Lacks social interest.
25. Lacks loyalty in relationships.

10

THE ELEVEN POINT TREATMENT PLAN FOR SEX OFFENDER PROGRAMS

Name: _____

INTERVENTIONS: (cont)

INITIATED DATES		TARGETED DATES

J. Utilizes the 5 Step Strategy to:
 1. Care review.
 2. Listing of events.
 3. Identify reaction to each event.
 4. Select and use cycle model format.
 5. Develop a summary cycle of each victim type and composite cycle.

K. Other task assignments as assigned:

OUTCOMES:

COMPLETION DATES		TARGETED DATES

A. Demonstrates understanding of general assault cycle concept.
B. Demonstrates identification of general cycle.
C. Demonstrates identification of his own cycle, 4 Stage, 6 Stage, and others as deemed appropriate.
D. Demonstrates how he used his cycle behaviors in his daily lifestyle.

5. **GOAL:** Offender displays changes in lifestyle characteristics. This goal pertains to recovery factor #7.

INITIATED DATES		TARGETED DATES

CHANGE IN LIFESTYLE BEHAVIORS
Lifestyle behaviors refers to the specific and general tendencies or patterns of behavior. These include:

A. Antisocial
B. Narcissistic
C. Borderline
D. Schizoidal
E. Obsessive-Compulsive/Passive-Aggressive

9

THE ELEVEN POINT TREATMENT PLAN FOR SEX OFFENDER PROGRAMS

Name: _____

OBJECTIVES: (cont)

INITIATED DATES   TARGETED DATES

26. Lacking in close friendships or manipulates friendships.
27. Projects blame onto victim for antisocial acts.
28. Uses religiosity as a cover-up.

B. Narcissistic behavioral characteristics that need changed.
1. Grandiose fantasies.
2. "Me first" attitude/behavior.
3. Attitude of superiority.
4. Brags and exaggerates about accomplishments.
5. Egotistical (inflated sense of self-worth).
6. Stuck-up or snobbish.
7. Exaggerated sense of self-importance.
8. Distorted sense of entitlement.
9. Unrealistic expectations.
10. Displays self-pity ("poor me" attitude).
11. Is overtly concerned by and overly reactive to criticism.
12. Inconsiderate of others.
13. Self-centered.
14. Grandiose behaviors.
15. Envious.
16. Strives for control through power.
17. Pleasure seeking behaviors.
18. Demanding.
19. Fears situations where his/her deficiencies will become known to others.
20. Uses religiosity to enhance "good person" image.

11

THE ELEVEN POINT TREATMENT PLAN FOR SEX OFFENDER PROGRAMS

Name: _____

OBJECTIVES: (cont)

INITIATED DATES   TARGETED DATES

C. Borderline behavioral characteristics that need changed.
1. Unstable lifestyle.
2. Seeks immediate gratification.
3. Poor impulse control (especially in sexual behavior and substance abuse).
4. Repeated suicidal ideation/threats/gestures/attempts.
5. Unstable, inconsistent, and/or intense relationships.
6. Marked intense moodiness with mood shifts.
7. Emotionally unstable.
8. Dependancy.
9. Over-attachment to others.
10. Enmeshed relationships.
11. Vacillates between over-idealizing and devaluing others.
12. Possessiveness.
13. Jealousy.
14. Unstable/vacillating self-image and self-identity.
15. Sensitivity to, or fear of real or imagined abandonment.
16. Fears situations wherein his/her thinking and behavior will become known and result in shame.

D. Schizoidal behavioral characteristics that need changed.
1. Displays flat/restricted affect.
2. Avoids people.
3. Develops superficial relationships.
4. Isolates self.
5. Alienates/distances others.
6. Emotionally withdrawn.
7. Unaware of feelings.
8. Lacks social skills.

12

299

THE ELEVEN POINT TREATMENT PLAN FOR SEX OFFENDER PROGRAMS

Name: _____

OBJECTIVES: (cont)

INITIATED DATES / TARGETED DATES

15. Repeated engaging in appetitive/addictive behaviors which have caused harm to self or others.
16. Uses religiosity as a means of self-absolution.

INTERVENTION:

A. Group therapy.
B. Psycho-educational group therapy.
C. Peer groups.
D. Wing and house meetings.
E. Task assignments.
F. Changing key belief system from the following criteria:
G. Identify specific behaviors that apply.
H. Identify underlying beliefs or cognitions with each targeted behavior.
I. Utilize cognitive behavioral interventions and in particular behavioral change formats.
J. Journaling monitoring the behavior.
K. Challenging and replacing distorted cognitions with appropriate beliefs.
L. Experimental experiential exercises.
M. Participates, cooperates and complies with therapeutic milieu (treatment environment).
N. Other task assignments _____

14

THE ELEVEN POINT TREATMENT PLAN FOR SEX OFFENDER PROGRAMS

Name: _____

OBJECTIVES: (cont)

INITIATED DATES / TARGETED DATES

9. Tends to prefer solitary activities.
10. Strong emotions experienced covertly.
11. Indifferent to praise.
12. Is covertly concerned by, and overly reactive to criticism.
13. Difficulties with reciprocating nonverbal emotional expressions.
14. Few, if any, close friends.
E. Obsessive-Compulsive/Passive-Aggressive behavioral characteristics that need changed:
1. Controls passively through feigned capitulation (fake surrendering), dependency, or inadequacy (another form of stubbornness).
2. Controls actively through perfectionism as an evasion.
3. Insistent and persistent about his/her beliefs and rituals.
4. Overly fastidicus.
5. Ruminates on matters which are discomforting.
6. Obsessively engages in fantasy.
7. Avoids mistakes by per severation or indecisiveness.
8. Ambivalent towards feelings of others.
9. Black-white thinking.
10. Expects any loss of control to result in extreme embarrassment or foolish appearance.
11. Behavior used to procrastinate.
12. Inherent conflicts between goals and methods used for attainment.
13. Covertly defiant, vindictive, spiteful toward others.
14. Reacts poorly to constructive criticism.

13

THE ELEVEN POINT TREATMENT PLAN FOR SEX OFFENDER PROGRAMS

Name: _____

OUTCOMES:

TARGETED DATES   COMPLETION DATES

A. Does not demonstrate the following antisocial behavior:

1. Exploitive (takes advantage of others).
2. Cheats (use of trickery, acts dishonestly).
3. Lies (purposefully and wholly untruthful statements).
4. Deceives others (deliberate concealing/hiding the truth, intentionally misleading).
5. Distorts information (through omission, adding to facts, or embellishment).
6. Secrecy.
7. Slyness/slick.
8. Operates on hidden agendas/motives.
9. History of conning.
10. Displays phoniness.
11. Disowns behavior.
12. History of cruelty towards others.
13. Currently displays cruelty.
14. History of sadistic behavior.
15. Current display of sadistic behavior.
16. Destructive.
17. Impulsive behavior.
18. Recklessness.
19. Victimizes others.
20. Lacks remorse for victims.
21. Lacks victim empathy.
22. Unstable work history.
23. Nonconforming, breaks rules and/or laws.
24. Lacks social interest.
25. Lacks loyalty in relationships.
26. Lacking in close friendships or manipulates friendships.

THE ELEVEN POINT TREATMENT PLAN FOR SEX OFFENDER PROGRAMS

Name: _____

OUTCOMES: (cont)

TARGETED DATES   COMPLETION DATES

27. Projects blame onto victim for antisocial acts.
28. Uses religiosity as a cover-up.

B. Does not demonstrate the following narcissistic behaviors:

1. Grandiose fantasies.
2. "Me first" attitude/behavior.
3. Attitude of superiority.
4. Brags and exaggerates about accomplishments.
5. Egotistical (inflated sense of self-worth).
6. Stuck-up or snobbish.
7. Exaggerated sense of self-importance.
8. Distorted sense of entitlement.
9. Unrealistic expectations.
10. Displays self-pity ("poor me" attitude).
11. Is overtly concerned by and overly reactive to criticism.
12. Inconsiderate of others.
13. Self-centered.
14. Grandiose behaviors.
15. Envious.
16. Strives for control through power.
17. Pleasure seeking behaviors.
18. Demanding.
19. Fears situations where his/her deficiencies will become known to others.
20. Uses religiosity to enhance "good person" image.

THE ELEVEN POINT TREATMENT PLAN FOR SEX OFFENDER PROGRAMS

Name: _____

OUTCOMES: (cont)

INITIATED DATES | COMPLETION DATES

5. Alienates/distances others.
6. Emotionally withdrawn.
7. Unaware of feelings.
8. Lacks social skills.
9. Tends to prefer solitary activities.
10. Strong emotions experienced covertly.
11. Indifferent to praise.
12. Is covertly concerned by, and overly reactive to criticism.
13. Difficulties with reciprocating nonverbal emotional expressions.
14. Few, if any, close friends.

E. Does not demonstrate the following obsessive-compulsive behavior:

1. Controls passively through feigned capitulation (fake surrendering), dependency, or inadequacy (another form of stubbornness).
2. Controls actively through perfectionism as an evasion.
3. Insistent and persistent about his/her beliefs and rituals.
4. Overly fastidious.
5. Ruminates on matters which are discomforting.
6. Obsessively engages in fantasy.
7. Avoids mistakes by per severation or indecisiveness.
8. Ambivalent toward feelings of others.
9. Black-white thinking.
10. Expects any loss of control to result in extreme embarrassment or foolish appearance.
11. Behavior used to procrastinate.
12. Inherent conflicts between goals and methods used for attainment.

18

THE ELEVEN POINT TREATMENT PLAN FOR SEX OFFENDER PROGRAMS

Name: _____

OUTCOMES: (cont)

TARGETED DATES | COMPLETION DATES

C. Does not demonstrate the following borderline behaviors:

1. Unstable lifestyle
2. Seeks immediate gratification.
3. Poor impulse control (especially in sexual behavior and substance abuse).
4. Repeated suicidal ideation/threats/gestures/attempts.
5. Unstable, inconsistent, and/or intense relationships.
6. Marked intense moodiness with mood shifts.
7. Emotionally unstable.
8. Dependency.
9. Over-attachment to others.
10. Enmeshed relationships.
11. Vacillates between over-idealizing and devaluing others.
12. Possessiveness.
13. Jealousy.
14. Unstable/vacillating self-image and self-identity.
15. Sensitivity to or fear of real or imagined abandonment.
16. Fears situations wherein his/her thinking and behavior will become known and result in shame.

D. Does not demonstrate the following schizoidal behaviors:

1. Displays flat/restricted affect.
2. Avoids people.
3. Develops superficial relationships.
4. Isolates self.

17

THE ELEVEN POINT TREATMENT PLAN FOR SEX OFFENDER PROGRAMS

Name: _____

6. GOAL: Offender displays insight into developmental/motivational dynamics and including sexual identity issues.
*This goal pertains to recovery factors #8, 9 and 10.

INITIATED DATES | TARGETED DATES

INSIGHT INTO ONE'S DEVELOPMENTAL AND MOTIVATIONAL FACTORS.
Insight into developmental/motivational dynamics refers to one's specific and motivational/developmental dynamics that propel the decisions to offend.

RESOLUTION OF DEVELOPMENTAL AND MOTIVATIONAL DYNAMICS.
Resolution of developmental problems and motivational dynamics to lesser degrees of intensity.

SEXUAL IDENTITY ISSUES.
Sexual identity issues are any issues involving sexual role confusion and/or traumas associated with sexual preference and selection.

OBJECTIVES:

A. Identify key developmental events (perceptions) that contribute to sex offending dynamics and increase autonomy/independence lifestyle.

B. Identify key motivational dynamics.

C. Resolve key changing one's perceptions of those developmental events and/or traumas.

D. Developing appropriate self structure.

E. Identify sexual identity issues.

F. Resolve any key motivational dynamics or core issues that feed the offending process.

G. Resolve the following issues:
1. Dependency
2. Insecurity
3. Rejection
4. Jealousy
5. Possessiveness

H. Resolve sexual identity issues and/or problems.

I. Resolve any type of inferiorities.

J. Develop the "new me" identity.

K. Develop appropriate worth and self concept issues.

L. Defuse any victim standing patterns.

M. Ensure that offender doesn't blame offending on the past.

20

THE ELEVEN POINT TREATMENT PLAN FOR SEX OFFENDER PROGRAMS

Name: _____

OUTCOMES: (cont)

INITIATED DATES | COMPLETION DATES

13. Covertly defiant, vindictive, spiteful toward others.

14. Reacts poorly to constructive criticism.

15. Repeated engaging in appetitive/addictive behaviors which have caused harm to self or others.

16. Uses religiosity as a means of self-absolution.

COMMENTS:

19

THE ELEVEN POINT TREATMENT PLAN FOR SEX OFFENDER PROGRAMS

Name: _____

OUTCOMES:

TARGETED DATES   COMPLETION DATES

A.   Has understanding of developmental issues.

B.   Has an understanding of the motivational factors.

C.   Has an acceptance (resolution to a lesser degree) of developmental events.

D.   Has an acceptance (resolution to a lesser degree) of motivational factors.

E.   Has an acceptance of appropriate sexual identity.

7.   GOAL: Offender will control his deviant behavior. *This goal pertains to recovery factor #11.

INITIATED DATES   TARGETED DATES

AROUSAL CONTROL
Control of deviant urges/arousal refers to the overall management of deviant responses.

OBJECTIVES:

A.   Assess deviant arousal.

B.   Track deviant urges/fantasies (self-report).

C.   Reduce deviant arousal patterns.

D.   Develop self-management tactics and strategies reducing deviant arousal and behavioral patterns.

E.   Develop appropriate arousal.

F.   Develop appropriate fantasies.

G.   Reduce excessive masturbation.

H.   Eliminate self-abusive sexual behavior.

22

THE ELEVEN POINT TREATMENT PLAN FOR SEX OFFENDER PROGRAMS

Name: _____

INTERVENTIONS:

INITIATED DATES   TARGETED DATES

A.   Develop genogram and present in group therapy.

B.   Write autobiography.

C.   Present autobiography in group.

D.   Task assignments.

E.   Take effects from core issues of developmental events/ motivational factors to all therapy groups to gain understanding and increase resolution to a lesser degree.

F.   Participates, cooperates, and complies with therapeutic milieu (treatment environment).

G.   Work through traumas by accessing memories and shifting underlying key central beliefs supporting detrimental perceptions to functional beliefs.

H.   Develop different appropriate coping response.

I.   Work through grief issues associated with developmental events and emphasize letting go processes.

J.   Develop functional coping responses to fulfill needs appropriate-y in RET.

K.   Develop self-nurturing patterns.

L.   Develop imageries associated with nurturing, worth and appropriate coping strategies.

M.   Instill appropriate self- worth/esteem/confidence/concept/ identity/ etc.

N.   Sort out worth through any sexual orientation confusion issues by refusing traumas, issues, choices, etc.

O.   Defuse patterns of anger, hurt, resentment, negativity, etc. via RET or Cognitive restructuring tactics.

P.   Emphasize Old Me/New Me concept and develop New Me identity.

Q.   Use guided imagery protocols.

R.   Inward Journey.

S.   Inner child work.

T.   Other _____

21

THE ELEVEN POINT TREATMENT PLAN FOR SEX OFFENDER PROGRAMS

Name: _____

OUTCOMES:

TARGETED DATES   COMPLETION DATES

A. Reduce and control of deviant impulses.

B. Reduce and control of violent/sadistic fantasies.

C. Reduce and control of masturbation to deviant fantasies.

D. Develop and maintain normal and appropriate fantasies.

E. Able to defuse deviant urges.

F. Able to defuse deviant fantasies.

G. Able to control deviant fantasies.

H. Able to cease self-abusive masturbation.

8.   **GOAL: Reduce and manage offenders psycho-pathology** *This goal pertains to recovery factor #12.

INITIATED DATES   TARGETED DATES

TYPE OF PSYCHOPATHOLOGY
Psychopathology refers to the specific mental health problems and dysfunctions, including paraphilias.

OBJECTIVES:

A. Identify any psycho-pathologies:

B. Resolve any/or reduce specified pathologies.

C. Utilize self-management in controlling pathologies.

24

THE ELEVEN POINT TREATMENT PLAN FOR SEX OFFENDER PROGRAMS

Name: _____

INTERVENTIONS:

INITIATED DATES   TARGETED DATES

A. Assess deviant arousal through phallometric measures.

B. Assess deviant arousal through inventories.

C. Assessment of deviant arousal through self-report.

D. Behavioral treatments:
  Covert sensitization
  Minimal arousal conditioning (MAC)
  Aversive conditioning
  Boredom therapy/satiation techniques
  Other _____

E. Group intervention and dynamics.

F. Cognitive restructuring techniques (i.e. RET, etc.).

G. Cognitive behavioral interventions (i.e. task assignments, appropriate/inappropriate fantasy work).

H. Imagery.

I. Victim empathy techniques.

J. Developing appropriate arousal through conditioning.

K. Other techniques.

L. Participate, cooperate and comply with therapeutic milieu (treatment environment).

M. Reduce excessive/self-abusive masturbation.

N. Develop deviant fantasy "crashers" (self-management interventions).

O. Develop appropriate normal social-sexual fantasy.

P. Other _____

23

THE ELEVEN POINT TREATMENT PLAN FOR SEX OFFENDER PROGRAMS

Name: _____

9. GOAL: To change offender's offense specific/global disowning behaviors. Disowning behaviors relate to any ways the offender uses to enable and/or avoid responsibility for his behaviors.
    *This goal pertains to recovery factor #13.

INITIATED DATES / TARGETED DATES

LEVEL OF DISOWNING BEHAVIORS
Level of disowning behaviors are the degree of and/or amount of irresponsibility in ways of distorted thinking and defenses or other dysfunctional coping strategies.

OBJECTIVES:

A. Identify offense specific disowning behaviors (cognitive distortions, defenses, activities, etc.).

B. Identify lifestyle or global patterns of disowning behaviors.

C. Change offense specific disowning behaviors with responsibility/appropriate behaviors.

D. Change global patterns with responsibility oriented behaviors.

E. Develop appropriate coping responses.

INTERVENTIONS:

A. Identify cognitive distortions globally and offense specific:

    1. Minimizing
    2. Denial
    3. Exaggeration
    4. Over-generalization
    5. Justifying (giving excuses or reasons to suggest the behavior is okay).
    6. Projecting blame/placing responsibility on others.
    7. Polarized (either/or) thinking.
    8. Selective memory (remembering only what he/she wants to remember).
    9. Displacing

26

THE ELEVEN POINT TREATMENT PLAN FOR SEX OFFENDER PROGRAMS

Name: _____

INTERVENTIONS: (cont)

INITIATED DATES / TARGETED DATES

A. Participate, cooperate and comply with therapeutic milieu (treatment environment).

B. Medications _____

C. Enforced medications _____

D. Suicidal contracts

E. Suicidal gesture contracts

F. Lapse contracts

G. Task assignments

H. Self-control/management interventions.

I. Self-mutilation contracts.

J. Behavioral contracts.

K. Group interventions.

L. Other interventions as deemed appropriate _____

M. Attend substance abuse abuse education program.

OUTCOMES:

TARGETED DATES / COMPLETION DATES

A. Reduced and/or managed non-sexual psycho-pathologies.

    1. Depression
    2. Drug abuse
    3. Alcohol abuse
    4. Suicidal behavior
    5. Psychosis
    6. Other _____

COMMENTS: _____

25

THE ELEVEN POINT TREATMENT PLAN FOR SEX OFFENDER PROGRAMS

Name: _____

INTERVENTIONS: (cont)

INITIATED DATES   TARGETED DATES

A.   Identify cognitive distortions: (cont)

10. Doing the opposite (i.e. becoming outwardly religious while actively offending).
11. Attitude of ownership (i.e. viewing others as personal property).
12. Intellectualizing
13. Suppressing or holding in feelings.
14. Anger/aggression to control.
15. Plays dumb.
16. Fabrication
17. Omission
18. Distortion
19. "Me first" attitude
20. Good guy syndrome
21. Objectifying
22. "Poor me" attitude
23. Undoing (making up for)
24. Excessive pride
25. Uniqueness (rules don't apply)
26. "Trash city" (everything is bad; why bother)
27. Victim role/portrays self as victim
28. Being superficial
29. Phoney fawning ("kissing up")
30. Procrastination (putting off)
31. "Who cares" attitude/apathetic
32. Passive-aggressive
33. "Know-it-all"
34. Paranoia as evasion
35. Unrealistic expectations

27

THE ELEVEN POINT TREATMENT PLAN FOR SEX OFFENDER PROGRAMS

Name: _____

INTERVENTIONS: (cont)

INITIATED DATES   TARGETED DATES

36. Personalization (inappropriately takes things personally)
37. Entitlement (I deserve to get all I want when I want it)
38.
39.
40.

Defensive structures:

41. Repression (unconscious elimination or "forgetting" information)
42. Suppression (conscious elimination or "forgetting" information)
43. Rationalizations (using reasons to justify one's position)
44. Projections (placing own blame/feelings onto someone else)
45. Reaction formation (engaging in opposite behavior)
46. Denial (not admitting to)
47. Displacement (discharging energy onto others)
48. Emotional isolation/insulation (withdrawal, alienating self from others)
49. Intellectualization (splitting off cognitively)
50. Self-pity
51. Detachment or dissociation - specify circumstances:
52. Other
53. Other
54. Other

28

THE ELEVEN POINT TREATMENT PLAN FOR SEX OFFENDER PROGRAMS

Name: _____

10. GOAL: Offender will develop and understand relapse intervention model, process and skills.
*This goal pertains to recovery factor #14.

INITIATED DATES | TARGETED DATES

RELAPSE INTERVENTION SKILLS
Relapse Intervention Skills are the specific coping strategies designated to help offenders identify offending cycle, triggers, cues, disowning behaviors, and specific skills that are used to defuse cycles and/or deviant responses.

OBJECTIVES:

A. Understand relapse prevention/intervention models and related concepts.

B. Identify assault cycle/relapse process.

C. Identify triggers/risk factors (high & low).

D. Identify relapse cues.

E. Identify AVE (Abstinence Volitional Effect) state of mind when lapsing.

F. Identifying dysfunctional coping patterns (Maladaptive Coping Response).

G. Develop functional coping (Adaptive Coping Response).

H. Identify lapse behaviors.

I. Develop automatic relapse intervention responses.

INTERVENTIONS:

A. Attend relapse prevention psycho-educational module.

B. Attend relapse prevention psychotherapy group.

C. Attend relapse advanced interventions group.

D. Complete relapse prevention/interventions workbook.

E. Complete relapse prevention/interventions task assignments.

F. Complete Safer Society Workbook on Relapse Prevention.

G. Attend peer groups.

30

THE ELEVEN POINT TREATMENT PLAN FOR SEX OFFENDER PROGRAMS

Name: _____

INTERVENTIONS: (cont)

INITIATED DATES | COMPLETION DATES

B. Identify defenses, global and defense specific.

C. Identify dysfunctional belief system

D. Identify any type of disowning behavior

E. Attend RET (Rational Emotive Therapy) group psycho-educational module

F. Task assignments

G. Group process

H. Any other psycho-educational modules deemed appropriate: _____

I. Appropriate application of cognitive restructuring within the therapeutic milieu (treatment environment).

OUTCOMES:

TARGETED DATES | COMPLETION DATES

A. Decrease in use of defenses.

B. Decrease in use of global cognitive distortions.

C. Decrease in use of offense specific cognitive distortions.

D. Decrease in use of disowning behaviors.

E. Understanding of the cognitive restructuring concepts and process.

F. Demonstrates application of cognitive restructuring process.

COMMENTS:

29

THE ELEVEN POINT TREATMENT PLAN FOR SEX OFFENDER PROGRAMS

Name: _____

11. GOAL: Offender will develop appropriate self-structure, self-esteem, self-image, self-confidence, self-worth, and self-concept based on non-deviant/victimizing behavior. *This goal pertains to recovery factor #15,

INITIATED DATES | TARGETED DATES

SELF-STRUCTURE IN GENERAL.
Self-structure refers to the internal/external perceptions of one's self. This includes one's self-worth, self-concept, self-esteem, self-image, level of confidence, etc.

OBJECTIVES:

INITIATED DATES | TARGETED DATES

A. Identify patterns and dynamics ("old me" identities) involving poor self-concept constructs including; work, image, inferiority, esteem, confidence, security, etc., that leads to compensation via offending.

B. Identify underlying perceptions and related key core beliefs of "old me" pattern.

C. Defuse dysfunctional patterns of "old me" via cognitive restructuring and cognitive behavioral experiential approaches.

D. Replace "old me" self-structure with "new me" identity or self-structure based on appropriate behaviors.

E. Balance inferiority versus superiority patterns.

INTERVENTIONS:

A. Learn to accept self as an offender.

B. Learn to generate self-worth and self-esteem through appropriate behavior.

C. Learn to generate self-confidence based on appropriate behavior.

D. Learn to generate positive self-concept based on appropriate behavior.

E. Learn to generate positive self-image based on appropriate behavior and exhibit no offending behavior.

F. Learn to change key core beliefs about inferiority problems in which the offender over-compensates by demonstration of superiority behavior to others.

32

THE ELEVEN POINT TREATMENT PLAN FOR SEX OFFENDER PROGRAMS

Name: _____

INTERVENTIONS: (cont)

INITIATED DATES | TARGETED DATES

H. Attend house and wing meetings.

I. Participate in therapeutic milieu (treatment environment).

J. Learn and identify behavioral cycle and continue work on recognition of his own cycle behaviors.

K. Maintain relapse intervention journal.

L. Identify and learn triggers and/or risk factors.

M. Identify and learn relapse cues.

N. Identify and learn relapse process.

O. Learn basic concepts of relapse intervention.

P. Learn appropriate coping skills.

Q. Learn appropriate relapse intervention.

R. Utilize cognitive behavioral task assignments as assigned.

OUTCOMES:

TARGETED DATES | COMPLETION DATES

A. Demonstrates knowledge of relapse intervention concepts.

B. Demonstrates appropriate use of relapse intervention skills on a consistent basis.

C. Sporadic (hit or miss) use or occasional (approximately once per week) demonstration of appropriate use of relapse preventions skills.

D. Demonstrates identification of triggers or high risk factors.

E. Demonstrates identification of cues.

F. Demonstrates identification of cycle and relapse process.

31

THE ELEVEN POINT TREATMENT PLAN FOR SEX OFFENDER PROGRAMS

Name: _____

DIAGNOSIS:

AXIS I

_____ 302.90	Paraphilias NOS male/female
	Features as follows:
	Age Range: Male _____ Female _____
_____ 302.40	Exhibitionism male/female
	Age Range: Male _____ Female _____
_____ 302.82	Voyeurism male/female
	Age Range: Male _____ Female _____
_____ 302.2	Pedophilia
	Age Range: Male _____ Female _____
	Specify if:
	_____ Sexually attracted to males
	_____ Sexually attracted to females
	_____ Sexually attracted to both
	_____ Limited to incest
	Specify type:
	_____ Exclusive type
	_____ Non-exclusive type
_____ 302.81	Fetishism - Specify:
_____ 302.84	Sexual sadism male/female
	Age Range: Male _____ Female _____
_____ 302.83	Sexual masochism male/female
	Age Range: Male _____ Female _____
_____ 302.30	Frotteurism male/female
	Age Range: Male _____ Female _____
_____ 302.3	Transvestic Fetishism
_____ 302.75	Premature ejaculation
_____ 296.xx	Major depression
_____ 300.4	Dysthymic Disorder
_____ 296.90	Mood Disorder NOS
_____ 315.9	Learning Disorder NOS
_____ 303.90	Alcohol dependency
_____ 305.00	Alcohol abuse
_____ 304.80	Poly substance dependence

34

THE ELEVEN POINT TREATMENT PLAN FOR SEX OFFENDER PROGRAMS

Name: _____

INTERVENTIONS:: (cont)

TARGETED DATES

INITIATED DATES

_____	G.	Attend and participate in group therapy relating to present experiences.
_____	H.	Attend and participate in psycho-educational modules.
_____	I.	Participate in the therapeutic milieu (treatment environment).
_____	J.	Complete task assignments.
_____	K.	Other task assignments designated:
_____		
_____		

OUTCOMES:

TARGETED DATES   COMPLETION DATES

_____ _____	A.	Develop appropriate sense of self-worth and self-esteem based on non-deviant/victimizing behavior.
_____ _____	B.	Develop appropriate self-concept and confidence based on appropriate behavior.
_____ _____	C.	Develop appropriate self-image based on appropriate behavior.
_____ _____	D.	Develop appropriate key core belief(s) to be able to live a functional non-deviant lifestyle.

COMMENTS:

_____
_____
_____
_____
_____
_____
_____
_____

33

THE ELEVEN POINT TREATMENT PLAN FOR SEX OFFENDER PROGRAMS

Name: _____

DIAGNOSIS:

AXIS I (cont)

Other: _____

_____

_____

_____

_____

AXIS II

_____ 301.70 Antisocial personality disorder

_____ 301.83 Borderline personality disorder

_____ 301.81 Narcissistic personality disorder

_____ 301.20 Schizoid personality disorder

_____ 301.22 Schizotypal personality disorder

_____ 301.9 Personality disorder NOS

_____ 319 Mental retardation, severity unspecified

_____ V62.89 Borderline intellectual functioning

Other: _____

_____

_____

_____

35

THE ELEVEN POINT TREATMENT PLAN FOR SEX OFFENDER PROGRAMS

Name: _____

AXIS III

_____

_____

_____

_____

_____

COMMENTS:

_____

_____

_____

_____

_____

_____

_____

_____

_____

_____

36

THE ELEVEN POINT TREATMENT PLAN FOR SEX OFFENDER PROGRAMS

Carole Metzger, MSW & Mark S. Carich, PhD

NAME _____   IDOC # _____

Reviewed with client, Signature / Date

_____
_____
_____
_____

Presenting problems

_____
_____
_____

Diagnosis
Axis I _____
Axis II _____
Axis III _____

Medication review dates

_____
_____
_____

Treatment Team Reviewed, Signature / Date

_____
_____
_____
_____
_____

© Metzger C and Carich MS, 1997. Reproduced with the permission of Mark S Carich.